Emotional Patterns

Fears, Emotional States and Created Patterns (Beliefs) by Disease, Disorder and Trauma

Formerly Healer Wisdom
Revision 1

VALERIA J. MOORE

Copyright ©2021 Valeria J. Moore

All rights reserved. Reproduction is permitted for brief passages.

ISBN Print: 978-1-7371275-4-3
ISBN Ebook:978-1-7371275-3-6

Published by Three Moons Publishing
Interior design by Valeria J. Moore
Cover by Valeria J. Moore

www.emotionalpatterns.com

This revision was done to put the book under Three Moons Publishing for printing through other distributors.

TABLE OF CONTENTS

ACKNOWLEDGMENTS -- 3
INTRODUCTION -- 4
HOW TO USE THIS BOOK -- 6
GROUPINGS OF DISEASE, DISORDERS AND TRAUMA ---------------------------- 10
DISEASES, DISORDERS AND TRAUMA -- 27
ABOUT THE AUTHOR -- 680
INDEX -- 681

DEDICATION

In loving memory of Crystal Stone

ACKNOWLEDGMENTS

I have to start with my life partner, Mike Read. Mike has listened to the endless typing over the many years that I have been writing. He has supported my work, advised me and corrected my grammar. He has endured my 3 a.m. mornings of coffee, meditation, and writing. Thank you, Sweetie.

Thank you to all of the wisdom teachers that have allowed me to walk with them through the ages.

I am deeply grateful to the first person that asked for a copy of the binder-clipped-coffee-stained-wrinkled original Healer Wisdom. That request started a journey that has lasted 15+ years and may go on for another 30 years.

A special acknowledgment to Barbara Milliken; she has been my friend, volunteer editor and advisor.

INTRODUCTION

The Journey

One of my key talents in life is collecting and organizing large volumes of data. When I was in high school, they gave students aptitude tests. These aptitude tests evaluate our innate abilities. The counselor would call us into the office and predict what we would excel at in life after graduation.

In 1968 my aptitude tests revealed that I would make a great mechanic or librarian. I can still remember the look of confusion on my counselor's face. The test results made no sense in 1968, but in 1996, the elements came together. My mechanical skill, coupled with my love of books and information, resulted in a degree in Computer and Information Sciences from the University of California.

Years later, when I had become a consciousness arts practitioner, a flood of new information about our emotional body and how it related to the physical body was coming in daily. I started to collect this information. Within a short period of time, I had stacks of papers, emails, sticky notes and books surrounding my desk. I decided to compile this information to use in working with clients. My focus was singular: developing my skills so I could help others. That compilation was nothing more than a collection of my notes in an unsophisticated format. After all, I was the only one using it until someone asked for a copy one day.

When I did the first version, the motivation was that inner quickening that prompts us with a call to action. I was working on a paper for Ph.D. course work when I awoke on a morning in September of 2005 to that inner knowing telling me I HAD to compile this information into a book, NOW. I didn't question that knowing. I then started that first official version of Healer Wisdom and not the dog-eared-coffee-stained-binder-clipped collection of papers I called Healer Wisdom.

The second version of Healer Wisdom reflected a new level of awareness for developing the material. I had trained in a process called Perceptual Awareness Technique. This technique accesses the wisdom of the soul. This process opened up a whole new layer of wisdom in understanding our emotional states and created patterns.

Over the years since publication of the Healer Wisdom 2.2, I continued to write new material as requested and fill in the holes in the information. I knew that I had more than enough new material written to publish the next version of Healer Wisdom. But I wasn't getting it done, and I felt like I was walking through wet cement. The new version was initially destined to be Healer Wisdom 3.0. However, it seemed I could not get Healer Wisdom 3.0 into book form.

Since the publishing of Healer Wisdom 2.2, I worked with new transformation processes that worked with the gut-mind and stuck instinctual fears. The personal transformation work I had done in that period also subtly changed the depth of the writing. Then one day, I realized that I needed to change the book's name to reflect the new information, and the title 'Emotional Patterns' was born.

I was ready to begin putting together the manuscript with the new title when I felt a drag. It felt like I had hit an invisible wall that drained all my energy. Over the last year, I had started working with a transformation process that worked from the heart-mind. The heart-mind transformation was again influencing my writing. I sat with the feeling stopping me, and I heard the word 'fears.' I acknowledged that I probably had fears. So I began working on transmuting those states of non-peace to peace. After bringing myself to a state of peace, I still felt that energetic sluggishness. I asked a couple of good friends what they thought. The answer was the same, 'fears.' Then, one morning, the light bulb went on while journaling and meditating. I needed to specifically address the fears held in a disease, disorder or trauma.

As I evolved in my transformation journey, my writing evolved. The passion for understanding the mind-body disease and disorder connection expanded to encompass the three minds; gut-mind, thinking-mind and heart-mind.

HOW TO USE THIS BOOK

This book is for anyone on a healing journey as either a healing arts professional or an individual exploring their foundations of non-peace (dis-ease). The information provides a catalyst of recognition that opens the doors to the next level of growth in a personal development journey. There are different aspects to each malady: Fears, Emotional States, Cross Indexing, and Created Patterns (beliefs).

Fears

At the core of every emotional state or created pattern (belief) is a historical trauma(s). Historical trauma is from our ancestry or a recent life experience. We frame our human experience of trauma within our familial, cultural, geopolitical, dogmatic or institutional rules. We build additional fears on top of a core fear. We layer innumerable created patterns (beliefs), emotional states and feelings upon those fears. Finally, we crystallize those emotional patterns, fears and created patterns in our bodies so we can live in a state of emotional 'heart peace.' The reality is that we have swapped one state of non-peace for another state of non-peace.

Emotional States

The nature of all diseases is that we have had an experience and not understood or learned the higher nature of the event. We have taken in the suffering and created an identity around the trauma. The value of the emotional states is that it references a conceptual grouping of created patterns within a vignette of behavior. Individual created patterns may be culturally biased in their wording orientation and may not resonate with the person. Emotional states allow for the translation into the respective value system. A person may resonate with all the emotional states or none or an aspect.

Emotional States may have a masculine or feminine nature. This does not mean that a woman can have only the feminine or a man only the masculine. It means that the feminine or masculine aspect of a person is reflected in that emotional state. A person may be out of balance with respect to the masculine or feminine aspects of self. For example, if the masculine is weak, then they have a lot of doubts. They doubt their abilities and capability to do things. There is a feeling of being intimidated by life, and moving forward is difficult. There is a fear of putting themselves out there because they 'know' they will fail, so they don't even try to accomplish things. With a weak masculine side, there is the need to show off attributes and accomplishments. There is a low value on others with a weak feminine side, and they are not giving. Instead, there is a predisposition to be selfish and greedy and be closed off from people. Also, the weak feminine does not take responsibility for their actions but blames others for their problems.

The power of disease-based change may come from within the emotional state itself. Beliefs come together synergistically and create an amplified experience within the body. For example, a person has the created pattern 'I hate Aunt Edith.' Along with that belief, there is a reason for the hatred. Maybe the belief is based on the fact that Aunt Edith betrayed them. So they believe 'Aunt Edith betrayed me.' Depending on the nature of the betrayal, the person may also believe that 'Women betray me.' All of the beliefs have a different vibrational quality that synergistically amplifies the energy of an emotional state. A single belief is limiting but may not produce a powerful shift. When multiple beliefs come together, they may create an energetic shift within the emotional state(s) sufficient to create dis-ease.

The goal of the Emotional State information is to facilitate the recognition of a pattern(s) before the disease happens. Awareness of that pattern opens the door to begin a process of change.

Cross-Indexing

The cross-indexing provides you with additional information during the discovery process. The energetic disease profile rarely exists in the human body without connection to another part of the body. The feeling associated with a created pattern, a fear or emotional state is not so discriminating that it targets one particular organ or group of cells. The cross-indexing connections point to similar fears, created patterns or emotional states that other diseases may have in common with the focus of your exploration. For example, a child hears something that wounded their heart. That 'something' was heard by their ears. An energetic block may have been created in their ears to prevent further hurt, which may produce maladies in their ears. What they heard may have felt like it was tearing them apart inside as a child. That same child may additionally experience difficulties with joints and connective tissue. Then many years later, if the heart has not been healed, heart disease may evolve.

Created Patterns (Beliefs)

A created pattern is a conceptual identification statement that underlies a behavior done over and over again. For example, a created pattern may be the ritual of drinking coffee first thing in the morning. The created pattern identifies as 'I must have my coffee first thing in the morning.' A created pattern may be feeling betrayed by "friends" repeatedly. The created pattern would then identify as 'My friends betray me.' This created pattern is telling a story of hurt and harm repeatedly to prove a victim's status. The ritual of drinking a cup of coffee in the morning may not be limiting. However, the feeling and the created pattern of being betrayed by friends may have locked this person into a cycle of victim identity. This created pattern may be limiting.

The term created patterns reflects a shift from the use of the word '**beliefs**.' Words carry energy, and one of the aspects of the word 'belief(s)' is that it does not globally imply ownership. All 'beliefs' are patterns of creation by the individual holding them regardless of the origin. Ownership, awareness of how their heart feels and the willingness to change a created pattern are essential if a person is genuinely committed to transmuting their state of non-peace.

The created patterns are worded as a person would say them in natural conversation as they are given. Natural language phrasing of a created pattern establishes resonance. Resonance is found in your heart, body or mind. You may feel a contraction in one or all of your minds when resonating with a statement.

Created patterns rarely exist in a singularity; they are layered. That layering happens as a consequence of an entrainment relationship. That relationship is fear. The foundation of all limiting created patterns is fear(s). You are hard-wired to respond to a physical threat with an instinctual response. An experience or a repeated experience of an instinctual response to a physical threat, and that response is not allowed to complete its process, that response will get stuck. When an instinctual response is stuck, we develop limiting created patterns that we believe keep us safe. To stay safe, we adapt our lives and responses to those patterns and create emotional states and multiple created patterns. The origin of those stuck responses is not always from your life experiences. Stuck responses may be passed down to you from your ancestry through a process of either conception trauma or epigenetics. Epigenetics is a change in how the genetic code expresses itself as opposed to actual genetic changes.

Wounded Creative Core

The wounding of our creative core is the adaption we made to survive institutional abuse. We are born with the ability to create and freely access inner wisdom, our creative core. As children, we are joy. However, institutions (schools, governments, familial, cultures and religious dogma) conform and perform behavior structures. These structures constrain the creative core and destroy joy through shame, humiliation, rejection, shunning and violence. When these constraint tools are used on a child, the creative core is wounded, and the creativity flow is severely impaired. I have named this trauma The Wounded Creative Core. The Wounded Creative Core is referenced throughout this book.

Wording

One of my favorite mind-body authors, Annette Noontil, wrote in a way that requires the reader to sit with the information and see what it means at a deeper level. The wording in the disease, disorder and trauma text is sometimes written to require the reader to 'sit' with what has been written. If the wording feels cryptic, close your eyes, holding the relevant phrase in your mind, and ask 'what does this mean' or 'what would be another way of stating this?' The answer will be what is energetically correct for you.

In Closing

The understanding of the thinking-heart-body mind connection and its part in creating diseases and disorders is still evolving. As such, Emotional Patterns will continue to evolve. I add new material to the online book at emotionalpatterns.com frequently. The online book also offers the ability to search for related maladies and symptoms or explore system-level categories, such as searching for all disorders in the Digestive System. Please see the information located on this website for accessing new information.

Index of individual disease, disorder and traumas is located at the end of the book

GROUPINGS OF DISEASE, DISORDERS AND TRAUMA

Abdominal
Abdominal Aortic Aneurysm
Abdominal Pain and Problems
Abdominal Sacrocolpopexy
Appendicitis
Colitis – Ulcerative
Constipation
Crohn's Disease
Duodenal Ulcer
Dysmenorrhea
Intestinal Problems
Intestine – Large Problems (Bowel)
Intestines – Blocked
Lumbar Hernia
Pelvic Organ Collapse/Prolapse
Stomach Ulcer (Peptic Ulcer Disease-Gastric)
Umbilical Hernia

Adrenals
Addison's Disease
Adrenal Fatigue
Adrenal Problems
EMF Sensitivity
Toxins – Cadmium

Allergies
Allergies – Dairy
Allergies – General
Allergies – Gluten Intolerance
Allergies – Hay Fever
Allergies – Wheat
EMF Sensitivity
Fear of Mold
Hives
Irritable Bowel Syndrome
Mold Sensitivity
Post Nasal Drip
Sinus Congestion – Chronic
Sinus Polyps
Sinus Problems
Stye
Tonsil Problems
Toxins – Mercury
Upper Respiratory Infection (URI)

Autoimmune Disorders
AIDS and HIV
Alopecia
Amyloidosis
Arthritis – Psoriatic
Arthritis – Reactive (Reiter's Syndrome)
Arthritis – Rheumatoid
Autoimmune Disorder
Autoimmune Hemolytic Anemia
B Cell – Abnormal Recognition
Cancer – Hodgkin Lymphoma
Celiac Disease
Chronic Fatigue Syndrome
Crohn's Disease
Diabetes Mellitus Type 1
Fascia Problems
Good Pasture's Syndrome
Hashimotos Disease
Huntington's Disease
Joint Problems
Lupus
Lyme's Disease

	Myasthenia Gravis
	Nephritis
	Neuritis
	Peripheral Neuropathy
	Polyarteritis
	Polymyositis
	Psoriasis
	Pulmonary Fibrosis
	Rosacea
	Scleroderma
	Sjogren's Syndrome
	Spleen Problems
	Stills Disease – Juvenile
	Toxins – Glyphosate
	Wounding of the Empathic Sense
Bacteria	**Blood Disorders**
Bacterial Infection	Anemia
Boils	Anemia – Pernicious
Conjunctivitis	Anemia – Sickle Cell
Duodenal Ulcer	Aneurysm
Gum Problems	Angiolipoma
Impetigo	Autoimmune Hemolytic Anemia
Infertility	B Cell – Abnormal Recognition
Joint Problems	Blood Disorders
Lymes Disease	Bruises
Meningitis - Bacterial	Cancer – Leukemia
Osteomyelitis	Cancer – Multiple Myeloma
Parasites	Cancer – Non-Hodgkins Lymphoma
Pyorrhea – Periodontitis	Candida
Stills Disease – Juvenile	Cardiovascular Disorder
Stomach Ulcer (Peptic Ulcer Disease-Gastric)	Cholesterol – High
Strep Throat	Circulation Problems
Stye	Diabetes
Tuberculosis	Hepatitis C
Upper Respiratory Infection (URI)	Hypotension
	Liver – Jaundice
	Polyarteritis
	Sepsis
	Spleen Problems
	Stroke
	Swollen Feet
	Temporal Arteritis
	Vasculitis
	Wegeners Granulomatosis
Bones	**Brain Disorders**
Bone Problems	Acoustic Neuroma – Left Side
Bones – Broken	Acoustic Neuroma – Right Side
Cancer – Multiple Myeloma	ALS or Amyotrophic Lateral Sclerosis or Lou

EMOTIONAL PATTERNS

Cancer – Osteosarcoma Clavicle Problems Fibula – Left Fibula – Right Kidneys – Amyloidosis Osteomyelitis Osteoporosis Paget's Disease Sciatica Scoliosis Shin Problems Slipped Disc (Herniation) Spurs Tibia – Left Tibia – Right Wounding of the Empathic Sense	Gehrig's Disease or Motor Neuron Disease Amyloidosis Aneurysm Brain Problems Brain Tumor Chronic Traumatic Encephalopathy (CTE) Concussion Dementia Depression with a history of abuse Epilepsy Focal Dystonia Headache Headache – Migraine Huntington's Disease Hyperactivity Insomnia Lack of focus (in school/studies) Memory Loss non-physical trauma Meningitis – Bacterial Meningitis – Fungal Meningitis – Viral Narcolepsy Nerve Problems Nervousness Neurosis Parkinson's Peripheral Neuropathy Pituitary Gland Problems Post Traumatic Stress Disorder(PTSD) Pseudo Tumor – Cerebri Restless Leg Syndrome Schizophrenia Senility Smoking – problems with quitting Spasmodic Dysphonia – (Laryngeal) Stroke Stuttering (non-developmental) Temple Pain or Pressure Tinnitus Tongue Problems Tourette's Syndrome Toxins – Aluminum Toxins – Glyphosate Toxins – Mercury Vertigo
Breast Disorders Breast Problems Cancer – Breast Post Mastectomy Problems	**Cancer** Brain Tumor Cancer Cancer – Basal Cell

EMOTIONAL PATTERNS

Radiculopathy of Left Breast Radiculopathy of Right Breast	Cancer – Bladder Cancer – Breast Cancer – Cervical Cancer – Colon Cancer – Esophageal Cancer – Hodgkin Lymphoma Cancer – Leukemia Cancer – Liver Cancer – Lung Cancer – Medullary Thyroid Cancer – Melanoma Cancer – Multiple Myeloma Cancer – Non-Hodgkins Lymphoma Cancer – Osteosarcoma Cancer – Ovarian Cancer – Pancreatic NeuroEndocrine Cancer – Prostate Cancer – Squamous Cell Cancer – Stomach Cancer – Urethral Sepsis Spleen Problems Toxins – Asbestos Toxins – Cadmium Toxins – Glyphosate Toxins – Polychlorinated Biphenyls (PCBs)
Circulatory Disorders Abdominal Aortic Aneurysm Amyloidosis Aneurysm Arteriosclerosis (Atherosclerosis) Artery Problems Atrial Fibrillation B Cell – Abnormal Recognition Behcet's Syndrome Bloating Blood Disorders Bruises Cancer – Liver Cardiovascular Disorder Chest Problems Circulation Problems Congestive Heart Failure Deep Vein Thrombosis(DVT) Edema Heart Problems Hypertension Hypotension Insulin Resistance	**Connective Tissue Disorders** Achilles Tendonosis-left Achilles Tendonosis-right Ankle Problems (pain, sprain, swelling) Carpel Tunnel Dupuytren's Contraction Fascia Problems Fibromyalgia Good Pasture's Syndrome Hand Problems Joint Problems Ligament Problems Marfan Syndrome Plantar Fasciitis Pulmonary Fibrosis Scoliosis Shoulders Slipped Disc (Herniation) Sprains Temple Pain or Pressure Tendon Problems Wrists

Leg Edema
Leg-Paralysis
Macular Degeneration
Mitral Valve Prolapse
Muscles – Cramps
Parathyroid Disease
Phlebitis
Polyarteritis
Reynauds Syndrome
Sepsis
Spleen Problems
Swollen Feet
Tachycardia
Temporal Arteritis
Thrombosis
Thrombotic thrombocytopenic purpura
Thiamine Deficiency
Toxins – Cadmium
Toxins – Glyphosate
Toxins – Mercury
Varicose Veins
Vasculitis
Vein Problems
Vertigo

Developmental Disorders
Attention Deficit Disorder
Autism
Lack of focus (in school/studies)
Tourette's Syndrome
Toxins – Glyphosate
Toxins – Lead
Toxins – Mercury

Digestive System
Abdominal Pain and Problems
Allergies – Dairy
Allergies – General
Allergies – Gluten Intolerance
Anorectic Bleeding
Anorexia
Anus Problems
Appendicitis
Appetite – Excessive
Appetite – Loss
Arthritis – Reactive (Reiter's Syndrome)
Biliary Colic
Bloating
Cancer – Colon
Cancer – Esophageal
Cancer – Liver
Cancer – Pancreatic NeuroEndocrine
Cancer – Stomach
Celiac Disease
Cirrhosis
Colitis – Ulcerative
Colon Problems
Constipation
Crohn's Disease

	Diarrhea
	Diverticulitis
	Duodenal Ulcer
	Epigastric Hernia
	Esophagus Problems
	Gall Bladder Problems
	Gallbladder Polyps
	Gallstones
	Gastritis
	Gastroesophageal Reflux Disease (GERD)
	Halitosis
	Hemorrhoids
	Hepatitis
	Hepatitis C
	Hernia
	Hiatus Hernia
	Indigestion
	Insomnia
	Intestinal Problems
	Intestine – Large Problems (Bowel)
	Intestine – Small Problems
	Intestines – Blocked
	Irritable Bowel Syndrome
	Leaky Gut Syndrome
	Liver – Jaundice
	Liver Problems
	Lumbar Hernia
	Mouth Problems
	Nausea
	Pancreas Problems
	Pancreatic Insufficiency
	Pancreatitis
	Pelvis Problems
	Stomach Problems
	Stomach Ulcer (Peptic Ulcer Disease-Gastric)
	Swallowing – Trouble
	Tongue Problems
	Tooth Infection
	Toxins – Glyphosate
	Vomiting
Ear Disorders	**Emotional Disorders**
Acoustic Neuroma – Left Side	Abused Child
Acoustic Neuroma – Right Side	ACOA-Adult Children of Alcoholics
Ear Infection – Chronic	Addiction – Alcohol
Ear Problems	Addiction – Chemical
Ears – Hearing Problems	Addiction – Cocaine
Hearing – Hyperacute	Addiction – Food
Hearing Loss (Deafness) – Left	Addiction – Gambling
Hearing Loss (Deafness) – Right	Addiction – Shopping

Labyrinthitis Tinnitus	Addiction – Smoking / Nicotine Adrenal Fatigue Agoraphobia Anorexia Anxiety Appetite – Excessive Appetite – Loss Attention Deficit Disorder Bedwetting Bi-Polar Syndrome Brain Problems Bulimia Depression Depression with a history of abuse Dizziness Fingernails – Biting Headache Headache – Tension Hyperventilation Insomnia Nervous Breakdown Nervousness Neurosis Obsessive-Compulsive Disorder Overeating – Compulsive Panic Disorder Peacemaker Post-Partum Depression Post Traumatic Stress Disorder(PTSD) Schizophrenia Sexual Assault – Adult Sexual Assaulter Suicidal Temporo-Mandibular Joint (TMJ) Weight Loss Panic Wounded Creative Core Wounding of the Empathic Sense
Endocrine System Disorders Addison's Disease Adenoid Problems Adrenal Fatigue Alopecia Amenorrhoea Anemia – Pernicious Autoimmune Disorder Bloating Cancer – Medullary Thyroid Cancer – Pancreatic NeuroEndocrine Cancer – Prostate	**Eye Disorders** Cataracts – Left Cataracts – Right Conjunctivitis Dry Eye Eye Problems Eyes – Nearsightedness and Farsightedness Floaters – Left Eye Floaters – Right Eye Lasik Surgery Reversal – Left Eye Lasik Surgery Reversal – Right Eye Macular Degeneration

Cardiovascular Disorder Diabetes: A Global View Diabetes Mellitus Type 1 Diabetes Mellitus Type 2 Endocrine System Problems Endometriosis Fibroid Tumors and Cysts Glaucoma Hair – Falling Out Hashimotos Disease Hyperthyroidism Hypoglycemia Hypothalamus Hypothyroidism Infertility Insomnia Insulin Resistance Libido – Underactivated Menstrual Problems Morning Sickness Neuritis Pancreas Problems Pancreatic Insufficiency Parathyroid Disease Pelvis Problems Peripheral Neuropathy Pineal Gland Pituitary Gland Problems Post-Partum Depression Prolapsed Bladder (Cystocele) Prostate Problems Testicle Problems Thalamus Problems Thymus Problems Thyroid Problems Toxins – Mercury Weight Loss – Insulin Resistance Wilson's Syndrome	Pinguecula Sjogren's Syndrome Stargardt's Disease Stye Toxins – Mercury
Face and Head Problems Acne Acoustic Neuroma – Left Side Acoustic Neuroma – Right Side Ethmoid Bone Face/Head Problems Frontal Skull Bones Hair – Ingrown Headache Headache – Migraine Jaw Problems	**Fungus** Athlete's Foot Candida Fungus Meningitis – Fungal Mucormycosis Thrush Upper Respiratory Infection (URI) Yeast Infection

Nose Problems Temple Pain or Pressure Temporo-Mandibular Joint (TMJ)	
Genetic Disorders Addiction – Alcohol Alopecia ALS or Amyotrophic Lateral Sclerosis or Lou Gehrig's Disease or Motor Neuron Disease Alzheimer's Anemia – Pernicious Anemia – Sickle Cell Behcet's Syndrome Bulimia Crohn's Disease Diabetes Diabetes Mellitus Type 1 Diabetes Mellitus Type 2 Dupuytren's Contraction Ehlers-Danlos Syndrome Gingivitis Graves Disease Growths – Skin Hair – Balding Headache – Migraine Huntington's Disease Joint Problems Kidneys – Polycystic Macular Degeneration Marfan Syndrome Mitral Valve Prolapse Multiple Sclerosis Muscular Dystrophy Myasthenia Gravis Paget's Disease Polymyositis Sjogren's Syndrome Spasmodic Dysphonia – (Laryngeal) Stargardt's Disease Stills Disease – Juvenile Toxins – Cadmium Vitiligo	**Heart Disorders** Arteriosclerosis (Atherosclerosis) Atrial Fibrillation Circulation Problems Congestive Heart Failure Heart Problems Hypertension Hypotension Insomnia Leg Edema Mitral Valve Prolapse Polyarteritis Swollen Feet Tachycardia Thiamine Deficiency Toxins – Mercury Vasculitis
Infection Abscess Appendicitis Arthritis – Reactive (Reiter's Syndrome) Bacterial Infection Bladder Infection Boils	**Inflammatory Disease** Acne Ankylosing Spondylitis Behcet's Syndrome Bronchitis Bursitis Colitis – Ulcerative

Cysts Ear Infection – Chronic Gastritis Gum Problems Hair – Ingrown Herpes Virus Simplex II Ingrown Toenail Left Big Toe Ingrown Toenail Right Big Toe Joint Problems Mucormycosis Pimples Pityros Pneumonia Sepsis Skin Problems Spleen Problems Tooth Infection Upper Respiratory Infection (URI) Urinary Tract Infection (Cystitis) Vaginitis	Conjunctivitis Crohn's Disease Diverticulitis Fascia Problems Henoch Schonlein Purpura Infection Inflammation Insulin Resistance Irritable Bowel Syndrome Joint Problems Liver – Jaundice Meningitis – Bacterial Meningitis – Fungal Meningitis – Viral Neuritis Osteomyelitis Pancreatitis Pleurisy Polyarteritis Polymyalgia Rheumatica Polymyositis Rosacea Sarcoidosis Skin Problems Spurs Stills Disease – Juvenile Temporal Arteritis Temporo-Mandibular Joint (TMJ) Wegeners Granulomatosis
Joint Disorders Ankylosing Spondylitis Arthritis Arthritis – Infectious or Septic Arthritis – Osteoarthritis Arthritis – Psoriatic Arthritis – Reactive (Reiter's Syndrome) Arthritis – Rheumatoid Baker's Cyst Bunions Bursitis Carpel Tunnel Cartilage Degeneration Charcot's Joints Dupuytren's Contraction Ehlers-Danlos Syndrome Elbow Problems Ganglion Cyst – Left wrist Ganglion Cyst – Right Wrist Gout	**Liver Disorders** Amyloidosis Cancer – Liver Cholesterol – High Cirrhosis Hepatitis Leg Edema Liver – Jaundice Liver Problems

Henoch Schonlein Purpura
Jaw Problems
Joint Problems
Knee – Left
Knee Problems
Knee – Right
Polyarteritis
Polymyalgia Rheumatica
Rotator Cuff
Scoliosis
Shoulders
Slipped Disc (Herniation)
Spleen Problems
Sprains
Stills Disease – Juvenile
Temporo-Mandibular Joint (TMJ)
Wrists

Lung Disorders
Asthma
Bronchitis
Cancer – Lung
Cardiovascular Disorder
Circulation Problems
Cough – Chronic
Coughing
Emphysema – COPD
Good Pasture's Syndrome
Lung Problems
Pleurisy
Pneumonia
Post-Nasal Drip
Toxins – Asbestos
Toxins – Polychlorinated Biphenyls (PCBs)
Tuberculosis
Upper Respiratory Infection (URI)
Wegeners Granulomatosis

Lymphatic System Disorder
Cancer – Hodgkin Lymphoma
Cancer – Leukemia
Cancer – Non-Hodgkins Lymphoma
Edema
Leg Edema
Lymphatic System Problems
Sarcoidosis
Sjogren's Syndrome
Thymus Problems
Toxins – Glyphosate

Miscellaneous
Accidents
Aches
Chronic Illness
EMF Sensitivity
Long Term Illness
Preemie Birth – now adult
Radiation Influence on Disease Creation
Sickness and Love
Sidedness
Tumors – Lipomas

Mouth Disorders
Adenoid Problems
Gingivitis
Gum Loss (Gingival recession)
Gum Problems
Gums – Bleeding
Halitosis
Jaw Problems
Mouth Problems
Periodontal Bone Loss
Pyorrhea – Periodontitis
Salivary Gland Problems

	Tongue Problems Tooth Infection Toxins – Mercury
Muscle Disorders ALS or Amyotrophic Lateral Sclerosis or Lou Gehrig's Disease or Motor Neuron Disease Back Back – Cervical (neck) Back – Coccyx Pain – Tailbone Back – Sacral – Lower Back – Lumbar (middle) Back – Thoracic (Back High heart) Epigastric Hernia Focal Dystonia Hernia Hiatus Hernia Hiccups Insulin Resistance Leg-Paralysis Lumbar Hernia Muscle Problems Muscles – Cramps Muscular Dystrophy Myasthenia Gravis Polymyositis Temple Pain or Pressure Thigh Problems Umbilical Hernia	**Neural Disorder** Acoustic Neuroma – Left Side Acoustic Neuroma – Right Side ALS or Amyotrophic Lateral Sclerosis or Lou Gehrig's Disease or Motor Neuron Disease Alzheimer's Brain Problems Chronic Traumatic Encephalopathy (CTE) Concussion Dementia Depression Focal Dystonia Huntington's Disease Insomnia Leg-Paralysis Meningitis – Bacterial Meningitis – Fungal Meningitis – Viral Multiple Sclerosis Muscular Dystrophy Narcolepsy Nerve Problems Neuritis Paralysis Parkinson's Peripheral Neuropathy Radiculopathy of Left Breast Radiculopathy of Right Breast Reflexive Sympathetic Dystrophy Syndrome Restless Leg Syndrome Sciatica Senility Slipped Disc (Herniation) Spasmodic Dysphonia – (Laryngeal) Stroke Stuttering (non-developmental) Toxins – Aluminum Toxins – Glyphosate Toxins – Lead Trigeminal Neuralgia
Nose Disorders Allergies – General Ethmoid Bone Fear of Mold Post-Nasal Drip	**Reproductive Disorder** Abdominal Sacrocolpopexy Abortion Complications Amenorrhoea Bloating

Rhinitis – when laying down at night Sinus Problems Snoring	Cancer – Cervical Cancer – Ovarian Cancer – Prostate Dysmenorrhea Endocrine System Problems Endometriosis Erectile Dysfunction Fallopian Tube Blockage Fibroid Tumors and Cysts Herpes Virus Simplex II Infertility Leucorrhea Low Progesterone Levels Menstrual Problems Morning Sickness Ovarian Cyst Ovarian Fibroids Ovaries – Polycystic Ovary Problems Pelvic Organ Collapse/Prolapse Pelvis Problems Post-Partum Depression Premenstrual Syndrome Prolapsed Bladder (Cystocele) Prostate Problems Pruritic urticarial papules and plaques of pregnancy Testicle Problems Vaginitis
Respiratory Disorders Adenoid Problems Allergies – Dairy Allergies – General Allergies – Hay Fever Asthma Chest Problems Cough – Chronic Coughing Emphysema – COPD Ethmoid Bone Fear of Mold Hyperventilation Nose Problems Pneumonia Post-Nasal Drip Pulmonary Fibrosis Rhinitis – when laying down at night Sarcoidosis Sepsis	**Sexual Disorders** Amenorrhoea Cancer – Cervical Erectile Dysfunction Herpes Virus Simplex II Infertility Libido – Under Activated Menopause – Difficult Prostate Problems Venereal Disease

Sinus Congestion – Chronic Sinus Polyps Sinus Problems Sleep Apnea Smoking – problems with quitting Snoring Tonsil Problems Toxins – Mercury Wegeners Granulomatosis	
Skeletal System Achilles Tendonosis-left Achilles Tendonosis-right Ankle Problems (pain, sprain, swelling) Ankylosing Spondylitis Arms – Left Arms – Right Arthritis Arthritis – Infectious or Septic Arthritis – Osteoarthritis Arthritis – Reactive (Reiter's Syndrome) Arthritis – Rheumatoid B Cell – Abnormal Recognition Back Back – Cervical (neck) Back – Coccyx Pain – Tailbone Back – Sacral – Lower Back – Lumbar (middle) Back – Thoracic (Back High heart) Bone Problems Bones – Broken Bunions Cancer – Leukemia Cancer – Osteosarcoma Clavicle Problems Ethmoid Bone Fibula – Left Fibula – Right Foot Problems Frontal Skull Bones Ganglion Cyst – Left wrist Ganglion Cyst – Right Wrist Hand Problems Jaw Problems Leg Problems Mastoiditis Maxilla Occipital Skullbone Paget's Disease Paralysis	**Skin Disorders** Acne Allergies – General Angiolipoma Arthritis – Psoriatic Blisters Bruises Calluses Cancer – Basal Cell Cancer – Melanoma Cancer – Squamous Cell Cysts Dandruff Eczema Facial Dandruff Fear of Mold Fingernails Fingernails – Biting Growths – Skin Hair – Ingrown Henoch Schonlein Purpura Hives Impetigo Ingrown Toenail Left Big Toe Ingrown Toenail Right Big Toe Itching Lip Problems Moles Pityros Plantar Wart Pruritic urticarial papules and plaques of pregnancy Psoriasis Pyrogenic Granuloma Rashes Rosacea Sebaceous Cysts Shingles Skin Problems Stye

Plantar Fasciitis Radiculopathy of Left Breast Radiculopathy of Right Breast Rotator Cuff Sciatica Scoliosis Shin Problems Shoulders Slipped Disc (Herniation) Sphenoid Bone Misalignment Spinal Stenosis Spurs Teeth Problems Temporo-Mandibular Joint (TMJ) Tendon Problems Tibia – Left Tibia – Right Toes Wrists	Toxins – Mercury Toxins – Polychlorinated Biphenyls (PCBs) Warts
Symptoms Anorectic Bleeding Appetite – Loss Atrial Fibrillation Bacterial Infection Bloating Constipation Cough – Chronic Depression Depression with a history of abuse Diarrhea Dizziness Dry Eye Erectile Dysfunction Fatigue Fever Headache Hyperventilation Inflammation Insomnia Itching Laryngitis Leg Edema Leucorrhea Muscles – Cramps Nausea Pain Rashes Right-Sided Negative Tendencies Sinus Problems	**Teeth** Gum Loss (Gingival recession) Teeth Problems Teeth – Upper Left 1st Incisor Teeth – Upper Right 2nd Molar Toxins – Mercury

Snoring Stuttering (non-developmental) Suicidal Swallowing – Trouble Tongue Problems Tonsil Problems Urinary Tract Infection (Cystitis) Vomiting	
Throat Disorders Adenoid Problems Cough – Chronic Laryngitis Snoring Strep Throat Swallowing – Trouble Throat Problems Tonsil Problems Vocal Cord Problems	**Urinary Tract System Disorders** Kidney Problems Arthritis – Reactive (Reiter's Syndrome) Bladder Infection Bladder Problems Bloating Cancer – Bladder Cancer – Prostate Cancer – Urethral Erectile Dysfunction Incontinence Kidney Stones Kidneys – Amyloidosis Kidneys – Polycystic Leg Edema Nephritis Prolapsed Bladder (Cystocele) Sepsis Swollen Feet Urinary Tract Infection (Cystitis)
Viruses AIDS and HIV Behcet's Syndrome Bronchitis Cancer – Cervical Cancer – Hodgkin Lymphoma Colds Conjunctivitis Cytomegalovirus Epstein Barr Syndrome Flu Hepatitis C Herpes Simplex (Cold Sores) Herpes Virus Simplex II Human Papilloma Virus (HPV) Infertility Laryngitis Measles Meningitis – Viral	**Weight** Anorexia Bulimia Overeating – Compulsive Weight Loss – Fear of Starvation Weight Loss – Insulin Resistance Weight Loss Panic Weight Loss – The Magical Thinking Diet Weight Loss – The Family Money Story and Weight - Overweight Weight – Under

EMOTIONAL PATTERNS

Mononucleosis Neuritis Parasites Sepsis Shingles Tonsil Problems Viruses	

DISEASES, DISORDERS AND TRAUMA

A's

Abdominal Aortic Aneurysm

Fears
- Fear of their life being nothing
- Fear of never being able to rise above or up
- Fear of never realizing their dreams
- Fear of never having a safe life
- Fear of acting on their feelings
- Fear of standing up
- Fear of defending themselves
- Fear of living
- Fear of rejection
- Fear of being trapped
- Fear of being forgotten

Emotional States
- False hopes about their life become too much to bear as their life wanes. They commit an inner suicide as the hurt and anger explode on the inside. What should have been joy becomes nothing but pain, anger, and hatred in the face of being powerless. The pain of living becomes too much. Held out to others as unworthy. Feels subjugated, humiliated and is possibly physically abused.

Cross Indexing: Abdominal problems, circulatory problems, PTSD, ACOA, and Physical Abuse

Created Patterns
1. I am not good enough.
2. I no longer wish to live.
3. I'm unworthy.
4. I am invisible.
5. I'm a punching bag.
6. Life is hate and evil.
7. Life is hard.
8. Life is sorrow.

9. My life is slavery and abuse.
10. I have no hope.
11. I can't change things.
12. I have no power.
13. There is no beauty in my life.
14. There is nothing sacred for me.
15. I have no identity.
16. I am faceless.
17. I am ugly.
18. I am trapped. The only way to get out is dying.

Abdominal Pain and Problems

Fears
- Fear of moving forward
- Fear of creativity
- Fear that they have already died inside
- Fear of flow
- Fear that they will be wrong
- Fear of rejection
- Fear of what might happen next
- Fear of being judged
- Fear of being wrong and missing out
- Fear of having happiness
- Fear of losing stuff

Teachings
- Feel safe when a mistake is made
- Happy
- Live without an unhealthy attachment to people
- Live without an unhealthy attachment to things
- Live without anxiety
- Live without needing things to feel good about yourself
- Live without needing things to feel important
- Live without worry
- Make good decisions
- Meet my needs without sacrificing relationships
- Put myself first
- Trust
- Trust my judgment
- Trust myself

Emotional States
- Cannot seem to get much going in life; feels like they're slogging through wet cement.
- There is no physical/ emotional/ mental/ creative energy.
- The connection to the flow of life has been lost.
- Out of sync with those around them – says the wrong things, makes the wrong decisions.
- Feels disheartened, anxious and worried that what they say and do is wrong.
- Always complaining; nothing is good enough, hard to satisfy, never happy with what people do for them.
- Lost the connection of Source as a child; does not hold a concept of a divine plan – experienced tragedies and continual negative events as a child.
- Feminine: Heartache – bound to earth cannot seem to get going – the energy just isn't there, no desire, no creativity. Lost the connection to the flow of life and cannot connect. Out of sync with those around them – says the wrong thing, makes the wrong decisions – disheartened and

worried about what they say and do may be wrong.
- Masculine: Bellyaching – always complaining – nothing is good enough. Negative, hard to satisfy – never happy with what people do for them. Lost connection to source as a child, does not hold a concept of the divine plan. Tragedies and continual negative events created source of negativity.
- Masculine: Head is in gut, head is always worried about what may happen and of course those things are always bad, closing down to the good things in life does not live in the present. So misses life.

Cross Indexing: Irritable Bowel Syndrome, Constipation, Diarrhea, Leaky Gut Syndrome, Ulcerative Colitis, and Diverticulitis

Repeating Patterns: Doesn't feel safe when a mistake is made, an unhealthy attachment to people or things, anxious, need things to feel good about themselves or important, worry, fails to make good decisions, does not put themselves first, sacrifices a relationship to get their needs met, lack of trust.

Created Patterns
1. _____ will leave me.
2. Bad things happen to good people.
3. God lets bad things happen to people.
4. I always do the wrong thing.
5. I always say the wrong thing.
6. I am afraid of losing _____.
7. I am always wrong.
8. I am anxious about _____.
9. I am depressed.
10. I am jealous of _____.
11. I am responsible for being understanding when _____.
12. I am responsible for helping when _____.
13. I am responsible for supporting _____ when _____.
14. I am unhappy.
15. I can't leave _____ any time I want.
16. I can't make a mistake and be safe.
17. I can't make good decisions.
18. I don't believe in god.
19. I don't trust _____.
20. I don't trust god.
21. I don't trust life.
22. I don't trust my judgment.
23. I don't trust myself.
24. I must sacrifice myself for others.
25. I need _____ (name of person and why).
26. I never seem to be able to make others happy.
27. I'm not free to do as I want.
28. If I worry about 'stuff' bad things won't happen.
29. It's always my fault.
30. Nothing is good enough.
31. Others come first.
32. Things are taken from me.
33. Who do you feel possessive about?

*Look at themes of fun, boundaries, trust, self-esteem, self-knowledge, self-love, self respect, self-pity, happiness, God, jealousy, judgment, decisions, responsibility, unmet needs, disconnection

Abdominal Sacrocolpopexy

Fears
- Fear of having to settle
- Fear of being second best
- Fear of having to follow others
- Fear of dreaming
- Fear of never living their dream
- Fear of unworthiness
- Fear of joy
- Fear of love
- Fear of having desires

Emotional States
- Knowing that they can't have everything so they adjust their desires and don't allow themselves disappointment by not stretching, stretching their vision of who they could be and what they will be if they were to stretch and move. They shut down the dreams very early. They just didn't allow themselves to think them; the dreams of what they can be. Sacrificed true nature to fit the expectations of those that had no dreams and could not dream a new way into being. Joy was expunged and creation died. Feels dead inside.

Cross Indexing: Pelvic Organ Collapse/ Prolapse, Wounded Creative Core

Created Patterns
1. I'm not good enough.
2. Everything I try falls apart.
3. The bottom has fallen out of my life.
4. I do not allow joy.
5. My dreams have died.
6. I am worthless.
7. I'm not allowed the good stuff.
8. Everything in my life is held together with string and paper clips.
9. I'm not creative.
10. Life is a bitch and then you die.
11. Everyone else gets what they want, why not me?
12. It's hopeless.
13. True love will never happen to me.
14. Love will only hurt you.

Abortion Complications

Fears
- Fear of being responsible for another life
- Fear of creative expression
- Fear of betrayal
- Fear of being discovered
- Fear of something being wrong
- Fear of not wanting to live
- Fear of guilt

Emotional States
- There is a wounding from abortion. The creative process has been cut short. There is an association of not having the burden of children to feed. Feels they cannot feed the children. Feels they cannot take care of them. Epigenetic/Ancestral wound. The wound of the mother. A deep heart pain.

Created Patterns
1. I can't move forward.
2. I am frozen in time.
3. Life isn't working for me.
4. I am hopeless.
5. Nothing is right.
6. Everything is out of balance.
7. All hope is lost.
8. I'm not good enough.
9. I am anonymous.
10. If I die no one will ever know I existed.
11. Too much, everything is too much.
12. I am overwhelmed.
13. I am lost.
14. I am tortured by just living.
15. Nothing ever works for me.
16. Everything and everyone is out to hurt me.
17. Nothing brings me happiness, only pain.
18. I am locked in a battle of life or death.
19. I always lose.

Abscess

Fears
- Fear of the past
- Fear that little can be done about who they are and where they come from
- Fear of being hurt
- Fear of the unknown
- Fear of being out of control
- Fear of letting go of what's toxic
- Fear of forgiveness
- Fear of flow or life
- Fear of happiness
- Fear of responsibility/ ownership
- Fear of injustice

Teachings
- Allow change in your life
- Forgive
- Forgive those that hurt me
- Hope
- Inner peace
- Letting go of past hurts
- Live without disappointment
- Live without holding a grudge
- Live without needing revenge
- Live without resentments
- Love yourself
- Make changes easily
- Release anger
- Rely on self for inner happiness
- Respect yourself
- Take responsibility for who you are
- Take responsibility for your actions
- Take responsibility for your life
- Trust
- Unconditional love

Emotional States
- Festering of past hurts and life disappointments.
- Feels life has misled them.
- Resented having to change when events required a change, the change created a challenge to their concept of self and self-worth that they could not reconcile.
- The loss led to resentments and in some cases the desire for revenge.
- The underlying resentment has caused people to leave their life. This has led to a feeling that they have been 'done wrong'. They have difficulty hanging onto friendships and a love relationship.
- Stuck in the resentment (holds onto old stuff) and won't move forward with their life.
- Replaces creativity with feelings of resentment.

Cross Indexing: Infections, Liver Problems, Gallstones, Gallbladder Problems, Skin Problems, Wounded Creative Core

Repeating Patterns: doesn't allow change in their life, doesn't forgive to stay safe, a feeling of hopeless, doesn't let go past hurts, lives with disappointment, lives holding a grudge, lives with a need for revenge, lives with resentments, does not love themselves, does not respect themselves, does not take responsibility for their actions, their life or their actions, does not understand or feel unconditional love.

Created Patterns
1. _____ hurt me.
2. Change isn't good, it doesn't get me anywhere.
3. He / She took my life from me.

4. I am a disappointment.
5. I am angry at _____.
6. I can never get back what I have lost.
7. I could have been _____.
8. I don't know how to let go of _____.
9. I hate _____.
10. I have no hope left.
11. I resent _____.
12. I want revenge against _____.
13. I'm not responsible for what happened; it's his / her fault.
14. I'm not wanted.
15. Life has disappointed me.
16. Life isn't fair.
17. Life ripped me off.
18. I don't love myself.
19. No one loves me.
20. People leave me.
21. There's no justice in the world.
22. When things change I always lose.

*Look at themes of self-respect, self worth, selfishness, resentment, revenge, anger, compassion, control, letting go, abandonment, unmet needs for love, rejection

Abused Child

Fears
- Fear of being hurt
- Fear that nothing will ever be better
- Fear of feeling hopeless
- Fear of being loved
- Fear of judgment
- Fear of defending yourself
- Fear of feelings
- Fear of touching
- Fear of being found

Emotional States
- Fear of being touched and fear of being untouchable. Fear of being scrutinized or judged gives rise to anger that happens in places that are not good – road rage can happen. Feelings of hopeless, worthless, discounted, judged, useless, invalidated, overpowered, unseen, giving up, and fighting. Where they can fight they become the bully.
- The benefit of abuse is that they get to stay in the family. If they try to stand up for who they are and be within their boundaries the judgment becomes more severe. They have no right to boundaries. They have no right to be angry. If they get angry they are isolated and rejected there is an energetic withdrawal of connection (which may be their concept of love).
- Association of love equaling backing down or hiding.

- Association of compromise equaling backing down or giving up.

**For additional information use the ACOA information (Adult children of alcoholics)

Cross Indexing: Physical Abuse, ACOA, PTSD

Created Patterns
1. Touching = pain
2. I'm not worthy of being loved.
3. I am constantly judged.
4. I am always being criticized.
5. I must be abused to be wanted.
6. I can't be angry.
7. I am hopeless.
8. I am worthless.
9. I am powerless.
10. I must always give in.
11. I must give up to be loved.
12. I must hide to be safe.
13. When I hide I can be me.
14. To be loved I must be hit.
15. Boundaries will get me hurt.
16. I am humiliation.
17. I am shame.

Accidents

Fears
- Fear of being present
- Fear of the heartlessness of others
- Fear of being unworthy
- Fear of suffering
- Fear of pain
- Fear of a purpose
- Fear of their inner self being seen
- Fear of their body

Teachings
- Be good enough
- Be in the now
- Be in your body and be safe
- Be present
- Be safe with new ideas
- Be wanted without the drama
- Creator definition and perspective of life purpose
- Creator's definition of my life purpose
- Forgive self
- God's Unconditional Love
- Joy
- Live in the now
- Live without punishment
- Be wanted without suffering

EMOTIONAL PATTERNS

- Be loved without suffering
- Love yourself without suffering
- Live without the drama
- Love yourself unconditionally
- Relax
- Speak your truth and be safe
- Trust
- Understand the perspectives of others

Emotional States
- Wanting something bad to happen.
- Wronged by another but won't yield. Too much anxiety. Holds self in contempt. Projection of awareness into the past or future…not in the now.
- Wrong direction in life. Narrow focus on options and other paths. Hardness with self.
- Sense of life purpose is forgotten.
- Feeling helpless in the face of challenges – a shut down occurs. Doesn't know what to do with the body or how to react emotionally.

Cross Indexing: Look at the body part injured in an accident for more information.

Repeating Patterns: not good enough, cannot be in the present, not safe in their body, not safe with new ideas, wanted without the drama, a sense of no life purpose, lack of self forgiveness, feels punished, must suffer to be wanted, can't relax, doesn't trust, does not understand the perspective of others.

Created Patterns
1. I am angry at _____.
2. I am bad.
3. I am disconnected from god.
4. I'm not good enough for _____.
5. I am no good.
6. I am tense about _____.
7. I am worried about _____.
8. I can take care of myself.
9. I can't speak my truth and be safe.
10. I can't defend myself.
11. I don't have a real purpose.
12. I don't love myself.
13. I don't trust _____.
14. I must hurt myself.
15. I must punish myself.
16. I need to hurt physically to be loved.
17. I need to hurt physically to love myself.
18. I need to prove others wrong.
19. I need to punish myself for _____.
20. I want something bad to happen.
21. I want to die.
22. I'm not good enough.
23. I'm not worthy.

24. It is safe to stand up for myself.
25. People always tell me what to do.
26. What is causing the stress?
27. When I hurt I get attention.
28. I must suffer to be good enough.
29. I must suffer to be wanted.

*Look at themes of worry, worthiness, unconditional love, understanding, true self, God, suicidal, self worth, self respect, loving myself, self-esteem, accidents, life purpose, conflict, anger, soul purpose, anxiety, fight or flight, confidence, creativity, sabotage, disconnection, feelings, stress

Aches

Fears
- Fear of being OK
- Fear that no one out there that cares
- Fear of responsibility
- Fear of inner self
- Fear of being well
- Fear of loving self
- Fear of injustice
- Fear of being forgotten
- Fear of not being touched

Teachings
- Be cherished
- Be honored
- Be in the flow of life
- Be loved
- Be respected
- Be safe to feel
- Creator's definition and perspective of past hurts, events and actions of others
- Creator's definition and perspective of responsibility
- Creator's definition of honesty
- Express myself without blame
- Forgiveness
- Get your needs met without pain
- God's Unconditional Love
- Joy
- Let go of past hurts
- Live without anger
- Live without bitterness
- Live without blame
- Live without feeling that everything you do is wrong
- Live without needing to control those around me
- Live without pain
- Live without pain to get attention
- Live without resentment
- Living in the now
- Love myself
- Nurture myself
- Successful

Emotional States
- There's a payback for illness.
- Used as an escape from responsibility.
- Feels one thing and says another.
- Love-hate relationship with self.
- Underlying hostility/ anger

Repeating Patterns: feeling unwanted, feeling dishonored, not in the flow of life, unloved, disrespected, feels blamed when they express their point of view, can't forgive, needs are only met with pain, feels unloved, can't let go of past hurts, must live with anger, must live with bitterness, must live with blame, feels like everything they do is wrong, lives with constant pain, needs pain to get attention, lives with resentment, cannot be present, does not nurture themselves, feels unsuccessful.

Cross Indexing: Chronic Illness, Accidents, long term illness

Created Patterns
1. Every time I try I fail.
2. Honesty will get you hurt.
3. I 'm not loved.
4. I am all alone.
5. I am angry at _____.
6. I am bitter towards _____.
7. I am disconnected from _____ (The person that loves them).
8. I am disconnected from god.
9. I am invisible until I hurt.
10. I am only loved when I hurt.
11. I am sad about _____.
12. I can't make _____ happen.
13. I don't have to _____ when I hurt.
14. I force people to pay attention to me by hurting.
15. I get blamed when things go wrong.
16. I hate myself.
17. I love myself.
18. I resent _____.
19. If you are responsible you are blamed when things go wrong.
20. Life is easier when I hurt.
21. Love is pain.
22. Nobody loves me.
23. People care for me when I hurt.
24. People pay attention to me when I hurt.
25. The only time I am loved is when I hurt.
26. You can't be honest with people.
27. You don't ever let people know how you truly feel.

*Look at themes of worry, worthiness, unconditional love, understanding, true self, God, suicidal, self worth, self respect, loving myself, self-esteem, accidents, integrity, success, car accidents, drama, unmet needs (love, recognition, attention, being important), truth, abandonment, control, letting go, creativity, feelings, sabotage

Achilles Tendonosis-left

Fears
- Fear of being wrong
- Fear that when people break they are left behind
- Fear of being out of control
- Fear of the unknown
- Fear of their dreams
- Fear of letting go

Emotional States
- Strong inclination to be right, wants to hold the lead in all things around them. They step forward with an intention of bringing out the protest so that they can see the strengths and weaknesses of the people around them. It's a way of staying safe.
- They drive other people nuts with their ideas of how to do things. They know how to do things they don't really know how to do. Stepping into the unknown – really the unknowing—fuels their false sense of security because if they know it all then they are seen as being needed.
- Wrong direction. Deep down they question their direction and why they have made the choices they have made. They very rarely allow themselves to see that part of themselves because if they do they will crumble. At least they fear that.
- Feels as if all their efforts to move forward are held back by circumstances and that they are barely able to tread water. Wants to do lots of things. Has lots of hopes and dreams but can't make progress toward them.

Cross indexing: tendons, ligaments, inflammation, left sided negative tendencies

Repeating Patterns: a need to be right, plays people, lack of flexibility, plays the 'know it all', lots of false starts.

Created Patterns
1. I must get my way.
2. People depend on me.
3. I'm always right.
4. I'm afraid I will be found to be wrong.
5. I don't change my mind.
6. I never get anywhere.
7. I'm not good enough.
8. I must stand my ground.
9. People see me as a leader.
10. I must be seen a right.
11. Something always stops me.

Achilles Tendonosis-right

Fears
- Fear of being connected
- Fear that they will never be allowed in the circle/ group/ community/ etc.
- Fear of peace
- Fear of calm
- Fear of going forward
- Fear of being trapped
- Fear of being present
- Fear of feeling
- Fear of letting go of an identity
- Fear of being seen
- Fear of letting go of the chaos-drama

Emotional States
- Jumps into chaos without a thought to the impact on their own peace. The ensuing drama creates a sense of numbness and disconnection. They then keep going in that same chaotic drama filled direction but numb out to survive and gets ungrounded.
- Long-term plans have been stopped. Feels resentment about the compromise but doesn't know how to express that without harming relationships. So there's a sense of playing the silent martyr.
- A sense of being thwarted and being stuck in wet cement. Seems to be going along with the flow but the flow feels like a trap. Wants to run but can't. Plays passive aggressive.
- Staying under the radar, hold back, hold down.

Cross indexing: tendons, ligaments, inflammation, right sided negative tendencies

Repeating Patterns: Keep the drama going, one drama quits and another begins, builds resentment at not getting their way, stuck, can't move forward.

Created Patterns
1. I must not be seen.
2. If I am seen I freeze.
3. I can't move forward.
4. I can't change.
5. Change is dangerous.
6. Change is hard.
7. I can't move.
8. I am stuck.
9. I am a martyr.
10. I am the victim.
11. I feel safe in chaos.
12. I feel safe within the drama.
13. I can hide in chaos.
14. I must stay down.
15. I let others hold me down.

16. I can't see a future.
17. Compromise = me losing

Acne

Fears

- Fear of finding peace within
- Fear that it's hopeless
- Fear of feeling unsupported
- Fear of love
- Fear of being seen
- Fear of feelings
- Fear of being bullied
- Fear of being ridiculed
- Fear of having their core self revealed
- Fear of standing up
- Fear of letting go
- Fear of being unworthy

Teachings

- Be good enough
- Be in the flow of life
- Be in the now
- Be safe expressing your feelings
- Be safe standing up
- Be seen and be safe
- Creator's definition of courage
- Creator's definition of justice
- Deserve
- Express feelings safely
- Face your problems
- Forgive
- Forgive yourself
- Joy
- Letting go of anger
- Live life with ease and grace
- Live without guilt
- Live without holding onto anger
- Live without needing to hide
- Live without shame
- Love myself
- Love myself unconditionally
- See your inner beauty
- Stand up for your self
- Truth

Emotional States

- Failure to thrive internally. Constantly looking for support and recognition. Concepts of love and nurturing have been poisoned. Looking outward for what they can get in terms of support and recognition.
- Unwilling to be seen by others. Courage is lacking. Visibility is painful. Their world feels hollow. Not living as an authentic self. Fear of being seen.
- Challenged by life. Life is a struggle. Being seen just makes it harder. Feels ridiculed, overwhelming shame. Feels judged and not seen for who they truly are.
- They have felt the stinging of an injustice. Anger turned inward…kept in. Could not protest or affect the injustice.
- Wishing they were someone else. Saw others getting their needs met and figured if they were someone else they would get their needs met.
- Cannot face up to the issues
- Must keep the past alive and does not move past old hurts. (Look at colon issues also)

Cross Indexing: Skin problems, head/face problems, infection, pimples

Repeated Patterns: not good enough, not in the flow of life, not present, doesn't feel safe expressing feelings, doesn't feel safe standing up, does not feel safe being seen, does not understand courage or justice, feels like they don't deserve, doesn't face their problems, doesn't forgive, doesn't feel joy, can't let go of anger, doesn't live life with grace and ease, feels guilt, holds onto anger, needs to hide, feels shame, does not love themselves, does not see their inner beauty, does not live in truth.

Created Patterns

1. I am angry at myself.
2. I am guilty of _____.
3. I am shamed by _____.
4. I am stupid and no good.
5. I can't accept who I am.
6. I can't face up to _____ (the issues).
7. I can't forgive myself.
8. I can't see the truth and be safe.
9. I can't stop people from blaming me.
10. I can't tell people how I feel.
11. I don't deserve.
12. I don't deserve to be treated like this.
13. I don't like myself.
14. I don't love myself.
15. I feel sorry for myself.
16. I hate myself.
17. I have been singled out for abuse/ humiliation/ shame/ridicule.
18. I must hide from others.
19. I never get what I want.
20. I want to die.
21. I wish I were someone else.
22. I'm not good enough.
23. I'm not loved.
24. I'm not respected.
25. I'm unworthy.
26. If I ignore a problem it will go away.
27. If I tell how I feel I will be ridiculed/ shamed/humiliated.
28. If I were someone else I would be happy.
29. Innocent people get blamed for the mistakes of others.
30. It's dangerous to stand up for yourself.
31. It's just not fair that this happened to me (what happened?).
32. Life is a struggle.
33. Life is hard.
34. My heart is broken.
35. No one likes me.
36. Nobody loves me.
37. People are mean to me.
38. The truth will hurt me.
39. Truth is whatever someone makes it.

EMOTIONAL PATTERNS

40. What is being denied?

*Look at themes of self-esteem, self worth, loving myself, unconditional love, justice, leadership, denial, anger, anxiety, approval, authenticity, beauty, body, boundaries, confrontation, flow, insecurity, joy, physical appearance, shame, needs (recognition, love, support, kindness, caring), broken heart, worthiness, truth, freedom, feelings, disconnection, conflict, awareness, appearance, stress

ACOA-Adult Children of Alcoholics

Fears
- Fear that they will never be free to have a life without hurt/ stress
- Fear that they will never have control of their destiny
- Fear of life
- Fear of being hurt
- Fear of the crazy
- Fear of parents
- Fear of fear
- Fear of being like their parents
- Fear of acting
- Fear of making choices
- Fear of connecting
- Fear of leaving
- Fear of letting go
- Fear of being like others
- Fear of loving themselves
- Fear of change
- Fear of intimacy
- Fear of fun and joy
- Fear of the truth
- Fear of knowing

Teachings
- Balance
- Be confident when making a decision
- Be connected to myself
- Be heard breathing and be safe
- Be myself
- Be safe when a project is finished
- Be visible and safe
- Being worthy
- Breathe and be safe
- Caring to myself
- Change with ease and grace
- Complete
- Cooperate
- Creator's definition and perspective of love
- Creator's definition and perspective of perfect
- Cry and be safe
- Deserve
- Express anger safely
- Express emotions safely
- Feel safe while being still
- Feel safe with others
- Feel safe with your emotions
- Fun
- Getting what you want
- Happiness
- Inner peace
- Joy
- Kind to myself
- Know what I am truly feeling
- Live being good enough
- Live without being a martyr
- Live without being a victim
- Live without being embarrassed by your family

- Live without constant crisis
- Live without constantly being on high-alert
- Live without feeling like a loser
- Live without having to keep the secrets
- Live without humiliation
- Live without shame
- Love myself
- Make a promise and keep it
- Make changes in my life and be safe
- Make mistakes and be safe
- Responsible
- Safe
- Say no
- Solve problems
- Spontaneous
- Structure
- Tell the truth
- Think for myself
- To be honest
- To be honest and be safe
- To finish a project
- To know truth when you hear it
- Trust
- Trust my inner voice
- Trust myself
- When it is appropriate to tell the truth

Emotional States

- Adult children of alcoholics guess at normal (functional) behavior.
- Adult children of alcoholics have difficulty following a project through from beginning to end.
- Adult children of alcoholics lie when it would be just as easy to tell the truth.
- Adult children of alcoholics judge themselves without mercy.
- Adult children of alcoholics have difficulty having fun.
- Adult children of alcoholics take themselves very seriously.
- Adult children of alcoholics have difficulty with intimate relationships.
- Adult children of alcoholics overreact to changes over which they have no control.
- Adult children of alcoholics constantly seek approval and affirmation.
- Adult children of alcoholics usually feel that they are different from other people.
- Adult children of alcoholics are super responsible or super irresponsible.
- Adult children of alcoholics are extremely loyal.
- Adult children of alcoholics are impulsive. They tend to lock themselves into a course of action without giving serious consideration to alternative behaviors or possible consequences. This impulsiveness leads to confusion.
- Adult Children of Alcoholics may be passive in the face of life's challenges.

Cross Indexing: Post Traumatic Stress Disorder, Addictions, Sexual Abuse, Thymus Problems, Temple pain/pressure, Adrenal Fatigue, Thyroid problems, Pancreas Problems, Liver Problems

Repeated Patterns: out of balance, lack of confidence, unconnected to self, feels unsafe being heard breathing, cannot be themselves, when a project is complete they feel unsafe, cannot be themselves, cannot feel safe when seen, feels unworthy, cannot breathe and be safe, cannot nurture self, change is difficult, does not know how to feel complete with something, does not know how to cooperate, cannot cry and feel safe, feels undeserving, cannot express anger safely, cannot express emotions safely, feels unsafe while being still, feels unsafe with others, does not know how to have fun and avoids it, does not get what they want and does not know how to get what they want, does not choose happiness, does not have inner peace, does not know joy, is not kind to themselves, does not know what they are feeling, plays the victim, plays the martyr, constantly embarrassed by family, lives in constant crisis, lives constantly on high-alert, feels like a loser, constantly having to keep the secrets, feels humiliation, lives in shame, does not love themselves, cannot make a mistake and feel safe, does not know how to feel safe, does not know how to say no, does not know how to tell the truth, does not know what truth is, does not trust their inner voice, does not trust.

Created Patterns

1. I can't stand still and be safe.
2. I am never safe.
3. I must always be doing something.
4. The only time I am safe is when I am alone.
5. I don't know what it is to feel emotions.
6. When people are angry I will be hurt.
7. I can't feel emotions and be safe.
8. I fear my anger.
9. I can't control myself when angry.
10. I can't express emotions and be safe.
11. I can't cry and be safe.
12. It is dangerous to feel.
13. I must be silent and strong.
14. I must always have a smile on my face.
15. I'm not in charge of my thoughts and feelings.
16. I am invisible.
17. I am helpless.
18. I must stay busy so I don't feel.
19. I must be perfect to be safe.
20. I must be perfect to be loved.
21. I don't know what it feels like to have fun.
22. I am angry at the world (The anger may be at specific individuals).
23. I don't know what it feels like to love myself.
24. I don't know what it feels like to be kind to myself.
25. I am a procrastinator.
26. I can't finish anything.
27. Promises are lies.
28. I don't know how to solve problems.
29. I don't know how to finish a project.
30. I don't know what it feels like to solve problems.
31. I don't know how to cooperate with people.
32. I can't focus on one thing at a time.
33. I don't know what structure feels like.

34. I don't have boundaries around my time.
35. When I don't finish things I am not safe.
36. I am a loser.
37. I am a goof off.
38. I am no good for nothing.
39. I can't survive in unfamiliar circumstances.
40. I must say what people want me to say to be safe.
41. I must do what people want me to do to be safe.
42. I must do what my parent says to survive.
43. I hate my parent (You may not be ready to forgive.
44. I don't know what truth feels like.
45. I don't know what honesty feels like.
46. I don't understand what it is to tell the truth.
47. I don't understand what it feels like to be honest.
48. I don't know what truth is.
49. I don't know what honesty is.
50. I don't know when to tell the truth.
51. I don't know when to be honest.
52. I don't know what it feels like to be safe.
53. I will die if I am honest.
54. I don't know what it is to be honest.
55. I don't know what it is to be honest with my feelings.
56. If I am honest people won't show their true feelings.
57. I won't be loved if I am honest.
58. I can't be honest and be safe.
59. I'm not safe dealing with the unfamiliar.
60. I can't say no when someone say's 'I love you'.
61. I'm not responsible.
62. I will do anything to be loved.
63. I can't speak my truth and be safe.
64. I can't speak honestly and be safe.
65. I won't be loved if I speak my truth.
66. I'm not good enough.
67. If you can't do it perfectly don't do it at all.
68. I must be perfect.
69. I caused my parent to be an alcoholic.
70. If I am not perfect then I must be punished.
71. If I am not perfect I am guilty.
72. I don't believe in myself.
73. I can't accept compliments.
74. I can't receive nice things from others.
75. I can't make mistakes and be safe.
76. I can't do anything right.
77. I am to blame for everything.
78. No matter how hard I try I will never win.
79. I am a mistake.
80. I must judge myself.
81. I must judge everything I do.
82. I am at fault for everything.

83. I am always wrong.
84. I don't know what it feels like to have fun.
85. I don't know how to have fun.
86. I don't know how to be spontaneous.
87. I can't have fun and be safe.
88. I don't know how to play.
89. It isn't safe to be spontaneous.
90. I can't ever show I am happy.
91. I am my job.
92. I can't separate myself from my job.
93. Having fun is dangerous.
94. I must always be on guard.
95. To have fun is to be vulnerable.
96. I don't know what it feels like to let down my guard.
97. It is dangerous to let down my guard.
98. I am embarrassed by my family.
99. I must keep outsiders away so that they will not know the truth.
100. I don't know what it feels like to have an appropriate healthy relationship with others.
101. Love is pain.
102. I must protect others from the truth.
103. I am invisible.
104. I'm not lovable.
105. I don't know who to trust.
106. I don't know how to trust.
107. I am always in danger.
108. I am powerless.
109. I must give away my power to be loved.
110. I don't love me.
111. I'm not worthy.
112. I hate/was betrayed/am angry at mother/ father/ creator.
113. The creator/ Father/ Mother abandoned me.
114. I have no boundaries around my personal space.
115. I don't know what it feels like to have boundaries around my personal space.
116. People who love me will hurt me.
117. All People leave me.
118. I will do anything to keep a relationship.
119. I constantly need approval to be loved.
120. I take care of others to be loved.
121. I can't rely on other people.
122. I must do everything myself to be safe.
123. If I don't control everything bad things will happen.
124. Controlling everything keeps me safe.
125. Nothing I do is ever enough.
126. I feel sorry for myself.
127. Things would be better if I were not here.
128. I must be perfect to be loved.
129. I am always in the way.
130. I must be good to be love.
131. I must earn my right to be loved.

EMOTIONAL PATTERNS

132. I must always say yes.
133. I am worthless.
134. I must work harder than everyone else around me.
135. I must do things to be special.
136. I must be special to be loved.
137. I don't belong.
138. I am alone.
139. No one understands me.
140. I must give away myself to be loved.
141. I must give things to people to be loved.
142. I am not accepted for who I am.
143. It's a mistake I was born.
144. I will never fit in.
145. I am guilty for everything.
146. I live in a fantasy world to survive.
147. I am afraid of people.
148. I am responsible for the world.
149. I carry the burden of _____ (family member).
150. I must take care of _____ (family member).
151. If I cause trouble someone will love me.
152. I can't do things right.
153. I mess up to get attention.
154. I must do more and more to be loved.
155. I do more than everyone else so I will be loved.
156. I don't know how to say no.
157. I am insecure.
158. I am always in trouble.
159. I must hide my feelings.
160. Feelings are dangerous.
161. I must not ask.
162. I must not tell.
163. I must not feel.
164. I am ashamed.
165. No one must ever know.
166. I must hide my shame.
167. I must protect the family secrets at all costs.
168. The family is sacred.
169. I must protect my mother from the outside world.
170. I must protect my father from the outside world.
171. I must lie to cover up what is going on at home.
172. It is OK to treat me poorly.
173. Change is hard.
174. I can't make changes easily.
175. It is OK to live in constant crisis.
176. I can't have what I want when I want it.
177. I don't understand the possible consequences of my behavior.
178. I can't plan for the things I want in life.
179. I'll never have what I want.
180. I can only see in the moment.

181. I can't be patient with others.
182. I'm not patient with myself.
183. I discourage easily.
184. It's hopeless.
185. I can't change things.
186. It's no use.
187. Things will never be better.
188. It's dangerous to try and change things.
189. _____ humiliated me.
190. _____ hurt me.
191. Being happy is selfish.
192. Change is dangerous.
193. Having a life purpose isn't safe.
194. I am a disappointment.
195. I am always a disappointment.
196. I am ashamed of myself.
197. I am disappointed.
198. I am disconnected from myself.
199. I am going to die.
200. I am humiliated.
201. I am punished for being happy.
202. I am shamed.
203. I can't be myself.
204. I don't know me.
205. I don't know what my authentic self is.
206. I don't know what my life is.
207. I don't realize my own success.
208. I have a broken heart.
209. I must do for others before I do for myself.
210. I must set high standards.
211. I will die if things change.
212. I will make a big mistake if I trust myself.
213. I'm not believed.
214. I'm not confident in myself.
215. I'm not proud of my own success.
216. If I listen to my inner voice I will be humiliated.
217. If I listen to my inner voice I will be shamed.
218. If I listen to my inner voice I will lose everything.
219. If I listen to my inner voice they will hurt me.
220. If I make a mistake I end up in jail.
221. If I make a mistake I will be humiliated.
222. If I make a mistake I will be shamed.
223. If I make a mistake I will end up broke.
224. If I make a mistake I will end up crazy.
225. If I make a mistake they will lock me up.
226. If I trust my inner voice I will die.
227. If I were myself I would be confused.
228. If no one believes me I will be punished/ beaten.
229. It's not safe to live my life.

230. Living my life purpose is selfish.
231. My feelings are wrong.
232. People that love me humiliate me
233. When I am happy I am guilty.
234. When I am happy I'm not wanted / loved.
235. If I cry I will be hurt.
236. Change is dangerous.
237. You must not look at things too closely.
238. It is dangerous to 'see'.
239. I will be hurt if I see.
240. Crying is a waste of time.
241. Crying is for babies.
242. I can only survive if I don't see.
243. I can't let them/him/her know I saw.
244. I must not see to hide the truth.
245. The eyes are the windows of the soul.

*Look at themes of workaholics, abandonment, abuse, acceptance, acknowledgment, anger, anxiety, approval, attention, authenticity, beingness, boundaries, burnout, calm, childhood, communication, confidence, control, denial, disassociation, failure, finishing things, freedom, grief, happiness, harmony, home, honesty, identity, intimacy, inner child, innocence, Joy, loving yourself, overwhelm, peace, punishment, relationships, self-esteem, self-knowledge, self-love, self-respect, self-worth, sexual abuse, shame, speaking up, stability, trust, victimhood, addiction, unmet needs (love, affection, attention, recognition, approval, belonging, being a child), broken heart, denial, disconnection, feelings, joy, physical abuse, power, rejection, sexual abuse, truth, stress

Acoustic Neuroma – Left Side

Fears
- Fear of mis-hearing what is said
- Fear that there is no way to get out of a bad situation
- Fear of letting go
- Fear of taking responsibility
- Fear of being forced to listen
- Fear of being unheard and judged for it
- Fear that if they are present to everybody they will be overwhelmed and their being overrun

Emotional States
- Hard loss that resulted from a miscommunication. Feelings were so raw that nobody turned back the clock or looked at the communication and took ownership. The heart was hurt and held onto the hurt, would not listen to the explanation or cause.
- Anger at being left. In reality they left. Ran away from some hard truths that they then blamed on others.
- Pressure to listen to those that won't listen themselves. Feels like they have to keep taking in other peoples words and no one listens to theirs.

Cross Indexing: growths, neural disorders, ear disorders

Repeating Patterns: Miscommunication, feels forced against their will, doesn't take responsibility directs it to others, wants to blame others, walks away from difficulties, powerlessness, worthlessness, yields to one in their insistence that they are right. Their way is always correct.

Created Patterns
1. I am not listened to.
2. I am forced to listen to the dribble of others.
3. My words are meaningless.
4. No one listens to me.
5. I am left out.
6. I get left behind.
7. I must run away when things get intense.
8. I miss what people are saying.
9. People judge me.
10. I am criticized for being myself.

Acoustic Neuroma – Right Side

Fears
- Fear of going below the surface of their being
- Fear that no one will listen to their "silliness" (deemed that by others)
- Fear of living
- Fear of connecting
- Fear of self-honesty
- Fear of responsibility
- Fear of being blamed
- Fear of being found wrong
- Fear of failing

Emotional States
- Shallowness of beliefs. No real depth to their personality or sense of being. They skim the surface of life with little understanding or knowing their sense of purpose as a human. They don't hear the call to a purpose or the call to meaning. They never eat the apple they just carry it around until it rots. They just sit in a situation of their life until it goes sour and then they "get" a new situation.
- They march to the beat of a drum that is broken. A broken drum creates a sound that is muffled and dull. It does not create a vibration that stirs the cells. Their gait through life does not connect them to others. They make a lot of noise but none of it creates bonds of connections with others.
- Horse laughter. They have a propensity toward loud ostentatious laughter. This is not nervous laughter. It is laughter that alienates others. It pushes people away and it is never triggered by a comical or gleeful situation. The laughter creates a boundary of sound that keeps them alone and safe. The sounds they make in life are dis-resonate.

- Blindsided. They feel blindsided by life. They never see that the consequences of their actions will create a reaction. When the reaction happens they act as if they have been blindsided. They do not follow the energy of their actions. They do not feel the responsibility of their actions. They then think they are under attack and people are sabotaging them. People are only responding to their actions.
- Failure to launch their life. They get in the way of their own life. They create obstacles that prevent them from a full expression of their talents. They don't get out of the way of their own obstacles and they slam head-on into their creation. For example, They overspend, then they must work to pay their debts. Due to the overspending, they never have the energy or money to develop those talents that create life energy.
- Creates a fear in others that they will be judged and that they will be wrong in their search for truth. Keeps searching for the ultimate truth. Wants no one to find fault with their truth. Fears being judged themselves.

Cross index: deafness, growths

Repeating Patterns: Self-sabotage, wounded creative core, doesn't see the results of their actions.

Created Patterns
1. I am judged by others.
2. I must defend my position at all costs.
3. No matter what I do I always fail.
4. I am never good enough.
5. What I do is never enough.
6. Bad stuff happens to me.
7. I'm not responsible.
8. I am under attack.
9. I am being sabotaged.
10. I am safe when I am alone.
11. No one likes me.
12. I don't fit in.
13. I don't belong.

Addiction – Alcohol

Fears
- Fear of dying
- Fear of their dark side
- Fear of feeling
- Fear of pain
- Fear of feeling trapped
- Fear of being not good enough
- Fear of self
- Fear of making the wrong choices
- Fear of having lost themselves
- Fear of confronting and healing their inner truth

- Fear of their senses
- Fear of letting go
- Fear of judgment
- Fear of feeling powerless in the presence of alcohol
- Fear of feeling powerless

Emotional States
- They feel as if they cannot survive. The environment is oppressive. It is without options and there is a deep sense of being unable to escape. A feeling of being trapped.
- That trapped feeling and a need to escape can come from constant scrutiny and judgment of their actions. The person feels the pain of worthlessness and being no good. They continue to bring the experience to justify their behavior. They see the alcohol as a way to survive this pain.
- They have a sense of doubting everything they do. They have no sense of what they do will be the right thing. They are trapped in a morass of doubt.
- There is a dread in their life. Every aspect of their life is filled with stress and demands. There is no flow in their lives. Their life is boxes, many boxes. Each of the boxes has its rigid demands. They run between the boxes to meet the demands of each box. There is a deep pain of not living an authentic life.
- There is a deep pain in their life that has no bottom. No matter how many times they confront it they have no skills for resolving their pain.
- There is sensitivity to everything around them. They are hypersensitive – born this way (skin, hearing, taste, etc.)—it is overwhelming. The alcohol dulls the hypersensitivity and emotions.

    **Use of alcohol-based medications during early life in the treatment of illness accompanied by a high fever may have contributed to the addiction.

Cross Indexing: ACOA, Wounded Creative Core, Depression, Addictions, PTSD

Repeating Patterns: stuck, overwhelmed, relationships are judgmental and angry, false values, no connection with nature, no connection with self, no joy, no control, powerless, everything hurts.

Created Patterns
1. I am trapped.
2. I can't escape.
3. I must stay in line.
4. I must do what others say.
5. I have no voice that is listened to.
6. I am always discounted.
7. I am judged.
8. Alcohol kills the pain of an unbearable life.
9. I do nothing right.
10. I doubt myself.
11. I am never right.
12. I am in pain.
13. I dread getting up in the morning.
14. I want life to end.
15. If I drink myself to death at least it is an acceptable form of suicide.
16. Everything hurts.

17. Everything is too much.

Addiction – Chemical

Fears

- Fear of being punished for their creative _____
- Fear that they will never be what they want to be
- Fear of being alone
- Fear of responsibility
- Fear of feeling worthless
- Fear of everything
- Fear of doing
- Fear of life energy
- Fear of the creative
- Fear of connecting to the creative
- Fear of pain
- Fear of being connected
- Fear of happiness and joy
- Fear of the unknown
- Fear of stopping
- Fear of their intuitive senses
- Fear of power
- Fear of not surviving

Teachings

- Access your inner wisdom
- Balance
- Be myself
- Be safe when a project is finished
- Be visible and safe
- Being Worthy
- Caring to myself
- Change is dangerous
- Complete
- Complete
- Cooperation
- Creator's definition of love
- Creator's definition of perfect
- Cry and be safe
- Deserve
- Express anger safely
- Express emotions safely
- Feel safe while being still
- Feel safe with others
- Feel safe with your emotions
- Feel welcome around others
- Feel what I am truly feeling
- Fun
- Getting what you want
- God's Unconditional Love
- Happiness
- I will die if things change
- Inner peace
- Joy
- Kind to myself
- Live in the now
- Live without being a martyr
- Live without being a victim
- Live without being embarrassed by your family
- Live without constant crisis
- Live without constantly being on high-alert
- Live without needing an escape from pain
- Love myself
- Make a promise and keep it
- Make mistakes and be safe

- Responsible
- Safe
- Say no
- Solve problems
- Spontaneous
- Structure
- Tell the truth
- Think for myself
- To be honest
- To be honest and be safe
- To finish a project
- To know truth when you hear it
- Trust
- When it is appropriate to tell the truth
- Whole
- Worthy
- Live without drugs / alcohol
- Be drug free
- Be alcohol free
- Live without craving drugs
- Live without craving alcohol
- Be in my body without drugs
- Be in my body without alcohol

Emotional States

- The person is isolated, alone and disconnected from Source. When in the presence of others they do not feel a connection. Blames others for problems. Negative thoughts. Procrastination. All of life comes through a filter of insecurity. A sense of constantly having to struggle to survive.
- The creative is shut down. Punished in childhood for being a child. They are now trying to find that aspect of self in an environment devoid of life force. Emotion and feeling shut down.
- Overwhelmed by repeated experiences of life pain – and no skills to cope.
- Very intuitive, very sensitive. Keep people out by distracting them with a colorful façade. Their true nature is covered to protect from the psychic pain of exposure. This distraction is also used to keep them feeling the wound of psychic pain.
- Trouble being accepted by others. Cannot maintain social relationships. Social activity based on drugs and alcohol. Identity-based on drugs and alcohol.
- This person has closed themselves off from a connection to Source. They experience a sense of isolation and aloneness, as if they are in a shell, and have difficulty with feeling contact with those around them. Thought processes tend to justify and maintain the sense of aloneness. This person does not accept responsibility, tends to blame others, procrastinate, and dwell in negative thoughts and actions. This person will experience insecurity as the filter for their life. They are constantly in a state of tension (which is really fear). An increase in the tension can lead the person to feeling terrified and that they are not going to survive. They shut down their source of renewing life force by disconnecting from Source and being in a constant state of insecurity. This emotional state may have had its roots in a dysfunctional household where a chemical addiction was integral. The person may suffer from headaches, endocrine system and lower intestinal issues (constipation, hemorrhoids, rectal cancer, etc.) beyond the other physiological issues that can be attributed to the chemicals.

- This person has locked themselves into an aspect of self that keeps them from experiencing creative childlike innocence. As a child, their playful innocence was not allowed expression and their childlike creative energy was suppressed, maybe forcefully, by those in authority over the individual. They are now spending their time trying, within that same emotional setting, to find a way to express the locked away aspect of self. They search endlessly, going only in circles, for the opening out of the lifeless, barren existence and into the creative childlike aspect of self. They have confined themselves to a life that is cold, drained of life force and vacant of emotion and feeling.
- Seemingly out of nowhere an incident of life happens to this person. This event, to them, is huge. They do not possess the skills or strength to free them from the emotional grip of psychic pain and move forward with their life. As they struggle to free themselves from the energetic and emotional grip of this event they are hit by another event. These events feel like they are piled upon each other and they can't get out from under the psychic weight of these events. They continue to struggle against this pain and the more they struggle the more they enter their shadow. They feel that no matter how hard they try they can't get out from under this psychic pain.
- This person puts on a facade to cover over their sensitive, intuitive nature. They are continually in motion. The movement is in a tight circle so that no one can enter their circle of movement. They keep the people around distracted and at a distance by presenting a bright colorful exterior. They are not moving on with life but stay locked in the just described pattern. They present a life that is hyper-busy. This is all done so that their hyper-sensitive nature is not exposed. This person is a very sensitive and intuitive individual. In their past they have been hurt by someone who exposed and diminished their hyper-sensitive nature. The psychic pain of that exposure was almost too much to bear. That incident of pain completely overwhelmed them. The pain is still there and if they stop moving they feel the pain, acutely.

Cross Indexing: Addictions- Gambling, Addictions – Smoking, ACOA (Adult Children of Alcoholics), Post Traumatic stress disorder, Headaches, Intestinal Problems, Liver Problems, Endocrine problems, Wounded Creative Core

Repeating Patterns: Not trusting self, out of balance life (work too much, etc), puts on airs of being someone else, unable to complete a project, feel safe being seen, feeling unworthy and making decisions or life moves that support that feeling, no self-care, doesn't tell the truth, doesn't know how to express emotions safely, can't stay still (feels unsafe), doesn't feel safe with emotions, doesn't feel safe with others, no inner peace, lives life as either a victim or martyr, they are on constant alert, feels death will bring them peace, has a constant crisis going, doesn't keep promises, doesn't or can't solve problems, life is unstructured, irresponsibility.

Created Patterns
1. All I have is my pain.
2. Bad things happen all the time to me.
3. Being creative is dangerous.
4. Creative people are rejected.
5. Creativity comes from pain.
6. Everyone is out to get me.
7. Everything bad happens to me.
8. Feeling too much will kill me.
9. I am a smoker/drug addict/alcoholic.
10. I am addicted to smoking/alcohol/drugs.

EMOTIONAL PATTERNS

11. I am afraid of everything.
12. I am afraid of the pain.
13. I am afraid to feel _____ (What are you afraid to feel?).
14. I am alone.
15. I am an addict.
16. I am angry at myself.
17. I am bored.
18. I am depressed.
19. I am disconnected from god.
20. I am going to die.
21. I am guilty of _____.
22. I am helpless.
23. I am helpless to change anything.
24. I am hopeless.
25. I am inadequate.
26. I am insecure.
27. I am living a lie.
28. I am no good.
29. I am not good enough.
30. I am only loved if I am someone else.
31. I am powerless to do anything.
32. I am powerless to solve _____ (What is the challenge you face that seems overwhelming?).
33. I am terrified of finding out who I really am.
34. I am too weak.
35. I am too weak to handle the pain.
36. I am too weak to quit smoking/drinking/taking drugs.
37. I am too weak to stop.
38. I am worthless.
39. I believe what others say about me.
40. I can only be creative when I'm tortured.
41. I can only be creative when I am drunk / high/ out of control.
42. I can't be creative and be accepted.
43. I can't control myself.
44. I can't cope without smoking/cigarettes/drugs.
45. I can't feel and be safe.
46. I can't do it alone.
47. I don't accept myself.
48. I don't know how to accept nurturing.
49. I don't know what it feels like to be happy.
50. I don't know what it feels like to be nurtured.
51. I don't know what joy is.
52. I don't know what nurturing is.
53. I don't love myself.
54. I don't trust others/men/women/family/etc.
55. I don't want to remember.
56. I don't like who I am.
57. I hate myself.
58. I have no control over my life.

59. I must always keep moving or I will get hurt.
60. I must not let anyone see who I am.
61. I need alcohol/drugs to kill the pain.
62. I need the approval of others.
63. I run away from conflict.
64. I run away from inner conflict.
65. I would rather feel nothing than feel my pain
66. I'm not good enough.
67. I'm not happy.
68. I'm not worthy.
69. Idle hands are the playground of the devil.
70. If I feel too much, I will die.
71. If I let people see the true me, they will hurt/reject me.
72. It hurts to feel.
73. It is all hopeless.
74. It is dangerous for me to feel.
75. It is dangerous to play.
76. It is not OK to feel.
77. It is not safe to be close to another person.
78. It isn't safe for me to feel.
79. It's hopeless.
80. It's too much (what is the 'IT').
81. Life is no picnic; you have to just suck it up.
82. Life is nothing but struggle and pain.
83. My alcohol/cigarettes/drugs are my friends.
84. My anger is dangerous.
85. My feelings overwhelm me.
86. No matter how hard I try, nothing will ever change.
87. No one talks to me.
88. Nothing good will ever happen.
89. Other people are to blame for all the bad things that happen to me.
90. Others have power over me.
91. People hurt me.
92. Playing/Being creative is sinful.
93. Playing/Being creative is the playground of the devil.
94. The drug/ alcohol has power over me.
95. The world is a terrible place.
96. There is no reason for living.
97. There is so much pain in this world.
98. There's no time for play, you must work.
99. What's the use?

*Look at themes of workaholics, abandonment, abuse, acceptance, acknowledgement, anger, anxiety, approval, attention, authenticity, beingness, boundaries, burn out, calm, childhood, communication, confidence, control, denial, disassociation, failure, finishing things, freedom, grief, happiness, harmony, home, honesty, identity, intimacy, inner child, innocence, Joy, loving yourself, overwhelm, peace, punishment, relationships, self-esteem, self knowledge, self-love, self respect, self worth, sexual abuse, shame, speaking up, stability, trust, victimhood, addiction, energy, unmet needs (love, affection, attention, recognition, approval, belonging, being a child), broken heart, disconnection, feelings, joy, physical abuse, power, rejection, sexual abuse, truth, stress, addictions

Addiction – Cocaine

Fears
- Fear of the illusion being real
- Fear of reality
- Fear of being present
- Fear of compassion
- Fear of losing everything
- Fear of responsibility
- Fear of pain
- Fear of life
- Fear of connecting for fear of loss
- Fear of being powerless
- Fear of their senses
- Fear of feeling out of control

Emotional States
- Very narrow view of the world creates stress when that narrow view is corrupted. Malformed ideas of reality keep them focused on an illusion instead of a place where they are grounded. Reality is painful. It hurts too much for them to read a newspaper. They cannot be present for the pain of others because of their own psychic and emotional pain.
- Long-held ideas of what was reliable have come crashing down in what felt like a deliberate sense to destroy their world. They look to blame others for the destruction. But this destruction is just realities in the cycle of life.
- There is a building of pain in layers. They have a feeling that they can't share with anyone the pain of their life. They must keep this to themselves. In reality, there is no one. They have pushed away all those that at one time were close. The pain seeped into and colored all of who they were.

Cross Indexing: Addictions, PTSD, ACOA, Depression, wounded creative core

Repeating Patterns: situations of powerlessness, steers clear of responsibilities, sensitive to the noise of urban/suburban life, easily over stimulated, cannot relax, loss is overwhelming, repeated failures in job/relationships, when they sit quietly pain floods their senses.

Created Patterns
1. My way is the only way.
2. Feels out of control when not in control.
3. I have no power.
4. It's dangerous to be responsible.
5. The world hurts.
6. It hurts to be around others.
7. I can't shut out the world.

8. I can't keep up.
9. I must hide/escape.
10. I can't depend on anyone.
11. Life is painful.
12. There is too much pain for me to bear.

Addiction – Food

Fears

- Fear that food will be withheld if they are hungry
- Fear of being trapped
- Fear of violence
- Fear of being hurt
- Fear of anger
- Fear of being present
- Fear of not having enough
- Fear of never being enough
- Fear of being invisible
- Fear of being me
- Fear of too much energy
- Fear of letting go
- Fear of not giving enough
- Fear of receiving
- Fear of eating
- Fear of love
- Fear of feeling
- Fear of failing
- Fear of being like their parents

Emotional States

- A free nature or inner will that is undaunted by the call of authority is suddenly trapped in violence. They feel like there is no way out of the hatred, anger, and demeaning demands. They cannot move. They can find a little escape by connecting to the time before the violence as a way to survive.
- A perpetual sense of lack. They have a void in their life that is a bottomless pit. They will throw endless amounts of what is missing into the pit and it is never deemed good enough or it is not even seen. This becomes a cycle – They try to fill the void—can't do it—drop down into feelings of hopelessness/ worthlessness/ invisible—this builds a stress—stress is relieved by utilizing a previous association that has been made as to how to relieve the stress and feel better for a short time—then the cycle starts again based upon what the association is (possible connections to guilt and shame).
- Petty annoyances build and create a nervous energy that only gets relieved by continual eating. There is no cognitive ability to release the energy of the annoying emails, bills, noises in the environment, etc. There is no outlet for hyper-energies. May have felt that as a child. The food was a way of focusing the hyper energies that would get you punished if they were resolved in another way.

- Can't let go. This includes hurts, losses, grief, etc. It's like hanging onto these things creates the justification/ validation of their existence. If someone dies they hang onto what connected them to that person. If they are hurt they hang onto the hurt and won't forgive.
- There can be compulsive quality to eating that is not a food addiction but a false association with an emotion. For example: Sugar/ Sweets=Love, Sweets=acceptance, Sweets=feeling special, Sweets = connection, ice cream = release of stress, large evening meals = connection to mother (this is stuck grief).

Cross Indexing: Other addictions, ACOA, Post Traumatic Stress Disorder.

Repeating Patterns: Out of time – not present, surrounded by angry bitter people, constant sense of lack, relationships that demean, eats to feel something good — immediate guilt afterwards, do things for others to fill the hole but their giving is not seen or acknowledged, cycles through grief and loss.

Created Patterns

1. I am in danger.
2. I am unsafe.
3. I am stuck/ frozen.
4. I am humiliated.
5. I am someone's slave.
6. I am missing something.
7. The world is a violent place.
8. I am not good enough.
9. I am worthless.
10. My life is a bottomless pit of _____.
11. I feel guilty about everything.
12. I am shameful.
13. I get punished if I am not eating.
14. I can't let go.
15. I can't forgive.
16. My grief is the reason for living (identity).
17. I can't let go of the hurt. My hurt/pain is the reason I live. I must punish the ones that hurt me by showing them how much they hurt me. I must get even.
18. When I eat bread/potatoes/pasta I am safe/nurtured/mothered.
19. Being heavy is how I am strong.
20. Being heavy is how I stay safe.
21. Don't ask, don't tell, and don't feel.
22. Eating is my greatest fear.
23. Eating kills the psychic pain.
24. Eating takes my inner peace.
25. Food always makes me feel good.
26. Food equals love.
27. Food is how I love myself.
28. Food is the friend that never fails me.
29. Food keeps me from feeling.
30. Food will make me feel better.
31. Food will solve any problem I have.
32. I am a failure.
33. I am afraid of my feelings.

EMOTIONAL PATTERNS

34. I am an embarrassment.
35. I am ashamed of how I look.
36. I am ashamed of myself.
37. I am consumed by food.
38. I am depressed.
39. I am disconnected from The Creator / God.
40. I am full of rage at _____.
41. I am my father.
42. I am my mother.
43. I am overwhelmed by anxiety.
44. I am powerless to control my eating.
45. I am shamed for not being good enough.
46. I can never fill the void inside of me.
47. I can never get enough.
48. I can never have a relationship.
49. I don't know how to be safe with my feelings.
50. I don't know how to control my eating.
51. I eat to keep from feeling.
52. I hate myself.
53. I have been betrayed.
54. I have no control.
55. I have no one close to me.
56. I hide behind my body.
57. I must stuff my feelings.
58. I need armor to protect me from abuse.
59. I resent /am angry at _____.
60. I substitute food for love.
61. I think about eating all the time.
62. I want out.
63. I'm not lovable.
64. I'm not loved.
65. I'm rejected / reviled.
66. It dangerous to feel.
67. It is dangerous for people to see who I truly am.
68. It is dangerous to feel.
69. My eating protects me.
70. My feeling overwhelm me so I eat.
71. No one likes me.
72. No one sees the real me.
73. No one supports me.
74. People don't like me because I am overweight.
75. When I eat I feel guilty.
76. When people make fun of me I eat.
77. You can always rely on food.

Addiction – Gambling

Fears
- Fear everyone will see they are worthless
- Fear of being indicted
- Fear of loss
- Fear of being worthless
- Fear of being unacceptable
- Fear of the truth
- Fear of real life
- Fear of being blamed
- Fear of responsibility
- Fear of death
- Fear of failure
- Fear of valuing themselves
- Fear of peace
- Fear of letting go
- Fear of feeling out of control

Teachings
- Live without needing to win
- Be good enough
- Be balanced
- Be worthy
- Live without yourself worth coming from winning
- Live without needing to be somebody
- Love myself
- Unconditional love
- Let go
- Be in control
- Be loved without winning at gambling
- Live without needing to be special
- Be loved without being special
- Live without the high gotten from winning

Emotional States
- Regret as to how they have handled their affairs in prior roles has led to a deep sense of guilt and grief at the loss they have caused. Worry that they are perceived as less than insignificant. Histrionics created by the misery that they have created lead them into unsavory relationships that are perceived or feel like a level of acceptance.
- Joyous methods of communication make the world appear rosy and wildly successful for them when in fact the opposite is true. They are constantly chasing an illusion that is more a phantom with no basis in reality. This often results in a nightmarish outcome that quickly is glossed over or run away from. There is no completion or resolution in their life.
- Childish needs and playful ideas replace responsible adult actions. The concept of responsibility is denied and reasoned away in the light of their need to be joyful and happy without regard to the legitimate needs of others to whom they have obligations. The spotlight is always on them and the spotlight is all about them being in center stage as the center of attention.
- Hostile images menace their inner horizons – always threatening them with impending doom. They think their death is imminent and so they play their life as if it is a continual game of roulette, always on the edge of catastrophic failure or glorious success. They are always being chased by the inner demons of failure, worthlessness, chaos and self-loathing.

Cross Indexing: Addictions, ACOA, Depression, Bi-Polar, Parkinson's, and Restless Leg Syndrome

Repeating Patterns: Needs to win, feels not good enough/unworthy, life is out of balance, self-worth is based on winning, actions and speech are anchored in needing to be somebody, doesn't love themselves, needs to be in control, can't let go

Created Patterns

1. Everyone loves a winner and I must keep trying to be a winner to be love.
2. Gambling makes me feel good.
3. I am depressed.
4. I am going to die.
5. I am special when I gamble.
6. I can't control myself.
7. I can't finish anything (outside the gambling table).
8. I can't let go of what is not good for me/what is toxic.
9. I can't wait I must have it now.
10. I don't know how to complete anything.
11. I feel alive when I gamble.
12. I have no choice I must gamble.
13. If I win big then I'll be _____(happy/loved/respected/wanted).
14. I'm not good enough.
15. I'm not worthy.
16. The only way to be loved will be to be a winner.
17. While gambling I am in control.

Addiction – Shopping

Fears

- Fear of letting go (shopping gives a momentary feeling of 'having')
- Fear of anger
- Fear of depression
- Fear of people
- Fear of being hurt
- Fear of the unknown
- Fear of intimacy and connection
- Fear of going home with the bags
- Fear of being challenged
- Fear of being judged
- Fear of not shopping
- Fear of not being loved or accepted
- Fear of having things take away
- Fear of being wrong

Emotional States

- Fundamental concepts of how life "is" are very skewed – doesn't know how to make things work and feels like a square peg in a round hole or vice-versa. Hurts by early life people create an unknown in their life as to what is normal and what isn't. They are in a constant state of confusion and trying to figure out how to behave and what they are supposed to do. They live life in a big state of anxiety.

- Wants to run away. Feels a strong urge to run. Life events create the need to run away. Doesn't feel safe with people. Finds no comfort with them. There is no basic sense of security in any relationship. Things provide safety. The things provide a place to be, in their mind, safe from people. They equate the dopamine hit with security and they get that with a new dress or pair of shoes.
- Justification of control; No one seems to get that they need to do something that feels of value. The shopping gives them a sense of value. They feel like no one understands them and they hate being questioned or challenged in their habits and ways. The shopping gives them that space or respite from the judgment of others. They feel free and safe. Holding onto and having things – more and more – that feels safe. They may never wear or use the things they buy but they give them a sense of security.
- Association of feeling loved to shopping.
- Wearing something new gets them acceptance and love
- They possess, they own it and no one can take it away from them, childhood trauma around having what was theirs continuously taken away. A sense of loss and having to fill the void.

Cross Indexing: Obsessive Compulsive Disorder, addictions

Repeating Patterns: Refuses leftovers (food, clothing,etc), Over spends, shops to relax then feels anxious and out of control after they buy things, Out of balance, feels a lack of inner peace, perspective is out of alignment – feels like they don't belong and do things that support that feeling, relationships fail to due to out of body (not present and ungrounded), anxiety, confusion, haunted by memories that recreated feelings of hurt and rejection, thinks others will pick up the responsibilities.

Created Patterns
1. I am lost.
2. Everyone is against me.
3. I don't belong.
4. Everything I do is wrong.
5. I must run away.
6. I am alone.
7. People will hurt me.
8. People leave me.
9. When I buy things I feel good.
10. I am in control when I shop.
11. I am judged.
12. I can't ever do anything right.
13. I feel at peace when I buy things.
14. I feel loved when I buy things.
15. I am special when I wear something new.
16. I am accepted when I wear something new.
17. People take things from me.

Addiction – Smoking / Nicotine

Fears
- Fears being treated like a toy (objectified)
- Fear of letting go of anger
- Fear of letting go
- Fear of color in life
- Fear of making decisions
- Fear of going forward
- Fear of being held responsible
- Fear of purpose
- Fear of being present
- Fear of commitment
- Fear of failing
- Fear of feeling
- Fear of pain
- Fear of being out of control
- Fear of memories
- Fear of feeling worthless
- Fear of making friends

Emotional States
- Hostile thoughts toward others distract and consume. It leads them into non-productive space that endangers their jobs and other relationships. Unable to let go of that aspect. Can't forgive and move on.
- Dwelling in their being of non-presence. They have a feeling of no motivation, interest or passion in anything around them. There's just a feeling that they are biding time in an existence. There's not a sense that they are missing anything. No desire to change – smoking gives them that pleasure center element that they don't get anywhere else. Life is dull and lifeless. Not a depression.
- Bounces all over the place with ideas – thoughts are up and down. They have a constant divergence in decision making. They will look at an issue and see the negative and then see the other side. This keeps them frozen in a state of non-decision. They have more or less failed in their life, any real direction of thought or movement is squashed. Fear of change, moving forward and decision making. Does not like to write emails or letters, there's a danger in putting anything in writing.
- The leanness of soul: a lightness of purpose has kept them from a deep sense of need. They have not known how to be present in the sense of a real life – always just barely touching the surface. They present a facade of depth and wisdom but it is only that which they surmise without challenge to convention. They do not look further. When forced to look further they escape behind vague statements that make them look wise without really making a commitment in speech.
- Failure to create what they want in life. A continual sense of running up against a brick wall. Feelings of anger and frustration resulted in a persecution that was blown completely out of proportion.

Cross Indexing: Addictions, Lung Problems, Cancer – Lung, Emphysema

Created Patterns

1. Cigarettes help me deal with stress.
2. Feeling too much will kill me.
3. I am a smoker.
4. I am addicted to smoking.
5. I am afraid of the pain.
6. I am afraid to feel _____ (What are you afraid to feel?).
7. I am bored.
8. I am going to die.
9. I am helpless.
10. I am helpless to change anything.
11. I am powerless to solve _____ (What is the challenge you face that seems overwhelming?).
12. I am too weak.
13. I am too weak to handle the pain.
14. I am too weak to quit smoking.
15. I can't control myself.
16. I can't cope without smoking/cigarettes.
17. I can't let myself have fun.
18. I can't quit smoking.
19. I don't accept myself.
20. I don't know how to/what it feels like to nurture myself.
21. I don't know how/what it feels like to deal with stress without smoking.
22. I don't trust others/men/women/family/etc.
23. I don't want to remember.
24. I have no control over my life.
25. I run away from conflict.
26. I run away from inner conflict.
27. I smoke to be accepted.
28. I smoke if I feel too much.
29. If I smoke all the bad stuff will go away.
30. If I smoke it will all go away.
31. If I feel too much I will die.
32. I'm not good enough.
33. I'm not worthy.
34. It is dangerous for me to feel.
35. It is not safe to be close to another person.
36. It's hopeless.
37. It's not OK to take care of myself.
38. It's too much.
39. My anger is dangerous.
40. My cigarettes are my friend.
41. My feelings overwhelm me.
42. Others come before me.
43. Smoking is how I take care of myself.
44. When I smoke I am accepted.
45. When I smoke I am being selfish.
46. When I smoke I am doing something for me.

Addison's disease

Fears
- Fear of disconnection from their secrets
- Fear that if they let go there will be no one to catch them as they fall into the abyss
- Fear of connection with the divine
- Fear of overwhelm
- Fear of out of balance
- Fear of feeling worthless
- Fear of being attacked
- Fear of defending themselves
- Fear of change
- Fear of anger
- Fear of being seen
- Fear of rejection
- Fear of the divine
- Fear of saying no
- Fear of being alone
- Fear of loving self
- Fear of inner peace
- Fear of living life
- Fear of being abandoned

Teachings
- Balanced
- Be at one
- Be wanted
- Be safe
- Complete
- Connected to the Creator
- Flow
- Get your needs met
- Happiness
- Joy
- Let go
- Live knowing all is in divine order
- Live without feeling overwhelmed
- Live without chaos
- Live without feeling rejected
- Live without feeling under attack
- Live without feeling unwanted
- Live without needing secrets
- Live without self anger
- Love myself
- Move forward with your life
- Take in only energies that are good for me
- Trust myself
- Trust others
- Unconditional love
- Be valued
- Whole
- Worthy

Emotional States
- Undying love for someone they cannot have. Have lived for years with the secret of this love. The quest for this love has reached mythic proportions. It is really their disconnection from god that they are feeling – severe pain felt at the separation – never reconciled or at peace. Soul body-mind (awareness or consciousness) always in turmoil, always in torment.
- Heart and body in a state of anxiety caused by a continual sense of feeling overwhelmed by everything. Chakras are blown wide open in an unhealthy way. Does not have the skills to move to a place of balance. Out of balance – too much of everything coming at them.
- Feels thrown away – incurred a personal attack that was bent on destroying them. They have no boundaries to withstand such an attack. Energy systems in response to the attack went into overload to repel the attack. Fear that it will happen again has kept that over response going.

Cross Indexing: Autoimmune disorder, Adrenals, Adrenal Fatigue, Heart problems, Liver problem, Endocrine System

Repeating Patterns: abandoned, life out of balance, feels unwanted, feels unsafe, doesn't trust others or self, doesn't get their needs met, lack of inner peace, stays stuck – doesn't move forward, feels rejected by friends/family/boss, will invent and keep chaos going, feels under attack, feels angry at self, exposes themselves to situations and people they know are not good for them, needs to keep secrets which create chaos.

Created Pattern

1. Change is dangerous.
2. I am alone.
3. I am always disappointed.
4. I am angry at myself.
5. I am denied what I desire in life.
6. I am disconnected from god / creator.
7. I am invisible.
8. I am no good.
9. I am nobody/nothing.
10. I am not seen.
11. I am of no value to anyone.
12. I am overwhelmed by life.
13. I am rejected.
14. I am tormented.
15. I am under attack.
16. I am worthless.
17. I can never get what I want.
18. I can't defend myself.
19. I can't let go of _____.
20. I can't move forward.
21. I can't say no.
22. I don't believe in myself.
23. I don't know how to feel anger/love/sadness/joy/etc.
24. I don't know what love/anger/sadness/joy/etc. feels like.
25. I don't love myself.
26. I don't trust myself.
27. I must be hard on myself.
28. I must keep the secret.
29. I must try hard to be noticed.
30. I must work really hard to be seen.
31. I will be alone the rest of my life.
32. I will never be good enough.
33. I will never be happy.
34. I will never have a life's partner.
35. I will never have inner peace.
36. I will never have someone that loves me.
37. I will never have true happiness.
38. I will only have one true love.
39. I'm not good enough.
40. I'm not good enough for god / creator.

41. I'm not good enough to be loved.
42. I'm not wanted.
43. It's not safe to feel anger/ love/ sadness/ joy/ etc..
44. My life is a failure.
45. My life is chaos.
46. No one loves me.
47. Nothing I do ever seems to work out for me.
48. Nothing is good enough.
49. People are out to destroy me.
50. People attack me.
51. People that love me abandon me.
52. Something always blocks me from getting what I want.
53. What is it that you are feeling that you do not understand?

*Look at themes of abandonment, anger, anxiety, approval, attention, attack, blockages, boundaries, conflict, confrontation, direction, control, denial, disassociation, emotions, failure, feelings, relationships, soul mates, martyr, now, overwhelm, past, peace. Self worth, secrets, self-esteem, self-love, unconditional love, unmet needs (love, affection, attention, recognition, approval, belonging, being a child), broken heart, denial, disconnection, joy, power, rejection, energy, movement, relationships, stress

Adenoid Problems

Fears
- Fear of being invisible
- Fear of being out of alignment / out of sync/ out of breath(life)
- Fear of being unwanted / unloved
- Fear of disappointment
- Fear of speaking up
- Fear of being alone
- Fear of failure
- Fear of knowing they are wrong

Teachings
- Be in the flow
- Love myself
- Unconditional love
- Yield to life's changes and be safe
- Accepted
- Live without feeling rejected
- Be wanted
- Breathe and be safe
- Be listened to
- Talk and be safe
- Speak your truth and be safe

Emotional States
- Failure to receive the acknowledgment in life. This acknowledgment creates the feeling of being unneeded and unwanted. Has an unloving family. They present a headstrong attitude to cover up disappointments.
- Needs of being loved/feeling loved are not being met. They stop the feeling before it gets started. Choices made based on family control have stopped the freedom of their heart to get what they need to feel loved.

Cross Indexing: Throat Problems, Tonsils, Ear Problems, Nose Problems, Mouth Problems, Lymphatic System

Repeated Patterns: lack of inner peace, does not feel love for self, change becomes unsafe, situations, where they feel unaccepted/rejected/unwanted, when they speak up they feel unsafe, could also be experiencing chronic lung issues/allergies because of a feeling it is unsafe to breathe.

Created Patterns

1. I am a failure.
2. I am alone.
3. I am in the way.
4. I am rejected by _____.
5. I am unwanted.
6. I can't breathe and be safe.
7. I can't talk and be safe.
8. I must be strong to protect myself.
9. I must be unyielding to be safe.
10. I must not let anyone get close to me.
11. I'm not loved.
12. I'm not wanted.
13. It's not safe to hear.
14. Love is pain.
15. My father doesn't want me.
16. My mother doesn't want me.
17. People don't listen to me.
18. People don't want me.

Adrenal Fatigue

Fears
- Fear of the unknown
- Fear that if they don't get out they will die
- Fear of change
- Fear of being under attack
- Fear of not being good enough
- Fear of the quiet / calm
- Fear of being caught not knowing
- Fear they can't change their situation
- Fear of not being approved
- Fear of being present
- Fear of being wrong
- Fear of being lost and alone

Teachings
- Say no
- Have fun
- Have people listen to me
- Relax
- Be balanced
- Be nurtured
- Trust
- Listen to the needs of others
- Safe in my body
- Care for myself
- Trust that my needs will be met
- Let others help me
- Ask for help
- Gratitude
- Express gratitude
- Creator's definition of gratitude
- Reverence
- Express reverence

- Right action
- Balance my work and personal life without punishment
- Get my needs met
- Receive love

Emotional States

- Fear of change which creates a state of hyper-alert, feeling like they are under attack when things change (fight or flight response). This can be a simple job function. There is an over-reaction to all changes.
- Fear of not being good enough and therefore not loved/wanted produces a background anxiety/fear that is always there and sometimes is the predominant feeling.
- Hooked on stress and stress-inducing chaos.
- Repeats the same stress-inducing behaviors because if they don't they will feel guilty for letting others down.
- Uses artificial stimulants to keep the energy high (caffeine or other).
- The more they do the more they feel approved of/wanted.
- Lifelong hyperactive behavior as a consequence of childhood loss of nurturing.
- Uses chaos as a form of nurturing and getting needs met.
- A life full of stresses (high-pressure job, lots of demands on time, always busy, always out of breath, lots of sighing).
- Not present with people and their needs and subsequently doing extraneous things that don't really achieve what needs to be done and this just creates more stress and a sense of not being good enough.
- A sense that they will be found out to have done something wrong…always on guard.
- Fear that they may lose everything, so there is a tight hold that resists change.
- What this person truly wants in their life gets lost in the chaos-they never have time to attain goals, emotional growth, spiritual growth, taking care of their physical.

Cross Indexing: Tachycardia, ACOA, Post Traumatic Stress Disorder, Weight-over, Thoracic area of back, shoulder problems, Neck, leaky gut syndrome, depression, toxins, sleep problems-Insomina, Adrenal Problems, attention deficit disorder

Repeated Patterns: Life out of balance, attracts lots of chaos, on constant high alert (may have a diagnosis of PTSD), overreact to changes in life, uses stimulants to keep the energy high (caffeine/red dye), aren't present, hyperactive, don't feel safe in their body, don't practice self-care, do not trust their needs will be met, lack of inner peace.

Created Patterns

1. Bad things happen when there is change.
2. Change is dangerous.
3. Everyone else is better than me.
4. I am alone.
5. I am guilty of doing something wrong.
6. I am guilty of letting people down.
7. I am taken advantage of.
8. I am tired.
9. I can never slow down.

10. I can't ask for help and be safe.
11. I can't depend on others to help me.
12. I can't let anyone find out _____ (what's the fear).
13. I can't say no.
14. I don't ever seem to do the right thing.
15. I don't ever seem to say the right thing.
16. I don't have time to do fun things.
17. I don't love myself.
18. I don't trust that my needs will be met.
19. I have given everything I have to give.
20. I have no energy left.
21. I have nothing left to give.
22. I must always do more to survive.
23. I must always keep my guard up.
24. I must do it myself for it to get done.
25. I need the approval of others to be good enough/wanted/loved.
26. I will be punished if I do something wrong.
27. I'll have fun when my work is all done.
28. I'm not wanted.
29. If I am punished I am shamed.
30. If I am selfish I will be punished.
31. If I have just a little more time I can make it even better.
32. If I keep moving/doing I will be safe.
33. If I stop I will die.
34. If I take care of myself I will be considered selfish.
35. It isn't safe for me to take care of myself.
36. No one listens to me.
37. People don't listen to me.
38. People take and never give anything in return.
39. People in authority will hurt me (mother/ father/ boss/ etc).
40. The more I do the more I am wanted/ loved.
41. There's never enough time to do the things I want to do.
42. There's never enough time to take care of myself.
43. Things don't get done if I don't do them.
44. Work comes before everything.

*Look at themes of gratitude, safety, fun, boundaries, trust, self-esteem, self-knowledge, self-love, self respect, self-pity, workaholic, change, unmet needs (fun, play, creativity, nurturance, and approval), worthiness, spirituality, soul purpose, sex, power, manifesting, disconnection, domination, control, letting go, stress

Adrenal Problems

Fears

- Fear of the unknown
- Fears trusting self
- Fears being shamed

- Fears being unworthy
- Fear that right around the corner there is a trap
- Fear of being powerless to stop violence
- Fear of change
- Fears defeat
- Fear of what could happen next
- Fear of being under attack
- Fear of not being good enough
- Fear of the quiet / calm
- Fear of being caught not knowing
- Fear they can't change their situation
- Fears things will never change (nothing they can do, bad things will happen)
- Fear of not being approved
- Fear of being present
- Fear of being wrong
- Fear of being lost and alone

Emotional States
- Start and then a sudden stop. Their fears and lack of belief in themselves stop anything from happening.
- Feels hopeless. Believes things will never get better or change. Despair of the heart. Those feelings are suppressed.
- Sense of well-being is shattered when a truth once held secret is revealed causing an emotional meltdown. The illusion they have been living has been destroyed.
- They have memories of violence / foul play/crime they incurred that haunt them. They live with the threat of violence…fight or flight.
- Lives a justification for wrong actions taken against them that caused harm. They believe they deserved the harm and so they must be bad.
- Constantly haunted by exhaustion. They are overwhelmed by not being able to do it all.

Cross Indexing: Kidney problems, endocrine system problems, post traumatic stress disorder, ACOA, Adrenal fatigue

Repeated Patterns: depression, secrets get revealed, constant fear of violence, feels they deserve to be hurt, victim or martyr, constantly having bad things happen, a feeling they can't change things, doubts self and doesn't support themselves in the face of adversity, no energy to stand.

Created Patterns
1. Bad things happen to me.
2. Everything is hard.
3. I am a victim.
4. I am afraid of _____.
5. I am bad.
6. I am depressed.
7. I am going to be attacked.
8. I am going to be hurt.
9. I am going to die.
10. I am hopeless.

11. I am jealous of _____.
12. I am powerless.
13. I am without hope.
14. I am worthless.
15. I can never stop.
16. I can't do anything.
17. I can't let people know how I feel.
18. I deserve to be hurt.
19. I don't believe in myself.
20. I don't care what happens to me.
21. I feel defeated.
22. I must be ready to defend myself against violence.
23. I must do it all.
24. I must earn love.
25. I must earn my right to be here.
26. I must hunker down to survive.
27. I must prove myself.
28. I must save the world.
29. I will never be good enough.
30. I'm not good enough.
31. If I do anything it will make it worse.
32. Life is a burden.
33. Life is hard.
34. My heart is broken.
35. Nothing will ever change so what's the use.
36. *What are you afraid of failing at? Who made you feel that way?*
37. *Who am I to think I can do anything about this?*
38. You must struggle/ work hard for success/ power/ position/ money/etc.

Aging – Difficulties

Fears
- Fear that others will die before them (friends and/or family)
- Fear of shame and/ or embarrassment
- Fear of death
- Fear of pain
- Fear of life
- Fear of the flow of life
- Fear of starting over
- Fear of looking inward
- Fear of being alone
- Fear of receiving
- Fear of acceptance
- Fear of change

Teachings
- Compassion (Inner peace in the face of suffering)
- Be in the flow
- Creator's definition and perspective of aging
- Receive love from all of creation
- Receive life force
- Love myself
- Live without struggle
- Let go of the heartache
- Let go
- Be at peace with each cycle of human life
- Grace
- Live with ease and grace
- Age without disease

- Age without pain
- Joy
- Happiness

Emotional States

- They believe death is inevitable. They believe they will grow old and die. Feels that they must physically fall apart at some point.
- Feels life has defeated them and worn them down. They have fought and struggled against the flow. They have resisted the flow of life and as a consequence life force has been drained.
- The heart is broken. All their dreams are broken. No energy to build new dreams. The ego is invested heavily in the illusion.
- The heart is hardened and indifferent to the things that give life. Has shut down the renewal of life force. Doesn't see a purpose for living. Has disconnected from source and those things that revive and nourish.
- Worn out witness to the extremes of humanity – depleted their ability to care. Friends have died and they want to die also. They do not believe they have a reason to be here. They feel all alone.

Cross Indexing: Alzheimer's, Memory Problems, Dementia, Senility, Arthritis, and Osteoarthritis

Repeating Patterns: Depression, can't receive, life is a struggle (events occur makes this their reality), can't let go of the losses that created heartache, fights the cycle of human life, feels as if they have lost control of their life, feels vulnerable because of their aging body, feels invisible – no longer a productive part of the world, unresolved issues in their life cause a state of non-peace in their hearts and body. Complains about everything, everything is wrong.

Created Patterns

1. All I have ever done is work hard and got nowhere.
2. Death is inevitable.
3. Every day is a fight just to maintain the status quo.
4. Getting old means getting sick.
5. I am a failure.
6. I am all alone (friends/family have passed).
7. I am alone.
8. I am defeated.
9. I am depressed.
10. I am getting old.
11. I am in the way.
12. I can't allow myself to be dependent on someone else.
13. I don't have a purpose.
14. I hate/am angry at/have been betrayed by/want revenge on/ am bitter at/have a grudge against _____.
15. I have never realized any of my dreams.
16. I have no reason for living.
17. I just don't care anymore.
18. I must struggle to live.
19. I regret _____.

20. I wake up each day and wonder what isn't working now.
21. I want to die.
22. I'm a burden on my family/friends.
23. I'm just circling the drain.
24. I'm just waiting to die.
25. I'm next to die.
26. If you care you get hurt and angry and I can't do anything about it anyway.
27. It would be better if I died.
28. It's a good day when I can get out of bed.
29. It's no use anymore.
30. It's not OK to grow older.
31. It's one thing after another.
32. Life is a hard and then you die.
33. Life is a struggle.
34. Little by little my body parts just quit working.
35. Living is fighting a losing battle.
36. My heart is broken.
37. No one around me understands what it is to get old.
38. The older I get the less I am worth.
39. The older I get the sicker I get.
40. We all grow old unless you die first.

Agoraphobia

Fears
- Fear of being overwhelmed
- Fear of anything outside of the hardened walls they have created around themselves
- Fear that they have wasted the learning their soul intended
- Fear of feeling guilty
- Fear of being powerless
- Fear of being out of control
- Fear of being hurt
- Fear of being attacked
- Fear of rejection
- Fear of wanting and getting
- Fear of the unknown
- Fear of depending on others
- Fear of their heart

Teachings
- Be valued
- Be safe
- Be safe alone
- Be safe in crowds
- Be safe in public
- Be safe outside
- Be safe with angry people
- Be safe with the unknown
- Be wanted
- Complete
- Creator's perspective and definition of right and wrong
- Creator's perspective of father
- Creator's perspective of mother
- Creator's unconditional love
- Defend yourself appropriately
- Deserve
- Feel loved by others
- Forgive
- Forgive yourself
- Happiness
- Joy

- Live without fear of ridicule
- Live without feeling attacked
- Live without feeling guilty
- Live without the fear of losing control
- Living an authentic life
- Living in the now
- Nurtured
- Release the trauma of the past
- Release trapped fear of the unknown
- Trust
- Whole
- Worthy

Emotional States

- Lives a facade that everything is wonderful. Underneath the facade are feelings of overwhelming guilt. Feelings of being powerless and having no control.
- Being out in public causes a feeling of being in immediate danger. Feels a loss of power and incapable of defending self.
- Has been harmed as a consequence of physical appearance or feminine aspects of self.
- Believes they are dirty, disgusting, stubborn or selfish. Feels rejected. Believe they don't deserve good things. Live in isolation to play out that deprivation.
- Fear of the unknown. Fear that if they go outside their circle of safety they will not be able to get back and they will perish.
- Feels that there is nothing they can depend on. Foundations are built on fear. Internal battle of anger tries to destroy the foundation of the life they built.
- Lives a role that is rigid. The role is a wall to keep them safe. But, the role works to sabotage their safety and they fear losing control.
- Intense fear of relationships. Unable to defend themselves. Wounded by family and/ or community. Heart connections are shut down.

Cross Indexing: Depression, ACOA, Post Traumatic Stress Disorder, Weight-over, Weight-under, Thymus problems, heart problems

Repeating Patterns: a sense of extreme vulnerability out in public, under attack, feels guilty for feeling under attack, feelings of being out of control, lack of inner peace, brings in angry people, sees danger with being in the open.

Created Patterns

1. Angry people are dangerous.
2. I am afraid of being alone.
3. I am afraid of losing control.
4. I am afraid that if I am needed I will freeze.
5. I am angry at _____.
6. I am dangerous.
7. I am depressed.
8. I am different from everyone else and they make fun of me.
9. I am dirty/ stubborn/ selfish.
10. I am guilty of _____.

EMOTIONAL PATTERNS

11. I am helpless.
12. I am in danger.
13. I am inadequate.
14. I am not safe.
15. I am not safe outside of the house.
16. I am overwhelmed by the world outside my house.
17. I am out of control.
18. I am powerless.
19. I am powerless to change things.
20. I am rejected/ ridiculed.
21. I am worthless.
22. I can't cope.
23. I can't defend myself.
24. I can't depend on anyone.
25. I can't forgive _____.
26. I can't forgive myself.
27. I can't trust myself.
28. I can't trust people.
29. I don't deserve.
30. I don't fit in.
31. I don't have the ability to _____.
32. I don't know how to be safe.
33. I don't know how to defend myself.
34. I don't know what is right and wrong.
35. I don't know what it feels like to be safe.
36. I don't know what it feels like to defend myself.
37. I don't really exist/ I am not real.
38. I have absolutely no control.
39. I have been abandoned by _____.
40. I have nothing to stand on.
41. I want to die.
42. I will lose control if I go outside.
43. I'm no good.
44. I'm not worthy.
45. If I am seen I will be in danger.
46. If I get angry I am dangerous.
47. If I get angry I may lose control.
48. If I get overwhelmed I will lose control.
49. If I go outside I will be attacked/ hurt.
50. If I go outside I will die.
51. If I lose control I may hurt someone.
52. If I lose control they will lock me up.
53. My mother / father abandoned me.
54. Nothing is real.
55. Outside of my house it is dangerous.
56. People are dangerous.
57. People hurt me.
58. People make fun of me.
59. The unknown is dangerous.

60. The unknown is right outside the door.
61. The unknown will hurt you.
62. The world is dangerous.
63. There is nothing here for me.

*Look at themes of intuition, letting go, control, guilt, overwhelm, abandonment, allowing, anger, anxiety, attack, authenticity, beingness, blockages, co-dependence, danger, depression, doubt, enjoying life, flow, forgiveness, now, freedom, grounded, letting go, love, rejection, sabotage, safety, self-esteem, self-knowledge, self-love, self-worth, trapped, trust and authenticity, power, unmet needs (safety, nurturance, being wanted, childhood innocence, and support), shame, confidence

AIDS and HIV

Fears
- Fear of rejection
- Fear that there is no life that this is just a cruel cosmic joke
- Fear of being themselves
- Fear of abandonment
- Fear of love
- Fear of being alone
- Fear of being shamed
- Fear of guilt
- Fear of god
- Fear of being good enough for inner peace
- Fear of life
- Fear of being judged

Teachings
- Awareness of the needs of others
- Be at peace
- Be hopeful
- Be myself
- Compassion (inner peace in the face of suffering)
- Forgive self
- Forgiveness
- Live being good enough
- Live without anger
- Live without blaming others for our problems
- Live without criticism
- Live without having to keep secrets
- Live without shame
- Love myself for who I am
- Loving self
- Respected
- Responsible
- Successful
- Supported
- Unconditional love
- Wanted
- Worthy

Emotional States
- Longing for the past when life was simpler and there wasn't rejection, fear, and abandonment for being who you are.
- Left without support. Feels all alone. Has been abandoned by all who said they love them but don't. Found love to be false. Love is betrayal. Love equals loss.

- Not allowed to see who they are. Forced to be something their not to keep up appearances in the community. Shame is the result if you don't keep the secrets.
- Heart is broken by rejection. Loss of hope. Depressed. Feels denied of life. Holds others to blame. Does not want to take responsibility for their actions.
- They feel they have gone against the teachings and laws of 'god' and must be punished for their sin and transgressions. A patriarchal presence that condemns and judges.

Cross Indexing: Virus, Herpes-Simplex II, Herpes Simplex I, Shoulder Problem, Rotator Cuff, Arm problems, Autoimmune Disorders, Left Sided Negative Problems, Right Sided Negative Problems, ACOA, Arms –Right, Arms – Left, Brain Problems

Repeating Patterns: lack of inner peace, doesn't trust self, finds themselves unsupported over and over, depression, loneliness, victim or martyr, no sense of belonging or purposes.

Created Patterns

1. As long as I am sick I don't feel guilty.
2. Getting close to another is dangerous.
3. Having sex is wrong.
4. I am a disappointment.
5. I am afraid of myself.
6. I am alone.
7. I am always disappointed.
8. I am an abomination before god.
9. I am angry at _____.
10. I am angry at/ hate/ resent bitter toward.
11. I am ashamed of who I am.
12. I am bad.
13. I am being punished by god.
14. I am condemned and criticized by my father/mother/ who else?
15. I am depressed.
16. I am disconnected from god / creator.
17. I am going to die.
18. I am guilty.
19. I am guilty of having sex.
20. I am humiliated.
21. I am not worthy.
22. I am punishment for my parent's sins.
23. I am ashamed.
24. I am sinful.
25. I am unlovable.
26. I am wrong.
27. I believe what others tell me.
28. I blame _____ for _____.
29. I can't be myself.
30. I can't fight this.
31. I can't stop others from hurting me.
32. I deserve to have AIDS/HIV.
33. I don't count.
34. I don't deserve to live.

EMOTIONAL PATTERNS

35. I don't like who I am.
36. I hate myself.
37. I have a broken heart.
38. I have been betrayed by _____.
39. I have disobeyed god.
40. I have sex to feel wanted.
41. I have sinned before god.
42. I let others control me.
43. I must be punished.
44. I must be sick to punish myself.
45. I must believe what others tell me to be accepted / wanted.
46. I must die for my sins.
47. I must die to prove my parents/ mother /father right.
48. I must keep the secrets.
49. I want to die.
50. I will go to hell.
51. I'm not at peace.
52. I'm not good enough.
53. I'm not worthy of being alive.
54. It is better to die than get old.
55. It's hopeless.
56. Life is not worth living.
57. Life is suffering and betrayal.
58. Love is a lie.
59. Love is abandonment.
60. Love is betrayal.
61. Love is loss.
62. My father doesn't love me.
63. My feelings are hurt.
64. My mother doesn't love me.
65. My sexuality is wrong.
66. No one understands me.
67. Nobody cares about me.
68. People that love me leave me.
69. People that love me lie to me.
70. There is no one to help me.
71. There is no peace for the wicked.
72. What are the family issues?
73. You must be a certain way or no one will love you.

*Look at themes of life purpose, body, health, beauty, feelings, relationships, unmet needs (love, approval), and broken heart

Allergies – Dairy

Fears
- Fear of being hurt
- Fear of failing at life (bigger than failing an exam)
- Fear of not making everyone happy
- Fear of being trapped
- Fear of being mistreated
- Fear of being bullied
- Fear of being questioned
- Fear of letting go
- Fear of being powerless
- Fear of intimacy
- Fear of growing up
- Fear of being judged
- Fear of feeling unwanted

Teachings
- Be free to meet your own needs
- Be respected as an adult by parents
- Be safe around conflict
- Forgive those that have hurt me
- Have a compassionate father / mother
- Have a loving father / mother
- Keep my father's love and be true to myself
- Keep my mother's love and be true to myself
- Let go of past hurts
- Live without being criticized
- Live without being cut down
- Live without being ridiculed
- Live without having to please others
- Meet your needs and not be hurt by others
- The difference between Creator's divine law and man's laws
- Love myself
- Unconditional love
- Be wanted
- Be respected
- Stand up for myself and be loved
- Creator's definition and perspective on God's law

Emotional States
- Person has milky sweet kindness but churning inside because they cannot reconcile their needs with the demands of someone in authority.
- Trapped in a relationship and they can't escape (parent, sibling?).
- Heart is very big and is an easy target for the hurts that are expected.
- Just want people to be nice to you.
- Bottled up emotions-unable to explain how they feel to someone in authority.
- Can't see the future getting any better-just can't seem to make it work with the other person.
- Hurting inside from emotional hurts.
- Holding onto the hurts and can't forget and can't let go.
- Wanting more out of life than they are getting; they think they lack power.
- Willing to be whatever someone wants them to be to avoid conflict.
- Had an ancestor with much monetary worth. All of their support and nurturing was paid for. Nothing was given.
- They are afraid of what it is to be nurtured. False association to nurturance. Nurturance = Danger. Afraid to let anyone near them that would nurture them. Holds others to a level of scrutiny and evaluation before they can come near.

Cross Indexing: Asthma, All Allergies, Weight-over, Intestinal problems, leaky gut syndrome, Irritable

Bowel syndrome, Sinus problems

Repeating Patterns: lack of self-care, treated like a child by parents, when there is a conflict there is a feeling fear, feels constantly criticized or judged by others, feels unwanted in social settings, constantly suppresses what they need to the needs of others, feelings of powerlessness, uses empathic sense to be what others want them to be.

Created Patterns

1. Conflict makes me sick at my stomach.
2. Everyone else has all the luck.
3. Everyone hurts me.
4. I am afraid of my mother/father.
5. I am aggravated by _____.
6. I am holding my father/mother to the obligation of loving me.
7. I am irritated at _____.
8. I am obligated by god's law to my father.
9. I am obligated by god's law to my mother.
10. I am trapped.
11. I can't ever seem to please my father/mother.
12. I can't forgive the hurts.
13. I can't let go.
14. I can't let go of the hurts.
15. I can't let my parents know how I feel.
16. I can't question my father / my mother.
17. I can't stand my ground around my father/ mother.
18. I hate my father/ mother.
19. I hate myself.
20. I have a soul obligation to my father/ mother.
21. I don't love my father/ mother unconditionally.
22. I love my father and don't want to lose him; they are all I have.
23. I love my mother and don't want to lose her; they are all I have.
24. I must avoid conflict at all costs.
25. I must be what my parents want me to be.
26. I must deny my heart.
27. I must deny myself.
28. I must obey god's law or I will go to hell.
29. I must obey my parents.
30. I resent my father.
31. I ruined my mother's life.
32. I should have been thrown away at birth.
33. If I am myself, my mother/father won't approve/love me / want me.
34. If I stand up to my father I will be cut down / ridiculed /criticized.
35. I'm angry at my father.
36. I'm grieving my father.
37. It is God's law that I must obey my parents.
38. My father/mother can't be trusted.
39. My father hurt/betrayed/abandoned me.
40. My mother betrayed me.

41. My mother didn't love me.
42. My mother didn't want me.
43. My mother hurt me.
44. My mother wishes I had never been born.
45. Nothing I do is ever good enough.
46. Nothing will ever get any better; it will always be this way.
47. People are mean to me.
48. People in authority hurt me.
49. They will disown me if I'm not obedient.

*Look at themes of power, boundaries, peace, self-worth, trapped, speaking up, self-esteem, self-respect, loving myself, father, mother, and freedom, trust, power, unmet needs, and emotional abuse

Allergies – General

Fears
- Fear of attack (self and others)
- Fear that if they step out they will be attacked
- Fear of self
- Fear of failure
- Fear of standing up
- Fear of feeling worthless
- Fear of life
- Fear of breathing
- Fear of people
- Fear of dying

Emotional States
- The body feels poisoned. Hostile feelings toward others. They feel like they are under attack. Fear for personal safety – old patterns of physical abuse from childhood. Didn't understand what was expected. The rules were constantly changing. So there is a hyper-alert feeling of being constantly under attack or looking for the attack to happen.
- Inner anger derived from carelessness and has to deal with the ramifications. Beats self up for being less than perfect and making mistakes.
- Has high standards that they cannot meet themselves but expect others to meet. They put on a façade that they are at that level. The hypocrisy of their standards – doing and saying something they are not – pulls at their identity. They are very critical and judgmental of others. All of life's failure, no matter how small, are annoying and irritating to them.

Cross Indexing: All allergies, nose problems, toxins, EMF sensitivity, Sinus problems, Asthma, PTSD, ACOA, ancestral/ epigenetic, digestive disorders, fear of mold

Repeated Patterns: Constantly looking out for the next attack, non-present and makes careless mistakes, boundaries are confused.

Created Patterns

1. I am afraid to cry.
2. I am afraid to live my life.
3. I am kept from _____.
4. I am powerless to make changes.
5. I am stifled.
6. I am under attack (by whom?).
7. I can't change _____.
8. I criticize myself.
9. I don't allow myself to cry.
10. I don't have permission to cry.
11. I don't understand my feelings of _____.
12. I must always defend myself.
13. I need permission to cry.
14. I'm being attacked.
15. If I start to cry I will never stop.
16. I have been poisoned.
17. I am angry at _____.
18. Life is dangerous.
19. People annoy me.
20. People are critical of me/what I do /what I say.
21. People attack me.
22. People irritate/ aggravate me (all people or just specific ones?).

Allergies – Gluten Intolerance

Fears

- Fear of not getting through (completing) anything they try
- Fear of being irrelevant
- Fear of their own power
- Fear of starving
- Fear of being a burden
- Fear of flow
- Fear of not being in control
- Fear of being left out
- Fear of the unknown

Emotional States

- No one cares that you have an opinion or that you have your own identity of power. Unfamiliar territory creates (inner plane) a panic. They do not know they are powerful and pull back so that they will not be seen. Constantly striving for a higher vibrational plane.
- Fear of famine, of not having food. Shame, guilt, and feeling you are a pain the ass, a burden, one more mouth to feed. Intolerant of those that were hungry. Ancestral. Once wheat bread was available intestines could not digest.

- Misdirected intention, lack of inner peace and flow, tries to change things with will instead allowing a flow.

Cross Indexing: All Allergies, Weight-over, Intestinal problems, leaky gut syndrome, Irritable Bowel syndrome, pancreas problems, and toxins (look at all)

Created Patterns

1. I am unloved.
2. My boundaries are ignored.
3. My boundaries are over run.
4. I am powerless.
5. Who I am is ignored.
6. The unknown is dangerous.
7. I must be unseen to be safe.
8. I am lost.
9. I am nobody.
10. I am shameful.
11. I am guilty.
12. I am a burden.
13. I must get my share.
14. I must have mine before others.

Allergies – Hay Fever

Fears
- Fear that if they are heard breathing they will be hurt
- Fear of breathing
- Fear of life
- Fear of the flow of life
- Fear of love
- Fear of feeling worthless
- Fear of people taking from you
- Fear of letting go
- Fear of failing their mission
- Fear of being hurt
- Fear of joy
- Fear of attack

Teachings
- Breathe safely
- Listen to my inner guidance
- Be safe when accessing your inner guidance
- Make decisions in alignment with my life purpose
- Be seen safely
- Live without expecting your heart to be broken
- Breathe in the joy of life
- Living life with ease and grace
- Be in the flow
- Be in the now
- Worthy
- Loving yourself
- Be honored
- Respected
- Live without being taken advantage of
- Relax

- Live without feeling under attack
- Honor my grief
- Allow myself to grieve

Emotional States
- Breathing too deeply is dangerous.
- Life is a struggle.
- No in and outflow of life.
- Trying to expand and grow; someone/something is stopping you.
- Being stopped from your heart's desire.
- Heart is wounded and feels trapped; heart was not cared for and discarded by someone.
- Feeling of not being worthy of being loved.
- Feeling of being discarded and overlooked.
- Someone else takes credit for your work.
- Fear or a sense that you are headed in the wrong direction to achieve your life's higher purpose.
- Holding on tightly to ideals that are misaligned with your greater spiritual reality.
- Lost focus; off on a tangent.
- Unresolved grief.

Cross Indexing: Asthma, All Allergies, Weight-over, Intestinal problems, leaky gut syndrome, Irritable Bowel syndrome, Sinus problems

Repeating Patterns: chronic breathing issues, lack of inner peace, doesn't trust self, gets hurt over and over in relationships – expects it to happen, can't find the joy in the simple things of life, does stuff that says I don't love or respect myself, gets taken advantage of, feels under attack by the universe, doesn't honor the grief process.

Created Patterns
1. Being seen is dangerous.
2. Breathing the air will make me sick.
3. Crying is wrong.
4. I am afraid of _____.
5. I am angry at _____.
6. I am being attacked by _____
7. I am dependent on others to tell me what to do.
8. I am guilty of _____.
9. I am headed in the wrong direction.
10. I am trapped and can't find a way out.
11. I am under attack.
12. I am unhappy.
13. I can't breathe and be safe.
14. I can't cry.
15. I can't hear my inner voice.
16. I can't speak to the creator.
17. I don't know how to access my inner guidance.
18. I don't know how to take care of myself.
19. I don't know the difference between myself and others.
20. I don't know what is safe.

21. I don't know where I am headed in life.
22. I have been discarded.
23. I let others make my decisions for me.
24. I must compromise what I want to make others happy.
25. I must do what others say to be liked / loved / wanted / approved / needed.
26. I must hide my grief.
27. I must make compromises to be wanted.
28. I must make compromises to get things done.
29. I must sacrifice my values to get where I want to be later.
30. I need an excuse to cry.
31. I want revenge against _____.
32. I want to get even with _____.
33. I'm not loved.
34. I'm not worthy.
35. I'm not worthy of being loved.
36. If I change I will lose the love in my life.
37. If I do what I really want I will lose what I love.
38. If someone hears me breathing they will annoy / hurt me.
39. It is dangerous to breathe.
40. It is dangerous to breathe the air.
41. It isn't safe to cry.
42. Life is hard.
43. Life's a struggle.
44. Listening to your inner voice is dangerous.
45. Love is pain.
46. My heart is broken.
47. No one wants me.
48. Nothing I do is of value.
49. People take advantage of me.
50. Someone is always waiting to attack me.
51. What I say and/or do is ignored.
52. What/Who I love hurts me.

*Look at themes of life purpose, worthiness, attack, abuse, acknowledgement, approval, beingness, boundaries, flow, self-esteem, self worth, self knowledge, self respect, grief, past lives, memory, trust, power, unmet needs of recognition, defenses, grief

Allergies – Wheat

Fears
- Fear of being out of control
- Fear of taking anything in
- Fear of living
- Fear of abandonment
- Fear of being unloved / unwanted
- Fear of others telling them what to do
- Fear of others knowing your truth

Teachings
- Allow and value the ideas of others
- Be accepted for who you are
- Be around others and not be stressed
- Be in the flow of life
- Be listened to
- Be myself
- Be open to different ways of doing

- Fear of being seen
- Fear of no one listening

- things
- Be open to the ideas of others
- Be safe with being seen
- Be safe with feelings
- Being in the now
- Express your feelings safely
- Get what I need to be nurtured
- Joy
- Live in the now
- Live without a rule for everything
- Live without being a martyr
- Live without being a victim
- Live without being harried
- Live without controlling everything around me
- Live without having to meet the expectations of others
- Live without rules
- Love myself
- Nurture myself
- Receive love
- Safe with change

Emotional States

- Fear of loss of control.
- Only living half a life.
- Pressured to conform to restrictive role expectations (job, family, community).
- Not in the flow of life.
- Keeps self from being nurtured.
- Constantly arguing and rejecting the ideas of others.
- Holds rigid and structured beliefs.
- Extreme kindness/ sweetness to others; self-sacrificing to cover over feelings of hostility.
- Unmet needs in early life for nurturing.
- Gives off the aura of being harried/ frenetic energy- this is a smokescreen that keeps them from being seen.
- Everything is stop and start – the frenetic energy keeps them having to look at self and feelings.
- Guilt

Cross Indexing: Leaky gut syndrome, pancreas problems, allergies, bladder problems, asthma, skin problems, celiac disease, ACOA, Wounded Creative Core

Repeating Patterns: doesn't allow in new ideas, feels unaccepted for who they are (stressed in the company of others), lack of inner peace, feels their not being listened to – yet they shut others out, no self-care, not present in the moment, victim and/or martyr, need to control those around them, doesn't receive, stresses out at change.

Created Patterns

1. _____ is constantly after me for something.
2. _____ irritates me.
3. Change is dangerous.
4. Expressing my feelings/ thoughts is dangerous.
5. God let me down.
6. I am a victim / martyr.
7. I am abandoned by _____.
8. I am afraid of my anger.
9. I am aggravated by _____.
10. I am dangerous when I am angry.
11. I am invisible.
12. I am out of control.
13. I am overlooked.
14. I am powerless.
15. I am powerless to stop others from hurting me.
16. I am trapped.
17. I am unhappy with life.
18. I am worthless.
19. I can't do what I want to do.
20. I can't ever please _____.
21. I can't let go of my grudge against _____.
22. I can't stomach _____(who?).
23. I don't know what I what to do in life.
24. I don't know who I am.
25. I don't love myself.
26. I don't trust God.
27. I have no value.
28. I must argue with others to prove my worth.
29. I must be right.
30. I must be right to prove I'm good enough.
31. I must control my emotions.
32. I must control my environment.
33. I must control my feelings.
34. I must do what others tell me to do.
35. I must hold my feelings in.
36. I must never show who I truly am.
37. I must prove myself.
38. I must put on a happy face to be safe.
39. I must sacrifice for others.
40. I mustn't let anyone see how I feel.
41. I never get to do what I want to do.
42. I don't know what I want to do so I put others first.
43. I'm not valued by/ respected by _____.
44. I'm not wanted by _____.
45. If I agree with everyone I'll be safe / love/ wanted/ accepted /approved of.
46. If I don't conform I will _____ (lose my job, be rejected, be ridiculed, etc).
47. If I express my feelings I am out of control.
48. If I stay busy no one will see me.

49. If things change I'm not safe/ I get hurt.
50. My feelings were hurt by _____ and I can't forgive.
51. No one listens to me.
52. Others before me.
53. People stress me out.
54. Safer to not be seen.
55. There is only one way to do things.

*Look at themes of boundaries, control, emotions, running away, self-esteem, self-worth, self-respect, change, soul purpose, unmet needs, anger, feelings, fear, joy, judgment, power, rejection, defenses

Alopecia

Fears
- Fear of persecution
- Fear of the future
- Fear of pain
- Fear of needing to be needed
- Fear of looking inward
- Fear of intimacy
- Fear of love
- Fear of life in its many forms
- Fear of being unloved
- Fear of feeling worthless
- Fear of never having or being enough
- Fear of being judged
- Fear of others attacking

Teachings
- Accepted
- Balance
- Be compassionate (inner peace in the face of suffering)
- Be flexible
- Be good enough
- Be in the flow
- Be yourself and be safe
- Change easily
- Connected to Creator / God
- Creator's definition and perspective of power
- Deserve
- Give
- Happiness
- Have enough
- Have other choices
- Know who you are
- Listen to your inner voice and be safe
- Live without a façade
- Live without being critical of others
- Live without expecting to be hurt by those you love
- Live without expecting to fail
- Live without fear of others
- Live without judging others
- Live without judging others by how they live
- Live without judging others by where they live
- Live without love being conditional
- Live without needing to better than others to be good enough

- Loving myself
- Open heart
- Open to change
- Open to new ideas
- Receive
- Respectful of the path of others
- Safe and protected
- Unconditional love
- Wanted

Emotional States

- Unhappy with who they are, resist change, afraid that someone will get too close and see who they are and that scares them. Lives on the surface.
- Lacks compassion for others. Thinks harshly of others with a diminished capacity in life. Highly critical of people in poverty, with addictions and limiting attitudes.
- Wants what they cannot get, not just material goods. In relationships, they fall in love with someone that does not return their love. They set themselves up to be hurt fulfilling the belief that people they love always hurt them. This pulls them into a spiral of hurt, pain, and depression. This is a cycle. They did not get their needs for love and acceptance met as a child.

Cross Indexing: Aging, Hair-falling out, hair-balding, endocrine system disorders, genetic

Repeating Patterns: lack of inner peace, feelings of unworthy, never have enough, doesn't listen to or trust their inner voice, expect to be hurt by those they love, fear of others (this may be ancestral), continual judging, closed to new ideas – immediately shuts down anything that comes in, does not feel safe.

Created Patterns

1. I always get the seconds.
2. I always have to settle.
3. I am a failure.
4. I am depressed.
5. I am disconnected from god/ creator.
6. I am in danger.
7. I am unhappy.
8. I am vulnerable.
9. I am weak and will be hurt.
10. I can't ask for help.
11. I can't let people get close to me.
12. I don't know who I am.
13. I don't like myself.
14. I don't love myself.
15. I have a broken heart.
16. I have failed life.
17. I have to settle for second best.
18. I must be critical of people that could hurt me to protect myself.
19. I must point out what is wrong with people, otherwise I am like them.
20. I must prove I am better than others to feel good.

21. I need to be better than others.
22. I never get what I want.
23. I never have enough.
24. I'll never be as good as _____.
25. I'm not good enough.
26. I'm not lovable.
27. I'm unworthy.
28. Love always has strings attached.
29. Love is pain.
30. My heart is broken.
31. No one loves me.
32. People I love always let me down.
33. People I love hurt me.
34. People that get close to me hurt me.
35. People with addictions are dangerous.
36. Poor people are dangerous.

*Look at themes of relationships, peace, happiness, joy, acceptance, allowing, authenticity, beauty, change, class systems, compassion, depression, God, judgment, love, loving yourself, rejection, self-worth, self-esteem, unconditional love, unmet needs, broken heart, consumerism/always wanting more, empathy, jealousy/envy, power, romantic love relationships, worthiness

ALS or Amyotrophic Lateral Sclerosis or Lou Gehrig's Disease or Motor Neuron Disease

Fears
- Fear of letting go
- Fear that they have traveled a road to their own doom
- Fear of changing course
- Fear of falling
- Fear of the unknown
- Fear of accomplishment
- Fear of the rules

Emotional States
- Junked ideas pile up in the corners of their life like rotten garbage that has not been taken out. They have not let go of concepts or ideas that they know do not work in their life. Fostered concepts in others that will be proven unreliable. Whole areas of their lives look like plains of darkness. They refuse to journey into the darkness and they refuse to clean out piles of junked ideas. They fear falling into the abyss if they let go. They fear dropping into the darkness of the unknown. Ancestral: trauma of choice — either choice would result in death.
- Feels as if getting anywhere in life is like scaling a vertical cliff of sheer basalt. There is nothing to hang on to and it is almost impossible to drive a piton into the rock, so they climb. Hardly ever do they win or accomplish what they set out to do. That is their feeling. Unwritten rules of behavior have kept them constrained. They can only climb that wall one

way or not at all. Ancestral trauma: if they go another way or take a different path to the top of the cliff they will be hurt or die.

Cross Indexing: Swallowing-trouble, muscle problems, nerve problems, Wounded Creative Core

Repeating Patterns: depression, doesn't let go of stuff that doesn't work – keeps doing the same thing expecting a different result, continual sense of failing.

Created Patterns

1. No one knows how to listen to me.
2. Life is a struggle.
3. Life is hard.
4. If you don't struggle it's not worth it.
5. Things should never come easy.
6. If it's easy it's not worth anything.
7. There's only one way to do things.
8. I will die if I stay where I'm at.
9. I can't win.
10. I can't let go.
11. I'm never enough.
12. My accomplishments are never enough.
13. People don't listen to me.
14. I fear change.
15. I am paralyzed with fear.
16. I have no control of my life.
17. Someone has taken my power (who?).
18. It is better to concede than fight.
19. It's not safe to relax and go with the flow.
20. Day by day I am losing my power.
21. People take my power from me.
22. The loss of my power is the loss of my life.

Alzheimer's

Fears
- Fear of tomorrow
- Fear of institutions
- Fear of being trapped
- Fear of being forced against their will
- Fear of giving in
- Fear of being told what to do
- Fear of their anger
- Fear of being out of time
- Fear of being seen a failure
- Fear of being diminished
- Fear of letting go

Teachings
- Allowing
- Be in control of your body
- Be in control of your life
- Be in control of your thoughts
- Be in the flow
- Be trusting of others
- Capable of handling my life
- Competent
- Experience life in new ways with joy
- Forgive
- Handle challenges without anger

- Fear of being ripped off
- Fear of being hurt
- Fear of being out of control

- Handle change without anger
- Happiness
- Have the power to make change
- Joy
- Let go
- Live feeling reassured
- Live without anger
- Live without feeling overwhelmed
- Manage successfully
- Self-reliant
- Supported
- Trust my decisions
- Trust myself
- Valued

Emotional States

- Longtime hatred of established ways has built resentment deep within the thoughts. This animosity is from cultural mores that have dictated behavior. They have "obeyed" the cultural mores but held a deep unsaid and for the most part deep resentment toward these mores. Church, institution, family, etc. have said you "must" be this or you must do that or you must feel that.
- Unsaid words holding deep directions not taken. Hollow acquiescence to life. The penalty is too high for them to be otherwise. It's too hard to know that they have not answered the deep primal yearnings of their cells.
- Warnings from other went unheeded. Hateful speech (bigotry, racism, misogyny, etc.) raced through their being. Remnants of a legacy left in the DNA with no home no landing place. Confusion. Words unfelt floating to the surface of awareness. Ancestral DNA finds no resting place in this life.
- Failure. Life has been a series of failures that have led to biased opinions toward others. Strong sense that others have failed them instead of having failed and taking responsibility for those failures.
- Hard-won victories over obstacles have created bitterness at the ease of others. They don't realize they have created the obstacles. They pontificated about their hard life and that others should suffer the way they do/have.
- Justice denied. Feels deep resentments. These are resentments of the mind. Holds negative attitudes that create a maelstrom of anxiety in and around them. They hold things tight to their chest because they fear revealing too much of them for fear of being "ripped off" and justice denied again. This is a loop. The pattern is repeated in their life.
- There is a watery aspect of their nature. The water is an overflow of emotions. They will retain water and have issues with edema and other maladies that reflect a buildup of fluids. The emotions are overwhelming and they don't know how to express them so the emotions build up and get reflected in wet maladies.
- Strong emotions of hatred and-or a lack of fulfillment in their life. A deep sadness fills their being and the past is mired in sadness. Wrong impressions created the sadness. Communication that went awry tumbled over in their mind and became hatred.

Cross Indexing: Dementia, Senility, depression, hypertension, aging, wounded creative core

Repeating Patterns: lack of inner peace, cycles thoughts of hatred and feelings of injustice, creates a life of struggle, blames others for their failures, stuck to thoughts and behaviors dictated by institutions.

Created Patterns
1. I am angry at _____.
2. I am depressed.
3. I am going to be hurt by others.
4. I am helpless.
5. I am helpless to change things.
6. I am overwhelmed.
7. I am powerless.
8. I am powerless to change things.
9. I can't be angry at _____.
10. I can't cope with life.
11. I can't face life anymore.
12. I can't let go of the past.
13. I don't trust myself.
14. I have been overrun.
15. I'm not in control of my life.
16. I'm not supported.
17. It is hopeless.
18. It is safer being in my world.
19. It's easier to be somewhere else.
20. Life is overwhelming.
21. My life is being taken away from me.
22. My life is out of control.
23. Other people must tell me what to do.
24. People don't trust me.

Amenorrhoea

Fears
- Fear that they are on the edge of dying
- Fear of starvation
- Fear of no control
- Fear of being nothing
- Fear of love

Emotional States
- Under extreme stress to the point where the body thinks it is in danger and may not survive. This may be ancestral and damage to the endocrine glands happened during grandmother's gestation.

Cross Indexing: Endocrine System Disorders, menstrual problems

Repeating patterns: Anxiety, possible eating disorders, wounded creative core

Created Patterns
1. I must survive.
2. I must sacrifice everything to survive.
3. I must starve to survive.
4. I don't love myself.
5. I can't change things to be better.
6. I am helpless in the face of overwhelming forces.
7. I'm not here, there is no me.

Amyloidosis

Fears
- Fear of attack
- Fear of hating themselves
- Fear that everyone else hates them
- Fear of being defenseless
- Fear of injustice
- Fear of retribution
- Fear of letting go
- Fear of being trapped
- Fear of self

Emotional States
- They are unable to mount a defensible defense against an attack. The defense is thwarted and when it is there is a feeling of being wronged. The initial attack was based on something they needed that was at the time justified within them. They can't let go of the feeling of being wronged or the thoughts of anger and there is a cycle. They then punish themselves over and over. Not grieving the original wound that created the second. They have broken a sacred vow.

Cross Indexing: Arthritis – Rheumatoid, Crohn's Disease, Colitis – Ulcerative, Bone Problems

Created Patterns
1. I can't defend myself.
2. I have been wronged and then I was made out to be the bad person.
3. I have been falsely accused.
4. I must punish myself forever. What I did was justified in doing.
5. I will never forgive or be forgiven.
6. The only way out of this suffering is to die.
7. I let people think they are right and then I do what I need to do.
8. I must harm myself to make amends.

9. I hate myself. I hate the person accusing me but I can't get away from them.

Anemia

Fears
- Fear that someone else's truth will hurt them
- Fear of peace
- Fear of success
- Fear of being seen
- Fear of not being good enough
- Fear of joy
- Fear of relating
- Fear of not being better than
- Fear of being present
- Fear of being alone
- Fear of being worthless
- Fear of love
- Fear of betrayal

Emotional States
- Just can't get it right. Always feels like their efforts are short of getting the right solution/answer/direction. They don't see that they are actually the one undermining their efforts. They can't allow themselves those successes or peace. Every time they put themselves out there they go into fear. The fear of being found to be lacking is always there.
- Hearsay is how they live. They scan the horizon for an opportunity to repeat hearsay that brings them attention; a news story that is not quite right, gossip that has gotten distorted, etc. They long to be seen but not seen. They get seen by being interesting through the stories of others where they have no aspect of self that is to be shared. This keeps the real them from being unseen.
- Not there of joy. Avoids the things that bring joy. When invited to play they have work to do. When attending a party they will head for the kitchen to become part of the serving staff or one of the cooks. If forced to mingle or be among people for recreation they will find ways of escaping; a headache, alcohol, etc.
- Fosters a need to be right which creates a defensiveness in others.
- Constant searching for the answer to their aloneness – there is a haunting quality to their existence a sense of being barely there – the physical body is latent. Desires are solitary. Yields little in the winds of life.

Cross Indexing: Spleen Problems, Bone Problems, Blood Disorders, cancer, HIV/AIDS, rheumatoid arthritis, kidney disease, Crohn's disease, and inflammatory diseases

Repeating Pattern: Gives all they have to a relationship – then they play out a sense of ownership of that individual – then they are alone, lack of inner peace, no self-care (includes loving themselves, resting when needed, etc.), creates scenarios of unworthiness, hasn't allowed themselves joy or a comfort with themselves.

Created Patterns

1. Each day is a struggle.
2. Everyone else has a good life but not me.
3. God hurt me.
4. God is punishing me.
5. I am angry at _____.
6. I am angry at the world.
7. I am depressed.
8. I am going to die.
9. I am rejected by _____.
10. I am unhappy.
11. I can't change things.
12. I can't get past the pain.
13. I can't see things getting better.
14. I don't get to have fun.
15. I have a broken heart.
16. I have been betrayed by my mother / father.
17. I have no luck.
18. I should never have been born.
19. I want to die.
20. I will never realize my dreams.
21. I'm not good enough.
22. I'm not lovable.
23. It's hopeless.
24. Life is a burden to be endured.
25. Life is hard and mean.
26. Life is pain.
27. No one can help me.
28. No one understands how much I hurt.
29. Things will never change.
30. I am angry at myself.
31. I am devoted to _____.
32. I can't control _____.
33. I don't like myself.
34. I don't love myself.
35. I hate myself.
36. I have to control _____ or they will leave me.
37. I let _____ happen and I blame myself.
38. I must be right.
39. I must control _____.
40. I must control others to be safe.
41. I must do it myself or it to be right.
42. I never get what I want.
43. I'm not enough.
44. I'm not good enough.
45. Nothing is ever done right.
46. There is no joy in life.

Anemia – Pernicious

Fears
- Fear of letting go
- Fear of getting caught
- Fear of life
- Fear of living
- Fear of being seen
- Fear of pain
- Fear of being present
- Fear of injustice
- Fear of someone getting more than them
- Fear of their anger
- Fear of joy
- Fear of not being good enough

Teachings
- Inner peace
- Loving yourself
- Unconditional Love
- Be in the flow
- Live without life being a burden
- Live without life being painful
- Live without life being a continual challenge
- Live without carrying the ancestral burden of life being suffering
- Joy
- Divine Order

Emotional States
- Running. Always running. Arms are full of what they are holding onto. Frantic energy of hanging onto the old and dead images of the past. No desire to carry on with life. Hard lessons in this life. Wants to not be seen – they want to disappear into the earth. Feels like they can't carry the load of life. Too much pain – holds onto beliefs that are hollow, high regard for false idols. Has an approach that if 'I could only be like him/her life would be better'. They are not really 'in' their life. They don't love themselves.
- Haunted by the past. They cling to long-dead memories and bring them into their present as if they were still alive. Joined in this by others they strengthen the hold the past has and think they will crumble if they did not have the dead in the now.
- Gender imbalances drive them nuts. They see the unfairness and biases toward their gender and this almost more than they can bear. They have stuffed these feelings to survive. Occasionally, they will work their way to the surface in a flash of anger.
- Their life is one big juggling fest. One minor distraction and everything will come raining down from its suspended position. They hold out their juggling skills as a badge of honor but in essence, they are keeping away joy and life.
- No desire to carry on with life. Hard lessons in this life. Wants to not be seen – they want to disappear into the earth. Feels like they can't carry the load of life.

Cross Indexing: Anemia, Spleen Problems, Blood Disorders, Autoimmune diseases, HIV, Diabetes Mellitus Type 1, Crohn's Disease

Repeated Patterns: lack of inner peace, creates a burdened life full of struggles, and continually sends joy away.

Created Patterns
1. _____ abandoned me.
2. I am always in pain.
3. I am depressed.
4. I am helpless to change things.

5. I don't have the energy to live anymore.
6. I don't love myself.
7. I don't understand how to get what I want in life.
8. I have given up.
9. I never made anything of myself.
10. I want to die.
11. I want to quit.
12. I'm not nurtured and cared for.
13. I'm not wanted.
14. If I am seen someone will expect something from me.
15. Life is a burden.
16. Life is a struggle.
17. Life is pain.
18. Life is too hard.
19. Love is pain.
20. No one understands me.

Anemia – Sickle Cell

Fears

- Fear of a crisis in their culture that will destroy them
- Fear of joy
- Fear of life
- Fear of living
- Fear of not being good enough
- Fear of their anger
- Fear of pain
- Fear that things will never change
- Fear of peace
- Fear of letting go of their anger
- Fear of betrayal

Teachings

- Whole
- Fun
- Joy
- Play
- Inner peace
- Let go
- Let go of the anger that holds their pain
- Let go of the anger at God/ The Creator
- Live without pain
- Live without betrayal
- Live without needing someone else's approval to be loved
- Complete
- Acceptance
- Be in the flow
- Compassion (inner peace in the face of suffering)

Emotional States

- Heartsick – Heaviness to life. Joy is not there. No ability to move forward with their heart's desire to be what they want to be. They have a deep longing for acceptance and love. Happiness eludes them. They feel like they are not good enough.

- Headstrong and angry – raging at the fates. This person came into the world with that anger. They want other people to hurt as much as they do. Anger is due to a sense of helplessness at not being able to change their condition.

Cross Indexing: Anemia, Blood Disorders, Spleen Problems, Ancestral / Epigenetic

Repeating Patterns: lack of inner peace, sabotage what they want in life, hang onto anger, a feeling of betrayal by others – people leave when the anger becomes too much.

Created Patterns
1. Each day is a struggle.
2. Everyone else has a good life but not me.
3. God hurt me.
4. God is punishing me.
5. I am angry at _____.
6. I am angry at the world.
7. I am depressed.
8. I am going to die.
9. I am rejected by _____.
10. I am unhappy.
11. I can't change things.
12. I can't get past the pain.
13. I can't see things getting better.
14. I don't get to have fun.
15. I have a broken heart.
16. I have been betrayed by my mother / father.
17. I have no luck.
18. I should never have been born.
19. I want to die.
20. I will never realize my dreams.
21. I'm not good enough.
22. I'm not lovable.
23. It's hopeless.
24. Life is a burden to be endured.
25. Life is hard and mean.
26. Life is pain.
27. No one can help me.
28. No one understands how much I hurt.
29. Things will never change.

Aneurysm

Fears
- Fear that they are too weak to bring joy into their life
- Fear of not being good enough

- Fears joy
- Fears inner peace
- Fear that there will never be enough
- Fear of letting go
- Fear of letting new information in
- Fear of having happiness taken from me
- Fear of hurt
- Fear of pain
- Fear of listening to others
- Fear of being left
- Fear of connection

Emotional States
- Hole in their life – something missing. They can't quite seem to fill the hole to achieve happiness. They feel like they are never quite good enough. They feel as if they have stopped short of their goals. Self-hatred for the situation they were born into. Physically can't meet the expectations of their life. Works (physical) beyond what would be expected of a human.
- Would like to be someone else. Can't accept who they are. Doesn't allow themselves inner peace or joy. They have trouble letting go. They feel like they never get the answers to their questions. They are closed off to the answers. Early influences closed them off to the flow of answers.
- Stuck in disappointment. No joy. If they let go of the disappointment they have to face themselves. The journey of getting to the core of their disappointment is too overwhelming.

Cross Indexing: Stroke, Brain Problems, Blood Disorders, ACOA, Arteries, Veins

Repeating Patterns: lack of inner peace, keeps cycling through scenarios that create disappointment, keeps trying to fill a gigantic hole in their being with no success.

Created Patterns
1. I am angry at _____.
2. I am disappointed.
3. I am never satisfied.
4. Everything always falls short.
5. I must work hard to be happy.
6. I work hard and never get anywhere.
7. If I were someone else it would be different.
8. I can't let go.
9. No one gives me the answers I want to hear.
10. I can't hear what people are telling me.
11. I am stuck.
12. I can't change anything.
13. I can't let go of _____.
14. I can't say no.
15. I don't deserve.
16. I am empty.
17. I am alone.

18. I have been abandoned.
19. I don't like myself.
20. I don't love myself.
21. I hate who I am.
22. I hate my family.
23. I can't change.
24. Change is dangerous.
25. I must do everything.
26. I must please everyone.
27. I never have any fun.
28. I will never be happy.
29. I'm not good enough.
30. If I could just be someone else I would be happy.
31. Life is a disappointment.
32. Life is just too overwhelming.

Angiolipoma

Fears

- Fear that they can't ask for what they need in life
- Fear of being caught
- Fear of being wrong
- Fear of not being good enough
- Fear of pain
- Fear of hurt
- Fear of betrayal
- Fear of feeling
- Fear of life
- Fear of letting go
- Fear of change
- Fear of knowing
- Fear of intuition

Emotional States

- Yields to no one. Ensconced in their position. Will not budge. Lost in the field of ideas that are not their own and not based in the truth of their life. Has no way of finding the edge of the field. Always wandering. Taking what they see as the "way" it is.
- Hardness. They feel a sense of rigidness in their perceptions. Nothing allows them to soften. They bang up against hard walls so they have to be hard to survive. They are constantly pushing up against hard walls. There is no sense of flow. Only obstacles.
- Correctness. Always a need to be correct. Hollow answers surround their correctness. Those hollow answers give them a perceived purpose at its core there is a deep heart pain of hurt caused by a betrayal of values.
- A narrowness of vision only allows so much to enter. They have intuitive knowingness but they shut it down to just a narrow flow, to the point where it has lost all real information or meaning.

This stems from their inability to integrate that level of information so that it is helpful. So they are constantly shutting down to avoid truth.

Cross indexing: skin problems, blood problems, growths

Repeating Patterns: Creates trauma/drama in relationships and life situations that create hardship for themselves and others. Self-sabotage, stubbornness, and shallow personality. Doesn't allow access to feeling – only shows the surface – no depth. Stuck, holds ideas that have lost truth, hitting truth against a brick wall, lack of inner peace. Betrayed. Must be correct, shuts out the flow of ideas and life force.

Created Patterns
1. Life is hard and you must be hard to survive.
2. I must make life a struggle to be relevant.
3. I am right.
4. I am perfect.
5. My approach is the only one that matters.
6. I don't change my position on ideas.
7. Just because some says it doesn't make it right.
8. People betray me.
9. I am stuck.
10. I can't change.
11. Change is dangerous.
12. I must go along with what others say.
13. I must be hard/ rigid/ unyielding.
14. I am always hitting a wall.
15. Life is hard.
16. Life is a struggle.
17. I must be right even if I am wrong.
18. I am betrayed by _____.
19. People betray me.
20. I have betrayed myself.
21. I have betrayed others.
22. I can only know so much.
23. Too much info is bad.
24. Truth is not truth.
25. I can never know what's right.
26. Right is what I say it is.

Ankle Problems (pain, sprain, swelling)

Fears
- Fear of seeing it through
- Fear of being out of control
- Fear of being unsupported
- Fear of being questioned / challenged
- Fear of letting go

Teachings
- Good enough when challenged
- Good enough
- Intelligent
- Self-Worth
- Self Esteem

- Fear of things not getting better
- Fear of their intuition / knowing
- Fear of listening
- Fear of being wrong
- Fear of inner peace
- Fear of being right even when they know they are wrong
- Fears failing
- Fear of not being good enough
- Fear of being unwanted / unloved
- Self Love
- Accepted without proving my intelligence
- Receive
- Flexibility
- Guilt

Emotional States

- Lack of control over the direction of their life.
- Unhappy and wants change but can't seem to change course.
- Hanging onto the wrong things thinking that things will get better if they just keep going down their current path.
- Second-guessing the outcome, that second-guessing is not coming from the intuitive and it leads them in the wrong direction.
- Hears only half the story and makes decisions before all the facts are known.
- Hates to be seen as wrong so they will try to cover over the mistakes and not take responsibility for the wrong direction/ errors.

Cross Indexing: Leg problems, Feet problems, Right or Left-sided negative tendencies, Sarcoidosis

Repeating Patterns: lack of inner peace, doesn't listen to their inner voice – chooses the wrong path – then doesn't change course, defends their wrong position at all costs.

Created Pattern

1. I am a failure.
2. I am afraid of failing.
3. I am angry at people that doubt me.
4. I am overworked.
5. I am stupid.
6. I am wrong if I am challenged.
7. I can only be good enough if I am right.
8. I don't want / can't hear someone else's opinion.
9. I must be intelligent to be accepted.
10. I must prove I am good enough.
11. I must prove my intelligence.
12. I must prove myself.
13. I'm not needed / wanted / valued / liked.
14. I'm not valued.
15. I'm not worth anything.
16. I'm not worthy.
17. Issues of being inflexible.
18. People that doubt me question my integrity / intelligence / path.
19. People think I am stupid.

20. People think I don't know anything.
21. There is no relief from the burden of life.

Ankylosing Spondylitis

Fears
- Fear that they will be defined, put in a box
- Fear of letting go
- Fear of failing
- Fear of knowing too much
- Fear of seeing too much
- Fear of disobeying the rules
- Fear of change

Emotional States
- Lack of reality. A sense that if they just keep going in this direction it will get better. They get focused on one path. Don't look at the other alternatives that could be a solution. Rigidly holds to one way of looking at the world. Feels that they hold the right worldview.

Cross Indexing: Inflammation, Arthritis, Arthritis-Osteoarthritis

Repeating Patterns: Keeps doing the same thing time after time even though it's a time of failure. Life is pretty much the same. Lives in a world that doesn't change because they don't let it.

Created Patterns
1. Change is dangerous.
2. My way is the best way.
3. I know best.
4. People lie, they make stuff up.
5. If I work hard, it will be OK.
6. Nothing matters except what I say.
7. I can't forgive or forget.
8. I can't let go.

Anorectic Bleeding

Fears
- Fears being struck by family
- Fear that there is no choice but to take the abuse
- Fears trusting others
- Fears trusting self
- Fear of change

- Fear of joy
- Fear of freedom
- Fear of not doing their duty
- Fear of letting go
- Fear of peace

Emotional States

- Hollow promises to self lead to self-demotion and denigration. Life is joyless. The joys are always being taken by self. High levels of resistance to change. Afraid to discharge one's duty. Feels helpless to let go of duty must hang on to it at all costs. There is a horror deep in their being of being discharged from their duty. Loud noises from within create the chaos and confusion that harness the energy of fear. This stops them from freedom.

Cross Indexing: Anus Problems, Colon problems, Intestinal problems, Cancer-colon, hemorrhoids

Repeating Patterns: lack of inner peace, doesn't honor their own needs, positions of duty control their life.

Created Patterns

1. I am angry at _____.
2. There is no joy in life/living.
3. I must never forgive.
4. I must be in control.
5. I can't let go.
6. I don't know how to let go.
7. I can't get anywhere.
8. I am frustrated by _____.

Anorexia

Fears
- Fear of the disappointment of life
- Fear of not being freed by knowing the illusion
- Fear of the shell they show
- Fears judgment
- Fear of life
- Fear of inner peace
- Fear of nurturing
- Fear of being invisible
- Fear of losing the story (identity)
- Fear of trusting others and self
- Fear of being themselves
- Fear of not being good enough
- Fear of being unwanted / unloved

Teachings
- To be nourished
- To be nurtured
- Trust
- Take care of myself
- Live feeling nurtured
- Be valued
- Be happy
- Live without feeling out of control when eating
- To harmonize food with your body
- Be accepted
- Live without judging my weight
- Be loved
- Love myself

- Fear of being out of control
- Fear of their flesh/ body
- Fears their body keeps them from being loved

- Unconditional love
- Live being myself and being loved
- Live without needing to make my self worth equal my weight
- Accept my body
- Be good enough
- Be seen and be safe
- Be accepted
- Live without being a victim
- Live without depression
- Creator's perspective and definition of body weight

Emotional States
- The promise of life is hollow. Plainly aware that everything is an illusion. Disillusioned with life. Life offers no alternatives to their psychic pain.
- They feel as if they are held up to constant scrutiny. They want to be transparent or invisible. Jumps into situations that they have absolutely no idea what they are doing and when it fails they punish themselves.
- Wants to die. Feels like they are headed for destruction. They are held out as an example to others. Looks at life through the eyes of a child. They can't grasp what people are doing. They only know it doesn't feel good and the attention hurts. Stunted emotional growth – unable to please parent(s).
- Self-rejection, self-hatred, rejection of nurturing, not grounded, mother relationship is skewed.

Cross Indexing: Bulimia, Depression, Obsessive Compulsive Disorder, Addictions – Chemical, Anxiety

Repeating Patterns: lack of inner peace, lack of self-nuturing, lack of self-care, lack of loving self, food is an enemy, depression, victim/ martyr.

Created Patterns
1. Being fat is disgusting.
2. Being fat is horrid.
3. Fat people are ugly.
4. I am a mistake.
5. I am a victim.
6. I am depressed.
7. I am fat.
8. I am not accepted.
9. I am used by others *(who are the others?)*.
10. I can never be good enough for others.
11. I can never please my mother/father.
12. I can't eat and be happy.
13. I don't love myself.
14. I don't trust myself.
15. I don't trust others.
16. I hate myself.

17. I must be invisible.
18. I must be perfect.
19. I must be perfect to be accepted / loved / wanted.
20. I must be someone else to please people.
21. I want to die.
22. I'm not good enough.
23. I'm not good enough for me.
24. I'm not wanted by my mother / father.
25. If I am skinny I am in control.
26. If I control my eating I control my life.
27. If I looked like someone else I would be loved.
28. Life is a disappointment.
29. My body is ugly.
30. My mother hates me.
31. No one wants me for just me.
32. Nothing ever seems to work for me.
33. People are just out for what they can get from you.
34. The thinner I am the closer I am to being perfect.
35. The thinner I am the more beautiful I am.
36. The thinner I am the more I am loved.

Anus Problems

Fears
- Fears the contraction of sadness
- Fears forgiving
- Fears letting go
- Fears being seen as not enough
- Fears being unloved
- Fears being threatened
- Fears being powerless
- Fears loving self
- Fears pain
- Fears being themselves
- Fears not being punished
- Fears freedom
- Fears peace and calm
- Fears not pleasing others

Teachings
- Let go
- Be in the flow
- Joy
- Unconditional Love
- Harmony
- Live without feeling threatened
- Forgiveness
- Live having your needs met
- Live without having to please others
- Happiness
- Joy
- Love myself
- Unconditional love

Emotional States
- Inability to let go of something that needs to be "done" or end. Early potty training involved punishment. High level of intolerance for people. All interactions with people are very impatient. Must hold in the impatience. Punishment is how they get love. Guilty of not doing the right thing and pleasing. Can't do what they want to do. Feels guilty about wanting to end something. A recurring problem of not being able to do what they want.
- Survival is threatened by outer conditions and they feel powerless in the face of this threat.

Cross Indexing: Colon, Hemorrhoids, Anorectic Bleeding

Repeated Patterns: impatient with people – impatience builds – becomes irritation, creates situations where they are punished and then they feel loved, lack of inner peace, created a life where they feel threatened, lack of the selfs (self-love, self-care, self-nurturance).

Created Patterns
1. I am threatened by _____.
2. I am powerless.
3. I can't forgive _____.
4. I can't do what I want to do.
5. I am guilty of not doing the right thing.
6. I must please others.
7. When I am punished I get love.
8. Love is pain.
9. I must be punished.
10. I am powerless to _____
11. I don't know how I am going to survive.
12. Everything is falling apart around me.
13. I doubt my inner voice.

Anxiety

Fears
- Fear that life has too many expectations and they will fail
- Fears self
- Fear of intuition
- Fear of being present
- Fear of god
- Fear of failure
- Fear of things not getting better
- Fear of being overwhelmed
- Fear of doing
- Fear being trapped
- Fear of uncertainty
- Fear of being alone
- Fear of being unsupported
- Fear if change
- Fear of love
- Fears the heart

Emotional States

- Can't reconcile the inside with the outside...spiritual with the physical. The physical world (material) creates an inner tension when this person gets too close to the awareness of the higher self.
- Fear of the pain of failure. Influence of others puts pressure on the person to act in a way different from their inner guidance. This person knows their needs are not being met. They have a feeling of failure when their own needs are not being met. They feel trapped and do not feel like they can change.
- There is a feeling of overwhelm and that they are in a deep dark pit. The tools they have used in the past are no longer working. They feel nothing is making their circumstance better. The harder they work at trying to change things through the use of the creative-intuitive or nurturing the worse their condition seems to get. This state may be reflective of the individual being in parenting situation that is frustratingly difficult. They feel trapped and there is no way out.
- What has supported this person is now wrapped in uncertainty. They are faced with having to make choices. Everything they know, their foundation, is now reflecting inconsistencies. Their means of self-expression has been shredded. What they have learned now appears rigid and hard. Response to their needs feels cold and mechanical. They feel very alone and unsupported. There is no real place for them to go to feel support from someone else...that is what they see and feel. They have lost sight of love and tolerance of self. This person is not allowing in the power of intuition and self-trust to move them through this life transition. There is a fear of looking at the alternatives. All that they have relied on is not there so they revert into confusion
- The first broken heart is the source of anxiety. The first broken heart is when the one they love most in the world hurts them, breaks their trust. They then replicate that pattern of not being worthy of love. Never allowing themselves to love.
- The experience of anxiety is the heart trying to send a message, information, and the person in their separation from knowing their heart has suppressed messages from the heart.

Cross Indexing: Agoraphobia, Panic Disorder, Depression, ACOA, Obsessive-Compulsive Disorder

Repeated Patterns: depression, not honoring the journey, lack of inner peace, ignoring the inner voice of intuition, lack of trust of self, painting themselves into a spiritual corner, not adapting to life's changes, don't trust.

Created Patterns

1. Change is dangerous.
2. Change isn't safe.
3. Bad things are going to happen to me.
4. Decisions are dangerous.
5. Everything falls apart.
6. Everything is a mess.
7. I am alone.
8. I am angry at _____.
9. I am bitter toward _____.
10. I am depressed.
11. I am dying.
12. I am helpless.
13. I am jealous of _____.
14. I am lost.
15. I am overwhelmed.

16. I am trapped.
17. I am unsupported.
18. I can't change anything.
19. I can't depend on anyone or anything.
20. I can't let go of _____ (what will happen if you do?).
21. I can't move.
22. I can't wait for the solutions.
23. I don't belong.
24. I don't know where to turn.
25. I don't know who I am.
26. I don't love myself.
27. I don't trust myself.
28. I don't trust others.
29. I expect more from myself that others.
30. I give away my power away.
31. I have no choices.
32. I must be better than others.
33. I must have things now.
34. I want to die.
35. I'm not empowered.
36. I'm not important to God.
37. I'm not in my power.
38. I'm not protected.
39. I'm not safe.
40. I'm not secure.
41. I'm stuck.
42. If I make a decision I will get hurt.
43. If I make a decision it will be wrong.
44. My intuition has failed me before.
45. No one cares about me.
46. No one listens to me.
47. No one loves me
48. No one understands me.
49. Nothing I do works.
50. There is no one to help me.
51. There is no way out.
52. Using my intuition is unreliable.

Appendicitis

Fears
- Fear of being trapped
- Fear of letting go
- Fear of anger
- Fear of dying
- Fear of secrets
- Fear of people in authority

Teachings
- Be safe
- Be in the flow
- Have boundaries
- Let go
- Forgive
- Be able to let go of frustration

- Fear of life
- Fear of standing up
- Fear of being forced to do against their will
- Fear of having something held over their head

- Be able to let go of anger
- To have choices
- Live without feeling trapped
- Live without feeling people are out to get you
- Live having your needs met
- Live without thinking authority will hurt you
- Live without feeling bound by rules
- Live without having people keep secrets from you
- Speak your truth and be safe

Emotional States
- Stuck in a dead end situation; does not appear to be a way out.
- Won't let go of the bad stuff that has happened to them; holding anger.
- Angry at people withholding what they need.
- Anger at hidden choices/agendas that are not revealed; which limited the ability to meet needs.
- An inner desire to push and speak back to authority figures but holds the inclination-and pressure builds.

Cross Indexing: Wounded Creative Core, Abdominal Problems, Throat Problems, Intestinal Problems, Ear Problems, Infection

Repeated Patterns: lack of inner peace, keeps hold of resentments/anger/betrayals, creates life situations of no-choices.

Created Patterns
1. Everyone is out to get me.
2. I am afraid of life.
3. I am afraid of the people that have authority over me.
4. I am being pushed around by _____.
5. I am dependent on others to meet my needs.
6. I am overwhelmed by the fear of _____.
7. I am angry at _____.
8. I am trapped.
9. I can't forgive.
10. I can't get my way.
11. I can't get what I want.
12. I can't let go.
13. I can't speak up when faced with an authority figure.
14. I hate being told what to do.
15. I hate people (which people?).
16. I must be something I'm not to please people (who?).
17. I must shut up and be quiet.
18. I never get what I want.
19. I resent / bitter toward / angry at / etc. _____.

20. I will never get out of _____.
21. I'm not safe.
22. If I speak back I will be hurt.
23. If I speak back I will be punished.
24. It's not safe to say what I truly feel.
25. Life is full of rules that make me unhappy.
26. No one listens to me (who doesn't listen to you?).
27. People keep secrets from me (who?).
28. There's too much pressure on me to be something I'm not.

Appetite – Excessive

Fears

- Fear of being unable to change things
- Fear of getting close (intimacy)
- Fear of letting go
- Fears feeling unworthy
- Fears peace and balance
- Fears nurturing themselves
- Fears control
- Fears feelings
- Fears rejection
- Fears being unloved

Emotional States

- Foresaw/foreseen instances of non-compliance to the way things "ARE" creates anxiety. No hope to change the way things "ARE" created a vacuum of life. No sense that there is any other way. Won't let go of the way things "ARE".
- Long awaited rewards leave them numb, feeling unworthy and off balance. Their balance always feels off. They feel as if they do "X" they'll be balanced. The imbalance equals excesses are balanced by eating. Since they are always off balance they are always trying to feel balanced by eating.

Cross Indexing: Weight-Over, Addictions-Food, Weight Issues

Repeated Patterns: out of balance, lack of inner peace, lack of the selfs (self-love, self-care, self-nurturance, self-acceptance).

Created Patterns

1. I have no control.
2. I am being controlled by others.
3. I am out of balance.
4. I always do things to extremes to be safe.
5. I must eat to be safe.
6. I am numb.

7. I am unworthy.
8. Nothing satisfies me.
9. I am never sated.
10. My life is empty.
11. I must eat to feel in control.
12. I can't let go.
13. I am not protected.
14. _____ will hurt me.
15. I am not accepted.
16. People reject me.
17. I feel safe when I eat.
18. Food is safe.
19. I feel loved when I eat.
20. Food is love.
21. I'm not loved.
22. I'm not nurtured.
23. Food protects me.
24. The heavier I am the safer I am.
25. I must be heavy to be safe.
26. I must eat to keep from feeling.
27. My feelings are wrong.
28. I must not feel.
29. The more I feel the more I must eat.
30. When I eat I can ignore my feelings.

Appetite – Loss

Fears

- Fears being present
- Fears the heartlessness of others
- Fears responsibility
- Fears looking within for answers
- Fears being powerless
- Fears life
- Fears having to give
- Fears connection that is not giving to them
- Fears knowing
- Fears intimacy
- Fears criticism

Emotional States

- Congealed narcissism. Deep into oneself as the source of all. Rarely look outside of themselves for inner support. Holds everything outside at a distance. As if they were planets circling a sun. They are warmed by their own presence until one day the veneer cracks. A look in a mirror, a look at a reflection in a shop window and they are horrified at the presence of someone they do not know.

- Worried. Futurization of what may be a strong sense of accountability for what may go wrong. Continual projection kills the life force in the present. Ancient attitudes flood into the present and render them powerless.
- Hurrying through life pretending they don't see those that judge and criticize. They blow past them yet those same people reach deep into their being laying the roots that siphon off life force and get substantiation by criticizing others.

Cross Indexing: Depression, Anxiety, Bulimia, Anorexia, Aging, Weight Issues

Repeating Patterns: parasitic relationships – they get life force from others, focuses on the past or future – not present, lack of inner peace, no sense of inner self.

Created Patterns
1. I am depressed.
2. I distrust _____.
3. I'm not good enough.
4. I am going to die.
5. I want to die.
6. I don't trust myself.
7. I don't trust others.

Arms – Left

Fears
- Fears peace
- Fears being in situations of tension
- Fears the balance of give and receive
- Fears being trapped by the stuff of life
- Fears being forced against their will
- Fears letting go of the female ancestral story
- Fears their concept of the divine is wrong

Emotional States
- Out of balance with the sister (right arm). Fairly nothing can be done when there is a failure to compete. They feel as if they drop and break things-the things of life: relationships, jobs, finances. They feel a heaviness with these things and often feel they are not strong enough to hang on or hold them.

Cross Indexing: Right and/or left sided negative tendencies, Carpal Tunnel, wrists, Hand problems

Repeating Patterns: out of balance, lack of inner peace, everything is a competition, lack of inner strength, can't hang onto a job/relationship, doesn't enjoy life, lack of harmony with the women in their life.

Created Patterns
1. I don't believe in the creator.
2. The creator abandoned me.
3. The creator doesn't exist.
4. I can't embrace life.
5. I can't hang onto what I have.
6. I can't get what I want.
7. It's dangerous to reach for what I don't have.
8. I must carry the burden of hatred/anger/bitterness/failure felt by my mother/ex-wife/wife/daughter.

Arms – Right

Fears
- Fear of being unable to protect themselves and others
- Fear of movement
- Fear of showing self-care
- Fear of receiving
- Fear of not being better than
- Fear of getting what they want
- Fear of losing the pity story
- Fear of having to depend on themselves
- Fear of letting go of the ancestral male story

Teachings
- Loving yourself
- Be nurtured
- Unconditional Love

Emotional States
- Holding themselves to a higher standard than others. They expect more of themselves than others do. Feels that expectation keeps them at a distance and safe from others so that others won't see they are not good enough.
- Not aligned with reality. Holding out for things that are never going to happen. The scope of what is expected and the effort being made to get it are not in alignment.

Cross Indexing: Right or Left-Sided Negative Tendencies, Wrists, Carpal Tunnel, Hand Problems

Repeating Patterns: Plays the poor pitiful me, unrealistic expectations, holds themselves out as not good enough, needs someone else to take care of them, lack of the selfs (self-care, self-nurturance, self-love, self-acceptance).

**Trans-generational wound of not being able to protect

Created Patterns
1. Exercise is too much trouble.
2. I can't take care of myself.

3. Everyone else comes before me.
4. I must be better than everyone else.
5. I expect more of myself than others expect of me.
6. I must carry the burden of hatred/anger/bitter/failure felt by my father/ex-husband/husband/son.

Arteriosclerosis (Atherosclerosis)

Fears
- Fear of getting what they want
- Fear of letting go
- Fear of being wrong
- Fear of joy
- Fear of not being good enough
- Fear of being unloved
- Fear of being irrelevant
- Fear of change
- Fear of being controlled
- Fear of self preservation

Emotional States
- Desire is suppressed. They feel they cannot have what they want. No one gives them what they want. What they receive will never meet their expectations. They are always disappointed.
- Holds on. Won't let go when it is time. Holds on when even hanging on hurts them in many ways. Has made many enemies by hanging on to what is needed to serve others. By hanging on they have hurt others.
- Holdout hope-beyond-hope that things will come around to their view. Won't let go of needing to be right. Unjustly, hanging on to what they expect of life. Life expectations are based on false ideas that hold a fantasy world.

Cross Indexing: Hypertension, Blood disorders, heart problems, addictions – smoking, kidney problems

Repeating Patterns: never satisfied, must be right, false ideas (their concept of perfection) with no connection to reality, make up what they want to believe.

Created Patterns
1. Everything stops me from getting what I want.
2. I am disappointed by _____.
3. I am worthless if I am not perfect.
4. I can't see how good things are.
5. I know more than others.
6. I must be perfect.
7. I must be perfect to be loved.
8. I must be perfect to be seen.
9. I must tell others what to do or they will do it wrong.

10. I will be punished if others do it wrong.
11. What are the issues of inflexibility and rigidity?
12. When I am perfect _____ (what happens?)

Artery Problems

Fears
- Fear of telling the truth
- Fears being lied to
- Fears lies creating blame
- Fear of blame
- Fear of letting go
- Fears joy
- Fears being trapped
- Fears feeling
- Fears someone will reveal the secrets
- Fear that someone will know what they hold in their heart
- Fear of listening to others
- Fear of being wrong
- Fear of letting someone else control them
- Fear of standing in their truth
- Fears powerlessness
- Fears being forced into giving
- Fear of giving and not receiving in kind

Emotional States
- Unyielding. Yields to no one, feels that if they do they give up a piece of identity. When pushed they will stiffen their resolve and refuse to see wisdom. They will only see the threat to their identity.
- Hatred. Inflamed passions without reason and not rooted in desire. Hatred without cause or foundation. No harm has been done to them. Simply a deep-rooted hatred. Genetic. They have always known this hatred.
- Weakness. Weakness of the "heart". This does not imply a physical weakness of the heart but it does imply a weakness of character that is soft. They take no stance. When confronted or challenged they wilt. They lose "heart". There is no resolve to persevere in their own way.
- Cannot say "I love you" without feeling weak and losing life force. They feel as if they are handing over their power to someone else.
- Never does anything wrong. Is always right. They must get it right or they feel impotent and powerless.

Cross Indexing: Veins, ACOA, Blood Disorders, Heart Problems, Arteriosclerosis

Repeated Patterns: very stubborn – consistently refuses to listen to other wisdom, must be right, loving someone is weakness, feels stuck and has no idea how to get out (couple that with stubbornness and the flow of joy is impaired), feels as if feeling is a weakness and creates a weak position, feminine-masculine imbalance to giving and receiving.

Created Patterns
1. I am forced to lie.
2. I am responsible for everything.
3. I am stuck and have to accept this.
4. I can't tell (What secrets are you holding?).
5. I hold all the secrets.
6. I lost my childhood to _____.
7. I was never allowed to be a child.
8. I'm distracted.
9. I'm not free to feel.
10. People/Stuff gets in my way and stops me.
11. There is no joy in life.
12. There is no way out.

Arthritis

Fears
- Fears being forced against their will
- Fear of reprisals if they don't give
- Fears being wrong
- Fears life
- Fears letting others see their emotions
- Fears not being heard
- Fears being overrun
- Fears being invisible
- Fear of giving and giving with no reciprocity

Emotional States
- Does for everyone else and not themselves. Gives to others. This is how they stay relevant and needed. Fears disappearing. Shows up unexpectedly to 'help'. They were taught to always pitch in and help. They were never allowed to be idle or just be part of party. May have been regarded the servant within the childhood family structure.
- Repeatedly forced to do manual work against their will.

Cross Indexing: Joint problems, arthritis-Rheumatoid, arthritis-Osteoarthritis, arthritis-Infectious

Repeating Patterns: Disappears into the kitchen to cook and clean at parties. Refuses to be part of the party. Will do what they are forced to do but will hurt themselves in the process.

Creative Patterns
1. I am angry at being forced to 'do' against my will.
2. I am always right in what I think.

3. I am angry at _____.
4. I am depressed.
5. I am going to die.
6. I am never good enough.
7. I am never wrong.
8. I can't forgive _____.
9. I have no right to be angry.
10. I have to be right.
11. I must be right.
12. I must never let people see I am angry.
13. If I am wrong I will be rejected.
14. If I am wrong no one will ever listen to me.
15. If you compromise you give in and you are weak.
16. It is wrong to be angry.
17. My anger keeps me safe.
18. No one is ever good enough.
19. Nothing is ever right.
20. The story of my life is I'm not good enough.
21. What are the issues of rage?
22. What are the issues of rigidity/inflexibility in your life?

Arthritis – Infectious or Septic

Fears

- Fears being unsupported
- Fears feelings
- Fears aging
- Fears powerlessness
- Fears being out of control
- Fears being dependent
- Fears not being good enough
- Fears creativity
- Fears criticism
- Fears being their own person
- Fears being taken advantage of
- Fears being in the limelight
- Fears inner violence being justified

Emotional States

- Loss of support for spiritual growth. Weakened feminine; intuition, creativity, and compassion have shut down. Masculine energy in their life is insisting on the person anchoring in the material world at the expense of their spiritual growth.
- Afraid of the unknown parts of self. Afraid of getting close to the tough stuff. Getting close to the emotions is overwhelming and they pull back.
- Emotions are out of control. They are having trouble functioning in day to day life.

- Out of sync with the world. Confused and overwhelmed. Heart is wounded and doesn't know where to go to put it back together.
- Helps others tirelessly at the expense of their own ego. Diminishment of self. Holds tight to being right about helping others that then take advantage of them. Is continually being drained by others that take and never give. Holds tight to being the way they are in the world. Does not want to adapt to new information or new facts that would change existing ideas or attitudes.

Cross Indexing: Joint Problems, Arthritis – Osteoarthritis, Arthritis-Rheumatoid, Arthritis

Repeating Patterns: lack of inner peace, lack of the selfs (self-love, self-acceptance, self-nurturance, self-care), wades deep into the inner punishment of guilt, giver.

Created Patterns
1. Emotional work is painful.
2. Feelings are painful.
3. Getting old means you can't do things.
4. I am afraid of my emotions.
5. I am angry at/resent _____.
6. I am getting old.
7. I am going to die.
8. I am going to fall apart.
9. I am helpless.
10. I am lost.
11. I am no good.
12. I am overwhelmed by my feelings.
13. I am rejected.
14. I can't control my emotion.
15. I can't control myself.
16. I can't receive.
17. I can't take one more thing (What is it that you can't take one more of?).
18. I don't know how to nurture myself.
19. I don't know how to take care of myself.
20. I don't know what I feel.
21. I don't understand what is expected of me.
22. I must do what my partner says to be loved/respected/wanted/supported.
23. I must guess at how to behave.
24. I'm not good enough.
25. I'm not OK alone.
26. I'm not protected.
27. I'm not supported.
28. It is too hard to feel.
29. Love is pain.

Arthritis – Osteoarthritis

Fears
- Fear that their time will be taken from them
- Fears others
- Fears their feelings
- Fear of being blamed
- Fears not being good enough
- Fear of not having enough
- Fears letting others close to their story
- Fears being overrun
- Fears letting go
- Fears being used by others
- Fears an identity of overt power
- Fear being dependent on others
- Fears being heard
- Fears being in control
- Fears intimacy
- Fears change and authority
- Fears being vulnerable

Emotional States
- Self-punishment behaviors. The feminine aspect is wounded. Compassion and nurturing others is shut down. Person may be controlling / harsh / bitter/ judgmental. Believes they are the victim. Conversely, they overdo for others without regard for their own needs. They still believe they are the victim.
- Out of control. Energy is scattered. There's an inner anger. No one is hearing them. They feel as if they have no energy.
- Stressed to perform flawlessly. They feel like they are in the spotlight. Performance is a façade. No one gets close enough to them to see the real self. Projects a façade of truth, light, and love. The energy to keep the façade up is wearing them down.
- Living in their head. Imbalance of the masculine analytical and the feminine intuitive.
- Puts on a façade to cover up their deep unhappiness. Won't let anyone see who they truly are.
- Holding hatred of their mother or father. Old anger that destroys flexibility and understanding. Feels betrayed by father and/or mother.
- Rigid and inflexible in their ideas. Cannot compromise.

Cross Indexing: Joint Problems, Arthritis – Rheumatoid, Arthritis, Arthritis-Infectious

Repeating Patterns: Victim/Martyr, not heard by the feminine (women in their lives), loss of energy, out of balance, when they are in public they can't seem to disappear, giving but with rules, giving exceeds their physical abilities.

Created Patterns
1. Emotional work is painful.
2. Feelings are painful.
3. I am a martyr.

4. I am a victim.
5. I am afraid of my emotions.
6. I am angry at _____.
7. I am bitter toward/ angry at/ hate / resent/ jealous of _____.
8. I am forced to bend to someone else's will.
9. I am fragile.
10. I am insecure.
11. I am overwhelmed by my feeling.
12. I am sad/ unhappy.
13. I can't do enough to make people happy.
14. I can't forgive _____.
15. I don't know how to be happy.
16. I hate _____.
17. I have no energy.
18. I must hide the truth.
19. I must sacrifice myself for others.
20. I will never be enough.
21. I will never have enough.
22. I will never heal.
23. I'm not protected.
24. It is dangerous to be angry.
25. It is too hard to feel.
26. It's the fault of others I am unhappy.
27. No one believes me.
28. No one listens to me.
29. Other people blame me for their problems.
30. There is never enough.

Arthritis – Psoriatic

Fears
- Fears being heard
- Fears emotions that are couched in being an adult
- Fears growing up
- Fears adults
- Fears responsibility
- Fears letting go
- Fear of the unknown
- Fears that they will never have enough
- Fears relationships where they are not dependent
- Fear of responsibility
- Fear of injustice
- Fears being the last one to know

Emotional States

- Childlike wisdom keeps them focused on being a child. There is a failure of the consciousness to grow with the body. Lost in the wilderness of life that does not connect with a childlike value system with the expectation of adult attitudes. Sense of justice is seen from their perspective as a child. There is not a balance of give and take within the scope of events. They feel like no one listens to their point of view.
- Huge need to let go of the imbalanced. Can't let go of the past and hangs on, this creates the imbalance. Unwritten aspect of self creates aspects of self that cannot be reconciled. There is an unknowing. Like a big dark, hole in the center of their being. They feel as if the hole cannot be filled.
- Purpose is at odds with what has been created. Emotional growth stopped due to trauma of what was supporting them.

Cross indexing: Joints, skin, arthritis, autoimmune disorders, inflammatory disorders

Repeating Patterns: Relationships take over the role of parent. Boss is like a father or mother. They are often discounted in the roles the play in relationships. Wounded creative core. Lack of inner peace. Child like approach. Justice must be a perfect balance of take.

Created Patterns

1. No one listens to me.
2. If I never grow up no one will take me seriously.
3. I don't want responsibility.
4. Justice is what I say it is.
5. Right and wrong are what I say it is.
6. I can't let go.
7. I feel empty.
8. My heart is numb, I don't feel.
9. The past defines me.
10. I am out of balance.
11. I expect everyone to give me what I want.
12. Why can't people be nice?
13. I must hang onto the past.
14. I am unsupported.
15. I am owed.
16. The world isn't fair.
17. I must stay a child to be loved and wanted.
18. I am ignored.
19. I must yell to be heard.
20. I have no life purpose.
21. I am supported/ unwanted.

Arthritis – Reactive (Reiter's Syndrome)

Fears
- Fears change
- Fear of too much overrunning them
- Fears being controlled
- Fears being out of control
- Fears new
- Fears letting go
- Fears being vulnerable
- Fears being unsupported
- Fears not being good enough
- Fears getting it right
- Fears losing their connection to the ancestors

Emotional States
- Headed in the wrong direction. Feels like nothing ever works. Feminine side is not developing.
- Feeling of barely hanging on emotionally.
- Lack of foundation for principles. Their value system is built on sand. They want to be able to shift and change their inner truth in whatever way serves them at that moment.
- Fear that nothing they touch will be good enough. Old out of date ideas creates the dynamic for nothing they do being good enough. What they do gets rejected because it doesn't reflect an enlightened/modern form of thinking. They won't change. They have gotten stuck in a method of learning that doesn't let them bring in new information. Nothing makes sense so it is discarded. They lost the ability to follow linear learning. Because if they take on new thoughts it will say that the people they love and their passed ancestors are wrong. This will dishonor their memory. They need to protect the illusion.
- Longing for the 'good ole days'. Stuck in a time and era where the vibrations were denser and can't move into higher vibrational ways of thinking. As such they have little to contribute.
- Leaning on others to support them. They have sacrificed their independence for support – doesn't know any other way. Uses this to hang onto people in their life. A sense of grasping.

Cross Indexing: Autoimmune Disorders, Polyarteritis, Infection, Urinary Tract Infection

Creative Patterns
1. Being a woman means you will be dominated.
2. Change is dangerous.
3. Change will destroy what I know.
4. I am barely hanging on.
5. I am going to fall apart.
6. I can't learn anything new.
7. I can't let go.
8. I can't take one more thing (What is it that you can't take one more of?).
9. I don't know what I believe.
10. I don't know what is important.
11. I don't know what my inner truth is.

12. I must give up myself to be supported.
13. I must pay a price to be supported.
14. I must please people to be accepted / loved / taken care of.
15. I'm not good enough.
16. I'm not important.
17. I'm not valued.
18. My parents/ grandparents were always right.
19. Nothing ever works.
20. Why change if the old ways are good enough?
21. Women are weak.

Arthritis – Rheumatoid

Fears
- Fears being hurt by hostile intentions
- Fears inner peace
- Fear of joy
- Fears pain
- Fears life
- Fears feeling vulnerable
- Fears being overrun
- Fears their feelings
- Fears being attacked
- Fears being irrelevant
- Fears being wrong
- Fears authority
- Fears the creative core
- Fears being out of control
- Fears being unsupported
- Fears being overwhelmed
- Fears powerlessness
- Fears letting go

Emotional States
- Creative expression through movement and speaking is stopped. Their enjoyment of life has been stifled. There is no inner peace. Anger festering at the person that stopped their joy.
- Life is a burden to be endured. Lacks courage of convictions. Closed down and so no hope of change.
- Expressing and feeling emotions are suppressed. Poor boundaries. Does not trust intuition. Creative energies are stopped.

Cross Indexing: Joint Problems, Arthritis, Arthritis-Osteoarthritis, Arthritis-infectious, Restless leg syndrome

Repeating Patterns: Wounded creative core, stuffs their feelings, feels like they have to fix others, doesn't trust the inner voice or feelings, lack of inner peace, feels under attack by people in power or authority needs to stuff their feelings as a consequence, takes on duties or burdens that don't belong to them, feels powerless to change things, lack of creativity (wounded creative core) stops them from finding solutions that are maybe outside of the box or circumvent those in authority.

Creative Patterns

1. Creativity is dangerous.
2. Everything is out of control and I must fix it.
3. I 'm not supported.
4. I am a victim.
5. I am angry at /bitter toward/ resent _____.
6. I am helpless to change things.
7. I am overwhelmed by life.
8. I am powerless.
9. I am responsible for everything.
10. I can't forgive _____.
11. I can't speak my truth and be safe.
12. I don't know what joy is.
13. I don't trust people in authority.
14. I have been expressing/feeling strong emotion of _____ for a long time (these are negative emotions: hatred/ resentment/ anger/ revenge/ sorrow/ grief/ bitterness).
15. I have no control.
16. I must always wear a smile.
17. I must be perfect.
18. I must hold it all in.
19. I must judge myself.
20. I must never let people see who I am.
21. I want vengeance against _____.
22. I will be hurt if I let people see me cry.
23. It isn't safe to feel.
24. Life is a burden.
25. Life is all work and no play.
26. My survival is dependent on my doing my duty.
27. No matter what I do I will never be able to make it better.
28. People in authority are mean.
29. People in authority ridicule me.
30. People in authority will hurt me.
31. Playing is frivolous and doesn't get the job done.
32. The good things are always taken away from me.
33. The grief is so overwhelming I want to die.
34. What has caused you to close down?
35. What is the grief you feel?
36. Where ever I go I am attacked.
37. You must work to survive.

Asthma

Fears

- Fears being irrelevant
- Fears the fire in their heart
- Fears being overrun
- Fear of failing
- Fear of being seen
- Fears having time on their hands
- Fear of change
- Fear of stepping outside the box
- Fears their purpose
- Fears life
- Fears that they can't change
- Fears conflict
- Fears depending on others
- Fear of breathing
- Fear of crying
- Fear of letting others down
- Fear of being vulnerable
- Fears being unloved / unwanted
- Fears not being good enough
- Fear of pain
- Fear of being used
- Fear of saying no

Teachings

- Allow the flow of the universe
- Balance
- Be good enough
- Be in the flow
- Breathe and be safe
- Complete
- Creator's definition and perspective on success
- Cry safely
- Delegate responsibilities to others
- Depend on others
- Happiness
- Have good boundaries
- Joy
- Know what needs to be really done
- Let go
- Let go of obstacles / burdens
- Live without feeling like a failure
- Live without feeling overwhelmed
- Live without forcing things to happen
- Live without having to please people
- Live without needing to keep up appearances
- Lovable
- Loved
- Receive
- Say no and be safe
- Say no without guilt
- Success
- Trust others to handle responsibilities
- Whole

Emotional States

- Takes on more than they can handle which creates a feeling of overwhelm. They feel like they carry burdens and have obstacles to overcome. Lack of confidence and fear of failure.
- A feeling of can't get it all done creates a feeling of anxiety. Feels like there's no time to catch their breath. Blind to the fact things can be done differently. Locked into one way of doing things.
- High profile; seen by a lot of people with high expectations of them. Excessive work hours to keep up appearances. Has trouble getting to the real work that needs to be done. Doing what others what you to do. No room to breathe and no room to live.
- Deep questioning going on about the reason for life. Doesn't understand why they are here and what it is they are supposed to be doing.
- Breathing in sorrow – sadness – rejecting life. Feels as if they are drowning in demands of the life they have created. No respite or break from incessant demands.

EMOTIONAL PATTERNS

Cross Indexing: Lung Problems, Hypertension, Heart Problems, Allergies, Allergies-Hay fever, Shoulder Problems, Back Lower, Back Upper, ACOA (Adult Children of Alcoholics), Foot Problems, Anxiety

Repeating Patterns: lack of inner peace, creates jobs/relationship/home life/community life that creates overwhelm and they can't see a way out of the overwhelm, people pleaser, depression, they have shut down real living, don't get enough rest.

Created Patterns

1. For things to get done I must make it happen.
2. Friends always try to use me.
3. I am alone.
4. I am always tired.
5. I am depressed.
6. I am dominated by mother/ father.
7. I am going to die.
8. I am responsible for the world.
9. I am trapped.
10. I can handle anything.
11. I can't accept myself.
12. I can't be me.
13. I can't breathe and be safe.
14. I can't cry and be safe.
15. I can't do _____ myself.
16. I can't go home until the work is all done.
17. I can't let people down.
18. I can't say no.
19. I can't tell people what I think/ feel.
20. I can't walk away from someone asking for help.
21. I don't like myself.
22. I don't love myself.
23. I have to carry a heavy load.
24. I have to constantly prove I am good enough.
25. I hold myself to a different standard.
26. I must be a success to prove _____ wrong.
27. I must be better than everyone else.
28. I must be good at everything.
29. I must be helped to do _____.
30. I must constantly improve myself.
31. I must do it all to be loved / wanted / respected / needed.
32. I must keep my pain (physical or emotional) to my self.
33. I must meet the expectations of others to be loved / wanted.
34. I must prove I am worthy.
35. I must work harder than everyone else to be good enough.
36. I never have enough time to enjoy my life.
37. I'm not good enough.
38. I'm not good enough for me.
39. If I cry I will be hurt.

40. My family uses me.
41. No one believes me if I hurt.
42. No one cares about me.
43. People depend on me to make things happen.
44. Things must be done my way to be right.

*Look at themes of trust, trapped, support, strength, speaking up, sensitivity, over-sensitivity, self-love, self-knowledge, self-pity, self-respect, self-worth, responsibility, power, overwhelm. Letting go, father, mother, happiness, boundaries, overwhelm, unmet needs for recognition, anxiety, confidence, rejection

Athlete's Foot

Fears
- Fear of being nothing in the world
- Fear of letting go
- Fears being wrong
- Fears change
- Fears criticism of their direction
- Fears being challenged

Emotional States
- They have taken resentment into themselves, held it in. They will filter their choices and direction in life based upon the old resentments that they hold. This has become a part of their identity.

Cross Indexing: Thrush, Candida, Yeast Infection

Created Patterns
1. I can't move on from feeling resentment.
2. I can't let go of how I feel.
3. My ideas are the way it should be.
4. Why should I look at stuff in a new way? The old way is fine.
5. Change is not always good.
6. Why should I question my direction? It has always worked before.

Atrial Fibrillation

Fears
- Fears connection
- Fears that no one will ever rescue them
- Fears intimacy

- Fears being out in the world
- Fear of being seen
- Fear of rejection
- Fears being out of control
- Fear of inner peace
- Fear of creativity
- Fears being unloved
- Fears pain
- Fears feeling unworthy
- Fear of change
- Fear of attack
- Fear of failing
- Fear of deserving
- Fear of feeling used

Emotional States

- Heart wanders and wonders from thing to thing not really hanging on. Doesn't allow themselves the attachment of the heart. Compromises their worth. 'I can't have the really good stuff.' A feeling of being failed by the luck of their birth. Doesn't allow themselves to see beyond the Plexiglas that they put around their world. They can see the world enough to operate but can't access what's outside the Plexiglas walls.
- Desire is unmet. Keeps themselves small. They have a big self in a small enclosure wanting to get out. Many dreams as a teenager/young person that did not materialize. Deep disappointment at the failure of not achieving their dreams. The dreams were a heart's desire. May have put those dreams to others and were disappointed at the rejection.
- A heart out of control

Cross Indexing: Heart Problems, Tachycardia, Stroke, Congestive Heart Failure, Hypertension, Thyroid Problems, Graves Disease, Addictions – Alcohol, Sleep Apnea

Repeating Patterns: lack of inner peace, wounded creative core, has one failed situation after another, lack of discretion in business and relationships – makes bad judgment calls, leads a small life, has a dream that seems like it is out of reach, out of balance, doesn't easily move on when it is time to go, doesn't ask for help when it is needed, feeling of being unloved seep into intimate relationships, boundaries with mother and/or father.

Created Patterns

1. Love hurts.
2. I am worthless.
3. I am not good enough.
4. Loving yourself is sinful.
5. I'm unlucky.
6. Change is dangerous.
7. New things are dangerous.
8. I can't get what I want.
9. I must stay invisible to be safe.
10. I get attacked for wanting.
11. I get attacked for dreaming.

12. I am a disappointment.
13. I am a failure.
14. I never get what I want.
15. I am invisible.
16. I get passed over for good things.
17. No one sees me.
18. I am trapped by those around me.
19. I can't love.
20. People I love hurt me.
21. People I love leave me.
22. I'm not good enough to be seen.
23. I am not connected to anyone.
24. No one loves me.
25. People only want me for what I do for them.

Attention Deficit Disorder

Fears
- Fear no one loves them
- Fear of hurting
- Fear of pain
- Fear of the unknown
- Fear of knowing
- Fear of their inner voice
- Fear of having no purpose
- Fear of their creative core
- Fear of feeling guilt
- Fears feeling vulnerable
- Fear of not being good enough
- Fear of being blamed
- Fear of the shame
- Fear of standing still
- Fear of their body

Teachings
- Adapt to the energy of others
- Allowing
- An identity not based on doing
- Balance
- Be at peace
- Be focused
- Be in the now
- Be in your body and feel calm
- Be seen and be safe
- Be still
- Be valued
- Calm your mind
- Creator's definition and perspective of balance
- Creator's definition and perspective of love
- Creator's definition and perspective of truth
- Feel safe around others
- Feel safe being still
- Feel safe in the darkness
- Focus on one thing at a time
- Forgiveness
- Know my life purpose
- Let go
- Letting go of needing to do many things at once
- Live a life of honesty to self
- Live an authentic life

- Live without chaos
- Live without fear of blame
- Live without fear of shame
- Live without overwhelm
- Live without shame
- Loving yourself
- Still your mind
- To be calm

Emotional States

- Hard to stay in their body. The body is a painful place to be. This pain creates fear. Energies are scattered.
- Afraid of the dark…afraid of the unknown. Fear for personal safety in the dark.
- Because they cannot see the outcome of an action there is a fear of the future. The future appears as a black hole to them.
- Looking for the justification of life. They have no idea why they are here and they don't want to be in the body or here.
- Scattered thoughts, scattered energies. Energy fields were fragmented early in life by an overload of the senses caused by fear.
- Wants a balancing of a wrong. Feels overridden by guilt for wanting retribution.
- Doesn't allow anyone to find a place to connect with them. Connections to others are uncomfortable. They feel hostility towards others.
- Doesn't want to communicate from the authentic self. Sees a threat and they become afraid of being vulnerable. So they keep the focus away from self.
- No trust in self. So they do many things. With doing many things there is a hope for validation of at least one thing.
- Running away from the nightmares. Afraid someone will see who they are or are not. They don't want to be found lacking.
- Wants to not be seen so they keep moving. If they keep moving they can't be held responsible or questioned. Fear of blame and shame.
- Nothing is clear to them. They are conflicted so to keep the anxiety of inner conflict managed they do many things at one time. Sometimes these actions are in opposition to each other. But they keep the streams of action separate. They don't see the opposition. They have needs or wants that are being denied. So they settle but still have an inner desire for what has been denied.

Cross Indexing: Anxiety, Post Traumatic Stress Disorder, Insomnia, ACOA

Repeating Pattern: feels uncomfortable around others, lack of inner peace, must keep doing, must keep moving, can't let go, immersed in chaos, PTSD patterns, shame and blame, overwhelmed, out of body or not present,

Created Patterns

1. I am alone.
2. I am different.
3. I am guilty.
4. I am overwhelmed.
5. I am shamed by.

6. I am to blame when things go wrong.
7. I am vulnerable when I sleep.
8. I can't handle being responsible for _____.
9. I can't tell people how I truly feel they will laugh at me.
10. I don't belong.
11. I don't fit in.
12. I don't know what is true.
13. I don't trust myself.
14. I don't trust others.
15. I don't want people close to me.
16. I get blamed for stuff that is not my fault.
17. I have been wronged by _____.
18. I have no purpose.
19. I have to do many things to be good enough.
20. I know don't know what to do with my body.
21. I must keep busy to be safe.
22. I must keep moving to stay in control.
23. I must stay invisible.
24. I resent _____.
25. I want out of this body.
26. I want revenge against _____.
27. I'm not good enough.
28. I'm not safe.
29. I'm not valued.
30. If I keep moving no one will hurt me.
31. If I work really hard I will be valued.
32. If I worry about the future nothing bad will happen.
33. It isn't safe being in my body.
34. It isn't safe to stay still.
35. No one understands me.
36. People hurt me.
37. People that get close to me hurt me.
38. Something will get me in the darkness.
39. The darkness is dangerous.
40. The future holds danger.
41. The human body is chaos.
42. The unexpected is dangerous.
43. The unknown is dangerous.
44. The world is overwhelming.

*Look at themes of divinity, anxiety, balance, beingness, overwhelm, calm, life purpose, authenticity, body, change, communication, decisions, flow, future, insomnia, integrity, now, overwhelm, peace, polarity, purpose, self-esteem, self-worth, stress, past lives, spirituality, worthiness, joy, unmet needs, anxiety, fight or flight, boundaries, disconnection, feelings, grief, power, rejection, soul contracts, soul purpose, energy

Autism

Fears
- Fears pain
- Fears hurting
- Fears others
- Fear of not being able to speak out
- Fear of authority
- Fear of dying
- Fears feelings
- Fears connections
- Fears losing their parents
- Fears being forced against their will
- Fears suffering
- Fears being thrown away
- Fears being trapped
- Fears their body
- Fears living
- Fears making any noise
- Fears being touched
- Fears people will hurt them
- Fears being unprotected
- Fears doctors
- Fears being poisoned
- Fears letting go

Teachings
- Creator's definition and perspective of the events, actions and people causing the soul wound (on the child) or soul memory
- Spiritual understanding can be learned without leaving the body
- Learn about our spiritual nature without withdrawal from the body
- Being in the body is a path to learning and achieving spiritual at-one-ment
- Safe to feel
- Safe to be seen
- Safe to swallow
- Safe to be touched by others
- Safe to see
- Wanted
- Live without fear of being hurt
- Live without fear of being abandoned
- Live without fear of what will be seen
- Live without fear of doctors
- Live without fear of being poisoned
- Live without fear of illness
- Recover from an illness with ease
- Be in the body and be safe
- Get our lessons in the human body without being wounded
- Trust
- Forgive those that hurt you
- Inner Peace
- Live without having to hide
- Live without taking on the thought forms of the past
- Let go of past life neural patterns
- Let go of the need to control

Emotional States
- Soul wound of profound grief and fear from cellular memory or a past life. In this cellular memory/past life, they were unable to speak out, unable to be heard – child held great fear at death.
- Emotions of fear were so overwhelming that feelings and sensory input went into shutdown. This memory is held in the cellular memory/past life. A feeling that no one is there to save them from the trauma event. The cellular memory of that trauma has been triggered.
- Soul lesson of the Higher Self wanting to let go of the illusionary 'reality' that have connected them so deeply into the 3rd plane. Spiritual understanding is the objective of the Higher Self.

Cross Indexing: Wounded Creative Core, Ancestral/ Epigenetic

Repeating Patterns: a feeling unsafe, a feeling of overwhelm, a feeling of too much sensory stimulation, fear of being hurt, fear of doctors, fear of poison, fear of their bodies, no trust, no inner peace, needing control.

Created Patterns
1. Bad people will hurt me.
2. Bad people will kill my mother/ father.
3. Bad things are going to happen to me.
4. Feeling is dangerous.
5. Getting a shot means I have been poisoned.
6. Getting a shot means I will die a painful / horrible death.
7. Getting medicine means I have been poisoned.
8. Getting medicine means I will die a horrible / painful death.
9. God abandoned me.
10. God has sent me to hell.
11. I am bad otherwise I would not be tortured /hurt.
12. I am being punished by god.
13. I am disconnected from god.
14. I am forced to do things against my will.
15. I am going to be abandoned.
16. I am going to be hurt.
17. I am going to be tortured again.
18. I am going to see others suffer.
19. I am going to suffer.
20. I am nothing.
21. I am of no value.
22. I can do nothing to stop them.
23. I can't bear to see the pain of others.
24. I can't get away.
25. I don't trust people.
26. I don't want to be in a human body.
27. I don't want to feel life.
28. I must escape.
29. I will be thrown away.
30. I will die a painful death.
31. If I keep very quiet they won't hurt me.
32. If I keep very quiet they won't hurt me as much.
33. Illness means I will die a horrible/painful death.
34. It is god's will that my child is autistic.
35. It isn't safe to be touched.
36. It isn't safe to feel.
37. It isn't safe to hear.
38. It isn't safe to see.
39. It isn't safe to swallow.
40. My father did not save me.
41. My father let bad things happen to me.

42. My father will be killed.
43. My mother did not save me.
44. My mother let bad things happen to me.
45. My mother will be killed.
46. No one can help me.
47. No one can protect me.
48. Nothing can be done to stop them.
49. Nothing I do will stop them from hurting me.
50. People use me.
51. Sores mean I have been poisoned.
52. Sores mean I will die a horrible / painful death.
53. The doctors will hurt me.
54. The doctors will kill me.
55. The human body is nothing but pain.
56. The human body is overwhelming.
57. The needles will kill me.
58. The needles will make me sick.
59. The only escape from the pain is to leave the body.
60. The pain is too great.
61. The pain of being hurt is overwhelming.
62. The pain of living in a human body is too great.
63. The world is a bad place.
64. They let people hurt me.

*Look at themes of pain, boundaries, abandonment, balance, body, control, forgiveness, God, grief, guilt, higher self-connection, loving yourself, now, oneness, purpose, truth, victimhood, spirituality, worthiness, joy, unmet needs, anxiety, fight or flight, boundaries, disconnection, feelings, grief, power, rejection, soul contracts, soul purpose

Autoimmune Disorder

Fears
- Fear of attack
- Fear of authority
- Fear of breaking the rules
- Fear of being trapped
- Fear of stepping out of the box
- Fear of being vulnerable
- Fear of feelings
- Fear of being seen
- Fear of hurting
- Fear of pain
- Fear of feeling unworthy
- Fears feeling good
- Fear of others
- Fears powerlessness
- Fear of being overrun

Teachings
- Whole
- Complete
- Be safe to feel
- Joy
- Happiness
- Creator's definition of control
- Hope
- Live an authentic life
- Forgive
- Inner Peace
- Stand up and be safe
- Cry
- See others as Creator sees them
- Recognize the at-one-ment of life
- Be in the flow of universal

- Fear of not being enough
- Fear of the dominant dogmatic institution
- Fear of being happy
- Fear of life
- Fear of being nothing
- Fear of letting go

consciousness
- Creator's definition of justice
- Let go of the anger in your body
- Grieve
- Trust
- Nurture myself
- Live without being depressed
- To have life options
- Be worthy
- Live without resentments
- Respect self
- Love self
- Live without needing revenge to protect self
- Respecting others

Emotional States

- Their role in life is defined, possibly by a dogmatic institution. Very structured role in the community. They must look 'this' way, act 'this' way, be 'this' way, believe 'this' way, etc.
- They don't see any way out of the situation.
- Presents a façade to the world
- Emotional hurting inside. Feelings of not being allowed to live an authentic life. Longs to be someone else. Not happy. Has never felt whole or complete with their needs.
- Sees themselves as better than others. Wants to believe this. It gives them a false purpose for being. Otherwise, they feel worthless.
- Lots of emotional sadness. Lots of tears. Unable to get out of the pity party – poor me. Hostility held toward a source of feminine nurturing. Turns the anger inward to create tears to get nurturing from that source.
- Inflamed at the world. Anger kept tightly controlled. Inside there is a rage. Lost contact with other feelings. Anger coats everything. Probably started as a child. How to get even with those that hurt them has been their life focus.

Cross Indexing: Wounded Creative Core, Alopecia, Arthritis – Psoriatic, Arthritis – Reactive (Reiter's Syndrome), Arthritis – Rheumatoid, Autoimmune Hemolytic Anemia, B Cell – Abnormal Recognition, Cancer – Hodgkin Disease, Celiac Disease, Chronic Fatigue Syndrome, Chron's Disease, Diabetes Mellitus Type 1, Fascia Problems, Good Pasture's Syndrome, Huntington's Disease, Joint Problems, Lupus, Parkinson's, Polyarteris, Sjogrens Syndrome, Spleen Problems, Stills Disease – Juvenile, Hypertension, AIDS, Endocrine System Disorder

Repeating Patterns: lack of inner peace, in and out of abusive relationships, victim/ martyr, wounded creative core (early feelings of being under attack), depression, doesn't trust self or others, inner anger, attacking themselves.

Created Patterns

1. _____ hurt me.
2. All people are interested in is protecting themselves.
3. Everything is out of control.
4. Feelings are dangerous.

EMOTIONAL PATTERNS

5. I always attack myself.
6. I am a victim.
7. I am angry at _____.
8. I am being attacked from all sides.
9. I am better than others.
10. I am depressed.
11. I am never enough.
12. I am picked on.
13. I am sinful so I must suffer.
14. I am totally helpless.
15. I am unfairly prosecuted/ criticized/ judged/ condemned.
16. I am worthless.
17. I can't cry and be safe.
18. I can't defend myself.
19. I can't tell the difference between friends and enemies.
20. I don't care about anyone.
21. I give up.
22. I give up, it's no use, and nothing will change.
23. I hate _____.
24. I have no inner peace.
25. I know who the enemy is.
26. I must be what is expected of me or I will lose everything.
27. I must do what people tell me to.
28. I must do what the church tells me to do.
29. I must put on a pretty face.
30. I over-respond when I am under attack.
31. I resent _____.
32. I resent/ hate / am angry at?
33. I sacrifice myself for the blood of Christ.
34. I shut down when confronted by _____.
35. I want to get even with _____.
36. I will never be happy.
37. I'm judge, jury, and executioner.
38. I'm not enough.
39. I'm not worthy of living.
40. If I disobey the church I will burn in hell.
41. If I disobey the church I will lose my family/ children/life.
42. If I stand up for myself I will be hurt/put down / ridiculed.
43. If I were to be who I truly am I would hurt someone.
44. It is easier to die having lived a life of obedience than be happy.
45. It is easier to die having lived a life of obedience than do what I want.
46. It's hopeless.
47. It's not OK to let people see you cry.
48. Life is unfair.
49. Most people have got it all wrong.
50. My father is _____.
51. My mother is _____.
52. No one will ever see it my way.
53. People are out to get me.

54. People must always see the smile.
55. People/ parents hurt children just to be mean.
56. Standing out is dangerous.
57. The odds are against me.
58. The only way to survive is to do nothing.
59. There is no way to defend myself.
60. There's no use trying anymore.
61. *What can't you forgive?*
62. *Who can't you forgive?*

*Look at themes of trust, trapped, self-love, self-knowledge, self-pity, self-respect, self-worth, father, mother, happiness, boundaries, life purpose, loving yourself, right, unmet needs (recognition, anxiety, confidence, rejection, power, and justice), health, feelings, disconnection, emotional abuse, control, letting go, receiving, grief

Autoimmune Hemolytic Anemia

Fears
- Fear of secrets being revealed
- Fear that people will walk away from them when they know you are sick
- Fears joy
- Fears living
- Fear of dying
- Fear of letting go
- Fear of intimacy
- Fear of being overrun
- Fears feeling
- Fear of never having enough
- Fear of being wrong
- Fear of losing the story

Emotional States
- Keeps secrets. Puts on a huge persona of half-truths that sound complete. Living is torn into two desires: Life/live or no life/die. Always being pulled back from the choice of die by grief that holds their life in place. A grief that fills the inside of the shell of their humanity.
- Yields to no one. Holds their thoughts as being sacred, well developed and infallible. Warmth is fake. Tries to make the leap to heart from numbness but always falls back into the chasm of darkness. Has no answers to their darkness. Always grasping at abundance. There is never enough. Never feels secure in the financial aspect of living. Always a hustle to make it. Feels like they have just run a race; out of breath and then they are told they have not finished the race and they have to run some more.

Cross Indexing: Anemia, Autoimmune disorders, toxins, liver problems, kidney problems

Created Patterns

1. I must not let anyone see who I am.
2. I mustn't let people know everything; I must keep the power my secrets give me.
3. I must die, I must live.
4. I must never forget.
5. I must hold on at any costs.
6. I can't let go.
7. If I let go I will never be loved again.
8. If I let go I will fall into a chasm of nothingness.
9. Without my grief I am nothing.
10. I must be right to be safe.
11. I am numb.
12. I never have enough.
13. I must hustle to eat.
14. I must grab at what comes my way.
15. I never get to rest.
16. I am always so tired.
17. My heart only feels loved in the darkness of my grief.
18. I am without hope.
19. I must wear my wound to be seen.
20. I must sacrifice myself to my grief.

B's

B Cell – Abnormal Recognition

Fears
- Fears attack
- Fear of the next big crisis
- Fears being overrun
- Fears not being good enough
- Fears being cast in a box
- Fears sameness

Emotional States
- Sees the stuff of life through a distorted lens. Perceives through a value set that applies a distortion to interactions with others.

Cross Indexing: Scleroderma, Multiple Sclerosis, Lupus, Diabetes Mellitus 1, and Arthritis – Rheumatoid

Repeated Patterns: out of balance, seen as odd by others, perspective is skewed, under attack and invaded.

Created Patterns
1. Life is too much.
2. I am overwhelmed.
3. I am going to give up.
4. Nothing I do is good enough.
5. Others do not see me.
6. I am not good enough.
7. I can't protect myself.
8. No one understands how I see things.

Back

Fears
- Fear of letting go
- Fear of not seeing danger coming
- Fear of change
- Fear of their creativity
- Fear of being unsupported
- Fear of being overrun
- Fear of their outside voice
- Fear of feelings being known

Emotional States

- Yields to no one – back up against a wall and still will not let go. Holds the memory of old grudges and old ways that no longer work. The grudges don't protect and the old ways do not create, they only hold them stiffly in place while the world just detours around them.
- Beliefs that will not be reconciled hold or anchor them to a place they think is solid and reliable. Then one day the rock is no longer solid and no longer dependable as an anchor. What they believed to be how they supported themselves is gone.

Cross Indexing: All Back categories, spinal stenosis, slipped disc

Repeating Patterns: head says one thing and the heart says another – heart and head are incoherent, feels unsupported, wounded creative core that feels its dangerous to create solutions not sanctioned by linear thought.

Created Patterns

1. I am frustrated by _____.
2. I am overwhelmed by the feelings of _____.
3. I am responsible for _____.
4. I can't express my feelings if I do I will be rejected.
5. I can't get _____ off my back.
6. I can't handle my feelings.
7. I can't stand up for myself.
8. I must support _____.
9. I'm afraid to be seen or heard.
10. I'm not supported.
11. It's not OK to let people see how you feel.
12. People will laugh at me if I say what I am thinking.
13. You must keep your feeling to yourself.

Back – Cervical (neck)

Fears

- Fear of being unsupported
- Fear of being vulnerable
- Fear of being bullied
- Fear of standing up
- Fear of defending themselves
- Fears peace
- Fear of letting go

Emotional States
- Thinking and ideas are not supported. This person is derided and put down for their ideas. This person keeps their anger to themselves when being put down. Pretends to be dominated by the people putting them down. But, inside there is a seething anger.

Cross Indexing: All Back categories, spinal stenosis, slipped disc

Repeating Patterns: lack of inner peace, feminine and masculine is out of balance, behaves the ways others want them to – inauthentic in their behavior, compassion is stifled and rarely shown, stiffness reflected in opinions that can have the effect of hurting and alienating people.

Created Patterns
1. I'm not accepted.
2. I can't give into others when they are wrong.
3. I can't forgive _____.
4. Who or what can't you forgive?
5. What are the issues in your life of inflexibility or rigidity?
6. I can't show my feelings, people will think I am weak.
7. I am being forced to do _____.
8. I have to hold my head up high.

Back – Coccyx Pain – Tailbone

Fears
- Fear of being alone
- Fears being take advantage of
- Fear of being unsupported
- Fears success
- Fears moving forward
- Fears being out of control
- Fears of dominant women (mother, grandmother, sister, ex-wife, etc.)
- Fear of driving away the family
- Fear of change
- Fear of growth
- Fears someone will usurp them
- Fears people will walk away
- Fears there will not be enough
- Fears not being enough
- Fears being unloved
- Fears being powerless
- Fears betrayal
- Fears pain
- Fears being hurt
- Fears failing

Teachings
- Abundance
- Balance between when to ask for help and when to do it myself
- Be in a mature relationship
- Comfortable
- Creator's definition of abundance and mine are the same
- Creator's definition of happiness
- Creator's definition of right and wrong
- Creator's definition and perspective of my current of life
- Creators love
- Enjoy life
- Finish a project
- Flow with the currents of life
- Get my needs met
- Happy
- Have a relationship with myself
- Joy
- Let go of grudges

- Fears rejections
- Fears being responsible

- Let go of past hurts
- Let go of the grudges/ sludges
- Let go of what no longer serves me
- Recognize what is not working in my life
- Responsible for myself
- Satisfied
- Soul purpose
- Support others
- Supported
- When to help others and when to ask for help

Emotional States

- Worry that life will never be any better, that they will always be stuck in the mud. They will be unable to get out the dirt. The dirt equals the baseness of their life. There is an anguish to this worry.
- Justification in their need to be in control of the family. Feels family is out of control and they need to play the dominant role in keeping people in check.
- Unknown women have meted out control in their desire to rule the roost (ancestral) – "undies in a bunch syndrome".
- Generations have been left without a family leader because the prior model of family dominance was so alienating. Now there's a sense of being rudderless – there is no place for the family to come together.
- There is a winding/wound energy of having felt like their life has gone in circles and they keep repeating the same cycle over and over. Doesn't release family from familial patterns but keeps repeating them – prohibiting change and growth.
- Restriction of the free flow of energy to the roots or foundation –family/ tribal/ community relationships.
- Deeply unhappy with life.
- Can't let go of ideas that are not working/ Can't recognize what those ideas are.
- Holding onto a lack of self-reliance.
- Scarcity – lack of abundance.
- Needs not being met.
- The focus is on what they don't have.
- Goals are not being realized.
- Not achieving the goals that will get them what you want.
- Not knowing what they want.
- Lack of confidence in the Universal Intelligence/ creator to help them with the fundamental needs.
- Want to be taken care of.
- Feign independence while waiting for someone to take care of them.
- Dependent mindset and assume others are dependent on them.
- Lack of love for self.
- Unable to let go of the grudges and past hurts.

Cross Indexing: All Back categories, spinal stenosis, slipped disc, Adrenal Problems, Kidney Problems,

EMOTIONAL PATTERNS

Bladder Problems, Sciatica, Appendicitis, Large intestine, candida, Hip Problems, Pelvis Problems

Created Patterns

1. _____ betrayed me.
2. _____ hurt me.
3. _____ is a pain in the ass.
4. Being seen/visible is dangerous.
5. I am a failure.
6. I am always a day late and a dollar short.
7. I am always on the short end of the stick.
8. I am angry at _____.
9. I am being held back.
10. I am never satisfied.
11. I am not good enough.
12. I am not good enough to get things done.
13. I am only loved when I fail (the phrase was really 'screw up').
14. I am unhappy.
15. I can't complete a project.
16. I can't do _____ on my own someone else will have to do it.
17. I can't ever get things done.
18. I can't let go because no one will let me.
19. I can't support myself.
20. I can't take care of myself.
21. I don't love myself.
22. I don't trust the creator to meet my needs.
23. I don't want anyone looking to me for help.
24. I don't want to be responsible for my life.
25. I feel cheated by life.
26. I have a grudge against _____.
27. I need permission to make changes.
28. I need someone else to take care of me.
29. I need to be in a relationship where I am taken care of.
30. I never get what I want.
31. I never have enough.
32. I never seem to get anywhere.
33. I will never be happy.
34. I will never get what I want.
35. If I am responsible then I lose my life.
36. If I complete something then I will be held responsible.
37. If I don't get it done someone else will do it.
38. If I get something completed then I will be seen/ visible.
39. If I let go of _____ who will I be?
40. If I tell people what I am doing they will take advantage of me.
41. If I tell people what I am doing they will take it from me.
42. Life is a struggle.
43. Life ripped me off.
44. No one support me.
45. People let me down.

46. Someone else needs to take care of me.
47. There is safety in failure.
48. There's never enough to go around.

Back – Lumbar (middle)

Fears
- Fears being creative
- Fears being made the scapegoat for someone else's gain
- Fear of the rules
- Fear of letting go
- Fear of new thinking
- Fears change
- Fears authority

Emotional States
- High ideals of self-create inflexibility in their lives. The rules cannot be broken even by those around them without creating great amounts of anxiety.

Cross Indexing: Wounded Creative Core, All Back categories, spinal stenosis, slipped disc

Repeating Patterns: obeys the rules at all costs, the rules create stress, gets really anxious when around others that don't obey the rules, stuck in old ways of thinking and behaving.

Created Patterns
1. I am guilty.
2. I can't support myself.
3. I can't trust _____.
4. I'm not confident that I can do _____.
5. I'm not good enough/ strong enough.
6. I am going to die.

Back – Sacral – Lower

Fears
- Fears being heard
- Fear of being manipulated
- Fears being seen
- Fears un-belonging
- Fears being hurt
- Fears pain

- Fears being trapped
- Fears a positive attitude
- Fears being taken advantage of
- Fears weakness
- Fears letting go of the story
- Fears failing
- Fears being alone

Emotional States

- Lack of ability to be heard. If they are heard, they won't be seen. If they are seen they won't be heard. This person feels they can have one but not both. Unworthy of belonging. If they speak they are bad and they feel they will be hurt.
- Gripes, lots of gripes. Unable to be free. Feel locked into this…there doesn't seem to be a release from where they're at. They need to be done.
- Carrying their "weight" and having to do so much. Wants to unload. Tired of the pressure to "do" and be. If they're strong they can do everything. They must be strong all the time and then they hit a wall.

Cross Indexing: All Back categories, spinal stenosis, slipped disc

Repeating Patterns: invisible, unheard, doesn't belong, condemns themselves when speaking, stuck into repeating patterns of speech – repeats the same stories over and over, burdened, pressured, must stay strong.

Created Patterns

1. I am a failure.
2. I am all alone and have no one to help me.
3. I am going to run out of money.
4. I am in the wrong job, city, relationship, body, life, etc.
5. I can never ask for help.
6. I don't have enough money to pay my bills.
7. I failed at _____.
8. I must always do it myself.
9. I want out of _____.
10. I will never have any money.
11. I'm not supported financially.
12. I'm not supported in my relationship.

Back – Thoracic (Back High heart)

Fears

- Fear of betrayal
- Fear of carrying a burden until they die
- Fear of attack

- Fear of being unsupported
- Fear of being trapped
- Fear of responsibilities
- Fear of nothing to do
- Fear of becoming nothing
- Fear of confrontation
- Fear of the rules
- Fears rejection
- Fears being unheard
- Fears being seen
- Fears letting go of the burden
- Fears letting go of the story
- Fears not deserving
- Fears being vulnerable

Emotional States

- A shield has been created over the back heart to stop the wounding of unseen acts of betrayal.
- This is the heart space – stiffness and inflexibility in the face of stress and/or danger – freeze. Anger and resentment toward the source become hardened.
- Anger at what is supposed to support you and be safe. Anger at what is supposed to love you but just hurts you.
- A weight pushes them down. There is a weight of family obligation that keeps them from feeling their own presence and height. They feel compressed into a small space that does not allow them to move from what has been pre-ordained by family.
- Wrong-headed ideas plunge them into situations where they literally brute force their way through a situation. Instead of going around the wall they insist on breaking down the wall with their bodies.
- An unyielding flow of responsibilities. They are always responsible for everything and when there is a slowdown in responsibilities they create more responsibilities. The need for responsibilities to be safe.
- They have a Jones. (Urban slang for a state in which one experiences strong desire or attraction.)
- Knots in the stomach give them knots in their back. Anxiety in any confrontation in life causes the shoulders to brace for the onslaught of life's blows.
- Questions whether it is safe to be flexible. Can be seen but not heard. Feels that if they are heard they are violating the rules. Feels shameful. Feels accused if they speak. Feels invisible. When not heard feels rejected…shoved away. This person then pouts. Has the pity party. They then leave to go to a place where they will not be seen or heard until someone comes to bring them back. They feel that if they don't withdraw then no one will ever make an effort for them. They get recognition and acknowledgment by holding a feeling of being unheard.

Cross Indexing: Back categories, skeletal system, spondylitis, arthritis, slipped disc

Repeating Patterns: lack of inner peace, keeps themselves small, family rules (ruled), burdened, taking care of others at the expense of self, solves challenges with sheer will of strength, life and identity is defined by responsibilities, buckles under in the face of any confrontation.

Created Patterns

1. I am unsupported.
2. I carry the weight of the world on my shoulders.
3. What are the burdens in your life?
4. I am responsible for the world.
5. I am frustrated by _____.
6. Love is only given to those that deserve it.
7. I am expected to lie about my feelings.
8. I can't ever say how I truly feel (What will happen if you do?).
9. I can't forgive.
10. It's not safe to be flexible.
11. I must freeze to be safe.
12. I am in danger if I move.
13. I am in danger if I don't move.
14. I am invisible.
15. If I am heard, I am unsafe.
16. If I am seen, I am unsafe.
17. I am the victim.
18. I must run away and be the victim.
19. I must make others feel shame.
20. I must make other feel bad like I feel.
21. I get seen when I am unheard.
22. I am angry at _____.
23. I resent _____.
24. People that love me hurt me.
25. I am unloved.
26. I am unsupported.

Bacterial Infection

Fears
- Fears being unneeded
- Fears rejection
- Fears others
- Fears being told what to believe
- Fears letting go
- Fears feeling unloved
- Fears feeling unwanted

Teachings
- Be Accepted
- Creator's definition and perspective of trust
- Creator's definition and perspective of truth
- Forgiveness
- Letting go
- Live trusting others
- Live without expecting to be hurt
- Live without guilt
- Live without rejection
- Live without the fear of rejection
- To be needed
- To be valued
- To be wanted

- Trust
- Unconditional love

Emotional States
- Wanting to be needed. Feels rejected. Does not trust others. Rejects others. Does not trust what others say.
- Truth is variable. It becomes whatever they want to make it.

Cross Indexing: Reference the part of the body infected, Lyme's Disease, Meningitis-Bacterial

Repeating Patterns: unaccepted, untrusting self and others, the truth is a moving target, unforgiving, won't let go, expects to be hurt, guilt, rejected, unneeded, unwanted, unloved.

Created Patterns
1. I am alone.
2. I am guilty.
3. I am guilty for _____.
4. I am guilty for everything.
5. I am in danger when I am questioned.
6. I am rejected because I am guilty (guilty of what?).
7. I am rejected by _____.
8. I can't let go.
9. I don't know where I belong.
10. I don't trust others.
11. I don't want to be around other people.
12. I have been betrayed by _____.
13. I must be right.
14. I regret _____.
15. I'm not needed.
16. I'm not valued.
17. I'm not wanted.
18. My life is full of regrets.
19. Truth is whatever someone wants it to be.
20. When I am rejected I am hurt.
21. You can't trust people.

*Look at themes of authenticity, truth, betrayal, forgiveness, integrity, letting go, loving yourself, rejection, trust, truth, unmet needs (recognition, anxiety, confidence, rejection, power, and justice), stress

Baker's Cyst

Fears
- Fear of the world
- Fear of righteous indignation in their face

- Fear of intimacy
- Fear of their anger
- Fears rejection
- Fear of being hurt
- Fear of dismissal
- Fear of pain
- Fear of hurt

Emotional States
- Desire to run and hide from the world. Latent hostility renders them motionless in the face of their deep anger—the anger is held in the facile tendrils of their connective tissue. It is with each tensing or movement of connective tissue that they encounter a flare of anger.
- Joining in joint efforts to confront hostile joint efforts are obtuse and unproductive. They cannot connect with another person without a poisonous energy coloring the efforts between them. This could play out in a marriage, partnership or family connection.
- Hides their anger, encapsulates it. When someone gets close to it they shut down.

Cross Indexing: knee problems, arthritis, back – thoracic (Back High Heart)

Repeating Patterns: run away and hide, anger at inflexible friends or relatives, cycle back through anger, irrational confrontations, connections are filled with trauma-drama, emotions are on high alert, anger is always at the surface.

Created Patterns
1. I must run away.
2. I must hide.
3. I am angry at _____.
4. I must fight back.
5. I must be vigilant.
6. People are always trying to hurt me.
7. The world is a dangerous place.
8. I am so angry I can't move.
9. I must hide my anger to be safe.

Bedwetting

Fears
- Fear of being heard in the night
- Fear of being harmed in the night
- Fear of mother
- Fear of father
- Fear of the night
- Fear of being unloved
- Fear of rejection

- Fear of speaking out
- Fear of being ridiculed
- Fear of being hurt
- Fear of pain
- Fear of shame
- Fear of others
- Fear of family
- Fear of powerlessness
- Fear of being unworthy

Emotional States

- Hiding long held soreness of spirit. Unable to express past hurts. Expression of past hurts would render them to ridicule.
- Love is non-existent. Family is codified in abuse as a means of control and stability. There is no place for solace and standing in one's power becomes a point of attaching within the family circle.
- Passive aggressive shaming of family. Ancestral norm for the family.
- Hyper vigilance caused the person to freeze. The fear is deep and unrelenting. Being heard in the night was dangerous. The night did not bring sleep it brought monsters and torture.
- Unrelenting authoritative yelling (parents / teachers) left no place for peace. There was no one to trust. There was no way to gain power and hence peace. Huge energy envelops and held as a non-protective cocoon. Suspended. Frozen. Cannot respond to the needs of the physical.

Cross Indexing: ACOA, PTSD, Insomnia, Abused Child

Repeating Patterns: depression, lack of flow, lack of peace, doesn't talk much, won't talk about what hurts, fear being laughed at, unloved, family is controlling, doesn't nurture or care self, shame, on constant alert, lack of sleep, untrusting of self and others, powerless, worthless, surrounds themselves with stuff.

Created Patterns

1. I am afraid of my father/mother.
2. I am angry at _____.
3. I have been hurt by _____.
4. I want revenge against _____.
5. I never get what I want.
6. I'm not loved.

Behcet's Syndrome

Fears

- Fear of attack
- Fear of not having enough energy to fight

Teachings

- Unconditional Love
- Live without pain

- Fear of family
- Fear of their own anger
- Fear of life
- Fear of being present
- Fear of speaking
- Fear of asking questions
- Fear of joy
- Fear of being alone
- Fear of being nothing
- Fear of peace
- Fear of feeling
- Fear of needing support
- Fear of being hurt

- Live without anxiety
- Speak and be safe
- Be valued
- Be lovable
- Inner peace
- Joy
- Trust
- Forgiveness
- Receive
- Give
- Letting go
- Love myself
- Unconditional love
- Be balanced
- Allow others into your life and feel safe
- Live without being judged
- Live without needing permission
- Be in the flow
- Do the right thing at the right time
- Trust your inner voice

Emotional States

- Fight or flight feeling, very much on hyper-alert status. Doesn't know how to check the overreaction response in their body. Feels an ongoing background anxiety. Flow of life is shut down. Spent a lot of childhood being afraid of what might happen. Often heard the phrase 'If you don't do this you will get whipped'.
- Angry
- Un-level, off-kilter perception by the person of the events surrounding them. This person is always a little off. They never quite synchronize to the perceptions or thoughts being conveyed by those around them. This creates anxiety around interaction with others and a low-level background anxiety.
- Hyperactive attention to the details. Doesn't see the big picture. Gets lost in the details, again creating a situation where they miss the point and then create the anxiety. Told to do tasks without ever being told why. Never allowed to ask.
- They were punished if they asked 'why'.
- Feels lonely – no inflow – no connection – no joy – isolation. Does not know how to connect with others. There's a basic distrust. They get up each day and keep living. Strong independence. Heart is closed off so they close themselves off from the rest of society.

Cross Indexing: this disorder can affect many parts of the body, reference the body part that is affected, circulatory disorders, vasculitis

Repeating Patterns: run or hide or both, alone, no flow of life, lack of peace, heart is shut down, doesn't let themselves depend on anyone, disconnected from others, anger, doesn't ask questions, lives in the minutiae, out of balance, hyperactive, no real understanding of give and take, unloved, judged.

Created Patterns

1. I am angry at _____.
2. I can't let go of my anger.
3. I don't trust others.
4. I am alone.
5. Being alone is safer.
6. People are hurtful.
7. People hurt me.
8. If I do it myself no one will hurt me.
9. If I do it myself no one will reject me.
10. I am rejected.
11. I'm not loved.
12. I don't trust myself.
13. I am always doing the wrong thing.
14. I can't ask.
15. If I get it wrong I will be hurt/ punished/ rejected.
16. If I question I will be punished.
17. I must do what I am told.
18. I don't have permission to be myself.
19. I don't have permission to _____.

Bi-Polar Syndrome

Fears
- Fear of not knowing what to know
- Fear of the inner voice
- Fear of the inner struggle
- Fear of their body
- Fear of their thoughts
- Fear of being not good enough
- Fear guilt
- Fear of feeling unaccepted
- Fear of joy
- Fear of love
- Fear of being trapped
- Fear of no way out
- Fear of letting go
- Fear of others
- Fear of being boxed
- Fear of being out of control
- Fear of hell
- Fear of mother
- Fear of father
- Fear of living
- Fear of making mistakes

Teachings
- Balance
- Be accepted
- Be good enough
- Create with joy and ease
- Be in the now
- Be reliable
- Be safe in your body
- Be trusted
- Be creative and be balanced
- Be creative and be safe
- Be confident in your actions
- Calm
- Feel safe in the present
- Forgive yourself
- Forgiveness
- Happiness
- Joy
- Letting go
- Live without anger
- Live without depression
- Live without guilt
- Live without hatred

EMOTIONAL PATTERNS

- Fear of creating
- Live without needing to keep secrets
- Live without projecting that bad things will happen
- Live without needing to run away
- Live without hating people in authority
- Love myself
- Still your mind
- Trust myself
- Trust
- Unconditional love
- Allow myself to be happy
- Live without trying to find a way out

Emotional States

- Running away. Needs to escape the body. Mind is nervous with uncomfortable thoughts. Lack of self-esteem and self-worth. Extreme thoughts of hatred early in life about a parent/person in parental authority. Then extreme guilt about the hatred. Thoughts were/ are held obsessively.
- Made a mistake early in life and could not forgive themselves. The guilt ate at their consciousness and became a repetitive thought. A parent or religious dogmatic entity reinforced the guilt. They were too afraid to admit the mistake so the guilt continued to build.

Cross Indexing: Addictions, Depression, Anxiety, Obsessive Compulsive disorder, Suicidal

Repeating Patterns: out of balance, unaccepted, joyless, worthlessness, unsafe in body, untrusting of self and others, wounded creative core, nervousness and anxiety, can't let go, unforgiving, not in the present, anger, depression, guilt, hate, keeps secrets, worry that bad things will happen, running away, loveless, monkey mind, unhappy, always searching for a way out.

Created Patterns

1. Everyone thinks I am crazy.
2. Everyone thinks I can't be trusted.
3. God is going to punish me.
4. I am a sinner.
5. I am always messing stuff up.
6. I am angry at _____.
7. I am angry at people for categorizing me.
8. I am angry at people for judging me.
9. I am bad for hating someone.
10. I am depressed.
11. I am going to hell for the bad thing(s) I have done.
12. I am guilty of _____.
13. I am out of control.
14. I can't be helped.
15. I can't change.
16. I can't control my thoughts.

17. I can't do anything right.
18. I can't forgive myself.
19. I can't get away from the guilt.
20. I can't tell anyone about the bad things I have done.
21. I don't know how to talk to people without making them mad.
22. I don't know what I want.
23. I don't understand people.
24. I hate _____.
25. I hate my father.
26. I hate my mother.
27. I must get away from everything around me.
28. I must keep my secrets or bad things will happen.
29. I must punish myself.
30. I need to escape.
31. I need to get away.
32. I need to hide.
33. I want out of my body.
34. I want to die.
35. I'm not good enough.
36. I'm not good enough for god.
37. If I make a mistake I will be hurt.
38. If I make a mistake I will feel guilty.
39. If they find out about my mistake I will be _____.
40. It is not safe being in a human body.
41. It is wrong to hate someone.
42. My father hurt me.
43. My mind won't stop.
44. My mother hurt me.
45. No one understands me.
46. People put me down because I am different.
47. The human body is painful.
48. The only time I feel sane is when I am creating.
49. When I create I get very negative.
50. When I create then I feel out of control.

*Look at themes of self-esteem, self-worth, father, mother, guilt, mind, mistakes, inner child, balance, polarity, anger, betrayal, body, calm, childhood, feeling, flow, God, left out, letting go, loving yourself, unconditional love, authority, goals, creativity, motivation, negativity, paranoia, punishment, suicidal, confidence, artist, unmet needs, control, creativity

Biliary Colic

Fears

- Fear letting go of anger
- Fear of nothing being right
- Fear of things being right

- Fear of being different
- Fear of rejection
- Fear of not getting needs met
- Fear of feeling hopeless
- Fear of kindness
- Fear of the feminine
- Fear of life
- Fear of joy
- Fear of disappearing
- Fear of pain
- Fear of being hurt
- Fear of not being good enough

Emotional States
- Stuff not working leads to intense frustration and anger. Won't step back from the edge of their anger and lets it take over.
- A jaundiced view of the world. Believes that things are wrong all the way around.
- Enveloped in anger in childhood they internalized the anger of one near them in an effort to fit in and get approval.
- Feels hopeless and frustrated at their need for emotional support that never quite meets what they expect.
- Nurturing is blocked. Won't allow others to give them 'feel good' kudos or support. Won't give it to themselves either.

Cross Indexing: Gallstones, Gallbladder problems

Repeating Patterns: short fuse, falls apart when things don't work, negative speech about the world and people, anger, molds their anger to what others feel, lack of inner peace, no self-nurturing, doesn't accept or give.

Created Patterns
1. Nothing ever works for me.
2. I don't fit in.
3. Everything is wrong.
4. I have never been happy.
5. I am angry all the time.
6. I am hopeless.
7. I am worthless.
8. No one loves me.
9. I am unsupported.
10. I am unknown.
11. I am invisible.
12. I'm not worthy of being touched.
13. I don't deserve nice things.
14. I can't ever get what I want.
15. Everyone is out to get them.

16. If someone does something nice for me they expect something in return.
17. It's either black or white, right or wrong, there is no middle ground.
18. I am in pain.
19. I am not good enough.
20. I feel validated by anger.
21. I feel loved when people are angry at me.

Bladder Infection

Fears

- Fear of letting go of what is toxic for fear of losing something/ someone you love
- Fear of playing
- Fear of losing
- Fear of seen as slacking
- Fear of conflict
- Fear of standing their ground
- Fear of rejection
- Fear of hurt
- Fear of pain
- Fear of authority
- Fear of letting go
- Fear of authority
- Fear of being out of control
- Fear of being wrong
- Fear of being challenged
- Fear of their inner wisdom/voice
- Fear of intimacy

Emotional States

- Failure to hold one's values in the face of conflict. Wants more value in life. All of play must have a value. It is never play just for the sake of play.
- Unnatural ability to see past the B.S. in people. This renders them toxic to others who find it really hard to be around them and communicate with them. The B.S. detector does not take the energy of compassion into consideration. This creates an energy of rejection.
- Holding anger. Anger with an underlying theme of not good enough. Made to feel hurt — hurt feelings — held in. Wants to make someone else take responsibility for their hurt feelings.
- Everything is tiring. Held in high esteem by those around them. They let go of the right course to be right and joined those not right to be wrong. They feel let down by the people in power around them. Always holding them to a higher standard of knowing. Unable to be who they want to be and let go of the pain in their hearts.
- A desire to control and be in control. Being in control keeps them safe. They can see the bad things coming and hold it all in and together. Unwilling to let go of the past. Shows themselves to be highly agitated at the small annoyances of life. All of life irritates them.
- Anger at being challenged or questioned.
- Intuitive but they don't acknowledge it.

- Throws up walls to communication.

Cross Indexing: Urinary Tract Infection, bladder problems, infection

Repeating Patterns: Controlling anger, constantly disappointed by people, irritation, lack of inner peace, values are variable, believes in what will create a win

Created Patterns
1. I am angry.
2. I must be in control.
3. I must hang onto the past.
4. I am tired.
5. I'm not good enough.
6. I'm not responsible for others feelings.
7. I must win.
8. I am unworthy.
9. I am always right.
10. People let me down.
11. I can't let go.
12. If I let go bad things will happen to me.

Bladder Problems

Fears
- Fear of being cast away
- Fear of confrontation
- Fear of criticism
- Fears disappointment
- Fear of being blind-sided and harmed by the action
- Fear of being useless
- Fear of the unknown
- Fear of being powerless
- Fear of being overrun
- Fear of letting go
- Fear of shame
- Fear of humiliation
- Fear of being trapped
- Fear of being vulnerable
- Fear of deserving
- Fear of change
- Fear of moving on
- Fear of peace
- Fear of the future
- Fear of being out of control

Emotional States

- If they let go they fear the ramifications. They fear shame and humiliation. There is a longing for freedom to let go of toxic emotions held in check.
- A desire to have something that they don't think they will ever be able to have. They get what they don't want.
- Wants things the way they used to be. Wants to hang onto the past even though it is decaying.
- Hard liner ideas that are unyielding to an ideology that was based in a concept that is an anachronism of the past, haunted by the idea that their life would be better if people would just adhere to the old ways.

Cross indexing: Kidney problems, urethritis, bladder infection, urinary tract infection, Cancer – lung, Cancer – bladder

Repeating Patterns: They keep emotions to themselves, especially emotions that are negative. They appear to always have a sunny disposition. Pulls up the past as the gold standard. Shuts off the flow of new ideas. No inner peace. Longs for the good ole days.

Created Patterns

1. I am pissed at _____.
2. Sexual feelings are wrong.
3. I will be punished if I am sexual.
4. It is wrong to have sex.
5. I worry over money/job/health.
6. I can't release things/ideas/beliefs I don't need.
7. I must keep order to keep control.
8. I always get what I don't want.
9. I am afraid I will be hurt if I speak my truth.
10. If I express my feelings I will be hurt.
11. I am shameful.
12. I am humiliated.
13. I can't say how I feel.
14. Things/ life was better before _____.
15. The past is not past.
16. Change is dangerous.
17. Change is wrong.

Blisters

Fears

- Fear of letting go of something that has outworn its usefulness
- Fear of letting go of something that is a defeating habit
- Fear of doing something that has a different result than what you expect
- Fear of emotions
- Fear of injustice
- Fear of letting go

- Fear of being vulnerable
- Fear of being overrun
- Fear of being wrong

Emotional States
- Irritating emotions bubbling to the surface, related to how they are perceived. That perception crosses boundaries. Those emotions are always very close to the surface.
- Justice is lacking. Wants to let go of what is bothering them but if they do then a wrong will not be righted. Herculean effort to stop something from happening at their own expense.

Cross indexing: skin problems, viruses, herpes, impetigo, shingles, eczema

Repeating Patterns: injustice, violated, anger in irritating situations

Created Patterns
1. I make things harder than they should be.
2. I am vulnerable.
3. What is the unresolved anger in your life?
4. I am irritated by _____.
5. They always _____ which irritates me.
6. I feel a sense of injustice by _____.
7. People think they can walk all over me.

Bloating

Fears
- Fear of not getting enough of what you need
- Fear of weakness
- Fear of powerlessness
- Fear of being vulnerable
- Fear of being out of control
- Fear of being seen
- Fear of their anger
- Fear of the creative
- Fear of joy
- Fear of criticism
- Fears being with others
- Fear of their inner voice
- Fear of letting go
- Fear of intimacy
- Fear of creativity
- Fear of dying

Emotional States

- Letting go of emotions creates a fire that feels like it is out of control. Loss of strength in the face of this fire, puts out the fire. Fire that is held within is continually put out by the water of emotions. The stronger the fire the more water is needed to put out the fire. The fire is the fire of passion. Passion of the sacred, passion of the creative fires, inflames the artist. The fire that consumes the lover. The fire built by injustice. The fire of anger in the face of powerlessness. The last fire of releasing the physical. The fire is unsafe. The fire makes you vulnerable. The fire burns away the identity. Once the fire starts you have no control. That is why the fire must be extinguished. The water is the emotions or feelings that hold the fire in check.
- Stuffs their feelings. Doesn't know how to process
- Possible trauma of having one's sexuality criticized or the joy a creative endeavor destroyed.

*When the flames of passion cannot be lived and the water of emotion suppresses that passion then you have gas, if you drown the flame you have water – edema, congestive heart failure.

Cross Indexing: Constipation, irritable bowel syndrome, menstrual problems, allergies-gluten intolerance, cancer – colon, cancer – ovarian

Repeated Patterns: No flow, lack of inner peace, wounded creative core, doesn't feel like they can control their emotions, doesn't feel safe with others, keeps feelings to themselves, communicates at a surface level, inauthentic, intuitive guidance is silenced.

Created Patterns

1. I am stuck.
2. I can't make changes in my life.
3. I have to suck it up.
4. I must make do with what I have and not complain.
5. I must swallow my feelings.
6. My life will never be good.
7. I have to live with things the way they are.
8. Sex is dangerous.
9. Losing control is dangerous.
10. My anger is dangerous.
11. Losing control will kill me.
12. Being creative is dangerous.
13. If I express my sexuality I will be rejected.
14. Desiring sex is dangerous.
15. If I express my creativity I will be shunned.
16. Holding the water keeps me from dying.
17. Having emotions is dangerous.
18. Feeling emotions make me out of control.

Blood Disorders

Fears
- Fear of the flow of life
- Fear of understanding the cycle of life
- Fear of knowing the balance of the cycle
- Fear of moving
- Fear of change
- Fear of joy
- Fear of life
- Fear of love
- Fear of the future
- Fear of being positive
- Fear of being powerless
- Fear of pain

Emotional States
- Unwilling to see that the flow of their life has become stagnant. They have become the undead. They neither experience the joy of living or the sadness of living. The natural state of life has become non-energetic. The dynamic tension of life has been shelved. They live in an existence of a tight cycle — the life energy has become devitalized.
- Blood carries the breathe, it carries nurturance, it carries the toxins of your fears, it carries the inebriation of your happiness, love, and joy. Blood is the messenger of your body's state of being.
- Blood will carry the expansion or contraction of frequencies. The frequencies are the feelings which when felt in the body create emoting or emotion. The blood carries those frequencies to the organs of the body. The changes in the frequencies create a change in the internal pressure and the flow of life force.

Cross Indexing: Anemia, Anemia – Pernicious, Anemia – Sickle Cell, Aneurysm, Angiolipoma, Autoimmune Hemolytic Anemia, B Cell – Abnormal Recognition, Bruises, Cancer – Leukemia, Cancer – Non-Hodgkins Lymphoma, Cardiovascular Disorder, Circulation Problems, Diabetes, Hepatitis C, Hypotension, Liver – Jaundice, Polyarteritis, Sepsis, Spleen Problems, Stroke, Swollen Feet, Temporal Arteritis

Repeating Patterns: no joy, no love, fears, contracted heart, worry, eating that lowers the vibration, darkness in their living.

Created Patterns
1. I don't love myself.
2. There is no one I love.
3. I am powerless to _____.
4. I am angry at _____.
5. I am depressed.
6. I hate myself.
7. I can't accept change easily.

8. I am afraid of _____.
9. Life is painful.
10. I don't deserve to be happy.

Boils

Fears

- Fear of loving yourself
- Fear of accepting yourself
- Fear of never being enough
- Fear of not good enough
- Fear of being criticized
- Fear of being wrong
- Fear of being present
- Fear of being unloved
- Fear of hurting someone
- Fear of losing themselves in the needs of others
- Fear of the future
- Fear of authority
- Fear of pain
- Fear of anger

Emotional States

- Failure to please those around them leads to an internal anger. 'I can't do anything right', 'Nothing I do is good enough', 'Why am I even here', 'How can I make people love me'…these are the internal tapes running in their head. The anger boils to the surface when confronted with their perceived shortcomings. But, the poison of that anger cycles backs down without being expressed until it is hardened and expresses itself as rejection.
- There is a deep stress. A stress that questions the continuation of life. The biological system is stressed about the systems of survival…food, shelter, clothing, nurturance.
- A deep ancestral poison of hatred. The hatred gets pushed down and bubbles its way to the surface. At its core is an abuse by the authority figures (father, mother, clergy, etc.).
- Yields nothing (and gives up everything) to be loved. Holds those around them hostage in the way they are seen by others and themselves.

Cross Indexing: Reference the body part affected, bacterial infection, hair – ingrown, cyst, impetigo, stye

Repeating Patterns: Anger at feeling like they are always wrong bubbles to the surface, keeps the anger flowing, toxins build up in the body instead of being released, stress, food/housing/job insecurities.

Created Patterns

1. I am angry at _____.
2. I am afraid to express my feelings.
3. What feelings need to be let out?

4. I hate _____.
5. I'm not good enough.
6. No one loves me.
7. I'm not good enough to be loved.
8. I must hide my anger.
9. Nothing I do is good enough.
10. I can't do anything right.
11. I want to disappear.
12. Survival is hard.
13. Living is hard.
14. My hatred protects me.
15. My anger protects me.
16. My hatred defines me.

Bone Problems

Fears

- Fear of being shown their true self
- Fear of authority
- Fear of being bullied
- Fear of moving
- Fear of being usurped
- Fear of not being good enough
- Fear of being unsupported
- Fear of being out of control
- Fear of being controlled
- Fear of being hurt
- Fear of life
- Fear of the flow
- Fear of being present

Emotional States

- Lack of perception. Hones in on the wrong causes. They look at the world through how it fits into their agenda. They don't hear or see anything else. There is no understanding beyond the surface. There is never insightful understanding.
- Wrongheaded. Stubbornly refuses to hear the opinion and direction of others. Dances about an issue for which they do not have the answers. So they won't have to listen to someone else.
- Resents that others seem to know more. Unless they feel like they own it they will not listen. That resentment is connected to worthiness. They must know and be the dominate voice or they are not good enough.
- Direction is off the cliff. Do or die. Drives an idea until it is no longer valid. Its validity was in question from the beginning.

Cross Indexing: Ankle Problems (pain, sprain, swelling), Ankylosing Spondylitis, Arms – Left, Arms – Right, Arthritis, Arthritis – Infectious or Septic, Arthritis – Osteoarthritis, Arthritis – Reactive (Reiter's

Syndrome), Arthritis – Rheumatoid, B Cell – Abnormal Recognition, Back, Back – Cervical (neck), Back -Coccyx Pain – Tailbone, Back – Sacral – Lower, Back – Lumbar (middle), Back – Thoracic (Back High heart), Bones – Broken, Bunions, Cancer – Leukemia, Clavicle Problems, Ethmoid Bone, Frontal Skull Bones, Ganglion Cyst – Left wrist, Ganglion Cyst – Right Wrist, Hand Problems, Jaw Problems, Occipital Skull bone, Pagets Disease, Shin Problems

Repeating Patterns: resentment, out of balance, structure, stability, foundations, letting go, stuck, rigid, martyr, telling them what to do, unsupported.

Created Patterns

1. I must punish myself.
2. I must resist authority.
3. I won't let people tell me what to do.
4. I can't move away from what is not good for me.
5. I must freeze/stay still to survive.
6. If I do anything I will make it worse.
7. I can't move away from this situation.
8. I'm not supported.
9. I have to stay and take it.
10. I am off balance when _____.
11. I am manipulated by _____.
12. I can't move forward.
13. I must be strong all the time.
14. I have to stay and _____.
15. What is the situation in life that they can't control?

Bones – Broken

Fears
- Fear of having to depend on others
- Fear of having no one to support you
- Fear of being alone in your stand
- Fear that what you believe will isolate you
- Fear of being out of control
- Fear of being controlled
- Fear of letting go
- Fear of moving forward
- Fear of change
- Fear of being wrong
- Fear of making decisions
- Fears being diminished
- Fears being vulnerable
- Fears not belonging
- Fears being present

Teachings
- Letting go
- Letting go of past hurts
- Live without resentment
- Forgiveness
- Change with ease
- Change and be safe
- Live without being told what to do
- Live without feeling your ideas are devalued
- Live without needing to blame others
- Valued
- Live with a sense of belonging
- Belong
- Trust
- Trust my intuition
- Live without feeling life is a contest

- Fears the flow of life
- Fears being ripped off
- Fears being unwanted
- Fears judgment
- Fear of not being good enough
- Fear of authority

- Live without needing to feel justified
- Be in the flow
- Make changes and be safe
- Make decisions and be safe
- Live without being stuck in old ways of thinking
- Accepting of new ideas
- Accepting of new ways of doing things

Emotional States

- Hard on themselves, hanging onto the past; resentment of self. Unwilling to let go of the resentment. Resents self for not taking the path/ opportunities that would have supposedly led to a better life.
- Anxiety around the little things of life. Doesn't feel in control.
- Wants to move forward but they feel like they are being pulled in two different directions; staying in the old ways (past) or moving in a forward (new direction). Very conflicted about this new direction.
- Holding out for change to make their life better but they never allow the change in.

Cross Indexing: the bones broken, osteoporosis, accidents

Repeating Patterns: Can't let go, hangs onto resentment, can't forgive, doesn't make changes easily, doesn't feel safe with change, needs to be told what to do, feels their ideas are devalued, blames others, doesn't feel valued, doesn't feel they belong, doesn't trust others or self, needs to feel justified, doesn't allow themselves to feel the flow, doesn't feel they can make decisions and be safe, doesn't accept new ideas or ways of doing things.

Created Patterns

1. _____ is getting what I should have.
2. Bad things will happen.
3. Change can be dangerous.
4. Everyone is against me.
5. I am alone.
6. I am justified in my resentment.
7. I am not going to do what they tell me.
8. I am out of control.
9. I can't let go.
10. I can't move forward.
11. I can't trust god / creator.
12. I can't trust my instincts.
13. I don't belong.
14. I don't belong anywhere.
15. I don't know who to trust.
16. I don't love myself.
17. I don't trust _____.
18. I must be this way.

19. I must judge myself.
20. I must push back against those in authority to be heard / seen / acknowledged.
21. I must win.
22. I must worry about the future to keep bad things from happening.
23. I resent _____.
24. I resent being told what to do.
25. I'm not good enough.
26. If I give in then I'm not good enough.
27. If I give in then people make fun of me.
28. If I give in then they win.
29. If I had only _____ my life would be wonderful / better / happier / richer.
30. If I make a mistake I will be laughed at.
31. If I make a mistake I will never live it down.
32. If I move forward I will be seen as stupid.
33. Life is out of control.
34. My life is shattered and I blame _____.
35. My life would be better if _____.
36. My resentment of _____ protects me.
37. People are always telling me what to do (who?).
38. People in authority don't listen to me (who?).
39. People think they need to tell me what to do (who?).
40. There is no one there for me.
41. What are you pushing against?
42. When things change I am not wanted.
43. Why change? The old ways are safe.

*Look at themes of resentment, authority, future, resentment, anxiety, change, control, disassociation, feelings, flow, forgiveness, future, intuition, judgment, letting go, loving yourself, regret, self esteem, self worth, trust, unconditional love, rebellion, disconnection

Brain Problems

Fears
- Fear of having their heart broken by deception
- Fear of being alone
- Fear of disconnection
- Fear of being lost
- Fear of letting go
- Fear of knowing
- Fear of dying
- Fear of confusion
- Fear of people knowing
- Fear of being out of control
- Fear of memories

Emotional States
- Disconnected from action and feelings
- Repetitive circular thoughts that create an energetic burden and tension. This creates safety. Circular thoughts never really resolve themselves.

Cross Indexing: Acoustic Neuroma – Left Side, Acoustic Neuroma – Right Side, ALS or Amyotrophic Lateral Sclerosis or Lou Gehrig's Disease, Brain Tumor, Chronic Traumatic Encephalopathy (CTE), Dementia, Epilepsy, Focal Dystonia, Headache, Headache – Migraine, Hyperactivity, Insomnia, Senility, Parkinson's, Smoking – problems with quitting, Spasmodic Dysphonia – (Laryngeal), Stroke, Stuttering (non-developmental), Temple Pain or Pressure, Tinnitus

Repeating Patterns: won't let go, acts without thinking or over thinking without acting, often actions and thoughts are disconnected from feelings

Created Patterns
1. If I know I will die.
2. Knowing too much is dangerous.
3. What are you afraid to feel?
4. I am confused by _____.
5. I can't see clearly _____.
6. I must keep things to myself.
7. I am unable to control my life.
8. I am out of control.
9. It's not safe to remember (What will happen if you remember?).
10. I am disconnected.
11. I don't feel feelings.
12. I act without thinking.
13. I over think everything and then do nothing.

Brain Tumor

Fears
- Fear of the unknown and no control
- Fear of masculine energy
- Fear of being unsupported
- Fear of being betrayed
- Fear of life
- Fear of balance, flow and peace
- Fear of creativity
- Fear of choice
- Fear of power
- Fear of change
- Fear of the future
- Fear of being alone
- Fear of disconnection

- Fear of being lost
- Fear of letting go
- Fear of knowing
- Fear of dying
- Fear of confusion
- Fear of people knowing
- Fear of being out of control
- Fear of memories

Emotional States

- Life's possibilities and a sense of security and protection have been destroyed by a masculine energy in their lives (self-masculine energy or someone with strong masculine energy). Their state of dependency on this masculine energy/personality was suddenly changed, possibly by an act that seemed violent in its nature. Instead of developing the skills needed to be self-sufficient they fell back into old behaviors of dependency. This need to be dependent took over and their life force is being drained away. The resources needed to rebuild this person's life force are being blocked by them. They block these resources by falling into patterns of anger, blame and a belief of having been betrayed.
- This person is self-centered and self-serving and disregards the needs of others. Their pride and arrogance has pushed them out of balance. They have based their life on soaking up other people's energies both the negative and positive. They have literally sponged off of others. This person will consistently straddle all types of values in order to receive the energy of others. When faced with the prospect of having to depend upon their own energies they feel as if their life force is being drained away. They will become emotionally (and maybe physically) cold and lifeless.
- This person has stopped growing and developing in their life. They are stuck in the period of their life that represents a time when they did not have the option for self-expression. They were kept from creating and sharing their inherent gifts with others. Any movement was just a reflection of looping back into the same experiences and ways of being in the world. There is a sense that the situation will never change/get better. Their will bends to this way of being. It is easier to live life in the way it has always been than trying to make a change.
- This person has a fear of choice, personal power and the principles/values that have been used to build their life. These fears have taken control of their mind. The fear is based on outmoded ideas. This person has difficulty setting boundaries and loses their power due to the fear. They get glimpses of the fact that the fear is an illusion but they think that getting to that place of awareness is like reaching the horizon; they will never get there. There is a sense of confusion because the fear is based on a part of their life experience that they do not understand from their past.
- A high state of agitation and anxiety around feminine qualities of creativity, being receptive, emotional, nurturing side of self. This person cannot 'unwind' enough to be able to nurture themselves. Their anxiety prevents them from giving in to the sense of the authentic feminine self. They are out of alignment with the true self. The anxiety is focused on what has been, currently happening and will happen. There is an intense fear of sudden change. The sudden change, that is feared, is a futurized projection created by the worry and anxiety. The person does not feel like they can control the anxiety. The energy of anxiety will occasionally release and when it does there's a sense of being out of control. The futurization then projects upon all facets of the person's life creating more anxiety and agitation. Then the cycle of 'anxiety-worry-release-out of control' repeats itself. This is a cycle of increasing intensity.

Cross Indexing: Cross Indexing: Wounded Creative Core, Acoustic Neuroma – Left Side, Acoustic Neuroma – Right Side, ALS or Amyotrophic Lateral Sclerosis or Lou Gehrig's Disease, Brain Tumor, Chronic Traumatic Encephalopathy (CTE), Dementia, Epilepsy, Focal Dystonia, Headache, Headache – Migraine, Hyperactivity, Insomnia, Senility, Parkinson's, Smoking – problems with quitting, Spasmodic Dysphonia – (Laryngeal), Stroke, Stuttering (non-developmental), Temple Pain or Pressure, Tinnitus, cancer

Created Patterns

1. _____ betrayed me.
2. _____ will never get better.
3. Bad things are going to happen.
4. Being creative is dangerous/ waste of time/ frivolous.
5. Change is dangerous.
6. Choice is dangerous.
7. Feelings are dangerous.
8. I am alone.
9. I am angry at _____.
10. I am hopeless.
11. I blame _____ for _____.
12. I can't support myself.
13. I don't know how to support myself.
14. I don't know how to take care of myself.
15. I don't know what I believe.
16. I don't know what it feels like to take care of myself.
17. I don't know what my values are.
18. I don't know who I am.
19. I don't trust myself.
20. I hate men.
21. I have been abandoned by _____.
22. I must look out for myself first.
23. I must not let others see how I feel…what will happen if you do?
24. I must stay in control to be safe.
25. I must stay the same to be safe.
26. I must worry about things to keep bad things from happening.
27. I must worry to keep control over things.
28. I need someone else to take care of me.
29. I'm not protected.
30. Life is out of control.
31. Life will never change.
32. Making decisions is dangerous.
33. Men hurt me.
34. My _____ (mother/father/etc) hurt me.
35. My needs come first.
36. No one wants me.
37. Sudden changes hurt me/people.
38. The world revolves around me.

39. There's no way out.
40. You can't make a living being creative.

Breast Problems

Fears

- Fear that the people around them bear only a false love
- Fear they are being used for what they give
- Fear of intimacy
- Fear of connection
- Fear of rejection
- Fear of receiving
- Fears feeling unwanted
- Fear of feeling unloved
- Fear of the feminine
- Fear of creation
- Fear of feeling guilt
- Fear of subjugation
- Fear of disappearing
- Fear of losing the story / identity

Teachings

- Nurture myself
- Put my needs before others
- Honor my needs
- Care for my children and meet my needs
- Value myself
- Be important
- Live my life without being my mother
- Be valued
- Be honored
- Live putting my needs first
- Recognize my needs
- Recognize I have needs
- Be nourished
- Live letting others find who they are without my interference
- Live without needing to overprotect others
- Live without needing to take care of others

Emotional States

- Breast Pain – heart not connected to sexuality. The disconnection of love from sexual energy. The heart says I tried that love connection to sexual energy before and got severely wounded. So the heart disconnected from sexual energy. So the heart and sex became disconnected from the need of closeness. Being close became too painful. The sexual energy feels like their needs will never be met. So the sexual energy may be shut down to keep from feeling the depression that follows. Sexuality is just another place for rejection.

Cross Indexing: Wounded Creative Core, Cancer-Breast, Post Mastectomy, Cancer-ovarian, Radiculopathy of right and left breast

Repeating Patterns: Doesn't nurture themselves, puts others needs before theirs, doesn't feel important, gets love when they take care of others, overprotects others, must take care of others to feel wanted.

Created Patterns

1. It's not safe being a mother.
2. I will die if I become a mother.

3. I must protect my child at all costs.
4. My children always come before me.
5. I must take care of others before myself.
6. I am guilty if I take time for myself.
7. Others come before me.
8. I come second.
9. I don't have a voice.
10. I am my mother.
11. I'm not important.
12. I am only loved when I take care of others.
13. I am a victim.
14. I am a martyr.
15. I don't know any other way of being in the world.
16. Taking care of others is all I know.

Bronchitis

Fears

- Fear of never knowing when to stop
- Fear of stopping
- Fear of never knowing when to stop to keep it together
- Fear of breathing
- Fear of being heard breathing
- Fear of powerlessness
- Fear of emotions
- Fear of letting go
- Fear of being seen
- Fear of speaking out
- Fear of pain
- Fear of attack
- Fear of judgment
- Fear of trusting authority
- Fear of being alone

Emotional States

- Hard-won victories in life have left this person feeling bereft and full of guilt. Those victories were couched in pain. The love they sought turned to a pile of poo. Hardness began to creep in around the edges as the pain of those victories colored the world vision.
- Jumping to conclusions has left the person unhappy and angry at being thwarted when they put their opinion out into the open. They get challenged and diminished at what they see as their truth. They feel judged and uncomfortable in their own skin. They feel dishonored and that their perspective is not being seen.
- Long-held beliefs of anarchy and conspiracy join to create a front of distrust and inability to see a bigger picture of how their fears have created the distrust. Their conceptual foundation is faulty.
  *Ancestral: goes to a time when there was a loss of a world where there was trust in authority.

- Joint efforts have died. Heroism has died. The knight in shining armor is either very late or he is not coming. Figures out that they are alone with themselves and they have to save themselves. Leads to some hard lessons and feelings of loss of what they had been taught.
- Nervous energy consumes them. Their heart beats rapidly in a continual state of high alert. Looking out for what might come next. Yet they sabotage themselves and create the "what comes next".

Cross Indexing: Lung Problems, ACOA, Pneumonia, Viruses, Coughing, Asthma, Allergies, COPD

Created Patterns

1. I am afraid to breathe.
2. Breathing will get me killed.
3. I can't let them hear me breath.
4. I can't change things.
5. If I cry I will be hurt.
6. It's my fault things are upset.
7. I must be quiet or I will get hurt.
8. I can't let go of _____.
9. I must stay invisible to stay safe.
10. I am not allowed to cry.
11. I must keep my tears silent.
12. I never got to cry for _____.
13. My grief was taken from me.
14. My tears will tell the truth.
15. If I speak the truth they will kill me.

Bruises

Fears

- Fear of not knowing what to feel
- Fear of being in the world
- Fear of looking inward
- Fear of feelings
- Fear of being present
- Fear of balance
- Fear of looking
- Fear of opening their eyes
- Fear of being in the light
- Fear of understanding at a deeper level

Emotional States
- A sense of being out of balance with the feminine and masculine which brings a lack of awareness of the relationship to the things and/or people around you.
- Lack of body awareness. Doesn't know how they fit in the world.

Cross Indexing: Blood disorders, hepatitis C, Leukemia, Left and/or Right-sided negative tendencies

Repeating Patterns: always running into things, didn't see that there.

Created Patterns
1. I need to punish myself.
2. I'm no good.
3. I am clumsy.
4. I don't belong.
5. I don't fit anywhere.
6. I'm always running into things.

Bulimia

Fears
- Fear that anything they take in will make them ugly
- Fear of inner peace
- Fear of rejection
- Fear of being wrong
- Fear of self
- Fear of knowing
- Fear of owning their stuff
- Fear of responsibility
- Fear of never being enough
- Fear of inward reflection
- Fear of creativity
- Fear of not being thin enough
- Fear of being out of control
- Fear of being unloved / unwanted

Emotional States
- Rejects what they are told as a form of getting even or retaliation. Does not know how to reach an inner peace. Feels wrong all the time, so they reject themselves.
- No sense of their own identity or how to achieve a sense of identity. They mirror another and the frequency of that other is out of harmony with their true nature.
- There is a deep hole within that longs for a heart-based life, a life connected to a deep sense of purpose and soul awareness. But, the disharmony of their walls keeps them from recognizing that what they need is already within them.

Cross Indexing: Anorexia, Obsessive Compulsive Disorder, Appetite-loss, Addictions, Anxiety, and Wounded Creative core

Repeating Patterns: self-hatred, doesn't belong, depression, lack of creative expression.

Created Patterns
1. I can't accept myself.
2. I'm not good enough unless I am thinner.
3. I can't control myself.
4. I can never measure up.
5. I can't meet others expectations.
6. I hate myself.
7. I am disgusting.
8. I am ugly and fat.
9. My needs are never met.
10. If I was skinnier I would be loved.
11. I can quit eating.
12. I am out of control.
13. I will never have enough.
14. I will never be loved because I am ugly and fat.

Bunions

Fears
- Fear of hostile people stopping them from doing what they want
- Fear of fear
- Fear of change
- Fear of deserving
- Fear of the future
- Fear of not being good enough
- Fear of being wrong
- Fear of moving
- Fear of being seen

Emotional States
- Long-held beliefs of inaction stop them from moving forward in life to their detriment. Inaction, thought to be safe, is actually an action that often does not yield what they want or keep them safe. When things go sideways because they did nothing they then feel the need to punish themselves.
- Wild ideas about how the world will "get" them or wreak havoc upon their life have kept them holed up in one corner of their life. They don't see the corners of the room. They hide in obscurity wanting to never be seen.

EMOTIONAL PATTERNS

Cross Indexing: Foot problems, leg problems, left or right-sided negative tendencies

Created Patterns
1. I am constantly in fear of _____.
2. I can't just up and change everything.
3. I have to be the stable one.
4. I am afraid of change.
5. Change is dangerous.
6. I must stay the course at all costs.
7. I am stopped from ever having what I want.
8. It is better to do nothing.
9. What if something goes wrong?
10. I'm not good enough.
11. If something good happens it's not for me.
12. Good things happen to those that wait.
13. I'm always at fault.
14. I'm always wrong.

Bursitis

Fears
- Fear of moving in the wrong direction
- Fear of making decisions
- Fear of being wrong
- Fear of failure
- Fear of letting go
- Fear of inner peace
- Fear of being forced against their will
- Fear of being overrun
- Fear of shame
- Fear of being undeserving
- Fear of ownership
- Fear of being present
- Fear of being judged
- Fear of being unloved / unwanted
- Fear of the chaos drama
- Fear of being out of control

Emotional States
- Repeated wrong directions in the past have set up a fear of going in the wrong direction again. They fear their own decision making and failures but can't seem to stop the repeated pattern of false directions. Once started they don't seem to be able to change course.

- Highly sensitive or emotionally charged situations create chaos and they desire to flee but they are frozen in the space.
- Repeatedly forced to move in an unwanted direction. There is an inner resistance that builds into anger. The anger also encompasses unexpressed feelings of not having strong enough boundaries and/or the will to stop the repeated misalignment of movement.
- Shame based on a need to have and being told that it was shameful to ask or want.
- Half-way relationship with life. Doesn't want to commit completely to anything.
- Unable to be present, yields to all. Justified in letting go because they found that if they took a position they would be judged without mercy. It is a way that they create a defensible border without establishing a border.
- Wild ideas of love and romance based on baseless foundations yield incompetence and incomplete results. Wants warmth and connection but has no idea how to achieve.
- Wants to be left alone but doesn't know how to push people away without drama. Any direction they take is usually filled with emotions that are over the top.
- Wrong ideas about everything lead to a heightened sense of failure. They push away and yell.

Cross Indexing: joint problems, area of body affected, inflammation

Created Patterns

1. I am angry at/hate/resent/bitter toward _____.
2. I have lost control of _____.
3. I am helpless to change the situation.
4. Things never go my way.
5. I am anxious about _____.
6. If I just hold on it will go my way eventually.

C's

Calluses

Fears
- Fear of change
- Fear of not being able to protect yourself
- Fear of having to fend off an attack
- Fear of being overrun
- Fear of being seen idle
- Fear of being hurt
- Fear of new
- Fear of thinking outside the box

Emotional States
- Continual hurts result in a hardening of their boundaries (an overreaction). Does not deal with the issue, just lets it keep pushing at them.
- Repetitive actions that are out of balance.

Cross Indexing: skin problems, reference the location of the callus

Created Patterns
1. I can't fight back; I have to keep taking it.
2. People keep trying to hurt me
3. My direction in life is hurtful
4. I can't seem to balance my life

Cancer

Fears
- Fear of living
- Fear of being in alignment
- Fear of a toxic non-peace
- Fear of peace
- Fear of being present
- Fear of belonging
- Fear of emotions
- Fear of god
- Fear of failing
- Fear of undeserving
- Fear of doctors

Emotional States
- Looking for acceptable form of suicide
- Out of sync with the world. Always off cue.
- Wrong time wrong place wrong action

Cross Indexing: All the cancers and the body part affected

Created Patterns
1. I want to die.
2. I am out of sync with everyone else.
3. I don't know where I belong.
4. I don't know how to fit in.
5. I am angry at/hate/bitter toward/ resent _____.
6. I am sad about _____.
7. The cancer will kill me.
8. I hate my body.
9. I am angry at having cancer.
10. God is punishing me.
11. I am a failure (What have you failed at? Who made you feel that way?).
12. I must be perfect.
13. I am not worthy of being healed.
14. I have been expressing/feeling strong emotion of _____ for a long time (these are negative emotions: hatred/resentment/anger/revenge/sorrow/grief/bitterness/rage).
15. I have to believe what the doctor tells me.
16. I would rather die than upset my doctor.
17. I must resist the medical profession.

Cancer – Basal Cell

Fears
- Fear of creativity
- Fear that hope is lost
- Fear of injustice
- Fear of being hurt
- Fear of betrayal
- Fear of letting go
- Fear of being overrun
- Fear of being present
- Fear of being vulnerable
- Fear of pain
- Fear of never having the magic
- Fear of being rejected
- Fear of being unloved / unwanted

- Fear of their identity
- Fear of feeling powerless
- Fear of authority
- Fear of seeing self
- Fear of seeing outside the box
- Fear of being blamed
- Fear of attack
- Fear of being left out

Emotional States

- Fire in the belly. Anger and creativity have blended. The creativity felt by this person can be destructive. They feel like they need that destruction to get their needs met. Their expression of self is laced with anger. Deep sense of injustice. They feel like they have been intentionally hurt by others. Feels stripped of their motivation to make things right. They think that if they try they will be hurt again. They hold grudges.
- Free expression of their nature is inhibited. Must be – put on a face — to be who they are not. Inability to move past limitation of the heart. More interested in maintaining the status quo despite the inner psychic pain held in their being. Heart is wounded but not from a failed relationship but from life. Their being came in with sparkles and 'life' has one by one put the sparkles out. They are on a quest to recover the sparkles – the magic of living what they once felt.
- Random (perceived) sequence of events has led them to a knowing of self (who they are) and they don't like what they see – this is the little self/egoic self. They do not like themselves. The stories are the person. It keeps them from getting into their true inner self/higher self. The stories are everything.'
- Weakness: Doesn't want to be seen as weak. They've lost contact with the inner truth of their being – buried in dogmatic layers and consumed by the layers. Dogmatic layers of religiosity that are carried like a heavy mantle are not strength but erode the will to get to their true inner self.
- Pomposity: Heart is pompous, trumped-up sense of self – done so they can't see themselves – no substance – have a tendency to take on the ideas and feelings of others — that way they stay away from having to be honest about their own interior landscape.

Cross Indexing: Skin problems, growths, cancer, moles, part of body affected

Repeating Patterns: betrayal, abandonment, frustrated desire, stays in the box but wants out, heart keeps getting broken, doesn't feel a life purpose, everything about life is hard, feels creative desire is lost, truth is a moving target

Created Patterns

1. I am angry at _____.
2. I break everything I touch.
3. Life is unfair.
4. I get blamed for everything bad.
5. People are out to get me.
6. I must put on a happy face.
7. I must be who others want me to be.
8. If I let others see who I truly am they will hurt me.
9. Life is out to get me.

10. I don't like myself.
11. I must tell me who I am.
12. I am weak and powerless.
13. I must believe what others tell me to believe.
14. I am at the mercy of others.
15. Life is a joke and I am the butt of all jokes.
16. Just when I think I am safe someone attacks me.
17. I am hopelessly underwater with everything.
18. I have no sense of balance; it feels like it's always one extreme or another.
19. I am always left out in the cold.

Cancer – Bladder

Fears

- Fear of life
- Fear they will never know peace
- Fear of presence
- Fear of being unworthy
- Fear of being penniless
- Fear of success
- Fear of failure
- Fear of defeat
- Fear of being left
- Fear of abandonment
- Fear of being diminished
- Fear of rejection
- Fear of being invisible
- Fear of being powerless
- Fear of being unloved / unwanted
- Fear of being judged
- Fear of letting go
- Fear of being caught lying
- Fear of disappointment
- Fear of feeling lost
- Fear of making decisions
- Fear of peace
- Fear of not deserving

Emotional States

- Failure to yield to the forces of life, felt they could be changed through prayer or divine intervention. Would not acknowledge the divine power of the cycles of being. Would try to change and then be devastated that nothing altered its energy/force of direction. This led them in a dark direction of habit that yields no fruit.
- Wanted to be known (a reputation of grandness) and failed. Wanted to be pointed to as a paragon of success. They did this in superficial ways and achieved nothing. Heartfelt defeated

and depressed. They did not recognize the true path to sunshine is by being a path of higher Truths (this is capitalized for a reason) for others. Feelings of confusion and loss overwhelm this person.
- Hopelessly left out of the circle. Always excluded from the inner decision making done by family, bosses, partners, etc. Feels excluded and rejected with no value. Their opinions are not sought and they feel invisible.
- Hard pressed to know why others don't look up to them. Their authority is ignored. They are not referenced or revered. They seek that as validation and love. What they look for they can never find or achieve.
- Choices made early in life are deemed without merit. Judged as stupid and denigrated by those closest to them. Hurtful statements by those others have been/are held. Will not walk away. Holds onto archaic ideas of family and heritage. Old ways are not always good ways. They are a way — not THE way. This has not fit with the true inner identity and they are constantly having to fit in where they know they are lying to themselves and all others. This creates an inner anguish that gets unresolved. Pop ideas are grabbed onto as a way of differentiating and continuing that search for little truths. Their identity is built on a series of little truths that lead to a continual series of disappointments and anger. They will never find peace on this path.

Cross Indexing: Bladder problems, cancer

Created Patterns
1. God has forsaken me.
2. God abandoned me.
3. I am lost.
4. I am confused.
5. One must pray to be healed.
6. One must pray to receive god's word.
7. God will save me.
8. I have no power on my own.
9. I only have the power god gives me.
10. My prayers are unworthy.
11. Nothing I try works.
12. I have nothing.
13. I am depressed.
14. I do not belong.
15. I don't know where I belong.
16. I am always left out.
17. I am not good enough.
18. I am worthless.
19. I am rejected.
20. I am invisible.
21. I am loved when I am spoken about.
22. People ignore me.
23. I make bad choices.
24. I must hang onto the hurts.
25. I can't forgive.
26. People take advantage of me.

27. The old ways work why not keep them.
28. I have no peace.
29. Good things are not for me.
30. My life is a lie.
31. I am always trying to figure out where I fit.
32. I am not good enough to live.
33. I must keep searching, it's out there.
34. 'T'ruth comes from someone else; I am too stupid to know 'T'ruth.
35. I have been misled and I am angry at myself for allowing it.

Cancer – Breast

Fears

- Fear of not being good enough
- Fear of a lack of knowledge
- Fears being unloved / unwanted
- Fear of life being easy
- Fear of being taken advantage of
- Fear of letting go
- Fear of being out of control
- Fear of failure
- Fear of living
- Fear of joy
- Fear of stopping
- Fear of rejection
- Fear of change
- Fear of the mother
- Fear of being undeserving
- Fear of being irrelevant
- Fear of being unworthy
- Fear of saying no
- Fear of receiving
- Fear of being judged
- Fear of losing self
- Fear of the unknown

Teachings

- Creator's definition of loving your mother
- Deserve
- Get my needs met
- Get my needs met without feeling guilty
- Good enough
- Joy
- Let others take responsibility
- Letting go
- Letting go of my mother's paradigm
- Like to be happy
- Like to be heard
- Live life with ease
- Live my life without permission from others
- Live without being judged
- Live without being my mother
- Live without feeling rejected
- Live without needing to control others
- Live without needing to punish yourself
- Love myself
- Make changes and be safe
- Make changes easily
- Nurture myself
- Put myself first and not feel guilty
- Receive
- Say no
- Take care of myself
- Trusting others to do it right
- Unconditional love
- Worthy
- Honor my mother without having to

live her values

Emotional States

- Feeling they will never be good enough. Spends their energy on nurturing those around them to be good enough. Rejects caring extended to them by others. Feels like they are not good enough to be loved.
- Caring becomes caring too much becomes controlling. Sacrificing themselves for others. The sacrifice is actually a way of controlling others.
- No joy in life. There's a responsibility and duty to make sure everyone else's needs are met. They are constantly playing catch up with the needs of their physical body. Life is a struggle. Juggling family and career to make everyone happy. Frantic quality to their life.
- Disillusioned with self-image. Rejection of self. Feeling of failure.
- Going in circles. Making no real change. But, they put in a lot of effort.
- Fear and/or hatred of the personal mother. Fear of becoming like their mother.

Cross Indexing: Post Mastectomy, Cancer-ovarian, Radiculopathy of right or left breast, Breast Problems

Repeating Patterns: looking for love, acceptance, and approval outside of self, feels undeserving, goes in circles looking to get their needs met, takes on all the responsibility, plays out their mother's paradigm, creates being rejected, goes into guilt if they put themselves first, doesn't trust others to do it right.

Created Patterns

1. Change is dangerous.
2. Everyone else comes first.
3. Everyone takes advantage of me.
4. Getting sick is how I get nurtured/ loved / get attention.
5. I am a doormat.
6. I am afraid I will be like my mother.
7. I am afraid of cancer.
8. I am not accepted.
9. I am not loved and cared for.
10. I am responsible for everything.
11. I am taken advantage of by my family/ others/ people at work.
12. I am worthless.
13. I can ask for what I want and get it.
14. I can't say no.
15. I can't love myself or others.
16. I don't know how to give love.
17. I don't know how to make change.
18. I don't know how to or what it feels like to nurture myself.
19. I don't know how to receive.
20. I don't know how to take care of myself.
21. I don't love myself.
22. I hate/am angry at my mother.
23. I hate/angry at/ want revenge on/have a grudge against/ bitter against _____.
24. I know how to live without being judged.
25. I know what I need.

26. I know what makes me happy.
27. I must be punished.
28. I must get sick to get time for myself.
29. I must lose my breast(s) to be honored/seen.
30. I must protect my children at all costs.
31. I must sacrifice myself for my children.
32. I must sacrifice myself for others.
33. I must serve others.
34. I must suffer.
35. I must take care of others before tending to myself.
36. I need permission to get what I want.
37. I resent being a woman.
38. I want to die.
39. I'm not worth loving.
40. I'm not worthy.
41. If I am happy someone will take it away from me.
42. If I don't do it who will?
43. It is a sin to put myself first.
44. It is my duty to make sure everything is taken care of.
45. It is wrong to be happy.
46. Keeping people away from me keeps me safe.
47. Men use me.
48. No matter what I do I will never be good enough.
49. People judge me.
50. People listen to what I need.
51. Spending time on me is selfish.
52. The unknown is dangerous.
53. There's no time for me.
54. What are your boundary issues?
55. Women must suffer.

*Look at themes of acceptance, anger, approval appreciation, blockages, body, boundaries, mother, father, forgiveness, giving, guilt, healing, judgment, loving you, protection, self-esteem, self-worth, sexuality, spiritual growth, unconditional love, worthiness, unmet needs, shame, control, letting go, feelings, physical stress, joy, judgment, receiving, stress, spirituality, worthiness

Cancer – Cervical

Fears

- Fear of intimacy
- Fear of being vulnerable
- Fear of being hurt
- Fear of god
- Fear of being alone
- Fear of being powerless
- Fear of their darkness
- Fear of pain

- Fear of authority
- Fear of authority that blocks/ destroys their creativity
- Fear of being unsupported
- Fear of being used
- Fear of being creative
- Fear of love

Emotional States

- This person presents a sunny, happy personality for all to see. Below the surface of their bright demeanor, there is darkness. This person stops short of self-fulfillment. They will let people only see the sunny side of their nature. They will not go very deep with their relationships and keep them at a surface level. They refuse to deal with anything unpleasant. They keep a tight lid on the darkness below the surface. This person may be hiding depression and may possibly be on anti-depressants. Relationships are used to keep this person from looking at themselves. They invest themselves in the lives of the other people. This may manifest itself as criticism, manipulation and being judgmental. This approach to relationships won't be seen by the other person until they have gotten hooked into the relationship. When the relationship begins to unravel the person will develop another relationship quickly to replace it. This person doesn't feel safe in relationships.
- This person is characterized by being obedient to authority without question. They have a passive and docile nature. They think that by being that way in the world they will always be protected and taken care of. But, there is an aspect of this person that is working to kill off the outward docile obedient nature. There is a repressed sexual nature to this person. They believe they have overcome the docile obedient aspect of self and then it comes back. They then express themselves in assertive ways that reject the docile nature leaving a bit of personal destruction in their wake. It's either all or nothing.
- This person is tightly wrapped in their family and/or ancestry. They can't allow themselves to think or behave outside of what is expected from their family. If they behave or explore outside of what the 'family' expects they believe that their behaviors will result in bad things happening to them. They will be punished for not doing what is expected of them. This would result in further reinforcement of their beliefs that they must do what is expected of them. They are bound by their family obligations and genetic ties.

Additional Notes: Cervix is between the vagina and the uterus. That transition from love to creativity…creativity based in love…creativity based in passion…must pass the cervix for that to happen. Creativity feeds spiritual growth. What is the fear if the spirit should grow? So the core question is 'what is the block that has been created'? What is blocking this person's creativity?

Cancer is a deep hurt, longstanding resentment, deep secret or grief eating away at self, carrying a deep hatred. Is there no love in the sexual relationships? Is there a deep resentment being carried due to an intimate relationship? What aspect of their creative self-was stopped as a child and not allowed to flower and reach expression? Without the creative expression the soul hungers, the ego becomes frantic and tries to fulfill the soul's needs. How does cervical cancer serve them? What changes have happened in their life since the diagnosis? What are they now paying attention to or avoiding? Who may have left their life or entered it?

It is one thing to be creative but it is another to carry out creative thought. This is the balance between the masculine and the feminine. The feminine carries the creative spark and the masculine takes the creative spark and makes it a reality. It is the masculine that wields the paint brush but it is the feminine that has the vision.

Cross Indexing: Cancer, Cancer-Ovarian, Herpes Simplex I, Wounded Creative Core

Created Patterns
1. Cancer is my punishment for being sinful.
2. I am always disappointed.
3. I am angry at _____.
4. I am bad.
5. I am better than/less than men.
6. I am depressed.
7. I am evil.
8. I am hopeless.
9. If I am myself no one will love me, I will be abandoned.
10. I am powerless to stop men from hurting me.
11. I am powerless to stop men from taking advantage of me.
12. I am sinful.
13. I hate _____.
14. I hate men.
15. I have been abandoned by _____.
16. I have been betrayed by _____.
17. I must always be the good one.
18. I must be hurt to be loved.
19. I must be punished if I disobey my mother/ father/ family.
20. I must be what others want me to be to be liked/ loved.
21. I must do what others expect me to do.
22. I must hurt them before they hurt me.
23. I must leave a relationship before I get in too deep.
24. I must stay in control to be safe.
25. I must suffer.
26. I must suffer for being sinful.
27. I only get to be me when I am sick.
28. I only make time for myself when I am sick.
29. I resent _____.
30. I'm not creative.
31. If I do nothing I stay safe.
32. If I fall in love I will be hurt.
33. If I make my own decisions I always screw up.
34. It isn't safe to make decisions.
35. It's all or nothing.
36. Men hurt me.
37. No one ever leaves me alone.
38. Others are to blame for my problems.
39. Relationships hurt.
40. The pain is dangerous.
41. The pain will kill me.
42. What stops this person from doing what they love?

43. Who hurt you deeply that you have not been able to forgive?

Cancer – Colon

Fears
- Fear that they do not have the energy to change things
- Fear of losing
- Fear of being unsupported
- Fear of the creative
- Fear of the feminine/women
- Fear of attack
- Fear of being out of control
- Fear of emotions
- Fear of their heart feelings
- Fear of abandonment
- Fear of being alone
- Fear of letting go
- Fear of not knowing what is toxic

Teachings
- Whole
- Complete
- Experience the divine nature of our sexuality
- Trust
- God's Unconditional Love
- To be connected to Source
- Be safe with men
- Be safe with women
- Listen to your inner voice
- Trust your feelings
- Know what is illusionary in life
- Be creative
- Trust myself
- Feel wanted by mother / father
- Forgiveness
- Release old anger
- Release old hurts
- Relax around men
- Relax around women
- Feel worthy
- Stand up for yourself appropriately
- Creator's definition of friendship
- Be loved
- Creator's definition of love
- Let go of what is not good for me
- Be safe without needing to control
- Trust in the Universal Intelligence
- Trust in the Universal flow
- Trust in the divine plan
- Inner Peace
- Balance

Emotional States
- Sexual energy is connected to the need to 'win', sex is a game. The focus of their sexuality has been to 'win'. Sex was set up as a game and the goal of the game was to have as many sexual encounters as possible. Out of sync with their shifting values. Unsuccessful at long-term relationships.
- Has discovered that their relationships (business and personal) are all an illusion. Their relationships have no real substance. No one is really there for companionship or support. The foundation of their life appears to not really be there.

- Has been betrayed by the feminine in their life. Believes women cannot be trusted. Questions whether they are worth loving. Feels abandoned by the feminine. Do not trust themselves.
- Feminine aspects of self experience extreme anxiety. Does not let go of the hyper-alert state. Repression of spiritual energies to balance the feminine and masculine energies. Tightly controls their masculine energies to keep their life in control.
- Disconnected from Creator. They are sad and depressed. This person has closed themselves off emotionally and experiencing life.

Cross Indexing: Cancer, Irritable Bowel Syndrome, Colitis-Ulcerative, Diverticulitis, Colon problems

Repeating Patterns: untrusting, feels unsafe with men/women, doesn't listen to inner voice, disconnected from the heart, doesn't trust their feelings, can't differentiated between what's real and unreal, wounded creative core, feelings of being unwanted by one or both parents, doesn't know how to let go of old anger or old hurts, sense of unworthiness, must be in control to feel safe, lack of inner peace.

Created Patterns
1. A relationship is about sex only.
2. Being creative is a waste of time.
3. Getting too close to god is dangerous.
4. God has abandoned me.
5. I am alone.
6. I am angry at/hate/want revenge against/bitter toward _____.
7. I am depressed.
8. I am disconnected from source/ god/ creator.
9. I am going to die.
10. I am out of sync with those around me.
11. I am sad.
12. I am unloved.
13. I am unprotected.
14. I am worthless/ unworthy.
15. I can let go of what is not good for me.
16. I can't defend myself.
17. I can't have a long-term relationship.
18. I can't let go.
19. I can't trust men.
20. I can't trust women.
21. I don't know how to be in a relationship.
22. I don't know how to defend myself.
23. I don't know what it feels like to defend myself.
24. I don't know what love feels like.
25. I don't know what love is.
26. I don't trust god.
27. I don't trust my intuition.
28. I don't trust myself.
29. I have been abandoned.
30. I have no real friends.
31. I must be hyper-vigilant around men so I won't be hurt.
32. I must get as much sex as I can to win.

33. I must win to be good enough.
34. I resent _____.
35. I want to die.
36. I'm not good enough.
37. I'm not good enough to be loved by god.
38. If I let go everything will be out of control.
39. If I let go then I will be hurt.
40. Life is about getting as much sex as you can.
41. Life is not worth living.
42. Men will hurt me.
43. My mother doesn't want/love me.
44. My mother/wife/feminine relationship hates me.
45. No one loves me.
46. Now that I'm old no one pays attention to me.
47. Old people have no value.
48. People use me.
49. Sex is a game.
50. Source/ god/ creator abandoned me.
51. When you get old people just throw you away.
52. When you get old you are worthless.
53. Women betray me.
54. Women hurt me.

*Look at themes of relationships, allowing, balance, beingness, blockages, competition, control, letting go, denial, fear, self-worth, flow, giving, loving yourself, trust, support, spiritual growth, unmet needs (affection, trust, support), conflicting motivations, peace, power, worthiness

Cancer – Esophageal

Fears
- Fear of being stuck
- Fear of being forced to swallow their anger
- Fear of being present
- Fear of living
- Fear of the future
- Fear of being vulnerable
- Fear of letting go
- Fear of letting go of the toxic in their life

Emotional States
- Finds life to hard to swallow. Everything gets stuck when they refuse to take it anymore.
- A sense that they don't belong in this life. That they are forced to be part of something that they don't want and didn't create.
- Overheated imagination brings in layers of confusion and doesn't know whether to take it or let it go.

- Won't let go of those things that are not good for them. Pretends to go along with the program and that holds them in a kind of limbo; not totally rejected and not totally taken in. What they do holds them in a space of toxicity.

Cross Indexing: GERD, Esophagus problems, Cancer

Repeating Patterns: won't let go of what is toxic, stuck, life is hard

Created Patterns
1. I must suck it up.
2. I must never complain.
3. I must swallow all of my pain.
4. Expressing my feelings is dangerous.
5. I will be seen as weak if I express my feelings.
6. I am stuck.
7. I can't let go of what is not good for me.
8. Life is hard.
9. I am confused.

Cancer – Hodgkin Lymphoma

Fears
- Fear that all is hopeless
- Fear of deserving
- Fear of flow
- Fear of being overrun
- Fear of feeling safe
- Fear of success
- Fear of life
- Fear of the present
- Fear of inner peace
- Fear of owning their life

Emotional States
- Rough life has created a negative approach to how they see life. Life has had a scramble quality to it. Scramble to pay bills, get a job, keep a job, cheating spouse, early and close relative death, etc. Doesn't know how to defend themselves or have a life that is in balance. They set in motion forms of self-sabotage or self-destruction to stay safe. Feels safer sabotaging their life and dealing with that than owning their life and moving forward.

Cross indexing: Epstein Barr syndrome, viruses, lymphatic system, cancer, Addictions-chemical, AIDS, Cancer-Non Hodgkin's Lymphoma

Created Patterns

1. I can't accept myself.
2. I'm not accepted.
3. I must always prove myself.
4. I use sarcasm to keep me from feeling the pain of my life.
5. I have had too much loss and the way to handle it is stick it in a box.
6. I can't ever get things evened out.
7. I have no peace. There is never a space for peace.
8. I am constantly having to upright the next chaotic disaster.
9. The only time I have any peace is when I am sick. Then life leaves me alone.

Cancer – Leukemia

Fears

- Fear that they have nowhere to go to be lifted up
- Fear of the lies
- Fears betrayal
- Fear of things being taken
- Fear of their anger
- Fear of being empty
- Fear of being nothing
- Fear of being vulnerable
- Fear of being trapped
- Fear of dying
- Fear of life
- Fear of the unknown
- Fear of not being able to let go of the things that have happened

Emotional States

- Desire and what they want are suppressed. They feel that the joy of life has been denied. Hatred and anger are suppressed so long ago they are forgotten but hatred and anger has been woven into the fabric of their identity. Goes on the attack but in essence they are attacking themselves. Deep seated confusion about the why of existence has led to an underlying depression. The support – the foundation of their being – does not get it. Moves through life searching. Is seen as having the answer but has no answers to their own questions.

Cross Indexing: Cancer, Blood Disorders, Lymphatic System, ancestral/ epigenetic

Created Patterns

1. I am angry/ bitter toward/ hate/ resent _____.
2. I am depressed.
3. I am not free to feel _____.

4. I am stuck.
5. I am totally helpless/ powerless to change this.
6. I did not get a childhood.
7. I don't know how to be happy.
8. I don't love anyone.
9. I don't love myself.
10. I give up.
11. I had to grow up before I wanted to.
12. I want to die.
13. I was forced to be an adult to soon.
14. I'm not happy and my life is not happy.
15. It is hopeless.
16. It's futile to try.
17. What burden of knowing do you carry?
18. What did you lose your childhood to?
19. What secrets are you holding?
20. I don't understand the why of my existence.
21. I never get what I want.
22. I must attack first.
23. Life is a huge question.

Cancer – Liver

Fears

- Fear that the anger and hatred cannot be released
- Fear of feeling powerless in the presence of their anger
- Fears loss of power
- Fear of themselves
- Fear of anger
- Fear of the creative
- Fear of the feminine
- Fear of rejection by the feminine
- Fear of space-time to be
- Fear of presence
- Fear of blame

Emotional States

- Prolonged hatred of someone with a sense of having to restrain themselves from violence. This could be ancestral. Anger/hatred that makes no sense to their current life. That hatred is right below the surface.
- Born too soon. Cut off from the nurturing needed as a babe. The expression of anger has/had no where to go. It becomes the essence of their being. Creative efforts are often thwarted: started, stopped, never completed and feelings are hurt in the process.

Cross Indexing: Cancer, Liver Problems, Addictions-Chemical, Hepatitis, Cirrhosis

Repeated Patterns: wounded created core, feelings are hurt over and over, unresolved circular anger/hatred, difficulty completing projects. Projects anger at others and blames those others or outside forces for the problems in their life, feelings of failure and blame, loses power and a sense of self in the face of the creative/feminine.

Created Patterns
- I am headed to hell so I'm going to take my time getting there.
- Everything I build is built on sand.
- I hate _____.
- I can't let go of my anger/hatred of/at _____.
- I blame _____ for _____.
- I am powerless to do anything about _____.
- I have this anger and nowhere for it to go.
- I am going to die.
- I am angry at _____.
- The doctor says I am going to die.
- I have resented _____ for a long time.
- I allow others to hurt me.

Cancer – Lung

Fears
- Fear of being left
- Fear that they will always be sad
- Fear of being unsupported
- Fear of looking beyond themselves
- Fear of success
- Fear of their feelings
- Fear of being unaccepted
- Fear of being seen
- Fear of betrayal
- Fear of breathing
- Fear of being hurt
- Fear of being ripped off

Emotional States
- People they love pull the rug out from under them because of their narcissistic tendencies that their needs come first. They never see the other side of those that pulled the rug.
- Depressed at never being able to keep a success for very long. They reach a certain pinnacle of accomplishment and then it all falls apart. They blame the failure on others and feel unsupported.
- Won't let go of past glories that went nowhere. They almost had the brass ring but the merry-go-round broke. They look to others to fix the merry-go-round but no one comes to save them so they can get the brass ring.

- Highly idealized concepts of self and the small accomplishments keep their thoughts small. They stay locked in ghetto/cultural thoughts of bigotry and bias which keeps them locked into small accomplishments and failure at the next level.
- Strong matriarchal influence has/had a lot of distrust and hate. Genetic or ancestral wounding of betrayal and grief that led to extreme poverty of spirit and feelings. Deprivation that becomes hate and anger in the ancestry.

Cross Indexing: Additions-chemical, Addictions-smoking, cancer, lung problems, Emphysema, Tuberculosis

Created Patterns
1. I am being smothered by _____.
2. I must hurt others before they hurt me.
3. I must take advantage of others before they take advantage of me.
4. What have you been grieving?
5. People are going to take things from me.
6. My needs must always be met first.
7. I must get them before they get me.

Cancer – Medullary Thyroid

Fears
- Fear of standing in their truth
- Fear of violating injustices will never stop
- Fear of attack
- Fear of pain
- Fear of hurt
- Fear of their anger
- Fear of injustice
- Fear of love
- Fear of betrayal
- Fear of being wrong
- Fear of hope

Emotional States
- Let's others destroy their concept of right and wrong. Afraid to stand and speak the truth of whom they are. Long term hatred of one who has wronged them. Long held anxiety around the hatred has led to calcification of strong emotions that have nowhere to go. Long held suspicion that others were involved in the wrong doing have created a lack of trust and a sense that there is no justice. There has been an involvement of institutions with no feeling of justice done. The wrongs were institutionalized. Has sacrificed their life and what they could have had for this committed sense of seeking to right a wrong(s). Has needed love but has shut it out because of this strong and impenetrable lack of trust.

EMOTIONAL PATTERNS

Cross Indexing: Thyroid Problems, Endocrine System Disorders

Created Patterns

1. I can't make my own choices.
2. I make wrong choices.
3. Making a choice is wrong.
4. I am powerless to make the right decisions.
5. If I speak the truth I will be destroyed.
6. I hate _____.
7. I have been wronged by _____.
8. I have no justice.
9. I can't forgive or let go.
10. I don't trust.
11. I have been betrayed.
12. The powers that be are out to get me.
13. I must have justice at any cost.
14. I can't trust others to not hurt me.
15. I long for the feeling of hope.
16. There is no joy in living.
17. I can't fight back.
18. No one listens to me.
19. The cancer is a plot to kill me.
20. They want to keep me quiet.

Cancer – Melanoma

Fears

- Fear being present
- Fear of hopelessness
- Fear flow of life
- Fears not being responsible
- Fears living a facade
- Fear of being wrong
- Fear of not belonging
- Fear of being nothing
- Fear of not being good enough

Emotional States

- Heaviness in their being. The world weighs on them. It feels like the world is closing in on them. They feel pressed/a pressure to present a presence to the world that is not them.
- Wrongheaded view of self and their place in the world. Has a hard time seeing how they belong despite the fact that they have predefined roles (mother/ father/sister/ brother/ son/ daughter/ career/ etc). They still feel unfulfilled in how they see themselves.

Cross Indexing: Skin Problems, Cancers

Repeating Patterns: judged and judging, burdened, heavy heart, overwhelmed, critical sense of a need for perfection, unworthy, feels never enough

Created Patterns
1. I must be perfect.
2. I am perfect / I'm not perfect.
3. People always die from melanoma.
4. I am inadequate.
5. I am unworthy.
6. I must be who I am not.
7. People see me in ways that are not true.
8. People see me the way they want to see me without regard to who I am or what I want.
9. I don't belong.
10. I don't know how to be myself.
11. I will never be enough for _____.
12. The world is too much.

Cancer – Multiple Myeloma

Fears
- Fear of the truth
- Fear of not dying
- Fear of self
- Fear of life
- Fear of being nothing
- Fear of giving
- Fear of receiving
- Fear of being wrong
- Fear of no pain
- Fear of injustice
- Fear of belonging
- Fear of letting go of their identity
- Fear of not suffering

Emotional States
- 500 ways of doing something and the person chooses one that is fraught with self sabotage. The person brings that self sabotage home and brings everyone there into their drama of self sabotage. The self sabotage brings them attention. They are afraid that if they don't do this they will completely disappear…be nothing but a ghost.
- Holds a pattern of nervous energy. The nervous energy equals being lost. Don't know what to do with themselves and what they have to do to give. Patterns of self-deceit weave them into the nervous energy to make a fabric that they swaddle themselves in like a blanket.

- Long ago a wish was made to not be something, to not do something and they got what they didn't want. Wrong choices and regrets fill their waking hours. Never giving their daydreams of regret to the sea to forgive and wash clean. Wrongness in their neural channels became ingrained despite evidence to the contrary that they were practicing the definition of insanity.
- Warm salt tears stream from eyes that see only the pain in life. Anchored in the pain they survive there, never seeing the joy. They see only the woe. Unrelenting hardships make life unbearable and death is a desired release. Wrong choices are declared no choices.

Cross Indexing- Cancer-Lymphoma, Cancer-Leukemia, Blood disorders, bones – broken

Created Patterns

1. I can't stand up for myself and when I do I just get knocked down.
2. I have no life in me to fight back against injustice.
3. I have no strength to defend against invasion.
4. What I thought would work in life was all wrong. I am all wrong.
5. I sabotage everything I touch. I need to do that to feel loved and wanted.
6. I don't know where I belong or even if I want to try and belong.
7. I am always wrong. I can't forgive myself for being wrong.
8. Life is pain and suffering. There is no joy, no respite from the suffering.

Cancer – Non Hodgkins Lymphoma

Fears

- Fear of being unloved
- Fear of attack
- Fear of being unworthy
- Fear of no purpose
- Fear of being nothing
- Fear of living
- Fear of being trapped
- Fear of struggle
- Fear of losing their identity
- Fear of no peace
- Fear of peace
- Fear of injustice
- Fear of joy
- Fear of powerlessness
- Fear of light
- Fear of duty
- Fear of obligation

Emotional States

- Anger at someone that was supposed to be a substitute in their life for love and affection – early in life – left a gaping hole in their sense of well being. Often the desire to live was impacted by lack of purpose created by the gaping hole.

- Long held beliefs about their worth and constitution are without statutory beingness. Gentleness has withered and died in the face of the continued assault.
- Without merit. Their whole life feels as if it is without merit. Nothing in their life can be pointed to as distinctive. Feels like nothing of noteworthy in their presence on the planet.
- Longing to enter another realm of existence to feel free of the binds of this life. There is a sense of feeling shackled. There is no freedom to explore or be human. This was brought on by a lifetime of obligatory duty and responsibility – each day had no color.
- Walking into a place of the unknown – makes them feel alive – there is a sense of deadness in their being — the idea of heading into dying is at its core fascinating — it is an accepted adventure — because they are unable to break the binds of their existence as it is.
- Tired of fighting. Forces in their life cause a continual struggle. Forces are loud and overwhelming. Doesn't know how or have the energy to stand up and stop the abuse. There is a quality to the 'forces' that seem to drain their life force.
- Revelations about their past caused a complete undoing of their identity. Unable to feel a grounding or footing in the now formlessness of their identity. There is nothing for them to grab onto and they feel like a balloon…floating above a car lot when the string has been cut. Left holding the bag. Has a pattern of having to clean up the chaos and drama of others.
- Wild malformation of their identity has created manifestation of drama that borders on lunacy. They have no basis in fact or truth of information. This has been a repeated pattern their whole life and they are tired. They long to escape. They long for silence in their mind and in their blood.
- Wondrous hope sparkled in their mind one day and then the vision of that hope was destroyed by childhood monsters. Violence marred the scenery and they were left with remnants of a tattered life that was without hope. Joy became a shadow at the horizon that was never reachable. Warnings of injustices created a sourness in their being.
- Remnants of a past haunt their thoughts. Deep regrets and anger at the power that held them. Feels as if they are in a whirlpool of this energy that they cannot escape.
- Willing their life to end. Vapidness of their life gives it little hope or value. The avenues to change feel blocked. They struggle a little bit and then give up.
- Windowless world (they don't see the rich canvas of a life to be lived). There is no light only a darkness to their days. Jealous of others who appear to be able to move through their life with joy and love. Kindness has not been the experience of their life. They have a filter that interprets everything as without light.

Cross Indexing: Cancers, Lymphatic System Disorders, Blood problems, Wounded Creative Core

Repeating Patterns: Stays working at one job (usually repetitive) so that they don't have to think about life. Lives a life circumscribed by a sense of duty and is rote. Wounded creative core. Gives up easily on challenges. Holds jobs that are invisible (truck driver, janitor, nurses' aides, clerical, etc.). Works to pay the bills and can't see a way out to enjoy life…live. In relationships with people that only want them for what they can do for them. Trauma-drama.

Created Patterns
1. I have been abandoned.
2. I am unloved.
3. I am under constant attack.
4. I have nothing to live for.
5. I have nothing in my life.
6. I have achieved nothing in my life.

7. I have no hope.
8. Life is like a lead weight.
9. Life is a prison.
10. Life is bleak.
11. I am tired of the struggle.
12. I'm only seen when people need me.
13. I am angry at _____.
14. People that love me betray me _____.
15. I don't know who I am.
16. I am lost.
17. I have no purpose.
18. I am worthless.
19. My worth has no purpose.
20. I am under attack.
21. I attack myself.
22. I am trapped.
23. My life is nothing but duty to someone else's concept of how I should be.
24. I have no life.
25. I want to die.
26. I am a slave.
27. I must fight to just exist.
28. Life is a continual struggle.
29. Life is chaos.
30. I have no foundation, no identity.
31. Life is unjust.
32. People blame me for stuff I didn't do.
33. I regret _____.
34. I give up.
35. Life is darkness.

Cancer – Osteosarcoma

Fears

- Fear of not being good enough
- Fear of risk
- Fear of peace
- Fear of being invisible
- Fear of being seen
- Fear of leaving the box
- Fear of letting go
- Fear of being hurt
- Fear of joy
- Fear of being vulnerable
- Fear of being told what to do
- Fear of the flow of life
- Fear of giving

- Fear of feeling

Emotional States

- This person lacks a sense of wholeness, they always feel like something is missing in their life and they are always trying to achieve in order to achieve 'wholeness'. They will say things like "when I do this, I'll _____". The blank is what they think the (w)hole is about. No inner peace.
- They live silently. They feel (and it is) that no one sees them. They lead little lives with little thoughts — never reaching for their grandness of being. Deeply afraid to step into that space. It is their objective not to be seen. Not to see that inner self. They fear that a vision of the inner self will take them into a place of ridicule and shame. The separateness they live is how they stay safe.
- They don't let go of a hurt they felt very deeply — this could be ancestral — they have come into this life bearing that wound and may have repeated that wound. The resentment is carried deeply. Holds out that the perpetrator will pay. It is they that pay for holding the energy of deep resentment.
- They struggle with honesty. They cannot feel joy. No deep sense of happiness. What they show the world is only skin deep, they stuff the emotions deep inside. Deeply resents people telling them what to do. There is an extreme energy of protection. They fear that others will hurt them.
- Shields themselves from life. They do not yield to the flow. They pull their strength from a place of resistance as opposed to a place of love and flow. They have little or no comprehension of the divine order and flow of the universe. They want all expansion to cease. They resist the inevitable nature of all that is and all that will be.
- Adjust to nature – all of nature must be controlled and manipulated for the collective profit. The earth is to be used to support man. Their belief that they can take and take and not give back – giving has never been part of their experience – out of balance feminine. A taking nature – masculine nature is me first and the others be damned. Wants to be left alone to wallow in their self-pity. This is part of the taking and taking pulls inward. The self-pity is a way of taking from others.
- Heartless nature of their life – they go through their life with no heart to what they do. There is a rote nature to their life. They do not feel the joy of a beautiful sunset or the joy in the seeing and hearing a child's laughter. Their life is unconnected – no heart – no emotion – no love—no feeling attached to the feeling. They are the living dead – they feel nothing when they feel.

Cross Indexing: Cancer, Bone Problems

Created Patterns

1. I resent my life.
2. I will never have inner peace.
3. Something is missing in my life.
4. I am incomplete.
5. When I _____ I will be happy.
6. Just when I think I am _____ something happens (what happens?).
7. Achievement is how I am happy.
8. Doing is how I am love.
9. I can't complete anything.
10. Everything I do is done half-way.

11. I get love/attention when I mess up.
12. I'm not loved.

Cancer – Ovarian

Fears
- Fear of the inner child
- Fear of their own hatred of self
- Fear of loving themselves
- Fear of the power of the feminine
- Fear of duty
- Fear of creativity
- Fear of authority and rule
- Fear of joy
- Fear of finding the meaning in life
- Fear of receiving
- Fear of no purpose
- Fear of being unworthy
- Fear of being judged
- Fear of loss
- Fear of abandonment

Emotional States
- There was never the opportunity to honor and create the childlike center of her being. A place of play and innocence never seemed to be important, duties came first.
- Creativity was corralled by convention – wild exploration of what was possible was cut off; 'you can't do that, it doesn't follow the rules'.
- Hard won pleasures give no pleasure. She works hard to get things and then finds they are worthless and have no meaning. The inward journey gets short circuited by rules.
- Born into a world where every essence of control and power had to be fought for. Expected to meet the needs of others before self. Made to feel worthless and powerless as a method of obedience to the system. If she tried to slip out of the system she is abandoned and judged, betrayed by her own kind. Uniqueness and difference were not tolerated. Felt thwarted in her efforts to be herself (loss of creativity and expression). Only finds self through sickness.

Cross Indexing: Cancers, Wounded Creative Core

Repeated Patterns: Won't let others near their ideas, hides them to keep them safe. So they lead a life of half way success. May experience shelter/housing insecurity. Lack of inner peace – may have experienced the loss/death of loved ones. Relationships and/or jobs that diminish worth. Feels something is missing in their being that can't be replaced. Often ill.

Created Patterns
1. I am angry for letting others tell me what to do.

2. I'm not allowed to have needs.
3. Only their needs are importance.
4. I must serve others.
5. Others come before me.
6. I don't know how to take care of myself.
7. I don't know how to nurture myself.
8. No one is there for me.
9. Women must take care of others before themselves.
10. I hate myself.
11. I'm not good enough.
12. I'm not worthy.
13. I'm rejected.
14. I'm ostracized.
15. I'm alone.
16. Being vulnerable is dangerous.
17. Being a woman is wrong.
18. I am nothing.
19. I am invisible.
20. It is dangerous to create.
21. I deserve nothing.
22. I deserve cancer.
23. I am a victim.
24. I'm not supposed to have anything.
25. I'm responsible for my mother's anger.
26. I'm responsible for my mother.
27. I'm to blame for everything.
28. No matter what I do I am to blame.
29. I deserve to lose everything.
30. I am going to die.

Cancer – Pancreatic NeuroEndocrine

Fears

- Fear of loving self
- Fear of authority
- Fear of their anger and hatred of authority
- Fear of their inner pain
- Fear that nothing will ever release them
- Fear of disappointment
- Fear they will not achieve their purpose
- Fear of trusting others
- Fear of being wrong
- Fear of staying still
- Fear of being alone
- Fear of failure
- Fear of being seen as less than

- Fear of being taken advantage of

Emotional States

- Always looking for the higher truth of our nature. But in the search false paths are taken that lead to anger, frustration, and inner conflict. All of life appears disappointing in that light but all boils down to a lack of love for self. There is a sense of endless searching for a truth that is within but the truth is too frightening and painful. So the person never starts and continues to look for that truth in the outward manifestation of the inner truth which is simply a reflection. Holding all others in that reflection the search for self-love is never achieved.
- Held to very high standards by themselves and community. Needs that elevation to survive. Lost their concept of self very early in life, always a sense that life had a higher calling, that they are being raised for that sacrifice and that their life was not their own.
- Unwritten rules become the Quixotic banner of life. Nailed to the cross. Lack of reality in knowing who they are. Their basic nature is to not trust. Long held betrayals have created a deep lasting connection to believing that others are not there for their ideals. Unwavering devotion to their ideals, as those have not failed them.

Cross Indexing: Cancer, Pancreas problems, Endocrine system disorders, Addictions (chemical, alcohol, etc.)

Created Patterns

1. I can't be wrong.
2. If I am wrong I will be humiliated.
3. If I am wrong I will be shamed.
4. I am angry at _____.
5. My life is in service to others.
6. I must be of service to others.
7. I must wear the facade all the time.
8. I can't let others see who I am.
9. I must always be right.
10. I am unloved.
11. I don't love myself.
12. I have to keep moving.
13. I have to keep performing.
14. There is no rest until I know all truth.
15. I can't be alone.
16. I can't be alone with myself.
17. I am alone.
18. I am superior to others.
19. People that challenge me are stupid.
20. I can't trust others.
21. People betray me.
22. People take advantage of me.
23. My life is not my own.

Cancer – Prostate

Fears
- Fear of authority and the system
- Fear of being stopped in their creation by authority
- Fear of being invisible
- Fear of being powerless
- Fear being challenged
- Fear of being out of control
- Fear of intimacy
- Fear of blame

Emotional States
- Passive-aggressive. Holds lots of anger at a system from which he derives his livelihood. Sees the system as unresponsive and bloated. Feels ineffective and diminished within that system. Can't seem to get out of that system.
- Lack of knowledge and understanding. Judgmental approach. Judging an issue before all is known. Gives an appearance of strength and dominance. Holds a complete lack of regard for others if challenged for judgments. Gets really angry when challenged.
- Wrapped around a pole. Life seems like a big accidental wreck. Hard to see who wins and who loses. Bitterness at a relationship and how it turned out. Doesn't have a clue how to unravel the mess without letting ego go down the drain. Needs their pride as their identity.

Cross Indexing: Cancer, Prostate Problems

Repeating Patterns: In and out of relationships that haven't worked, blames someone else's ego when the blame should be theirs, stuck in the beauty of themselves. Anger, lack of inner peace, passive aggressive, ineffectual, powerless.

Created Patterns
1. I know what's best.
2. I must judge a situation before it gets out of control.
3. I must put people in their place.
4. People who challenge me are stupid.
5. I am angry at _____.
6. I resent _____.
7. Life is a mess.
8. Nothing works out for me.
9. Women/Men do not know how to be in a relationship.
10. I only attract women/men that care about themselves.
11. I am bitter toward _____.
12. Why should I change? It's their fault.

Cancer – Squamous Cell

Fears

- Fear of emotions
- Fear of people that run unchecked over them
- Fear of change
- Fear of giving
- Fear of not receiving
- Fear of being unheard
- Fear of betrayal
- Fear of attack
- Fear of being taken advantage of
- Fear of being wrong
- Fear of being unloved
- Fear of freedom
- Fear of happiness
- Fear of being less than

Emotional States

- They are being held hostage by their emotions. And one person is the source of those emotions. Childhood anxiety created a dynamic of fixation. This dynamic created emotional frustration of never being able to accomplish what they wanted. Their life frustrations were expressed and couched in manipulative efforts toward others to get what they felt they needed. The need was deep and visceral.

Cross Indexing: Cancers, skin problems, cancer – melanoma

Repeating Patterns: spinning in their emotions, manipulative, doesn't get what they want, feels as if people are out to get them

Created Patterns

1. I am angry at god.
2. I resent god.
3. Everyone else is wrong and I am right.
4. Life is out to get me.
5. I never get what I want.
6. I am unloved and I have to manipulate people to get what I need.
7. I am frozen in a state of need.
8. I must use others to get what I need.
9. I have no friends.
10. I walk straight but everyone else tries to push me off the path.
11. Happiness is only a dream.
12. The world is full of jerks and I am always up against them.
13. The world is out to get me.
14. I resent people who have what I want.
15. It's OK to take from people who have what want.

16. I am entitled to _____.

Cancer – Stomach

Fears
- Fear of guilt
- Fear that nothing they do will make it better
- Fear that what they take in has a price to be paid
- Fear of shame
- Fear of seeing other points of view
- Fear of feelings
- Fear of being whole
- Fear of presence
- Fear of success
- Fear of hurt
- Fear of pain
- Fear of deserving
- Fear of being unworthy
- Fear of the secrets
- Fear of decisions
- Fear of life

Emotional States
- Competing ideas pull at this person. The juxtaposed ideas pull the person apart. Long forgotten crimes of the soul lead to guilt and shame. Long held beliefs fall out of favor and are replaced with ones inducing guilt and shame. These changes in view narrow the perception of the world to nothing more than a tiny slit in the wall.
- Hollow hatred rings like a bell through their being. No one person knows how to reach through the hatred and into the core of their intense feelings. The hatred becomes a focus. It is a focus of their life.
- Wounded by the nature of their lives. A life that intentionally hurt their being. A life that was focused on their personal destruction. The destruction of an identity or an individuality.
- The star of the show has faded and is no longer relevant. They had stardom but its luster burned too bright and it could not be assimilated. Yet they continue to grasp at the stars but do not understand the light. They think they can contain the light. They don't realize you have to either be the light or reflect it. They want to put the light in a box.

Cross Indexing: Cancer, cancer-esophagus, stomach problems

Created Patterns
1. I want to get even against _____.
2. I want revenge against _____.
3. I can't ever get anywhere.
4. Good things are for others not me.

5. I never get a break.
6. You have to stay with what is safe.
7. You stay safe by doing what you have done over and over.
8. I hate my family.
9. No one understands me.
10. Everyone hurts me.
11. Everyone puts me down.
12. I'm a nobody.
13. I am worthless.
14. I hate the people that have hurt me.
15. It's safer if you don't see everything.
16. It's safer if you don't know everything.
17. I'm being pulled apart.
18. I can't make a decision.
19. I am guilty.
20. I am shameful.
21. I hate _____.
22. I'm not good enough to live.
23. I am being destroyed by life.

Cancer – Urethral

Fears

- Fear of authority
- Fear of the revenge they seek
- Fear of being creative
- Fear of their inner voice
- Fear of their truth being unheard and unwanted
- Fear of their anger
- Fear of being heard
- Fear of being betrayed
- Fear of the opposite sex
- Fear of letting go
- Fear of people
- Fear of god
- Fear of being unwanted
- Fear of being unloved
- Fear of being take advantage
- Fear of being powerless

Emotional States

- Creative / nurturing / intuitive aspect is being ignored / suppressed. Stopped by intense anger. Feels spiritually blocked. Ability to express intense emotions so they will be heard is blocked. Feels betrayed by their family.
- Hatred of the opposite sex.

- Ability to forgive is shut down.

Cross Indexing: Cancer, Bladder Problems

Created Patterns

1. I am angry at /hate/ resent/ bitter toward _____.
2. Men/women are mean.
3. I hate men/women (this is All as opposed to some).
4. Men/women betray me (This is ALL as opposed to some).
5. _____ has betrayed me.
6. God betrayed me.
7. I am disconnected from god.
8. I have been deceived by _____.
9. No one listens to me.
10. No one cares about me.
11. I am ignored.
12. I have been betrayed by my family.
13. I am powerless.
14. People take advantage of me.
15. _____ is to blame for _____.
16. I am abandoned.
17. I am pissed at _____.
18. I don't trust _____ (myself/ father/ mother/ men/ women/ family/ ???).
19. My family doesn't listen to me.
20. I don't know how to nurture myself.
21. I can't speak my truth.

Candida

Fears

- Fears being lied to
- Fear of being cast aside
- Fear of change
- Fear of movement
- Fear of the truth
- Fear of authority
- Fear of losing
- Fear of letting others down
- Fear of failure
- Fear of joy
- Fear of a purpose
- Fear of living
- Fear of disapproval
- Fear of being alone
- Fear of being judged

- Fear of inner voice
- Fear of leaving the box
- Fear of letting go
- Fear of pride being hurt
- Fear of flow
- Fear of receiving
- Fear of responsibility
- Fear of blame
- Fear of creativity
- Fear of being unworthy

Emotional States

- False promises of things to come lead to dead ends. Heard from parents. Those failed promises lead to resentment and distrust. Locked ideas set in that create rigidity and dysfunction. The ideas are based on the old ways instead of movement and growth within a dynamic system
- Hard-won favor with a superior has created a loss of integrity and self. They have witnessed themselves doing things that have not served them but serve another. They have left their sense of self and integrity in a hole by the side of the road and the hole got covered up by a road crew.
- Joy has turned to ashes. Short-lived accomplishments have created sadness. A narrow vision of goals and objectives has a short-sightedness to them that quickly unravels. The goals are heartless and have no connection to the soul and that deep sense of self.
- A need to be something they're not based on someone else's values. Keeps them locked into a paradigm of old ideas that have stagnated and ruined relationships. Leaving them alone and all they have left are these old and irrelevant values and beliefs, Hard-won.
- Won victories have left them in a vacuum — alone with no one around to balance their life. So they reside in a place of imbalance. Their decision to stay in the rigidity of that isolation. The yeast infection creates more isolation — distances people.
- Higher awareness is thwarted. Heart hangs on to limiting ideas that keep the person safe. Judges others from the limiting ideas held by the heart. Judges all around him/her to stay safe. Doesn't trust higher awareness and higher concepts of thought. Needs to reconcile thinking to the environment and prior life experience. Won't get out of the box.
- Unable to let go of a past grievance. The grievance keeps the person stuck in time. Won't listen to reason about this issue. Is unforgiving – an issue of honor and personal value is at stake. Won't let go of an issue/grievance around lack – scarcity – something taken from them, has created a harden view of life. Faults all of their scarcity issues around the one event in their life.
- Unable to hear that others care for them. Very nervous around others, feels judged. Doesn't know how to deal with judgmental feelings. Holds others accountable for a lack of judgment. Shuns the judgment of others when he/she is lacking.
- Holds others accountable for his/her failures. Can't see that their own limitations have created the failures. Wants others to fix it for them. They won't hold the responsibility – blame shifts to others.
- Longs for the good 'ole days. Things were better then…. Does not create. Creativity requires new thinking—new Yearning of the heart to heal all wounds that narrow the heart. Holds grudges toward those that have created that narrowing. Unwanted sexual energies become annoying. Instead of channeling the energy into creativity the energies are ignored or tamped down. The warmth of the rise of those energies creates an inner chaos. Gentle outward nature belies an anger below the surface that causes an inner fire that will eventually burn the inner organs. The anger is at one's self. They needle. They poke at little things that are insignificant and unworthy

of recognition in an effort to deflect from the core of their irritation. The core of inner agitation is a hatred of self of having been born unworthy.
- Unyielding evidence that they lived a wrong life. A life that brings them no joy. They have forgotten the purpose and feel lost in the wilderness of their life.

Cross Indexing: Adrenal fatigue, fungus, chronic fatigue, fibromyalgia, Yeast Infection, Thrush, Athlete's Foot

Repeating Patterns: doubt, needing approval, feeling overrun, unable to give…feeling depleted, victim

Created Patterns
1. Everyone else is to blame.
2. Everyone else's needs come before mine.
3. I am powerless.
4. I can't accept who I am.
5. I can't handle change.
6. I don't know how to be in balance.
7. I don't know what balance is.
8. I don't love myself.
9. I doubt myself.
10. I must control things to keep safe.
11. I must keep things the same.
12. I resent _____.
13. I'm not accepted.
14. What is out of balance in your life?

Canker Sores

Fears
- Fear of being wrong
- Fear of being unable to speak words to defend themselves
- Fear of being guilty
- Fear of failure
- Fear of being in the flow of life
- Fear of shame
- Fear of rejection
- Fear of loving self
- Fear of not being enough
- Fear of being judged
- Fear of being unloved

Emotional States
- Justified in everything they say and do…even if it is wrong. The wrong becomes guilt which still gets defended as justified.

- Wrong headedness. Plunges headlong into fool hardy ventures that yield nothing except chaos and-or acrimony. Doesn't want to hear about their misdeeds. They're always right and someone else caused the failure.
- Wrong space, wrong time, and wrong relationship. Judgment always outside of themselves. Feels actions are warranted. The sore is how they repent when they inwardly know they are wrong but to save themselves from shame they never admit it.
- Early issues with getting what need from family based on what they didn't take in.
- They are more prone to take guidance from an outside source other than their own guidance. Never looking within for sustenance.

Cross Indexing: Behcet's disease, Celiac disease, HIV/AIDS, Inflammatory Bowel Disease, Reactive Arthritis, virus, cold sores, colds, herpes-simplex I, area of body affected

Created Patterns

1. I'm afraid I will do something wrong.
2. I am overworked and don't know how to change it.
3. I am angry/hate/bitter toward/want revenge against _____.
4. I can't face my shame.
5. I am ashamed.
6. I am guilty.
7. To be judged is to be unloved.
8. I am unloved when I feel guilt.
9. I must always be right.
10. I fear being judged.
11. I am worthless.
12. I must hide my face.
13. I must hide my shame.
14. I'm not worthy of being loved.

Cardiovascular Disorder

Fears

- Fear of betrayal
- Fear of heart hurt/wound
- Fear of their heart-stopping
- Fear of not achieving their life purpose
- Fear of not achieving their hearts yearning
- Fear of love
- Fear of being unloved
- Fear of being hurt
- Fear of letting their anger out
- Fear of inner peace
- Fear of not being good enough
- Fear of being in one place for long
- Fear of being different

- Fear of having things taken

Emotional States
- Holding anger in your heart for someone that betrayed a trust. They were hurt and can't let go of the hurt no matter how much it hurts them.
- Hardened attitudes towards others, bigotry, prejudice (ancestral biases) that hold the person in a space of non-peace, non-love, non-flow.

Cross Indexing: Heart Problems, Veins, Arteries

Repeating Patterns: chooses spaces where there is a sameness of culture, bigotry, racism, anger, not letting go, doesn't love self, closed to new ideas and ways of thinking, closed to better ideas, closed to change, lack of inner-peace

Created Patterns
1. I'm not good enough.
2. I am going to die.
3. I must be better than everyone else.
4. I can never stop.
5. Why are you driven to compete and achieve?
6. I must have it now.
7. Someone will get it before me and I will lose.
8. I want it now.
9. If someone is better than me then I am no good.
10. I am irritated by uppity people.
11. People that are different are wrong.
12. I am angry at _____.
13. I am unloved.
14. I don't love myself.
15. I have been betrayed.
16. People different from me are always trying to take something away from me.

Carpel Tunnel

Fears
- Fear of life
- Fear of a life doomed to repetitive work that fails the heart
- Fear of having purpose
- Fear of making a decision
- Fear of listening to their inner guidance
- Fear of stopping
- Fear of change
- Fear of their creativity
- Fear of letting go

- Fear of powerlessness
- Fear of being irrelevant

Emotional States
- Doesn't know what to do with their lives. Feels like they have lost a sense of purpose. Lets the fates decide their destiny.
- Non-dominate side: Doesn't know how to get what they need or want. So they do what hurts them to survive.
- Dominate side: Can't think to a place of change. They hate their job but they don't give themselves the space to see what else they could do.

Cross Indexing: Wrists, Left or Right sided negative tendencies, hand problems, arms-right, arms-left, arm problems

Repeating Patterns: Wounded Creative Core, doesn't change – does the same thing over and over expecting a different result, doesn't see how to change things – spins into that thought.

Created Patterns
1. Life isn't fair.
2. I am powerless to change things.
3. I have to do it all.
4. What are the issues of inflexibility in your life?
5. I always get the short end of the stick.
6. I never get a fair shake.
7. I am stuck.
8. I am afraid to move forward.
9. Change is dangerous.
10. I am powerless to change.
11. I can't compete.
12. I get really uncomfortable around competitive people.
13. I betray myself to pay the bills.

Cartilage Degeneration

Fears
- Fear of joy
- Fear of being unprotected from criticism
- Fear of flow
- Fear of stopping
- Fear of not carrying the load
- Fear of stepping up
- Fear of their outside voice
- Fear of life
- Fear of letting the burden go

- Fear of feelings
- Fear of not taking the responsibilities
- Fear of being invisible
- Fear of being never enough
- Fear of my emotions
- Fear of my anger
- Fear of loss
- Fear of being seen
- Fear of never being busy

Emotional States

- Life is wearing thin. Needs to rest, feels like they are always working. Tired of putting up with a lot from others and wearing thin.

Cross Indexing: Arthritis, Arthritis – Osteoarthritis, joint problems

Created Patterns

1. I am worn out.
2. Life is hard.
3. Life is too much of a burden.
4. I am burdened by life.
5. I always carry a heavy load.
6. I must work hard to survive.
7. I never go where I want to go.
8. I must go where others want me to go.
9. I must do what others want me to do.
10. I put up with a lot.
11. People are expecting something from me.
12. People are always asking for more of me.
13. People assume that I will take the responsibility.
14. I am always the responsible one.
15. I'm invisible.
16. People take advantage of me.
17. I only make enough to survive.
18. I only get enough to survive.
19. I can't take much more.
20. I am always at the breaking point.
21. I must keep my anger to myself.
22. I mustn't upset the balance.

Cataracts – Left

Fears

- Fear of seeing who you no longer are

- Fear of being wrong
- Fear of letting go
- Fear of new ideas
- Fear of consequences
- Fear of powerlessness
- Fear of driving their own destiny
- Fear of the joy of life
- Fear of the future
- Fear of disappointment
- Fear of injustice
- Fear of being left out
- Fear of being forgotten
- Fear of being unloved
- Fear of change

Emotional States
- Justified in their position and won't see other ways, options, or ideas.
- Closed to the exploration of new things, doesn't want to see them.
- Failure to take responsibility for the events they set in motion. Refused to see the consequences then and now.
- Hard ideas about others created envy and jealousy with their parents.
- Helpless or powerless to change the ideas of others to get them to see what they want them to see
- Mouse like approaches have left the person feeling that unreasonable people have kept them from their life. Unable to see past the facade others have created to hold power.
- Unwilling and unyielding energies have moved life in an inexplicable direction that hindsight still does not recognize. The responsibility is unknown.
- Failure to see that no one is going to look at them for their uniqueness and joy (not there). When looking outside one's self the person does not see the possibility that they can be happy, vibrant, and creative. False hopes about what they will see in the future cause them to not want to think or dream of the future. Deep disappointments have created deep heartache. Deep sense of injustice at the way they feel they have been treated.
- Heart and eyes are energetically connected. What one sees goes to the heart. Not enough love to go around and they are always left out. Those around are unwilling to hear them. Feels unneeded for self. Would rather not know that others are needed.

Cross Indexing: Eye problems, Cataracts-Right

Repeating Patterns: stuck, refuses to take responsibility, feels left out or forgotten, feels unneeded/unwanted, gets what they do not want, finds themselves in places they don't want.

Created Patterns
1. I am stuck.
2. Change is bad.
3. I am not responsible for someone else's issues.
4. Change is dangerous.
5. I am left out of everything.
6. I am unloved.

7. There's not enough for me.
8. I am unseen.
9. I am powerless.
10. I must hide to be safe.
11. I am forgotten by others.
12. I am forced to do things against my will.
13. No one needs me.
14. No one wants me.
15. My wishes are ignored.
16. No one sees things my way.

Cataracts – Right

Fears
- Fear of seeing what you can no longer do
- Fear of the future
- Fear of being judged
- Fear of powerlessness
- Fear of heart hurt
- Fear of being wrong
- Fear of the unknown
- Fear of being nothing
- Fear of being control
- Fear of religious institution

Emotional States
- High intensity analysis of one's life by another yielded a fear and anger at their judgment and scrutiny. This left the person feeling powerless at the confrontation and shutting down the vision that the confrontation created.
- New visions (imagery) of the world and future leave the person feeling lost, overwhelmed and confused by the information. The visual information becomes a blur and undefined tangle.
- Heart connection. A heart wound created great sadness at something unwanted.
- Long held beliefs are invalid and seeing the truth of those beliefs holds the person hostage. Letting go of those beliefs creates panic and unknowing. The eye is tired of having ideas counter to their "truths" exposed or revealed. So the eye hides. Looking into the future the person would see their own mortality and end. Religious views run headlong into the higher self (may be ancestral).
- Long held ideas of being nothing have created a feeling of stagnation. Nothing is going to change and nothing can be seen that would change it. A feeling that they have been up against an incredible and overwhelming power and control that they cannot be present in. The very existence produces fear and they look down to exist in the energy of that control and fear.

Cross Indexing: eye problems, cataracts-left

Created Patterns
- I don't want to see the future.
- The future is dangerous.
- I don't see any future for myself.
- I use knowledge to be better than others.
- I am afraid of the future.
- I am (alone, sad, angry....) in the future.

Celiac Disease

Fears
- Fear of having to stuff their anger
- Fear of the anger at what they have to take
- Fear of being overwhelmed
- Fear of expressing feelings
- Fear of too much
- Fear of heart hurt
- Fear of rejection
- Fear of decisions
- Fear of action
- Fear of being in the flow
- Fear of putting themselves first
- Fear of being powerful
- Fear of people
- Fear of change
- Fear of connection to their divinity
- Fear of an identity without being a victim
- Fear of being lost
- Fear of losing the pain
- Fear of attack
- Fear of not belonging
- Fear of the choice between right and wrong
- Fear of being unworthy
- Fear of people
- Fear of being stepped on

Teachings
- Creator's definition of the difference between right and wrong
- Live without pain/sickness
- Be in relationships without your story
- Live without your story
- To be nourished by life
- Nourish myself
- Nurture myself
- Receive nourishment
- Receive nurturing
- Enjoy life
- Joy
- Trust
- Loved
- Happiness
- Cherished
- Change easily
- Let go of past hurts with ease
- Feel safe being creative
- Be honored for my uniqueness
- Be in the now
- At one
- Be healthy
- Take the world in with joy and wonder
- Be safe with different energies
- Be safe with people
- Be safe
- Be cherished without pain/sickness
- Be loved without pain
- Be in the world without needing to cry
- Trust your inner guidance for answers
- Be comfortable with not knowing the

- answers
- Live without feeling under attack
- Let go of pain
- Live without ridicule
- Be honored for your creativity
- Honor yourself
- Good enough
- Cry and be safe
- Live without being sick
- Integrate the energy of my personal power
- Be safe with my personal power

Emotional States

- Heightened sense of awareness. Feels over stimulated at times. Shuts down parts of life so they don't feel so overwhelmed. Feelings are bottled up, which creates a heightened sense of pain. All emotions are sent to the intestines to get needs met through pain. Over stimulation causes a feeling of anxiety/fear that then is sent into the gut.
- Feel like they have always been crying in this world. Feelings have been hurt frequently leading to crying. Everything seems to hurt. They feel like they are always on the threshold of tears. Rejection is sent into the body to stifle the tears.
- There is a difficulty between right and wrong and they feel torn in two.
- Feeling of being lost in a linear world that requires masculine linear thought. Tends to stay in the creative.
- Application/being in a masculine oriented world creates an inner tension that hurts. Because they are coming from the creative they always feel like they are out of sync or 'off' from the world around them.

Cross Indexing: Allergy-wheat, Osteoporosis, bone pain, muscle cramps, anemia, Alopecia, intestinal problems, irritable bowel syndrome, Crohn's disease, skin problems, restless leg syndrome

Repeating Patterns: weaves a story and tells the story over and over, doesn't know how to nourish self, unmet needs (nurturing, loved, wanted, respected, honored), being rejected, sense of powerlessness, victim, lack of honesty in relationships, wounded creative core, feels unsafe with people, love is equivalent to pain, spends a lot of time crying, does not trust their inner guidance, feels not good enough, feels sick a lot.

Created Patterns

1. Change is dangerous.
2. Creator doesn't love me.
3. I always do the wrong thing.
4. I am a victim/martyr.
5. I am afraid of life.
6. I am always sad.
7. I am angry at being forced to live like this (like what?).
8. I am being foolish when I cry.
9. I am being poisoned by _____.
10. I am constantly being attacked.

EMOTIONAL PATTERNS

11. I am lost.
12. I am never good enough.
13. I am overwhelmed by _____.
14. I am overwhelmed by life.
15. I am ridiculed.
16. I am sad.
17. I am under attack.
18. I can never make a living being creative.
19. I can't let them see my pain.
20. I don't belong.
21. I don't know the creator's love.
22. I don't know what's bad for me and what isn't.
23. I hate myself.
24. I hate/ resent/ bitter toward/ angry at _____.
25. I have trouble keeping friends.
26. I hold onto the pain to keep safe.
27. I must be logical to make a living.
28. I must change myself to be what others want me to be.
29. I must keep my feelings to myself.
30. I must protect myself from _____.
31. I must stay away from people to be safe.
32. I must take the abuse to be wanted / needed / loved.
33. I need the pain to protect me.
34. I never know what to say or do.
35. I use the pain to focus on me.
36. I'm a slave.
37. I'm not good enough.
38. I'm not good enough for people to bother with.
39. I'm not happy and I don't know what to do to be happy.
40. I'm not honored.
41. I'm not loved.
42. I'm not respected.
43. I'm not wanted.
44. I'm sick to the pit of my stomach.
45. I'm the one that gets picked on all the time.
46. I'm the whipping boy.
47. If I get better then no one will pay attention to me.
48. If I show how I am feeling I will be ridiculed.
49. If they see me cry, they win.
50. Making decisions are dangerous.
51. My pain/sickness keeps me safe.
52. No one listens to me.
53. No one really loves you, they use love to get something they want.
54. No one wants me around.
55. Pain/Sickness is how I stay in my body.
56. Pain/Sickness is the only way I get treated kindly.
57. People are always trying to hurt me.
58. People are mean.
59. People expect me to be something I'm not.

60. People expect too much of me.
61. People make fun of me.
62. People overwhelm me.
63. People take advantage of me.
64. People that love me hurt me.
65. The pain/sickness is how I get my needs met and hide from others.
66. The world confuses me.
67. There's always a price to be paid when people are nice to you.
68. Things will never change.
69. When I am creative I am put down.
70. When I am in pain/sick people leave me alone.
71. When I cry I am rejected.
72. Whenever I try to do something nice I always get hurt.
73. Whenever I try to do something nice it is always wrong.

*Look at themes of unmet needs (feeling nurtured and loved when wounded, being wanted, respect, honored), truth, relationships, rejection, receiving, power, joy, self-worth, self-respect, victimhood, self-esteem, unconditional love, resentment, power, pain, oneness, letting go, intuition, honesty, friendship, freedom, stress

Cellulite

Fears
- Fear of never having enough
- Fear of seeing
- Fear of being unloved
- Fear of disapproval
- Fear of sabotage
- Fear of being judged
- Fear of being abused
- Fear of never being enough
- Fear of not being seen
- Fear of being diminished
- Fear of being creative
- Fear of being in charge of their destiny
- Fear of making decisions
- Fear of getting outside of the box
- Fear of being seen
- Fear of happiness
- Fear that things will be taken away
- Fear of success
- Fear of following through
- Fear of being present

Teachings
- Feel complete
- Criticism
- Control of others
- Blocked creativity
- Influenced by others
- What others think of you is important
- Fear of success
- Taking control of your life
- Let go of the past
- Live in the now
- Being accepted
- Accepting others
- Happiness
- Joy
- Filled with peace
- Being satisfied
- Be enough
- Be good enough

Emotional States

- Wishing things were different than they are. Always wanting more than they have. Never satisfied with life. Must have what they see (envy, jealousy).
- Buried in the details of life. Can't move beyond or see beyond the details to see the big picture.
- Doesn't like self. Wants to be recognized for something they're not. Always striving for something they don't have the inclination to achieve.
- Feels as if people judge them. Feels treated unkindly. Play the victim role. Life has been hollow promises. Unmet needs from childhood.

Cross Indexing: aging, skin problems, bulimia, anorexia

Created Patterns

1. _____ is critical of me (who).
2. _____ lied to me.
3. Good things are taken away from me.
4. I am angry at myself.
5. I am criticized for being creative.
6. I am jealous of _____.
7. I am judged by others.
8. I am ugly.
9. I can never get enough.
10. I can't control my life – others must do it for me.
11. I can't create and be safe.
12. I can't do anything right.
13. I can't hold onto happiness.
14. I do what others tell me to do.
15. I don't ever feel like I have enough.
16. I don't ever feel satisfied.
17. I don't know where I belong.
18. I don't deserve.
19. I hate my body.
20. I must be perfect to be accepted.
21. I must be perfect to be worthy.
22. I must do what is tried and true.
23. I must tell people what to do to keep them safe.
24. I never feel as if something is completed.
25. If I am creative I will be ostracized/hurt/made fun of.
26. If I am wrong I will be rejected.
27. If I get attention I will be hurt.
28. If I try looking at the big picture I will get lost.
29. I'm not worthy.
30. It is safer being invisible.
31. It is wrong to be happy.
32. People are always criticizing me.
33. People must do what I say to do the right thing.

34. Success is dangerous.
35. They promise and then they don't deliver.
36. What others think of me is important.
37. When eating I am never full.
38. I am never satisfied.
39. Women with cellulite are ugly/old/disgusting.

Charcot's Joints

Fears
- Fear of letting go
- Fear of moving
- Fear of being unwanted
- Fear of not belonging
- Fear of not having their needs met
- Fear of giving
- Fear of being taken advantage of
- Fear of being unloved
- Fear of never having enough
- Fear of having to please others
- Fear of the struggle
- Fear of living
- Fear of injustice
- Fear of not dying
- Fear of undeserving
- Fear of joy
- Fear of listening
- Fear of nothingness

Teachings
- Be in the flow
- Complete
- Deserve
- Get your needs met
- God's love
- Happiness
- Have your needs met
- Joy
- Let go of grudges
- Let go of resentments
- Listen to the needs of others
- Listen to your body
- Live life free of emotional burdens
- Live life with ease
- Live life without grudges
- Live without being a victim to get my needs met
- Live without being taken advantage of
- Live without feeling like being under attack
- Live without thinking God is punishing me
- Stand up for myself
- Whole
- Your voice heard

Emotional States
- This person has difficulty moving. They feel trapped by their own emotions and an overwhelming need to wallow in self-pity. They hold themselves to a different standard than others. Poor me feelings. They hold resentment for those that don't play into the self-pity.
- Unmoved by the needs of others; centered on self. Unable to take the idea that others may have needs too. All inflow and no outflow of energy. Energy comes in and stops. This person's needs will never be met as long as they don't do something for others. Had unmet needs as a child.

- Wanting to let go of the need to make other people happy. Knows that they are playing the role of people-pleaser and it really frustrates them but they don't know how to stop. The people-pleasing behaviors have an aura of compulsion…I can't stop myself.
- Desire to leave the planet-everything is too hard. They feel like they have been singled out for injustice and a life that is unfair. They don't want to do life anymore.

Cross Indexing: Peripheral Neuropathy, Joint Problems, Nerve problems, bone problems, osteoporosis, ALS

Created Patterns
1. Change is dangerous.
2. Change is difficult.
3. Everyone else's needs before mine.
4. Everyone ignores me.
5. Everyone picks on me.
6. Everything I try is the wrong thing.
7. God does not hear my prayers.
8. God hates me.
9. God is punishing me.
10. God knows I don't deserve the pain I'm in.
11. I am angry at _____.
12. I am going to die.
13. I am responsible for making everyone happy.
14. I am trapped.
15. I can't change.
16. I can't make a decision.
17. I can't stand up for myself.
18. I can't tell how I feel.
19. I deserve to come first.
20. I don't belong.
21. I don't feel like doing anything anymore.
22. I don't trust my intuition.
23. I don't trust myself.
24. I don't trust what my body is telling me.
25. I have no say in anything.
26. I hold a grudge against _____.
27. I resent _____.
28. I want to die.
29. I'm a martyr.
30. I'm a victim.
31. I'm always under attack.
32. I'm not good enough.
33. If I don't make people happy _____.
34. If I don't take care of myself no one else will.
35. If I share my feelings I will be _____.
36. It's a sin to have bad feelings toward someone.
37. It's every person for themselves.
38. Life is a struggle.

39. Life is hard.
40. Life is unfair.
41. Life is unjust.
42. My needs come first.
43. No one hears me.
44. No one understands how I feel.
45. No one understands the pain I'm in.
46. No one wants to hear that I am in pain.
47. People don't respect me, why should I respect them?
48. People should give me a break because of my problems.
49. People should understand I can't _____.
50. People take advantage of me.
51. There's no way out.
52. You can't just change direction.

*Look at themes of victimhood, struggle, selfishness, self-pity, self-respect, self-worth, boundaries, self-esteem, pain, health, boundaries, unmet needs, disconnection

Chest Problems

Fears
- Fear of giving in
- Fear of getting inspired
- Fear of not getting their needs met
- Fear of living
- Fear of the flow of life
- Fear of love
- Fear of giving
- Fear of being ripped off
- Fear of being unaccepted
- Fear of being invisible
- Fear of heart hurt
- Fear of being powerless

Emotional States
- Gives into others who won't let them have their way. Feels unfulfilled with life. Frets that they are giving away their energy for very little in return.

Cross Indexing: Lung problems, Pneumonia, Bronchitis, Cancer-Lung, Emphysema, Pleurisy

Repeating Patterns: Doesn't love self, gives in, doesn't give love or positive acknowledgment.

Created Patterns
1. I'm not accepted.

2. I must be invisible.
3. I must stay quiet.
4. I must stay still to be safe.
5. I am powerless to change things.
6. What is the fear you can't get past?
7. I can't control my world.
8. Love hurts.
9. I am vulnerable to being hurt.
10. People hurt me.
11. I am drowning in grief.
12. The grief will never end.
13. If I allow myself to feel grief.
14. I don't love myself.
15. I am afraid of _____.
16. I am grieving _____.
17. I give up in the face of challenges.
18. Life is hopeless.
19. I am unloved.
20. Complimenting people is a waste of time.

Cholesterol – High

Fears

- Fear of disappointment with life
- Fear of being forever unhappy
- Fear of being present
- Fear of hurt
- Fear of pain
- Fear of reflection
- Fear of the inner self
- Fear of connection
- Fear of loss
- Fear of betrayal
- Fear of being unloved
- Fear of being invisible
- Fear of attack
- Fear of joy
- Fear of heart hurt

Emotional States

- Unrecognized pain. Pain of the psyche. Pain of being in a world that challenges the senses. Pain that overwhelms and must be hidden from view. Pain that has no outlet but saps true joy, the true sense of the joyous inner core. Psychic pain that when you get close to it feels like a leaden weight pressing in on your chest. They keep the world and all it is at the skin outside level. They hold back warmth, true warmth, true connection. They show up in the friendship/relationship and go through the motions without truly feeling. They do not give that energy of their being. They bear the pain of friendship lost. They bear the pain of relationships that bore out betrayal. Betrayal of death. Betrayal of loss. Betrayal of confusion.

Cross Indexing: Blood Disorders, Liver Problems

Created Patterns
1. I'm not supposed to be happy.
2. I'm not lovable.
3. I must be invisible.
4. I must protect myself.
5. I can't let anyone in.
6. Why are you building walls to protect yourself?
7. I have been expressing/feeling strong emotion of _____ for a long time (these are negative emotions: hatred/resentment/rage/bitterness/ grief/ sorrow/ anger.
8. I can't express love and joy easily.
9. I can't communicate love and joy easily.
10. It's not safe to be open with others about how I love myself.
11. I don't love myself.
12. It's not safe to tell a man/ woman I love him/ her.

Chronic Fatigue Syndrome

Fears
- Fear of being seen
- Fear of taking in life
- Fear of change
- Fear of being present
- Fear of responsibility
- Fear of being judged
- Fear of being outcast
- Fear of life and living
- Fear of being forced against their will
- Fear of being undeserving
- Fear of being not worthy
- Fear of receiving
- Fear of being alone
- Fear of speaking

Emotional States
- Learns the hard way. Fights being brought into a new awareness. Longs to not be constantly challenged by what is new. Struggles to keep up. The resistance creates great stress at a physical level. Hopes, beyond a passing thought, that the challenges will just go away. Really feels out of time (sync) and does not belong in 'this' here and now.

- Holds others to a higher standard and wants them to take the responsibility since they are better capable of dealing with 'stuff'. Diminishes themselves. The fear of being responsible is overwhelming and draining. The responsibility creates fear of being judged and sentenced – to be avoided at all costs – that feels really dangerous.
- Journey of life is hard. Feels like every step is filled with lead. Movement (Emotional and physical) is very difficult. Wants to do the world their way. Feels like they are being forced into a world they did not make and therefore they don't want to do it – sense of injustice. They feel forced against their will in a world not of their making.
- The state of being spiritual and the state of being physical are in conflict with each other. There is an incoherence. There may have been a shock (fall, accident) early in life or an epigenetic challenge that created the incoherence. There is an intense awareness of this separateness in the two minds which creates a dynamic that takes a lot of energy to focus – the minds bounce together momentarily and they bounce apart – there is a constant struggle.
- The person exudes warmth and caring towards others. But can't care for themselves. In a constant struggle of worthiness. Caring for others gives others gives them a false sense of worth — and the 'sugar' high fades quickly and then there is a feeling that there is no reciprocation – feeds the unworthiness.

Cross indexing: Fibromyalgia, Depression, Chronic Illness, Fatigue

Created Patterns

1. I am alone.
2. I am abandoned.
3. I stay safe by doing nothing.
4. It's easier to give up.
5. It is dangerous to speak up.
6. It's hopeless.
7. It's no use.
8. I am constantly trying to prove myself.
9. I will never be good enough.
10. I want to die.
11. I have been expressing/feeling strong emotion of _____ for a long time (these are negative emotions: hatred/resentment/rage/bitterness/ grief/ sorrow/ anger).

Chronic Illness

Fears

- Fear that they have been/ will be left behind
- Fear of being unaccepted
- Fear of being unwanted
- Fear of letting go
- Fear of being trapped
- Fear of being unloved
- Fear of change
- Fear that things will never change

Emotional States
- Unwanted. A chronic illness brings acceptance. That identity of being unwanted may be held in the ancestral DNA as the result of a trauma or "way" of thinking.
- An awareness that there is no real way out of suffering, so they might as well suffer with what they have now.

Repeating Patterns: stuck, untrusting, feeling unloved, pushes the illness to feel loved, illness is an identity, unwanted rigid thinking, suffers to be loved and accepted

Created Patterns
1. I can't change.
2. I can't trust the world.
3. I must have _____(disease) because _____(person) needs me to.
4. I must be sick to be loved.
5. I have been expressing/feeling strong emotion of _____ for a long time (these are negative emotions: hatred/resentment/rage/bitterness/ grief/ sorrow/ anger).
6. Why can't you express emotions?
7. I don't get _____ unless I am sick.

Chronic Traumatic Encephalopathy (CTE)

Fears
- Fear of false paths
- Fear of their history being lost
- Fear of the goose chase
- Fear of false gods
- Fear of time
- Fear of connection
- Fear of no choice
- Fear of being trapped
- Fear of disappointing others
- Fear of a false life
- Fear of being forced to do things against my will
- Fear of having to hurt myself to please others
- Fear of having to hurt myself to be accepted

Emotional States
- Desire to have an impact, to do something, leads to a false path, one of little value.
- False impressions of 'god' are seen as salvation. But no one is quite sure what you are being saved from.
- Halting levels of chaos that create momentary space and time for self. Holding out for the time and space for self.

EMOTIONAL PATTERNS

- There is a feeling of no choice. That the only way out is to hurt themselves. They are locked in to one direction by those around them. They do not want to disappoint. Injuries are the only safe way out.

Cross Indexing: Brain Problems, Concussion, ALS

Created Patterns
1. God is a lie.
2. Everyone who talks of god is lying.
3. I must have chaos to have peace.
4. My life is a lie.
5. I can't change anything.
6. I can't make things better.
7. There is no space for me
8. I must do what others tell me to do to belong.
9. I have no control of myself.
10. I am a slave.
11. I keep hitting my head against a brick wall.

Circulation Problems

Fears
- Fear of having made or making poor choices
- Fear of joy
- Fear of light
- Fear of love
- Fear of happiness
- Fear of joy
- Fear of living
- Fear of too much
- Fear of letting go
- Fear of not being good enough
- Fear of being seen as good enough
- Fear of being forced against their will

Emotional States
- Lack of joy, lack of love, not finding that place where they can access those feelings. A darkness, like a wall, block them from the light, the light of joy the light of love which gives life to the life spirit.

Cross Indexing: Veins, Arteriosclerosis, Artery Problems, Cardiovascular Disorder, Heart Problem

Repeating Patterns: depression, heart feels a heavy sadness that veils their vision, sense of doom, pity party

Created Patterns

1. I am overloaded.
2. I can't quit.
3. I can't let go.
4. I must prove myself.
5. I don't love myself.
6. I never have any fun.
7. There is no time for fun.
8. I don't love myself.
9. I put myself down to be safe.
10. I hate my life.
11. I must do what I don't want to do.
12. Nothing will ever be good.
13. I am not loved for who I am.
14. I am unwanted.

Cirrhosis

Fears

- Fear of losing the battle
- Fear of losing everyone
- Fear of the loss of respect and / or honor
- Fear of hurting themselves
- Fear of heart hurt
- Fear of that they might live
- Fear of powerlessness
- Fear of their anger
- Fear of defeat
- Fear of no freedom
- Fear of being forced against their will
- Fear of destroying myself
- Fear of being vulnerable

Emotional States

- They have scars from self-inflicted wounds that have not truly healed. They have emotionally covered up those wounds. Those wounds are still there influencing their identity. This covering up creates an issue with their ability to filter their emotions. Hot emotions keep coming up and pushed down because they are not free to express them in a situation where someone else holds all the power.

Cross Indexing: Cancer – Liver, Hepatitis, Liver Problems, Addiction – Alcohol, Liver - Jaundice

Created Patterns
1. I must give in to be safe.
2. I feel defeated.
3. I am trapped and I have no freedom.
4. I am powerless and other people force me to obey them.
5. I must hold my anger or it will destroy my life.
6. People in authority put me down.
7. I don't know how to react appropriately. Everything is jumbled up.
8. I am hurt by those that should love me.
9. I must keep how I feel hidden to be safe.

Clavicle Problems

Fears
- Fear of having to carry the burden
- Fear of receiving
- Fear of being taken for granted
- Fear of being nothing
- Fear of being seen as lacking
- Fear of being wrong
- Fear of being seen as dependent
- Fear of never having enough
- Fear that things are not what they seem
- Fear of being off balance
- Fear that they are missing something in life

Emotional States
- Feels as if everyone else is complaining.
- Left: They give too much and get nothing in return that they expect. They expect gratitude. But what they get is little in comparison to their expectations.
- Left: They feel like what they do falls into an empty space. Unseen, unrecognized, unknown and unacknowledged.
- Right: Untried waters lead to disaster. Starts something new and doesn't have the skills to do what needs to be done. Refuses to take instruction from someone else.
- Right: Hard headed.
- Right: Wants more than they have and doesn't have the ability/skills to get it.

Cross Indexing: Shoulders

Repeating Patterns: over-giving beyond their abilities, taken for granted, selfish.

Created Patterns
1. I don't know how to share.
2. I must keep what I know to myself.
3. I learn things the hard way.
4. Nothing is simple for me.
5. I resent super positive happy people.
6. I know what's best.
7. No one seems happy at what I do.
8. Everyone should look out for themselves.
9. You can't depend on others.

Colds

Fears
- Fear of being misunderstood
- Fear of their truth being held to be worthless
- Fear of being different
- Fear of being unacceptable
- Fear of change
- Fear of emotions
- Fear of seeing the good
- Fear of having the good take away
- Fear of being undeserving
- Fear of hearing what they don't want to hear
- Fear of having to give in to get along
- Fear of not being good enough

Emotional States
- Holds a negative approach to life (impairs the immune system). That negativity gives them a sense of superiority.

Cross Indexing: Virus

Repeating Patterns: Gives in to what someone else wants, doesn't listen, isn't heard, sees the downside to everything, stuffy person

Created Patterns
1. I am angry/hate/bitter toward/resent _____.
2. It is dangerous for me to be angry.
3. I am confused.
4. I don't know where to go.
5. I always get sick in the fall/winter/spring.

6. Being sick gives me permission to rest.
7. I am unacceptable.
8. I am smarter than most people.
9. No one understands me.

Colitis – Ulcerative

Fears

- Fear of what they will never have
- Fear of losing their sense of self
- Fear of their emotions
- Fear of deception
- Fear of being exposed
- Fear of being heart hurt
- Fear of being trapped
- Fear of obligation
- Fear of expectations
- Fear of becoming nothing
- Fear of letting go
- Fear of never being able to be what they yearn for
- Fear of not being good enough
- Fear of being unloved
- Fear of making decisions
- Fear of being wrong
- Fear of being overrun

Teachings

- Allow the flow of the universe
- Balance the feminine and masculine aspects of self
- Be creative
- Be yourself
- Complete
- Deserve
- Express my feelings and be safe
- Feel safe when being creative
- Forgiveness
- Live without being a martyr
- Live without being a victim
- Live without believing you have to sacrifice
- Live without expecting people to betray you
- Live without expecting people to hurt you
- Live without having to conform to what others say
- Live without using anger to protect myself
- Live without using grudge to protect myself
- Live without using resentments to protect myself
- Make decisions and feel secure
- Make mistakes and be safe
- Release grudges
- Release resentments
- Say no
- Support
- Whole
- Worthy

Emotional States

- Faced with issues of identity based survival.
- Dealing with overwhelming dark emotions.

- They feel deceived by information that led to a dark night of the soul.
- Wants to hide from the dark emotions.
- They hide their true feelings from others.
- They have closed themselves off from support.
- They feel trapped by the emotions and isolation.
- Creative is not being expressed.
- Feels trapped between expectations and their inner desires.
- They are on a path that they believe will yield knowledge and wisdom which would lead them to happiness. A sudden event plunged them into a dark night of the soul. They are facing strong and powerful emotions that are overwhelming. They are faced with issues of identity-based survival. They feel deceived and angry by the information that led them to the choices that triggered this dark night. They want to hide from the power of these emotions but that same power is forcing them out of hibernation or hiding.
- This individual is surrounded by dark emotions. They cover over and protect their true inner self from those around them. They have closed themselves off from the support. They live in isolation avoiding the emotions/feelings that cover the core of their being. They feel trapped by this isolation and their negative feelings. This person has done work on resolving the negative emotions/feelings and all they have done is stirred them up so they are now on the surface. This has not resolved the feelings, only made them more apparent. These feelings stem from the conflict between what is expected of them by friends/family/job/relationship/society and their inner desires and needs. The creative/intuitive aspect of self is not being expressed.

Cross Indexing: Intestinal problems, Irritable Bowel Syndrome, Diverticulitis, Crohn's Disease, Leaky Gut Syndrome

Repeating Patterns: Wounded creative core, doesn't accept help from others, depression, martyr, victim-hood, lack of understanding, un-trusting, lack of self-worth, feeling unloved, doesn't forgive, feels trapped, has unmet needs(love, respect, acceptance, support and inner purpose), doesn't trust their decision making, conflicting motivations, out of balance with the feminine and masculine, betrayal by others, hurt by others, uses anger as a protection, uses grudges as a protection, uses resentment to protect themselves, mistakes make them feel unsafe, boundaries are out of balance.

Created Patterns
1. _____ deceived me.
2. Being 'normal' is very important to me.
3. Being creative is dangerous.
4. Being different is dangerous.
5. I am a martyr.
6. I am a victim.
7. I am alone.
8. I am angry at _____.
9. I am critical of others.
10. I am going to die.
11. I am trapped.
12. I can't be angry and be safe.
13. I can't express myself.
14. I can't forgive.
15. I can't make decisions.

EMOTIONAL PATTERNS

16. I can't release my anger.
17. I can't say no.
18. I can't see the good in others.
19. I don't honor my needs.
20. I don't know what is good for me.
21. I don't like myself.
22. I don't respect myself.
23. I don't trust my intuition.
24. I don't trust myself.
25. I feel sorry for myself.
26. I make poor/bad choices.
27. I must always be nice.
28. I must be like everyone else.
29. I must do what others expect of me.
30. I must judge others to be safe.
31. I must never let my feelings show.
32. I must sacrifice myself for others.
33. I must take care of others before myself.
34. I'm not good enough/worthy.
35. I'm not respected.
36. If I don't look at the problem it will go away.
37. If I ignore the problem it will go away.
38. My anger protects me.
39. Nothing will ever change.
40. Others come first.
41. People deceive me.
42. People hurt me (who hurt you and what do you think that was about?).
43. People make fun of me.
44. People take advantage of me.
45. I am shamed.
46. I am humiliated.
47. I am stifled by _____.
48. I am oppressed by _____.
49. I am defeated.
50. I'm not loved.
51. Nothing I do is good enough.
52. I must have order.
53. If I don't worry bad things will happen.
54. I have been expressing/feeling strong emotion of _____ for a long time (these are negative emotions: hatred/resentment/rage/bitterness/ grief/ sorrow/ anger) .
55. I make poor/bad choices.
56. People deceive me.
57. I am critical of others.
58. I must judge others to be safe.
59. I don't know what is good for me.
60. They deceived me.
61. If I don't look at the problem it will go away.
62. If I ignore the problem it will go away.
63. I don't trust myself.

64. I don't trust my intuition.
65. I can't see the good in others.
66. People hurt me (who hurt you and what do you think that was about?).
67. I am trapped.
68. I am alone.
69. Nothing will ever change.
70. Being creative is dangerous.
71. People make fun of me.
72. I'm not respected.
73. I can't forgive.
74. My anger protects me.
75. People take advantage of me.
76. I must do what others expect of me.
77. I can't say no.
78. I don't like myself.
79. I don't honor my needs.
80. I must take care of others before myself.
81. Others come first.
82. I feel sorry for myself.
83. I am a victim/martyr.
84. I must sacrifice myself for others.
85. I don't respect myself.
86. I'm not good enough/worthy.
87. Being different is dangerous.

*Look at themes of victimhood, understanding, true self, trust, self-esteem, self-worth, self-respect, self-pity, Now, Love, acceptance, artist, creativity, decisions, forgiveness, trapped, creativity, unmet needs (love, acceptance, respected, recognition, support, and inner purpose), denial, decision making, boundaries, conflicting motivations, expression, relationships, stress

Colon Problems

Fears
- Fear of making decisions
- Fear that whatever they do will never be enough
- Fear that what they get for nurturance is not enough
- Fear that who they are is not enough
- Fear that nothing will ever be right
- Fear of letting go
- Fear of confusion
- Fear of being out of control
- Fear of not knowing what is toxic
- Fear of honesty
- Fear of inner peace
- Fear of being in danger

Emotional States
- Hard decisions that force actions/conclusions that don't support being at peace — no outcome is going to work.

Cross Indexing: Intestinal Problems, Crohn's Disease, Diverticulitis, Celiac Disease, Intestines – Large, Intestines – Small

Repeating Patterns: Unable to let go of what is bad for them, no longer serves them, confusion, needing to be in control, confused about what is bad for them, feels unsafe.

Created Patterns
1. I can't let go.
2. I don't know what to do.
3. If I lose control_____ (What will happen?).
4. I can't release and move on.
5. I must stay still to stay in control.
6. I don't know what is toxic.
7. I can't let go of what is bad for me.
8. I can't be honest with myself.
9. I can't be honest with others.
10. I am never at peace.
11. Nothing is safe.
12. I hate _____.
13. I resent _____.

Concussion

Fears
- Fear of change
- Fear that they are leading a cursed life
- Fear of their inner voice
- Fear of being wrong
- Fear of being challenged
- Fear of being blamed
- Fear of being humiliated
- Fear of ownership
- Fear of getting what they want
- Fear of attack

Emotional States
- Blocks self from receiving new information. Does not go within to access the wisdom of the inner self. Shuts out the information that runs counter to their current set of beliefs and ideas. They are imprisoned in an old paradigm of thinking.
- Sees things one way and won't entertain the idea that there might be alternative points of view. Sees a destiny or a path of outcome and will not consider the possibility of change.
- Takes no ownership of self.

Cross Indexing: CTE, Brain Problems, Parkinson's

Created Patterns
1. I must do what others tell me.
2. My identity makes people like me.
3. I can't have what I truly want.
4. I cannot feel my heart.
5. I can never relax.
6. I must always be on guard.

Congestive Heart Failure

Fears
- Fear of the future loss of love
- Fear of heart hurt
- Fear of being unworthy
- Fear of the future
- Fear of being still
- Fear of the flow of life
- Fear of being out of control
- Fear of being powerless
- Fear of being vulnerable
- Fear of the wrong others do
- Fear of others breaking the rules
- Fear of the manipulated truth
- Fear of being manipulated
- Fear of information that triggers emotions
- Fear of struggling through life
- Fear of facing self
- Fear of responsibility
- Fear of being worthless
- Fear of being irrelevant
- Fear of the magic of life

Emotional States

- The feminine aspect of this person is very sensitive. What people think and say is taken seriously to heart. This person identifies with the external world paying attention to others perceptions instead of looking inward. Their sense of self-worth is based on what others think. So this person is constantly looking for self-validation outside of themselves. They do not do a good job at relaxing and may put themselves in situations that are aimed at inducing relaxation. But the situations all feel artificial and contrived. There is a feeling of rigidity and unable to bend or flow with the surroundings and the people in their life. This person has lost the joy in their life. Relationships that started off feeling supportive have become a power game and a battle for control. Their sensitivity is kept to themselves. They repress the feelings they have when something hurts them. They feel inadequate at every turn of their lives and they are constantly seeking self-validation. This person suffers from exhaustion and feels emotionally drained. They have had bitter confrontations in their relationships and this drains them emotionally. The constant worry and fear also present a draining of the life force. This person feels shame and guilt for actions that are actually the fault or design of others.
- When this person was a child the truth was distorted by the parenting adults in their life to be whatever the person wanted it to be. Now as an adult this person is very confused as to what is truth. They don't understand the lines between manipulated information for gain and 'what is truth without influence'. Spirituality was manipulated and now there is confusion as to their true spiritual nature. They have the beliefs built from childhood that feel disconnected from what they perceive from outside sources. This person has/is receiving a down pour of spiritual concepts. But, they are not 'getting' the truths and the information flows away. They have faced or are facing emotional changes that are tough ones. This person demonstrates emotional outbursts that are couched in confusion and a lack of wisdom. Their emotions feel overwhelming. This person feels as if they are struggling. They may have aspects of self that are unyielding. This person may have depression from repressed and unresolved anger.
- The masculine aspect of this person feels as if their life is moving at a fast pace. The fast pace is designed by them to keep from having to face their fears. The running keeps them from having to confront fears and/or taking responsibility for their actions. Their emotions are expressed with intensity. They seem to always be experiencing some sort of intense emotion. Again this is all a smoke screen from having to face fears and/or taking responsibility for their actions. Even while they are living this fast paced life there is heartache they feel from not being accepted. This individual is out of balance in their life. They are mostly out of their body and living only in the upper part of their body. This person may suffer also from lower body issues: lower back, intestinal, sexual organs, legs, knees, feet, etc. in addition to the cardio-pulmonary issues of congestive heart failure. They have no spiritual grounding.
- This person's ideas of how they are motivated and their source of life force are antiquated. These ideas loom so large in their thoughts and how they present themselves in the world that they are often called to task for their 'old-style' of thinking. They feel inferior or insignificant. They are ignored by others around them. This person has a negative self-image. This person feels anxiety over a perceived threat or challenge to attitudes, perceptions or beliefs. They are constantly facing emotional turmoil. The emotional turmoil signifies depression or anger. This individual's emotions erupt based on cloudy thinking that reflects a lack of wisdom and confusion. This person has been given opportunities to create and manifest a magical life that shifts and grows their world view. But, they let that opportunity fly away.

Cross Indexing: Adrenal Fatigue, Adrenal Problems, Tachycardia, Hypertension, Hyperthyroidism, Heart Problems

Created Patterns
1. Being in my body is dangerous/painful/hurts.
2. Change is dangerous.
3. Change means bad things will happen.
4. Change only creates chaos.
5. Compassion is for weak-kneed liberals.
6. Compassion just encourages bad behavior.
7. Disappointment hurts.
8. Doing what others say will only get me hurt/in trouble.
9. Everyone else always gets the lucky breaks.
10. Feelings are dangerous.
11. God abandoned me.
12. God let me down.
13. Good things always pass me by.
14. Good things never happen to me.
15. I am always afraid of _____.
16. I am always disappointed by others.
17. I am angry at mother/father/_____ (who else).
18. I am ashamed of _____.
19. I am depressed.
20. I am disconnected from god.
21. I am going to die.
22. I am inadequate.
23. I am no good.
24. I can't handle disappointment.
25. I do things for others to be loved/ respected/ wanted/ accepted.
26. I don't deserve good things.
27. I don't know how to bring joy into my life.
28. I don't know how to handle rejection.
29. I don't know how to live an authentic life.
30. I don't know how to relax.
31. I don't know how to take care of myself.
32. I don't know what a balanced life feels like.
33. I don't know what balance is.
34. I don't know what joy feels like.
35. I don't know what joy is.
36. I don't know what truth is.
37. I don't love myself.
38. I don't trust god/source.
39. I don't trust myself.
40. I don't trust others.
41. I have been manipulated by _____.
42. I must always take care of others first.
43. I must control the people around me to get it done right.
44. I must fulfill the needs of others to be love.

EMOTIONAL PATTERNS

45. I must make things happen or nothing will ever get done.
46. I must take the blame for the bad things done by others (family/friends/co-workers).
47. I need recognition to feel good about myself.
48. I never have good luck.
49. I resent _____.
50. I resent authority.
51. I take everything seriously.
52. I will never feel good/joy again.
53. I work hard to be recognized/ accepted.
54. I worry about _____.
55. I'm not any good anymore.
56. I'm not good enough.
57. I'm not lovable.
58. I'm not loved.
59. I'm not respected.
60. I'm not worthy.
61. If I feel there is chaos.
62. It is easier to be somewhere else (not being present in your body).
63. It is OK to manipulate others.
64. It is OK to manipulate the truth.
65. Life is a struggle.
66. Life moves too fast.
67. Love is pain.
68. My life is a disappointment.
69. My mother/father manipulated/betrayed/lied to me.
70. No one takes me seriously.
71. People always disappointment.
72. People are always trying to change me.
73. People are dangerous- they hurt me.
74. People close to me betray me.
75. People don't do what they say.
76. People don't listen to me.
77. People in authority are bad.
78. People in authority can't be trusted.
79. Rejection hurts.
80. Relationships hurt.
81. The joy is gone from my life.
82. The needs of others come before me.
83. Things must be done my way or they fall apart.
84. Truth is whatever you make it.
85. What other people think of me is important.
86. When I feel bad things happen.
87. When you get old you are powerless.
88. When you're old no one listens to you.

Conjunctivitis

Fears
- Fear of seeing what hurts
- Fear of violation
- Fear of their anger at what they see
- Fear of seeing the whole
- Fear of seeing the shadows
- Fear of injustice
- Fear of facing their feelings
- Fear of the outside world
- Fear of people
- Fear of balance

Emotional States
- Inflamed at what they are seeing. What is being seen goes to the heart. There is a lack of understanding.
- Feels like they are unable to protect themselves from what they are seeing. They see the surface and it causes them to feel angry or irritable. (Ancestral / epigenetic recognition of the events that have not been learned from.)
- Daylight is never shined into the corners. There is need to keep attention focused on one thing and not look around at what else is there. But the dust and shadows are still there and as they close in they make themselves known which creates an irritation that they just won't go away.

Cross Indexing: Eye Problems, Infection, Inflammation, Dry Eye, Allergies, Cold

Repeating Patterns: Sees only truth that serves them and gets irritated when others truths make themselves known.

Created Patterns
1. Life is unfair.
2. Everywhere I look things are wrong.
3. I see the pain of the world.
4. I am angry at being here.
5. What keeps you from seeing the good in the world?
6. What is it that you don't want to look at?
7. Not seeing is how I stay safe.
8. I'm sorry I was born.
9. I see injustice everywhere.
10. God's messengers are ridiculed.
11. It's not safe being a messenger of god.
12. I'm not worthy of being god's messenger.
13. There is nothing in the shadows to see.
14. I am irritated by _____.
15. I am afraid of _____ and being seen by _____.
16. I am frustrated by _____.

17. I am angry at _____.
18. I want to shut out _____ (What is going on around you that you don't want to see?).
19. The world is full of bad.
20. I don't want to see things that make me feel bad.
21. I can't protect myself from the bad in the world.
22. I see bad things happening everywhere.
23. People hurt each other without cause.

Constipation

Fears
- Fear of giving
- Fear of letting go of what is no longer useful
- Fear of not having enough
- Fear of letting go
- Fear of being out of control
- Fear of joy
- Fear of the future
- Fear of change
- Fear of being wrong
- Fear of bad things happening

Emotional States
- Withholding of the heart; caring compassion, praise, connection, etc. Holds back all nurturing to themselves. Unwilling to share to have joy.
- Demands they be in control

Cross Indexing: Digestive System disorders, Bowel Problems, Intestinal Problems, Colitis-Ulcerative, Abdominal Pain

Repeating Patterns: Relationships based on getting needs met. Doesn't express caring and gets rejected.

Created Patterns
1. I can't let go of _____.
2. I am afraid bad things will happen.
3. If I worry over stuff bad things won't happen.
4. What keeps you from saying what you want to say?
5. I am afraid things will go wrong.
6. I am afraid of change.
7. I must do things my way.
8. My way of doing things is the only way to do them.
9. Against all odds I must carry on.
10. I have been expressing/feeling strong emotion of _____ for a long time (these are negative emotions: hatred/resentments/anger/sorrow/bitterness/grief/rage.

11. I have to be on top of things.
12. It's my job to prevent bad things from happening.

Cough – Chronic

Fears
- Fear that what they have done will have repercussions
- Fear of life
- Fear of change
- Fear of breathing
- Fear of flowing with life
- Fear of others getting too close
- Fear of being put upon
- Fear of being overrun
- Fear of completing a project
- Fear of success
- Fear of presence
- Fear of being in the now
- Fear of injustice
- Fear of things that too easy

Emotional States
- Failure to thrive. Constant struggle with life in the face of commonality. They make it hard. No joy in their life. Constantly looking for the hard side of things. Even if it was easy they would make it hard.
- The cough is a warning to others to keep away. The cough creates a boundary that keeps people a cough away – the message is stay away from my space. It is a way of getting the space that they feel they need. Probably has a person in their life that nags them and has expectations put on how they spend their time.
- Hurries through everything. They behave more like a hummingbird, flitting from here to there. Not really holding onto anything for any length of time. If they stay still for too long then someone will put expectations on them.
- Inappropriate gestures of gratitude spill over into aspects of their life that can create chaos and a need to run away. Example: They give a gift to someone that is inappropriate and this then creates a feeling of boundaries crossed.
- Knowing they can do better and they don't. Life is always half done – they start projects that are always incomplete with a wide variety of excuses to go along with it.
- Sour methods and mood render their world a sour place, always looking for the sour hard candy instead of the sweet and creamy. They never see the sweet and creamy only the sour and hard.
- Hardly has a grasp, always feels as if things are slipping from their grasp and they are mystified at every time it happens. Don't see the real essence of missed opportunity. Scared to death of success.
- Wrongfully accused in their life they retreated into a shell of half answers to life challenges.
- Holding out for the brass ring – "I'll get the next great thing, it's just around the corner". Never in the moment, always projecting out beyond the present.

Cross Indexing: Coughing, Respiratory disorders, Lung disorders, throat disorders, sinus problems, allergies

Repeating Patterns: Makes things harder than they need to be. Over thinks situations — spins into the emotion of injustices. Misses opportunities. Can't hang onto things.

Created Patterns
1. Life is hard.
2. Everything conspires to defeat me.
3. I always lose.
4. I can't ever seem to get things right.
5. I always fail.
6. I can't hang onto things.
7. I am wrongly accused.

Coughing

Fears
- Fear that they can't relax and allow life to flow
- Fear of having to be on guard
- Fear of moving forward
- Fear of change
- Fear of being out of control
- Fear of intimacy
- Fear of heart hurt
- Fear that things will not get better
- Fear of being judged
- Fear of no space for self
- Fear of making decisions
- Fear of no voice
- Fear of choices
- Fear of not being seen
- Fear of feeling
- Fear of not knowing the future

Teachings
- Be in the now
- Be safe with my feelings
- Express my feelings and be safe
- Forgive myself
- Forgive others
- Good enough
- Honor my feelings
- Live my inner truth without fear
- Live without always having the answers
- Live without criticism
- Live without doubting myself
- Live without emotional confusion
- Live without putting myself down
- Live without the fear of being criticized
- Open to new ideas
- Recognize my inner truth
- Release criticism
- Release past hurts
- Respect myself
- Say what I feel easily
- Stand up for myself
- Trust myself

Emotional States
- Being pulled in a direction and then pulling back due to your own limiting thoughts.
- Witnessing an evolution of heart that gives one pause…hesitant emotions…emotions seem to have a life of their own. Looking for control of those emotions and there is a sense of no control.
- Unable to let go of thoughts around a relationship – thoughts seem to have taken over.
- Half-hearted attempts at commitment (relationship, job, etc)
- Anxiety around change.
- Anxiety around letting go of a lifestyle. This lifestyle may have been a place where you were living, relationship change, job change, etc.
- Wants to control emotions but they seem to be in control.
- Realization that things are not what they appear and the created illusion does not serve you. The situation is not good enough and it does not appear to improve in the future
- Self critical
- Afraid to let go of the reference to / framework for decisions that no longer serves you. This framework could be based in jealousy or wanting what someone else has.

Cross Indexing: Chronic Coughing, sinus problems, post-nasal drip, colds, bronchitis, lung problems, throat problems

Created Patterns
1. Change isn't safe.
2. I always get hurt in relationships.
3. I am afraid that I will be criticized.
4. I am always being criticized.
5. I am annoyed at _____.
6. I am not in control.
7. I am overwhelmed by change.
8. I can't be free to be me.
9. I can't cope with the changes happening.
10. I can't make a decision and stick with it.
11. I can't take it all in.
12. I can't talk about my feelings.
13. I choke on my feelings.
14. I don't seem to have a say in anything.
15. I don't understand my feelings.
16. I doubt myself.
17. I expect myself to be better than others.
18. I have high expectations of myself.
19. I make decisions quickly and then I regret what I have done.
20. I must always have the answers.
21. I must control what I feel otherwise I will _____ (be hurt/ make a bad decision/ let someone down/ be let down/ be disobedient/ not honor my parents).
22. I must criticize myself before someone else does.
23. I must find my mistakes before others find them.
24. I must judge myself before others judge me.
25. I need recognition to be wanted/ loved/ honored/ respected.

26. I'm not appreciated.
27. I'm not good enough.
28. I'm not loved.
29. I'm not recognized.
30. If I say what I feel I will be hurt/ made fun of/ rejected/ criticized.
31. If I stand my ground I will be hurt.
32. Life is choking me.
33. Love hurts.
34. My feelings betray me.
35. My feelings confuse me.
36. Nothing I ever do is right.
37. Relationships never work out for me in the long run.
38. What is causing the nervousness?
39. What is the hesitation?

*Look at themes of doubt, allowing, discernment, emotions, feelings, freedom, judging, love, perfectionism, relationships, self-respect, self-worth, unmet needs (recognition, love), relationships, parenting, jealousy

Crohn's Disease

Fears
- Fear of having to take on the ancestral anger
- Fear of letting out their emotions
- Fear of their anger
- Fear of anger
- Fear of being vulnerable
- Fear of not balancing the scales
- Fear of letting go
- Fear of everything
- Fear of being hurt
- Fear of moving forward
- Fear of living
- Fear of seeing out beyond the space they are in
- Fear of getting outside the box
- Fear of abandonment
- Fear of powerlessness
- Fear of rejection
- Fear of giving and/ receiving
- Fear of not being good enough
- Fear of being wrong
- Fear of being manipulated
- Fear of false people
- Fear of nice people

Teachings
- Calm
- Cared for
- Creator's definition of giving
- Feeling fortunate
- Fun
- Honored
- Hopeful
- Joy
- Let go of what no longer serves you
- Live without anger
- Live without pain
- Live without revenge
- Loved
- Nurtured
- Peaceful
- Receive
- Recognize the Divine Presence within
- Release anger
- Release revenge
- See the big picture
- Self Nurturance
- Trusting others
- Trusting self
- Welcomed
- Worthy

Emotional States

- Hot temper, an inner heat, inflamed emotions that do not flow from the body. Uses the term 'that just burns me up'. When this person is angry it is an inappropriate level of anger. The overreaction is a backlash to the fear heaped on the person as a child.
- Doesn't know how to release or clear anger.
- This person feels it is wrong to express emotions so they stay bottled up inside.
- Mental focus is on hostility, punishment, and wants revenge.
- Intense anger has taken over sensory perceptions that would give pleasure; taste, smell, touch.
- Fear that someone will find out how afraid they are of everything and everyone. Puts up a shield to keep people out but the same shield keeps things in.
- Wants acknowledgment. They feel ignored. They feel unfortunate. Lack of interest in life; depressed.
- Hard worker, acknowledged for attention to detail. Doesn't look up and see the rest of the world. Only lets little bits of life inside.
- Energy systems are easily over stimulated causing a feeling of rawness. Deep anxiety. Rejects life.

Cross Indexing: Kidneys, Intestinal Problems, Lower back, Colitis-Ulcerative, Irritable Bowel Syndrome, Bloating, Celiac Disease

Created Patterns

1. _____ abandoned me.
2. Change can be dangerous.
3. Everyone else gets all the luck.
4. I am abandoned by _____.
5. I am afraid I will miss something that could hurt me (work related).
6. I am angry at _____.
7. I am depressed.
8. I am ignored (who ignores you).
9. I am powerless to stop people from hurting me.
10. I am rejected by _____.
11. I am vulnerable.
12. I can never meet _____ expectations (who).
13. I can't give.
14. I can't receive.
15. I don't love myself.
16. I don't put myself into situations where I can't trust.
17. I don't trust others.
18. I hate _____.
19. I hate myself for not standing up to _____.
20. I hide in my work.
21. I must keep my feelings hidden.
22. I must protect myself from others.
23. I must punish myself for feeling bad things about others.

24. I want revenge on _____.
25. I'm not accepted.
26. I'm not acknowledged.
27. I'm not worthy.
28. If I don't trust a situation I walk away.
29. It's hopeless.
30. Its _____ fault for _____.
31. Making changes is just too risky.
32. My anger protects me / keeps me safe.
33. My job is who I am.
34. My work is everything to me.
35. I can't let go of past hurts.
36. New ideas are not safe.
37. No one even knows I am alive.
38. Nothing I ever do is right.
39. People always want something from me.
40. People manipulate me using guilt.
41. People never mean what they say.
42. People that like/love me hurt me.
43. The details keep me safe.
44. There's always a price to pay when someone is nice to me.
45. There's no reason to go on living.
46. Things never work out for me.
47. Why me?

Cysts

Fears

- Fear that what they feel cannot be let out
- Fear of heart hurt
- Fear of being unsupported
- Fear of being unloved
- Fear of being unwanted
- Fear of being out of control
- Fear of letting go
- Fear of emotions being seen
- Fear of being vulnerable
- Fear of change
- Fear of attack
- Fear of the truth
- Fear of having my freedom taken

Emotional States

- Guarded sense of holding everything still. Not changing yields nothing. Denies to others that they are guarded. They hide behind the guarding.

- Projections of their reality stumbles into others and it feels like walking on rocks with bare feet. Uncertain, unsure. Deep sense of hatred is held toward another and encapsulated, put away. Look at the part of the body for clues. Example: Pilonidal Cyst occurs at the base of the spine. This would be the area of the root chakra. There is a connection of family and ancestral roots. The base of spine also holds Kundalini energy. The Pilonidal Cyst is usually an infection. Infection is probably caused by bacteria. Bacteria has the energy of rejection, needing to feel needed, and not trusting. One could look at a parent or other authority relationship and see if there is a deep belief that that person is keeping them from growing and achieving by withholding support (praise, acceptance, etc.) and rejects what they have tried to do.

Cross Indexing: Sebaceous Cysts, Polycystic Ovaries, Kidneys-polycystic, Ganglion cyst, Ovarian cyst, Baker's cyst

Repeating Patterns: Feels a lack of trust, holding their tongue and being untruthful, sucking it up, stuffing their feelings.

Created Patterns
1. I feel sorry for myself.
2. Why can't you forgive those that have hurt you?
3. Nobody loves me.
4. _____ hurt me.
5. I must keep my feelings to myself.
6. I can't release _____ (Anger, rage, hate, bitterness, resentment).
7. I must keep others from knowing how I feel.
8. I must hide how I feel.
9. I must protect myself form others.
10. I don't trust myself/others.
11. People try to tell me what to feel.
12. People try to tell me what to do.

Cytomegalovirus

Fears
- Fear of feeling devastated by feeling worthless
- Fear of attack
- Fear of blame
- Fear of being diminished
- Fear of being unworthy
- Fear of heart hurt
- Fear of life
- Fear of loss
- Fear of what others say
- Fear of being out of control
- Fear of authority
- Fear of shame
- Fear of humiliation

- Fear of being unloved
- Fear of being unwanted
- Fear of powerlessness
- Fear of being alone
- Fear of having things taken

Emotional States
- Under attack
- Weaken ability to attack
- Blamed for the inability of other to reach their goals
- Worthless: sense of self-worth is very low. Ancestral patterns of gender. Fears around leaving relationship
- No connection to a sense of oneness /divine /life sustaining force

Cross Indexing: Viruses, Herpes, Mononucleosis

Repeating Patterns: Wounded Creative Core. Boundaries are tested frequently. Gender role from a past era is adhered to which embraced shame and humiliation as part of the moral system.

Created Patterns
1. I am ashamed.
2. I am humiliated.
3. I am worthless.
4. I am unloved/ unwanted.
5. I can't be who I want to be.
6. I am under attack.
7. I can't fight back.
8. Others are stronger than me.
9. I can't do that I'm a woman/man.
10. Men/women don't do those things.
11. I can't take care of myself.
12. I don't believe in a higher power.
13. I am alone.
14. I can never get what I want; someone else always takes it from me.

D's

Dandruff

Fears
- Fear of feeling
- Fear of being found lacking
- Fear of being found wrong
- Fear of being found not good enough
- Fear of letting someone being better
- Fear of being out of control

Emotional States
- Stops themselves from loving themselves. They nit-pick about the perceived imperfections they have. Outwardly they nit-pick the way others do things. There is an anxious quality to a sense of "just let me do it, so it's right" feeling. They see the world in black and white terms of right and wrong…there's no grey areas or places of compromise.

Cross Indexing: skin problems, facial dandruff

Created Patterns
1. Things must be done a certain way.
2. I can never be wrong.
3. I am always right.
4. I can't accept myself.
5. I'll never be good enough.
6. I am right in the way I want things done.
7. People just never get it right.

Deep Vein Thrombosis (DVT)

Fears
- Fear of being judged
- Fear of change
- Fear of moving forward
- Fear of the future
- Fear of decisions
- Fear of choice
- Fear of being hurt
- Fear of the flow of life
- Fear of leaving the box

Teachings
- Being in the flow
- Learn life's lessons with ease and grace
- Make decisions and be safe
- Be open to new ideas
- Be open to new ways of thinking
- Allow

Emotional States
- Running in circles not getting anywhere, not looking outside the circle for answers
- Refusing to take new directions or new paths to achieve what they want and desire; life is stagnant
- Unresolved anxiety that keeps a person in stagnation; indecision causes the anxiety to build – keep trying the same thing expecting a different result

Cross Indexing: Leg Problems, Thrombosis, Arteriosclerosis, Diabetes, Diabetes Mellitus I, Diabetes II, anxiety, pelvis problems

Created Patterns
1. I can't go forward with my life.
2. I am afraid of the future.
3. Bad things are going to happen.
4. I don't understand what people want from me.
5. I can't go forward.
6. I can't make decisions.
7. Making decisions are dangerous.
8. I will be hurt if I make a decision.
9. I don't understand what people want from me.
10. I don't understand life.
11. I never get anywhere, something always stops me.

Dementia

Fears
- Fear of the past
- Fear of being embarrassed
- Fear of feeling shamed
- Fear of being unwanted
- Fear of the unknown
- Fear of what happens next
- Fear of being forgotten
- Fear of someone else before them
- Fear of letting go
- Fear of pain
- Fear of being helpless
- Fear of being hopeless
- Fear of not being the center of attention
- Fear that if they give there won't be anything left for themselves

Emotional States

- They make sure their needs are met before others, but do not follow through to the needs of others, all one-sided. There is a sense of the world revolves around them.
- Concept of self is the focus, look to themselves as the 'I' of the world, always sees how a situation revolves or involves them, cannot be left out.

Cross Indexing: Alzheimer's, Senility, Memory Loss, Aging

Repeating Patterns: Selfishness, the world is all about them. Demands attention, demands a vulnerable person meet their needs, must be the center of attention.

Created Patterns

1. It is hopeless.
2. I am helpless.
3. Life is too painful.
4. I can't forgive myself.
5. I can't forgive others (Who are the others?).
6. Life is a struggle and I am tired of it.
7. I am angry at/hate/ want revenge against/bitter toward _____.
8. My needs come first.
9. I must be the center of attention.
10. Others need to help me.
11. It's all about me.
12. Others get their needs me through me.

Depression

Fears
- Fear of there being no purpose to life
- Fear that what is real is all an illusion
- Fear of life flow
- Fear of being hopeless
- Fear of their anger
- Fear of recognizing loss
- Fear of being nothing
- Fear of the creative core
- Fear of being authentic
- Fear of expressing emotions
- Fear of being overrun
- Fear of intrusion
- Fear of receiving
- Fear of being trapped
- Fear of being wrong
- Fear of being found and seen

Teachings
- Be safe with my feelings
- Live without being depressed
- Joy
- Live with hope
- Live feeling supported
- Creator's Unconditional Love
- Live within my power
- Acknowledge you have the power to change
- Be safe with change
- Live without feeling a failure
- Be safe when a mistake is made
- Allow the flow of the universe
- Be in the now
- Living my authentic self
- Love myself

- Fear of doing anything
- Fear of losing their identity
- Fear of powerlessness
- Fear of being unsupported

- Feeling worthy
- Live feeling safe
- Live life with joy
- Know I am guided, protected and loved
- Whole
- Complete
- Knowing your life has a purpose
- Knowing there is a divine plan
- Knowing that you are part of a divine plan
- Live feeling connected to Creator
- See outside of myself
- Creator's definition of compassion

Emotional States

- A sense that it is hopeless; no one understands or cares. Their insecurity has drained life force. The ability to give and receive has been stopped. Self-worth tied up in outward appearances.
- Apathetic toward life (Anger turned inward).
- Unexpressed grief from loss.
- Quickly judges a situation and moves into a new situation that is really the same (relationships, jobs, geography, etc.). When they finally see the illusion they have created they go into a holding pattern and do nothing.
- Suppression of inner needs to comply with societal/ cultural/ family expectations. Fears the loss of love and support if they lead an authentic life. Feels misunderstood.
- There is a sense that it is hopeless to express needs and feelings. No one really understands. This individual feels lost and all attempts at expressing needs are felt to be a waste of time. This person does not know where to turn and they feel like they are wandering in a space of insecurity. There is nowhere for them to turn and that lack of support makes them feel hopeless. The creative, nurturing, intuitive aspect of self is being overshadowed by a fear based in insecurity. This feeling has drained their life force. This person lashes out at those that are trying to help and refuses to receive (assistance, love, compassion, support) from others and in the process deprecates themselves. The energies of the masculine and feminine is out of balance, They are not able to give and receive in a holistic way. Their physical appearance has been a source of objectification via stereotypical assumptions as to intelligence and worth. For example: a physically attractive woman with blonde hair is objectified for her beauty and is considered not very bright. Her entire concept of self-worth is tied up in her outward appearance; this is a trap that she does not know how to get out of. Any movement out of that stereotyped role is thwarted by the people around them, she is only seen as one thing and one thing only. She is constantly reminded of this by her social structure.
- This person has taken multiple jumps in new directions in a way that reflects no forethought as to the outcome. They have entered a new situation (relationship, job, venture, geography, etc.) looking for something that they think they are missing. They quickly judge the new situation and move out of it quickly. The judgment is based on a childlike basis of decision making. There was an aspect of self that as a child was left incomplete. This has been their history. Then one day they took one of these ' jumps' into a new direction and saw the outcome of this new move. They 'saw' that it was very much the same as the other moves in their life. So instead of moving into the new situation and working through the lessons of life to be gotten there, they pulled

themselves up above the situation and moved into a place of stasis. They don't know what to do at this point. They are suspended above the life situation. This act of stasis will or has triggered a dark night of the soul.

- This person has experienced a loss of power (relationship, job, life situation, etc.) and they are suppressing the pain of that loss. Unexpressed grief is the thread of emotion throughout their being. The individual is being torn between the values of two different worlds. One of these worlds has very rigid and structured societal expectations that must be complied with or there are harsh penalties. This person's inner world is in direct contradiction with this societal expectation. So they suppress their true inner needs and put on an outward appearance of compliance. But, inside there is a quiet desperation being played out that does not appear to have a solution. If they play out their needs they will lose what they perceive as a source of support and love. This person feels like no one understands them. They have a masculine energy in their life that is trying to 'fix' this person's unhappiness. That act is actually causing the psychic pain to increase because the masculine energy is going after the wrong thing. The person then withdraws even more into the darkness to hide from the 'fix-it' attempt.

Cross Indexing: CTE, PTSD, ACOA, Heart Problems, Intestinal Problems, Brain Problems, Adrenal Fatigue, Sexual Abuse, Bi-Polar, Depression with history of abuse

Created Patterns
1. Change isn't safe.
2. I always get hurt in relationships.
3. I am afraid that I will be criticized.
4. I am always being criticized.
5. I am annoyed at _____.
6. I am not in control.
7. I am overwhelmed by change.
8. I can't be free to be me.
9. I can't cope with the changes happening.
10. I can't make a decision and stick with it.
11. I can't take it all in.
12. I can't talk about my feelings.
13. I choke on my feelings.
14. I don't seem to have a say in anything.
15. I don't understand my feelings.
16. I doubt myself.
17. I expect myself to be better than others.
18. I have high expectations of myself
19. I make decisions quickly and then I regret what I have done.
20. I must always have the answers.
21. I must control what I feel otherwise I will _____ (be hurt/ make a bad decision/ let someone down/ be let down/ be disobedient/ not #honor my parents).
22. I must criticize myself before someone else does.
23. I must find my mistakes before others find them.
24. I must judge myself before others judge me.
25. I need recognition to be wanted/ loved/ honored/ respected.
26. I'm not appreciated.
27. I'm not good enough.

28. I'm not loved.
29. I'm not recognized.
30. If I say what I feel I will be hurt/ made fun of/ rejected/ criticized.
31. If I stand my ground I will be hurt.
32. Life is choking me.
33. Love hurts.
34. My feelings betray me.
35. My feelings confuse me.
36. Nothing I ever do is right.
37. Relationships never work out for me in the long run.
38. What is causing the nervousness?
39. What is the hesitation?
40. I don't want to feel.
41. Feeling hurts.
42. It hurts to feel.
43. I am depressed.
44. I don't know what joy is.
45. I don't know what joy feels like.
46. It's no use.
47. Things are beyond my control.
48. I'll never be able to be enough can never do enough
49. Life is too painful.
50. I am powerless to change.
51. I am failure.
52. I am afraid I will fail.
53. It is hopeless.
54. I am helpless to change things.
55. I want to die.
56. It's useless.
57. I give up.
58. I am angry at.
59. I've wasted my life.
60. I make all the wrong choices.
61. I should have (what 'should have' is limiting your life).
62. I am weak.
63. I must be what everyone else wants me to be.
64. I am only loved for my beauty.
65. I get love by being beautiful.
66. I am only loved because of _____.
67. I am only love when I do for others.
68. I don't know how to love myself.
69. I don't know what it feels like to love myself.
70. I hate myself.
71. I'm worthless.
72. I am in a dark night of the soul.
73. There is no place for me to turn.
74. God has abandoned me.
75. I am abandoned by.
76. I feel sorry for myself.

77. I must do what others tell me to do or I will be hurt.
78. I can't meet people's expectations.
79. People expect too much from me.
80. I am lost.
81. I have no direction.
82. Things will never get better, so I may as well die.

*Look at themes of abandonment, acceptance, allowing, balance, beingness, burn out, denial, ego, fear, flow, forgiveness, giving, grief, insecurity, joy, letting go, overwhelm, peace, resentment, trapped, true self, depression, unmet needs (recognition, love, respect, being listened to, support and encouragement), shame , self denial, broken heart, creativity, denial, fear, feelings, receiving, stress, trust, worthiness, grief

Depression with history of abuse

Fears
- Fear of being forced to be something they're not
- Fear of being forced to do against their will
- Fear of hopelessness
- Fear of being unloved
- Fear of being unwanted
- Fear of disconnection
- Fear of feeling their body
- Fear of feeling emotions
- Fear of pain
- Fear of receiving
- Fear of living
- Fear of being powerless
- Fear of overwhelm
- Fear of remembering
- Fear of being terrorized
- Fear of being hurt

Emotional States
- Separation is created by the sense of hopelessness and when there is a sense of separation outside of the body—a feeling that there is no connection to what is happening with the body – this gives rise to an incoherence that yields depression as a symptom – numbness would be a way of surviving a body that is being abused – there is a feeling of duality in the existence. 'I have a body but I am not part of the body – I am separate and distinct.' Transformation cannot take place unless there is an awareness of the numbness in the body – this brings the focus to momentary unified awareness. The person that has been abused will not stay with a sensation long enough to work through a healing transformation. They contact a sensation and immediately retreat into numbness and back to separation. Now they have moved to the head. They acknowledge that there was a feeling but the feeling moved into the head very quickly – staying numb is survival.
- How does depression keep someone safe? The sadness is the person's identification with life and security. Nurturance was pain, hurt and violation. The sadness keeps a person from the felt sense in the body. So the sadness keeps others from seeing the real pain of physical violation. The

person does not have to feel the pain of the stored trauma in the body. He won't have to feel the terror of living. No one will see the weakness and shame. They have an idea that people will see them as powerful. The thought process being that they will think I am powerful and not know that I am powerless. This will keep others away and by default keep away the pain and hurt. They will be left alone. Being near others bring on overwhelm. Being overwhelmed leads to freezing – terror is freezing. The freezing keeps the memories from being triggered. There is a fear that when you get close to the place of remembering the experience of trauma the feeling of that trauma (terror, rage, helplessness) will be recreated. An aversion response is stimulated and the safety of flight response is triggered.

Cross Indexing: Depression, ACOA, Sexual Assault, Concussion, CTE, Addictions

Repeating Patterns: Has a lot of illnesses, the body is trying to reconnect. Uses drugs to cope. Relationships are surface only and when they being to fall apart the person will run — applies to career, school, intimate partners, children. Will have injuries or illness and does not really experience discomfort.

Created Patterns
1. I am hopeless.
2. My heart is numb.
3. I don't feel.
4. Feelings are dangerous.
5. I am alone.
6. I am unloved.
7. I am unwanted.
8. I am powerless.
9. I am out of control.
10. I must run away to be safe.
11. I must freeze to be safe.
12. People hurt me.
13. I am depressed.
14. Being depressed is safety.
15. I am weak.
16. I am shame.

Diabetes

Fears
- Fear of disconnection
- Fear of not conforming and performing
- Fear of the feminine power
- Fear of honoring the feminine
- Fear of disappointment
- Fear of their shadow
- Fear of the joy of life
- Fear of feeling

- Fear of letting go
- Fear of belonging
- Fear of not belonging
- Fear of their feelings
- Fear of authority
- Fear of not being good enough

Emotional States

- The emotional state of diabetes at the global level (global level diabetes energy would be the vibration held by a community/ region/ country) may be about our disconnection from the Mother Earth. Our ancestral cultures have either abandoned or been driven away from connection to the earth. Food is one of the principles of feminine nurturing and we are disconnected from that source of nurturing. We no longer raise our own food or do work in a community to meet the food needs of that community locally. We are not connected to the source of our food. Our disregard for the source of our food represents a lack of honor for what nurtures us. We have lost the sacredness of our food by poisoning the earth with pesticides and fertilizers. If the food we eat is toxic then the source of nurturing our bodies, food, creates a toxic energy that cascades throughout the entire body from a poisoned feminine energy.
- Underlying bitterness and anger at the disappointments the world has presented. Expectations were unrealistic to begin with. There is a seething darkness deep inside of them.

Cross Indexing: Diabetes Mellitus Type I, Diabetes Mellitus Type II, Endocrine System Problems, pancreas problems

Created Patterns

1. I am ashamed of _____.
2. I am disappointed in life.
3. I am disconnected from the creator.
4. I am numb.
5. I am sad all the time.
6. I can't express my emotions and be safe.
7. I can't feel.
8. I can't forgive _____.
9. I can't release _____.
10. I don't belong.
11. I don't get to be angry.
12. I don't know how to safely express my anger.
13. I have been expressing/feeling strong emotion of _____ for a long time (these are negative emotions: hatred/resentment/anger/rage/bitterness/grief/sorrow/revenge /regret / despair).
14. I have never found a place where I am happy.
15. I have to believe what doctors tell me.
16. I must show people that I am good enough.
17. If I ignore the diabetes it will go away.
18. If it's done my way.
19. It's dangerous to feel.
20. My life should have been different.

21. The doctors don't know what their talking about.
22. There is no joy/happiness in my life.
23. What truth about diabetes are you denying?
24. Why do you criticize others?

Diabetes Mellitus Type 1

Fears
- Fear of loss
- Fear that they have done nothing with their lives
- Fear of authority
- Fear defeat
- Fear of joy
- Fear of judgment
- Fear of shame
- Fear of taking the time to nurture themselves
- Fear of receiving
- Fear of connection to the earth
- Fear of depending on others
- Fear of receiving
- Fear of looking weak
- Fear of their anger
- Fear of failure
- Fear of their inner self
- Fear of play
- Fear of being asked to help others
- Fear of not having enough
- Fear of not being enough
- Fear of change
- Fear of disappointment
- Fear of obligation
- Fear of hear hurt
- Fear of judgment
- Fear of being unloved
- Fear of being unwanted

Teachings
- Accepted
- Allowing fun in my life
- Allowing joy in my life
- Ask for help
- Be balanced
- Be nurtured
- Being safe when having fun
- Care for myself
- Complete
- Creator's definition of the flow of life
- Flexibility
- Get my needs met
- Have fun
- Joy
- Laughter
- Let others help me
- Letting go and being safe
- Letting go of outmoded ideas
- Listen to the needs of others
- Receive
- Receive love
- Relax
- Say no
- Trust
- Trust that my needs will be met
- Whole

Emotional States
- Has worked hard to make something of themselves and they feel like they are still struggling-no sense of accomplishment.
- Dogmatic approaches to life in general prevents joy from entering-rigidity / judgmental-no in and outflow; judgmental attitude may be in response something that has caused them to feel shame.
- Does not know how to derive pleasure from the senses – food is taken on the go and is usually fast / junk food; lack of beneficial movement; accumulation of toxins in the body, no regular awareness of the beauty in nature, etc.

- Won't let someone else help them in their needs or goals.
- Rigid dogmatic concepts create a trapped animosity in the cells that has no where to go and stops the enjoyment of life, this trapped animosity will create drama.
- Continual striving for what they don't have; creates an inner stress which shuts down the flow of life. No inner sense that they have succeeded.
- No joy in their life.
- Lost the connection to their divine nature; has lost the awareness of the inner self.

Cross Indexing: Diabetes, Adrenal fatigue, Diabetes Mellitus type II, Arteriosclerosis, Kidney problems, eye problems, cataracts, weight-over, addictions-smoking, heart problems, congestive heart failure, tachycardia, pancreas problems

Repeating Patterns: Has achieved in their career/job but doesn't feel the accomplishment. They feel like they have to work harder, creates situation that are shameful, must do everything themselves. Does not go out in nature willingly — doesn't see it out. Looks for happiness outside themselves but never finds it. Doesn't play finds every excuse to not play…really doesn't know how and when forced to be in the play space shuts down/freezes. Holds onto outmoded ideas or ideas that are just wrong and won't let go. Turns a deaf ear to those in need. Has no idea how to get their needs met.

Created Patterns

1. There is no god.
2. There is no spirit.
3. I have no joy.
4. I must have _____, I must have more.
5. I must do it myself.
6. I'm not good enough.
7. I am worthless.
8. I am judged.
9. I must judge to be safe.
10. Nothing makes me truly happy.
11. Bad things happen when I am not in control.
12. Change is dangerous.
13. Change is unnecessary.
14. Feelings are dangerous.
15. God doesn't listen to me.
16. God is for everyone except me.
17. Having fun is a waste of time.
18. I am a failure.
19. I am ashamed of _____.
20. I am beaten down.
21. I am disconnected from god.
22. I am going to die.
23. I am heartsick at how life has disappointed me.
24. I am powerless to make things better (what things?).
25. I am run down.
26. I am to ashamed to talk to god.
27. I am wrong (this is the fear).
28. I can do it all myself.

29. I can't be beholding to anyone else.
30. I can't let go of the past hurts.
31. I can't seem to accomplish anything.
32. I can't trust others to do it right.
33. I don't deserve.
34. I don't have time to take care of myself.
35. I don't need anyone else to help me.
36. I don't want to owe anyone anything (fear of needing others).
37. I have given up on being a success.
38. I have given up on getting anywhere in life.
39. I have nothing to laugh about.
40. I have to connect to God through someone else.
41. I must be right.
42. I must be successful.
43. I must do it myself.
44. I must judge others before they judge me _____.
45. I must stay in control to keep on top of things.
46. I stay safe when I judge others / situation.
47. I want more than I can get.
48. I work and work and never seem to get anywhere.
49. I'm not accepted.
50. I'm not good enough.
51. If I ask for help I am weak.
52. If people help / support me then they want something from me.
53. Life is a disappointment.
54. Life is a struggle.
55. Life is hard.
56. My body is just a means to an end.
57. My feelings always get me in trouble so I don't have them.
58. My feelings overwhelm me so I ignore them.
59. My way is always better.
60. New ideas are a waste of time / dangerous.
61. No one supports me; I have to do it all myself.
62. Nothing I do ever seems to work out the way I had planned.
63. People always let me down.
64. There is no god.
65. There is no possibility I am wrong.
66. When I depend on others I get hurt.
67. When I finally do get a little ahead I lose it all.
68. Work before play.
69. You are what you do.

*Look at themes of safety, fun, boundaries, trust, self-esteem, self-knowledge, self-love, self-respect, self-pity, workaholic, change, joy, life purpose, reflection, feeling, awareness, unmet needs, success, shame

Diabetes Mellitus Type 2

Fears
- Fear of joy
- Fear of play
- Fear of humiliation
- Fear that they will be punished for not adhering to the rules
- Fear of shame
- Fear of betrayal
- Fear of being creative
- Fear of being trapped
- Fear of feeling lost
- Fear of the future
- Fear of the unknown
- Fear of the letting down others
- Fear of failing
- Fear of control
- Fear of living
- Fear of learning
- Fear of change
- Fear of their inner wisdom
- Fear of their heart
- Fear of feelings
- Fear of disappointment
- Fear of letting go
- Fear of being unaccepted
- Fear of living an authentic life
- Fear of not being good enough
- Fear of their creativity
- Fear of authority

Emotional States
- Shut down child-like innocence. Out of balance feminine energy. No permission to play or experience joy. Creative is suppressed. Does not have alternatives for nurturance. Has been humiliated, shamed, or betrayed associated with creative/ nurturing from a trusted source.
- Cannot see the forest for the trees. Feels lost. Future looks dark. Shut off from nurturing. Feels trapped.
- Controlled by the responsibilities they have taken on. Does what their family wants them to do. Barely holding their world together. Feel like they carry a heavy load.
- Relinquished control of their life. Control of their life was given up to have some peace. Given up on the game of life.
- Not in touch with their feelings and emotions. Pretend to be something they're not. They feel no joy. Feel dead inside.
- Fear of the unknown as a consequence has thrown away the opportunity to grow mind, body and spirit. Taken the safe path. Fear of risk. Suppressed the need for joy. Fear of change. Uses aspects of life as an excuse to stop growth.

- Suppresses the intuitive. Sacrificed spiritual growth to be accepted. Afraid of losing everything if they embrace spiritual growth. Let themselves be controlled by others. Afraid of their own power.

Cross Indexing: diabetes, Diabetes Mellitus Type 1

Repeating Patterns: Wounded Creative Core, all work and no play, tends to not want friendships with women, disconnected from nature, doesn't go to parks or out in nature.

Created Patterns
1. I give up.
2. I have no control, I am controlled by others.
3. All work and no play – I must get the work done before I can relax.
4. I am shamed.
5. I am humiliated.
6. I hate my mother/grandmother.
7. I hate my father/grandfather.
8. You can't trust women.
9. I am lost.
10. I am trapped.
11. I don't know how to get my needs met.
12. I am afraid of change.
13. Being spiritual is dangerous.
14. I am disconnected from my heart.
15. I must be responsible.
16. I am disconnected from my heart.
17. Feelings are dangerous.
18. Being different is dangerous.
19. Being vulnerable is dangerous.
20. Better the devil I know than the devil I don't know.
21. Change is dangerous.
22. Feelings are dangerous.
23. I am ashamed of _____.
24. I am dangerous.
25. I am disappointed in life.
26. I am disconnected from the creator.
27. I am numb.
28. I am sad all the time.
29. I can't express my emotions and be safe.
30. I can't feel.
31. I can't forgive _____.
32. I can't release _____.
33. I don't belong.
34. I don't get to be angry.
35. I don't know how to safely express my anger.
36. I don't know what being nurtured feels like.
37. I don't know what joy is.
38. I don't trust myself.

39. I have been holding onto /feeling strong emotion of _____ for a long time (these are negative emotions: hatred/resentment/anger/rage/bitterness/grief/sorrow/revenge).
40. I have never found a place where I am happy.
41. I let others tell me what to do.
42. I must be accepted to be loved.
43. I must do what others tell me to have peace.
44. I must do whatever it takes to be safe.
45. I must give in to have peace.
46. I must give up myself to have peace.
47. I must hide who I truly am.
48. I must hold things together.
49. I must not be different.
50. I must sacrifice happiness to stay safe.
51. I must sacrifice myself to be safe.
52. I must show people that I am good enough.
53. I need to be accepted by _____.
54. I'm beaten down by life.
55. I'm not nurtured.
56. I'm not safe with change.
57. If I am creative people will hurt me.
58. If I ignore the diabetes it will go away.
59. If it's done my way everything will be OK.
60. It isn't safe to create.
61. It isn't safe to play.
62. It's too late to make changes.
63. Listening to your intuition is dangerous.
64. My life should have been different.
65. No one appreciates me.
66. Psychic skills are dangerous.
67. The doctors don't know what their talking about.
68. The unknown is dangerous.
69. There is no joy/happiness in my life.
70. What truth about diabetes are you denying?
71. Why do you criticize others?
72. Women betray/hurt me. (Which women have betrayed or hurt you?)
73. You can't make a living being creative.

Diabetes: A Global View

Diabetes at the global level may be about our disconnection from the Mother Earth. Our ancestral cultures have either abandoned or been driven away from connection to the earth. Food is one of the principles of feminine nurturing and we are disconnected from that source of nurturing. We no longer raise our own food or do work in a community to meet the food needs of that community locally. We are not connected to the source of our food. Our disregard for the source of our food represents a lack of honor for what nurtures us. We have lost the sacredness of our food by poisoning the earth with pesticides, herbicides and fertilizers. If the food we eat is toxic then the source of nurturing our bodies, food, creates a toxic energy that cascades throughout the entire body from a poisoned feminine energy. Our food is no longer food. It is chemicals and our bodies see the chemicals as toxins.

Diarrhea

Fears
- Fear of not getting what they want
- Fear of not deserving
- Fear of giving
- Fear of injustice
- Fear of not being able to change things
- Fear of authority
- Fear of having to stay in the box
- Fear of being overrun
- Fear of being forced against their will
- Fear of the unknown
- Fear of failure
- Fear of giving in

Emotional States
- Anger at those that would keep you bound to a certain or specific way of doing things. Their way is not your way. You don't get what they want.

Cross Indexing: Intestinal Problems, Celiac Disease, Allergies-Dairy, Allergies-Wheat, Colitis-Ulcerative, Irritable Bowel Syndrome, Abdominal Problems

Repeating Patterns: Taking what's being thrown at them and then instead of taking care or pushing it back they walk/run away.

Created Patterns
1. I want to be done with _____.
2. I can never get what I want.
3. What is it that you can't accept in your life?
4. I need to get away from _____.
5. I can't make things different.
6. I have given up trying to make things better.
7. Life is unfair.
8. Nothing ever works out my way.
9. I am unable to give.
10. There is no justice in the world.
11. I'm afraid of what will happen next.

Diverticulitis

Fears
- Fear of hanging onto what is toxic
- Fear of letting go of what is no longer of value (might need it someday)
- Fear of feelings
- Fear of speaking their truth
- Fear of being authentic
- Fear of letting go
- Fear of the unknown
- Fear of the future
- Fear of change
- Fear of the new
- Fear of inner peace

Emotional States
- They take what is good use it up, and then hang onto what is toxic. Toxic old ways and ideas that no longer have a function or place in the world.
- Short-sighted concepts that lead down a rabbit hole and offer no way out.

Cross Indexing: Colitis-Ulcerative, Irritable Bowel Syndrome, abdominal problems, Inflammation, Leaky gut syndrome

Repeating Patterns: Stays stuck in a pattern of old stories that color all of what they say and do. They think it works but it keeps bringing in the energy of the same — no newness — the endeavor will eventually die. Tells the same stories over and over. Stuck — won't give newness a change. Hangs onto what no longer serves.

Created Patterns
1. I can't say how I truly feel.
2. If I tell the truth something bad will happen.
3. I can't be around other people and be safe/OK.
4. What are the issues of anger and/ or resentment you are hanging onto?
5. Change is to be feared.
6. I feel out of peace.
7. I am stuck.
8. I can't let go.
9. If I let go there is nothing to replace it.

Dizziness

Fears
- Fear of listening to their heart
- Fear of too much

- Fear of the future
- Fear of feeling
- Fear of the creative
- Fear of being ignored
- Fear of not being listened to
- Fear of being overrun
- Fear of being taken advantage of
- Fear of being out of control
- Fear of being out of balance
- Fear of a life purpose
- Fear of their anger

Emotional States
- The what ifs become overwhelming. The energy of feeling overwhelms the intellect or the energy of intellect (thinking) overwhelms the feelings. There is a push-pull between the thinking mind and the feeling mind. This results in confusion as to what to do next.

Cross Indexing: Vertigo, Ear Problems, Labyrinthitis, Neural disorders, Brain problems

Repeating Patterns: Looks to the thinking mind to tell them how to feel and ignores the heart until the feeling in the heart demand recognition. Wounded Creative Core.

Created Patterns
1. Everyone else comes before me.
2. I am overloaded.
3. I don't know how to cope.
4. I don't know what balance feels like.
5. I don't want to accept things as they are.
6. I don't want to cope anymore.
7. I have no direction in life.
8. I have no sense of a life purpose.
9. My life is out of control.
10. My life is out of balance.
11. What are the issues of anger and/or resentment?
12. I don't know what to feel.

Dry Eye

Fears
- Fear of crying
- Fear of being vulnerable
- Fear of attack
- Fear of the unknown
- Fear of expressing feelings

- Fear of the flow of life
- Fear of being wrong
- Fear of not being perfect
- Fear of judgment
- Fear of moving forward
- Fear of feeling
- Fear of being seen as weak
- Fear of not being good enough

Emotional States

- LEFT – They do not feel protected from the things they see. They feel like the outside world bad things are on their doorstep. This causes thoughts that are always on the lookout – unfocused on what should be focused on – doesn't relax into the flow. Narrows the vision to just see what is in front. Doesn't feel safe in expression of feelings.
- RIGHT – Feelings and actions are out of sync, they do not work together. This leaves them vulnerable when that out of sync condition doesn't go well. So they over compensate and try to do things perfectly. That perfectionism can stop them from getting anything done.

Cross Indexing: Eye Disorders

Repeated Pattern: Self criticism to the point of stopping progress. Does not take the next step to realize their potential. Always stops short.

Created Patterns

1. I can't cry.
2. I can't feel.
3. I am numb.
4. I must keep a stiff upper lip.
5. It's wrong to express your feelings.
6. Expressing feelings shows a lack of class.
7. Showing your feelings make you weak.
8. I am afraid of the pain of my feelings.
9. If I show my feelings people will ridicule me.
10. If I feel I will fall apart and everyone depends on me.
11. Real men don't cry.
12. It is dangerous to cry.
13. People are superior to me.
14. I feel bad about myself most of the time.
15. I am sad most of the time.
16. I am suspicious when people look at me.
17. I am suspicious when people look at my work.
18. I'm not worthy/not good enough.
19. I can only see what my mother sees.
20. I must be perfect to be safe.
21. I'm my own worst critic.
22. I don't do things right.
23. I can't get things done.

Duodenal Ulcer

Fears
- Fear of being in trouble
- Fear of being wrong
- Fear of attack
- Fear of inner wisdom
- Fear of change
- Fear of being powerless
- Fear of being out of control
- Fear of life
- Fear of not understanding
- Fear of giving
- Fear of listening to others
- Fear of stepping outside the box
- Fear of the future
- Fear of change
- Fear of what is underneath the surface

Emotional States
- Lack of perception and sense that there is no depth to life. It is only on the surface. They will see only the face and not what is behind it. They don't see underlying emotions or motivations. When they miss these states of information, wrong actions are done.
- They feel like they always get it wrong. Lack of control and power.

Cross Indexing: Stomach Ulcer, Digestive disorders

Repeating Pattern: In a constant state of hyper-awareness and does not trust the intuitive senses. Hangs onto old ideas to keep them safe, but they don't. Has trouble being empathetic or compassionate.

Created Patterns
1. I can't trust myself.
2. My ideas are wrong.
3. The world is not a nice place.
4. I must be on guard.
5. My intuition is always wrong.
6. The old ways are best.
7. Change is dangerous.
8. I am always wrong.
9. I am powerless to make things better.
10. I am out of control.
11. I don't see underlying motivations.
12. I don't understand other people's feelings.

Dupuytren's Contraction

Fears
- Fear of heart hurt
- Fear of pain
- Fear that their handle on life is slipping away
- Fear that life is always going to be lemons
- Fear that life is just struggle
- Fear of being cast away
- Fear of disappointment
- Fear of powerlessness
- Fear that the truth is manipulated
- Fear of the truth
- Fear of attack
- Fear of people
- Fear of ownership
- Fear of success
- Fear of being outdone
- Fear of having things taken
- Fear of my feelings
- Fear of intimacy

Emotional States
- Generalized dissatisfaction with life. Always on the edge of a funk or feelings of depression. Past yearnings never materialized and they always felt alone in their desires and needs. This hardened and became anger and borderline hatred.
- Bitter disappointments and conflicts brought back childhood experiences where they felt powerless in the face of disappointment. Extreme upset was met with feeling discarded.
- Justifications were used like a noose to strangle truth. They felt a constriction throughout the body when confronted with situations of defending the truth. Knowing familial/parental truths were dangerous.
- They hold their feelings out and then close them off whenever there is a perceived threat. They stay contracted for as long as the threat is there. They become defensive and put up shields. The threat is often generalized and includes broad categories of people.

Cross Indexing: hands, joint problems, Connective disorders, joint disorders, ancestral/epigenetic

Repeating Patterns: Career and relationships end in disappointment. Puts the creation of those repeated patterns outside of themselves. Someone else is always at fault.

Created Patterns
1. Life is disappointing.
2. Life is hard.
3. Success is always just out of reach.
4. I am depressed.
5. I am bitter at _____.

6. I am unwanted.
7. Someone is always trying to best me.
8. I can only share so much.
9. People use my feelings against me.
10. The truth is dangerous.
11. People discount my feelings.
12. The harder I try to hang on the faster things slip away.
13. The harder I work at at relationship the worse it gets.
14. The harder I work at a job the worse it gets.
15. I can't hang onto good things.

Dysmenorrhea

Fears
- Fear of rejection
- Fear others will know you are having a period
- Fear of the shame of being a woman
- Fear of feeling
- Fear of heart hurt
- Fear of being unloved
- Fear of never being enough
- Fear of being shamed
- Fear of not being punished
- Fear of the feminine
- Fear of living
- Fear of the flow of life

Emotional States
- Their heart is encased in concrete as they harden themselves against hurt and rejection, love that never comes or is never enough.

Cross Indexing: Reproductive Disorders (female)

Repeating Patterns: Sets themselves up for rejection in relationship.

Created Patterns
1. I am angry at myself.
2. I must be punished.
3. I can't release the shame.
4. Women are evil.
5. Women are dirty.
6. It is wrong to be born a woman.
7. I am ashamed of _____.
8. What are the issues of shame in your life?

9. Women must suffer.
10. I can't forgive myself.
11. I don't love myself.
12. If I can't love myself how can someone else love me?

E's

Ear Infection – Chronic

Fears
- Fear of angry voices that kill joy
- Fear of betrayal
- Fear of angry voices
- Fear of failing
- Fear of not doing what authority wants
- Fear of misunderstanding
- Fear of letting go
- Fear of toxic people
- Fear of being unloved
- Fear of being unheard
- Fear of duty
- Fear of obligation
- Fear of heart hurt
- Fear of pain
- Fear of conflicting information
- Fear of confusion
- Fear of chaos
- Fear of being overrun
- Fear of mean people
- Fear of being trapped
- Fear of normal
- Fear of being out of control
- Fear of authority
- Fear of failing
- Fear of being worthless
- Fear of being ripped off

Emotional States
- Failure to meet the expected outcome of others. Meets the expectation of others to be secure. But the expectation vocalized wasn't the true outcome expected. So there was a perceived failure. Wants to be known as effective and efficient as a standard of their identity. So there is a conflict between what they heard and what was meant (or unsaid but expected to have been understood).
- Just won't let go of the idea that where they come from was OK. The toxic energy of the home was masked in pus. The words in the home were based in the toxicity of anger, hatred and betrayal. There was/is a misaligned motivation for staying connected. People around them were covered in the toxicity of the emotions. No love or caring — only duty and the perception of what that implied.
- Nothing made sense and it always hurt. Conflicting ideas that always felt like you are damned if you do and damned if you don't. The world felt/ feels jumbled. No safety anywhere. Health was/is impaired in other ways. Lost reason and no boundaries.

- The voices heard are mean. The sound feels hard and harsh. Hopeless sense that it can't be stopped – no escape. There is a sense that nothing is ever right. Everything you hear is wrong. So there's always a sense of trying to find normal in a not-normal world. The adult will duplicate that world because this is where survival is at. Always guessing at the non-normal normal. Inner conflict is created. That conflict becomes the source of security.

Cross indexing: Ear problems, Infection, Chronic Illness

Repeating Patterns: Relationships end in betrayal and great loss. Sex is used as a way of controlling a relationship. Creates drama and chaos to be safe — hides within it. Wounded Creative Core.

Created Patterns
1. I must always be nice.
2. Sex is a way to be nice.
3. I am unheard.
4. The wrath of god is always around the corner.
5. People that are powerful will hurt me.
6. When there is chaos I must hide.
7. People that love me are mean and hard to get along with.
8. Change is constant.
9. The world is unstable.
10. When people fight I am safe.
11. People betray me.
12. People rip me off.
13. I must be on alert to not get hurt.
14. People are mean.
15. I always fail.
16. I am worthless.
17. I must work harder to be as good as others.
18. The way it is, is the way it should be.
19. Words hurt.
20. I don't know what is normal.
21. I have no idea what is right.

Ear Problems

Fears
- Fear of being different
- Fear of learning the truth if they listen
- Fear of ideas that are different
- Fear of being challenged
- Fear of being wrong
- Fear of people that are different
- Fear of being seen as different
- Fear of not being understood

- Fear of not being heard
- Fear of hearing
- Fear of heart pain
- Fear of not belonging

Emotional States
- Prejudice toward others that are different.
- Prejudice toward ideas that are different from their own. Sees themselves as having the perfect logic in their forgone conclusion.

Cross indexing: Heart Problems, Vertigo, Dizziness, Labyrinthitis, Ears-hearing Problems, Kidney problems, Hearing loss

Repeating Patterns: Avoids situations of difference (leans toward environments of sameness; racial, career, gender/community).

Created Patterns
1. Nobody listens to me.
2. I don't want to listen to others.
3. Hearing is dangerous.
4. It is dangerous to hear.
5. I want to shut the world out.
6. Nobody hears what I have to say.
7. Everything is going to fall apart.
8. I am prejudiced against _____.
9. I don't understand what people are saying to me.
10. What do you not want to hear?
11. I don't want to hear the pain of my heart.
12. People that are different are risky/ dangerous.
13. People that are different are wrong.
14. People that are different don't belong.

Ears – Hearing Problems

Fears
- Fear of giving
- Fear of heart hurt
- Fear of understanding the pain of others
- Fear of listening
- Fear of presence
- Fear of being in the now
- Fear of life
- Fear of the flow of life
- Fear of judgment

- Fear of attack
- Fear of overwhelm
- Fear of chaos
- Fear of my anger
- Fear of hearing the truth of others
- Fear of being hurt by what others say

Emotional States

- RIGHT – Lack of understanding, not lack of intellectual understanding but lack of compassionate listening.
- LEFT – Lack of listening to what is said. Interprets through their own filters instead of "hearing" the essence of what is being said.

Cross Indexing: Aging, Ear Problems, Hearing loss, Infection

Repeating Patterns: Misinterpret something that is said, hears only a partial statement and not the whole information. Jumps to conclusions before all the facts are understood. Judgmental. Feelings of impatience. Feelings of anxiousness and wanting to run away from people that are talking.

Created Patterns

1. I am in danger.
2. I will be hurt if I hear.
3. You must hear things my way.
4. What are the advantages of not hearing?
5. I shut down when the chaos is overwhelming.
6. I am angry at what I am hearing.
7. I don't want to hear what is going on.
8. I can't tolerate what I am hearing.
9. I hear what I want to hear.
10. People have wrong ideas.
11. I can't hear what people say if its not my way of thinking.
12. There is no one else's truth just mine.

Eczema

Fears

- Fear of being overrun
- Fear of being trapped
- Fear of a continued life
- Fear of living
- Fear of feeling hopeless
- Fear of the unknown
- Fear of the future
- Fear of change

- Fear of letting the creative in
- Fear of intimacy
- Fear of heart hurt
- Fear of kind people
- Fear of betrayal
- Fear of never being enough
- Fear of never having enough

Emotional States

- Wants to be let alone so they can do their own thing. Someone is always bugging them – irritating–diverting their attention from the things they want to be doing. Won't be allowed to be their own person in their own time and space. Feels irritated by life in general. The demands of being human; job, relationships, eating food, securing shelter –the basics are irritating.
- The union of body and soul are incomplete. Joint exploration into the heart by body or soul yields conflicting and disparate functional approaches which causes inner conflict and yields a life of little meaning and purpose. No longer feels any drive to exist. The conflict between body and soul have worn them out.
- Journeying into the unknown – all of life – creates a sense of hopelessness. The lack of clarity in where they are going and what to do next is frightening as 'hell'. They want the road map. Without any hope of a predictable life they panic and freeze. They believe that their next step will be a step into the abyss. Tightness of thought. Holds to a tight path that does not allow creativity or transcendent thought to enter.
- Warmth causes pain. Association of kindness to abusive outcome in a relationship. Does not trust people that present kindness – pushes away affection and kindness. Everything is muddled. Confusion is their constant companion. Deep sense that nothing good will ever happen to them and they are doomed to a depressing life.
- Genetic inclinations have created symptoms of greed. The instinct to survive has been mal-adapted to feel safe only if surrounded by lots of everything. They must have more money, more house, continual more – strong need to have it all or they die. They lack moderation in their life. Everything is taken to a level of excess. There is no balance. There is no sense of boundaries.

Cross Indexing: Skin Problems, Liver problems, Adrenal fatigue, Temple pain/pressure, Wounded Creative Core

Created Patterns

1. _____ hurt me.
2. I am being stopped from doing _____.
3. Something always gets in the way of my success.
4. I am overly sensitive.
5. I am angry at _____.
6. I resent _____.
7. I am constantly on the lookout for danger.

Edema

Fears
- Fear of letting go
- Fear of change
- Fear of moving
- Fear of feelings
- Fear of not being good enough
- Fear of their creativity
- Fear of judgment
- Fear of their heart's yearning
- Fear of being wrong
- Fear of hopelessness
- Fear of being authentic
- Fear of vulnerability

Emotional States
- False hopes and expectations around people and situations. Puts values into people and situations that are not held by others. Doesn't see the wisdom and then creates their own truth. Jumps without measuring the depth of the water. Creates own understanding – not based in the collective – based in ego. Holds self out as the paragon of virtue. Wants to be faultless. Wrongs others to elevate self.
- Chides mother. Hopeless sensing of self. Wanders around with an unknown sense of direction. Belittles others to elevate self. Unwilling to let others know they have a sense of self. Feels helpless in moving forward. Wanders if things will ever get better.
- Adjustment to life is unyielding (doesn't budge). Wants things to be their way. Feels they have been denied the opportunity for bigness or grandness in their life. Hurts others in their quest for bigness. Wants to be seen and known. But they really have nothing to share. They come from the skin/surface and not the heart.

Cross Indexing: part of the body affected, bloating, circulatory problems, kidney problems

Created Patterns
1. I feel sorry for myself.
2. I can't let go of what is no good for me.
3. If I move I will be hurt.
4. Feelings are painful.
5. I must keep myself from feeling.
6. I can't let myself feel.
7. I must keep my emotions bottled up.
8. I am not good enough.
9. I am not good enough to be creative.
10. Taking risks are dangerous.
11. I can't have my heart's desire.
12. Listening to my heart is risky.

Ehlers-Danlos Syndrome

Fears
- Fear of god
- Fear of wholeness
- Fear of their divine nature
- Fear of the inner wisdom
- Fear of understanding their divine nature
- Fear of being punished
- Fear of themselves
- Fear of disconnection
- Fear of aloneness
- Fear of nothingness

Emotional States
- A desire to die. A strong belief held from before birth that the human form was inherently sinful (ancestral memory).
- It is the will of god that I be punished (ancestral memory). Fear of god. Feeling that I sinned before god. God will take what is precious to me. God will crush me.

Cross Indexing: Joint Problems, Autoimmune disorders, Lupus

Created Patterns
1. Bad things always happen to me.
2. Being human is sinful.
3. God abandoned me.
4. God betrayed me.
5. God hates me.
6. God wants to destroy me.
7. I am angry at _____.
8. I am disconnected from god.
9. I am not good enough.
10. I can't stand up for myself.
11. I carry the sin of all men.
12. I have no purpose.
13. I have sinned before god and I must suffer.
14. I must do what others tell me to do to be loved / wanted.
15. I resent _____.
16. I want to die.
17. I was born as an example of what happens to sinners.
18. It is god's wish I must suffer.
19. Nothing I do will ever be enough.
20. Nothing I do will ever make it better.
21. People run over me.

Elbow Problems

Fears
- Fear of being taken advantage of
- Fear of being weighed down
- Fear of being irrelevant
- Fear of not being seen
- Fear of becoming nothing
- Fear of change
- Fear of ideas that are different
- Fear of injustice

Emotional States
- RIGHT – as you achieve accomplishments in your life there is a desire to give to others. This gets out of balance when the giving moves from being selflessness to wanting recognition. Feels burden when there is no recognition. The giving is no longer heart-based but 'I' based.
- LEFT – Rejection of the wisdom of others – judging what others have offered as being judgmental and with no merit. Feels burden by the opinions of others.

Cross Indexing: Arms, Left & Right-sided tendencies, Joint problems

Repeating Patterns: Involved in Charity/community activities that start off with good intentions but become a burden.

Created Patterns
1. _____ is leaning on me.
2. People rely on me.
3. What are the issues of inflexibility in your life?
4. Status quo is good/safe.
5. It is dangerous to change.
6. I will lose _____ if I change
7. I can't ever be better than I am right now.
8. I am not every going to be good enough.
9. Change is dangerous.
10. Change is risky.
11. I can't change direction.
12. Change means you are out of control.
13. New ideas are threatening.
14. Give people an inch they will take a mile.
15. I judge others to be safe.
16. Nobody listens to what I have to say.
17. People should be grateful for what I do.
18. People think they are entitled.

EMF Sensitivity

Fears
- Fear of being overrun
- Fear of living
- Fear of life
- Fears connecting to others
- Fear of joy
- Fear of the sweetness of life
- Fear of not deserving
- Fear of leading a flat life
- Fear of their heart
- Fear of not being disappointed

Emotional States
- Jousting with life. Constantly trying to move past the heartache of a life that disappointed. Nothing ever feels familiar enough to be at ease. Constantly questioning their existence as if walking into their home is a stranger's experience. No attachment. Feels un-grounded. Feels disconnected.
- Hard and narrow views strangle the opportunity for connection and happiness. Always snuffing out a connection that would bring their humanness into focus. Hard on themselves and always judging their existence with "Why am I here". Feels depressed; rarely bring happiness or laughter into their space. Brings in people that are that way also.
- Joyless life. Feels no joy. Constrained. A nice thing is forbidden. A joy is forbidden, a sweet is forbidden. The sin of their ancestors flows through their veins. Gradual relinquishment leads to a feeling that their soul has demised.
- Hurt sensation in the heart that yields no response, feels a deadness. They yield nothing to others. Has a non-specific migration of attitude. Thoughtless as they respond. No interpretation or integration of thoughts so they don't hurt. There's little else they want in life other than being left alone.
- Creates aloneness by alienating people.

Cross Indexing: Allergies

Repeating Patterns: Sets up life situations that disappoint, works to manipulate people and situations to feel more in control/safe. Cycles feelings of why am I here to blah (a deadness or nothingness). Heart is closed to joy – allows themselves to feel hurts.

Created Patterns
1. I am disappointed.
2. Nothing ever goes my way.
3. I am unhappy.
4. I am depressed.
5. People don't like me.
6. I make life hard.
7. Life is hard.

8. It's wrong to have good stuff.
9. I always say the wrong thing.
10. I am alone.
11. I can't have nice things.
12. I am joyless.
13. Life is joyless.

Emphysema – COPD

Fears

- Fear of being heard breathing
- Fear of pain
- Fear of suffering
- Fear of living life
- Fear of not being worthy
- Fear of being different
- Fear of being overrun
- Fear of being rejected
- Fear of being different
- Fear of being noticed
- Fear of being diminished
- Fear of listening
- Fear of letting go and moving forward

Emotional States

- Back is against the wall. No where to turn and no one to help them. They feel separated from that deep inner sense of knowing. They are not looking for their purpose. There is an acquiescence to the work of survival. There is a gnawing sense that they are blocked from seeing the light of their being. The search is out of the question. They would be judged and rejected. They are coerced to accepting the prevailing "way" and not question.
- Chopped into little pieces by someone who is always on the attack. They feel destroyed by life and the lies. They want to hide. They hide in their life by being the backroom accountant, the bus person, etc. Invisible. At its core is a deep sense of anger at a life possible for others but not for them.
- Wrong headedness dominates. They stubbornly refuse to listen to the ideas and concepts of others. They feel diminished by the ideas of others as they are better than theirs. Their value is in being right. They take joy at seeing others wrong.
- Nothing helps to hold life in place. When life changes (as in the cycle of life) they grieve and do not stop grieving. They cannot bear the inevitable change. The grief never resolves it is always just at the surface. The grief becomes an identity.
- Too much anger. Anger that has been built into the ancestry. Anger at how life has failed them. A continual struggle to run from the truth of how they don't take responsibility for the failures.

Cross Indexing: Lung problems, Cancer-lung, tuberculosis, Addictions – chemical, Addictions – smoking

Created Patterns

1. I am unworthy to live.
2. I can't be myself.
3. I am unworthy.
4. My grief is killing me.
5. The grief is too much.
6. I am afraid to really live my life.
7. I can't be better than _____.
8. _____ betrayed me.
9. Others are always telling me what to do.
10. I don't get to think for myself.
11. Others come before me.
12. I am second.
13. I am last when getting my needs met.

Endocrine System Problems

Fears

- Fear of change
- Fear of attack
- Fear of the future
- Fear of inner peace
- Fear of the unknown
- Fear of being wrong
- Fear of their inner voice
- Fear of being independent
- Fear of authority
- Fear of the rules
- Fear of knowing one thing and the rules/authority say something else
- Fear of decisions
- Fear of saying no
- Fear of abandonment
- Fear that nothing is right
- Fear of letting go
- Fear that there will never be enough

Emotional States

- What you hear you don't believe, what you see you don't trust, what you know you think is not true, what you sense is wrong. Feels that they cannot know what is true based on their senses.
- Presents the past as relevant to today. They refer to the past and apply to the today issues, whether it is relevant or not. Feels that any new thoughts will just create chaos.
- Short term fixes to problems that then create the chaos again and/ or create long term problems that will then be addressed with a short term fix. They make no long term plans. Even when

there is plenty there is a sense of lack (bills are unpaid, repairs are not done, medical care is delayed, etc.) They always have a crisis or chaos running in their life. Their life is always off balance with no peace.

Cross Indexing: Addison's Disease, Adenoid Problems, Adrenal Fatigue, Alopecia, Amenorrhoea, Anemia – Pernicious, Autoimmune Disorder, Bloating, Cancer – Medullary Thyroid, Cancer – Pancreatic NeuroEndocrine, Cancer – Prostate, Cardiovascular Disorder, Diabetes Mellitus Type 1, Diabetes Mellitus Type 2, Endometriosis, Fibroid Tumors and Cysts, Hair – Falling Out, Insomnia, Insulin Resistance, Pancreas Problems, Prostate Problems

Repeating Patterns: Wounded Creative Core, always second-guessing themselves, difficulty with being decisive.

Created Patterns
1. Bad things are going to happen.
2. I am a/the savior.
3. I am not enough.
4. I am only comfortable in a crisis.
5. I am only important when I save people.
6. I can never slow down.
7. I can't be at peace/ relaxed.
8. I can't live without crisis.
9. I can't live without drama.
10. I don't know what balance is.
11. I have to do things to be important.
12. I keep busy to keep from feeling.
13. I must always prove myself.
14. I must earn the right to be loved.
15. I need a crisis to motivate me.
16. I need to needed.
17. I never have enough.
18. I will never be enough.
19. I'm a pessimist.
20. I'm in danger.
21. If I stop (slowdown) my life will fall apart.
22. It will never change.
23. My identity is chaos/crisis.
24. My life is out of balance.
25. Nothing is safe.
26. People need me to control chaos.
27. The more I do the more important I am.
28. I always have to say yes.
29. I have to do everything.
30. I am abandoned by _____.
31. I am overloaded.
32. I can't say no.
33. I am a martyr.
34. I must sacrifice myself for others.

35. If I say no _____ (what will happen?).
36. I don't know how to say no.

Endometriosis

Fears
- Fears making decisions
- Fears being wrong
- Fears humiliation
- Fears being ridiculed
- Fears their creativity
- Fears trusting themselves to judge
- Fears being unwanted
- Fears depending others
- Fears their body

Emotional States
- A creation for which you have lost control and it is now a problem, this creation is an idea/concept only and has not produced anything. The concept is never going anywhere because it is not trusted or believed in. Feels unsure of their ideas and feels humiliated if they fail.

Cross Indexing: Reproductive Disorders (female)

Repeating Patterns: Not trusting self, start and stop new projects, wounded creative core.

Created Patterns
1. It's someone else's fault.
2. I am sad about _____.
3. What is the deep sadness you feel?
4. What is the shame you feel?
5. I'm not wanted.
6. I'm not enough.
7. I am expendable.
8. Boys are better than girls.
9. I should have been a boy.
10. I don't love myself.
11. I can't depend on anyone.
12. I'm not lovable/ loved.
13. I can't let go of the past hurts.
14. I don't trust myself.
15. I never have good ideas.
16. I'm not creative.
17. I'm always wrong.
18. Everyone is better than me.

Epigastric Hernia

Fears
- Fear of being out of control
- Fear of being powerless and weak
- Fear of being weakened by what they take in
- Fear of being weakened by others in control
- Fear of guilt
- Fear of being wrong
- Fear of taking the wrong side

Emotional States
- Loss of control in social situations – saying and doing that which makes them feel guilty. Saying the wrong thing at the wrong time. Acting from a place that is socially inappropriate.
- Holds everything in perfect control before interacting with others. Has thought out everything before it is said and sits in the justification of those things even though they hurt others. When they can't control the situation, they feel angry. Yields no ground in their position. Feels they have the higher ground.

Cross Indexing: Intestinal problems, Muscle problems, abdominal problems, Digestive System

Repeating Patterns: Needing to be in control in social situations. Says the wrong thing in social situations. Feels out of control when they are not the center of attention. Doesn't let people get really close. Feels uncomfortable with intimacy.

Created Patterns
1. I lose power when I am around others.
2. I must control the situation.
3. I am guilty of hurting others when I am right.
4. I can't trust others to help me.
5. I am confused at the ideas of others.
6. I am confused that others do not see me as right.
7. I am always the center of attention.
8. People look up to me.
9. I am better than others.
10. I shut out others to stay safe.

Epilepsy

Fears
- Fear of being outcast

- Fear of saying the wrong thing
- Fear of being alone
- Fear of hopelessness
- Fear of losing
- Fear of fighting for the wrong thing
- Fear of being out of balance
- Fear of chaos
- Fear of their anger
- Fear of being out of control
- Fear of living
- Fear of life and the struggle
- Fear of being wrong
- Fear of being unloved
- Fear of being unwanted
- Fear of rejection

Emotional States

- Hard-won respect makes them believe they have to fight for everything. Every quest in life feels like a battle. Fight or lose. Even the most mundane things become a huge instinctual response to prevail over.
- Genetic energetic preferences create a strong energetic polarization in the energy fields. High ideals fought for are based in fantasy.
- They reach for the fruit from the tree and they can never quite pick it. They can touch it, smell it and reach it. But their hand stops just before pulling from the tree. They stop short because picking the fruit will throw their world out of balance. There's peace where they are at now and if they introduce something new they believe chaos will ensue. They feel like they are standing on thin ice.
- Spinning energies inside create an endless looping of desire and feelings of hopelessness. One minute their life is hope, energy, love and life and then in the next moment hopelessness loops in to create chaos. Ancestral anger at powers they could not conquer or control with no boundaries.
- The ancestral wound of extreme fear from being and feeling outcast and the transmission of the unresolved fear. Brain is highly activated for survival prior to death and that activation is unresolved then there is a transference of that survival fear to another that survives and the epigenetic field is altered. The ancestral transmission is then triggered by either a physical wound or intense feelings of no control that activate the epigenetic trauma.

Cross Indexing: Brain Problem

Created Patterns

1. I must punish myself.
2. I want to die.
3. I must hurt myself.
4. There must be a better way.
5. Everything is so hard.
6. Life is a struggle.
7. I'm not good enough.
8. I never do anything right.

9. I must be punished when I make a mistake.
10. I don't love myself.
11. I don't know how to show others I love them.
12. I am disconnected from the world around me.
13. I don't trust people.
14. I don't trust myself.
15. I'm not lovable.
16. I am rejected.
17. I can't depend on myself.
18. I am vulnerable.
19. I am afraid of myself.
20. I hurt others.
21. People near me get hurt by me.
22. I must disappear and be invisible.
23. People run away from me.
24. I am unwanted and unneeded.
25. I am a freak.
26. I must always live on the edges never seen.
27. I am an outcast.
28. I am a cast off.
29. I am damaged goods.

Epstein Barr Syndrome

Fears

- Fears their family/authority
- Fear of the divine inner self
- Fears struggling
- Fears being abandoned
- Fears the heart hurt
- Fears pain
- Fears ridicule
- Fears being unworthy
- Fears being seen
- Fear of being attacked
- Fear of being still
- Fear of not moving

Emotional States

- Slow-burning within, a repressed anger felt in the first chakra. Hatred within the family that prevented the divine expression of who they are. Held up to ridicule for attempts at expression of their divine nature. This warped their view of the world around them. It became unsafe to express the divine self. They would have been subjected to ridicule and shame if they did. Worked to find safe outlets but still felt anger which turned inward. Feels unsafe within their family.

- Warns that they could be the last to know. Feels embattled by life and living. Needs support and feels abandoned in the quest. Warns others to stay away by putting on a facade or bravado to the pain of their life. Brings self into focus rarely. Loses focus on own inner truths and reacts to the world from the facade or bravado.
- Held out to others as an example of what not to do. Ridiculed. Nothing they do is of value in the eyes of others and it is judged as worthless before its value is truly evaluated. Hide to survive and not be ridiculed. Feels disrespected and worthless.
- Bound to the concept of nothingness. If they stay nothing then they will not be attacked or seen which would bring on an attack. Feels under siege by all of life. Doesn't know how to defend self, so it feels as if they have to attack themselves so that they won't be attacked by others.
- There's a doing too much. If they do too much they stay safe in their overwhelm. The overwhelm is a form of protection. Kneels down at the feet of those seen to be greater and of more power. Fears that if they are not obsequious they will be killed. Feels helpless when using a facade in the presence of power and authority. Has no strength in the face of power and if found lacking, will attack themselves.

Cross Indexing: Virus, mononucleosis, fatigue, flu, adrenal fatigue, tachycardia, congestive heart failure

Created Patterns

1. What is the prolonged stress that has you worn down?
2. What feelings can't you release?
3. I must work hard to be loved/accepted / good enough.
4. I'm not good enough.
5. I must be better than others to be loved/accepted / good enough.
6. Life is hard.
7. Life is a struggle.

Erectile Dysfunction

Fears
- Fear of being alone
- Fear of their mother
- Fears being out of control
- Fear of an identity
- Fear of being wrong
- Fear of overwhelm
- Fear of being overrun
- Fear of intimacy
- Fear of being powerless
- Fear of injustice
- Fear of guilt
- Fear of being judged
- Fear of being ripped off

Emotional States

- Lack of control in their influence over others. No sense that others listen to their needs but are only focused on getting what they can from them. There is no equality in their relationships, feels like no one is listening. Their relationships are all give and take – no balance of give and receive. It's all one way or the other. Strong sense that they are wrong. There is a strong undercurrent of wrong to all they do. They are always second-guessing their decisions, their thoughts, their actions. Weak sense of self. Ungrounded in their connection to the body. Their senses overwhelm and they checkout and shut down. Too much information and a sense of not being able to process and make sense of the steady flow.
- Holds a deep sense of guilt around close intimate relationships. Intimacy feels wrong. Pleasure is a bad thing and sexual pleasure is even worse. Condemned. Deep ancestral condemnation around sexuality. Sense of sexuality derived from mother – maternal line. Sex becomes a betrayal. Feels helpless in the face of maternal energy. A sense of powerlessness will envelop the person.
- Feels cheated of their inheritance. They feel like a piece of them was taken by an injustice in the world. They feel like they were judged as a consequence of this injustice.

Cross indexing: Aging, Hypertension, Reproductive Disorders (male), Endocrine System Disorders, stress, atherosclerosis or diabetes

Repeating Patterns: Mother has a powerful influence over the success of relationships. They lost out on wealth because of poor decisions that were made in a sense of powerlessness to change things.

Created Patterns

1. I'm all mixed up about sex.
2. I am afraid of having sex.
3. I resent being expected to perform.
4. I am afraid of my mother.
5. I am no good.
6. My mother didn't want me.
7. Sex makes me feel guilty.
8. Sex is wrong.
9. Sex makes me feel like I am betraying my mother.
10. I am betrayed by women.
11. I am powerless.
12. The world is unfair, life is unfair.
13. I get ripped off by others.
14. I am guilty.
15. I have no say over anything.
16. I'm not listened to.
17. People take from me.
18. I must take from others before they take from me.
19. I am always wrong.
20. I am not good enough.
21. The world is too much.
22. Sex is dirty.

23. I am judged.

Esophagus Problems

Fears
- Fear of being unloved
- Fear of being unwanted
- Fears needs will never be met
- Fear of never having enough
- Fear of never being enough
- Fear of the world around them
- Fear of not knowing what's good and what is bad
- Fear of being out of control
- Fear of being vulnerable

Emotional States
- Feels that they can't discern what is good for them to take in and what isn't, so they take it all in to be safe.
- Being forced to swallow intense emotions they cannot express.

Cross Indexing: GERD, Cancer-Esophagus, Stomach Problem, Indigestion

Created Patterns
1. I don't know what to take in.
2. I don't know what is good for me.
3. I distrust everyone and everything.
4. I can't ask for what I need.
5. I must manipulate others to get my needs met.
6. I must swallow my pride/pain/feelings.
7. I can't say how I truly feel.
8. I don't believe in a creator.

Ethmoid Bone

Fears
- Fear of authority
- Fear of change
- Fear of being wrong
- Fear of people that know more than I do
- Fear of learning and growing
- Fear of powerlessness
- Fear of being too weak to stand in their ideas

Emotional States
- Refuses knowledge or learning that will help them grow. They resent information thrust at them. They close themselves off to anything that is not their idea. Feels that taking the wisdom of others weakens their control and power. They resent others that think they know more than others. Wisdom has to smack them in the face before they get it.

Cross Indexing: Sinus Problems, Nose problems, face/head problems

Created Patterns
1. I resent teachers/bosses/etc. (anyone that tells them what to do).
2. I resent authority.
3. I resent people who are more educated.
4. People don't know what they are talking about.
5. I've got to learn it the hard way.
6. Nothing comes easy for me.

Eye Problems

Fears
- Fear of being unaccepted
- Fear of being unwanted
- Fear of losing themselves to get needs met
- Fear of being hurt by what they see
- Fear of planning for the future
- Fear of responsibility
- Fear of injustice
- Fear of shame
- Fear of being seen
- Fear of connecting with others
- Fear of being taken advantage of
- Fear of inner seeing
- Fear of being undeserving
- Fear of happiness
- Fear of the future
- Fear of living a life of not getting their needs met

Emotional States
RIGHT EYE
- The right eye holds the ability to see the future (not precognition). A person with right eye issues wants to be accepted and wanted but they do so in such a way that they give up their own determination. They let others determine the hike they will take, the vacation they will go on or the person they will date. They may have even taken a vocational or career direction that others "saw" for them and then probably resented or hated every minute of it. A person with right eye

issues may have trouble setting goals or having a dream of a future accomplishment. The very idea of planning a vacation or setting goals leaves them confused and overwhelmed.
- Sees the injustice that's felt in having to be the one responsible for holding the balance (sets up the dynamic for repressed anger and resentment).
- Letting others plan their fun so they don't have to engage fully and feel responsible for their lack of enjoyment.
- Holds the energy of being slighted, not being understood, and wanting to be recognized, fear of losing sight of the inner me.
- People will lose sight of them, forget them. Feels forgotten.
- They get dumped and feel shameful.

LEFT EYE
- The left eye holds the ability to see the past (not retro-cognition). A person with left eye issues will have difficulty remembering events of the past. When they do remember past events they may be missing large chunks of information. Sometimes the experiences of the past are seen through a filter that changes the events and changes the feelings around the event. An uneventful and fun family reunion may have been seen as a horrible crisis and remembered that way. The person experiencing faulty memories may have experienced degradation in their vision very early in their life and may have had a childhood of abuse or ancestors that were abused.
- Fears of disrupting the balance in the group consciousness.
- See with a distance, feels disengaged.
- They do not engage the feelings of others. They create a distance so that we don't connect at the understanding level of what motivates others.
- They retreat from a situation (within) to create a distance.
- They feel overwhelmed by other peoples 'stuff'. A way of creating a boundary which causes a person to be seen as aloof and not caring.
- They see people as they want them to be and then when they aren't as how they want them to be, they cycle back into the feelings of being unappreciated. Selfish energy.

THIRD EYE
- Asks that they look into their heart for the sound of pain that requires them to open their third eye to see.
- There can be a fear of letting the true god-mind in.
- **Class System Energy of Seeing (lower, middle, upper, etc. emerging from feudal systems or religious systems for control and power)**
    o When they see nice things they are taken away
    o The person can't see good things, because they are not for them
    o Seeing good things hurt
    o Seeing color is wrong
    o Seeing nice things is rejection
    o Seeing nice things is being not good enough
    o If they do get what they want they don't deserve it and they get no pleasure from it
- Class system of denial of good things and pleasure:
    o Can't be showy, no color and can't be seen
    o Religious ethic of a sparse existence to keep the masses in check
    o Promotion of the ethic that feeling undeserving keeps you safe and pious.

What Stops Future Vision:
- A feeling that if they plan they will be disappointed. A feeling of not being good enough, didn't allow themselves the good stuff. Fear of living, fear of future vision, fear of being happy, fear of being seen, fear of planning the future. Fear that if they get the things they want they will have no life.

**Heart and eyes are energetically connected…what you see goes into the heart. Gets felt in the heart and when the feelings become trauma the eyes becomes a filter for what is seen.

Cross Indexing: Pink Eye, Dry Eye, Conjunctivitis, Glaucoma, Heart Problems, Nearsightedness and Farsightedness

Created Patterns

1. It is dangerous to see the truth.
2. If I can't see it then it didn't happen.
3. I'm not going to have fun until I'm not judged anymore.
4. I've never seen things right..
5. I must see things my way or not at all.
6. I am afraid to see the truth.
7. I am a victim.
8. I will lose my vision as I get older.
9. I am angry at others for not seeing the truth.
10. I must stop seeing the truth to not be angry.
11. I must stop seeing.
12. I am angry at others for not seeing the truth.
13. It isn't safe to be angry.
14. I don't have permission to be angry.
15. I don't have the right to be angry.
16. I know how to be appropriately angry.
17. I know what it feels like to appropriately angry.
18. If I see the truth I will not be liked.
19. If I see the truth I will be alone.
20. I will be rejected/cast-off if I see the truth.
21. If I see the truth I will lose the people I care about.
22. It isn't safe to speak my truth.
23. I don't have the right to think for myself.
24. I must be obedient.
25. I can never do enough to be good enough.
26. I can never do enough to please god/those in authority.

Eyes – Nearsightedness and Farsightedness

Fears
- Fear of seeing
- Fear of seeing the divine
- Fear of seeing emotions

- Fear of seeing who we are
- Fear of aging
- Fear of dying
- Fear of inner vision
- Fear of intuition
- Fear of being like your parents
- Fear of being seen
- Fear of your secrets being known
- Fear of being unprotected
- Fear of being hurt
- Fear of witnessing suffering
- Fear of shame
- Fear of humiliation
- Fear of rejection
- Fear of crying
- Fear of being vulnerable

Emotional States

Eyes carry the energy of our stuck grief, the anger of betrayal, the witness to suffering, the fear of others seeing who we truly are, our relationship to divine source, the loss of self-confidence, the loss of trust, loss of control, ancestral aging patterns and the ancestral patterns of how our physical eyes relate to inner 'seeing'. The crystallization of these states becomes the filter through which we see the world and the energy of vision.

Our ancestors believed that a blind person had the gift of inner seeing. A person employed as 'seer' by a ruler was often blind or blinded to enhance their inner vision. This pattern may have had its roots in Greek Mythology when a prophet from Thebes was blinded by the goddess Hera. The prophet made the mistake of giving Hera, Zeus's wife, the answer to a question that made her angry. Zeus could not change the man's blindness so he gave him the gift of foresight. Additionally, there is the ancient Greek belief that if you are blind you have seen a God or Goddess. Blindness was a punishment for looking upon the Divine; it also signified the knowledge that comes from contact with the Divine. The symbol of the American justice system is represented by The Lady Themis, a blindfolded woman from Greek Mythology, who had the gift of intuition. One of the messages from that symbol is that to know truth one has to be blind to physical world influence and go within for the answers. Themis was also the goddess of the Oracle of Delphi. Our ancestral collective consciousness gave us the patterns, as an example, that "I must lose my eyesight to know God", "To be close to God I must lose my eyesight", "To know the truth I must be blind", "To have psychic sight I must be blind" or "If I see the truth I will be punished". I have often heard people in their 40's say 'the eyes are the first to go' and 'My life is half over'.

The collective consciousness around aging and vision loss imply the pattern that with each birthday over 40 you head into physical decline and chronic physical deterioration until your die. Around age 40 the muscles that focus the eye begins to stiffen. This inflexibility in the eye muscles leads to the need for 'readers'. I asked someone one day why they thought their vision acuity had declined to the point of needing 'readers'. The response was 'My mother needed them at my age and I'm just like my mother'. The follow up conversation yielded patterns that as we age our vision will decline and that physically we will have the same experiences as a parent or ancestor. The created pattern 'the eyes are the first to go' may have another root. This statement may have as its source the physical progression of death. Up until the early 1900's the average life expectancy in the United States was 40. During the death process there will be times when a person may appear to be staring off into space and their eyes have a glassy appearance. At this point they may be experiencing hallucinations. When the eyes become glassy and fixed death usually occurs within a few hours. So the euphemism may have had more to do with the life expectancy and a method for anticipating someone's death in our recent past than the actual aging and vision loss as few people made it past age 40.

A person may feel as if someone looking them in the eyes will expose their vulnerabilities. Eye contact would make this person fearful and anxious. Being able to look someone in the eyes is used as a societal measure of whether a person is telling the truth or not. A person fearful of eye contact may have low self-esteem and believe themselves to be sinful, bad or not good enough. They believe that if someone looks them in the eyes the person will 'know' they are not good enough. In the American business world when meeting a new client, job applicant, or vendor it is often noted if they looked you in the eyes. A job applicant that does not make eye contact may not be considered for the job on that basis alone. A judgment is immediately made that they are hiding something. Poor vision supplemented with glasses would create a level of protection for a person fearing eye contact. This aspect of societal interaction is not true for all cultures. Eye contact in some cultures is considered rude and demonstrates a lack of respect. Additionally, the lack of ability to make eye contact is demonstrated in aspects of pervasive development disorders.

In dysfunctional family environments children are often the focus of violence. The violence created suffering for those that witnessed the violence as well as the person that has been physically abused. A child's emotional survival often meant not 'seeing' the suffering. The created patterns developed in this environment would have had the theme of losing your vision to keep from suffering or seeing the pain. Violent behavior demonstrated by a parent is often acted out in school and other social settings by an abused child. A child may be told don't ever hit anyone with glasses (I was). To a child this means violence is OK as long as the other party is not wearing glasses. To a child beleaguered with school, family and social violence glasses become a way of protecting themselves. This would have led to the created patterns focused around a vision loss requiring glasses to stay safe. For example; "People that wear glasses are safe", "my glasses keep me safe", "people that can't see are safe", "If I don't see bad things happen, I will be safe", "I would rather suffer than see the one's I love suffer"," I will be hurt if I see"," I can't bear the pain of watching others suffer", "If I don't see the pain it is not there", or "I can't see the pain of others and survive", etc. I have found the created patterns of shame and humiliation related to reading and writing may be held in the eyes. A feeling of academic shortfall is a form of public humiliation and shame. A child that is humiliated and/or shamed by a parent, teacher or classmates when they read or write may hold that energy in their eyes. A child will connect reading and writing to shame, humiliation and a lack of self-confidence. A parent that drives a child to excel academically is often sending the message that no matter what you do you will never be good enough. An aspect of shame and humiliation is anger or rage at having been shamed or humiliated. In the states of humiliation or shame we must not express the rage. This experience in a person's life would yield created patterns of "No matter what I do I will never be good enough", "when I read/write I will be shamed or humiliated", "it isn't safe to read", "it isn't safe to write"," I am always wrong", "I can't be angry", etc. Wearing glasses as a result of poor vision may become a means to acceptance and recognition.

A person that wore glasses in high school was usually stereotyped as being studious, geeky and socially inept. This person was not one of the beautiful people or the 'in' crowd in high school. If someone needed assistance with homework or passing an exam the people stereotyped as being studious were sought after for assistance and hence became wanted, even if it was for only a couple of hours over algebra problems.
There is a created pattern that any display of emotions is a sign of weakness and vulnerability. Dysfunctional parenting that did not allow for the expression of emotions is often the result of learned behavior from their parents and their parents learned it from their parents. A child's crying may have been frequently stifled by parenting that comes from this pattern. A child may have heard "I'll give you

something to cry about", "Don't cry, everything is going to be OK", "Big boys don't cry", "Your being a cry baby" or "Stop it you big crybaby". This child's parent did not learn how to meet the emotional needs of another person. The crying of a child causes the parent to revert back to the parenting model of their own childhood. The energy of pain, grief, or loss is then stopped in the eyes when the need to cry is halted by fear.

Story: I decided it was time to work on myself. I had worn glasses since I was 11 years old. The unlayering of the created patterns held by my eyes had some 'interesting' side effects. Within seconds of the unlayering my right eye became inflamed and painful. I wore an eye patch for two days because just blinking hurt. Additionally, I was in this state of overwhelm and my heart rate and blood pressure increased dramatically. I wasn't effective at getting the physical stuff to resolve. After 3 days I asked someone to help me. A friend used kinesiology to track back to the core of my eye discomfort. I had unlayered what she perceived to be a tangled knot of energy in my brain stem that was rage. The rage tracked to an incident in the womb. This tangled knot did not have a created pattern that could be intuited to start unraveling it. I felt a bit better after my friend used a series of kinesiology procedures. The eye inflammation reduced by about 50%. Then I traveled back to Tacoma and a friend said she had learned this technique for pulling energy. She placed two fingers lightly at the base of skull and immediately my pulse rate dropped, my eye cleared and the energy released. I had not told her what my other friend had seen and she described with the same exact words what she was seeing in my brain stem. When I visualize what my two friends were seeing I perceived a mass of tangled worms in a hard-packed ball. The mass was made up of the chemistry of emotions passed to the fetus in the womb. **End of Story**

A mother experiencing an event of emotional upheaval in a pregnancy will bath the fetus with the chemicals of those emotions. If a mother experiences the loss of someone close to her during the pregnancy she will bath her child in the chemistry and the energy of grief. If an expectant mother finds out her husband has been unfaithful during the pregnancy she will bath the fetus in a wide array of emotional chemicals and energy. A wide array of emotions (betrayal, abandonment, grief, anger, rage, rejection, loss, etc.) experienced at one time creates a feeling of overwhelm. In this state of overwhelming emotions the mind goes into freeze. There may be no bonding with the infant when it is born because of being frozen in overwhelm. Consequently, the child will be looking for a source of acceptance, love, and bonding in their life. What did this tangled mass of patterns held in place by rage have to do with eyes? The brain stem controls the blood pressure, heart rate and eye movement. The brain stem is the first brain structure in the developing fetus. If the mother felt overwhelm and fear of preservation/survival this energy and chemistry would have affected the brain stem of the developing fetus. The mother may have stuffed her rage for the sake of survival. In America we have statements about anger that reflect the impact on the eyes 'I'm so angry I can't see straight' and ' I'm so angry I'm seeing red'. When I looked at the energy of this mass those statements were aspects of the rage that had been held there.

Created Patterns
1. I am angry at _____ for _____.
2. I feel betrayed by others.
3. I feel betrayed by.
4. If I can't see I can't see the pain of others.
5. If I let others see who I am I will be shamed/ humiliated / rejected / abandoned.
6. If I let people see who I am they won't see me at all.
7. I am invisible to others.
8. I am not worthy of seeing.
9. I am worthless.
10. I am not in control; everything I see is chaos and mayhem.

11. I must give up my vision to have inner sight.
12. I must give up my vision to know the divine.
13. I must be blind to know truth.
14. I will lose my vision as I age.
15. I must be like my mother/ my father.
16. If I wear glasses I can hide.
17. If people see my eyes they will know I am worthless.
18. If I wear glasses I won't be beat up.
19. I am acknowledged as intelligent with glasses.

F's

Face/Head Problems

Fears
- Fear of the future
- Fear of the struggle
- Fear of hardship
- Fears defeat
- Fear of being invisible
- Fear of being judged
- Fear of not belonging
- Fear of being unknown
- Fear of humiliation
- Fear of being wrong
- Fear of not being in control
- Fear of not being good enough

Emotional States
- Facing destiny is a struggle. Not wanting to face what god has given you. Does not want to face the future.
- Living in a dream/ fantasy. Does not face up to reality. Feels un-centered in life.
- Disappointed with what you see in the mirror. Feels disappointment and defeat shows in their face. Depressed at what is in the mirror. Their face shows them what they have been denying.
- No one sees them for who they are. Identity issue. Can't see past the physical form of the face. Feels lost and unknown.

Cross Indexing: Skin problems, Aging, Temple Pain/Pressure

Created Patterns
1. I am ashamed of myself.
2. I am depressed.
3. I am disappointed in myself.
4. I am going to die.
5. I am humiliated by _____.
6. I am rejected by _____.
7. I can't be myself around others.
8. I can't face doing _____.
9. I can't face looking at _____.
10. I can't seem to ever get it right.
11. I don't like/ love myself.
12. I hate what I see in the mirror.
13. I have to be someone I'm not.
14. I must be better than everyone else.

15. I must be something I'm not.
16. I must maintain an image of control/perfection / being on top of everything.
17. I must meet the expectations of others to loved/needed/ wanted.
18. I need the recognition of others to be wanted/needed/loved.
19. I'm not good enough.
20. I'm not safe.
21. I'm not wanted.
22. If _____ I lose face.
23. If I am myself no one will like me.
24. No one sees the real me.
25. Others are better than me.
26. The future is scary.
27. The way people see me hurts.
28. What in your life can't you face (situation, person, or something)?
29. What others think of me is important.

Facial Dandruff

Fears
- Fear of being present
- Fear of being in the now
- Fear of not being good enough
- Fear of making decisions
- Fear of being responsible
- Fear of being an adult
- Fear of going forward

Emotional States
- Longing to be somewhere else and knowing that they can't (self-imposed rules). Journey not taken—holding themselves to a different standard than others. Needing to prove themselves. Not yielding to their needs. They get up every morning and can't face their true self.
- Hoping that some miracle will come along and make their decisions for them. They are waiting for the wave of the magic wand to make it all better. Frustration that their life has gotten nowhere in the comparison to others and/or family.

Cross Indexing: Face/Head problems, dandruff

Repeating Patterns: Finds repeated excuses for not taking the road of expansion. Contracts to stay safe: Financial investments, family, relationships. Buys those lottery tickets as the safe path to cure all of your problems.

Created Patterns
1. I am never good enough.
2. Life is better in other places.

3. I am disappointed with me.
4. Nothing I do is right.
5. Someday someone will save me.
6. I need the short-term gain to be successful.
7. I'm not good enough.
8. I am fed up with life.

Fallopian Tube Blockage

Fears
- Fear of the mother
- Fear of running out of time
- Fear heart hurt
- Fear of never being enough
- Fear of being criticized
- Fear of their creative energies
- Fear of being themselves
- Fear of being vulnerable
- Fear of being authentic
- Fear of not letting go
- Fear of being unsupported
- Fear of moving fast enough
- Fear of failure
- Fear of dying
- Fear of being unable to meet expectations

Emotional States
- Starts projects and can't seem to complete them. Mother issues – highly critical mother – feels as if she can never do enough or be enough. Mother blocked balance of masculine and feminine.

Cross Indexing: Infection, Pelvic problems, infertility

Repeating Patterns: Wounded Creative Core

Created Patterns
1. Something bad is going to happen.
2. I must protect myself from evil.
3. What are the mother issues?
4. What is the shame?
5. I am always criticized when I create.
6. Whenever I do anything good it is always torn down.
7. I can't finish a project.
8. If I do something it is never good enough.
9. Anything I do is never good enough.

10. I must hide.
11. Something always stops me.

Fascia Problems

Fears
- Fear of attack
- Fear of being wrong
- Fear of not hearing correctly or misunderstanding
- Fear of being off balance
- Fear of being taken advantage of
- Fear of being misunderstood
- Fear of being ridiculed
- Fear of anger
- Fear of being truthful

Emotional States
- Holds anger in communication where they feel like they can't say anything that is right. They acquire a guarding, tightening of the body to brace for the next onslaught of being found wrong. They feel under attack.

Cross Indexing: Plantar Fasciitis, Ehlers-Danlos Syndrome, Fibromyalgia, Hernia, Marfan Syndrome, Arthritis – Rheumatoid

Created Patterns
1. I am under attack.
2. I must guard myself.
3. I am not respected.
4. I am taken advantage of.
5. I am always wrong.
6. I am angry at.
7. I can't be angry.
8. I can't speak my truth.
9. I am bullied.
10. People make fun of me.
11. People can't communicate and make sense.
12. I misunderstand people when they try to tell me what to do.

Fatigue

Fears
- Fear of receiving

- Fear of never being enough
- Fear of inner peace
- Fear of self-fulfillment
- Fear of not being able to please people
- Fear of being still
- Fear of not doing enough
- Fear of not working hard enough
- Fear of living
- Fear of saying no
- Fear of inner wisdom
- Fear of letting someone else take over
- Fear of letting go of responsibility
- Fear of letting go

Emotional States
- Very poor sense of personal boundaries. Gives and gives. Feels fearful of receiving.
- Not being on the right path and expending energy for which there is no purpose, no desire. Actions, hence energy, are expended in ways that do not create peace or balance. Feels lost and unsure what to do next so they just keep doing the same thing.
- Action directed in an instinctual pattern with no real purpose or peaceful outcome.
- Out of balance feminine and masculine.

Cross Indexing: Chronic Fatigue, Chronic Illness, Fibromyalgia, Epstein Barr Syndrome, Virus, Depression, Cancers

Repeating patterns: chronic pain, lack of sleep, over stimulation, fear of loss, brain won't shut down when trying to get quiet time, continually pushes the envelope in terms of physical abilities, works past the point of a healthy endurance, lack of awareness of the body's needs and nurturing, doesn't self-nurture.

Created Patterns
1. I am bored.
2. Life is too hard.
3. I want/need to be left alone.
4. People want too much from me.
5. I am fried with my job/ relationship.
6. Who/what do you give your energy away to?
7. What are the boundary issues?
8. I am too tired of living.
9. I must keep going to meet the needs of others.
10. I don't need much, just a cup of coffee.
11. I can't say no.
12. If I listen to my inner voice I would never get anything done.
13. I don't trust my inner voice.
14. I have to fix it, if I don't no one will.
15. If I don't do it, it won't get done.

Fear of Mold

Fears
- Fear of attack
- Fear of where they live
- Fear of being overrun
- Fear of being invisible
- Fear of being unwanted
- Fear of being unloved
- Fear of speaking their truth
- Fear of standing up
- Fear of being authentic
- Fear of not being who others want them to be
- Fear of the rules
- Fear of authority

Emotional States
- Wrong process for being in the world. Yields but doesn't. Fear that something they need to trust is going to attack them. Feels unsafe in their house. Feels under attack. Not safe within themselves. Feels like they attack themselves. Other people won't leave them alone. Feels forgotten and as if what they want doesn't matter.

Cross Indexing: hair loss, anxiety, overweight/weight gain, nasal congestion, respiratory issues

Repeating Patterns: Constantly looking for mold. Doesn't rest until every surface is examined. Passive aggressive response to the actions of others that overrun their boundaries.

Created Patterns
1. I am under attack.
2. No place is safe.
3. I have no peace.
4. People forget what is important to me.
5. I trust no one.
6. I must keep my feelings to myself.
7. I am in danger.

Fever

Fears
- Fear of letting go
- Fear of being dismissed
- Fear of not being respected
- Fear of not being taken seriously
- Fear of not being honored

- Fear of being overrun
- Fear of being seen
- Fear of being controlled
- Fear of being trapped
- Fear of being unprotected

Emotional States
- Feels anxious and inflamed at the cavalier response to a person's being. They take them for granted. Their feelings are not considered.

Cross indexing: viruses, bacteria, infection, blood disorders, endocrine system problems

Repeating Patterns: Weak boundaries being overrun. Plays a subservient role in jobs. Gets passed over for promotions to management positions.

Created Patterns
1. I am angry at _____.
2. I can't let go of _____.
3. I must hang onto _____.
4. I am burning mad about _____.
5. I must protect myself from _____.
6. People always tell me what to do.
7. I'm nobody.
8. People don't think I have a brain.

Fibroid Tumors and Cysts

Fears
- Fear of their creativity
- Fear of their feminine nature
- Fear of spiritual awareness
- Fear of being ridiculed
- Fear of being diminished
- Fear of being discounted
- Fear of people
- Fear of criticism
- Fear of the creative
- Fear of speaking up
- Fear of doing anything outside of conform and perform

Emotional States
- Lack of connection to a sense of the divine. The feeling of expansion when in an experience of inspiration has never been recognized as a connection to our divine nature. Life on earth is the end of it all. Not spiritually inclined, no awareness of spirituality.
- Lack of creativity doesn't connect or resonate with art, music, etc. Life is a grey suit. Feels that the creative is off-limits to them.

Cross Indexing: Reproductive System (female), growths, cysts, Ovarian Fibroids, Ovary Problems, Ovaries-Polycystic, Wounded Creative Core

Repeating Patterns: Gets criticized for an endeavor and they stuff the reaction.

Created Patterns
1. I have been hurt by_____.
2. _____ betrayed me.
3. Women are inferior to men.
4. Boys are better than girls.
5. I hate being a woman.
6. I get criticized.
7. There is no god.
8. There is nothing beyond this life.
9. People are mean.
10. Other people judge me.
11. Everyone is critical of what I do.
12. Every time I try to do something creative I am stopped.

Fibromyalgia

Fears
- Fear of change
- Fear of freedom
- Fear of attack
- Fear of not being controlled
- Fear of being invisible
- Fear that things will never change
- Fear of being forced against their will
- Fear of being trapped
- Fear of authority
- Fear of rules
- Fear of standing up in their truth
- Fear of having no rights or standing
- Fear of being ignored
- Fear of the unknown

- Fear of the future
- Fear of not dying
- Fear of being overrun
- Fear of hope
- Fear of being forced against their will
- Fear of guilt

Emotional States

- Forced to do something against their will. If they resist there is danger. Ongoing effort to control this person via sex. Fear of dying if they defy those in authority. Energy of anger, fear and frustration is turned inward. Their truth is ignored despite requests for help. Feeling of being objectified. Feel they have no rights.
- Fear of the unknown. Life looks really dark. They are in the grip of overwhelming fear. Very low energy and little clarity. Feelings of being overwhelmed and threatened. Safer to stay in the fear than make change.
- Lives in a fantasy world. Inner world is safe. Fear of the light. Fear of new ideas.
- There is a struggle against a barrier imposed by others in authority over this person. The individual is forced to do something against their will. If they resist and break through the barrier danger awaits. There is an ongoing effort to tame the person's sexual energy: attempt to dominate and control via sex. There is an intense fear that if they break the barrier they will die or be in grave danger. There is an intense internal struggle to fight this control within the structure that has been imposed. The energy of anger, fear and frustration expended on the internal struggle is turned inward. Their truth is ignored or not seen despite the request for help. They feel as if they have no rights and no freedom. There is a feeling of being objectified.
- They are caught in an emotional storm. There is nothing to stop the strong feeling of fear of suppressed emotions; anxieties, guilt, and unknown have surfaced. Things look really dark and overwhelming fear grips the heart. Something unknown is emerging from the unconscious. There is a feeling of walking through life with very low energy and little clarity. Feeling of being threatened and overwhelmed. Change is perceived as jarring. It is safer to stay in the fear even though the change could release one from the grip of the strong emotions based in fear.
- Running away from reality, preferring to live in the fantasy world. There is a retreating into the safety of their inner world. There is a fear of bringing light into their world. Fear of new ideas that would open them up to new ways of being. Emotional and Spiritual growth has been cut short/stopped. Heart is heavy with dread. Feels like no one really listens to their plight. They feel invisible in so much of what they do.

Cross Indexing: Fatigue, Fascia Problems, Adrenal Fatigue, Epstein Barr, Depression

Created Patterns

1. Change is dangerous.
2. Freedom is dangerous.
3. I am afraid of _____.
4. I am angry at _____.
5. I am depressed.
6. I am guilty of _____.
7. I am not wanted.
8. I am nothing.

9. I am overwhelmed by _____.
10. I am owned by _____.
11. I am powerless.
12. I am useless.
13. I am worthless.
14. I can't be in the world and be safe.
15. I don't know how to forgive.
16. I don't know how to slow down.
17. I have no control over my life.
18. I must do what others tell me to do to be safe.
19. I must earn the right to be loved.
20. I must earn the right to live.
21. I must not forgive so I can stay safe.
22. I resent _____.
23. I want to die.
24. I'm not worthy.
25. It is safer to hide than be in the world..
26. It would be easier to die than face my life.
27. Life is too overwhelming.
28. No one believes me.
29. No one hears me.
30. People are going to hurt me (this is ALL as opposed to SOME people will hurt me).
31. The world is a dangerous place.
32. The world is a scary place.
33. The world is unsafe.

Fibula – Left

Fears
- Fears being alone
- Fear of challenge
- Fear of giving in
- Fear of being forgotten
- Fear of love
- Fear of dying
- Fear of heart hurt
- Fear of change
- Fear of being trapped
- Fear of being abandoned
- Fear of not being good enough
- Fear of losing their identity and control
- Fear that life will never be pain-free
- Fear that life is one continuous painful struggle

Teachings
- Accepting
- Allowing
- Balance receiving and giving
- Be balanced without pain
- Be flexible
- Be in the flow
- Be listened to
- Be loved without being pain
- Be true to myself
- Be who I am and be accepted by my family
- Be who I am and be safe
- Forgiveness
- Get your needs met without pain
- Give to others
- Good enough
- Let go of the ancestral roles
- Letting go

- Live without being a martyr
- Live without being a victim
- Live without feeling imprisoned
- Live without needing to defend my position of power
- Live without using martyrdom to feel powerful
- Live without using victimhood to feel powerful
- Love yourself
- Stand up to adversity and be safe
- Unconditional Love

Emotional States

- Feels helpless in the face of adversity. Takes on the victim/martyr role. Gains power from their pain. Hardened position.
- Fear of being left behind. Fear of dying from being left behind. Playing out ancient ancestral fears of when someone was injured they were left to die. Feels unworthy.
- Pain is there to bring an out of balance state back to balance.
- Uses the pain/ victim-hood/ martyr to get what they want. Feels in control when using that identity.

Cross Indexing: Leg Problems, Left Sided Negative Tendencies, Fibula – Right

Created Patterns

1. I have been abandoned.
2. I am going to die.
3. I can't do what I want.
4. I'm not good enough.
5. I am left behind.
6. People don't slow down for me.
7. I get left behind.
8. I can't keep up with others.
9. I'm a prisoner.
10. I can't move forward.
11. I have never been free to do what I want.
12. I can't defend myself.
13. My mother/ father did it this way so why change?
14. New ideas are not necessarily good ideas.
15. Change is dangerous.
16. I am sad.
17. I am unhappy.
18. I am depressed.
19. I am alone.
20. Love is pain.
21. The only time people listen to me / love me is when I am hurt.
22. No one listens to me.

23. No one is there for me.
24. I am my mother/father.

*Look at themes of victimhood, power, boundaries, martyr, right, allowing, flow, forgiveness, family, abandonment, ancestors, confrontation, confidence, control, judgment, letting go, loving yourself, now, self-esteem, self-worth, trapped, unconditional love, unmet needs (acknowledgment, attention), boundaries, defenses, power

Fibula – Right

Fears
- Fear of the rules
- Fear of authority
- Fear of leading
- Fear of living
- Fear of connection
- Fear of intimacy
- Fear of self
- Fear of feelings
- Fear of being judged
- Fear of getting their needs met or seen
- Fear of guilt
- Fear of not being good enough
- Fear of not doing their duty
- Fear of not meeting their obligations
- Fear of people's demands on them
- Fear of trusting themselves

Emotional States
- This person holds themselves to a different standard. Doesn't know how to break the behavior of judging themselves. This is a standard created in childhood by an exacting parent who may have been rigid and unyielding.
- Follows others without thought to where they are going.
- Loses themselves in details. Uses the details of life (job, family, household) to keep from living life. They will become singularly focused on a task and pay no attention to the needs of self.
- This person speaks hollow words. They say they are going to do something and it never happens. They give 'lip service' to those around them; a form of passive aggressive behavior that allows them to hide from having to deal with issues of self.

Cross Indexing: Leg Problems, Right-Sided Negative Tendencies

Created Patterns
1. There's no time for me.
2. I must put the needs of others before mine.

3. I must watch myself or I will be seen as selfish.
4. I must judge myself before someone else does.
5. If I do something for myself I am wasting time.
6. It is wrong to waste time.
7. It is wrong to take time for myself.
8. I am guilty (of what?).
9. I'm not good enough.
10. I must do what others tell me.
11. I can't think for myself.
12. The decisions of others are always better than my decisions.
13. I must take care of everyone.
14. I am responsible for everyone.
15. I must give people what they need so they will leave me alone.
16. Feelings are dangerous.
17. I must make promises to people to get them to go away.
18. I must tell people what they want to hear.
19. I don't trust myself.

Fingernails

Fears

- Fear of being around people
- Fear of being bullied
- Fear of being ridiculed
- Fear of being vulnerable
- Fear of criticism
- Fear of authority
- Fear of failing
- Fear of letting go
- Fear of attack
- Fear of being hurt

Emotional States

- Feels vulnerable, insecure, doesn't know how to behave in social situations.

Cross Indexing: Hand problems, Fingernails – Biting

Repeating Patterns: Finds themselves in bullied situations (school, work, family). Doesn't know how to handle being bullied.

Created Patterns

1. People in authority over me hurt me/ betray me/ take advantage of me.
2. I can only see what's in front of me.
3. I am just hanging on.

4. I can't protect myself.
5. I am vulnerable.
6. I am afraid of people.
7. I am only safe when I am alone.
8. People bully me.

Fingernails – Biting

Fears
- Fear of being hurt
- Fear of being worthless
- Fear of authority
- Fear of failing
- Fear of being found lacking
- Fear of not being enough
- Fear of being seen
- Fear of standing up

Emotional States
- Can't protect themselves from abuse, if they try there is more abuse. Feels trapped and unable to escape…cornered.

Cross Indexing: Fingernails, hand problems, ACOA, Abused child

Repeating Patterns: Adult child of alcoholics, abusive home, bites their nail to relieve the building stress from living in an unsafe environment.

Created Patterns
1. I never get what I want.
2. I want to destroy myself.
3. Nothing will ever change.
4. If I don't get the little stuff taken care of I will be hurt.
5. If I don't take care of all the details I am a failure.
6. I want revenge toward my parents.
7. If I stay busy no one will notice me.
8. I am frustrated at _____(What is causing the frustration?).
9. If I try and protect myself I will be hurt.

Floaters – Left Eye

Fears
- Fear of being out of control
- Fear of getting old
- Fear of losing their eyesight
- Fear of losing their faculties
- Fear of the flow of life
- Fear of being wrong
- Fear of seeing their life in ruins

Emotional States
- There is a breaking down of the sense of perception of what they think they perceive, what they have relied on in the past is changing. The old is no longer whole. This breaking down has the effect of casting a shadow or influences how they see the world. They don't allow for the flow of change. Feels that if they stop the change by being critical, then nothing is good but they feel in control of a process that is out of their control.

Cross Indexing: Aging, Eye Problems, macular degeneration

Created Patterns
1. I am falling apart.
2. I must judge to be safe.
3. I've got to slow the world down. Things are changing too fast.
4. My perception no longer seems to be right.
5. What I see I don't like.
6. I am getting old.
7. The whole world is falling apart.
8. Nothing is good about getting old.
9. There is nothing good about the world.
10. I can only see the bad stuff.

Floaters – Right Eye

Fears
- Fear of memories
- Fear of having to deal with the past
- Fear of being present
- Fear of being in the now
- Fear of being responsible
- Fear of being an adult
- Fear of seeing the difficult stuff

Emotional States
- Resistance to truth in the present that is the cumulative effect of past truths. Feels the past should be forgotten.

Cross Indexing: macular degeneration, eye problems, aging, floaters-left eye

Repeating Patterns: Ignores the stuff of life — credit card bills, mounting debt, repairs to the house/car/self. Doesn't take the needed steps to reverse course.

Created Patterns
1. People have it all wrong.
2. Memories are not always good for you.
3. If I ignore it, it will go away.
4. Stuff get better by itself.
5. Life is just too much.
6. I can't keep up.
7. I don't want to see the bad stuff.
8. I don't want to remember what has happened before.

Flu

Fears
- Fear of being trapped in a cycle of nothing
- Fear of being unworthy
- Fear of the future
- Fears being vulnerable
- Fear of being overrun
- Fear of being taken advantage of
- Fear of boredom
- Fear of letting go
- Fears of never being able to escape
- Fear of great expectations
- Fear of failure
- Fear of being put down by others

Emotional States
- Conflict has kept them from understanding their true goals in life. They are more focused on knowing short term information just to get through a day than looking at the big picture of their life. They feel held down by the mundanity of friends, family, and community. It feels like they have been doing the same thing for centuries.
- Desire to not let go of the past. Held firmly in the grip of anxieties and loss from a time of no worth. Feelings of no worth follow them like a dark cloud over their head. Judged unworthy by

people of no standing. Yearns to be somewhere else. Helpless to not be in their space. Driving expectations to exceed expectations so they can be worthy, so they won't fall short.
- Clearly not qualified to have expectations of life. Too concerned about where they are not. Holds themselves down. Fires out at others when they can't get up. Highly idealized concepts keep them from achieving.

Cross Indexing: virus

Created Patterns
1. Bad things are going to happen.
2. It's all bad out there.
3. The world is a bad place.
4. Life is just too much.
5. There is no one to take care of me.
6. I don't know how to be nurtured.
7. I don't know how to be nourished.
8. I don't know how to be cherished.
9. Everybody is going to die.
10. I am overwhelmed by life.
11. I am being smothered by work/ family.
12. I can't stand my life.
13. I want out.
14. I am the victim.
15. I am overrun.
16. I am taken advantage of.

Focal Dystonia

Fears
- Fear of being out of control
- Fear of not being relevant
- Fear of authority
- Fear of being creative outside the rules
- Fear of being wrong
- Fear of being vulnerable
- Fears visualizing and hearing about it
- Fear of doing anything without a problem to solve

Emotional States
- Need to control but feels out of control, so keeps trying harder.
- Critical at a micro-managing level, tries to take over a project that is not theirs, doesn't allow others to create and feels really vulnerable when they don't know what is going on. Can't visualize an outcome of a creative project. Shuts down hearing the solution — doesn't get it.

Cross Indexing: Parkinson's Disease, Brain Problems

Repeating Patterns: Won't do a creative project unless it has a purpose. Needs to stay safe. Creativity is confined to a solution to a problem.

Created Patterns

1. I am in control.
2. I am out of control.
3. When I do things my way I am happy.
4. I give people advice to make it better.
5. I must show people how to do it right.
6. I must not make a mistake.
7. I will get hurt if I get it wrong.
8. I never get it right.

Foot Problems

Fears

- Fear of no peace
- Fear of not doing
- Fear of not working
- Fear of moving forward
- Fear of being stopped
- Fear of being stuck
- Fear of being tied to the old ways
- Fear of the unknown
- Fear of the future
- Fear of being taken advantage of
- Fear of falling
- Fear of failing
- Fear of being out of balance
- Fear of not pleasing everyone
- Fear of disappearing
- Fear of their worth not tied to doing
- Fear of trusting others and self

Emotional States

- They feel like they have high expectations that can't be met. A need to always be working. Feel like their always putting up with a lot. Feels as if they are wearing thin.

RIGHT FOOT

- Not being allowed to move forward. Feels bound to the past. Needs flexibility in the answers. A sense that if they move forward they step into nothing.

LEFT FOOT
- Plays the role of the peacemaker. Is always balancing. It always feels like they are walking the tight wire. It is deeply ingrained that if you make two people get along then you are safe. If there is no peace there is no safety and no balance. As the Peacemaker you give up part of yourself with each peacemaking until there is very little of yourself.

Cross Indexing: Bunions, Left or Right sided tendencies, Leg Problems

Created Patterns
1. I am afraid to step forward in my life.
2. I am afraid to go forward with my life.
3. I am so confused I can't go one-way or the other (What is the confusion?).
4. I am in the wrong place.
5. I am afraid of making the wrong decision (What happens if you make the wrong decision?).
6. I am going the wrong direction.
7. Others stop me from going forward with my life (who are the others?).
8. I am stuck.
9. I hate having to deal with life (bills, relationships, job, etc.).
10. I must constantly be moving to be safe.
11. There is never enough time in the day to get things done.
12. The more I get done the better I am.
13. The more I do the more I am liked / loved / wanted / valued.
14. I don't trust the universe to provide.
15. I must make things happen.
16. I don't trust god.
17. I don't trust others.
18. I don't trust my inner voice.
19. There are people standing in my way.

Frontal Skull Bones

Fears
- Fear of being blamed
- Fear of the brick wall
- Fear of planning
- Fear of looking forward
- Fear of moving forward
- Fear of seeing too much
- Fear of having to hold the secrets
- Fear of being seen

Emotional States
- Doesn't see what needs to be done in time to avoid disaster. Keeps running headlong into the same issue over and over. Hits the wall and then blames the wall as they bang their head on it. Feels like they are not responsible for their obstacles in life.

Cross Indexing: face/head problems

Created Patterns
1. I never get anywhere.
2. There's always a wall in my way.
3. Someone is always stopping me.
4. If I see too much I will die.
5. If I don't do it I won't be blamed when it goes wrong.
6. Something always stops me.
7. If I do something I will be seen.
8. I must not move.
9. I need to be invisible.

Fungus

Fears
- Fear of attack
- Fear of being blindsided
- Fear of happiness being taken
- Fear of the unknown
- Fear of not having unknown needs me
- Fear of cooperating with others
- Fear of carrying the burdens
- Fear of being the only one responsible
- Fear of being submissive
- Fear of not being in control
- Fear of their own creativity and insight
- Fear of safety
- Fear of being trapped
- Fear of not hurting
- Fear of never having enough
- Fear of being hopeless
- Fear of moving
- Fear of allowing
- Fear of change
- Fear of being authentic and being safe
- Fear of being overrun
- Fear of being looked down upon

- Fear of memories
- Fear of disappointment

Emotional States

- Feels creepy, feels like most of life has an unnerving quality to it that blocks light, joy and happiness. Always on guard, always searching but can't see what they think is there that prevents their happiness.
- Unknown developments create nervousness. Feels unlucky. Feels like they can never get what they want. But they never express what they want, it sits there wasting away unseen to the world.
- Joint participation with others feels like a struggle. No true concept of partnership. Feels like they are the one carrying the load and pulling a tremendous weight. They don't allow. Their manner is dominant and subversive. They create the energy of no partnership.
- Holds the light out in front of them like a beacon that can never be reached or achieved. They sit in darkness and refuse to see the light within. They think that it is only on the outside and not for them.
- Healthy optimism turns to jaded expression in the same sentence. Battling dualistic concepts that raise joy and then dash it. Hostile concepts of a human's true nature is their platform for life. They have been cautioned and so they fly back and forth between the two hoping to find safety. When they get to one concept or the other they still feel unsafe.
- Forever running. Running from the inside pain of darkness. "If I do this or if I eat that or if I go there it will all take me away from what haunts me". They wear a tattoo of their pain for the world to see. Their pain holds them and prevents them from living.
- Jinx, judge, jury. Doesn't want time to be there. Wants – is always wanting, craving and trying to fill the void of that craving – the pit that cannot be filled. Hibernates as a way of justifying the wanting and craving. Sweetness (the good stuff of life) is for others not them and outside and only creates pain and misery.
- Errant ideas are unfocused and grow into dead end caves of hopelessness and instead of turning around and going back to the opening of the cave into light they keep bumping into the cave wall thinking that with a little more effort it will open.
- Hard on themselves and others. Belittles! Feels justified in knocking down others and other ideas. Even their own. Stagnant. They don't move they just rot within their judgment.
- There is no light. They feel in the dark. They are not being who they are and they are angry.
- Overrun. Killing me softly. A desire to not be free. Being held in place by the dysfunction. If they lets go of the dysfunction they will unravel. The dysfunction is the identity dysfunction. Intolerance of the world. Old stuff.
- Lack of initiative in making needed changes.
- Lack of motivation in cleaning up the waste.
- Hanging onto the past.

Cross Indexing: Body part affected, constipation, liver problems, Candida, itching, adrenal fatigue, diabetes, cancer

Created Patterns

1. Change is too much work.
2. Changing things won't make it better.
3. I am conflicted by _____.
4. I am disappointed by _____.

5. I am disappointed in myself.
6. I can let go of the past.
7. I can't change.
8. I can't forgive _____.
9. I resent _____.
10. I resent being taken advantage of.
11. I was _____ then (a time when you felt things were better).
12. If I change my way of thinking I disrespect/ dishonor my family / mother / father.
13. Just because it's new doesn't mean its better.
14. Movement is too much work.
15. No one loves me.
16. Nothing is good enough (and you have to remind people of it).
17. People disappoint me.
18. People take advantage of me.
19. The past is better than the present.
20. Things are good the way they are.
21. Things fall apart when changes are made.
22. Things were better when _____.

G's

Gall Bladder Problems

Fears
- Fear that someone would be better than them
- Fear that someone will have something they don't
- Fear of things not being done their way
- Fear of being taken advantage of
- Fear of people taking things
- Fear of abandonment
- Fear of not being in control
- Fear of change
- Fear of growing
- Fear of being not enough

Emotional States
- Pushing back against experiences that should be viewed as learning. Feels entrenched, stubborn, in their position. Instead they fall back into a very rigid idea that the experiences are there to prove them inadequate. The experience crystallizes as points of anger turned to bitterness. Keeps trying to make others have their value set.

Cross Indexing: Gallstones, Liver Problems, Digestive Problems, Gallbladder Polyps

Created Patterns
1. I am angry at _____.
2. I am bitter toward _____.
3. I must make things my way.
4. It's my way or the highway.
5. Nothing ever changes.
6. People take things from me.
7. What is being taken away from you?
8. I am abandoned by _____.
9. If I don't make things happen they fall apart.
10. Why should I learn from the crazy stuff others do to me?
11. I am not in this world to makeover people. They should just do what they are supposed to do.

Gallbladder Polyps

Fears
- Fear of not being good enough

- Fear of being unloved
- Fear of being unwanted
- Fear of their anger being seen
- Fear of someone knowing they are angry
- Fear of their anger
- Fear of their brokenness
- Fear of authority and the rules

Emotional States
- They don't like themselves. They have turned their anger inward. Something happened to them as a child that made them not feel good about themselves. They have a sense of feeling broken, not whole. This was reinforced by training later in life.
- Feelings of bitterness are compartmentalized, stuck away so no one can take that from them.

Cross Indexing: Gall Bladder problems, Wounded Creative Core

Created Patterns
1. I don't like myself.
2. I am broken, no good.
3. My parents treated me as if they wished I would go away.
4. I am unwanted / unloved / unneeded / left behind.
5. I am angry at how I was treated in childhood.
6. I must guard myself from people who treat me badly.

Gallstones

Fears
- Fear of father/masculine
- Fear of letting go
- Fear of peace
- Fear of being unwanted
- Fear of being unloved
- Fear that there will be no retribution
- Fear that the scales will never balance
- Fear that others will not believe them
- Fear of guilt
- Fear that others see their pain
- Fear of being judged
- Fear of someone else winning
- Fear of losing
- Fear they will prove their father right

Emotional States

- Wants others to feel what they feel. Puzzled at why others are not seeking the same level of vengeance they are wanting because of the harm done. They have a bitter sense of wanting retribution for the bad things that have been done. Lies to make the wrong seem worse to others to build the intensity of it so they can sway the judgment of others.
- They want nothing more than to let go of the grip of anxiety they feel. There is a deep fear of a wrong they committed that will come to the surface. They are afraid they will be found out. There is a sense of guilt that must be born – maybe for the rest of their life. They know they will never be whole and they will never be able to live a life free of the burden they carry.
- Wound up in criticisms. Constantly criticizing and judging others so they can be safe from what others might say. Always on the offense otherwise someone else will win and they will become nothing. Winning is not sweet. Winning is hard and bitter. They can never stop and hold the accomplishment. There is a father's voice that says 'you'll never do it, you will always be a worthless loser'.

Cross Indexing: Gallbladder Problems, Wounded Creative Core, Gallbladder Polyps, Liver Problems

Created Patterns

1. Having feelings make me weak and stupid.
2. I am bitter toward _____.
3. I am envious of _____.
4. I am jealous of _____.
5. I am unloved.
6. I can't be myself.
7. I can't forgive _____.
8. I can't just allow things to happen.
9. I don't know how to forgive.
10. I don't trust myself.
11. I must be someone else.
12. I must hide my feeling.
13. I must listen to others to be accepted/ safe.
14. I'm not good enough.
15. I'm not worthy.
16. If I give in then things go wrong.
17. If I give in then there is chaos.
18. If people want what I have I have to keep giving.
19. If people want what I have they have to pay for it.
20. It is safe to listen to my inner voice.
21. It isn't safe to feel.
22. Listening to my inner guidance will get me into trouble.
23. My mother/father abandoned me.
24. My mother/father did not want me.
25. My way is the right way.
26. People only want me for what I can do for them.
27. People take advantage me.

Ganglion Cyst – Left wrist

Fears
- Fear of new ideas
- Fear of being wrong
- Fear of being found to be lacking
- Fear of not being good enough
- Fear of growing
- Fear of change
- Fear of being unloved
- Fear of being unaccepted

Emotional States
- Restricts new ideas with old prejudiced concepts. Will kill a new concept before it has unfolded to understanding and knowing. Feels the new could prove their foundation to be wrong. Feels threatened by new information.

Cross Indexing; cysts, skeletal system, joint problems, wrists

Repeated Patterns: Shuts down, kills new ideas by pulling back into a defensive mode and taking the life force out of a new idea or concept.

Created Patterns
1. I must criticize and tear apart new ideas. If they are true they will stand up, if not they will go away.
2. I want new ideas to fail so that my foundation of beliefs is safe.
3. I don't want to understand an idea within the sense of knowing, it must be logical.

**May change based on the location of cyst in the wrist. This is based on a thenar location.

Ganglion Cyst – Right Wrist

Fears
- Fear of not being the victim
- Fear of losing their victim identity
- Fear of being unloved
- Fear of choice
- Fear of making the wrong decision
- Fear of not being believed
- Fear of being disrespected
- Fear of creativity

Emotional States

- (right wrist just below thenar) Competing ideas that conflict with creativity, creates rigidity in your life. Can have an association with prostate or uterine issues. Feels that neither idea is right and so they choose neither to not be wrong.
- Emotions have hardened which are tied to rigidity. Holds out the cyst as evidence of their wounding. Self induced rigidity and inflexibility keeps them from making major needed changes in their life. Feels that if they make changes they will lose their victim identity. Gives them an outward excuse for not engaging your creative energies. Feels like they have to have physical evidence of their victimhood.

Cross Indexing: wrists, joint problems, cysts, skeletal disorders

Repeating Patterns: Wounded Creative Core, victim

**May change based on the location of cyst in the wrist. This is based on a thenar location.

Created Patterns

1. Being creative makes me vulnerable.
2. If I use my creative energies I will be ridiculed.
3. I must be rigid to protect myself.
4. If I keep myself from being creative it allows others that space and focus.
5. I must sacrifice myself for others.
6. Change is not possible for me. I've got to stay the course to be safe.

Gastritis

Fears

- Fear of knowing their hatred for 'mothering'
- Fear of mother/ maternal presence
- Fear of feeling good
- Fear of the unknown
- Fear of life
- Fear of growing
- Fear of living
- Fear of being wrong
- Fear of being unloved
- Fear of feeling devastated
- Fear of trusting others
- Fear of anger

Emotional States

- Warmth of feelings has gone. They are left with a cold aching contraction. Heartache became a stomach ache. Held themselves and others to a standard that has been violated. They left the realm of knowing to a place where everything was questionable. What they took in gave them no solace and soon turned cold and hurtful. Their values were being gnawed around the edges and called into question. Feels under attack by the maternal. They take in the anger from the maternal or nurturing source and it becomes self-destructive.

Cross Indexing: Infection, stomach problems, Ulcers-Gastric, Cancer – Stomach, Colitis, Anemia, indigestion, bloating

Created Patterns

1. I'm not sure about anything.
2. The world is a dangerous place.
3. I am not good enough.
4. I'm afraid of _____.
5. Everything I do is wrong.
6. I get hurt by the people I love.
7. I must punish myself when those that love me are angry.
8. People fail me.
9. I must swallow other people's anger.
10. Nurturing is hurtful.
11. What is supposed to make me feel good is all wrong/painful/destructive.

Gastroesophageal Reflux Disease (GERD)

Fears

- Fears saying no
- Fear of guilt
- Fear of knowing too much
- Fear of growing
- Fear of rocking the boat
- Fear of changing a relationship from mutual passive-aggressive
- Fear of change
- Fear of letting go
- Fear of space that leads to the creative
- Fear of placing yourself first

Emotional States

- Overrunning of boundaries. They are striving to understand themselves, spiritually and someone keeps overrunning their boundaries. Interrupts their internal reflections and understanding to leave to have the interrupter's needs met. This someone feels left behind and wants to slow them down and be part of what they are experiencing. They feel guilty if they don't honor the request for time by the other person. So they give up their understanding of self for harming – builds an irritation with every interruption. They feel guilty if they say 'no'.

Cross Indexing: Esophagus Problems, Digestive system disorders, Gastritis, stomach problems

Created Patterns

1. I can't decide what is good for me.
2. I am afraid to make changes and move forward with my life.
3. I am stuck.
4. I must manipulate others to get love.
5. I can't express myself.
6. I swallow my pain.
7. I can't face my pain.
8. What in your life burns you up?
9. Someone is always interfering with my creative time / me time.
10. I allow others to interrupt my me-time to have harmony.
11. I feel guilty if I declare my space.
12. I must meet the needs of others before meeting my own.

Gingivitis

Fears

- Fear of their world collapsing in on itself
- Fear of overwhelm
- Fear of being overrun
- Fear of motion forward
- Fear of completion
- Fear of the creative
- Fear of being wrong
- Fear of saying no
- Fear of losing an identity that does is not responsible
- Fear of failure
- Fear of not being invisible

Emotional States

- All their needs are sidelined by a feeling of overwhelm that when faced with an ongoing challenge they can't do it. They feel that the entire structure will collapse. So they put off doing anything.

Cross Indexing: Gum Problems, Pyorrhea, Gums-Bleeding

Created Patterns

1. I am a procrastinator.
2. I can't finish anything.
3. Promises are lies.
4. I don't know how to solve problems.
5. I don't know how to finish a project.

6. I don't know what it feels like to solve problems.
7. I can't focus on one thing at a time.
8. I don't know what structure feels like.
9. I can't say no.
10. I'm not safe if I finish.
11. I am a loser.
12. I am a goof off.
13. I am a failure.
14. I am no good.
15. I don't know how to overcome the weight of meeting the expectations that are placed on me.
16. I am afraid I will fail.
17. I am irrelevant to meeting the expectations of my life.

Glaucoma

Fears

- Fear of being wrong
- Fear of needing others
- Fear of being out of control
- Fear of the conform and perform
- Fear of being forced to obey
- Fear of having others come before them
- Fear of being ignored
- Fear of being disrespected
- Fear of not being first
- Fear of being challenged
- Fear of being unsupported
- Fear of the box
- Fear of being disappointed

Emotional States

- Incorrect assumptions about life. Holds hate. No way to understand why their attitudes don't work. Feels out of control and nothing is safe. Wants to be allowed to do what they want to do without ramifications and resent being told they are wrong. Holds anger at parents. Needs to be patronized (revered) as the holder of knowledge. Insensitive to the needs of others.
- Wants to be allowed to fly — unwilling to take the measures needed to learn to fly. (This is a metaphor. They are looking to have grandness in their life but unwilling to do the work to get there.) Resents the restrictions of having to work and earn the right to be something or do something. Will not put in the commitment to make stuff happen. The world owes them a living. Wants the justification of why they should adhere to society rules — resents societal rules.
- High expectations of the people around them. The people in their world can never meet their expectations and so they feel let down and disappointed. Wants to be led to the answers does not want to use their own energy to understand or learn. They want it given to them.
- Yielding to authority makes them angry. Hates being wrong. Wants life on a silver platter. Inability to walk in the path of others. Feels constrained by the rules. Sees the world in terms of how can I get around this so that I make my own rules. Does not want to take orders from anyone.

Cross Indexing: All diabetes information, knees/legs/feet, peripheral neuropathy, heart issues

Created Patterns

1. I hate _____.
2. Nothing works out for me.
3. The world is not a safe place
4. I feel like everything is out of control.
5. Who are people to correct me?
6. I know more than most people and I should be looked up to.
7. I deserve to _____.
8. The world owes me.
9. I'm never wrong.
10. I make my own rules so I don't have to do what anyone else says.
11. I have been expressing/feeling strong emotion of _____ for a long time (these are negative emotions: hatred/resentment/anger/rage/bitterness/grief/sorrow/revenge/ grief).
12. What truth about yourself are you denying?
13. Who are you holding a grudge against?

Good Pasture's Syndrome

Fears

- Fears being taken advantage of
- Fear of flow
- Fear of allowing
- Fear of being out of control
- Fear of being taken advantage of
- Fear of joint efforts
- Fear of that someone else will sabotage them
- Fear of being hurt
- Fear of not being enough
- Fear of trusting others
- Fear of not being heard
- Fear of having to explain what they need
- Fear of ridicule
- Fear of responsibility
- Fear of failing

Emotional States

- Leans into the wind. Always going against the flow. Feels like life is a struggle so they have to struggle in all they do. Always working to make a solution to a problem harder than it should be by taking the hard way. Always warrants less attention to the details that yield the direction and creates consistent sabotage.

- Joint endeavors fail miserably. Hard-won sympathies are squandered in their attempt to justify failures. They sabotage their lives in all things requiring other people to work or act cooperatively. Fails to notify or tell others of their intentions and then gets angry when no one reads their mind and the situation fails. Feels better as the lone-ranger. Doesn't trust others to do their fair share. Feels like they will take the credit for their work, so they don't play.

Cross Indexing: Autoimmune, kidney problems, connective tissue disorders, lung problems

Repeating Patterns: Victim

Created Patterns

1. I can't seem to cooperate with others.
2. People don't understand me.
3. I can't hold things together.
4. People misunderstand me.
5. People should know what I need.
6. People should know what happens next.
7. People should take responsibility.
8. I am not responsible for other people's failures.
9. I don't seem to be able to get a good partner.
10. I can't work with others.
11. I am disappointed when others don't know what I need.
12. I am disappointed when others don't step up.
13. The details are not important.
14. When I fail it is someone else's fault.
15. Other people sabotage my efforts.

Gout

Fears

- Fears being unloved
- Fears being abandoned
- Fear of being dominated and controlled
- Fear of conflict
- Fear of disharmony
- Fear of being wrong
- Fear of letting others in
- Fear of not being needed
- Fear of rejection
- Fear of not being acknowledged

Emotional States

- They failed at a relationship that became impossible in time. They kept trying to play catch up and they kept failing until it was no longer possible. Feels hopeless and out of sync.

- They allow themselves to be controlled by another so they can keep the relationship on a peaceful plane and small resentments build. Feels anxious when there is conflict or conflicting ideas.

Cross indexing: Kidneys, Arthritis, sprains, osteoarthritis, metabolic disorders, plantar fasciitis, bursitis, overweight

Created Patterns
1. I am angry at the world/at_____.
2. I must control the world around me.
3. Everyone else is wrong.
4. I must do everything for it to be right.
5. I can't get _____ to love me.
6. The people I love most reject me.
7. I keep trying to get their love and I fail.
8. My life is out of control.
9. I must have outer peace at the cost of my own inner peace.
10. I am controlled by others.
11. I let others control me so no one gets mad.
12. I have a lot to lose if I don't let them control me.

Graves Disease

Fears
- Fear of being used
- Fear of being out of sync and unable to fit in
- Fear of not belonging
- Fear of others seeing their weaknesses
- Fear of the flow of life
- Fear of being loved
- Fear of giving love
- Fear of being outside the box
- Fear of being authentic
- Fear of their creativity
- Fears being wrong
- Fears the space of silence
- Fear of being hurt
- Fear of betrayal
- Fear of being challenged
- Fear of not being worthy

Emotional States
- Fear of being vulnerable. Living situation not nurturing. No giving and receiving. No creativity. No movement or growth. Creativity makes you vulnerable. Rigidity in the way they must live their life. Fear of living an authentic life. Lots of structure and rules. Life has no joy. Feels

creative through the accomplishments of others and then expresses their jealousy at their accomplishments.
- Walled off from others. No one else's way is right, only their way is right. Feels insecure if things are not done their way. If they try to break out of rigidity then they get knocked back into their 'place'. Talks excessively to create a barrier.

Cross Indexing: Thyroid Problems, Autoimmune Disorders, Hyperthyroidism

Created Patterns

1. _____ has hurt me.
2. _____ betrayed me.
3. _____ use me.
4. Being creative is dangerous.
5. Being honest is dangerous.
6. Being vulnerable is dangerous.
7. Change is dangerous.
8. I am being attacked.
9. I am depressed.
10. I am not any good.
11. I am worthless.
12. I can't listen to what others have to say.
13. I can't speak my truth.
14. I can't trust others.
15. I don't know how to give.
16. I don't know how to receive.
17. I don't know what joy is.
18. I don't trust people.
19. I must do things my way to be safe.
20. I must dominate a conversation to be safe.
21. I must protect myself from _____.
22. I should die.
23. If I am creative people will hurt me.
24. If I am myself people will hurt me.
25. If I am myself people will make fun of me.
26. Listening is dangerous.
27. My way is the right way.
28. People use me.
29. Speaking the truth is dangerous.
30. The world is unsafe.

Growths – Skin

Fears

- Fear of being rejected
- Fear that no one will ever see their pain

- Fear of being seen as lacking
- Fear of being seen as imperfect
- Fear of being seen as flawed
- Fear of being seen as broken
- Fear of being unworthy
- Fear of being relegated to nothing

Emotional States
- They wear their feeling of being unworthy on the outside. The feeling has pushed from deep within to the surface for you to take a look at. The feeling of being unworthy is so deep it feels hard-wired into your identity. Everything they do is in a field of feeling a sense of already rejected.

Cross indexing: Moles, warts, cysts, sebaceous cysts, spurs, skin tags, viruses, genetic

Repeating Patterns: victim

Created Patterns
1. I am angry at _____.
2. I resent _____.
3. I can't believe creator would help me.
4. I was hurt by _____.
5. I can't forgive _____.
6. I am unworthy.
7. I am rejected.

Gum Loss (Gingival recession)

Fears
- Fear of letting go
- Fear of disappointment
- Fear of presence
- Fear of revealing their creative self
- Fear of the conform and perform
- Fear of feeling
- Fear of dominate masculine energy
- Fear of being questioned
- Fear of their inner pain
- Fear of living
- Fear of life
- Fear of anger
- Fear of losing their victim/martyr identity
- Fear of being powerless
- Fear of saying no
- Fear of space

- Fear of being nothing

Emotional States

- Anger over inability to let go of a relationship. Anger is disappointment of self and is projected onto others.
- Has not been able to let go of past and create a new present. Creative, nurturing and intuitive aspect of personality needs to move to the surface. Unexpressed anger over having to perform according to society's definition of their role in life.
- Stopped feelings…doesn't want to feel. They feel vulnerable.
- Person has shut off the feminine aspect of self. Relationship problems. Suffers from tunnel vision.
- This person is angry. There is something in their life that needs to be removed. They have attempted, several times, to cut ties or sever a relationship. These efforts have been marked by intense emotion. The anger has a lot of energy to it. This anger is around a disappointment of Self and the anger has been projected onto others. This relationship had/has an emotional, physical, and spiritual connection.
- The feminine aspect of this person's nature (nurturing, creativity, intuitive, loving) is wanting more of a role in their life. This person may be starting over and in the process going through purification through changes of belief systems and opening to higher spiritual knowledge. There is an unexpressed anger or rage coming from a masculine aspect of or in this person's life. This person feels overpowered and oppressed by this energy. There is martyr energy prevalent and they have not taken responsibility for their own life yet. This person feels locked into a role defined for them by their culture/society. They have not yet figured out how to release the past and create a new present.
- This person feels like they have a core of stability and security on a material level. They get things done. But, there is a flow of emotions that they can't seem to protect themselves from. They work really hard at keeping themselves from feeling. The effort to keep from feeling is a rote way of dealing; they bury themselves in work, classes or a creative effort. They have a routine of projects that keep them from feeling. The effort to do this sometimes fails and they are left feeling open and vulnerable…it takes a lot of energy to hold back the rain.
- The feminine aspect (nurturance, caring nature, intuitive) of this person is closed-minded and as a consequence their vision is restricted. There is a relationship that is in need of being mended. The difficulty in this relationship has gotten out of hand and the problems associated with it appear to go on without end. This person has a spiritual awareness. The relationship needing mending has represented an ending or death. There is a sense of being judgmental around this relationship. They have pondered this situation but their tunnel vision has prevented them from seeing that they are the ones being negatively affected by this disharmony. They may feel emotional or physical pain as a result of this relationship.
- The masculine aspect of this individual is carrying a heavy burden in their heart. There is an aspect of this person's life that is causing them great difficulties. This person is going the wrong direction. They are retreating in the face of being close to accomplishing their goals. Their path has been marked by personal stubbornness, disharmony and unhappiness. This person has used this way of being in the world to control others. They have taken on responsibilities belonging to others and in so doing avoiding dealing with their own stuff. They then interpreted this as being the long suffering martyr. Their beliefs were based on being 'practical' and frugal.
- Not considering the foundation or source of words before they are spoken. The words can have no merit and therefore can have a negative value. These vacant words can carry an energy that delays the implementation of getting things done.

EMOTIONAL PATTERNS

Cross Indexing: Periodontal Bone Loss, Teeth Problems, Gums-Bleeding, Pyorrhea, Gingivitis

Created Patterns
1. I don't know how to carry through on decisions.
2. Angry people are dangerous.
3. Angry people will hurt me.
4. Being seen is dangerous.
5. Breaking the rules is dangerous.
6. Confrontation is dangerous.
7. Feelings are dangerous.
8. Feelings make me vulnerable.
9. I am a martyr.
10. I am a victim.
11. I am afraid of looking stupid.
12. I am angry at _____.
13. I am bitter towards _____.
14. I am disappointed in myself.
15. I am guilty of _____.
16. I am intimidated by others.
17. I am powerless to change things.
18. I am taken advantage of.
19. I can't forgive _____ (myself-who else?).
20. I can't let go of what is bad for me.
21. I can't make my own decisions.
22. I can't say no.
23. I don't know how to follow through.
24. I don't know what is good for me.
25. I don't trust myself.
26. I don't trust others.
27. I doubt myself.
28. I hate _____.
29. I have let myself down.
30. I must be frugal.
31. I must be practical.
32. I must do what I am told to do.
33. I must follow the rules.
34. I must judge others to be safe.
35. I must work hard to make things happen.
36. I must work hard to survive.
37. I push others away from me to be safe.
38. I take on others responsibilities/duties.
39. If I do something wrong I will be rejected/wrong/laughed at/shamed.
40. It is dangerous to make a mistake.
41. It is hopeless.
42. It is my duty/responsibility to help others.
43. Judging others keeps me safe.
44. Life is a burden.
45. Life is a struggle.

46. My anger keeps me from looking at my SELF.
47. My anger keeps me safe.
48. My anger protects me.
49. My emotions/feelings overwhelm me.
50. My way is best.
51. My wounds protect me.
52. People who yell are always right.
53. Taking risks is dangerous / stupid.
54. Things will never get better/change.
55. What happens if you finally let go?
56. I am confused about what needs to be done next.
57. What I say has no merit.
58. I say things I shouldn't.
59. I gossip and spread false information.
60. When I say false/meaningless words I alienate people and they will not help me or listen to me.
61. I don't get things done because I don't have the forethought about what is needed to get it done.

Gum Problems

Fears

- Fear that people will not allow them to have peace
- Fear of moving
- Fear of completion
- Fear of peace
- Fear of doing
- Fear of being forced against their will
- Fear of being pestered

Emotional States

- They must be pressed to move. They feel a deep reluctance. They only 'do' when the danger of not doing is greater than the danger of putting off. Danger = Consequences/Risks

Cross Indexing: Gums-Bleeding, Gum Loss, Pyorrhea, Heart Problems, Diabetes, Kidney problems, Alzheimer's, Asthma, Osteoporosis, and Cancer.

Repeating Pattern: Passive Aggressive

Created Patterns

1. I don't know how to carry through on decisions.
2. I perform best under pressure.
3. I need a deadline to get things done.
4. If I don't do it, it will just go away.
5. It's safer to just not do anything.
6. I must be forced to act.
7. I am forced to do things against my will.

8. I'll just do enough to get people off my back.

Gums – Bleeding

Fears
- Fear of making decisions
- Fear of attack
- Fear of not being good enough
- Fear of failing
- Fear of not being able to perform
- Fear of being lost
- Fear of no place to be
- Fear of criticism
- Fear of letting people down

Emotional States
- Life is a pressure cooker of anxiety, unmet expectations and disappointment. There is never enough time to get done what is expected and other things start to not get done.

Cross indexing: Gingivitis, Gum Problems, Pyorrhea, Gum Loss

Created Patterns
1. I can't be happy.
2. Bad things happen when I make decisions.
3. I must do something about not getting things done
4. I can't get it all done in one day. People are pressuring me and I cannot meet their expectations.
5. My life is falling apart.
6. I am under attack for not being able to get it all done.

H's

Hair – Balding

Fears
- Fear of being powerless
- Fear of mortality
- Fear of losing their prowess
- Fear of being rejected
- Fear of dying
- Fear of being ineffective
- Fear of being unworthy

Emotional States
- Loss of power, loss of function, sign of mortality and aging, loss of youth, loss of agility, hurt that they are diminished and betrayed by nature. Lost sense of masculine action; risk, bold movement, adventures. Traded in the wild masculine for the security of civilization – feeling that they have been tamed.

Cross Indexing: Aging, Alopecia, Prostate Problems

Created Patterns
1. Baldness is not reversible.
2. I have hair loss.
3. I am unworthy.
4. I can't accept myself.
5. I don't love myself.
6. I am rejected.
7. It's genetic.
8. It runs in my family.
9. It's my mother's fault.
10. I am losing my power.
11. I do not have the energy to do what I need to do.
12. I am going to die which is something I see every morning in the mirror.
13. I have lost my desire for adventure and the newness of life.

Hair – Falling Out

Fears
- Fear of no control

- Fear of being vulnerable
- Fear of being wrong
- Fear of being challenged
- Fear of attack
- Fear of uncertain certainty

Emotional States
- They feel like you have lost their protection. The world has become unsafe with a change, with job, family, etc. What used to feel safe and secure, and feeling protected has gone.
- Inflexibility in their thinking to see the other point of view. They view their inflexibility as a power. The power is about control, domination and strength (outer strength and authority).

Cross Indexing: Alopecia, Endocrine Gland problems, stress, autoimmune disorders, polycystic ovaries, aging, weight loss, anemia

Created Patterns
1. I am powerless.
2. I depend/ trust others to keep me safe.
3. I am stuck and can't change things.
4. I am unsafe. I have no one or nothing to protect me anymore.
5. I am in control. I dominate the situation. I know better than everyone else.
6. People must do what I say as I am the authority.
7. I am inflexible and unwavering in my opinions. After all I am smarter than everyone else.

Hair – Ingrown

Fears
- Fear of being judged
- Fear of being shamed
- Fear of a long hidden secret being revealed
- Fear of being present
- Fear of their power
- Fear of attack
- Fear of disappointment
- Fear of being hurt
- Fear of their lack of confidence being seen

Emotional States
- Ancestral hidden shame. Possible fear of judgment if someone knew their truth. An ancestor's heart was broken (a romance, a betrayal). This heart break may have been passed to their children's children. They may be keeping a secret so that people will not see their vulnerability. They are afraid to let someone in that close. They will keep things hidden and their true motivation from being seen. They have the wrong idea about what vulnerability means. Looking

for the justification for showing self to others and can't find it. They hide their power and their ability to stand up for themselves. Feels a lack of self-confidence. Sense of power to make things happen is depleted; probably from an early trauma/ or ancestral trauma where they felt powerless to change what had happened.

Cross Indexing: infection, skin problems, pimples, face/head problems, genetic

Created Patterns
1. I am shamed.
2. I feel ashamed of everything and I don't know why.
3. I am afraid of what people will find out.
4. I constantly have the heartache of disappointment.
5. If I let someone in close they will discover my secrets.
6. If I let someone in close they will hurt me.
7. I can see no reason to open with others.
8. I am vulnerable to attack.
9. I don't think I can stand up to people.
10. If I play dumb and weak people will leave me alone.
11. I have no confidence in myself.
12. I am powerless to make this better.
13. I can't make anything work.
14. I must keep my lack self worth hidden.
15. I must keep my feeling of inadequacy hidden.

Halitosis

Fears
- Fear of being crowded
- Fear of being unworthy
- Fear of being overrun
- Fear of the future
- Fear of finishing
- Fear of being responsible
- Fear of knowing
- Fear of knowledge

Emotional States
- People invade their space and they don't know how to tell them to back off. They feel overrun and crowded.
- They don't feel like what they have to say is worth saying. They feel unworthy. They feel stupid at times especially if they say something that brings attention.

Cross indexing: Gastro-esophageal Reflux disease, Mouth problems, gingivitis, gum problems, infection, stomach problems, esophagus problems

****For those with the skill of smelling a disease, the a specific odor may indicate a specific disease

Created Patterns
1. I can't see what needs to be done.
2. If I worry _____ (what won't happen?).
3. I will never get anywhere.
4. I will never reach my goals.
5. If only I had _____ I would have reached my goals.
6. I am unworthy.
7. I want people to stay out of my space.
8. I am stupid when I offer an opinion that is out of alignment with what other think.
9. I should just keep my mouth shut. No one wants to hear what I have to say.

Hand Problems

Fears
- Fear of letting go
- Fear of being forced against their will
- Fear of the future
- Fear of change
- Fear of being wrong
- Fear of being undeserving
- Fear of their truth being challenged
- Fear of authority
- Fear of being giving without receiving
- Fear that they will be stopped from getting what they want

Emotional States
- Anger, frustration at being forced to do something against their will, etc. Any strong feeling present while they are using their hands, that feeling will be directed to your hands.
- They are hanging onto people, things, and situations that they have no control over. They don't feel like they can let go. They think that if they do let go bad things will happen/ they won't be loved.
- Can't hold onto the things they want in life. They don't know why those things slip through their fingers. They reach out, hold and then it's gone.

Cross indexing: Left & Right-sided negative tendencies, wrists, arm problems, carpel tunnel

Created Patterns
1. I am afraid of making mistakes.
2. I can't reach for what I want.
3. I must not be seen as incompetent.

4. I can't communicate verbally (Why can't you say what you need to say?).
5. I can't speak my truth.
6. I can't do what I really want to do in life.
7. No one gives without wanting something in return.
8. If I give I expect the favor to be returned.
9. People take advantage of me.
10. I must do everything myself.
11. I hate what I do for a living.
12. I wish I could do something else with my life.
13. People in authority over me hurt me/ betray me/ take advantage of me.
14. I can only see what's in front of me.
15. I am just hanging on.

Hashimotos Disease

Fears
- Fear of attack
- Fear of familial betrayal
- Fear of new ideas
- Fear of not belonging
- Fear of inner wisdom
- Fear of being nothing
- Fear of being unworthy
- Fear of being nothing
- Fear of responsibility

Emotional States
- Failure to move forward in life and feels under attack for not doing so. Misaligned values have kept the person locked into a pattern of behavior that limits their outlook. This limitation is based on limitations of the past. Holds others at a distance and judges them based on an outlook from the past. This judging has the effect of coming back as an attack on themselves. There is confusion when their worldview is cause for being under attack. They have said what they thought was true and then it was turned against them.
- Forgets to be allowed to know their own truth. Wanders from pillar to post only to hear it's not here, feels lost in a universe where they don't feel like they belong. Looking for their truth externally when they should be looking inward. Heart is bound to an innate sense of nothingness. Wants someone else (needs) to lead them out. Heart is worn out by being nothing. There is an energy of self attack with the feeling of worthlessness and not good enough. Responsibility feels like an attack. So there is a secondary gain of keeping responsibility away.
- Heart is wounded by the past. Heart holds the person hostage. They are trapped by their own woundedness. Their wounds become the reason for living — a justification. The wound wants to be to heal but there is a forcing of the search for justice that keeps the wound open.
- Justification for existence is found in their search (this is hollow). They are in a search for meaning and inclusion in a world that feels as if they do not belong.

- Being attacked for a desire to live in a place of fairness, balance and truth. A place where their perception of their needs are met.
- Surprise attack coupled with betrayal from those that are trusted.

Cross Indexing: Thyroid Problems, Autoimmune Disorders, Hypothyroidism, Inflammation

Created Patterns

1. I am under attack.
2. I don't love myself.
3. I am depressed.
4. What is the stress you are living under?
5. I must hide my illness.
6. I am powerless to make changes.
7. No one believes me.
8. No one listens to me.
9. I'm not good enough.
10. I can take care of myself.
11. Everyone is out to get me.
12. People sabotage me.
13. I am going to die.

Headache

Fears

- Fears losing control of emotions
- Fears letting energy of emotions go, needs to keep it in
- Fear of being in social situations
- Fear of being with other people
- Fear of meeting people
- Fear of being expected to talk to people
- Fear of not knowing what is expected of them next
- Fear of never being free

Emotional States

- The world is a tense place. Never know how they should be in the world. They do not know how to react or act. No training or exposure to the world before they left home. Led an isolated, restrictive, abusive childhood.
- Living conditions create stress. High pressure to perform in every aspect; work, home, relationships, no peace to relax or be. Longs to escape. A headache gives them an out.
- Hatred and anxiety haunt their presence. Can't be in the present. Memories pull them into the past. No control over what keeps surfacing. When they are not present they have no influence over the present either.

Cross indexing: Headache – Migraine, ACOA, Post Traumatic Stress Disorder, Temple pain/pressure, stress

Created Patterns

1. I can't control my feelings.
2. There's no good anywhere.
3. I'm better than other people.
4. I am frustrated that I have not done enough.
5. I can't face _____.
6. My life is out of control.
7. I can't forgive him/her for _____.
8. I can't get over being upset by _____
9. I feel like I'm going to explode.
10. I can't let go of the way things are.
11. I have been expressing/feeling strong emotion of _____ for a long time (these emotions: hatred/resentment/anger/rage/bitterness/grief/sorrow/revenge).
12. I live in constant unrelenting stress; my only out is a headache.
13. People are always pulling at me. They need me to do this or that. There is no peace.
14. I have no control over what happened to me.

Headache – Migraine

Fears

- Fear of loss
- Fear of phantoms (there is a sense that they are carrying the traumas of past ancestors)
- Fear of authority
- Fear of being accused of being wrong
- Fear of showing who they really are
- Fear of letting others down
- Fear of not meeting expectations
- Fear of being pulled in different directions
- Fear of attack
- Fear of being shown to be less than

Emotional States

- Inner conflict with being told what to do and knowing that their way would be the best way. They have to prove the other way wrong. Frustration / anger level is high and it is turned inward. They don't believe they have the power to express themselves to authority.
- Fear of being authentic self. Fear that they are not good enough. Fear of being judged. Fear of being vulnerable. Anxiety when in the spotlight.
- Never enough time. The lack of time creates a sense of failure. Failure produces anxiety because they can't meet the expectations of others.

- Being torn between two worlds, two culture, competing value systems and demands. They are expected to be one person at work and then be someone else at home and then yet again be someone else in the community or two cultures with concepts or mores that conflict.
- People in their life reflect back to them their non-acceptance of themselves. They struggle to be comfortable in their own skin and others remind them of that. They attack their appearance, what they say and what they do. They are always lacking this in a reflection of what they lack – self-acceptance.

Cross Indexing: ACOA, stress, Post traumatic stress disorder, headache

** Ancestral trauma of prolonged periods of loss and grief, creating emotional changes such as depression. Sense of hopelessness and helplessness that are enough to create epigenetic changes that affect serotonin production.

**An intense fear of loss or grief during pregnancy that affected serotonin levels of the mother.

Created Patterns
1. I must take things at my own pace.
2. I hate being pushed.
3. It is too dangerous to remember.
4. Everyone wants a piece of me.
5. I am afraid of doing something wrong.
6. I am afraid of everything.
7. Everything is my fault.
8. I can't handle pressure/stress.
9. I want control.
10. There is never enough time to get things done.
11. I can't say no.
12. People expect too much from me.
13. I must be perfect.
14. I must meet people's expectations.
15. I am a failure.
16. I must do what others tell me to do.
17. I don't trust myself.
18. I don't trust my intuition.
19. I fear the judgment of others.
20. I am rejected for who I really am.
21. I can't create who I really want to be.
22. Being seen is dangerous.
23. If I fail I am not good enough.
24. If I am wrong I will be rejected/not accepted/not love.
25. I'm not good enough.
26. I'm not worthy.
27. I must prove others wrong to be seen as valuable.
28. I must prove others wrong to be right.
29. I can't say no.
30. I don't have good boundaries.
31. I put pressure on myself.

32. I am going to die.

Headache – Tension

Fears
- Fears loss
- Fears the unknown
- Fear of something bad going to happen
- Fears not doing it all
- Fears being present
- Fear of attack
- Fear of being blindsided
- Fear of the future

Emotional States
- Forgets that they are human and have a limited capacity for doing. All doing consumes and there is no being. They forget or suppress their own physical, emotional and spiritual needs to meet the needs of others. They do this so they hold onto what they think they 'have'. A deep fear of loss. Their intense doing is a way of staying in control so that they won't lose what they think they 'have'.
- Life is a mystery and how it works, feels puzzled and confused by the energy and behavior. Constantly trying to make sense of things and as such is on guard/heightened state of awareness so that they can keep what they don't understand away. If they relax something will happen that they don't understand and it could hurt them.
- Life is a jumble and they are constantly trying to sort it out. They focus much of their physical and emotional on trying to sort out what feels continually unsorted. Failure to lead-there is the expectation that they are responsible for getting things done, for making 'it' happen, doing it all and when that doesn't happen there's an internal sense of tension created. There is always this underlying vague sense that something bad is going to happen if they don't do it all.
- Hopeless feeling of never going to get there, can never feel finished, never get to the finish line. Nothing feels completed. A sense that they are trapped in a cycle of hopelessness–will never get out. No pleasure in life. No relief from the trapped cycle.

Cross Indexing: Headaches, Headache-Migraine, stress, anxiety

Created Patterns
1. I must do it all, others are depending on me.
2. If I don't get it all done on time I am a failure.
3. I have no time for myself.
4. I have no time to be, I've got to do.
5. If I don't keep it all together I will lose everything.
6. I must do to stay in control.
7. I am afraid of losing _____.
8. I don't understand people/life/the world.

9. I have to stay vigilant to the potential of bad things .
10. I don't know what's going to get me but I have to be on guard for it.
11. I can't finish, get it done, on time, so I panic.
12. The situation is hopeless, I can't change this and I can't find a way out.

Hearing – Hyper Acute

Fears
- Fear of hearing too much
- Fear of being abandoned
- Fear of hearing pain
- Fear of hearing I am unwanted
- Fear of being unheard
- Fear of hearing anger
- Fear of hearing violence
- Fear of hearing I am unloved
- Fear of trusting your inner guidance
- Fear of listening to your inner voice

Emotional States
- In a hyper-aware state from birth. Born with intuitive centers on high alert to survive. They knew they were being born into a difficult environment. Discordant energy hurts; yelling, loud music. They need to know if there is going to be a loss or change to protect themselves.

Created Patterns
1. I am unloved/ unwanted.
2. I don't trust myself.
3. I don't trust my inner voice.
4. I am in pain when I listen.
5. I am unheard.
6. I must be on guard at all times.
7. If I know too much I will be safe.
8. If I don't know enough I will be unsafe.

Hearing Loss (Deafness) – Left

Fears
- Fears loud noise
- Fears the unknown
- Fears overwhelm
- Fears being unloved
- Fears intimacy
- Fears relationships
- Fears being accused

- Fears heart hurt
- Fears attack

Emotional States
- Adjustment to changes felt like a shock, not ready for the changes. Thought things would just continue the same. Modern world changes were overwhelming – shut down to keep out of overwhelm. Felt frozen in the expectation of more loud sounds. This feeling may have been present at birth. The sounds of the world were overwhelming with no context…the instinctual sense of survival set in – maybe epigenetic influence that loud noises = danger without context. They feel like they are being torn apart by what they are seeing and hearing.
- Childhood jealousy during play turned angry and violent. The caretaker (parent/ relative/ babysitter) anchored the feeling of being disobedient – not listening to commands. Protects self from not being loved. May run away from a relationship before they think those words would be spoken.

Cross Indexing: Joint Problems, Heart Problems, Ear Problems, Hearing – Loss

Created Patterns
1. I don't want to hear what is going on.
2. I don't love myself.
3. I am worthless.
4. I give up hearing to be safe.
5. I must sacrifice my hearing to be safe.
6. I'm not worthy.
7. I want to be alone.
8. I want to shut the world out.
9. I'm afraid to hear what's going on.
10. It's dangerous to hear what people say.

Hearing Loss (Deafness) – Right

Fears
- Fear of being unheard
- Fears being unwanted
- Fears being irrelevant
- Fears losing power
- Fears being diminished
- Fears judgment
- Fears overwhelm
- Fears having many masters
- Fears being manipulated
- Fears being taken advantage of by others
- Fears being worthless
- Fears being unloved

Emotional States
- Fights to have their ideas and opinions heard. Feels like their ideas are not valued by those around them. Feels constantly put down and de-valued. Feels like they are constantly beating their head against a brick wall to do what they believe is right. Feels like they are always in conflict with the will of others.
- Juried by others. Their life is constantly under examination and criticism by the people around them (family, friends, job relationships, etc). They feel measured against the individual criteria of each of those people and they can never please anyone. They don't know what standard to live by since there are so many. And it is safer to do what someone says but they don't know who.
- Constriction of sound – the level of sound being spoken by others is used as a means of manipulation by a person in their life. They strain to hear this person. It become convenient to turn a deaf ear – power struggle between the constrained speech (maybe whispering) and the other person they are speaking to.
- Feels like they are being torn apart by what they are seeing and hearing.

Cross Indexing: Ear Problems, Hearing – Loss, Heart Problems, Joint Problems

Created Patterns
1. I don't want to hear what is going on.
2. I don't love myself.
3. I am worthless.
4. I give up hearing to be safe.
5. I must sacrifice my hearing to be safe.
6. I'm not worthy.
7. I want to be alone.
8. I want to shut the world out.
9. I'm afraid to hear what's going on.
10. It's dangerous to hear what people say.

Heart Problems

Fears
- Fears letting go (identities that come from a heart that feels devastated)
- Fear of their memories
- Fear of cruel people
- Fears forgiveness
- Fears being abandoned
- Fear of shame
- Fear of humiliation
- Fear of being alone
- Fear of being locked in endless sadness
- Fears giving to self
- Fears receiving

- Fears not being able to give enough
- Fears being found lacking
- Fears disappointment
- Fears being unloved
- Fears losing external source of support
- Fears trusting others
- Fears being seen in need
- Fears chaos
- Fears heart hurt
- Fears having love taken

Emotional States

- The heart is about the ego grace of love. Someone hurts us and our heart is hurt. We love someone and our heart is happy. But the heart of the heart is the truth of love that moves us beyond the boundaries of ego grace.
- A sadness; the sadness is a place of non-struggle. There is a giving up.
- The heart is about giving and receiving. The Left atrium is receiving from others and the right atrium is about receiving from self. The mitral valve is a door between self and others (a boundary). The mitral valve not opening and closing properly would be a question of whether you should be giving or receiving, an issue of when to give and receive. If the heart is enlarged then there could an issue around emotional overwhelm.
- Heart Left Atrium – expectations of others lead to disappointment, what is received is less than what was expected (receives oxygenated blood – receiving from others)
- Heart Left Ventricle – energy to sustain is external, no joy from within of giving to self. (sends oxygenated blood out to the body)
- Heart Right Atrium – undeserving of receiving from yourself (nurturing, love, the "selfs") (de-oxygenated blood enters – receiving from self)
- Heart Right Ventricle – letting go of what needs to be changed (receives the de-oxygenated blood and then sends blood to lungs for oxygenation)
- Their heart has been hurt over and over again and trust is gone. They are fearful that their heart will be hurt again so they put up walls around allowing themselves the opportunity to be vulnerable.
- Doing for others to the point of being depleted. Giving and giving to others but not to self.
- People pleaser.
- They are missing balance that comes from honoring the wisdom of the heart through it's connection to a higher awareness.

Cross Indexing: Congestive Heart Failure, Teeth Problems, Ear Problems, Cardiovascular Problems, Veins, Arteries, Vision Problems

**Social/Cultural transitions will create trauma reflected in the heart. For example: when people started to marry for love instead of being told who they would marry, this created heart trauma. Marriage moved from being grounded in family and the security of the family within a culture or group consciousness to a heart energy it created a rift in the connections to family and societal mores.

Created Patterns

1. _____ betrayed me.
2. I must give and give to be wanted/ loved.
3. Everyone else comes before me.
4. I am anxious about _____.
5. I am burdened by _____.
6. I am denied love/good things/happiness/nurturing.
7. I am hurt but no one knows it.
8. I can't accept/receive love.
9. I can't accept _____.
10. I can't let go of _____.
11. I don't know what it feels like to be nurtured.
12. I don't trust people
13. I have been expressing/feeling strong emotion of _____ for a long time (these are negative emotions: hatred/ resentment/ anger/ rage/ bitterness/ grief/ sorrow/ revenge/ resentment).
14. I have a broken heart.
15. I have to bear the pain alone.
16. I have to hide my pain.
17. I must dwell on the negative so that bad things do not happen.
18. I was abandoned by _____.
19. I will never let _____ happen again.
20. I'm not loved.
21. Love hurts.
22. Love is dangerous.
23. I'm not cared for.
24. My heart is broken.
25. No one really cares about me.
26. They don't believe me.
27. To show my pain is to show them where I am vulnerable.
28. If I cry I will be hurt.
29. Change is dangerous.
30. You must not look at things too closely.
31. It is dangerous to 'see'.
32. I will be hurt if I see.
33. Crying is a waste of time.
34. Crying is for babies.
35. I can only survive if I don't see.
36. I can't let them/him/her know I saw.
37. I must not see to hide the truth.
38. The eyes are the windows of the soul.
39. If I love someone they will only hurt me
40. I can't let go.
41. If someone looks me in the eyes they will know (what truth are you hiding?).

Hemorrhoids

Fears
- Fears getting one more promise
- Fears no one sees what they need
- Fears letting go of what they shouldn't
- Fears being compelled to give

Emotional States
- Feels anger and frustration at not being able to get their needs met. But, they keep their needs to themselves. Not getting their needs met makes them tense and frustrated. They try to create a flow, manipulation, that gets their needs met and all they get is resistance and sabotage.

Cross Indexing: Colon, Anorectic-Bleeding, Anus Problems

Created Patterns
1. I am burdened by _____.
2. I can't let go (What can't you let go of?).
3. I am being pressured to _____.
4. I must hold it all in.
5. I can't let go of _____.
6. I am afraid of _____.
7. _____ makes me tense.
8. I never get what I want/need and when I ask for it I am met with million reasons why I can't have it.
9. I am angry that I give and give and never get anything in return. I feel frustrated that I don't know what else to do.

Henoch Schonlein Purpura

Fears
- Fears being ignored
- Fears not being taken seriously
- Fears confrontation
- Fears losing their victim identity
- Fears the present
- Fears the unknown
- Fears the future

Emotional States
- The person feels distance (could be an aspect of time) is the answer to everything. They run or put distance between themselves and the situation at hand. Wants to always view everything from a distance. Hatred of a relative that wants to force the person to look at stuff and not turn away or

run away from situations. There is a victim energy at play that wants to show the world they are under attack and someone is mean to them. The attack is stuck on the surface. Weak boundaries.

Created Patterns

1. I don't want to change.
2. I am angry at _____.
3. I am afraid of _____.
4. I hate _____.
5. I resent _____.
6. I am under attack.
7. I am the victim.
8. People try to force me to do stuff against my will.

Hepatitis

Fears

- Fears knowing
- Fears understanding
- Fears being wrong
- Fears being hurt
- Fears their injustice will be taken
- Fears letting go
- Fears the scales will never be balanced
- Fears feeling anything except hot emotions (anger, frustration, etc.)

Emotional States

- Hatred of a singular person became the focus of inflamed emotion. This person hurt them and they have never been able to let go of the anger/hatred and figure out why they did what they did. They stopped all understanding.
- Hostile information created a bit of crazy and agitation. Instead of allowing it to play through the emotions, they blocked all flow around it. The feelings crystallized into anger.

Cross indexing: liver problems, autoimmune disorder, virus, inflammation, Epstein Barr syndrome

Created Patterns

1. I don't want to change.
2. I am angry at _____.
3. I am afraid of _____.
4. I hate _____.
5. I resent _____.
6. Someone hurt me and I can't forgive or forget what they have done to me.
7. I don't want to know if they had a justification for hurting me.
8. I can't let go of how I feel. It's not up to me to make it right.

9. I let someone take my peace and it is up to them to give it back to me.

Hepatitis C

Fears
- Fears defeat
- Fears powerlessness
- Fears the big stuff
- Fears being seen
- Fears their feelings
- Fears boundaries
- Fears standing up
- Fears a heart that feels

Emotional States
- Unyielding need to have power in the most mundane of situations. Yet they cave in on the big stuff. No energy to do the big fights. Feels justice/justified in the little fights. Their quality of life is benign. Their life is not growing or effective. There is no sense of knowing in their life (this would represent a disconnection between minds). They feel they don't deserve a sense of power in their life. They live their life at the edge of nothingness. They feel no meaning to their existence. To be powerless is survival. To have boundaries will get you killed. Boundaries are dangerous. They control the minutia to be safe. Hopelessly numb to the world at large (Does not engage in the bigness of living. Does not engage in dialog or thought around politics, religion, world hunger, economy, environment, etc.). Does not feel they can affect the whole, so why bother.

Cross Indexing: Virus, liver problems, inflammation, infection, shingles

Created Patterns
1. I give up.
2. I can't change anything in a world that is really messed up, so why bother.
3. I am powerless to authority/people better than me.
4. I must control the little stuff of life.
5. I am always right when it comes to the little stuff of life.
6. I must listen to what my head tells me to do.
7. My life doesn't have meaning and I focus my energy on doing the little stuff. I don't feel a need or want to know or learn about who I am.
8. If I am powerless in the face of confrontation I will be safe.

Hernia

Fears
- Fears being vulnerable
- Fears revealing their secrets
- Fears being seen as week
- Fears people getting close
- Fears being put in a box
- Fears not being able to hide their secrets

Emotional States
- Under pressure to be more giving and open with others about their weaknesses and secrets
- Guilt keeps them being open about their weaknesses

Cross indexing: Intestinal problems, muscle problems, abdominal problems, Lumbar Hernia, Umbilical Hernia, Hiatus Hernia, Epigastric Hernia

Created Patterns
1. I am angry _____.
2. I am being burdened by _____.
3. I don't want to be close to _____.
4. I use my hernia to push people away.
5. I must punish myself.
6. I am so _____ I could just explode.
7. I can't hold it together.
8. I have secrets about how I am in the world and people are pressing to know more about me.
9. I have no inner strength and I feel like I could crumble at the least amount of pressure.
10. I don't want people to know me I feel like they want to psychoanalyze me and judge me and put me in a box.

Herpes Simplex (Cold Sores)

Fears
- Fear of attack
- Fear of not being good enough to speak their truth
- Fear of not being allowed to speak their truth
- Fear of being unwanted
- Fear of being criticized
- Fear of being overrun
- Fear of being intruded upon
- Fear of being responsible
- Fear of too much
- Fear of being put on the spot

Emotional States
- Feels under attack at how they are seen.
- Shuts down in the face of information that is unkind or unwanted.

Cross Indexing: Virus, Herpes-Simplex II, Shingles, Liver Problems, Hepatitis

Repeating Patterns: defensive, overwhelmed, people invade their space

Created Patterns
1. If I express my anger.
2. I carry a heavy burden.
3. I am overwhelmed with life.
4. I am overwhelmed with responsibilities.
5. I can't cope with life.
6. I resent having to be responsible for _____.
7. I am under attack.
8. People get me wrong.
9. I am seen as defensive.
10. I must defend myself against attack.

Herpes Virus Simplex II

Fears
- Fears being seen
- Fears being acknowledged
- Fear of flow
- Fear of life
- Fear of being present
- Fear of their divine nature
- Fears being not good enough
- Fear of there not being enough
- Fear of being stopped from what they want
- Fear of being unloved
- Fear of abandonment

Emotional States
- High anxiety around life and living. Hard on themselves. Looking for answers in the wrong places. Living in the wrong place /town/ city/ state. Their energy is out of resonance with their place of residence. Hates being seen. Believes that if they are seen no one will love them. Holds the wrong things to be of value. What they hold of value is in opposition to their core values. Unable to grasp that life is not about them. That they are only an element of the cosmology of life. Does not see a cosmology. Very shortsighted in their vision of the grand scheme/ wheel of life.

- Unexpected needs/desires keep them off balance. Indifferent to how their motivations affect others. Lives life on the edge of desire. Wants to be seen as good enough. Looks to others to balance them in a virtual way…vicarious living. Always just on the edge of coming into balance with their desire. But, does not go that next step taking them to balance.
- Wants more than they have. Hardly able to afford what they have. Never have enough. Nothing is good enough. Thinks that others should give it to them. Attracts others that believe they are not good enough so they work to be good enough for this person. But they will never be good enough because for this person they are never good enough. Unwilling to change. Sees nothing wrong with themselves. Its always the other person and they are stopped by the others that restrict their ability to get what they want (this is their perception).
- What did come through in the above information is that there is impairment of the root chakra. Our community/tribal connections affect the root chakra. You will want to look at worthiness, imbalance and confusion as to what to do next, dissatisfied, feels blocked, no self-acceptance, feels unloved and insecure.

NOTE: There is a common wisdom related to Herpes Simplex Type II that it is related to sexual guilt. That information did not emerge in this body of work.

Cross Indexing: Viruses, Herpes-Simplex, Shingles, Liver Problems

Repeating Patterns: Victim

Created Patterns
1. I need the disease to be accepted (by others with herpes).
2. I don't know what creator's unconditional love is.
3. I feel guilty about _____.
4. I am afraid of being in another relationship.
5. Sex is wrong/ sinful.
6. Sex is dirty.
7. I feel ashamed.
8. I can't say no.
9. I am being punished by god.
10. I hate myself.
11. I am anxious about _____.
12. I am angry at _____.
13. I want revenge against _____.
14. I am angry at my sexuality.
15. The virus is triggered every time I feel worthy.
16. The virus is triggered every time I feel unworthy.
17. I know the difference between my worthiness issues and the viruses' worthiness issues.
18. I know the difference between my abandonment and a virus's abandonment energy.
19. I have to pretend to be someone else to be loved.
20. I must run away from difficult situations.
21. The big picture of life is irrelevant to me, it doesn't change things.
22. If someone really sees who I am they won't love me. I am unlovable.
23. I have no belief that anything is bigger than the life I am in right now.
24. Life is always throwing a monkey wrench at me. It's one breakdown after another.
25. If I act a certain way someone will want me.

26. When things are chaotic I come into my own and feel in control.
27. I attract in partners that know I am not good enough and that they love me as long as I am not good enough.
28. I never get what I want in life.
29. I can't afford it but I will get it anyway.

Hiatus (Hiatal) Hernia

Fears
- Fears being treated like a child
- Fears the loss of adult power
- Fears being powerless
- Fear of happiness being taken away
- Fear of being lost
- Fear of becoming invisible
- Fear of becoming like their parents
- Fears life will be swallowed up by family
- Fears being caught living their own life
- Fears being caught not living their cultures values
- Fears being unloved or unwanted

Teachings
- Joy
- Creator's perspective on your culture

Emotional States
- Generational pain that is hard to swallow. Leaves no taste for life, joy is suppressed.
- Does not take the time to understand the perspectives of others / family. Reacts from a place of power being taken away. Feels at risk of being powerless.
- Let's others tell them what to do and think. To do otherwise dishonors the generational burden of pain being carried in the family. Family is everything – no room for personal power. Feels lost in the family structure.
- Living a life in contradiction of their parent's values. Rejects the values held by their parents. Feels their values are wrong.
- Punishes themselves by repeating behaviors that they know will make them sick…eating spicy food, drinking alcohol, etc….so they can feel something. Feels numb.

Cross Indexing: Lumbar Hernia, Umbilical Hernia, Epigastric Hernia, Hernia, Stomach problems, GERD, Cancer-Esophagus, Esophagus Problems

Created Patterns
1. _____ has left me feeling bitter.
2. Being myself would get me punished.
3. Family is everything.
4. I am bitter toward.
5. I am guilty of _____.
6. I am guilty of everything.
7. I am powerless around my parents/ mother / father / siblings.

8. I can't be happy if _____ is suffering.
9. I can't be happy if my mother / father/ _____ isn't happy.
10. I can't be who I am with my family and be safe.
11. I can't breathe around my family.
12. I don't understand what they want from me (who is the they?).
13. I have to live up to my parent's expectations.
14. I must do what my father says.
15. I must do what my mother says.
16. I must punish myself for disobeying.
17. I punish myself.
18. I will never be allowed to be myself as long as my parents alive.
19. I will never be as good as _____.
20. I'm not worthy.
21. If I try to be my own person I will be disowned by my family.
22. My mother / father make me feel guilty for _____.
23. The rules are constantly changing.
24. There's no room for me.
25. Things won't change because that's been the way it's always been.

Hiccups

Fears
Fears vulnerability
- Fears not saying the right thing in the right way
- Fears letting go
- Fears injustice
- Fears being shamed
- Fears being judged
- Fears retaliation for saying what they feel
- Fears being wrong

Teachings
- Calm
- Let go
- Creator's definition of emotions
- Be in control of your behavior
- Listen to your body's emotional cues
- Understand what your body is telling you
- Express my feelings
- Be loved
- Be lovable
- Live without fear of being wrong
- Be wrong and be safe

Emotional States
- Controls emotions, hard to keep it in, desire to express feelings keeps erupting. Doesn't know what to do with emotions or how to express appropriately. Doesn't understand what they are feeling. Experiences keep trying to jar the feelings loose that are stuck. Emotions are not expressed at the time it is appropriate.
- Holding out for justice, wants revenge or justice for a perceived slight to their honor. Feels diminished by the slight. Won't let go or forgive.
- Feels shame for making a mistake.

Cross Indexing: Nerve Problems, Diabetes Mellitus I, Diabetes Mellitus II, Constipation, Addiction – Chemical, GERD

Created Patterns

1. _____ dishonored me.
2. I am afraid to say anything.
3. I am angry at _____.
4. I am justified for being _____.
5. I am vulnerable.
6. I can never think what to say at the time I am challenged / hurt / disrespected / dishonored.
7. I can't express my emotions be safe.
8. I can't forgive _____.
9. I can't let go of _____.
10. I can't say what I feel.
11. I can't stop what I am doing.
12. I don't know when to stop _____.
13. I must keep a stiff upper lip.
14. I must keep my anger in.
15. If I am wrong I will be shamed / humiliated.
16. If I express myself I am wrong.
17. If I express myself I will be judged / criticized.
18. It is dangerous for me to express my emotions.
19. It's wrong to say anything about how you feel.
20. No one loves me.

*Look at themes of denial, control, emotions, feeling, letting go

Hip Problems

Fears

- Fear of being present
- Fears disconnection from ancestral roots
- Fears connection to family
- Fear of connecting to others
- Fear of a purpose
- Fear of nothingness
- Fear of their inner self
- Fear of change
- Fear of letting go
- Fear of lack of financial support (right)
- Fear of lack of emotional support (left)

Emotional States

- Ancestral loss. Person has experienced the loss of their ancestral identification

- Life feels dull and boring. There is a sense that they are just plodding through to make to the next day. There is a feeling of no energy, no passion, no interest. There is nothing that inspires.

Cross Indexing: PTSD, Leg Problems, Back – Sacral, Pelvis Problems

Created Patterns
1. Life is just one day after another.
2. There is nothing I really want to do.
3. There is not flow in my life.
4. I am afraid of making major decisions.
5. I have nothing to look forward to.
6. I have no one to lean on.
7. I am all alone.
8. I am not supported.
9. I have to do it all.
10. I can't accept what's going on right now.
11. I am all alone in my suffering.
12. I am all alone.
13. I don't know who I am.
14. No one wants me.
15. I am losing all my family.
16. I am losing all my friends.

Hives

Fears
- Fear of letting go
- Fear they don't know what's good and what's bad
- Fears not being good enough
- Fears that others will see they are not good enough
- Fear that no one will ever see what they have to offer

Emotional States
- Concludes that they need to not let go of the stuff that is bad for them. They feel as if they are not good enough at their job, parenting, school, etc. They replace one toxin for another and it has no place to go except outside of the body.

Cross indexing: shingles, virus, rash, inflammation, allergies, skin problems

Created Patterns
1. What are the hidden fears?
2. I am mistreated.
3. I must protect myself from others getting close.

4. I am afraid of _____.
5. I need to speak my truth.
6. I am trying to do something that I am really bad at and I am not good enough to be doing it.
7. I am stressed about being in a human body.

Human Papilloma Virus (HPV)

Fears
- Fear of being worthless
- Fear of overwhelming conflicting demands
- Fear of fighting back
- Fear of getting hurt
- Fear of pain
- Fear of being judged
- Fear of giving too much
- Fear of being just a little too creative
- Fear of creativity going outside the lines
- Fear of growing
- Fear of moving

Emotional States
- Creative energies and efforts have been deemed unworthy, not good enough. They let those feelings of unworthiness and being judged build. They shut the door on further creative efforts and withdraw.
- Uncommitted due to the hardship involved in moving forward. There's a sense that they need to put their life on hold. Feels stuck.

Cross Indexing: Virus, ancestral/ epigenetic, Cancer – cervical, Venereal Disease, Herpes, Warts, Vaginitis, AIDS & HIV, wounded creative core

Created Patterns
1. I am not good enough.
2. Every time I put myself out there someone judges me and tears me down. Then I can't fight back.
3. I can't let go and move on.
4. I am bitter toward people that tear me down.
5. I must hide from people that judge me.
6. I'm not going to work for what I want. If it doesn't happen easily it's not going to happen at all.
7. I must hold and stay put.
8. Not doing anything is better than getting hurt.

Huntington's Disease

Fears
- Fear of being forced to reveal their secrets
- Fears someone might need something from them
- Fears the box
- Fears being out of control
- Fears being controlled by others
- Fears the assumptions about who they are
- Fears being judged
- Fears being ignored
- Fears not being adored
- Fears change
- Fears becoming nothing
- Fears disappearing

Emotional States
- Childlike approach used to manipulate and control the world around them. Doesn't hear what other people try to tell them in regard to the need to change who they are. Wants people to be subservient to their needs. Wants to be left alone when their needs are not met–sulk. Sulking is used as a way of punishing those that resist the manipulation. High maintenance. Hardened ideas, inflexible, forceful manner and approach.
- Freely lets their hardness toward people be known. Doesn't want to know the view point of others. Knows that they can't always have their way and resents it. Resentment builds. Wants to be seen as the center. Needs to be the center otherwise they are unhappy. Hangs onto a glory long past.
- Heartfelt desire to not be needed by others, wants to be free of restrictions imposed on them by others. Does not allow others to exist or be without judgment. Collapses under the weight of their own judgment and decisions. Rigid attitudes about others. Feels people should get out of their way. Heart is walled off from the support and kindness of others in a reciprocal fashion. Jumps into the fire of controversy to be the center of attention. Few people want to be around them because of their way of being in the world. Feeds off the energy of others.
- Natural distinction between right and wrong is distorted. Confuses the principles of right and wrong. Thinks that right and wrong can be manipulated for their advantage. The concept of honor is lost. Patterning from a parental behavior. Heart is tender and easily wounded when values are exposed as being out of sync with the societal expectations.

Cross Indexing: Dementia, Alzheimer's, ALS

Created Patterns
1. Everything must be done my way.
2. Change is dangerous.
3. I deeply resent _____.
4. My life is hopeless.
5. I might as well die, it's hopeless.
6. Death would be preferable to living any longer.

7. I am always right and don't need the opinions of others.
8. I want to die.
9. I can't change things so I might as well die.
10. I have no control.
11. People ignore me.
12. I have to get people's attention somehow.
13. I must make people pay attention to me.
14. I am helpless to make change.
15. I am a victim.
16. I have lost everything.
17. Everything good is taken away from me.
18. It was easier being a kid.
19. I want to go back to being a kid.
20. Kids have it so much easier.
21. I expect people to do as I say.
22. I expect people to listen and do as I say.
23. When things don't work out as I planned the world is unsafe.
24. I am in danger.
25. It doesn't do any good to explain things to people.
26. No one cooperates with me.
27. I must get people's attention to be listened to.
28. I must punish others that don't do as I say.
29. I must punish others that don't listen to me.
30. People are stupid.
31. People must be told what to do.
32. Things were better when _____.
33. People take from me.
34. I don't want to support others.
35. I decide what is right or wrong.
36. Other people are wrong.
37. I must use others before they use me.
38. If I am wrong I will be hurt.
39. It's every man for himself.
40. I am always wrong.
41. I'm not good enough.
42. I can't have people depending on me.
43. Responsibility is bad.
44. I can't let go.
45. If I let go of the past then I will be hurt again.
46. People never mean what they say.
47. I can't forgive and forget.
48. I hate myself.

Hyperactivity

Fears
- Fears being judged
- Fears losing their freedom
- Fears slowing down
- Fears staying in one place
- Fears they will be trapped

Emotional States
- Keep moving to not feel, trying to run away from self. Sucks all the air out of the room with their anxiety. Lowered expectations of self creates actions that don't meet the expectations of others or self. If they keep moving no one will see the lapse in judgment. Feels no inner peace. Feels that if people are looking at the outer movements they won't look at the inside lack of self-confidence and judge them as not good enough.

Cross indexing: Brain problems, Attention Deficit Disorder

Created Patterns
1. I must have my needs met now but I can't make it happen.
2. I can't feel peace.
3. My needs are never met.
4. I never get what I want.
5. I never get what I need.
6. I must keep moving (What will happen if you don't?).
7. I don't know what peace feels like.
8. I will never have peace.
9. If I am already moving I can run away faster.
10. As long as I am out of control I am safe.
11. I must run away so I won't be found lacking.

Hypertension

Fears
- Fear letting go of what they know
- Fear of the unknown
- Fear of being put in the box
- Fear that they will lose everything if they answer the call of their soul
- Fear of being forced against their will
- Fear of being in groups
- Fear of being wrong
- Fear of inner peace
- Fear of being present

Teachings
- Living in the now
- Creator's definition of self-identity
- Be in the flow of the universe
- At one
- Joy
- Listen to my inner truth
- Recognize to my inner truth
- Live in alignment with higher self
- Be allowed to feel joy
- To feel emotions safely

- Fear of flow
- Fear of allowing
- Fear of being responsible and relied on
- Fear of being out of control
- Fear of being letting others down

- Transmute emotions into healing
- Transmute anger into forgiveness
- Forgive
- Forgive and be safe
- Be loved and accepted
- Creator's definition of my life purpose
- Live my life purpose
- Know my needs are met
- Creator's definition of responsibilities
- Meet my responsibilities and live my heart's desire
- Happiness
- Be of value based on the present
- Be of value for who you are
- Be honored and cherished
- Follow my heart's desire and be safe
- Follow my heart's desire and know that the universe will provide
- Live without worry
- Be comfortable with groups of people
- Feel accepted
- Know who I am
- Speak my truth and be safe
- Accept others without criticism
- Live without needing to criticize others
- Live a balance of meeting your mind, body and spirit needs
- Honor your parents/ mother /father and live your life purpose
- Worthy
- Live without needing to be in control
- Value your own thoughts
- Live without needing to please others
- Live my own identity without needing the past to define me
- Live without needing a façade to feel safe
- Live without needing to suffer
- Honor my ancestry and be true to myself
- Honor my parents and be true to myself
- How to receive criticism without feeling unworthy /not good enough
- Live without needing the approval of others
- Live without family shame

- Live without shame
- Put myself first

Emotional States
- Local (egoic) resistance to life purpose. Lack of alignment with higher self and egoic (local) self. Resistance by ego to the 'yearned for direction' of higher self creates an inner tension.
- Allowing others to determine your life's direction. May have a historical period in their current life of being forced to be something they did not want to be.
- Hanging onto emotional upheaval/ hurts/ disillusionments of the past. These emotions are bottled up and they don't allow themselves the healing needed. These emotions may transmute into other emotions; such as grief turning into hardened anger or depression.
- Confusion in working with people. Self definition is unclear, feels unsafe in groups of people. Doesn't know where they belong or where they fit in. Becomes stressed when looking for self-definition within a group or community. Often says and does the wrong thing.
- Future feels uncertain and full of failure. Doesn't feel the flow of life. Ego wants to withdraw, build the walls and pull up the drawbridge in anticipation of certain catastrophe. May be disconnected from feelings and/or feeling.
- They feel like they never do anything right. They go out of their way to prove that they don't do anything right the first time. Critical of others. Everything observed is met with how a person should do it differently or better…they are in essence sending out their own message of not being good enough. Holds really tightly to the perception of not being good enough. May have taken an occupation that they resent/dislike. Life is full of woulda/ coulda / shoulda's. They have a need to be in control.
- Lack of meaning in their lives. Looks for a reason to exist. Looks to others for that meaning. Wants to make others happy as a reason for living. Shuts themselves off from the guidance of their inner voice.
- Establishes their identity based on the past and not the present.
- May have had a cultural identification that includes poor personal boundaries.

Cross Indexing: Adrenal Fatigue, Kidney Disease, Heart Problems, Eye Problems, Feet Problems, Veins, Arteries, Blood Disorders, Cardiovascular Disorders

Repeating Patterns: worry (lives in either the past or the future), Out of the flow – tries to force people, events to go their way, doesn't listen to or hear their inner truth, out of alignment/ out of sync/ out of time, doesn't allow themselves joy, doesn't follow their heart, no inner peace, holds resentments and does not forgive, people-pleaser (ignoring their own needs, but this keeps them in control).

Created Patterns
1. Being selfish is shameful.
2. Being spiritual means abandoning my responsibilities.
3. Feeling is dangerous.
4. Good children obey their parents.
5. I always do the wrong thing.
6. I always say the wrong thing.
7. I am afraid of disappointing my parents if I live my life the way I want to.
8. I am angry at _____.
9. I am being pulled in different directions.

EMOTIONAL PATTERNS

10. I am depressed.
11. I am disconnected from Creator.
12. I am lost.
13. I am worthless.
14. I can't be who I want to be because _____.
15. I can't forgive _____.
16. I can't let go of _____.
17. I can't let myself feel.
18. I can't start over with what I 'do' in life, it's too late.
19. I could have been _____.
20. I don't know what I want.
21. I don't know what to do with my emotions.
22. I don't know what will make me happy.
23. I don't know what's best for me.
24. I don't know who I am.
25. I hate my work.
26. I have been expressing/feeling strong emotion of _____ for a long time (these are negative emotions: hatred/ resentment/ anger/ rage/ bitterness/ grief/ sorrow/ revenge).
27. I missed my chance at being someone / happiness/ (what else did you miss the chance at).
28. I must be in control of everything.
29. I must criticize myself before someone else does.
30. I must do what my father/ parents/ mother wants me to do in life.
31. I must do what others tell me to do.
32. I must hang onto the past to know who I am.
33. I must interfere with others to keep them from harm.
34. I must keep my feelings to myself.
35. I must keep up appearances.
36. I must make other people happy to be needed / have a purpose.
37. I must shut down my feelings to be what others want me to be (this includes body and spirit).
38. I must suffer to honor my ancestors / parents.
39. I never do anything right.
40. I never get to do what I want to do.
41. I only criticize to make people better.
42. I resent _____ for stopping me from _____.
43. I should have _____.
44. I will shame my family if I don't do what my parents want.
45. I would have _____ if not for _____.
46. I'm not accepted.
47. I'm not good enough.
48. I'm not good enough to be somebody.
49. I'm not worthy.
50. I've got responsibilities; I can't change my direction in life.
51. If I am corrected or wrong I am no good.
52. If I am happy I dishonor my parents.
53. If I do what I want I will be out on the street / homeless.
54. If I do what I want I won't be able to pay my bills.
55. If I do what I want no one will love me.
56. If I follow my inner voice I will lose everything.
57. If I listen to my inner guidance I will be laughed at.

58. If I listen to my inner guidance people are disappointed in me.
59. If I put myself first I am selfish.
60. If I put myself first I am shameful.
61. If I show my feelings, I will be seen as weak.
62. If I stand up for what I want I will be rejected/ shot down/ made fun of.
63. If you have feelings you will just be hurt.
64. It is selfish for me to do what I want.
65. It is selfish for me to think of myself.
66. Listening to my inner voice is dangerous.
67. My life has no purpose.
68. My life is empty.
69. My responsibilities come before me.
70. Nothing I do is ever good enough.
71. Nothing I do seems to make things better.
72. Things are only going to get worse.
73. Things were better when I was young.
74. What people are bothering you?
75. What situation is bothering you?

*Look at themes of boundaries, joy, flow, acceptance, anger, boundaries, business(career), career (business), criticism, depression, direction, domination, enjoying life, Father, Mother, Feeling, Flow, Forgiveness, Happiness, identity, joy, life purpose, love, loving yourself, now, self-esteem, self worth, worthiness, unmet needs (acknowledgement, approval, recognition of my uniqueness), shame, control, letting go, stress

Hyperthyroidism

Fears
- Fear of being rejected
- Fear of being unloved / unwanted
- Fear of being outside their circle
- Fear of being unimportant
- Fear of not being in charge
- Fears being excluded

Teachings
- Live without drama
- Inner peace
- Live without needing to save people
- Relax

Emotional States
- Unyielding capacity for needing to force their way through a situation/ task/ job/ etc. They need to move. Their focus becomes singular and they need to be part of and the driving force of what they are part of.
- Needs to be left on their own to sort out an issue otherwise they feel like they have been usurped and are no longer important. They feel like they have been shelved.
- Holds up everything to be included and will judge those that wanted to proceed as stupid (they will diminish them).
- Lack of ideas lead to an overwhelming confusion. It's as if they are under attack for being without knowing. They feel judged if they don't have the solutions.

Cross Indexing: Thyroid Problems, Hypothyroidism, Endocrine System Problems, Bowel Problems, Pain, Heart Problems

Created Patterns
1. I am angry at being overlooked.
2. I am powerless to get what I need.
3. I have been expressing/feeling strong emotion of _____ for a long time (these emotions: hatred/ resentment/ anger/ rage/ bitterness/ grief/ sorrow/ revenge).
4. I am not safe.
5. I am not protected.
6. I am in danger.
7. Drama is how I stay in control.
8. I have to do things to be important.
9. Things will never get better.
10. I am a savior.
11. I must save people.
12. I will never have inner peace.

Hyperventilation

Fears
- Fear of trusting others
- Fear of the unknown
- Fear of life being out of control
- Fear of being closed in
- Fear of being trapped in their choices

Emotional States
- Not taking in what sustains or gives them life. Life comes down to splitting hairs to stay in control and when one of those hairs breaks there is a feeling that the whole world is going to crash in around them. They freeze and can't breathe. They shut down life and want to not be there.

Cross indexing: anxiety, panic, stress, lung problems, asthma, pneumonia

Created Patterns
1. I don't trust things to work out.
2. Life is out of control.
3. I have no space to think.
4. The world is caving in on me.
5. I can't make this work, it will fall apart.
6. I have no options, I am trapped.

Hypoglycemia

Fears
- Fear of enjoying the company of others
- Fear of heart hurt
- Fear of intimacy
- Fear of being unloved
- Fear that they will never be enough
- Fear of knowing
- Fear of being wrong
- Fear of being challenged
- Fear of change
- Fear of being unneeded
- Fear of being nothing
- Fear of being used
- Fear that if they let go they will be destroyed

Emotional States
- Hard to get to know. Pushes people away. Afraid to let people into their heart. Has a neediness of those people that are with them to be told they are loved. But it is like filling a bottomless well. Short tempered.
- Wants a justification for everything, nothing is safe to know unless there is concrete proof by the experts that this is the way it is. It must be absolute — there is no allowance for gray only black and white.
- Lacks strength of conviction in what they do in life. Wants to be something they're not. Believes all their problems would be solved if they could just be that thing.
- Wants to be needed but can't find a place where they are. They create the illusion of a place for themselves and then the illusion falls apart. They see the emperor has no clothes and life becomes intolerable. They feel like their heart breaks a little each time.

Cross Indexing: Diabetes Mellitus I, Diabetes Mellitus II, Hepatitis, Kidney problems, Adrenal problems, Addictions – Alcohol

Repeating Patterns: Feels out of sync with the flow of everything around them, Doesn't forgive or let go of old wounds, Has never felt love from mother and/or father, Doesn't know how to experience joy, Doesn't know how to experience unconditional love from within them, Shuts down what others are saying and doesn't listen, Lack of inner peace

Created Patterns
1. People take from me.
2. No one loves me.
3. People hurt me.
4. I'm not loved.
5. God doesn't love me.
6. God betrayed me.
7. I'm not needed.

8. My heart is broken.
9. People use me.
10. I don't trust _____.
11. When I am told I am loved I don't believe it.
12. I am disposable.
13. I'm not accepted.
14. I'm not good enough.
15. I'm not worthy.
16. Life is hard.
17. People take advantage of me.
18. People rip me off.
19. I am angry at _____.
20. People close to me hurt me.
21. People use love to get what they want.
22. No one is good enough.
23. I must put down others to be good enough.
24. I must prove other wrong.
25. I must win to be seen.
26. I must win to be loved.
27. I am beaten down.
28. There's no hope of change.
29. Everything is black and white.
30. It's either right or wrong.
31. I must judge others to be safe.
32. My life sucks.
33. Things would be better for me if I could just do _____.
34. All my problems would be solved if _____.
35. I can't commit to _____.
36. I don't belong here.
37. Things never work out for me.
38. I can't let go.
39. I must leave before I am hurt.
40. I must reject/ push away fun.
41. I must reject/ push away good things – they will just be taken away later.

Hypotension

Fears

- Fear of receiving
- Fear that they are being allowed to just exist
- Fear that they will never be enough
- Fears being unloved and unwanted
- Fears being unworthy
- Fear of the masculine
- Fear that if they don't give they will die

Emotional States
- They are not learning and growing for themselves. They are giving their life force (energy) to someone else. What they get back in return does not grow their wisdom and joy. The source of love is not from within but outward. Giving more than they receive.

Cross Indexing: endocrine gland problems, anemia, heart problems, depression, cardiovascular disorders, blood disorders, arteries, veins

Created Patterns
1. I don't love myself.
2. I have no desire to do anything.
3. I don't care about doing the things of life.
4. I have no ambition or drive.
5. Nothing I do matters.
6. I just never have time to take care of myself.
7. I must give my time and energy to another to feel wanted/ loved.
8. There is nothing left for me at the end of the day.
9. My whole world revolves around someone else.

Hypothalamus

Fears
- Fear of stepping outside the box
- Fear of not fitting in
- Fear of the being trapped in the box
- Fear of having to obey
- Fear of authority
- Fear of having to live by the old ways
- Fear of being betrayed to the authority
- Fear of being controlled
- Fear of being wrong no matter what they do
- Fear of being misunderstood
- Fear of being wrong
- Fear of not being able to focus

Emotional States
- A heartless need for hope and salvation – not a heart feeling but a programmed expression by societal influences, an adherence to structure to fit. Possible religious convictions that have become epigenetic – the religious convictions may not be part of their life but they are there nonetheless. Won't let go of the need for salvation. Tromps through life with the question looming in the back of their mind – Will this save me? Will this make me better?

- Wanting to break free from all restraints. Bristles at rules. Heart feels bound by iron straps. As they push against rules/restrictions/boundaries anger builds against the coercive nature of authority. Anger then shows in inappropriate ways. May manifest as yeast or autoimmune. Becomes a self attack. Their body feels like a jail. Body feels limiting and restricting.
- Hatred at authority. Wants others to see their point of view. But they perceive that no one feels the intensity of their emotions in the same way. They harbor feelings of betrayal at those that don't see their justification at the injustice of authority. Those 'others' then become the object of their mistrust and betrayal.

Cross Indexing: ACOA, Anxiety, Overweight, Endocrine System Problems, Anorexia, Bulimia, Endocrine Glands, Diabetes, Insomnia, Wounded Creative Core

Created Patterns

1. I am extremely angry at _____.
2. I'm not free to feel or express my opinions.
3. I am anxious about _____.
4. I am sad.
5. I'm not supported emotionally/financially/physically/mentally.
6. I'm not safe speaking my truth.
7. What is your declaration of independence?
8. What is the chronic repeating pattern in your life?
9. When did you feel imprisoned and what did you do about it?
10. I'll show them I'll _____.
11. I'll show them I'll do whatever I want to do.
12. I'll eat whatever I want to eat.

Hypothyroidism

Fears

- Fear of peace
- Fear of letting go
- Fear of the present
- Fear of things not being the way they want them
- Fear of being judged
- Fear of not being good enough
- Fear of no drama
- Fear of hopelessness
- Fear of the unknown
- Fear of being outside their circle

Emotional States

- Wishing that things were better and yet they never are and they never do anything to make them better. Lack of willingness to let go of the past and move forward. Can't be present to the now. Can't see the future without it being like the past.

- Clings to the illusion of what is and is not. Makes up the illusion. Paints the world as they would like it to be. Holds fast to not knowing the past or present. Their inner world is safe. Feels justified in their illusion and persecuted by those that don't see the world their way. Those 'others' are dangerous because they want to destroy their illusionary world view. Underneath the illusionary is a deeply entrenched feeling of hopelessness.
- Feels out of control, unable to keep it together. Unable to keep it together. Feels like the world is a dangerous place. They live a delicate balance between living and not living. Strong inclination to hide in a metaphorical cave from the rest of the world. Less interested in the sensory feelings of the body's interaction with the world and those things that do not bring them into an awareness of the felt sense.
- Lack of trust of others outside the circle. Ability to distinguish characteristics that would be dangerous, so immediate distrust and judgment of others. Strangers are dangerous.
- Feeling uninspired. Depressed. Pity Party going on. It's always something, which keeps the person entertained. Feels tired. Feels trapped by their body. Feels like their playing whack-a-mole to keep from seeing the other side. So they don't see what a depressing human being they are. By not seeing that they are a depressing human being they don't have to deal with who they are. They feel that if they were forced to look at themselves they could not bear the pain. They could not bear the pain of looking at a life that has been wasted by not living an authentic life. There is too much pain to look at. By not looking at the pain, they stay confined and safe. They feel as if no one honors or wants to know about your true self, so you make up a life half-lived. The pain of that disrespect is too much to bear. They feel their pain would go unheard. They feel they would be all alone in a place of intense pain and fear being alone.

Cross Indexing: Endocrine System Problems, Thyroid Problems, Hyperthyroidism, Endocrine glands

Created Patterns

1. I can't get what I want.
2. Everyone else has all the luck.
3. I can't achieve my goals…who made you feel that way?
4. Everyone else's needs come before mine.
5. It's no use trying nothing I do ever works.
6. I don't know how to ask for what I want.
7. I'm not good enough to get what I want.
8. I can't forgive _____.
9. Nothing good ever happens to me.
10. I can't tell people what I want.
11. Change is dangerous.
12. I need things to stay the same.
13. I am going to die.

I's

Impetigo

Fears
- Fear of risk
- Fear of the unknown
- Fear of change
- Fear of the flow of lie
- Fear of knowing what is held inside
- Fear of knowing
- Fear of someone seeing they are wrong

Emotional States
- Failure to jump. Holds back. Sees life as one big risk. Won't step into the flow or energy of life. They are always guarding their heart in fear that someone will find it wrong. The heart holds little love but lots of fear. Judges that only they know what's right and they make that determination based on what they see from the very outside never looking inward. Their intuitive senses are blocked by fear.
- Holds life as one big exercise in futility. Everything is wrong. Any movement, any change, any advice, it is all met with a declaration of what is wrong. The declarations of "wrongness" area a shield that keeps them safe. They are always on the other side of that shield, hiding in the shadow.

Cross Indexing: fungus, bacteria, skin problems

Repeating Patterns: Wounded Creative Core

Created Patterns
1. I have to be the one to reign in others. They do stuff that is dangerous. Bad things will happen if I don't.
2. I can't be open with people they might think my ideas are wrong.
3. I must always be on guard to being wrong.
4. They determine what is right by the outside world.
5. Intuition is a waste, it can't be trusted and it is evil.
6. I must find what is wrong with stuff before it hurts me.
7. I must not be seen. I keep hidden by not stepping up.

Incontinence

Fears
- Fears change
- Fears the unknown
- Fears being successful
- Fears having what they want
- Fears losing the pity party victim identity
- Fears being unloved
- Fears abandonment

Emotional States
- Can't hold onto what they want to achieve. Feels like something always sabotages the direction they are headed.
- They can't get what they want because something always happens to take away their money.

Cross Indexing: Bladder Problems, Kidney Problems, Cystitis, Aging

Created Patterns
1. I am guilty of not pursuing my dreams.
2. I feel like I could explode.
3. I am tired of trying to control my emotions.
4. It seems like something is always taking my dreams away.
5. I abandon my dreams to make others happy.
6. My goals always have take the back seat.
7. If I achieve my goals I won't be love, people will leave me.

Indigestion

Fears
- Fear of attack
- Fear of letting go
- Fear of being hurt
- Fear of others being hurt and being blamed
- Fear of losing control
- Fear of being lost
- Fear of disappearing

Emotional States
- Holds their breath in intense situations. Eating becomes stressful when they are having to focus on others around them. The focus is an awareness of care and possible danger. Feels on edge, like the whole world could erupt at any moment.

- Unable to let go of a situation that is not theirs. A situation that in their judgment is uncomfortable and possibly dangerous to their health. They view the person as being at risk of harm. They do not understand the why of how this happens. There's no understanding of the reasoning. Feels powerless to effect a safe change.
- They don't mind their own business. They try to mold the world to what they believe it should be — their life force begins to look like an octopus trying to control and be in everything. Feels out of control and wrong if they don't do this.
- Hostility toward someone that has hurt someone you love. This person is still in the picture and you cannot reconcile the harm he/she has done.

Cross Indexing: Stomach Problems, GERD, Gastritis, Esophagus Problems, Ulcers, gall bladder problems, pancreatitis

Created Patterns

1. Everyone is against me.
2. I have to fight my way through life.
3. I am anxious about _____.
4. I am afraid I am going to lose my job.
5. I have no security.
6. The world is not safe.
7. I don't understand why I am here.
8. I don't understand the world, sometimes I feel really lost.
9. I don't understand what to do and how to do it.
10. I can't let go or move on from _____.
11. I must live for others so I stay safe and I keep them safe.
12. I project my worry into every meal.
13. I don't see why these things keep happening to me.
14. I know better than others and I can see how they are going wrong.
15. I must stay in control of my world.
16. I cannot forgive or let go.
17. I want revenge.

Infection

Fears

- Fear having to choose
- Fear of conflict
- Fear of attack
- Fear of confrontation
- Fear of peace
- Fear that they will do it wrong

Emotional States
- They are at war with some aspect of self (being torn between conflicting ideologies that create anger). They run away from the conflict preferring to "make nice" and make everyone happy. They keep hidden their inner struggle.

Cross Indexing: The part of the body infected would be the place where the conflicting ideologies are resident. Ancestral. Headache-Migraines

Repeating Patterns: no inner peace

Created Patterns
1. I am really angry at _____.
2. I feel annoyed at _____.
3. I am suspicious of _____.
4. I am torn between my ancestry and the world I live in now.
5. I am being torn in two.
6. I can't make anyone happy.
7. I am attacked for who I am.
8. I am attacked for what I believe.
9. I am under attack from my family.
10. If I run away from confrontation I will be safe.

Infertility

Fears
- Fear of rejection
- Fear of their creativity
- Fear of dying
- Fear of rules
- Fear of authority
- Fear of being trapped
- Fear of shame
- Fear of being unloved
- Fear of being unwanted
- Fear of the guilt
- Fear of being like your mother
- Fear of becoming powerless
- Fear of losing control of my destiny
- Fear of saying "no"
- Fear of being controlled
- Fear of things falling apart
- Fear of becoming invisible
- Fear of not being good enough

- Fear of the unknown
- Fear of intimacy

Emotional States

- Feminine: This person holds a dream that they have been nurturing and cultivating. This dream has self-generated boundaries around it. They walk away from their dreams/desires fearing rejection. This person is passive. They are not comfortable expressing their truth. They abandon what they want most in life because of what other people might think.
- Feminine: The feeling side of this person is restricted. They will only go so far with what they will feel. This person moves around aimlessly with no real sense of direction. They feel like and they state they have no control over the things of their lives. They believe that they are at the mercy of the winds of change. The relationship they have with others is described as 'phony'. Their efforts at interpersonal relationships are considered plastic and artificial. This person lacks confidence.
- Feminine: This person is dissatisfied with who they are. This person feels like they have major obstacles to overcome. This person cannot unwind and relax even when they take a break from their lives, which seem hectic and stressful. There is a continuous state of chaos/crisis in their lives. They have weak boundaries. This person feels like they have no support and are invisible. They don't feel as if anyone understands them and they are frustrated at their attempts to communicate their needs. They go to places where they can be immersed in higher consciousness (ways of thinking). But, instead of being in that higher consciousness they dwell on trivial matters that divert their growth. They throw away, waste, the opportunity for spiritual and creative growth. So instead of building up they tear themselves down. They throw away what could potentially nurture them. This process causes them to lose inner-strength. This person does not enjoy the nurturing aspect of who they are. The nurturing aspect of self feels pressured to perform…get things done. This person has given up a sense of self and self defense. They feel overwhelmed. They do not understand that the self they are showing the world appears to be weak and ineffective.
- Feminine: This person's sexuality is tied to a form of rigidness and narrow-mindedness. They have difficulty dealing with their issues around sexuality. This narrow-mindedness/rigidness is an obstacle or barrier to a free expression of their nurturing, creative aspect of self. They circumvent dealing with their sexuality issues by using rational or intellectual arguments. This person may work to get 'ahead' by means that are not in alignment with higher consciousness values. This person cannot seem to make their creative efforts happen. They are tied to the barriers they have created. This person tries to use the energies of the intellectual rational side to create. Any creative efforts they make reflect no inspiration and are observed as lacking talent.
- Feminine: They look to others for direction and guidance instead of looking within to create their own solutions. This person may use readings from an intuitive, tarot, or other tools of perception to get guidance. Use of these external sources of information side tracks them from doing their own self growth and listening to their inner wisdom. There is a preoccupation with this approach. This practice is hidden from others. This person's concept of a spiritual self is fragile. This individual may reflect ideas or attitudes of single-mindedness and frequently appear to be stubborn. There is a fear of making decisions or taking self-motivated action. This person has had experiences and/or heartbreak that has hardened them…made them rigid in their thinking. They don't move forward and are stuck in old ways of thinking.
- Feminine: This person may be sexually frigid. They feel walled in by their current situation/relationship and can't get out no matter where they turn. They may actively work to stay away from spiritual concepts. This person has repressed/unexpressed emotions. They feel as if

they have no opportunity for creative expression. They feel as if all opportunity for expression has fallen away. This individual is passive in their approach to the challenges of life. They have created a barrier to protect them from a situation or relationship. The barrier has also worked to keep this person locked in their way of being in the world. This person lacks confidence in being able to break the barriers. This person lacks the confidence to find creative personal solutions that facilitate breaking through the self-created barriers.

- Masculine: Not allowed joy as a child. As soon as they expressed joy, fun from the world of a child they were put down and put back in their place. There was a lack of solitude, alone time was the devil's playground. There was no place to let one's mind explore and create
- Masculine: In a relationship this person is connected to the excitement and chaos of what feels like an out-of-control situation. There is a strong sexual aspect in the early part of their personal relationships with girlfriend/boyfriend or wife/husband. It is the primary reason that this individual will have an initial bonding. They will use their innate masculine energies of assertive control to alter the situation/relationship to one of order and predictability. Once the excitement is gone, this individual leaves…maybe only emotionally but they are gone. They use the excitement of the relationship to not look at or deal with their own feelings and emotions. This individual is overwhelmed by the problems and decisions of everyday life.
- Masculine: This person has lost their grasp/understanding of their divine essence. They keep sending it away and it keeps showing up in their life as frustration. The frustration is an ongoing tension because they have to be constantly in control. They don't know how to integrate being a divine essence into their life. This is not something their ego can control. The basic personality (ego-self) needs to be in control. This person suppresses their inner feelings because feelings don't represent control. They probably heard from a parent that crying or unbounded joy was unacceptable. For example: 'stop that crying or I'll give you something to cry about'. Or this person was expressing the divine joyful innocence of being a child and they received a punishment or criticism as a consequence. They have shut off inner communication with higher aspects of self. This person shoves away the creative in life. They have to live according to the rules (someone else's definition). So they will probably be in professions that don't allow for creative solutions to problem-solving. There is an imbalance between body, mind and spirit. This person lacks belief in self. Creative solutions (outside of the rules) lead this individual to second-guessing and not trusting. They feel insecure in the face of creativity. .
- Masculine: This person has shut down/closed off the feminine aspect of self. This person has probably been hurt deeply by a female in their life (mother, wife, girlfriend, teacher, etc.). They have closed off the aspect of self that knows how to receive, honors the intuitive and actively creates. This person keeps a secret about that aspect of self. Closing off from this aspect of self has created an imbalance in the masculine energies. An imbalance in the masculine energies may have created a situation where this individual has hurt people. This imbalance may have created a tendency to be constantly active and 'doing' with very little real substance to the 'doing'. This individual conceals this aspect of self by not going beyond the self-imposed barriers that keep them from having to explore the reasons for shutting that aspect of self.
- Masculine: This person has convinced themselves that they have inner strength but it has no real substance. They keep their creativity contained. They feel alienated from the world. They have huge creative ideas but they are never 'born'. The ideas and plans are grandiose and ungrounded. The ideas stay in the creation stage. They never finish a project. This person may be dishonest and/or shun the hard work to make the 'great' ideas come to fruition. This person does not want anyone to depend on them for support or help. This person may be attractive physically but emotionally no depth.

Cross Indexing: Wounded Creative Core, Sexual Disorders, PTSD, ACOA, Addictions

Created Patterns

1. If someone looks me in the eyes they will know (what truth are you hiding?).
2. It isn't safe to feel.
3. Men are inferior/ better than me (what are your beliefs around men).
4. Men are more capable/ skilled than women.
5. Men are superior/better than women.
6. Men are worth more than women.
7. My feelings are dangerous.
8. My friends/family all betray me.
9. My life is a mess.
10. My needs don't matter.
11. New ideas are dangerous.
12. New ideas are overwhelming.
13. No matter how hard I try I can't seem to make things happen.
14. No matter what I do I will never be good enough-so why try?
15. No one cares for me.
16. Nobody ever gives me a chance.
17. Nothing I do is ever right.
18. Others take advantage of me.
19. People hurt me (who are the people).
20. People take advantage of me.
21. Responsibility leads to failure.
22. Sex is a sin.
23. Sex is all about power/control.
24. Sex is an obligation.
25. Sex is bad/wrong and Sex is good.
26. Sex is dangerous.
27. Someone/something is always holding me back.
28. Someone/something is always stopping from going forward.
29. Speaking my truth is not safe.
30. Stuff just happens to me.
31. The needs of others come before me.
32. There is something wrong with me every time I am intimate with someone they leave me.
33. There's never any time for me there's always something to be done.
34. There's never enough for me.
35. Things always go wrong for me.
36. Things are OK just the way they are.
37. Things never go well if I try to do it my way.
38. Things will never be better so doing it the same is best.
39. What is causing the stress in your life?
40. What needs are not being met?
41. What other people think is more important than what I think.
42. When I am intimate with someone they always want to control me.
43. When things change I am never good enough.
44. Women are superior/better than men.
45. Women must submit to sex in a relationship.
46. You must always follow the rules.

47. You must be punished if you break the rules.
48. I will have a child I do not want.
49. I do not want a child like me.
50. Children destroy your life.
51. Children take your life away.
52. I would be better off not having been born.
53. Having children means losing my mother
54. I can't create and be safe.
55. Having children means losing my freedom.
56. Children will trap me
57. I am guilty of _____ (what is the unresolved guilt in your life).
58. Women are inferior/ better than me (what are your beliefs around women).
59. I can't love a child unconditionally.
60. I'm not secure.
61. I am disconnected/separated from god/The Creator/Source.
62. I can't say no.
63. I am overwhelmed with _____.
64. What is causing the stress in your life?
65. What needs are not being met?
66. I am in competition with _____ for _____.
67. I can't do anything right.
68. Being a parent means giving up on your dreams.
69. Being creative is a waste of time.
70. Being creative is the devil's playground.
71. Being different hurts others.
72. Being different is wrong.
73. Being pregnant will hurt.
74. Being pregnant will kill me.
75. I don't belief in myself.
76. Breaking the rules is bad.
77. Change is bad.
78. Change means things are out of control.
79. Childbirth is dangerous.
80. Childbirth will kill me.
81. Childbirth/pregnancy means I am trapped…I have no options after that…I become someone else's slave.
82. Children destroy your life.
83. Children take your life away.
84. Children will trap me.
85. Confrontation is dangerous.
86. Confrontation is overwhelming.
87. Creation is dangerous.
88. Creativity is bad.
89. Feelings make you weak and vulnerable.
90. Give up knowing who you are.
91. Having a baby means my parents know I have had sex.
92. Having children means I am trapped.
93. Having children means I cease to exist.
94. Having children means I must do what others tell me.

95. Having children means losing my father.
96. Having children means losing my freedom.
97. I always come last.
98. I am afraid of being pregnant.
99. I am afraid of having a child.
100. I am afraid of my mother.
101. I am afraid of sex.
102. I am alone.
103. I am always wrong.
104. I am as good as any man.
105. I am being used by _____.
106. I am disconnected/ separated from god/ creator/ source.
107. I am guilty of _____ (what is the unresolved guilt in your life).
108. I am guilty when/if I have sex.
109. I am in competition with _____ for _____.
110. I am inadequate as a woman.
111. I am laughed at for my ideas.
112. I am misunderstood.
113. I am overwhelmed with _____.
114. I am powerless.
115. I am rejected.
116. I am ridiculed.
117. I am worth less as a woman.
118. I can do as much as any man.
119. I can let go of my hurts.
120. I can never do what I want to do.
121. I can only be creative when I have permission.
122. I can't do it beliefs.
123. I can't make decisions.
124. I can't protect myself.
125. I can't love a child unconditionally.
126. I can't say no.
127. I don't believe in myself.
128. I don't belong anywhere.
129. I don't know how to get my needs met.
130. I don't love/like/trust myself.
131. I don't trust others.
132. I have no control over my life.
133. I know how to nurture myself.
134. I must be perfect or I will be rejected/ criticized.
135. I must control my sexual partner.
136. I must give up 'myself' to be in a relationship.
137. I must only have sex when my parents say it's OK.
138. I never get what I want.
139. I resent/hate/bitter toward/angry at _____.
140. I want a relationship but I don't want sex.
141. I will die if I am pregnant.
142. I will die if I have a child.
143. I will lose _____ by having a child.

144. I would be better off not having been born.
145. I'm disconnected from source/ creator.
146. I'm invisible.
147. I'm no good at sex.
148. I'm not creative like _____.
149. I'm not safe.
150. I'm not safe when I sleep.
151. I'm not supported.
152. I'm not talented like _____.
153. If I allow someone close to me they will hurt me.
154. If I become a parent I give up 'myself'.
155. If I do something creative I will be rejected.
156. If I do something creative I will be seen and being seen is dangerous.
157. If I don't let anyone close to me then I won't get hurt.
158. If I forget then it will happen again (what's the 'it').
159. If I have sex I will get caught.
160. If I tell people my dreams they laugh at me.
161. If I tell people what I want they will laugh at me.
162. If you can't do it right/perfect then don't do it at all.
163. I'm not secure.
164. In a relationship all the other person wants is sex.
165. In a relationship I lose my identity.
166. In a relationship I must always give in.

Inflammation

Fears

- Fear of being destitute
- Fear of out of control
- Fear of expressing self
- Fear of being outside the box
- Fear of being seen
- Fear of stopping
- Fear of inner peace
- Fear of flow
- Fear of saying anything
- Fear of being vulnerable
- Fear of saying and doing the wrong thing

Emotional States

- Heavy sense that an emotion is about to surface. This is an emotion that is overpowering. The expression of this emotion is overwhelming and scary so it is stuffed. Even if the emotion is joy there is a fear you will be diminished or put down. An anger builds at not having a flow. Instead there is a blockage of the flow of feelings.

- Time out. A time out is needed. Too much activity and doing. There's no sense of when to stop. Must keep going and doing. Doesn't consider the body's limitation.

Cross Indexing: Inflammatory diseases

Created Patterns

1. I am angry at _____.
2. I am afraid of _____.
3. I must keep going and doing.
4. I'll just take an aspirin and I can keep going.
5. I can't express myself.
6. I scare myself with how strong I feel about things.
7. I get angry when I can't say what I think.
8. Old adage of being seen and not heard is constant and present.
9. I have no flow in my life.
10. Not enough energy but you keep going anyway to the point of utter exhaustion.
11. Anytime I express myself I get put down by myself.
12. I get put down by others and I can't say anything about it.
13. When I feel anger coming to the surface I push it down.
14. No one can see me angry; if they do I will be found wrong.
15. I must keep how I feel to myself.

Ingrown Toenail Left Big Toe

Fears

- Fear not being good enough
- Fear of never having enough
- Fear of moving/thinking outside the box
- Fear of using creative thought to get around obstacles
- Fear of change
- Fear of the unknown
- Fear of flow
- Fear of peace

Emotional States

- Junk fills their life. Junk science, junk TV, junk food, junk emotions, and junk friends – things/people/feelings with no intrinsic value but suck up their time and energy. Nothing of any real substance or value is in their life. The lack of flow, the lack of energy and the lack of movement keeps them in one place, even though it is a place of anger. Movement in any direction is fearful. There is no security in movement.
- Feels like they are kicking down the obstacles on the wrong path. Each obstacle they kick down brings frustration, anger and/or despair. There is little they feel like they can do to change the path or the obstacles – there is always something getting in the way. They feel like they are

always in a battle. The battle is all inside them. They see a problem as something to be tackled and beat to death instead of 'just' doing what needs to be done.

Cross Indexing: feet problems, liver problems, teeth issues, trigeminal neuralgia

Created Patterns

1. I must fight to accomplish anything.
2. I am in despair.
3. I am angry.
4. There is no flow to my life.
5. I am always kicking the furniture.
6. I am always running up against obstacles.
7. Something is always stopping me.
8. I can't get my goals accomplish because someone/something is always getting in the way.
9. I can't keep people out of the way.
10. I struggle to get things done and I am always pushing up against something.
11. My life has no real substance to it.
12. Everything, including me, is worthless.
13. My life is consumed by getting junk.
14. I am surrounded by stuff.
15. I spend my time with people that add no meaning or real friendship.

Ingrown Toenail Right Big Toe

Fears

- Fear of being judged
- Fear of attack
- Fear of peace
- Fear of love
- Fear of intimacy
- Fear of the creative core
- Fear of their soul's yearning
- Fear of being left behind

Emotional States

- Judgment and jealousy – mean-spirited people have troubled them all their life. They bring in people who are quick to judge and jealous of what they have done. They create an anger that cannot be expressed. They take directions that are not in alignment with who they are because of a need to reject the judgment of others.
- Peace is elusive. There is always a prompting to move away from where they have found a place of rest. It's the movement of necessity. They have to be practical yet the heart longs to be somewhere else. For example: a career that fills the bank account but not the heart or a marriage that brings security but not peace of mind or a heart connection.

Cross Indexing: feet problems, teeth & jaw problems, liver problems, trigeminal neuralgia

Created Patterns
1. I am not contributing to a higher purpose.
2. I am financially secure but I feel trapped.
3. Life is empty.
4. My relationships are wrong.
5. I long for a life of integrity and meaning.
6. I am bullied.
7. People try to take things from me.
8. I can't protect myself from his/her assaults.
9. I don't seem to be able to get away from bullies.
10. I am angry at _____.
11. I am going to go the wrong way just to get away.
12. I have no inner peace.
13. Life is always in turmoil for me.
14. I have found an easy place to be but it is wrong and the bullies always show up any way.

Insomnia

Fears
- Fear of the inner voice
- Fear of the memories
- Fear of the future (what might happen next)
- Fear of stepping outside the box
- Fear of upsetting the apple cart
- Fear of feeling
- Fear of remembering
- Fear of the night
- Fear of sleeping
- Fear of loud noises
- Fear of attack
- Fear of being hurt

Emotional States
- Witless, does not understand they are here for a reason and they are not reflecting on the nature of their beingness. Mind is reactive and plows through life. Shows up at a job, gets married, has a family all without introspection and understanding their nature. The soul demands their awareness as they try to fall asleep.
- Hard to know what or where they find a motivational purpose. Unfounded annoyances keep them up and upset their tummy. They don't feel or sense a higher purpose or direction.
- Pain becomes all-consuming. A small ache becomes huge and creates discomfort. The pain is a distraction from the space and quiet of sleep. For within the quiet of pre-sleep are memories that create angst.

- Sleeping is dangerous. When they sleep they feel vulnerable to attack. Bad things happen to them in their sleep. They must make sure everything is safe. They can't let anyone die in the night. They need to be on guard to protect others. They must protect the babies.
- Created pain pattern. There is an awareness of pain in their body when they lay down to go to sleep. A created pain pattern is pain that moves into a person's awareness when it is trigger by a specific set of external events, like laying down to go to sleep.

Cross Indexing: Endocrine problems, anxiety, depression, overweight, heart problems, indigestion, hypertension, pain, ACOA, Post-traumatic stress disorder, wrist problems, carpal tunnel, wounded creative core, aging

Created Patterns

1. I am guilty of _____.
2. I'm not good enough to get the job done.
3. I am being threatened by _____.
4. I'm not good enough.
5. If I stop thinking something bad will happen.
6. The only quiet time to think is right before I go to sleep.
7. I am vulnerable when I am sleeping.
8. I can never let down my guard.
9. The world is not safe.
10. I must always be on guard.
11. There is no one to protect me.
12. I will be hurt when I go to sleep.
13. I am afraid of _____.
14. I am going to die.
15. I must worry at night; I don't get a chance at any other time.
16. I have no purpose.
17. I have no direction.
18. I can't sleep.
19. The pain is everything.
20. The pain fills my brain.
21. I am the pain.
22. I don't know where I am going.
23. I must worry to keep bad things from happening.
24. The pain screams at me at night.
25. Finding out the reason for pain is hard it is easier to take a pill.
26. My memories are painful and I would rather not go there.
27. Sleeping is dangerous.
28. When I sleep I am vulnerable to attack.
29. I need to be on guard to protect the others.
30. I can't let anyone die in the night.
31. I can't turn my brain off.
32. When I sleep I am vulnerable.
33. I must keep my guard up.
34. There is no one to protect me.
35. If I sleep I will be hurt.
36. What is changing or could change in your life?

37. I must constantly protect myself.
38. I am overloaded.
39. I am depressed.

Insulin Resistance

Fears
- Fear of being publicly shamed
- Fear of being overrun
- Fear of receiving
- Fear of being trapped
- Fear of the future
- Fear of thinking
- Fear of stopping
- Fear of being present
- Fear of being hurt

Emotional States
- Held up to others as an example of what you should and shouldn't do. Shame and humiliation is the result. Laughing on the outside but crying on the inside. Joined by others in the laughter and wants to hide. No boundaries – overrun by life and all relationships. Feels depleted with no more to give but keeps giving.
- Long the embodiment of an idealized way of being in the world that does not meet reality. Hopes at some point the world will give way around them and they can stop living the idealized format for existence. Living that way is compulsive. They feel like they have no choices.
- Worried about everything around them. They can't let go of the past stuff and that becomes the foundation and justification for the worry. The worry distorts their image of their life reality.
- Run away thoughts about life. They can't stop the thinking. It's like a train that just keeps going. There's this outward sense of being in control but inside they feel completely out of control.
- Decreased sense of ownership for the stuff around them – a loss of connection to the world around them – a disconnectedness. There is an emptiness in their movements and a sense of duty bound functions – they are just going through the motions.

Cross Indexing: Diabetes Mellitus Type 2, Arteriosclerosis, Overweight, inflammation

Created Patterns
1. I am shamed.
2. I am humiliated.
3. I am an example of what not to do.
4. I must keep a facade.
5. I must not show people how I truly feel.
6. When I laugh it is false, I want to run away.
7. I must give to be wanted / loved/ cherished.
8. I am drained by relationships.
9. I have no choices.

10. I have to keep up with the Jones's.
11. I have to keep up appearances.
12. I can't let go.
13. I worry about everything.
14. My mind races and I can't stop it.
15. I am out of control.
16. I worry to stay in control.
17. I don't belong.
18. I am empty.
19. I am unconnected.

Intestinal Problems

Fears
- Fear of death
- Fear of being taken from
- Fear of letting go of toxic feelings
- Fear of letting go of fear
- Fear of letting go of anxiety
- Fear of flow
- Fear of giving and a fear they will not receive
- Fear of having take what is not good for them
- Fear of change
- Fear of rejection

Emotional States
- The flow of life energy is stopped. They feel that they don't have enough and so they don't give of what they do have. They feel like they need to keep their feelings and things to themselves and guard their feelings and resources against others.
- When they hold onto their feelings and things these attachments become devitalized, and take life energy to maintain. They begin to feel drained by their stagnate feeling or attachment to things.
- Rejects nurturance. Nurturance is toxic. Poor relationship with the mother.

Cross Indexing: Abdominal problems, Diverticultis, Crohn's Disease, Irritable Bowel Disease, Leaky Gut, Intestine's – Blocked, Celiac Disease, Colitis- Ulcerative, teeth problems, allergies

Created Patterns
1. Things must not change.
2. What is new in your life that is causing upset?
3. Change is threatening.
4. The unknown is dangerous.
5. Change is bad.
6. When things change I get hurt.
7. It's easier to keep things the same.

8. I must keep what I have, there won't be more to replace it.
9. I must keep my ideas and feelings to myself.
10. I must be on guard, others will take what I have.
11. I must hold onto what I have.
12. If I relax I will be hurt.

Intestine – Large Problems (Bowel)

Fears
- Fear of letting go
- Fear of conflict
- Fear of shame
- Fear of humiliation
- Fear of guilt
- Fear of being judged
- Fear of being wrong
- Fear of being hurt
- Fear of being out of control
- Fear of being overrun
- Fear of displeasing
- Fear of not enough
- Fear of not deserving
- Fear of feeling unworthy
- Fear of not knowing what is bad for them

Emotional States
- Tired of having to struggle to get what I need. I have to struggle to get what I need. They feel that if it's too easy they will die. Nothing is easy. When they struggle they feel like they have accomplished something. They feel that if it's not hard to accomplish then they don't deserve it and they can't have it. They feel as if it would it would not be theirs and it would be taken away. They feel as if they are not worthy unless they have worked for it. Fear of being homeless.
- Hanging on to the point where it hurts them.
- What is taken in is toxic and they play the people-pleaser. They just take it and then can't get rid of it fast enough.
- They have a lot of wisdom to share but they keep it stuffed inside. They keep quiet, fearful of guilt, shame, or humiliation. Fearful being judged as wrong. They hide who they are. They have a lot of guarding.

Cross Indexing: Intestinal Problems, Intestines Blocked, Intestines-small, Irritable Bowel Syndrome, Colitis, Crohn's Disease, Constipation

Repeating Patterns: Out of balance feminine energy of nurturance , loss of control, people-pleaser, weak boundaries, stuffs feelings, stiffness and discomfort around people

Created Patterns

1. I have to struggle to get what I need.
2. Taking care of yourself is selfish.
3. If I don't work for it, it doesn't belong to me.
4. I must work for everything I have.
5. I can't relax.
6. Life is hard.
7. I am selfish.
8. I must keep stuff to myself.
9. It's only worth something if you work for it.
10. I must keep others at arm's length by doing.
11. I am afraid of displeasing _____.
12. I can't release what is no longer useful.
13. I won't have enough.
14. I can't give up control.
15. What must you control? What can't you give up?
16. It is wrong to displease others.
17. I must hold on to _____ (my memories etc.).
18. I must fight to protect my memory.
19. I have no control.
20. I am irritated by _____.
21. I must not upset other people.
22. I must hold my upset in.
23. I can't let other people know I am upset.
24. I can't let people know what I need.

Intestine – Small Problems

Fears

- Fear of deserving
- Fear of rejection
- Fear that the good stuff will be taken
- Fears isolation
- Fears abandonment
- Fears not being a victim
- Fears confrontation
- Fears being present
- Fears their secrets being known
- Fear of being wrong
- Fear of being unloved / unwanted
- Fear of heart being broken

Emotional States

- Not good enough to take in the good stuff. Person downplays their experience of food. Tends to shy away from new exotic or cultural food experiences. There is a fatigue in the constant battle of worthiness. Fear of having the good stuff taken away. They feel rejected, unloved and alone.
- Feels as if no one listens to their needs. Feels hopeless and manipulated. Doesn't trust new things. On pity party.
- They do not make a heart connection with others. There is no sense of inner knowing, if its there they do not trust it. There is a lack of honesty with themselves that is reflected back to them by others.

Cross Indexing: Abdominal Pain and Problems, Intestinal problems

Created Patterns

1. What secret are you keeping to yourself?
2. I must keep the secret.
3. I can't be true to myself.
4. I am hopeless.
5. I don't trust myself.
6. I have been dishonest with others.
7. My heart is closed off so I won't be hurt.
8. No one cares about me.
9. No one listens, truly listens.
10. I will never be at peace.
11. I am afraid of those that always make me wrong.

Intestines – Blocked

Fears

- Fear of receiving
- Fear of the future
- Fear of being out of control
- Fear of attack
- Fear of nothingness
- Fear of knowing the souls wisdom

Emotional States

- Self-nurturance has stopped. There is a tenseness around allowing themselves to relax with others. High ideals keep them from stepping outside of their concepts of communication. So they don't connect, flow in a social situation.
- Higher level of understanding has been blocked. Old traumas must be resolved first and they are happy to allow the scar tissue to just be and grow. The pain of scars is more subtle than working to resolve a wound.

Cross Indexing: Intestinal Problems, Intestines Blocked, Intestines-small, Irritable Bowel Syndrome, Colitis, Crohn's Disease

Repeating Patterns: Passive aggressive, when they don't like something they just passively stop without notice or talking about it.

Created Patterns

1. I have been expressing/feeling strong emotion of _____ for a long time (these are negative *emotions: hatred/resentment/anger/rage/bitterness/grief/sorrow/revenge).
2. I must control my life or bad things will happen.
3. I can't relax around others.
4. It is dangerous to be open with people.
5. If you are open with people they will hurt you.
6. I am better than you.
7. I am more powerful when I keep things to myself.
8. I am afraid of making my head hurt.
9. Let sleeping dogs lie — don't stir up stuff that will create problems.
10. If I just ignore it, it will go away.

Irritable Bowel Syndrome

Fears

- Fear of being present
- Fear of the flow of life
- Fear of being challenged
- Fear of never being enough
- Fear of sharing their creative ideas
- Fear of meeting the expectations of connection
- Fear of being blamed
- Fear of stepping outside the box
- Fear of responsibility
- Fear of letting their luminous self be seen
- Fear of being destroyed down to their core

Emotional States

- A disease of the spirit. Total lack of connection with the divine flow of joy, happiness and all. It's easier to live for what will be or living what was. Feels no spiritual depth to living.
- Hot-Headed. Anger flies to the top of their reactions immediately upon being challenged. The anger masked their fear of being wrong. They immediately go into a place of fight to keep from being seen as vulnerable. Feels that they must protect their heart from being hurt.
- Short-term gains are sacrificed for long-term benefits. They always look at the immediate. Safety is in the immediate. What is at the end of their nose is all that is relevant. Feels unsafe seeing the consequence of their actions.

- Feels they will never be good enough. They stifle creativity. They shut down the flow of information that creates beauty, color and transcendence. They block it with anger. The fire in the belly is not a desire to create but the fire of anger to destroy.
- Warmth and nurturing are not part of their world. They came into the world being held at arm's length. They were given what they needed to survive and very little else. They made up a fantasy world where they got what they needed.
- Holds the world accountable for sins against them and they hold that anger inside of them. Without remorse for their part in those sins. They do not "see" their part. The body holds the truth and that truth rises up when the heart is reminded.

Cross Indexing: Diverticulitis, Crohn's Disease, Leaky Gut, Intestines – Blocked, Celiac Disease, Colitis – Ulcerative, Colon Problems, Wounded Creative Core

Created Patterns

1. I have no enthusiasm or drive (What made you feel this way?).
2. I can't trust anyone enough to be open about what I feel.
3. I must keep to myself.
4. I can't trust _____.
5. I hate myself.
6. I don't know who I am or why I am here.
7. I am unreliable.
8. I can't trust anyone else to help me.
9. I am good enough to receive/ be helped by others.
10. No one sees me.
11. Lack of being. Afraid to be fully present.
12. It's easier to live in the past.
13. It's easier to live in the future.

Itching

Fears

- Fear of losing the wound
- Fear of losing the story
- Fear of losing the victim identity
- Fear of not knowing who they are
- Fear of being nothing

Emotional States

- What's on the surface, what has come to the surface, what has come to the surface that they need to look at, what has come to the surface that the world needs to see? What awareness has come to the surface that is annoying? What renewed energy has come to the surface that calls for a healing?
- Refusal to acknowledge a truth of self that is thrown at them. New information has come to the surface that allows for a healing.

- They are 'itching' to know. An impulsivity and curiosity leads to an awareness before they are ready to hear / know/ see that information.

Cross Indexing: rash, hives, allergies, skin problems

Created Patterns
1. I never get what I want.
2. I am inadequate.
3. I am unworthy.
4. I deserve more than I am getting.
5. I don't like myself.
6. I don't like my life.
7. I am sometimes too curious.
8. I need to know the gossip.
9. I must find out what is hidden from view.
10. I must keep stuff down or it will hurt me.
11. I don't want to remember or think to hard about anything.

J's

Jaw Problems

Fears
- Fear of having to rearrange their worldview
- Fear of being embarrassed by their worldview
- Fear of having their paradigm changed
- Fear of not being able to fight back
- Fear of ideological changes that can't be challenged
- Fear of being out of control
- Fear of new ideas

Emotional States
- Unreasoned ideas that won't fly, they are expected to mull these over and accept them. Not open to new ideas and new influences. Feels that things have worked fine up until now why change.

Cross Indexing: TMJ, teeth, heart problems, joint problems

Created Patterns
1. I am angry at _____.
2. I want revenge against _____.
3. I can't say what I feel.
4. I can't speak my truth and be safe.
5. I don't know how to tell people what I feel.
6. I am biting off more than I can chew (What is so big you can't chew it?).
7. I want to control _____.
8. I can't tell people how I feel.
9. I am not free to express myself.
10. People expect me to take their ideas and support them.
11. I'm not open to new ideas.
12. I'm not open to taking in new things.

Joint Problems

Fears
- Fear of being flexible with their ideas
- Fear of change
- Fear of the unknown
- Fear of being ground down by incessant change
- Fear of nothing being reliable

- Fear of trusting what is now
- Fear of the present
- Fear of letting go

Emotional States
- Hardened ideas. Feels like they need to reject different ways of seeing things. Inflexible in the face of alternate approaches to things of life. They feel like it's worked up until now why change. Resistant to the advancement of civilizations (cultural mores, technology, medicine, science, etc.)

Cross Indexing: Arthritis, Gout, Charcot's, Elbow Problems, Knee problems, Arthritis-Rheumatoid, Left-Sided Negative Tendencies, Right-sided negative tendencies

Created Patterns
1. I resent _____.
2. I am hurt by _____ and I can't say anything about.
3. I can't let go of the past.
4. New ideas are not necessarily good ideas.
5. Change is hard.
6. I am constantly trying to protect/defend myself from somebody who thinks they have a better way
7. Change is dangerous/ risky.
8. I must do this, this way.
9. My way is better than others.

K's

Kidney Problems

Fears
- Fear of their secrets
- Fear of their secrets being exposed
- Fears failing
- Fears being criticized
- Fears being shamed
- Fears being a disappointment
- Fear of not being in control
- Fear of flow
- Fear of the lessons they must learn
- Fear of pain
- Fear of struggle

Emotional States
- Has lied to themselves about what is causing the condition. Feels that the nature of the flow of abundance is without real value in the world. Doesn't know how to release what is toxic. Doesn't know what is toxic. Keeps secrets that should see the light of day so they can be cleansed. The secrets have become toxic. The secrets create fear within them.

Cross Indexing: Bladder Problems, Incontinence, Urinary Tract Infection, Kidney – Polycystic, Kidneys – Amyloidosis, Sepsis, Nephritis, Asthma

Created Patterns
1. I must control everything around me.
2. I don't know what makes me happy.
3. I don't know how to choose what is bad and what is good.
4. I don't know what to let go.
5. My needs come before others.
6. When people do things for me I know I am loved.
7. Others needs come before mine
8. My anger overwhelms me.
9. I don't know what love is.
10. I don't know what love feels like.
11. I am insensitive to the needs of others.
12. I am angry at _____.
13. I resent _____.
14. I am constantly critical of other people/myself.
15. I am controlled by others.
16. I am guilty of _____.
17. I can't express my emotions or feelings and be safe.

18. I must control my life or bad things will happen.
19. I betrayed myself.
20. I must constantly prove I am better than everyone else.
21. I don't like myself.
22. I don't know what makes me happy.
23. I don't know how to be happy.
24. I don't know what to let go of.
25. I am a disappointment.
26. I am extremely upset by _____.
27. I have been expressing/feeling strong emotion of _____ for a long time (these are negative emotions: hatred/resentment/anger/rage/bitterness/grief/sorrow/revenge).

Kidney Stones

Fears
- Fear that there is something they don't know
- Fear of someone not listening to them
- Fear of being out of control
- Fear of being wrong
- Fear of being nothing
- Fear of someone being more powerful
- Fear of someone being smarter

Emotional States
- Disregard for others. Sees their attitudes and ideas as merely support. If it goes contrary to their approach then they are irrelevant and mindless twits. Holds themselves in very high regard. Very much a tunnel of thought and beingness. This is how they survive. The walls to that tunnel are impenetrable. They keep walking toward the train light but it never comes.
- Helpless to stop others. They feel ineffectual at influential contact. No one listens. There is a sense that they need to influence or alter the path of others to prevent an inevitable bad end. If the path is not how they perceive it then they think it is wrong.
- Hijacked. They feel like the life they have has been hijacked and destroyed by the influence of others. People stray from the mold they have placed them in and the result for their life to feel hijacked by others.
- Wrongful influences have caused them to feel as if life is out of control. They then pull back, hunker down and escape. Hardened ideas with no flexibility. They must be right.

Cross Indexing: Kidney Problems, Kidneys – Polycystic, Cysts

Created Patterns
1. People hold the fact that I am better against me.
2. I am better than everyone else.
3. I can't let go of _____.
4. I can't let go of hardened ideas.

5. I am always right.
6. I must be right.
7. Life is out of control, I must stay the course to stay in control.
8. When things get tough I run away.
9. You must be what I tell you to be.
10. No one listens to me.
11. If you don't do what I tell you, you are wrong.
12. I don't need to change; I am the one that is right.

Kidneys – Amyloidoisis

Fears
- Fear of being shamed / humiliated
- Fear of letting go
- Fear of being unloved
- Fear of failing
- Fear that life is out to get them
- Fear being blamed for the bad things that happen
- Fear of never being enough
- Fear that there will never be enough

Emotional States
- Resentment at having their stature diminished. A very public failure leads to intense self-criticism. This resentment is never let go and builds a toxin in the body that is not released but caves in on itself. No self love and needs are not met. Feels like the diminishment of stature is held against them and represents all the faults they feel they are blamed for. Everything in their life is tainted by this failure and that failure happens over and over.

Cross indexing: Kidney problems

Repeating Patterns: depression, business failures, blames others for their failures, feel life is stacked against them, wounded creative core

Created Patterns
1. I am a failure.
2. I am no good.
3. I can't do anything right.
4. I get blamed for everything.
5. I get no support to go forward.
6. I resent _____.
7. I don't love myself.
8. I am unloved / unwanted/ unneeded.
9. People hold my past against me.
10. I can't let go of _____.
11. I am stuck.

12. I am held back by others.

Kidneys – Polycystic

Fears
- Fear of being denied
- Fear of losing
- Fear of disappointment
- Fear of flow
- Fear of letting go
- Fear of men in authority
- Fear of being loved by family
- Fear of being manipulated
- Fears no real purpose to living

Teachings
- Be heard
- Be listened to
- Compassion (inner peace in the face of suffering)
- Express your feelings and be heard
- Express your feelings appropriately and be safe
- Happiness
- Joy
- Know the difference between family/father programs and your own thoughts
- Letting Go
- Live without being critical
- Live without criticizing myself
- Live without hatred
- Live without needing to be angry
- Live without pain
- Live without putting myself down
- Living without being a victim
- Loving myself
- Not identify with pain
- Recognize my own inner truths
- To know God/ Source is listening
- Unconditional love

Emotional States
- Hatred at something bigger than themselves. Feels totally helpless in the face of overwhelming energy. Feels that no one is listening and especially god. No one or no thing is helping. They ask the question with no answer; what makes the other person's pain so special that they get help and I don't?
- Pissed off at the world and can't or won't express their anger. Feels relationships, people they love and material things have been taken away. All of life has been wrong. Lots of negative energy.
- A need to let go but can't. I know I should – but I can't help myself. Puts self down. Self-criticism. Self hatred. Masculine energy generating the self hatred. Rejection of male role in life. Role identification is castigated.
- Doesn't know how to let go of the hatred. Surrounded by the generational source of the hatred. Negative love; believes love is always conditional. To let go of the hatred means 'he/she' would

lose family connections. Love is a very toxic energy in their life. They and the people around them carry their negativity with pride.
- Doesn't love themselves and ignores their needs. When they do that they become very frustrated at life. They don't self-nurture. They don't take care of themselves. Yet there is an out of balance state where they appear selfish but they are just trying to get their needs met. In reality they will never get their needs met because it is self love and that doesn't come from the outside. Those needs get encapsulated in disappointment and put away.

Cross Indexing: Kidney problems, cysts

Repeating Patterns: Depression, weight gain, exercise is never, compulsive eating to fill a void

Created Patterns
1. A man doesn't _____.
2. Being a man is _____.
3. Everything has strings attached.
4. Families are poison.
5. God can't hear me.
6. I am a victim.
7. I am all alone.
8. I am angry at the world.
9. I am depressed.
10. I am doomed.
11. I am going to die.
12. I am only loved if I _____.
13. I am overwhelmed by _____.
14. I am wrong.
15. I can't be helped.
16. I can't get a break.
17. I can't let go of the hatred.
18. I can't let go of what makes me angry.
19. I can't live up to the expectations of my father.
20. I can't show my anger.
21. I don't know who I am without my family.
22. I don't love myself.
23. I hate _____.
24. I hate myself.
25. I must criticize myself.
26. I must judge myself.
27. I want to die.
28. I'm critical of others.
29. I'm not good enough.
30. I'm not living up to my family's standards.
31. I'm not living up to my father's standards.
32. If I try changing I will lose my family.
33. Life is struggle.
34. Life is suffering.
35. Life is unfair.

36. Love is pain.
37. My feelings of hatred have taken over.
38. My life is wrong.
39. No one can hear me.
40. No one listens to me.
41. No one loves you unless they get something in return.
42. No one understands how I feel.
43. Nothing I do ever works out.
44. Other people are helped and I'm not.
45. People I love are taken away from me.
46. People with different ideas are wrong.
47. The things I want are always taken away from me.
48. To be loved by my family is to be poisoned.
49. I don't love myself.
50. I never get what I want.
51. I am unloved/ unwanted.
52. Others come first.
53. I am selfish.
54. I'm not good enough.
55. I am unworthy.
56. I am a disappointment.
57. I am disappointment.
58. Life is disappointment.
59. Can't let go of hurts.
60. Can't let go of being ignored.
61. Can't let go of being disrespected.

*Look at themes of letting go, pain, negativity, unconditional love, loving yourself, depression, abuse, calm, childhood, co-dependence, domination, energy, family, father, happiness, integrity, joy, dominance, pain, self-worth, self-esteem, relationships, unmet needs, control, letting go, emotional abuse, power, relationships, worthiness

Knee – Left

Fears

- Fear of being led astray
- Fear of being forced against their will
- Fear of pushing against the impossible
- Fear of being put upon
- Fear of being unworthy

Emotional States

- Unable to move the unmovable. Iconoclast person in their life holds tight to worn-out concepts of judicial harmony. This renders one's self incapable of adjusting to the disharmonious harmony.

- Pushing, with rigidity, to move through a difficult decision. Judgment about a life path skewed by difficult people causing a deviation in their direction. Doing their best to circumvent their influence but they keep interjecting their opinions. This causes a need to escape and do an end-run around their mouthiness. Feels irritated, frustrated and fatigued.
- Just won't let go of an idea that is nagging. The idea has no real foundation, creativity or merit. But it is causing a lack of tolerance. The idea is being forced on this person. It doesn't fit with their flow or direction. Feels diminished by the incessant spiraling negative thoughts.
- Left knee holds the hallmark of religious or spiritual faith. If the left knee is having trouble bending, ask the question what about your spiritual faith is intolerant?

**Anytime there is an impairment (injury) in the knees, ankles, legs, or feet this can reflect a lack of certainty in moving in a specific direction. Injuries give us time. They slow us down. They give us time to either let go of direction not taken or consider, in your own time, the new direction at hand.

**There is imbalance in the masculine and feminine. In the Right Knee there appears to be a dominant masculine energy. In the Left Knee there is a tendency to take on the opinion to please others, an out of balance feminine energy. Either way, when one 'side' is out of balance so is the other side. If someone injures their left knee then their right knee/leg will have to compensate. Which means that they will throw other aspects of the skeletal, muscular and tendon systems out of balance.

Created Patterns

1. When unexpected things happen I _____ (What are your feelings?) (How do you react?).
2. I can't have a woman/man tell me what to do.
3. I feel insecure in my life.
4. I feel stressed by _____.
5. Masculine/Feminine energy is out of balance.

Knee – Right

Fears

- Fears disappearing
- Fears change
- Fears being lost
- Fears success
- Fears that they will never be of interest
- Fears authority

Emotional States

- Everyone has more problems than me, I'll wait. Inflexibility in direction of life. Can't find their footing in a life path that fulfills their need for recognition and acknowledgment. Climbs the mountains in fruitless searches or dead-end ideas — all illusional glory and no real substance to the efforts made. Unwilling to do the planning necessary to make a choice/path a functional success. Individual success in creative endeavors is illusive. A need to balance the creative with the practical.

- Loss of habit. Change has shifted what was known and now there is a need to move in unknown directions. To bend to new energies in new ways. There seems to be an elusive direction that they need to move in but don't know what it is. So they don't move at all.
- Inflexibility in their direction in life. Can't find their footing on a life path that fulfills their need for recognition and acknowledgment. Climbs the mountains in fruitless searches or dead-end ideas – all illusional glory and no real substance to the efforts made. Unwilling to do the planning necessary to make a choice/path a functional success. Individual success in creative endeavors is elusive. A need to balance the creative with the practical.

Cross Indexing: Joint Problems, Left or Right-sided negative tendencies, Knee-left

Created Patterns
1. I can't have a woman/man tell me what to do
2. I can't stand up to people in authority
3. Feminine/Masculine energy is out of balance

Knee Problems

Fears
- Fears vulnerability
- Fears attack
- Fears being people coming up behind them
- Fears being forced to bend
- Fears being forced to submit
- Fears having to carry the burden of our collective trauma (family, tribe, community)
- Fear of the wisdom of soul
- Fear of change
- Fear of the creative

Emotional States
The strength of the knees is the ability to bend. Yet the weakest structural point in our bodies is the back of the knees. A small child, attacker or opponent in the field of contact sports can take a person down by a very small blow to the back of the knees. Our knees hold the energy of the risks we do not take in life. Our knees hold guilt, shame and embarrassment when forced into subjugation (religious, government, police, community, etc). They hold the inflexibility of our decisions – the rigid patterns of thought received from our ancestors.

How many of us have had something shocking happen and our knees have buckled…or as the saying goes 'my knees were knocked out from under me'. Our knees hold the shocks of life (the knees are shock absorbers). Our knees cushion our drop from a high place or when we go up or down an incline. Our knees hold us up as we carry the weight of our burdens. Do we feel the weight of life's burdens or do we move with grace and ease.

Love of movement is held in our knees. Do you look forward to learning a new wisdom? Do you look forward to a long walk or dancing? Our knees represent the coherence of our minds in movement. Are we open in our minds, but fear change or newness in our hearts or body?

Our bending knees allowed us to crouch and not be seen by the predator or enemy. Our ancient ancestors would gather at tribal communion around the fire to tell our hunting stories and we would crouch in a symbol of being no higher than those seated. We would rest and yet not rest as we crouched, always ready in that position. A knee that bends in communion with the tribe or with others protects the family/tribe by supporting the whole. The knee bends to embrace the vulnerability instead of bracing against the blows of life with a rigid harden stance. People whose knees bear the strength of purpose and direction embrace their vulnerability.

Some people live from their knees. One type of knee person will not bend. They are inflexible and stubborn. Their knees will be stiff and rigid. They will not alter their ideas in the face of new information. Their opinions are based in fear. They fear being vulnerable. The knees carry that vulnerability. A second type of knee person has worn-out knees. They have used their knees to push against life and hence their knees have worn out. They deceive themselves by always having to push against the flow of life. These people don't know how to use their skills of communication so they use their knees to push their way through life. These people assert their dominance by being a bully or being loud in their assertion of control.

There is a holding back in their life of creative endeavors. There is no heart for rejection or challenge. Cannot stand up to challenge or rejection.

Cross Indexing: Joint Problems, Left-Sided Negative Tendencies, Right-Sided Negative Tendencies, Knees – Left, Knees – Right

Created Patterns
1. If I give in_____(what will happen?).
2. I must have my own way.
3. I'm not flexible.
4. I'm not giving in to _____ (person/situation of authority).

L's

Labyrinthitis

Fears
- Fears weakness
- Fears being taken advantage of
- Fears listening to inner guidance
- Fears being their mother
- Fears being their father
- Fears being let down

Teachings
- Accept help from others
- Be Balanced
- Be listened to
- Calm
- Communicate my needs easily
- Creator's definition and perspective of balance
- Deserve
- Easily recruit the help of others without drama
- Express my anger and not be made wrong
- Forgiveness
- Give myself some down time
- Honoring my feelings
- Live without being hard on myself
- Loving myself
- Make changes easily
- Nurture myself
- Open to change
- Open to new ideas
- Receive
- Say no without guilt
- Still my mind
- To be listened to
- Understand my human limits
- Unconditional love

Emotional States
- Uses a Herculean effort to keep things balanced per their definition. Balanced in their world means keeping themselves going and meeting the needs of the people around them. This is not really balanced…their needs are not being met. The load is not being shared equally and this creates an anger based in a feeling of injustice.
- Too hurried to see that no one is helping. Feels tremendous stress and strain. Locked into this imbalance and doesn't hear information that says there's another way. No one moves to help correct the imbalance.
- The reward for much effort is way out-of-balance. Feeling tired, used and abused. This is a repeating pattern in their life.

Cross Indexing: Vertigo, Dizziness, Virus, Ear Problems, ACOA

Created Patterns
1. I am angry at _____ for not helping me.
2. I am ignored.
3. I am my mother/ father.
4. I am not good enough / I am good enough.
5. I am out of balance.
6. I am overwhelmed.
7. I can't relax.
8. I can't say no.
9. I demand more of myself than I expect from others.
10. I deserve / I don't deserve.
11. I don't have time to be sick.
12. I have to do everything.
13. I must meet the needs of my family before myself.
14. I must do everything myself.
15. I push myself too hard.
16. I am responsible for everything.
17. If I don't do it things will fall apart.
18. If I don't get it all done I am guilty.
19. If I want it done right I have to do it myself.
20. It takes too much energy to change.
21. It takes too much time to change.
22. It's not fair, I have to do everything.
23. Life is unfair.
24. My life is a balancing act.
25. No one does anything except me.
26. No one helps me.
27. No one helps me with the load.
28. No one listens to me.
29. There is no time to take care of myself.
30. Things won't change.
31. When I am helped they just do it badly so I won't ask them again.
32. When I ask for help I am ignored.

*Look at themes of stress, self worth, self esteem, anger, boundaries, anxiety, blockages, justice, acceptance, acknowledgement, balance, co-dependence, communication, control, energy, flow, forgiveness, loving yourself, power, relationships, responsibility, unconditional love, unmet needs, approval, receiving, relationships, stress, worthiness

Lack of focus (in school/studies)

Fears
- Fear of the unknown

- Fear of the bullies
- Fear of tests
- Fear of being shamed
- Fear of loud noises
- Fears being rushed – pressured
- Fears time

Emotional States

- Anger in school. Lots of unknowns. Lots of potential for being unsafe. This is a place where you detach because the amount of potential danger is overwhelming. Drift off (spacing out). Tests can be dangerous. There are always repercussions from a test done poorly – public shaming. Drifting off in school allows them to live in a different place in their head. Sudden sounds cause a freeze response. This keeps you safe by not allowing the unexpected to get too close. This alertness gives you time to move. In reality this freezing keeps them in one place. Keeping in one place keeps the paralysis. Lets you be invisible which keeps them from being attacked. Hide in plain sight which allows them to not have to fight. May feel rushed to make a decision by family and needs more information and time to make a decision. Family may push a sense of obligation.

Cross Indexing: ACOA, PTSD, Attention Deficit Disorder, Hyperactivity

Created Patterns

1. I'm not pretty/ handsome enough.
2. I don't have what it takes.
3. I'm obligated to my parents.
4. I must freeze to be safe.
5. I never have enough time.
6. I need to hide to be safe.
7. I don't understand the pattern of life.
8. I'm unworthy and empty.
9. I move things out of my way so I don't have to deal with it.
10. I get angry if I am forced to make a decision.
11. I then get left alone. Then I get nothing and I am let down.

Laryngitis

Fears

- Fear no one is listening
- Fear of being hurt if they talk
- Fear that talking is a waste of time
- Fear that anything they say will be held against me
- Fear of being guilty for what I say
- Fear of connecting with the hearts of others with their heart

Emotional States
- I am tired of talking. It feels like the harder they try to inform the less people listen or care. Lacks a connection that reaches the people they are talking to because they don't seem to listen or even want to listen.

Cross Indexing: Throat Problems

Created Patterns
1. I can't voice my opinions and be safe.
2. If I speak out I will be hurt.
3. I am overwhelmed by grief and have no way to let it out.
4. I am frozen with fear.
5. Anger has overtaken me.
6. I am overwhelmed by _____ and can't let it out.
7. If I cry no one will hear me or care.
8. If I ask for help.
9. It is dangerous to be who I truly am.
10. I am tired of talking.
11. No one listens.
12. My words are a waste of time.
13. I know what I am talking about and no one wants to hear it.
14. I can't seem to connect with people.
15. People turn away from me.

Lasik Surgery Reversal – Left Eye

Fears
- Fear that nothing they do will change what they see

Emotional States
- Giant expectations are still disappointments.

Cross Indexing: Eye Disorders, Lasik Surgery Reversal – Right Eye

Created Patterns
1. I am disappointed
2. Everything I see is unchanged
3. Everything I do changes nothing

Lasik Surgery Reversal – Right Eye

Fears
- Fear of a future they create
- Fear of the unknown
- Fear that they can create a future
- Fear of authority
- Fear of being present
- Fear of being forced to see what they don't want to see

Emotional States
- Unwillingness to see past the defined future. They have preconceived ideas of who they are based upon cultural/ancestral/family/group info. They set themselves in those places and carve out a role for themselves in that place.
- Tired. They don't want to do it. They have had to make so many changes in their life to accommodate others that they just don't want to see beyond where they are now.
- A dreamer. Problems in school. Abuse at home. Rigid father; "no-nonsense". Ancestral trauma. Grandfather was the dreamer and probably an alcoholic. The grandfather always had a better place to go, always a better job.

Cross Indexing: eye problems, nearsightedness or farsightedness

Created Patterns
1. I don't want to plan too far out.
2. I am _____(cultural heritage), I don't see myself as anything other than.
3. I define myself by my ancestral heritage and all that implies.
4. I have to do what others want me to do.
5. I can't seem to see past my work load.
6. I don't get my free time.
7. My life would be better if _____.

Leaky Gut Syndrome

Fears
- Fear of inner peace
- Fear that the toxic emotions they hold are poisoning them
- Fear that what they do to feel good is bad for them
- Fear of being to weak to keep everything in control
- Fear of letting go would create chaos

Teachings
- Complete
- Whole
- Fun
- Play
- Live in the now
- Allow for the flow of universe
- Joy
- Happiness
- Play for the sake of play
- Let go of anger

- Creator's definition of control
- Living a life authenticity
- Grateful for abundance
- Forgiveness
- Inner peace
- Creator's definition of compassion

Emotional States

- Keeps a tight control on everything; fears chaos. Feels that if they lose control they lose life force. Must make everything nice. People -pleaser.
- Play/ fun becomes a competitive exercise. Exploration and creativity are lost to 'you must be practical' parenting theme. Suppressed anger at having creativity confined. Feels like life must be run by the rules of the ancestral parenting book.
- Stuck in old ways of doing things. Growth has stopped. Life has no richness of experience or depth to it. Feels as if they are being put upon if people try to show them a different way.
- Cross Indexing: Constipation, Irritable Bowel Syndrome, Crohn's Disease, Intestinal Problems, Diverticulitis, Abdominal Problems, Wounded Creative Core

Created Patterns

1. Bad things happen to me.
2. Chaos is dangerous.
3. Everything I do fails.
4. Feelings are dangerous.
5. Good people never win.
6. Good things get taken from me.
7. I am a disappointment.
8. I am angry at _____.
9. I am going to die.
10. I am lost.
11. I am poor.
12. I am responsible if bad things happen.
13. I don't deserve abundance.
14. I don't deserve good things.
15. I don't know how to play.
16. I have no purpose if things fall apart.
17. I must always win.
18. I must make everything nice.
19. I must never stop.
20. I must stay in control to be safe.
21. I must win to be loved/respected/wanted/good enough.
22. I'm not good enough.
23. If I have money I will lose it.
24. If I lose I'm not any good.
25. If things fall apart I disappoint the people around me.
26. If things fall apart I have failed.
27. If you don't win you are a loser.
28. It is dangerous to feel.
29. Nothing I do every works.

30. Nothing will ever get any better.
31. Nothing works out for me.
32. Only losers stop.
33. Play is a waste of time.
34. The harder I try/work the worse it gets.
35. Work before play.

*Look at themes of childhood, peace, manifesting, abundance, creativity, authenticity, anger, authenticity, beingness, control, failure, feeling, happiness, joy, letting go, peace, problems, unmet needs (play, creativity, fun), control, creativity, peace, receiving, trust, stress

Left-Sided Negative Tendencies

Fears
- Fear of being forced to the wounded side of the masculine to survive

Emotional States
Aspects
- Hurt
- Depression
- Rejected
- Moody
- Defensive
- Fearful
- Insecure
- Worry
- Lazy
- Low Self Esteem
- Guilt
- Victim
- Needy
- Self Pity
- Loneliness
- Shyness
- Procrastination

Created Patterns
1. I'm better than others.
2. People should fend for themselves and not expect me to help them.
3. I must keep what I have.
4. I must have all I can get.
5. I don't need others in my life.
6. I don't want to share.
7. I like myself and like being alone so that I don't have to compromise or share.

8. Others are to blame for my problems.
9. I'm not responsible for the bad things that happen.
10. People see me as evil.
11. I let others take advantage of me.
12. I am a doormat.
13. Others are better than me.

Leg Edema

Fears

- Fear of heartbreak
- Fear of the future
- Fear of being alone
- Fear of letting go
- Fear of not being the victim
- Fear of the unknown

Emotional States

- Failure to move forward in life. Fear of what might happen if they do keeps them bound to the current experience. Fear that the next experience (the unknown) would be dangerous. Emotions don't get expressed. They get held in. The fear of going forward is the emotion held in the edema.
- Can't make the 'stuff' of life happen. They feel really frustrated by this. They move into the pity party and that stops them from addressing what's really going on. Holds themselves to a different standard for progress and movement. Wants to be known as good or good at what they do. So they put boundaries and borders around their 'way' of being so that they operate only within those confines. This keeps them safe from seeing the artificial standards and judgment they have institutionalized for themselves.
- They are held to a standard by those around them that they can't meet and they can't achieve. They have learned it is safer to stay in a constant state of failure than it is to actually move away from the judgment. They stay locked in a cycle of frustration. They can't walk away from the expectations of others. So they internalize their feelings of struggle and frustration by the standards and judgment of others.
- Hopelessly involved in a triangle of chaos. The triangle is made up of the parents and the adult child. Patterns of judgment and 'what if this happens' thinking block their joy. Ancestral patterns of creating only so much and then stopping for fear of being seen and having it taken away from you. Their chaos gets created by the constant tug of the adult child wanting to be something different and step out of the paradigm of rigid life control dictated by the ancestry. Feelings of hopelessness.
- Held out as someone who would never make it in life. Judged and judging. No warmth to life. Not living life the way they want to. Someone else dictates how their life should be so they can be safe.

Cross Indexing: Congestive Heart Failure, Kidney problems, Liver problems, heart problems, Wounded creative core

Repeating Patterns: in a relationship being controlled by parents/authority figure (live or deceased), constant source of trauma/drama

Created Patterns

1. I am stuck.
2. I can't move forward.
3. I must keep my feelings and ideas to myself.
4. I don't seem to be able to accomplish anything.
5. New is not helpful.
6. New causes chaos and confusion.
7. New is dangerous.
8. I can't ever seem to make things happen.
9. I must put walls around what I do otherwise all kinds of bad stuff will happen.
10. People think I am better than I am.
11. I'm always trying to meet the expectations of others.
12. I can't run fast enough to make others happy.
13. I can't make anyone happy.
14. I am judged.
15. Life is trauma/drama.
16. My family is nothing but chaos.
17. I must not be seen.
18. If I am seen I will lose everything.
19. I am controlled by my parents.
20. I am a failure.
21. I am controlled.
22. There is no joy to life.

Leg Problems

Fears

- Fear that no one will have you in their life
- Fear of being blindsided
- Fear of the stepping off into unknown
- Fear of being unsupported

Emotional States

- Whenever you look at legs, feet, ankles or knees you are looking at the foundation we stand on that propels our body. Our legs, feet, ankles or knees from a general stand point support us and allow us to ambulate. If legs develop physical problems or an injury does not heal properly what aspect of life has not been supportive. There is a saying 'had my knees knocked out from under me'. This would indicate that an unexpected event had left the person feeling blindsided, unsupported or unprotected. If this had happened in the past then the beliefs of 'I can't change, Change is dangerous, moving forward is dangerous, I can't move forward, I am unsupported' would have been built in this person especially if it had been reinforced or parent(s) had lives in constant turmoil.

Cross Indexing: Joint Problems, Left or Right-Sided Negative Tendencies, Hip Problems, Foot Problems, Back-Lower, Sciatica, Leg Paralysis

Created Patterns
1. I am afraid of moving forward with my life.
2. I am afraid of change.
3. Change is dangerous/bad/hurtful.
4. I don't understand _____.

Leg-Paralysis

Fears
- Fear of the hostile intentions of others
- Fear of doing
- Fear of their heart
- Fear of being nothing

Emotional States
- Impaired vision of the future has them frozen in space and time. They feel vulnerable and fearful that if they do anything they will create more harm. If they freeze and do nothing – then they will be safe and they will survive. Their direction is in the heart not in their legs but if they stop and don't move on anything the heart will not hurt as much.

Cross Indexing: Left Sided or Right Negative Tendencies, Leg-problems, stroke, sciatica, accidents, back, foot problems, hip problems, symptom, neural disorders, heart problems, all back maladies, paralysis

Repeating Patterns: Frozen in the direction they are headed.

Created Patterns
1. I must avoid _____ (what in your life are you avoiding).
2. I am afraid of _____ (what in your life are you afraid of).
3. The future is not happening.
4. All of what I desire and want in life is not happening.
5. I am doomed.
6. I am frozen, if I move I will be hurt.
7. I don't know where I am headed.
8. I have no future.

Leucorrhea

Fears
- Fear of being present in their life
- Fear that there is nothing more

Emotional States
- Desire has run its course and there is no longer an sexual desire. Sex thereafter is now an energy of invasion, it becomes a consensual assault, questions why sex is even part of a relationship. Finds it difficult to complete a creative project, loses the passion.

Cross Indexing: infection, bacteria

Repeating Patterns: Wounded Creative Core

Created Patterns
1. Sex makes me feel guilty.
2. I am powerless.
3. I am angry at my mate/men.
4. I don't want sex with my partner.
5. The relationship is done except for the perfunctory sex.
6. I don' want sex.
7. I feel dirty and unclean after sex.
8. Love for all the wrong reasons and in the the wrong places.
9. Love is a farce.
10. Men get what they want but I never do.

Libido – Under Activated

Fears
- Fear of love connected to sexual attraction
- Fear of being alone
- Fear that no one is really there
- Fear of being judged for their creativity
- Fear of authority judging them

Emotional States
- Heavy heart connection of creativity to wounds and/or emotional hurts. Creativity has been shut down. Creativity is seen as being a place of vulnerability. Heart and sexual feelings are connected — sexual energy construed as making one vulnerable to attack and exposure. The exposure takes on the form of ridicule or being put down — there's a degradation of self-worth by others. Feelings of low self-esteem. One or both parents ridiculed as a form of punishment in adolescent years. Their ideas and how they were in the world was ridiculed. So they withdrew from being

exposed to the offending parent(s) and created a facade for them and the world to see that kept them safe. That same facade is the energy that now resides in the heart and second (sex) chakra. May have issue with drugs/alcohol and hypochondria. Will be looking for physical issues to hide the lack of sexual energy. Shame was used as a parenting tool — sexuality is shame — set up situations in their life where shame was integral to their sexual experiences.

- Self-hatred and mutilation – ancestral energy of sexuality being integral to physical mutilation. Sexuality is seen as an obstacle to getting what they want. Sexuality seen as a form of repression and enslavement of the the body and hence an entrapment of the mind. Sexuality is not considered integral to the whole person but is seen as a very distant and separate aspect of self punished for being sexual. Hardened after years of sexual denial. Feelings of being helpless to change but in reality they don't want to change because this is safe. They hide in the heart wounds and deny the sexuality of self. Looks for the remedy outside of self but they will never find it.
- Letting go of personal idealism – The romantic ideas of love and sexual ideals, grounded in the fantasy of fairy tales, have provided fertile ground for disillusionment and frustration. Nothing ever meets those expectations. There is no knight in shining armor or rapturous maiden to make you feel like the knight or the knight to bring out the rapturous joyous maiden. These stereotypes from childhood stories became the expectations of a relationship. In time the romance fades and love born of the fairy tale ideals will fade. Life's joy is not found within but outward and there is a sense of can't get what I want and need. Then they move to 'why look anywhere else' and then there's a shutting down.
- Doesn't want to be forced into anything. Energetic shutdown. A protection against more babies. Ancestral—it was the duty to produce a male child and once it was done your obligation was done. Lack of desire – control of sexual relations meant no more babies.

Cross Indexing: Wounded Creative Core, Adrenals Repeating Patterns: brings in relationships of sexual incompatibility

Created Patterns

1. When I create people criticize me.
2. I am ridiculed.
3. I am not good enough.
4. I must have a sexual partner to be loved.
5. I must have a sexual partner to be good enough.
6. People in authority make fun of me.
7. I must lie to be safe.
8. I must not show people who I am.
9. When I love someone I am shamed.
10. To be loved I must be shamed.
11. For someone to love me I must be shamed.
12. Love is shame.
13. After I have sex I feel guilty.
14. After I have sex I feel humiliated.
15. After I have sex I feel shame.
16. After I have sex I feel degraded.
17. After I have sex I feel vulnerable.
18. After I have sex I feel afraid.
19. I must hurt myself to feel.

20. I must have sex to get what I want.
21. My prince/princess will show up someday and save me.
22. I expect my lover to be my prince/princess.
23. If I have sex I will be forced to have babies.

Ligament Problems

Fears
- Fear of having to control their hatred and anger
- Fear of being present
- Fear of their actions will be controlled
- Fear of being out of control
- Fear of responsibility

Emotional States
- Demands that they be the controlling person. They present themselves as knowing how to be in control and run the show. Feels unsafe if they are not in control even if they don't know what they are doing.
- Not paying attention and not present. Actions are unfocused and seen to be reactive. Doesn't know where their body is in the space they are in. Doesn't feel like they fit in their life. Their reactions and responses are awkward. Doesn't always know how to react.
- Let's others tell them what to do. They don't have to be responsible.

Cross Indexing: Tendons, muscles, Parkinson's

Repeating Patterns: Stays away from leadership or management roles. Plays a subservient role in a relationship. Always wants to be in control. Is the manager or boss of all activities – job, relationships, volunteers, communities. Says does things that are awkward and cause issues.

Created Patterns
1. I must control _____.
2. I am controlled by _____.
3. I can't control myself.
4. I am out of control.
5. I must stay in control to be safe.
6. People try to control me.
7. People try to tell me what to do.
8. I don't fit in this world.

Lip Problems

Fears
- Fear of saying the wrong thing
- Fear of being diminished
- Fear of having to hold the injustice in
- Fear of my heartbreaking
- Fear of dying from a broken heart

Emotional States
- They feel like they can't share what they know. Their speech is inhibited. There is a fear of being put down and stopped from speaking – their speaking is often interrupted and stopped by themselves or others. If it is them that stops there is a fear that they will be wrong. If it is someone else they fear being diminished.

Cross Indexing: cancer, canker sores, heart problems

Created Patterns
1. I am frustrated by _____.
2. I am afraid of saying the wrong thing.
3. I can't tell people what I know.
4. People judge me.
5. I am always wrong.
6. I am afraid I will say the wrong thing.
7. I can't share what I know.
8. I am always stopped from speaking.
9. People put me down.
10. What I have to say is not important.
11. Speaking my truth is hard.
12. Something stops me from speaking up.
13. I keep quiet to be safe.

Liver – Jaundice

Fears
- Fear they will be seen as a fraud
- Fear of happenstance
- Fear of being hurt
- Fear of pain
- Fear of confusion in a legacy familial wounding
- Fear of being unloved

Emotional States

- Can't figure out why they keep getting hurt. They store the anger or bitterness from those hurts. When they do this the toxic energy builds because they feel hurt they think there is something wrong with them and they are unwanted and unlovable.

Cross Indexing: Liver Problems, Hepatitis, Hepatitis C, inflammation, anemia, Addictions – Chemical, Addictions – Alcohol

Created Patterns

1. I can't just let things/people be.
2. I don't love myself.
3. I am angry at _____.
4. I can't let go of my bitterness.
5. People keep hurting me.
6. I am unlovable.
7. I am defective.
8. I am hurt.
9. I am unworthy and unneeded.
10. People pick on me.
11. I am depressed
12. My soul is in pain.

Liver Problems

Fears

- Fear of having to give your power to someone else
- Fears being forced to give in
- Fears no choices
- Fear of letting others get close
- Fear of trusting others with their love
- Fear of trusting others
- Fear of hardness (life)
- Fear of rejection
- Fear of pain
- Fear of being present
- Fear of not being good enough
- Fear of trusting their judgment
- Fear of powerlessness
- Fear of trusting self
- Fear of control (lack, out of, by others)

Emotional States

- Desire to let go and rip through life in the fast lane – not letting anything slow them down until they smash into the wall. Takes in substances to the point where they become toxic (food, drink and themselves). There is a feeling that excess will keep them from the pain of living. They don't stop long enough to see that they are just continuing a hurt that happened.
- Doubt about themselves leads others to doubt themselves. They don't see people are just reflecting their own emotional state. That doubt leads others to believe they are insincere and walk away. They set up their own hurt.
- Their judgment doesn't filter what is toxic and what isn't. They then let in toxic experiences that create chaos among those around them. When they can't filter the good from the bad they then lose trust.

Cross Indexing: Hepatitis, Hepatitis C, pain, skin problems, bruise, cancer-liver, Wilson's syndrome, weight-overweight, addictions-alcohol, eye problems, fatigue, lack of focus, leg edema, pancreas problems

Repeating Patterns: Loss of control in their lives and they just have to put up with it. They never seem to be able to make the life they want. They feel like they have no choices. There is a sense they have lost power: life is not what they want and they have no control.

Created Patterns

1. I am forced to give in.
2. I have no choice.
3. Whatever I do is wrong.
4. I never get what I want.
5. I'm not worthy of living.
6. I can't make the life I want.
7. I must criticize others before they criticize me.
8. I have no ability to change my life.
9. I don't trust others.
10. There is no magic to life.
11. I'm not in control of my life.
12. I am angry at/ bitter toward/ resentful of _____.
13. Everything is hopeless.
14. I have been expressing/feeling strong emotion of _____ for a long time (these emotions: hatred/ resentment/ anger/ rage/ bitterness/ grief/ sorrow/ revenge.
15. I doubt myself and fail.
16. I doubt myself.
17. I undermine myself.
18. People abandon me, I have abandoned myself.
19. I eat/drink to kill the pain.
20. My life is toxic.

Long Term Illness

Fears
- Fear of losing their identity
- Fear of becoming non-ill
- Fear they will be nothing without the illness
- Fear of having no place
- Fear of being unloved
- Fear of un-belonging

Emotional States
- The long term illness has become an identity. Depending on the ailment everything in their life is rearranged to reflect the strength of the illness. Life becomes a series of can'ts. Can't do this activity, eat these foods. Life develops a very tight circle of activities, food and people. Life is safe within the confines of their illness.

Created Patterns
1. I must suffer.
2. Christians must suffer.
3. Suffering makes me acceptable to god.
4. I must suffer to enter heaven.
5. I must be punished.
6. My suffering is the will of god.
7. I must accept the will of god.
8. My suffering is how I am close to god.
9. I don't know how to be close to god without suffering.
10. I don't know what it feels like to be close to god without suffering.
11. I must suffer to know god.
12. This disease is who I am.
13. I must deprive myself to be safe.
14. I will suffer if I don't deny myself.
15. As long as I am sick I will survive I will be safe.

Low Progesterone Levels

Fears
- Fear that the babies and children will starve first
- Fear of dying and having been nothing
- Fear that what they desire will never happen
- Fear that they are not enough

Emotional States
- This has a strong ancestral influence. Fear of starvation.

- Desire to create that which cannot be created. A dream that is perceived to be out of reach. Long lost desires surface like the waves of an ocean and then drop to leave a void in the energy of passion. Heartache that takes a person beyond this life. There is an ancient ringing that brings a sadness in the heart for which there is no explanation and no solace. Once the ancestral fear of starvation is resolved then there is a whiplash effect to eat as much as one can, which feels out of control – almost a greed.

Cross Indexing: Wounded Creative Core, Premenstrual Syndrome, Gallbladder problems, libido – under-activated, weight gain, ancestral/ epigenetic

Repeating Pattern: Life is feast or famine, they have finances that are good and then they are bankrupt.

Created Patterns
1. I could die at any moment.
2. There is never enough.
3. There is nothing from which to build.
4. I have nothing.
5. I am sad.
6. I feel as if I have lost everything.
7. I can't express myself and be safe.
8. I never get what I want
9. What I want is always out of reach
10. It's all or nothing.
11. Living a reckless life has done this.

Lumbar Hernia

Fears
- Fear of being stopped from doing what they want
- Fear of not being allowed to flow
- Fear of being criticized for reaching out to others
- Fear that they won't be seen a supportive
- Fear of being unloved
- Fear of being

Emotional States
- Holds back an open and sincere connection to others. Language and interaction are guarded. Not open to information coming through a connection to their soul wisdom. Won't let go to those things that keep them limited. Doesn't feel free to be themselves.
- Activities of giving to others are unsupported and they are made to feel guilty for doing it. So efforts at giving are feeble at best.

Cross Indexing: hernia, epigastric hernia, hiatus hernia, umbilical hernia, intestine problems, intestine-small, intestine-large

Created Patterns
1. Opening up to others is dangerous.
2. I don't connect with others.
3. I must hold back and be careful with what I say and do.
4. I don't trust my intuitive information.
5. I'm not free to be myself.
6. People will attack me if I am open.
7. I can't be myself.
8. I'm not free.
9. I am confined and restricted.
10. There is no color its only black and white.

Lung Problems

Fears
- Fear of their breath giving them away
- Fear of living
- Fear of breathing in life
- Fear that the life they breath in is toxic
- Fear of incompletion
- Fears being caught crying
- Fears being punished for being sad

Emotional States
- Grief has left them hollow and empty. They do not remember what they have lost but what it held was the promise of life to come that did not happen – attachment.
- Dance of life has left them without a true partner. They have people around them but they have not allowed them an intimacy of the soul. A deep sense that they have not lived their life in a way that sustains joy or depth.

Cross indexing: Tuberculosis, Cancer-lung, chest problems, pleurisy, bronchitis, pneumonia, emphysema, liver problems, heart problems

Repeating Patterns: Resentment and anger of being denied a life of experience with a friend / sibling/ etc. A sense of betrayal at this loss.

Created Patterns
1. I am only half alive.
2. I'm not worthy of living.
3. I must smother my grief.
4. I am being smothered.
5. I can't breathe freely.

6. There is no joy in living.
7. I am guilty of _____ (What are you guilty of?).
8. I am stuck in overwhelming _____.
9. I'm not allowed to cry.
10. I must hide my grief.
11. I can grieve and be safe.
12. I have been expressing/feeling strong emotion of _____ for a long time (these are negative emotions: hatred/resentment/anger/rage/bitterness/grief/sorrow/revenge).
13. I'm not loved.
14. I can never do things my way.
15. I am always wrong.
16. Love hurts.
17. I'm not accepted.

Lupus

Fears

- Fear of hopelessness
- Fear of heart hurt
- Fear that their nightmares are in their waking life
- Fear of their hatred
- Fear that they are wrong
- Fear of the unknown
- Fear of losing control
- Fear of being forced to be present
- Fear of hope – loss of identity
- Fear of the unknown

Emotional States

- This individual has moved into unknown territory of their unconscious. This individual is dealing with emotions and feelings that they do not understand. They have moved from one committed relationship (jobs, friends, spouse/significant other) looking for something that nourishes them. This nourishment is what they need to survive. They are looking to others to fulfill the angst of the unknown. They feel like their life has had many struggles, obstacles and disappointments. This person has a great deal of personal power. Their words and deeds can be very effective in both a positive and negative fashion. This individual is attracted to the energy of what they are not. They may be in relationships with people that they see as lacking assertiveness. When that person does not give them what they believe they need in the relationship they will leave. They will use their personal power to over react to small incidents and use that excuse to leave the relationship. In the process they may use their powerful verbal skills to further diminish the other person.
- This person has lost their hope in the midst of despair. This person has either a masculine aspect of self or a masculine presence in their life that is coming in and working to break down 'what they perceive' to be this individuals problems into smaller pieces. This masculine energy is doing what comes naturally wanting to solve the problem. As they do this their efforts are absorbed

into resentment and hatred. This negativity (blackness) spills out and absorbs the individual and the foundations that have nourished them. This person perceives their life as being very dark and negative.
- This person feels as if they have reached a critical point in their life and they are afraid of losing control. They may also feel insecure and a lack of support in their life. These feelings may have their foundation in temptation and guilt. They may feel that they have failed to reach a goal that they set for themselves. They are going through some difficult times and they are afraid of what is ahead of them. They have been or are involved in deeply painful relationships or unhealthy, destructive behaviors. They see their life in terms of having been full of obstacles and struggles. They feel depressed or strangled by the situation or person. They may be struggling against an obligation or responsibility. This person feels as if they are dying inside. They feel as if the situation is hopeless and they don't know how to get out of it. This person feeds off old, decaying ideas, rather than creative, alive new ones.
- Doesn't understand the emotions they are feeling. Looking for a relationship that nurtures them (job, friends, or significant other). If they don't get needs met external they leave.
- Has lost hope, feelings of despair. Help from someone trying to help results in resentment and hatred. Sees life as dark and negative.
- Afraid of losing control. Feels insecure and a lack of support. Feels like they have failed to reach goals. Afraid of the future. In relationships that are destructive. Feel depressed by a situation or person. Feels like they are dying inside. This person feeds off of what is old and decaying.

Cross Indexing: Autoimmune Disorders, Sjogren's Disease, Arthritis-Rheumatoid

**This person may also have food sensitivities, food taste change, sensitive to the impact of food on their energy system, changes in digestive system.

Created Patterns
1. I feel like giving up.
2. I am grieving _____.
3. I have been holding/feeling strong emotions of anger for a long time.
4. *What are the boundary issues in your life?*
5. I must control the world around me.
6. I resent _____.
7. I can't stop people from _____.
8. I have to work hard to please my parents/husband/sister.
9. My parents have to be proud of me.
10. Failing is fearful/ dangerous.
11. Failing is the end of the struggle.
12. Failing is a sin.
13. If I fail I earn god's anger.
14. I can't stand up for myself.
15. There's no way out.
16. I am disappointed with myself/others…*who are the others and what did they do to disappoint you?*
17. It would be much easier to die than go on living.
18. It would be easier to die than try and change things.
19. I have no purpose.
20. My life is meaningless.

21. Every time I try to do something I am stopped.
22. If I express my feelings I will be hurt/ridiculed/shamed/embarrassed.
23. My mother did not protect me.
24. I resent/hate/angry at/bitter toward my Mother/Father.
25. God abandoned me.
26. I am disconnected from god
27. God betrayed me.
28. There is no God
29. God is out to get me.
30. I am bad/evil.
31. I deserve to die for my sins.
32. My life is out of control.
33. _____ is overwhelming.
34. People deserve it when I am angry.
35. I deserve to be punished.
36. My anger keeps me safe.
37. My anger keeps me from getting well.
38. I am taken advantage of.
39. I must win or I am worthless.
40. I am a failure *(what made you feel that way and what does being a failure mean?)*.
41. People always fail me.
42. No one ever meets my expectations-they always let me down.
43. I can't trust anyone.
44. I'm in a no win situation.
45. I am depressed.
46. I am angry at _____.
47. I don't forgive myself.
48. I hurt _____.
49. It is hopeless.
50. Life is a continual struggle.
51. I am forced to _____ *(this person may be the caretaker for someone and they resent having to do that)*.
52. I resent _____.
53. I hate _____.
54. I hate myself.
55. I give up.
56. Life will never get better.
57. Life is hard/a struggle.
58. Feelings are dangerous.

Lyme's Disease

Fears

- Fear of their hidden anger and hostility
- Fear that they will be forced to be present
- Fear of being overrun/overwhelmed

- Fear of being rejected
- Fear of change
- Fear of letting go

Emotional States

- This person is tied to a situation or relationship for which they have no love. There is a feeling of no emotion related to this situation/relationship. They are behaving in an automatic way. They are acting without thinking things through. They are locked into a dance of rigid beliefs built upon an out of balance state in the masculine and feminine. This relationship or situation is a result of obligatory or relational bonds. The 'wooden' feeling inside may be a result of repressed anger from childhood abuse. As memories of childhood abuse surface their feelings/memories are denied and trivialized by family members.
- This person has left a situation that was supposed to be good and turned out to be an environment where they were faced with emotions holding a lot of energy and power. They took drastic means to get out of the situation. When they took the 'plunge' out of that situation they jumped into another situation that was equally overwhelming. This person feels as if their life is out of control and making change is hopeless. They sought help but have given in to the overwhelming emotions and moved away or rejected the source of change/help.
- This person has worked very hard at their work/career in an expectation that they will have a significant payoff (this could also apply to other aspects of a person's life, not just work). Their work was very detailed and precise. During their work they broke through barriers and limits. They laid the groundwork for significant career growth. All of the seeds they had planted were growing in precisely the way they had been nurtured. There was nothing in their life that appeared out of place or random. Everything appeared to be very much in control. But, this person was covering up feelings of not being good enough or having been rejected. They kept these feelings tightly covered up. They presented an outward appearance of being easy going and calm. Then one day the inner frustration, anger and perceived disappointment in Self built to a level they couldn't take it anymore and they walked away from what they had worked so hard to build. In the process they laid waste to what they had built, projecting their anger upon the situation. This destruction resulted in that aspect of their life made a blank. They moved on to something else and did not go back to that aspect of self (career, relationships, etc.).
- This individual is not letting go of dysfunctional methods of communication and behavior. They stand in one place (don't make the needed changes) and the problem grows to a monstrous size. The refusal to change their behavior becomes even more apparent as everything else around them continually changes they cling to the way they have always been.
- This person has an immature aspect of the masculine. Instead of moving forward and progressing toward goals, they are stuck in a rut. They feel as if they have not made any significant accomplishments in their life. By staying in a pattern of retrograde growth they feel safe and secure. This person may not have moved out of immature masculine aspects of their sexuality. They are going in circles repeating the same behavior over and over. They have perfected the rational and mental processes around this aspect of self as justification for their behavior. They do not stop and think about their actions beyond their immature masculine worldview.
- This person's flow of life energy is contained and has become stagnant. They are repeating the same negative emotions. They have not allowed any new energy/ideas into the flow of their life. They have limited themselves in how they express their creative, nurturing, intuitive aspect of self. This person has made an attempt to resolve the situation/beliefs/relationships that limit their understanding of themselves but, getting past the 'layers' and doing the cleanup necessary has been an overwhelming task. In reality they only went along the edges. They never got past the

- layers to get into the center of their being. They finally 'gave up' and immersed themselves in the limiting way they are leading their lives. They believe that things will never change and they will never get any better.
- On the outside this person gives the appearances of positive change good health, growth, healing, hope, vigor, vitality, peace and serenity which all convey that they have a sense of self-worth but, they are taking care of the needs of others and neglecting your own needs. They are repressing their own thoughts and emotions. They may be repressing or hiding emotions of guilt, depression, worry, feelings of being rejected and/or self-pity. There is a feeling of passivity in this taking care of others and neglecting themselves as if it is 'happening to you' as opposed to you 'letting it happen'. This person is being broken in two by the needs of self and taking care of the needs of others. They also have a sense that the feelings of being broken in the different directions is getting bigger. The events that give them that sense are getting more frequent and instead of being resolved the feeling is becoming large and maybe overwhelming at some point. This person may be hiding in being a workaholic. The workaholic behavior is just an attempt to deal with the building anger at being in this situation. They may have become critical of self and others. There may be a deep sense or duty related to familial/cultural/religious beliefs.
- Relationship issues. Not letting go. Masculine and feminine out of balance. Repressed anger from childhood abuse. Rejected by family when they bring up the childhood abuse.
- Attracts emotionally overwhelming relationships. Feels like their life is out of control. It is hopeless to make changes. They have rejected changes.
- They had their life all planned out. Everything was controlled. Feels not good enough and rejected. Inner frustration, anger and perceived disappointment at self. They have burned their bridges.
- Dysfunctional communication and behavior. Refuse to change.
- Immature masculine energy. Stuck in a rut. Feels safe and secure in their rut. Self-justified in their behavior.
- Life flow energy is stopped. Refused to change. Creative expression is limited. Emotional issues and behaviors related to relationships are too overwhelming to make changes.
- Needs of others come first. Repressed feelings of guilt, depression, worry, rejection and self-pity. Meeting the needs of others 'happens to them'. Hides in being a workaholic. Anger is repressed by the work. Critical of self and others. Deep sense of duty to family/ culture / religious beliefs.

Cross Indexing: Chronic Fatigue, Fibromyalgia, Infection, Bacteria, Autoimmune Disorder

Created Patterns
1. Angry people are dangerous.
2. Anything I do only makes things worse.
3. Being at work is safer than being at home.
4. Being sick gives me an excuse to take care of myself.
5. Change is dangerous.
6. Everything I try fails.
7. I am a failure.
8. I am a workaholic.
9. I am all alone.
10. I am bad.
11. I am evil.
12. I am going to die.

13. I am Lyme's Disease.
14. I am out of control.
15. I am wrong to be angry.
16. I deserve to be hurt.
17. I don't deserve happiness.
18. I don't know how to take care of myself.
19. I know I am loved when I am wanted/ needed.
20. I must be sick to take care of myself.
21. I must sacrifice myself for others.
22. I must take care of others to be loved/ needed.
23. I was a bad child.
24. I worry about _____.
25. I'm at fault for the bad things that happened to me.
26. I'm not good enough.
27. I'm not worthy.
28. If I am angry I am dangerous.
29. If I don't do it people will be hurt.
30. If I don't do it who will.
31. If I speak my truth I will be put down/called a liar.
32. If I tell people how I feel they will hate/ reject/ not like me.
33. It is dangerous to show my feelings.
34. It is easier to let others tell me what to do.
35. It is my duty to _____.
36. It is my duty/ responsibility to put up with the situation.
37. It is my duty/ responsibility to take care of the needs of others.
38. It will always be this way.
39. It's easier to walk away from a problem than solve it.
40. Lyme's Disease is a way out.
41. My decisions are always wrong.
42. My feelings are dangerous.
43. My problems are just too big for me to deal with.
44. My way is always right.
45. No matter how hard I work I get nothing from it.
46. No matter what I do I can't make it better.
47. No one can help me.
48. Nothing I do works.
49. Only good people deserve happiness.
50. People don't believe me.
51. The needs of others comes first.
52. The unknown is dangerous.
53. There is no way out.
54. Things will never get better.

Lymphatic System Problems

Fears

- Fear that they can't realize their dreams

- Fear of being trapped
- Fear of actually realizing their dreams
- Fear of overwhelming feelings
- Fear of losing their victim identity

Emotional States

- Ease of life has been lost. Whole sections of their life have had major upheaval leaving them feeling groundless. They feel held hostage to the circumstances otherwise they would run away.
- Feels helpless in trying to make any headway. Feels held to a higher standard than others and wants to leave.
- Head is full of creative ideas that are good ideas then they engage in acts of self sabotage to destroy how those ideas play out.
- So much chaos they feel confused and overwhelmed. They keep creating the chaos and confusion. They want to stay lost and un-found in the forest of chaos.
- Whole areas of their lives are under water. They don't feel as if they can stay afloat any more (water = emotions). They feel as if they are drowning in feelings of sorrow and grief.

Cross Indexing: Cancer – Hodgkin's Lymphoma, AIDs, Epstein-Barr Syndrome, spleen problems, thymus problems, tonsils, Cancer Non Hodgkin's Lymphoma

Created Patterns

1. I am a victim.
2. I am going to die.
3. I am not loved.
4. I can't stand up for myself.
5. I can't take care of myself.
6. I don't know when to say no.
7. I don't love myself.
8. I have no enthusiasm for life.
9. I have no peace or joy.
10. I over commit, a busy person always gets it done.
11. I resent/ hate/ angry at _____.
12. I'm not accepted.
13. I'm not good enough.

M's

Macular Degeneration

Fears
- Fear of being wrong
- Fear of losing control
- Fear of being required to be obedient
- Fear of not hearing the whispers about them

Emotional States
- A need to be right, what they see always has a component of something wrong with it. Nit Picky — this person will pick it to death. Loss of control of the big things in their life. Comes across as judgmental or criticizing.

Cross Indexing: Wounded Creative Core, Aging, eye problems, hypertension, addiction-smoking, heart problems, weight-overweight

Repeating Patterns: Comes across as critical and judgmental to people presenting ideas. Halts the flow by being rigid in how they perceive ideas, concepts, world views, etc.

Created Patterns
1. I see what I want to see.
2. I must see the flaws to do it right.
3. I must stop others from making mistakes.
4. My ideas are not usually changeable.
5. I need to know what to expect.
6. If you don't stay the course you have chaos.
7. Play is just a frivolous waste.
8. People need to not wander outside the lines.

Marfan Syndrome

Fears
- Fear that underneath it all there is nothingness
- Fear that they are nothing
- Fear that their concept of reality is unreal
- Fear of being
- Fear that is existence is without meaning

Teachings
- Accept without questioning peoples motives
- Allowing new ideas to be considered
- Be at peace
- Be flexible
- Be good enough
- Be heard
- Be in the now

- Be listened to
- Belong
- Change easily
- Deserve
- Feel listened to
- Feelings honored
- Fit in
- Giving
- Happiness
- Inner peace
- Joy
- Letting go
- Live in alignment with my values
- Live without feeling deprived
- Live without feeling hopeless
- Live without feeling powerless
- Live without feeling tormented
- Live without manipulating people to prove they care
- Live without needing pity to feel cared for
- Live without needing to prove others care for you
- Loving myself
- Make changes easily
- Receiving

Emotional States

- Long distance desires, what this person longs for is too far removed to be attainable. The desire is overwhelming…wanting what they cannot have.
- Peace is illusive. This person feels tormented; helpless to make things different, external torment, does not fit in with those around them.
- Sense of hopelessness that things will never change

Cross Indexing: Heart Problems, lupus, Arthritis-Rheumatoid, Polymyositis, Scleroderma, Ehler-Danlos Syndrome

Created Patterns

1. Change is dangerous.
2. I am alone.
3. I am depressed.
4. I am helpless.
5. I am respected.
6. I am too tired to go on.
7. I am tormented.
8. I can't change.
9. I can't have what I want.

10. I can't let others help me.
11. I can't make changes in my life.
12. I can't say what I want.
13. I can't speak my truth.
14. I can't talk about my feelings (why?).
15. I can't tell anyone what I want (why?).
16. I don't belong.
17. I don't deserve.
18. I don't feel like living anymore.
19. I don't fit in.
20. I don't have a purpose.
21. I don't have a reason for living.
22. I don't love myself.
23. I feel sorry for myself.
24. I need to do everything myself.
25. I resent _____.
26. I use pity to get my needs met.
27. I want to be left alone.
28. I want to die.
29. I'm not good enough.
30. I'm not worthy.
31. If others help me it is out of pity.
32. It's not safe speaking my truth.
33. Life is cruel.
34. New ideas are hurtful.
35. New ideas get me into trouble.
36. No one cares.
37. No one knows me.
38. No one listens to me.
39. People need to prove they care about me.
40. People pity me.
41. The old ways are the best ways.
42. Things are hopeless, they will never change.

*Look at themes of power, depression, flow, abandonment, acceptance, anger, change, boundaries, body, compassion, contentment, control, energy, judgment, letting go, lonely, love, unconditional love, loving yourself, now, pain, peace, rejection, self-worth, self-esteem, unconditional love, unmet needs, conflicting motivations, empathy, movement, power, receiving

Mastoiditis

Fears

- Fear of feeling forced to say words of hate
- Fear of trouble if they don't conform / comply
- Fear of being abandoned
- Fear of losing those around them
- Fear that everything they think they know is wrong

Emotional States
- Old thoughts and feelings of bigotry and intolerance have created a toxic energy in their body. Their body is attacking toxic thoughts that they have heard and repeated.

Cross Indexing: Ear Infection -Chronic, Ear Problems, Ears – Hearing Problems, Labyrinthitis

Created Patterns
1. I don't want to hear what's going on around me.
2. I am left out.
3. I am so afraid I don't understand.
4. I am intolerant of others.
5. People say things that are so wrong and then they won't listen to reason.
6. People that are different should stay in their place.
7. I am always right whether you want to listen or not.
8. I refuse to listen to others with ideas I don't agree with.

Maxilla

Fears
- Fear that their words are useless
- Fear of being powerless
- Fear of disappearing into nothingness
- Fear of not being good enough
- Fear of the juxtaposition – having to reconcile the two sides

Emotional States
- When speaking there is no distance or carry through to the words. The words do not create a sense of learning or informing. They feel disrespected and like nothing they say or do gets them acknowledgement. Their actions do not bring cohesion to a group. There is a sense of ineffectiveness. They never step back and say "What am I learning?".

Created Patterns
1. My words are weak and useless.
2. My thoughts are powerless.
3. I am worthless.
4. I must keep quiet; speaking is a waste of my time.
5. I am disrespected.
6. I fail at the efforts I make.
7. Nobody listens to what I say.
8. I do the wrong things.

Measles

Fears
- Fear of the global undercurrent of hatred*
- Fear of being worthless
- Fear of being unwanted
- Fear of not knowing what is next
- Fear of being out of control
- Fear of being hurt
- Fear of rejection
- Fear of being wrong
- Fear of being me

*There is a global cognition of resources becoming critically restricted throughout the world. When resources needed for life (water, air, shelter, food, and medical care) are poisoned or withheld there is a sense by the affected groups that a human life, their human life, has minimal worth. When a collective group believes they have been deemed unworthy a collective anger and hatred begins to build. The immune system of those groups and overlapping groups is diminished by this collective feeling of worthlessness, powerlessness, anger and hatred. The planet has experienced periods and pockets of the collective immune system being diminished in the past but it is my opinion that the planet has entered a new phase of diminished immunity. Our planetary systems are stressed due to climate change and pollution. Therefore the immunity or resiliency of the planet is impaired. Our children are very sensitive and they "feel" what the planet is experiencing. Our children are sensitive to the poisoned food, water and air.

Emotional States
- The taming of the creative core creates a woundedness. That wound is a message that their expression of self is not good enough. That they are wrong if their expression is their being then their entire being is wrong. They are unworthy.
- An unknowing, unlearned apsects of life have created confusion and pain.

Cross Indexing: Virus, ancestral/ epigenetic, wounded creative core

Created Patterns
1. I have no idea what people want from me and then they punish me for not knowing what I have never been told.
2. I cannot be me.
3. Someone is always telling me what to do.
4. I cannot express my feeling safely.
5. I am wrong so often I must not be any good. I am worthless.
6. There is no peace in my life.

Memory Loss non-physical trauma

Fears
- Fear disappearing into confusion
- Fear of not know who they are
- Fear that someone is taking their things
- Fear of what they see
- Fear of being left
- Fear of being embarrassed
- Fear of looking stupid
- Fear of not belonging

Teachings
- Inner peace
- Release the trauma of loss
- Release fear easily
- Letting go of hurt
- Live without secrets
- Be safe with truth
- See the truth of those who hurt me
- Creator's perspective of the events
- Living in the now
- Live without feeling alone
- Understand
- Live without needing to punish yourself
- Live with the memories without guilt
- Live without fearing the past
- Live without needing to know the past
- Being good enough
- Be in control
- Safe
- Live without the fear of dying
- To be heard
- To be seen
- Knowing you always have options
- Live without thinking I have been abandoned by God
- Live without the fear of punishment
- Live without the fear of overwhelm
- Release the fear of being powerless
- Live without being a victim
- Release the fear of the unknown
- Knowing that that is then and this is now
- Live without needing to be special
- Complete
- Whole

Emotional States
- Intense fear of death, fear of the unknown.
- Fear of being alone.
- Intense fear of separation from god / Mother / Father.
- Frozen with fear; no understanding of what they are seeing / experiencing.
- Overwhelmed with fear; doesn't know what to do next.
- Fearful that if seen there will be a punishment / hurt.

- They give no energy to the past and seal it off. The path to the memory has been altered and corrupted.

Cross Indexing: Post Traumatic Stress Disorder, Aging, Alzheimer's, ACOA, Dementia, Senility, Brain Problems

Created Patterns
1. I will never be safe again.
2. I did not see anything.
3. No one will find me.
4. I am alone.
5. I don't know who I am.
6. The past will hurt me.
7. Something horrible happened to me, otherwise I would remember.
8. I am afraid of what will happen next.
9. I can't stand up for myself.
10. I am powerless.
11. I am guilty.
12. I am not good enough to know the truth.
13. I am powerless to stop _____.
14. I have no control over anything.
15. If I stand up for myself I will be hurt / killed.
16. I must worry to keep bad things from happening.
17. Bad things will happen to me again.
18. I need to run away.
19. I have no options.
20. I will be punished for _____.
21. I must punish myself.
22. I am going to die.
23. It is hopeless.
24. No one sees me.
25. No one hears what I have to say.
26. I don't know what to do.
27. I don't understand what I am seeing.
28. I'm not good enough.
29. I am a victim.
30. I will never see _____ again.
31. I am disconnected from god.
32. God abandoned me.
33. God left me all alone.
34. I am going to die.
35. No one is interested in what I know or what I have to say.
36. I'm not respected.
37. I am invisible.
38. I am irrelevant.

*Look at themes of power, perceptions, abandonment, abuse, accidents, anxiety, attack, blockages, boundaries, control, denial, disassociation, fear, innocence, victimhood, releasing wounds, power,

physical abuse, control, letting go, stress

Meningitis – Bacterial

Fears

- Fear that no matter how much they resist it is futile
- Fear of being powerless in the face of an attack
- Fear of shame
- Fear of attack
- Fear of being shown to be wrong
- Fear of losing everything
- Fear of betrayal
- Fear of invasion
- Fear of violation

Emotional States

- Feels as if their lives have been invaded by people who communicate and speak things that attack them. The attack comes from within their circle of people they trusted. Family is very important and when the attack comes from within there is a sense of a death in how they connect with family.

Cross Indexing: Candida, Yeast Infection, Murcorycosis, Meningitis-Fungal, Meningitis -Viral, Inflammation

Created Patterns

1. I know everything I need to know.
2. I'm not open to anyone else's opinions or ideas.
3. I want out of here.
4. My guilt is killing me.
5. I want to die.
6. I am under attack by the people closest to me.
7. I have let people get under my skin and then those same people go out of their way to shame me.
8. My family hurt me and betrayed me.

Meningitis – Fungal

Fears

- Fear of making meaningless choices
- Fear of being irrelevant
- Fear of crumbling in the face of challenge
- Fear that there is no meaning
- Fear that their belief foundation is wrong

- Fear that what they have protected themselves with has cracked

Emotional States
- They can't protect themselves from an assault on old ideas and old ways. They find they can't defend the concepts they have live for so very long. They collapse in on themselves.

Cross Indexing: Candida, Yeast Infection, Murcorycosis, Meningitis-Bacterial, Meningitis-Viral

Created Patterns
1. I have been expressing/feeling strong emotions of rage for a long time.
2. What is it that you think that makes you angry?
3. I can't protect or defend my speech.
4. I am attacked for what I say.
5. I am under attack by those that would stop me from speaking.
6. At least I live my life with integrity and honesty.
7. The old way need to be protected, they keep us anchored in reality.
8. Old ways are safe ways even if they hurt us.

Meningitis – Viral

Fears
- Fear of getting catching a disease
- Fear that someone will find out that they're essence is worthless
- Fear that someone will be angry when they find out about the fraud
- Fear that what they are communicating is at its core worthless
- Fear that what they are communicating is hurtful
- Fear that they are powerless to stop the out of control situation they are in
- Fear that they will be found to be a fraud

Emotional States
- Unhappiness in current situation and wanting to die. Powerless to make the needed changes.
- Jumping on a horse and racing at high speed in a direction that will not take them to their true destination.
- Needing to go through life unchallenged. Needs to be the expert. Fearful of being found to be a fraud and really worthless.

Cross Indexing: Candida, Yeast Infection, Murcorycosis, Meningitis-Fungal, Meningitis-Bacterial, Inflammation

Repeating Patterns: Low self-esteem hides behind a facade of anger. Pretends to be sweet but there is a viper-ready to strike at any threat.

Created Patterns

1. I must be on guard against any attack.
2. I am powerless.
3. I want to die.
4. I change the lives of others to meet my needs and when I can't I am out of control.
5. When I'm not in control bad things happen.
6. I am worthless and in need.
7. My needs are never met so I control others to get those needs met.

Menopause – Difficult

Fears

- Fear losing their identity
- Fear of not suffering
- Fear of aging
- Fear of becoming worthless
- Fear of their anger
- Fear of change
- Fear of the struggle and strife
- Fear of the regret of what can no longer be

Emotional States

- Wounds of the uterus, grieving for what has been lost. Ancestral loss of child with stillbirth, miscarriage or abortion.
- Holds tightly to preconceived ideas of menopause passed to her from mother, grandmother, great grandmother who suffered. Suffering was their association with life and their sexuality. This concept was anchored in a religious dogma. To not suffer is an invalidation of the mother and grandmother. Life is a struggle and everything is pain. Held against their will. The uterus was held hostage by an ideologue that hijacked ownership of procreation. The uterus became the slave of the masculine patriarch until it was no longer viable. The onset of menopause triggers the anger at the masculine hostage taking and then the casting away.
- Unyielding nature of individual as they go through 'The Change' creates the energy of conflict within the body. A person with a personality that is rigid and unyielding finds change as threatening and dangerous. 'The Change' would set up the vibrational dynamic of struggle within as the person grapples with her own body's betrayal — 'The Betrayal' is triggering her feeling when change in her life created an unsafe place to be.
- Warning of death. Aging consciousness that once a woman reaches menopause she starts to become worthless, no value. She loses her beauty and the strength and power of her sexuality. That becomes a place of panic and the questions of 'How will I survive?' Panic, anxiety, lotions, creams and plastic surgery. It's done, no more period, identity of 'who am I now' looms large with no real answers.
- Juried and judged — decisions around her sexuality were judged and juried by the values of others. Her sexual wounds were very public…miscarriage, abortions, possible stillborn, etc. The

wounds of the uterus may be carried forward from the mother, grandmother, great-grandmother, etc. The uterus bears judgment, guilt, regret, frustration and shame of failed procreation from the ancestry. Failure to produce the 'right' kind of child. Heart is wounded by the judgment. Feels as if the wholeness of being is not see by others but judged based on the procreation. Despair in the heart.
- Justification of existence is gone. Value was derived from being female with an abundant uterus. Not in alignment with 'self'. Incoherence between the minds.

Cross Indexing: Endocrine System Problems, Low Progesterone, Aging, Premenstrual syndrome, Heart Problems, Bone Problems

Created Patterns

1. I am afraid of menopause.
2. I will get old.
3. I am rejected.
4. I am useless.
5. I am angry at my body.
6. I have no control over my body.
7. I'm next to die.
8. I am no longer sexy.
9. I am no longer desirable.

Menstrual Problems

Fears
- Fear of not being whole
- Fear of being broken
- Fear of a period being shame
- Fear of a period being embarrassment
- Fear of others knowing she is having a period
- Fear of banishment
- Fear of being cursed
- Fear of being a taboo
- Fear of being unclean

Emotional States
- Trouble letting go of what no longer serves. What was once creative and direction of growth no longer applies and they can't let go of the dead end. They feel as if they have lost opportunities for expansion into new ways of being.
- Feminine values are under constant attack by masculine energies in their lives. Their femininity is considered a shortfall and reduces their humanity. They are diminished for being female. They do their best to not be feminine but to be more masculine in their values and approach.

Cross Indexing: Dysmenorrhea, Premenstrual Syndrome, Amenorrhoea, Wounded Creative Core

Created Patterns
1. I am guilty of _____.
2. I am afraid of being a woman.
3. Being a woman is bad.
4. Women must be punished.
5. Women must suffer.
6. Being a woman is no fun.
7. I am afraid of pain.
8. Being a woman is painful.
9. I hate being a woman.
10. I must suffer.
11. I deserve to be punished.
12. I must be more like a man to be valued/worthy.
13. Men are better than women.
14. Women have their place.
15. I am under attack because I am a woman.
16. I can't be creative.
17. Something stops me every time I try to do a creative project.

Mitral Valve Prolapse

Fears
- Fear of having their heart violated
- Fear of losing what they love
- Fear that the warning was not heeded in time (possible ancestral wound)
- Fear of loving the wrong person (possible ancestral wound)

Emotional States
- A feeling of sinking into a place of suffocation. Panic as the area closes in around them. Genetic qualities lend a voice to a heart that is big and broken. A heart long known for being loving gives and gives and never receives and that heart loses hope that it will ever feel the same amount of love it gives. But this is a heart that is in fear. It gives love because it does not believe it is worthy of love. It hopes that by giving it will be recognized and receive adulation. But all this heart attracts is worthlessness.
- Heavy handed influences early in life trigger deeply held (ancestral) feelings of panic and not knowing where to run to be safe. Fear grips the heart and leaves a stain. Feelings of panic are coupled with hatred. Worn out phrases and platitudes circle the brain to write the excuses.
- They have to take back what they have given. To receive they must take from themselves which dis-empowers them.

Cross Indexing: Marfan syndrome, Ehlers-Danlos syndrome, Muscular dystrophy, Graves' disease, Scoliosis, Ancestral/Genetic, Heart Problems (see for additional description of mitral valve)

Created Patterns

1. My father's anger is justified.
2. My father is always right.
3. My father will kill me.
4. I must make excuses to survive.
5. I hate my mother.
6. My father only hurts me because he has to.
7. My father hurts me because I am bad.
8. I am bad.
9. I am worthless.
10. My love is worthless.
11. I must give and give, if I ever expect to be wanted/love.
12. I can't breathe.
13. I am being suffocated by life.
14. Life is out to kill me.
15. Life is punishment.
16. I live to prove my father is right.
17. I can't get a break.
18. I can't get a breath.
19. I must be deceived to be safe.
20. Only by being hurt can I feel worthy.

Mold Sensitivity

Fears

- Fear of ridicule
- Fear of attack by what protects them
- Fear of being invaded
- Fear of being overrun
- Fear of the little ones
- Fear of what you cannot see
- Fear that what you cannot see will kill you

Emotional States

- Harsh criticism of self in the face of perceived thoughts. Lets down their guard and then catches themselves. Halts their progress when they do that. Uncharacteristic warmth and friendliness creates alarm.
- Unwillingness to create a new place for themselves.
- A miscommunication creates emotions that stagnates and becomes toxic. Wrong process for being in the world. Yields but doesn't. Fear that something they need to trust is going to attack. Feels unsafe in their house, feels under attack. Not safe within self. Feels like they attack themselves. The other people won't leave them alone.

Cross Indexing: EMF Sensitivity, Allergies, Autoimmune disorders

Repeating Patterns: passive aggressive

Created Patterns
1. I attack myself for being stupid.
2. My body feels unsafe.
3. I give people what they think they want and then I do what I want.
4. I am self critical.
5. I must criticize myself before others do.
6. I must put myself down before others do.
7. I must stick with old stagnate places, just because they are old does not mean they are valuable.

Moles

Fears
- Fear of their own inner hostility
- Fear of feeling worthless
- Fear of being outcast

Emotional States
- Cautious optimism has turned into nothing. Leads to feeling of I am nothing. Self is connected to the external illusion.
- Holding onto past hurts of the heart that diminished their sense of worth.
- Haphazard guesses at circumstances have yielded disastrous results – they then call in their sense of poor self-worth when they have made bad decisions.

**Epigenetic = moles at birth connected to sense of self-worth in the ancestry

Cross Indexing: skin problems, Growths

Created Patterns
1. I am inadequate.
2. I am worthless.
3. I am unworthy.
4. What do you believe wrongly about yourself?
5. I am nothing.
6. My identity is defined by my circumstances.
7. Without my stuff I am nothing.
8. I have been hurt in such a way that I no longer want to exist.
9. I make poor decisions.
10. I am safe when I am nothing.
11. Being nothing is my identity.

12. I will never be somebody.

Mononucleosis

Fears
- Fear of authority
- Fear of their creative being seen
- Fear of being seen
- Fear of the good things
- Fear of being seen as outstanding
- Fear of worthiness

Emotional States
- Judged as incompetent by those around and in authority at an early age. Hid away talent and passion to be safe in the face of harsh criticism. Everything they did, by default, strove for mediocrity and invisibility. Even exciting activities were done in such a way as to be invisible to keep the harshness of exposure away. The presence of criticism was just too much to bear. So this person kept themselves in the shadows and away from the light of visibility. Long held negativity in the ancestry become the defacto wisdom of how a life should be safely lived, otherwise bad things would happen. Keeping yourself worthless was the only way to be – being in the stream of negativity was acceptance.
- Being seen was dangerous and they projected that to others around them. This would manifest as an attempt to keep everyone in their group invisible. If someone in the group was headed toward visibility they would feel like the whole group was at risk. They will do whatever it takes to not be unique, excel or be seen. They aim for neutral
- A feeling of worthlessness pervades everything. If they get a compliment it is followed with an apology of how it's not good enough. They demean themselves relentlessly. Choices are made based on a value of "can this provide me a sense of less than" or "this is good enough". Choices are not made based on "this is great and I deserve this wonderful thing". They don't feel like good things are a possible choice. Makes fun of themselves and their life choices so that those with negativity in their lives don't get their pound of flesh out of beating them up emotionally.
- They run and hide every time there is an opportunity to be seen. This keeps them in the background of their work. They can be overworked and run down (home and/or work). To not be seen and not be criticized they allow their boundaries to be overrun. They are seen as a work horse. Nothing spectacular but they get the job done. Predictable and unremarkable even when they are sick and exhausted.

Cross Indexing: Liver Problems, Flu, Virus, Colds, Strep Throat, Tonsils, Spleen, Epstein-Barr, Heart Problems, Anemia

Created Patterns
1. I feel unloved.
2. I am unworthy.
3. I am worthless.

4. I am angry at not being appreciated.

Morning Sickness

Fears
- Fear of getting up in the morning
- Fear of losing self
- Fear of losing their identity
- Fear of losing their body
- Fear of no one telling them the truth
- Fear that they have been duped

Emotional States
- Forced to let go of the singularity. Transition of going from one state to another.

Created Patterns
1. I am no longer me, my identity has been taken.
2. I have a hard time adjusting to change.
3. I need to hang onto what I have.
4. My needs aren't considered.
5. I come last.
6. No one helps me.
7. No one supports me.
8. The needs of others come before me.
9. I don't want to be pregnant.
10. Being pregnant is being forced on me.
11. Women are forced to be pregnant.
12. Pregnancy is a burden.
13. My life is a burden.
14. I'm not accepted.
15. I'm rejected by _____.
16. Children take away my freedom.
17. Being pregnant destroys my body.
18. I will die from childbirth.
19. I am being used by _____.
20. Pregnancy is dangerous.

Mouth Problems

Fears
- Fear of people openly hostile to their speaking
- Fear of what will come out of their mouth

- Fear that they cannot say what they want to say
- Fear of talking back to people that have said too much
- Fear that they have more on the line than they should
- Fears that what is toxic is disguised as nurturance

Emotional States
- Holding or speaking words that should not be spoken. Not being the observer in states where there is a choice of peace or non-peace.
- Taking in that which nurtures to excess. Too much food, too much to the point where it creates a numbness and awareness of the imbalance of giving and receiving.

Cross Indexing: Jaw Problems, TMJ, Gum problems, Tongue, Teeth problems

Created Patterns
1. I am afraid to move out of my comfort zone.
2. I must criticize others before they hurt me.
3. I don't like change.
4. Change is dangerous/ hurtful/ bad.
5. When I eat too much I no longer taste the food, I am numb. It no longer gives a sense of calm.
6. I speak to the point of numbness.
7. My words are meaningless and betray my sense of not being good enough.
8. What I take in and give out is out of balance to the point of toxicity.

Mucormycosis

Fears
- Fear of having to suffer idiots
- Fear of the blows of life
- Fear of not being supported
- Fear of life
- Fear of presence
- Fear of the next thing
- Fear of being in the silence and confronted with myself

Emotional States
- Long distance contact is illusive in the world of negative thoughts and emotions. Is not interested in hearing malformed thoughts that have you guessing as to whether there is a soul behind the mouth saying those things. The vital essence is tattered and full of holes like a moth-eaten sweater and has no integrity. The vital essence will fail at the most subtle of emotional breezes. Buffeted by life in a way that gave nothing for nurturance. Each whack took away and nothing ever rebuilt them. The assault was continually unabated with no recovery. Head driven ideals also destroyed the vital essence.

Cross Indexing: fungus, infection, body part affected

Created Patterns
1. I am beat up and have no space to me to recover.
2. There's nothing to build on all my foundations are gone.
3. I am helpless and powerless to stand up.
4. I have been beat up and spit out by the world. There is nothing left of me to sustain living.
5. I have nothing left to give.
6. I have no desire to live.
7. Everything has been taken.
8. There is no joy in living.

Multiple Sclerosis

Fears
- Fear of listening to the heart
- Fear that they will only see the disease and not me
- Fear that I will be shamed
- Fear of listening to the inner self
- Fear of being overrun
- Fear of being overwhelmed
- Fear of change
- Fear of being out of control
- Fear abandonment

Emotional States
- Disconnection between the needs of the heart and body and what it is being told by the brain. Overreaction to a perceived violation of boundaries. Epigenetic.

Cross Indexing: spasmodic dystonia, focal dystonia, genetic disorder, Nerve problems, Autoimmune disorders, Muscular Dystrophy, muscle problems

Created Patterns
1. Change is dangerous.
2. Controlling everything keeps me safe.
3. Everyone else gets all the luck.
4. God doesn't love me.
5. I am afraid of disappointing others.
6. I am depressed.
7. I am going to die.
8. I am guilty of _____.
9. I am out of control.
10. I am powerless/ I have no control / I am dominated.
11. I am responsible for _____.

12. I am worthless.
13. I blame myself for _____.
14. I can't communicate.
15. I can't forgive myself/ others.
16. I can't make changes.
17. I can't talk to others.
18. I can't change.
19. I can't take care of myself.
20. I don't listen to what others are telling me.
21. I don't deserve to heal.
22. I hate my mother/father.
23. I must be perfect.
24. I need someone else to take care of me.
25. I shut down my feelings to keep from being hurt.
26. I'm not good enough.
27. Life is out of control.
28. New things are scary/ threatening.
29. New things aren't safe.
30. Nothing I do is ever enough.
31. Others don't hear me.
32. Others don't listen to me.

Muscle Problems

Fears
- Fear of what is lost (or losing)
- Fear of weakness
- Fear of being powerless
- Fear of family
- Fear of being manipulated by others
- Fear of moving

Emotional States
- They are manipulated by others through DNA connections or what those DNA connections represent.
- They stay very still to not be seen. They hold themselves tight and on guard to be at the ready for what might happen next.

Cross Indexing: Adrenal fatigue, adrenal problems, bone problems, connective tissue disorders

Created Patterns
1. I can't move away from what is not good for me.
2. I must stay still to survive.
3. If I do anything I will make it worse.

4. I'm not supported.
5. I am frozen with fear.
6. Fear dominates me/my life.
7. I have to stay and take it.
8. I am manipulated by _____.
9. I must be strong all the time.
10. I can't move forward.
11. I am manipulated by _____.
12. I am guilty of _____.
13. I have not lived up to my own expectations.
14. I must run away.
15. I must not move.
16. I must stay on guard to not be hurt.
17. I am forced to do against my desires.
18. I am not responsible for what has happened.

Muscles – Cramps

Fears
- Fear of being confined and defined
- Fear of not being able to please everyone
- Fear of being guilty
- Fear of doing
- Fear of moving forward
- Fear of being run over
- Fear of having to relive the regrets in their life
- Fear of living a life with no purpose

Emotional States
- Jerked around in life to the point where they can't pivot fast enough to make everyone happy.
- They are not in the flow of life. Life energy is constricted. They are held back by feelings of guilt. Should'a, would'a, could'a. Guilt constricts their ability to move. They hold themselves back so that they don't make anymore guilt.

Cross Indexing: Muscle problems, arteriosclerosis, spinal stenosis, kidney problems

Created Patterns
1. I can't move forward in life.
2. I don't take orders from others.
3. I'll do what I want to do.
4. Nobody tells me what to do.
5. I am guilty of _____.
6. I am guilty for everything.
7. I can't make anyone happy.

8. I can't pivot fast enough.
9. I can't stop people at the boundaries of my space.
10. I am not joyous. In fact I don't know what joy is.
11. I am out of balance. I give more than I receive.

Muscular Dystrophy

Fears

- Fear of shame and humiliation
- Fear of being laughed at
- Fear of dying
- Fear of being killed for surviving
- Fear of being killed for assuming the power of the masculine
- Fear of hatred for who you are

Emotional States

- Ancestral out of balance masculine traits. Actions that were so extreme they changed the genes. Possibly a grandmother that was forced to take over all the duties of sustaining a family to survive. She took on the masculine role with an experience of severe fear and hardship.

Cross Indexing: Nerve problems, Muscle Problems, multiple sclerosis, ancestral/ epigenetic

Created Patterns

1. I must experience pain.
2. I have been expressing/feeling strong emotion of _____ for a long time (these are negative *emotions: hatred/resentment/anger/rage/bitterness/grief/sorrow/revenge).
3. I must stop myself from going forward.
4. I must stop myself from hurting someone else.
5. Day by day I am losing my power.
6. People take my power from me.
7. The loss of my power is the loss of my life.
8. I can't be a man.
9. I am too weak to be of any use.
10. I must be the man to survive.
11. I can't defend myself.
12. I must be the breadwinner to survive.
13. I must take care of my family at all costs.

Myasthenia Gravis

Fears

- Fear of the flow

- Fear of obstacles
- Fear of what they have done
- Fear of being rescued

Emotional States
- Weakened by guilt in their erroneous connection to their divine nature. They believe that 'god' has declared them guilt of imaginary sins. A religious dogma has taken their connection to the divine. They have let that dogma destroy their boundaries. They feel an inner false guilt.

Cross Indexing: Autoimmune disorders, genetic/ancestral, thymus problems, Nerve Problems, Face/Head Problems, Muscle problems

Repeating Patterns: A deep sense that they have been abandoned by god.

Created Patterns
1. I am sinful and should be punished.
2. I have failed god.
3. Being wrong keeps me safe.
4. I am guilty of breaking god's laws.
5. I fear change in life.
6. I feel like giving up.
7. Change is dangerous.
8. When things change I get hurt.
9. I am helpless to change things.
10. I am powerless to change things.
11. I have expressing/feeling strong emotions of grief for a long time.

N's

Narcolepsy

Fears
- Fear of breathing prana
- Fear of nothing being right
- Fear of what other might say
- Fear of too much happening at one time
- Fear of what you think
- Fear of self-attack

Emotional States
- Yielding to all until the weight becomes too much, crown chakra is impaired and the upward and downward pressure flow of energy is too much.
- Ridden hard and put away wet – this is a euphemism that describes working really hard for a period of time and then no care to refresh or heal the body. This creates a split in the energy expectations. One side is trying to keep it going and the other side is trying to shut down. There is a continuous push-pull of energies.
- Punishing themselves for meeting expectations.

Cross Indexing: Brain Problems, Sleep problems

Created Patterns
1. I wish I were somewhere else.
2. I can't/don't want to cope anymore.
3. I am tired of being responsible for _____.
4. I wish my responsibilities would go away.

Nausea

Fears
- Fear of being threatened with overwhelming emotions
- Fear that no solution will bring you into safety

Emotional States
- A rejection of what is perceived as nurturing that becomes toxic. The toxin has a heat and over activation of energy. Feels out of balance.

Cross Indexing: CTE, Concussion, labyrinthitis, vertigo, headache – migraine, flu

Created Patterns
1. I am afraid of _____ (something going on in the here and now).
2. I wish _____ had never happened.
3. What from the past don't you want to remember?
4. What emotions are you taking in that are not yours?
5. I must take the abuse.
6. I am forced to take in something that is not good for me.
7. I must take in 'toxins' to be accepted.

Nephritis

Fears
- Fear the lack of reason
- Fear letting go of the anger
- Fear of letting go of the injustice
- Fear of being unprotected
- Fear of not knowing right from wrong
- Fear of not know what is toxic
- Fear of ownership

Emotional States
- Toxins are not filtered out, what is not good for us is retained, failure to filter, lack of discernment, can't let go of anger and injustice. Made decisions that did not ask the question 'is this good for me?'. The decision turned out to not be good for them. The lack of discernment created anger and a feeling of injustice that inflamed their feelings. Then they did not let go of those feelings. They keep recycling the memory. Does not take ownership of the decision.

Cross Indexing: Urinary Tract Infection, Lupus, Kidney Problems, inflammation, Autoimmune disorders.

Repeating Patterns: Victim/ Martyr

Created Patterns
1. I am disappointed by _____.
2. I am a failure.
3. Life is unfair.
4. I am overwhelmed.
5. I am guilty of _____.
6. I fear _____.
7. I am to blame for _____.
8. I can't let go of old hurts.
9. I make bad decisions.

10. I am the victim of people who _____.
11. I am angry at the injustice of _____.
12. I don't know what's good or bad.

Nerve Problems

Fears
- Fear of communication being lost
- Fear of communication being confused
- Fear of communication being corrupted
- Fear of secrets being leaked
- Fear of communication being stopped
- Fear of your circuits being overloaded

Teachings
- Be in balance between your rights and the rights of others
- Be valued
- Calm
- Communicate with ease
- Creator's perspective of truth
- Focus on the now
- Giving
- Receiving
- Go with the flow
- Letting go of the past
- Listening to my inner guidance
- Live not over reacting
- Live up to my potential
- Live without being taken advantage of
- Live without confusion
- Live without resistance to your inner voice
- Take action
- Taking responsibility for your choices
- Trust
- Trust myself
- Trust others

Emotional States
- Global level – distortion / imbalance in the communication between feminine and masculine principle.
- Individual level-not listening to what is being communicated. Resistance to what the inner self is trying to get across. Resistance leads to confusion and disconnection.

Cross Indexing: Acoustic Neuroma – Left Side, Acoustic Neuroma – Right Side, ALS, Alzheimers, Brain Problems, Chronic Traumatic Encephalopathy (CTE), Concussion, Dementia, Depression, Focal Dystonia, Huntington's Disease, Insomnia, Leg-Paralysis, Meningitis – Bacterial, Meningitis – Fungal, Meningitis – Viral, Multiple Sclerosis, Muscular Dystrophy, Narcolepsy, Slipped Disc (Herniation), Spasmodic Dysphonia – (Laryngeal), Stroke, Stuttering (non-developmental), Parkinson's

Repeating Patterns: Out of balance give and take, Not present – out of present time, Out of the flow of life, Can't let go of the past, Doesn't listen to inner guidance, Over reacts – an over correction of boundaries, Not living up to their potential, Feels taken advantage of, Doesn't take responsibility for their choices/actions, Uses confusion as a survival strategy

Created Patterns

1. I am alone.
2. I am confused.
3. I am disconnected from everything around me.
4. I am intimidated by _____.
5. I am lost.
6. I always say the wrong thing.
7. I always do the wrong thing.
8. I am treated unjustly by others.
9. I can't move forward.
10. I can't seem to get things done.
11. I can't seem to hold focus.
12. I don't care if my actions hurt others.
13. I don't have a clear focus.
14. I don't know where I am headed in life.
15. I don't trust my inner voice.
16. I don't trust myself.
17. I don't understand _____.
18. I doubt myself.
19. I must get mine before it's all gone.
20. I need to make sure I always get what I want.
21. I overreact to _____.
22. I prefer my company over others.
23. I'm not valued.
24. I have a broken heart.
25. If I give something I expect to be compensated.
26. It is hard for me to get my point across.
27. It's their fault for getting in the way.
28. Life is unfair.
29. Others are to blame for _____.
30. People always want something from me.
31. People don't seem to understand what I am saying.

*Look at themes of giving, negativity, greed, calm, balance, blame, change, clarity, confusion, control, energy, judgment, letting go, listening, justice, now, pain, relationships, selfishness, understanding, unmet needs, conflicting motivations, boundaries, communication, stress, broken heart

Nervous Breakdown

Fears

- Fear of being without
- Fear of nothing left
- Fear of the future and the past

- Fear of being a disappointment
- Fear of failing

Emotional States

- Memories collide with the overwhelm of the present and there is no place to sort out the pain in the face of overwhelming demands. So they shut down. All senses are on overwhelm and overload. They have no skills for coping with 'overwhelm' or overload. Goes into confusion and they shutdown to survive. They freeze. That is a strategy that doesn't resolve the stress and they go into overload in a repeating cycle. Weak boundaries.
- May have someone in their life that holds them to a certain standard that they simply can't meet (narcissist). This person's standards and what they want from life are in direct conflict. This relationship is draining, demanding and denigrating. For example: you can't have self-esteem and inner peace in the face of draining demands without something needing to shift. If this person feels there is no way out they will go into survival strategies.

Cross Indexing: PTSD, ACOA, Suicidal, Brain Problems, Emotional Disorders, Anxiety, Panic Disorder

Created Patterns

1. I can't say what I'm truly thinking.
2. I am afraid of what will happen next.
3. The future is scary
4. I am depressed.
5. I am in a dark hole and I can't get out.
6. I have no power to change things.
7. I am completely overwhelmed by the present.
8. I am lost in the confusion of what to do about it.
9. I am grieving the loss of myself.
10. No one can help me.
11. It's hopeless.
12. I am helpless.
13. I am overwhelmed.
14. I am confused.
15. Bad things happened to me.
16. I don't see the point of living a life that I can't live.
17. I am frozen and I can't move.
18. If I move the whole world will collapse.
19. No one listens to how I feel.

Nervousness

Fears

- Fear of what might happen next
- Fear of forgetting something and being shamed
- Fear of not getting it right and being shamed

- Fear of someone's hostility at them not knowing

Emotional States
- Lack of discernment about what is a threat and what isn't. Everything has the potential for harming them. As a child the whole world was dangerous and overwhelming. They did not know how to keep control of the environment. Chaos was the rule.
- Exposure to the potential for harm (shame, humiliation, ridicule or physical harm) for what they know or didn't know. Unpredictable outcome to knowing.

Cross Indexing: Anxiety, ADHD, Panic disorder, agoraphobia, obsessive compulsive disorder, depression, suicidal, insomnia, ACOA, PTSD

Repeating Patterns: No Inner peace, see threats around every corner, memory loss, cycles into intense periods of worry

Created Patterns
1. People don't understand what I am saying.
2. I am afraid of the future.
3. I get confused.
4. Everything gets jumbled up.
5. Knowing is dangerous.
6. Not knowing is dangerous.
7. I don't know what will harm me.
8. Everything and everybody is a threat.
9. The world is an unpredictable and harmful place.
10. No one wants to hear me or listen.
11. I am confused and disoriented.

Neuritis

Fears
- Fear of being blocked
- Fear of being misunderstood

Emotional States
- Communication is misunderstood. What they see is clouded or unclear which creates anger/ irritation. If the emotions are with others it is a reflection of their own irritation. What they hear is confused or is unheard.
- Holds others accountable for their own state of confusion. The confusion is a strategy to stay safe. They use confusion to obfuscate what is really going on in their heads. Passive-aggressive.

Cross Indexing: Inflammation, Shingles, Herpes Simplex, Virus, Nerve Problems, Peripheral Neuropathy, Diabetes

Repeating Patterns: Victim/ Martyr

Created Patterns
1. I can't do anything because I get overwhelmed with feeling irritated.
2. I am overwhelmed with irritation.
3. People don't understand me.
4. When people look at me they don't see me. They see what they want to see.
5. Others are to blame for my confusion.
6. Sometimes I don't see the whole picture and it causes me problems. Then I get things wrong. I just created more confusion and chaos. I then stay safe.
7. I am angry at _____.
8. I am angry at _____ for not understanding me.

Neurosis

Fears
- Fear of an possible threat
- Fear of powerlessness

Emotional States
- Heightened sense of insecurity. This insecurity is actually the foundation upon which their identity is built. That identity is then self-diminished. There is a response to the self-diminishment that either is a focus on self-criticism or self perfectionism.
- A feeling of powerlessness and no control.

Cross Indexing: Obsessive Compulsive Disorder, depression, anxiety, panic disorder

Created Patterns
1. I am better than other and my needs come before others.
2. I am overloaded/ overwhelmed.
3. Life is too hard for me handle.
4. I can't quit.
5. I must _____ to be safe.
6. I must be perfect.
7. Everything has to be perfect.
8. I am disconnected from god / creator.
9. God doesn't exist.
10. I'm not good enough.
11. I am worthless.
12. I must be hyper-vigilant.
13. I am more intelligent than others and everyone else is not good enough.
14. There is no rhyme or reason to people. They defy understanding so they need to be suppressed.

Nose Problems

Fears
- Fear of having to take it regardless of what it is
- Fear of rejection
- Fear of never being enough
- Fear of never being right
- Fear of not being acceptable
- Fear of my inner voice

Emotional States
- They feel like they need to be someone else. So they go through life trying on personas. The person they were as a child and young adult felt as if they were always being rejected for being themselves. They always felt as they were wrong in what they said and did so they were someone else. Then maybe what they said and did would be OK.

Cross Indexing: Face/Head Problems, Sinus problems, Allergies

Created Patterns
1. I am overlooked.
2. No one sees me.
3. Life is no fun.
4. I don't want to take this in because I resent _____ (What is it that you resent? And why are you pushing back? Who made you feel like you needed to do that?).
5. I never listen to my inner guidance.
6. I always do stuff I know is wrong.
7. I need help and don't know how to get it (What prevents you from asking for help?).
8. I must get away from the responsibility of _____ (What responsibility are you trying to get away from?).
9. I am not worthy (Who made you feel that way?).
10. I can't be myself (What would happen if you were yourself? Who made you feel that you couldn't be yourself?).
11. I can't tell people I love them (Why can't you tell people you love them?).
12. I am unwanted.
13. I don't know how to enjoy me.
14. I don't like myself.
15. I don't want or love me.

O's

Obsessive-Compulsive Disorder

Fears
- Fear of not knowing
- Fear of life
- Fear of change
- Fear of standing up
- Fear of the unknown
- Fear of being vulnerable

Emotional States
- Needs confirmation that what they are doing is right so they go back to it again and again to either do it again or check it – lack of love – they would go back to the same source that should love them and they would get the same rejection over and over again. Hope springs eternal – so they would keep repeating the same behavior expecting a different result.
- Needs recognition and doing something over and over will get them the recognition they crave. Once it's reinforced the pattern locks into the chemistry of the brain and the same behavior. They have never been acknowledged or felt they have. Lack of warmth and love in early life.
- Created a behavior from a time of extreme emotional vulnerability and becomes a source of comfort. Doing a thing repeatedly lets them cope with feelings of stress caused by feeling vulnerable.
- Cutoff from the expressive feeling part of self. There is a need to bring some kind of feeling in…any kind of feeling. They use a physical movement repeatedly to bring in some kind of feeling even if it only a physical sense that may be painful. Being cutoff from the expressive, feeling aspect of self happened as a child. They were hurt or punished for the expression of being playful, innocent, open, and vulnerable.
- Came into this incarnation not really wanting to be here. They have an inner anger at the process of physical birth and the associated pain. The physical birth was an unexpected shock and led to intense fear. Did not have conscious realization that they were undergoing the birth process. Experienced a state of anxiety, confusion and pain during the birth process. Feeling of powerlessness in the face of trying to survive. Will probably have chemical imbalances, need energetic balancing and metabolic support.
- Lost a situation of being protected. The protection was actually just living in a limited reality. While living in that limited reality they led a life that was lacking involvement in nit grit of life. They were suspended and never really entered into the energy of living. Then an event in their life forced them to deal with LIFE. This created a surrounding energy of anger, fear, anxiety and frustration just to survive. This emotional state could also be representative of the birth trauma as well as a post-birth emotional process.

Cross Indexing: Neurosis, Body part involved (ex: handwashing), Anxiety, Panic Disorder, Depression

Created Patterns
1. Being creative is dangerous.
2. Being vulnerable is dangerous.
3. Change is dangerous.
4. Change will hurt you.
5. Emotions are dangerous.
6. I am angry at _____.
7. I am betrayed by _____.
8. I am just safer if I don't _____.
9. I am overwhelmed by life.
10. I am overwhelmed by people.
11. I am powerless to change things.
12. I can't get what I want.
13. I can't trust anyone.
14. I could die by doing _____.
15. I didn't want to be born.
16. I don't know how to face my feelings and be safe.
17. I hide in my confusion.
18. I know how to feel and be safe.
19. I should never have been born.
20. If I am creative I will be rejected/ put down/ be hurt.
21. If I am vulnerable I will be hurt.
22. If I react I am rejected.
23. It is dangerous to feel.
24. It is dangerous to live.
25. It is safer to hide from people.
26. Life hurts.
27. Life is dangerous.
28. People are out to hurt me.
29. People hurt me (this is coming from that wounded child).
30. People/emotions/feelings/change confuse me.
31. When I am confused/overwhelmed people leave me alone.
32. Where do you hide?

Occipital Skullbone

Fears
- Fear of being unable to discern
- Fear of having no parameters
- Fear of no rules
- Fear of violation of the rules
- Fears others will violate the rules

Emotional States

- Tense judgment surrounds everything; can't relate to anyone or anything without judgment. Must put everything within the context of their framework and how it relates with their standards.

Created Patterns

1. I must judge everything to be safe.
2. I'm safe when I have determined everything to be safe.
3. I can't relax if I do someone will judge me.
4. I am right and everyone else is wrong.
5. No one understands me.
6. I am hopeless, it is wrong to have hope.
7. People who don't get me are stupid.

Osteomyelitis

Fears

- Fear of intimate connection
- Fear of projected kindness and warmth from another
- Fear of losing their identity
- Fear of not knowing who they are
- Fear of familial manipulation

Emotional States

- Deep resentment of the conflicting ideas held between them and another but this conflict in ideas is a reflection of their own inner conflict. The conflict is very deep and born of a need to reconcile concepts from childhood that as an adult ceased to make sense. Yet these ideas are their history and foundation.

Cross Indexing: Diabetes, kidney problems, Sickle cell anemia, Inflammation, bone problems, bacteria

Created Patterns

1. I'm not supported.
2. I am angry at my life/the whole world.
3. Everything is so hard.
4. I don't see any way to make it better.
5. I don't see any way to make it safe.
6. I am conflicted by the world of my parents.
7. The old ways are not the right ways.
8. I can't let go and move on.
9. I need to move forward with my life but this old stuff holds me back.
10. My ancestral ways manipulate me into obedience and if I don't I lose my family support.

Osteoporosis

Fears
- Fear of institutionalized hatred
- Fear of becoming nothing
- Fear of having no place

Emotional States
- Unknown future has led them to question the past. Historic information now feels wrong. The foundations upon which they built their life is without merit or real value. Wraps this realization in a blanket of impending doom. Feels that if they are wrong then all is wrong. Moves into a space of judgmental-ism to be safe. The judgmental-ism is the only foundation they now feel.
- Helps others too much – gives their strength away. Willing to put more into others than themselves. Holds life away by always giving and deflecting from seeing they have no real substance. Hurts chip away at what they do have until nothing is left.
- Games are done. They have played games all their lives. Using the game to move around the center. The games extract a price… a toll. They give up part of themselves with each game played. Part of the game is helping others that don't need it. So there is a reciprocation of resentment.

Cross indexing: Addiction – Alcohol, Anorexia, Hyperthyroidism, Menopause, Adrenal Problems, Endocrine System Problems, Bone Problems, Aging, Chronic Illness and Kidney Problems.

Created Patterns
1. I am unsupported.
2. I can't defend myself.
3. I can't speak up and say how I feel.
4. I have nothing to depend on.
5. My world is falling apart.
6. I'm afraid to depend on others.

Ovarian Cyst

Fears
- Fear of being hidden
- Fear of their creativity being seen
- Fear that who they are is a lie
- Fear of being worthless
- Fear that nothing is safe
- Fear of rejection
- Fear of being unloved
- Fear of being unresolved
- Fear of not meeting your destiny

Emotional States

- Deep longing for the pairing – a coming together of souls – but instead there is only heart pain. Emotions are not safely expressed. Loss of control if emotions are expressed so they keep them tucked away. Incessant talking without really saying anything is how the space is filled and kept safe.
- Longing for help. Looking for someone in their life to voluntarily step forward to help. The help has to be volunteered otherwise they feel unloved. They have the expectations but don't ask. They feel rejected, unloved, unseen and unwanted if help is not offered. Yet they attract the very people in life who see only themselves. They attract people that only want to be listened to but not listen to others.
- Hollow hearing. People don't hear their words. People don't hear why they are talking to begin with. Yields to the louder voice in the room. Retreats to the corner when the loud voice starts. Doesn't seem to be able to just leave – heart freezes and hears nothing after that.
- Keeps the creativity hidden and out of sight. Lots of emotion around keeping it hidden. Keeping the creativity hidden keeps that aspect of self from being accessed. Controlling the prime directive of creation. The prime directive of creation is act or die. This urgency is kept bottled up. Emotions are restricted and encapsulated. There is a longing for communion and union.

*prime directive of the ovaries/egg in the ovary is union, creation from the union and expression

Cross Indexing: Ovaries – Polycystic, Ovary problems, Cysts, Ovarian Fibroids, Infertility, Wounded Creative Core

Created Patterns

1. Help comes at a price.
2. Having to ask means I am unloved.
3. I shouldn't have to ask.
4. I'm unheard.
5. No one listens to me.
6. I'm unloved.
7. I'm unworthy of connection.
8. I'm not good enough to be helped.
9. I'm not creative.
10. I can't ask for help without feeling guilty.
11. I have to give up something if I get my needs met.
12. The prime directive means I am trapped.
13. I must give up my life to be creative.
14. Creativity comes at a price.

Ovarian Fibroids

Fears

- Fear that if you let go there will be a death

- Fear that if you let go they will die
- Fear of connecting and learning
- Fear of the world being out of control
- Fear of confrontation
- Fear of allowing
- Fear of the flow

Emotional States

- Has jumped from one new beginning to another. Has a tendency to overachieve in order to get attention. That overachieving extends into their life path. They tend to emotionally detach from their life's path. They have changed directions on their spiritual path a number of times. It appears as if they are jumping from one thing to another. Again with no real attachment to what they have just experienced.
- Has repressed fears that keep breaking through the emotional wall of protection they have built for themselves. The wall has created a rigid way of being in the world. They think they are creating behaviors that keep them safe emotionally. But the fears continue to break through. When the fears break through they feel as if the whole world is falling apart. There is sense of helplessness in making any changes that keep the fear away.
- Emotional turmoil right below the surface. They give the appearance that they are calm and emotionally in control. Has an issue or truth that they are trying to avoid and are not facing. They feel like that if they do confront the issue or truth they could lose their 'life'. Life being literally the human life or life being the situation they are now in. They are getting insights from their unconscious about the situation but they move to distance themselves from having to face the issue.

Cross Indexing: Growths, Ovary Problems, Infertility, Ovarian Cyst, Ovaries – Polycystic, Wounded Creative Core

Created Patterns

1. Being a woman is bad.
2. Female sexuality is bad/evil/dirty.
3. I am afraid of being sexual.
4. I am not as good as a man.
5. I can never get what I want.
6. I can't be better than my mother.
7. I can't change things.
8. I can't do it.
9. I can't take care of myself.
10. I can't create and be safe.
11. I can't do as much as a man.
12. I can't let go of what is not good for me and be safe.
13. I can't play and be safe.
14. I don't believe in myself.
15. I don't know how to/what it feel like to let go of what is not good for me.
16. I don't know how to/what it feels like to be safe.
17. I don't love myself.
18. I don't respect myself.

19. I hate being a woman.
20. I hate myself.
21. I have been abused by _____.
22. I have been humiliated by _____.
23. I have been shamed by _____.
24. I know how to/what it feels like to play.
25. I must accept things the way they are.
26. I must be recognized to be accepted/ loved.
27. I must depend on a man to have enough.
28. I must depend on a man to have what I need.
29. I will lose everything if I do what's right.
30. I will never have enough.
31. I'll never reach my goals.
32. I'm not any good as a woman.
33. If I change things my life will be awful.
34. If I confront my issues I will be alone.
35. If I do what I know I must then I will lose everything.
36. If I get too attached to anything it falls apart.
37. I'm not loved.
38. I'm not respected.
39. I'm not safe.
40. It is painful to be creative.
41. Men are better than women.
42. Men come first.
43. My creativity is blocked.
44. My goals are always just out of reach.
45. My husband/ex-???????/boyfriend/_____ hurt me.
46. My husband/ex-???????/boyfriend/_____ betrayed me.
47. My sexuality has always gotten me into trouble.
48. Women are inferior to men.
49. Women are second class to men.
50. Women aren't responsible.
51. Women must have a man to be complete.

Ovaries – Polycystic

Fears
- Fear of being a woman
- Fear that they will be subjugated
- Fear of the creative
- Fear of criticism
- Fear of being rejected
- Fear of heart pain
- Fear of what they are will never be good enough
- Fear of not being a man

Emotional States
- Old suppressed anger/resentment / animosity at being a girl. Rejection of the feminine is in direct conflict with loyalty to another. Their loyalty to another makes them disloyal to self. They choose to run away from dealing with the conflicting beliefs and lose a part of their identity in the process. Takes on great burdens. May fall into self-deprecation, remorse and regrets if creative renewal is not part of their life.
- Can see the big picture but keeps being pulled down into the affairs of others. Has negative attitude that causes discomfort. Small things upset them. Takes the opinions of others personally. They work to reject the hurt which causes more hurt. The source of their support is out of balance.

Cross Indexing: Infertility, Wounded Creative Core, Ovarian Fibroids, Ovarian Cysts, Ovary Problems

Created Patterns
1. Being a woman means never being good enough.
2. Doing creative things is a waste of time (program being parroted from an influential source).
3. I am a perfectionist.
4. I am alone.
5. I am angry at _____.
6. I am inadequate as a woman.
7. I can be sexual and be safe.
8. I can't create on my own.
9. I can't do anything creative.
10. I can't do it.
11. I can't make it better.
12. I can't make things happen.
13. I can't trust men.
14. I don't believe in myself.
15. I don't know how to get my needs met.
16. I don't know how to get what I need.
17. I don't know what it feels like to get my needs met.
18. I don't know what it feels like to get what I need.
19. I don't love myself.
20. I don't trust myself.
21. I know what's good for me I just can't bring myself to do it.
22. I must be a man to be good enough.
23. I must be better than a man to be good enough _____.
24. I must do what others tell me to do.
25. I must listen to the opinions of others.
26. I must work hard to be accepted/respected/wanted.
27. I never get what I want.
28. I never have enough.
29. I never reach my goals-someone/something always stops me.
30. I resent _____.
31. I will never have enough.
32. I'm not accepted by others/ self.

33. I'm not as good as a man.
34. I'm not loved by others.
35. I'm not secure.
36. If I can't do it perfectly-I don't want to do it at all.
37. If I do something creative I will be rejected/ hurt.
38. If I don't put others first then I am seen as selfish.
39. If I'm not loyal what am I?
40. It's better if men control everything.
41. Men must make the decisions.
42. Nothing I do ever works out.
43. Nothing I do is enough.
44. Others come first.
45. The opinions of others is more important than mine.
46. There's never enough.
47. What's the use in trying?
48. Women are less than men.
49. Women are supposed to serve others.
50. Women aren't good enough.
51. Women aren't worthy of recognition.
52. Women must be subservient to men.

Ovary Problems

Fears

- Fear of losing their identity
- Fear of being alone
- Fear of not being wanted
- Fear of not holding up their part
- Fear of not knowing when to let go and move on
- Fear of failing
- Fear of being unwanted
- Fear of being unloved
- Fear of being blamed
- Fear of being taken advantage of

Emotional States

- They hold on too long and then they fail. They have an out-of-sync sense of timing. They're constantly giving and get nothing in return.

Cross Indexing: Ovarian Cyst, Ovarian Fibroids, Ovaries – Polycystic, Wounded Creative Core

Created Patterns

1. I am alone.
2. I am lonely.

3. I'm not respected.
4. I am unloved.
5. I don't know how to get love.
6. I am a failure as a woman.
7. I'm unlovable.
8. I am held back from what I need to do.
9. If I hold on too long I will fail.
10. If I don't make the deadline I will fail.
11. I always have to struggle to make things happen.
12. If I don't do my part nothing will get done.

Overeating – Compulsive

Fears
- Fear of being out of control
- Fear of rejection
- Fear of starvation when away from home
- Fear of being unsafe in unfamiliar surroundings
- Fear of having no food
- Fear of never being enough
- Fear of there never being enough
- Fear of being weak
- Fear of being unloved
- Fear of failing
- Fear of feeling

Emotional States
- As long as they are eating they are in control. The hunger feels like a sense of being out of control. As long as they are eating they have a boundary. The weight and the food are protection.
- They never have enough. They feel like there is this black hole of emptiness that needs to be filled and they can't seem to fill it. They are never enough and there is never enough to satisfy their hunger for belonging. They have a deep need to be part of something.

Cross Indexing: Weight Loss Panic, Weight-Under, Weight Loss – Insulin Resistance, Weight Loss – Fear of Starvation, Weight Loss – The Magical Thinking Diet, Weight Loss – The Family Money Story and Weight, Bulimia, Anorexia, Ancestral/ Epigenetic

Created Patterns
1. Being heavy is how I am strong.
2. Being heavy is how I stay safe.
3. Don't ask, don't tell, and don't feel.
4. Eating is my greatest fear.
5. Eating kills the psychic pain.
6. Eating takes my inner peace.

EMOTIONAL PATTERNS

7. Food always makes me feel good.
8. Food equals love.
9. Food is how I love myself.
10. Food is the friend that never fails me.
11. Food keeps me from feeling.
12. Food will make me feel better.
13. Food will solve any problem I have.
14. I am a failure.
15. I am afraid of my feelings.
16. I am an embarrassment.
17. I am ashamed of how I look.
18. I am ashamed of myself.
19. I am consumed by food.
20. I am depressed.
21. I am disconnected from creator / god.
22. I am full of rage at _____.
23. I am my father.
24. I am my mother.
25. I am overwhelmed by anxiety.
26. I am powerless to control my eating.
27. I am shamed for not being good enough.
28. I can never fill the void inside of me.
29. I can never get enough.
30. I can never have a relationship.
31. I don't know how to be safe with my feelings.
32. I don't know how to control my eating.
33. I eat to keep from feeling.
34. I hate myself.
35. I have been betrayed.
36. I have no control.
37. I have no one close to me.
38. I hide behind my body.
39. I must stuff my feelings.
40. I need armor to protect me from abuse.
41. I resent /am angry at _____.
42. I substitute food for love.
43. I think about eating all the time.
44. I want out.
45. I'm not lovable.
46. I'm not loved.
47. I'm rejected / reviled.
48. It dangerous to feel.
49. It is dangerous for people to see who I truly am.
50. It is dangerous to feel.
51. My eating protects me.
52. My feeling overwhelm me so I eat.
53. No one likes me.
54. No one sees the real me.
55. No one supports me.

56. People don't like me because I am overweight.
57. When I eat I feel guilty.
58. When people make fun of me I eat.
59. You can always rely on food.

P's

Pagets Disease

Fears
- Fear that nothing stands between them and death
- Fear of losing all hope
- Fear that they won't have anything
- Fears ownership
- Fears presence
- Fears allowing
- Fear of letting down their energy level
- Fear of their vulnerability

Teachings
- Allow
- Be flexible
- Be good enough
- Be myself
- Be valued
- Change easily
- Depend on my own inner resources
- Giving
- Go with the flow
- Happiness
- Joy
- Know who I am
- Listen to my inner voice and be safe
- Live being open to new ideas
- Live true to who I am
- Live using the energy of the divine
- Live without being overwhelmed
- Live without having to force things to happen
- Live without taking energy from others
- Love myself
- Make change without disrespecting my family / ancestry
- Nurturance
- Receiving
- Relax
- Renew my energy from divine Source
- Take responsibility for my choices
- To lighten up
- Unconditional love

Emotional States
- Holding everyone else responsible for their pain, heart pain caused by pushing to hard. Uses brute force to make things happen. Lack of flow. Nurturance is forced and devitalized.
- Very dense and heavy energy in the body. On a whole doesn't let others in – strong boundaries that push away help, nurturance, love, and guidance.
- Intensity – strong intensity with how they live their life. Scrutinizing energy that is completely focused outside of self.

- Feeds off of others for their strength. Hides from their true self by taking personality energy from others. They behave as someone else behaves and takes from them to make a personality aspect – false self.
- Highly sensitive – their feelings are very sensitive and they become afraid of anyone getting close enough to nurture and care for them. Afraid of their own nurturance as it might bring them criticism from others and this would hurt. They work to hide their sensitive nature. This keeps them from being hurt but also stops love, caring and nurturance from coming into their life.

Cross Indexing: viruses, bone problems, breast problems, chronic illness, wounding of the empathic sense

Repeated patterns: inflexibility, being good enough, not present, doesn't give, depends on outside resources for their well being, unhappy, lack of joy, feels lost and doesn't know who they are, doesn't listen to their inner voice, closed to new information, constantly in a state of overwhelm, forces things to happen(not in the flow), uses the energy of others to get things done, doesn't love themselves, fears that if they make changes their family will feel disrespected, doesn't know how to relax, doesn't take responsibility for their choices, doesn't nurture themselves

Created Patterns

1. _____ is to blame for _____.
2. By the time I take time for myself I can't relax.
3. Change is dangerous.
4. I am disconnected from others.
5. I am overwhelmed.
6. I can't be myself and be safe.
7. I can't let myself be nourished.
8. I can't let myself be pampered.
9. I can't let others help me.
10. I don't like myself.
11. I don't love myself.
12. I don't make changes easily.
13. I force myself to take time for myself.
14. I have a broken heart.
15. I have to be what others want me to be.
16. I have to do everything myself.
17. I have to hide who I am.
18. I must act like others want me to act.
19. I must be tough.
20. I must criticize others.
21. I must force things to happen.
22. I must judge others.
23. I must keep others out.
24. I must protect myself from others.
25. I never seem to get anything out of being pampered.
26. I'm not good enough.
27. I'm not valued.
28. If I allow things to happen they never will.
29. If I am myself I will be hurt.
30. If I take care of myself I will be seen as weak.

31. If I take the walls down I will be hurt.
32. It is wrong to be weak.
33. My way is the right way.
34. No one cares for me.
35. No one loves me.
36. Nothing ever makes me feel good.
37. Nothing is ever good enough.
38. People hurt me.
39. The façade allows me to fit in.
40. The façade keeps me safe.

*Look at themes of flow, pain, giving, receiving, energy, boundaries, body, identity, judgment, approval, denial, inner child, authenticity, blame, blockages, boundaries, change, connection, expression, flexibility, forgiveness, joy, happiness, pressure, relaxation, responsibility, right, broken heart, energy, unmet needs, true self, conflicting motivations, control, letting go, empathy, judgment, power, truth, authenticity

Pain

Fears
- Fear of being hurt
- Fear they will never make a difference
- Fear of having to look at one's truth
- Fear ownership
- Fear of learning
- Fear of knowing
- Fear of understanding

Teachings
- Live without guilt
- Live without pain
- Be free of pain
- Love myself
- Unconditional love
- Release anger
- Be loved
- Be worthy
- Be good enough
- Be balanced

Emotional States
- Pain is an indicator of being out of balance. The balance of their being is in accordance with their innate purpose. They are not doing that but are living in accordance with their fear.

Cross Indexing: The part of the body affected and look at the guilt held there, wounded creative core, ancestral/ epigenetic

Repeating Pattern: They have been ignoring the lessons they need to learn

Created Patterns
1. I am out of balance but there is no choice and I cannot change things.
2. My life purpose is irrelevant. I have to pay the bills.
3. I sabotage myself so that I never have the space to live my purpose.
4. I will fail if I do what I yearn to do.
5. There is no other way. The pain is the price I pay.

6. If I fail I will die/ be homeless / starve / be at the mercy of others.
7. I am angry at _____.
8. I am frustrated by _____.
9. Love hurts.
10. What is the pain telling you?
11. How would your life change if the pain wasn't there?
12. I am hard on myself.
13. I don't take care of myself.
14. I'm not worthy.
15. I must be punished.
16. I am guilty of _____.
17. What is out of balance in your life?

*Look at themes of pain, judgment, guilt, unconditional love, loving myself, balance, stress, Pain is a way of correcting out of balance aspects of self

Pancreas Problems

Fears

- Fear of deprivation of an identity
- Fear of deprivation of physical needs
- Fear of deprivation of love
- Fear of deprivation of belonging
- Fear of deprivation of joy
- Fear of deprivation of a life in balance
- Fear of deprivation of acceptance
- Fears deprivation of feelings
- Fears deprivation of their heart
- Fear of the joy
- Fear of the joy of success
- Fear of the joy of accomplishment
- Fear of the joy of happiness
- Fear of enjoying joy
- Fear of being caught
- Fear of being forced into work
- Fear of failing
- Fear of shame
- Fear of connection with the earth
- Fear of connection with your roots
- Fear of being trapped and enslaved
- Fear that there is no way to get away
- Fear of being worthless
- Fear of judging self to be unacceptable
- Fear of not deserving the good
- Fear of receiving
- Fear of giving
- Fear of disappearing into nothingness

Emotional States
- Lack of success. Held back by intense shame.
- Intense fear of family secrets being discovered. Pulls back from feeling they deserve the good in life.
- Childhood nurturing in a family life was disrupted by abandonment, death, religious attitudes and/or addictions.

Cross indexing: Wounded Creative Core, Ancestral / epigenetic, diabetes I & II, intestines-small, liver problems, addictions-chemical, parasites, nerves, hiccups, pancreatic insufficiency, diabetes, cancer – pancreatic neuroendocrine

Created Patterns
1. If I have joy I am a failure or a loser.
2. I am ashamed of _____.
3. I am a failure.
4. There is no joy in life.
5. I am disconnected from creator.
6. I am going to die.
7. I don't belong anywhere.
8. I don't get to be angry.
9. I don't have the right.
10. I don't know what joy feels like.
11. I don't want to feel.
12. I must criticize others before they criticize me first.
13. I resent _____.
14. I'm not good enough.
15. It is dangerous to feel.
16. It is dangerous to show emotions.
17. Life is no fun/ there is no joy in living.
18. Life is not sweet.

Pancreatic Insufficiency

Fears
- Fear that there will never be anyone that can help and they must do it alone
- Fear of being found a fraud
- Fear of being called out for their giving too much
- Fear of having to let go of what gave you love in the past
- Fear of giving to self
- Fear that they must give to be wanted

Emotional States
- Not digesting what is nurturing, rejects the mother.
- What they take in for nurturing is not what they need and it hurts them. They are left lacking the 'self' needs. They are punishing themselves for not being good enough and not solving the world's problems. They give their power and life force to people who they think need it more than they, so they can have a better life.

Cross Indexing: ACOA, Addiction – Alcoholism, pancreatitis, pancreas problems

Created Patterns
1. I need to solve the world's problems.
2. It's my responsibility to make everything right.
3. I must fix everyone's problems.
4. I must make it all better.
5. Everyone else comes before me.
6. I can't have fun until all my work is done.
7. Life is being responsible and doing it right.
8. I don't know how to accept the support of others.
9. I must make sure everyone else's needs are met before mine, then there is never enough for me.

Pancreatitis

Fears
- Fear of injustice
- Fear of hostility
- Fear of being shamed for the injustice
- Fear of failing
- Fear of loving themselves
- Fears being hunted down
- Fears hope

Emotional States
- Failure and being wronged. Long ancestral history of being wronged. The injustice soured life. Allowed no one to correct the wrong. Being the wronged identity is from which all decisions were/are made. Hollow attempts at breaking out of this method of living created a stress on the binds/binding of this identity. This created an internal collapse – anger and no trust of self. Long running desire to not be seen by others – so that their failures would not have the attention of others.
- Wholly unfounded life. Gender identification: the roles of being masculine or the role of feminine were confused within their life role (this is not homosexuality). This confusion is wrought in balance that gets skewed by the family and community. Responding from the feminine ideal in a situation creates a conflict within 'norms' of the family. And vice versa. Responding from the

masculine ideal in a situation creates a conflict within the 'norms' of the blood family and the native community. That balancing of feminine and masculine into an androgynous presence creates confusion and non-acceptance.
- Hedonistic. Lack of expansiveness in the rendering. Very narrow view of how things/ people/ world serve them. Won't let others into their world. They identify strongly with the pleasures. The pleasure in living is from what external stimulation can be gotten from other substances and people. This is all receive and no give.
- Gets great joy in a false giving. They give in anticipation of being accepted and loved that never comes back to them in what they want. They look to that vehicle for love and acceptance which is never forthcoming. They lack the self-love to give to themselves and find self-acknowledgment of who they truly are.

Cross Indexing: Gallstones, Digestive Disorders, Addiction – Alcohol

Created Patterns

1. I am shamed and humiliated.
2. My ancestors were shamed for who they were.
3. I make decisions that will bring shame and humiliation.
4. I must be the person they say I am.
5. I forsake my sense of self for what other say. That way I stay out of harms way.
6. I need to be invisible to be safe but the shame keeps bringing them forward.
7. When I meet the demands of the masculine energies I am then remanded to the feminine energies to be subservient and dominated.
8. I need to take what I want to be happy.
9. I don't love myself.

Panic Disorder

Fears

- Fear of being afraid
- Fear of harm
- Fear of bad things
- Fear of dying
- Fear of overwhelm

Emotional States

- Hyper aware sense of impending doom. The whole world is going to come down around their ears and they are in mortal danger. Having a misguided awareness that something really bad is going to happen. They are very sensitive to the emotional energies of the world and pick up the random screams of the world. They cycle that information in on themselves.

Cross Indexing: PTSD, Anxiety, Agoraphobia, Obsessive-compulsive disorder, wounded creative core and wounded empathic sense

Created Patterns

1. I am afraid of another panic attack.
2. I am out of control.
3. Something really bad is going to happen.
4. I am unreal.
5. The anxiety will kill me.
6. I am overwhelmed with fear.
7. I am overwhelmed with anxiety.
8. My secrets will kill me.
9. I must not let myself be afraid.
10. I am afraid I am dying.
11. I am always in fear.
12. I am responsible for everything.
13. I can't ever seem to get everything done.
14. If you want something done you give it to a busy person.
15. I am overwhelmed with responsibilities.
16. I am afraid of letting someone down.

Paralysis

Fears

- Fear of moving
- Fear of attack
- Fear that if they run they will die
- Fear of feelings
- Fear of pain
- Fear of doing
- Fear of doing something wrong
- Fear of being left to die
- Fear of being vulnerable and forgotten

Emotional States

- The fear of moving forward is overwhelming. They are frozen. Their heart is contracted and rigid. Life force is stopped. Feelings are numbed. They feel safe here – no more feeling – no more abuse – no more.
- Communication to and from their needs has been severed.

Cross Indexing: Leg paralysis, stroke, ALS

Created Patterns

1. I am overwhelmed with responsibility.
2. I want out of here.

3. If I stay really still nothing will hurt me.
4. If I stay really still no one will see me.
5. I am afraid of the future.
6. I am constantly one edge (Why/what makes you feel that way?).
7. The world is a really unsafe place.
8. I must protect myself.

Parasites

Fears
- Fear of frustration
- Fear that they will be taken over
- Fear of stopping others from taking them over
- Fear of being unloved
- Fear of being unaccepted
- Fear of being forced against their will
- Fear of being forced to give
- Fear of saying no
- Fear of the details

Teachings
- Accepted
- Balanced
- Creator's definition of boundaries
- Creator's definition of power
- Good enough
- Know what is not your highest and best
- Know what is your highest and best
- Live without being controlled
- Live without being dominated
- Live without being taken advantage of
- Live without feeling invaded
- Live without giving away your power
- Live without needing to meet the demands of others
- Live without needing to support others
- Live without being drained by others
- Live without taking on the thoughts of others
- Loving yourself
- Make your own decisions
- Say no and be safe
- Stand up for yourself
- Unconditional love
- Wanted
- Wanted without needing to give
- Being myself and get my needs met
- Complete
- Lovable
- Respected
- Control the thoughts coming into my mind

Emotional States
- Open to being invaded / lack of boundaries. Fear of stepping into their power. Fear that their boundaries or application of their power will cause them to lose love and/ or acceptance / or being wanted. So they allow others to feed off their energy. Weakened by the continual outflow.

Cross Indexing: Viruses, Bacteria, fungus

Repeating Patterns: Being in relationships where they are controlled and dominated. Within those relationships they are not allowed to have thoughts that are not someone else's thoughts. They are continually being taken advantage of.

Created Patterns
1. I am forced to do things against my will.
2. I am powerless to stop others from taking advantage of me.
3. I can't say no.
4. I do what people tell me to, to be loved / wanted.
5. I give in just to get along.
6. I let others take advantage of me to be loved / wanted / accepted.
7. I must be someone else to be loved.
8. I must do what I am told.
9. I must meet the demands of others.
10. I will do whatever is necessary to be loved.
11. I'm not good enough.
12. I'm not respected.
13. If I don't take care of others they will _____.
14. People are always trying to tell me what to do (who?).
15. People take advantage of me.
16. People take things from me.
17. The devil is in the details.
18. You must pay attention to the details.
19. You must sweat the small stuff.

*Look at themes of power, boundaries, acceptance, approval, balance, energy, family, freedom, judgment, love, loving yourself, relationships, self-esteem, self-respect, self-worth, speak up, unconditional love, unmet needs, energy, and power

Parathyroid Disease

Fears
- Fear justice will be taken or overridden
- Fear that the search for justice will be their undoing
- Fear that they will always be the one to carry the banner

Teachings
- Step into my power
- Be angry and safe
- Be seen and be safe
- Make my own decisions
- Live without resentments

- Fear of making decisions/ choices
- Fear of power
- Fear of making mistakes
- Live without grudges
- Make decisions
- Make a mistake and be safe
- Make choices easily

Emotional States
- Holds out hope that someone will come into their lives and take over control. They engage in confusion to manipulate others. There is no power or energy in the decisions they do make. Difficulty in making choices. Waffles back and forth on a choice. They gravitate to the wrong choices even when presented with choices that are the right ones. The need to be told what to do and what choices to make to feel safe. Ancestral.

Cross Indexing: endocrine system disorders, osteoporosis, kidney stones, abdominal pain, heart problems, thyroid problems

Repeating Patterns: They have a hard time making choices and their life reflects a stuckness. They have a tendency to communicate in ways that will keep them invisible.

Created Patterns
1. I have been angry at/angry about _____ for a long time.
2. I can't make decisions.
3. I am forced to do things I don't want to do.
4. I am powerless.
5. I must keep anger in or I could hurt someone.
6. I must do what I don't want to do.
7. I can't be angry and be safe.
8. I can't be wrong and be safe.
9. I am afraid of making a wrong decision.
10. I don't know how to choose what I want.
11. Everything I want is taken away from me.
12. I can't choose.
13. I am powerless to decide _____.
14. I was never allowed to decide for myself.
15. Someone else always tells me what to do.
16. I resent my indecisiveness.
17. I am jealous of _____.
18. If I get angry I could be dangerous.
19. I am invisible.
20. My heart isn't in it.

*Look at themes of authenticity, power, decisions, anger, balance, blockages, identity, independence, freedom, judgment, self-worth, self-esteem, self-love, unmet needs, anger, confidence, decision making freedom, power

Parkinson's Disease

Fears
- Fear of losing control
- Fear of the unknown
- Fear that they are living a life that is retribution for their sins
- Fear of not being able to provide
- Fear of not being able to do
- Fear of being trapped
- Fear of the inner voice
- Fear of their feminine side (ancestral)
- Fear loss of power
- Fear of failure

Emotional States
- Masculine aspect of self-reflects ways of thinking that are trying to control those around them, this just leads to failure with no one wanting to help facilitate that way of being in the world. This person needs to be in control. This need is from an intense fear of failing or falling down. So this intense fear keeps them from making decisions. The more they try to hold on the less control they have, a loss of power, and this leads to an internal panic. They have held on too tightly and lost their perspective, position, and balance. They see their life as being very difficult and progress has been very slow, if not impossible. This person feels unsupported and alone.
- There is a feeling of being trapped and they can't get out. They don't see a way of getting out of the current way of thinking. They believe that the trap they feel themselves in is the making of others. This person feels like there is a whole lot they want to do but they can't find a way of getting out of the trap they feel they are in. This person has basically put a lid on their inner self so that others could not get near (fear of being hurt) that vulnerable aspect of who they are. This probably happened as a child. That inner child wants to get out and grow into the holistic self. The different aspects of this person's self are kept separate and distinct instead of a blended whole.
- Used judgment that then became a deep abiding guilt. Didn't listen to the inner voices that were telling them to soften instead his comfort/discomfort zone took him in a different direction. Thought (ancestral) they were supposed to be that way. Does not trust the inner voice.
- Unable to communicate with clarity the needs of the heart to the brain-mind (thinking) and others and be heard. Unable to hang on to what they have and they feel powerless. Their needs get met by being out of control and powerless. They hang onto those around them through manipulation. Life is a struggle of hard disappointments.

Cross Indexing: CTE, Concussion, Brain Problems, Nerve Problems, Restless Leg Syndrome, Focal Dystonia

Created Patterns
1. Failing is not an option.
2. I am a failure.
3. I am afraid of _____ and I don't understand why.
4. The world is out of control.
5. I am alone.

6. I am not supported.
7. I am out of control.
8. I am powerless to make change in my life.
9. I can be seen and be safe.
10. I can't accept responsibility for actions.
11. I can't let others near me.
12. I can't make decisions.
13. I don't know how to be myself.
14. I don't know how to play.
15. I don't trust myself.
16. I must control my world.
17. I must protect myself from others.
18. If I let go I lose control.
19. If I make a mistake I will be hurt.
20. It is dangerous to fail.
21. It's everyone else's fault.
22. Life is a struggle.
23. Life is hard.
24. Making decisions is dangerous.
25. No one is there for me.
26. No one listens to me.
27. There is only one way to do things, my way, the right way.
28. There's no way out.
29. What I say is not important.
30. You can't trust anyone.
31. I am trapped.

Peacemaker

Fears

- Fear of hurt
- Fear of what they have to do to keep the peace
- Fear of chaos
- Fear of others being hurt
- Fear of the guilt when it gets out of control
- Fear of loud voices
- Fear of non-peace
- Fear of being attacked
- Fear of being the target
- Fear of being seen
- Fear of not being heard

Emotional States

- The peacemaker is always balancing; it always feels like they are walking the tight wire. It is deeply ingrained that if you make two people get along then you are safe. If there is peace there is safety.
- Not being heard has a balancing effect. If they are heard they will would fall over [no balance], they insulate themselves to the no response. If they are heard they are in danger of being a target and attacked. When feeling unheard there is a feeling of being invisible, worthless, uncared-for and unloved.
- The peacemaker gives up a part of themselves with each peacemaking until there is very little left for themselves.

Cross Indexing: Left foot, Hip Problems, Pelvis Problems, Pancreas Problems, Hearing Loss, ACOA

Created Patterns

1. I must make everyone happy.
2. I must bring peace to the people around me.
3. I feel safe when no one is yelling.
4. I must hold everyone together by making them happy.
5. If I just do this _____ everyone will be nice.
6. I must sacrifice myself for others.
7. I'm safe when no one listens to me.

Pelvic Organ Collapse/ Prolapse

Fears

- Fear that what is holding them together will fail
- Fear of family
- Fears things that are too easy
- Fear of memories
- Fear of inner peace
- Fear of not deserving
- Fears loss
- Fears false friends
- Fears trust

Emotional States

- Unwilling to move thru life without obstacles. Finds purpose in the obstacles by making things hard they find value. The conflict detracts from looking at the deep hurts they hold. Hurts so deep they try the core.
- A deep weariness at the music of life. It has never felt like a harmony but a symphonic clash of notes – everything hurting the ears. Noise – Noise with no purpose or direction or resolution. Has

never known a sweet note only those that are sour and makes ones spine quiver in recoil at the aberrant sound.
- Long forgotten memories rise up and fade away in a sea of constant struggle. They put them away and they come back to haunt and hurt. There is no peace. The pain of indignation and injustice will not leave and not return. Its energy holds a grip of anger.

Cross Indexing: Pelvis Problems, Reproductive Organs, Abdominal Sacrocolpopexy

Created Patterns
1. I'm not good enough to have good things.
2. I am the scum of the earth.
3. The bottom always falls out of everything I try.
4. I've got no reason to be here.
5. I'm not allowed good things.
6. I work hard and nothing comes of it.
7. I work and then I die.
8. Life leaves you with nothing and nowhere to turn.
9. People pretend they are your friends but they just want to take from you.
10. I'm hopeless.
11. I don't belong here.
12. Nothing I do is good enough.
13. Everything I try falls by the wayside.
14. Life's a bitch and then you die.

Pelvis Problems

Fears
- Fear of being overrun
- Fear of violation
- Fear of being hurt
- Fear of being sexual violence
- Fear that all will fail them

Emotional States
- The masculine is out of balance; is not protecting but instead abuses. Abuse can be abandonment or no loyalty to themselves. They give up their safety and self-protection to not be hurt.

Cross Indexing: Reproductive disorders, Digestive disorders, Excretory System disorders

Created Patterns
1. I am ungrounded and unfocused.
2. When I get into a situation where I am supposed to feel I get ungrounded and checkout.
3. Feelings terrify me.

4. What sexual feelings are blocked?
5. I give up. I am powerless to stop people from taking from me (This could be sexual, money, etc. Where power is found in their relationships.).
6. I sabotage my life.
7. People expect me to give and give without regard for me.
8. If I stand up for myself I will be hurt.
9. I can't protect myself.

Periodontal Bone Loss

Fears
- Fears those that are defiant
- Fear of defiance
- Fears trust
- Fear of responsibility
- Fear of life
- Fear of the cycles of life
- Fear of presence
- Fear of feeling
- Fear of change
- Fear of rejection
- Fear of being unloved

Emotional States
- This person is in a dark night of the soul or in alchemical language the Nigredo. This is a stage of growth where one enters their shadow; self esteem issues, fears, anger, grief, jealousy, etc. They can see the answer to their problems. They know that they need to move to a higher level of awareness and feeling. But, they are not moving. They are just watching the answers. There is a lack of belief in Self and trusting their inner knowing and spiritual strength. So they stay in the same place. They are anchored in the weak feminine aspect of their nature. This person has closed themselves off from the outside world and the help it could offer. This person may blame others for their problems. They are not taking responsibility for their life. This individual may be depressed and they are questioning their existence.
- This person is in the midst of an emotional downpour; many inner changes are taking place. As they have gone through the process of cleansing and purification suppressed emotions, fears, and anxieties have surfaced. This person is seeking knowledge and answers to their problems. But, they are finding it really difficult because they are so heavily immersed in the emotions. This person has attempted to put up a shield against the emotions by trying to avoid dealing with them. That isn't working. They feel really unprepared to face their problems.
- This person is going through the motions of emotional growth. There is a feeling of being dead inside…emotionless. They are acting out without fully thinking things through. Their reactions to the stuff of life are rigid and not nourishing. Ego is not talking to the inner self.

Created Patterns

1. Bad things happen when you change.
2. Change is dangerous.
3. Feelings can hurt you.
4. Feelings make vulnerable to attack.
5. God has abandoned me.
6. I am betrayed by _____.
7. I am betrayed by my feelings.
8. I am depressed.
9. I am disconnected from god.
10. I am going to die.
11. I am in a dark night of soul.
12. I am rejected.
13. I am worthless.
14. I can't forgive _____.
15. I can't let go of what is not good for me.
16. I don't trust god.
17. I don't trust my inner knowing.
18. I don't trust my intuition.
19. I don't trust myself.
20. I don't trust others.
21. I resent _____.
22. I want to die.
23. I will never get out of this hole I'm in.
24. I'm not good enough.
25. It is dangerous to feel.
26. It is hopeless.
27. It is safe to do nothing than to change.
28. My resentment keeps me safe.
29. No one cares.
30. No one loves me.
31. No one understands me.
32. Talking about what you feel is dangerous.
33. The unknown is dangerous.

Peripheral Neuropathy

Fears
- Fears being not liked/ hated
- Fear of thinking for myself
- Fear of the future
- Fear of moving
- Fear of no purpose
- Fear of not enough
- Fear of the heart wound

Teachings
- Accepted without approval from father/mother/family/spouse/etc
- Balance
- Creator's definition of a life purpose
- Creator's definition of gratitude/peace
- Creator's definition of responsibility
- Determine truth

- Fears living without hope
- Fear of exile
- Fear of not deserving
- Fear of success
- Fear of trusting
- Fear of inner peace

- Good decisions
- Good enough
- Gratitude
- Inner peace feels like
- Let go of what is not good for me
- Live without a façade
- Live without betrayal
- Live without the lies
- Live without worry
- Miracle feels like
- Own my decisions and be safe
- Safe in new environments
- Safe with new things
- Success
- Tell the truth
- Tell what is good for me
- Truth
- What is good for me

Emotional States

- Unheld expectations of where they would be by now holds the pain of where they have been. They are looking for a life that is inspired.
- Can't go forward with what you really want to do.
- Frozen with the fear of the unknown/ futurization (worry).
- Feelings are unsafe.
- Lack of love from someone you feel like you depended on.
- Made rigid by self-hatred/self-dislike.
- Lack of integrity to self and their life purpose.
- Lack of responsibility for decisions.
- Frozen in the fear of finding out you have a self that is responsible.
- Frozen in the role of not knowing which way to go – unable to make changes.
- Frozen from the fear of more heart pain if they move.
- Shut down of communication.
- Lack of abundance.

Cross Indexing: Diabetes, Vision Problems, High Cholesterol, Arteriosclerosis, Restless Leg Syndrome, Adrenal Problems, Joint Problems, Liver Problems, Sciatic, Carpal Tunnel, Hypothyroidism, Shingles, Celiac Disease, Wounded Creative Core, Pancreas problems

Repeating Patterns: Do not feel accepted and struggle with self-esteem. Feels off balance. No inner peace. Tends to hang onto to things, people and situation that are not good for them. Wants to feel that inspiration in their work but seems to have it for a bit and then it fades.

Created Patterns

1. Everything is a fake/façade.

EMOTIONAL PATTERNS

2. I am angry.
3. I am angry at the world.
4. I am depressed.
5. I am going to die..
6. I am hopeless
7. I am jealous of my mother.
8. I am stuck.
9. I am worthless.
10. I am wrong.
11. I can only succeed if I follow orders.
12. I can't give up my facade.
13. I can't go forward.
14. I can't go forward and I can't go backward.
15. I can't let go of what is bad for me.
16. I can't let go.
17. I can't succeed outside of tribe/family/community.
18. I don't deserve.
19. I don't deserve success.
20. I don't know how to live or be any other way.
21. I don't know how to make decisions.
22. I don't know what is good for me.
23. I don't know what truth is.
24. I don't know where I am going.
25. I don't know why I am alive.
26. I don't trust god.
27. I don't trust myself.
28. I don't trust people.
29. I don't understand my life.
30. I forgive _____.
31. I hate _____.
32. I hate myself.
33. I hate others (who?).
34. I hate people.
35. I have been betrayed.
36. I have never done anything that works.
37. I have never known peace.
38. I have no desire to continue this life.
39. I have no direction in my life.
40. I have no one I can depend upon.
41. I let others/people/family/_____ down.
42. I make everything up since it is all lies anyway.
43. I must do what my father/mother/family/spouse says to have money.
44. I must do what others/father/family/mother/etc do to be good enough.
45. I must do what others/father/family/mother/etc do to be successful.
46. I need approval from others to make changes.
47. I need others to validate me.
48. I want what others have.
49. I will never have what others have
50. I'm not accepted.

51. I'm not good enough.
52. I'm not worthy of miracles.
53. If I disobey I will fail.
54. If I try new things I will be hurt.
55. If I worry about bad things happening they won't happen.
56. It is dangerous to try new things.
57. Life is suffering.
58. Miracles happen for others and not for me.
59. My father/mother/family/spouse/etc betrayed me.
60. My heart is broken.
61. My life has no purpose.
62. New is dangerous.
63. No one loves me.
64. Nothing I do is good enough.
65. People/Mother/Father lied to me.
66. The façade keeps me safe.
67. There is no depth to my life.
68. There is no one worthy of my consideration.
69. There is no reason to try.
70. There is no truth in the world it is all lies- it is all betrayal.
71. Worry keeps me safe.

Phlebitis

Fears
- Fear of being wrong
- Fear that the wrong people control their life
- Fear of being trapped
- Fear that there is no way out
- Fear of the future
- Fear of secrets
- Fear of being a disappointment
- Fear of no purpose

Emotional States
- Veins carry the fear of the secrets they hold. This fear causes a constriction of the flow of life force. They are angry at having to keep information secret when it should be known and dealt with.
- As a child they were not allowed to have joy. Ancestral. It was always taken away to make room for the anger and disappointment felt by the adults.

Cross Indexing: DVT, Vasculitis, Thrombosis, Vein Problems, Artery Problems

Created Patterns

1. I am trapped.
2. There is no way out.
3. There is no solution.
4. I am angry at _____.
5. I am always worrying about _____.
6. Bad things happen when _____.
7. I am stuck.
8. I can't ever get things right.
9. I have no purpose. Why am I here?
10. There is no joy in my life. I am fearful all the time.

Physical Abuse

Fears

- Fear of being creative
- Fear of being wrong
- Fear of authority
- Fear of themselves
- Fear of pain
- Fear of being hurt
- Fear of not belonging
- Fear of isolation
- Fear of those they love will hurt them
- Fear that they must be hurt to be loved

Emotional States

- Their creative core must be broken and wounded to not be sinful. They must be hurt to stop their creative desires and thoughts. They feel that creativity is wrong and they brought it on themselves.

Cross Indexing: Wounded Creative Core, ACOA, PTSD

Created Patterns

1. When I am beat I am safe.
2. By being physically hurt I feel something else.
3. I am sinful and must be taught to obey.
4. The pain reminds me of my obligations.

Pimples

Fears
- Fear that who they are is wrong
- Fear of the shame of being seen
- Fear of the inner self
- Fear of accepting themselves
- Fear of being accused

Emotional States
- Shamed at being seen. Stuck in ways of thinking that don't move them forward. These thoughts are focused at how they see themselves or others see them, which is one in the same. Whenever they get seen they go into shame or embarrassment.

Cross Indexing: Skin Problems, Acne, Growths, Infection, Wounded Creative Core

Created Patterns
1. I am frustrated by _____.
2. I am angry at _____.
3. I hate myself.
4. I don't like myself.
5. I don't love myself.
6. People think they can say anything they want to me. When they do I feel like I am under attack.
7. I must hide to be safe.
8. I am invisible.
9. I keep recycling the same thoughts. I am stuck.

Pineal Gland

Fears
- Fear of being unable to move
- Fear of wrath
- Fear of a fear that shuts down the senses
- Fear of knowing
- Fear of being outcast for knowing

Teachings
- Be in the flow of life
- Creative
- Have permission to create
- Know my own truth
- Know when I am making the right choices
- Know when I am making the right decisions
- Live being true to myself
- Live in the now
- Live without confusion
- Make changes and be safe
- Make changes easily
- Recognize my divine gifts

- Recognize who I am
- Understand the difference between ego-mind and higher self-direction

Emotional States
- Blocking of higher consciousness and awareness. Institutions deemed that higher awareness wisdom evil, wrong and stupid. So they block it to stay safe and stay within that box. These institutions have them under their control. That control blocks the expression of the transcendent.

Cross indexing: Wounded Creative Core, Depression, Insomnia, Brain Problem, Neural disorders, Alopecia, Endocrine system disorders, Erectile Dysfunction, Low Libido

Repeating Patterns: Doesn't flow with life, has a tendency to block or put up barriers to the flow. They don't think they can create so they avoid creating…everything is by the book. They rely on others or institutions for their inner truth. They do not look inward. The inner voice is shut out and down.

Created Patterns
1. My power has been taken by others (parents/ school/ religious dogma/ government/ etc.).
2. Change is dangerous.
3. I am confused.
4. I can't hear my inner voice.
5. I can't shut my mind off and just be quiet.
6. I don't know what my life purpose is.
7. I don't know who I am.
8. I don't trust myself.
9. I must do things a certain way.
10. I must be the same as everyone else to fit in.
11. I need permission to be creative.
12. I will be punished by The Creator.
13. I'm not any good at creative stuff.
14. If I sit still and listen to my inner voice I will be hurt.
15. If I speak up I am laughed at.
16. If I speak up I am put down.
17. Listening to my inner guidance is dangerous.
18. Listening to my inner guidance will get me locked up.
19. My connection with The Creator is blocked.
20. New ideas are dangerous.
21. People make fun of me when I try to do anything creative.
22. People make fun of you if you are different.
23. There is no direct path to the Creator.
24. Why change things if they are working?

*Look at themes of creativity, power, intuition, artist, authenticity, blockages, change, clairvoyance, confidence, discernment, divinity, expression, flexibility, flow, God, Higher Self Connection, identity, imagination, integrity, intelligence, life purpose, oneness, passion, purpose, spirituality, truth and authenticity, soul purpose, power, intuition, expression, creativity

Pinguecula

Fears
- Fear that they will be replaced
- Fear of being unwanted
- Fear of being cast aside
- Fear of being invisible

Emotional States
- Has a hard time listening to other people ideas. Wants to jump in and give them what they think to dominate and control the narrative. They feel that their ideas have a firmer foundation and are therefore best.
- Holds themselves out as the example of right. They expect everyone else to follow their thinking and opinions and agree.

Cross Indexing: Growths, Eye Problems, Aging

Created Patterns
1. I am better than everyone else.
2. I am smarter than everyone else.
3. My ideas/ opinions are always right. Why would anyone do or think otherwise?
4. I know what's best for everyone.
5. How I see the world is how everyone else should see it.
6. I am right and everyone else is wrong.

Pituitary Gland Problems

Fears
- Fear of risk
- Fear of being held accountable
- Fear of missing an opportunity
- Fears humiliation / shame
- Fear of living their larger best selves
- Fear of being betrayed
- Fear of being invisible
- Fears that they will never be anything
- Fears lack of freedom
- Fears not being good enough
- Fears being caught expressing grief

Emotional States
- False hopes get generated by the promises of others. Then when the promises get broken no one is held accountable. Indifference to the emotional suffering of the person is the reaction by others.

This creates a lack of trust and a sense of betrayal that over time hardens into a protective shell against the creation of hope and or reliance on others.
- Minimal projection of needs-does not reach out to others for help and gives the impression that they are very self reliant and don't need others. Feels like that if they ask for help they will be denied and there's a sense of hopelessness in getting assistance – so why ask. Can be seen as 'cold' with no real warmth to others. 'Warmth' is seen, by this person, as a value of trust – cold is how they stay safe.
- Heart feels a sense of hopelessness that nothing will ever change. There's a cellular sense that the repeating pattern of life is hopeless – it ends the same way. There is the subconscious avoidance of putting themselves out there – take the easy road – secure – not living a larger life – stay in the background – a lack of connection with a purpose within the oneness.

Cross Indexing: Headaches, Headaches – Migraine, Insomnia, Depression, Anxiety, Thyroid Problems, Endocrine System Problems, Diabetes

Created Patterns

1. I always have bad luck.
2. I always miss opportunities.
3. I am afraid of recognition in groups.
4. I am unworthy of _____.
5. I can't accept recognition.
6. I have no destiny.
7. I must see the negative to stay safe.
8. I survive by not being seen.
9. I will be humiliated in front of people.
10. It is safer to stay in the background.
11. It is safer to stay in the shadows.
12. No one sees me.

Pityros

Fears

- Fear of wrong reactions
- Fear of being inappropriate
- Fear of letting go to be safe
- Fear of disobeying
- Fear of the rules

Emotional States

- Unable to let go of the past. Wants to hang onto it because it keeps them safe. If healing means letting go then they won't heal. Wants to be left alone to suffer. Doesn't want anyone pointing to their pain as evidence of their refusal to let go. The pain gets fed by the sympathy of others. Wants to overlook the elephant in the room and create a distraction so people won't see it. Past

keeps coming to the surface to be confronted and dealt with and let go. Heart anger. Irritated at past choices. They keep coming to the surface. Can't let go of self-blame.
- Unable to be at peace. Long-standing turmoil of the heart. Wants peace but can't get there. Wants release from the heart. Wants loneness. Wants the voidness where there is no anger, no pain, no heart pain, and no heart anger.
- Yielded to nothing. Hardness. Wants complete autonomy. Does not want to work for anyone else. Is irritated by the restriction and rules of institutions. Wants to be free. Feels burdened by life.

Cross Indexing: Skin Problems, Acne, Yeast Infection, Pruritic Urticarial papules and plaques of pregnancy, Wounded Creative Core

Created Patterns

1. I can't do any better.
2. I must do what is expected of me by others.
3. I must stop myself from being better than _____.
4. If I break the rules _____ (what happens).
5. I can't be better than _____.
6. I must settle to get by.
7. I want to do better.
8. I want to be in alignment with my higher self's purpose.
9. I am in alignment with my higher purpose.
10. My boundaries keep me safe.
11. I trust myself.
12. I am afraid of losing myself if I surrender into the Oneness.
13. I am limited by being a woman.
14. I limit my creativity.
15. I can allow myself so much and then I must stop.
16. I limit my feminine nature/ I limit who I am to be safe.
17. No matter how hard I work I can never get ahead — One step forward, two steps back. Look at the money language of your parents.
18. I must sacrifice _____ (what are you giving up and what are you getting in return).

Plantar Fasciitis

Fears
- Fear of being laughed at
- Fear of being responsible
- Fear of new ideas
- Fear of new ways of doing things
- Fear of authority
- Fear of self-determination

Teachings
- To allow change
- Live in the divine flow
- Be in the divine flow
- Forgive
- Be without fear
- Safe with creativity
- Make mistakes and be safe
- Be creative and be loved
- Be creative and be accepted
- Live without resentment

- Live without needing to judge
- Live without needing to criticize
- Live without fear of being criticized
- Trust others
- Live without being taken advantage of
- Be safe with others in authority
- Live without the fear of criticism
- Be loved
- Be good enough
- Be loved without judgment
- Live without needing to be in control
- Live without fear of being punished
- Higher self-perspective of your mother
- Higher self-perspective of your father
- Higher self-perspective of authority

Emotional States

- Fixed ideas that make for inflexible decisions and approaches to life. Holds others accountable - to blame-for the bad things that happen in one's life. Unyielding in the exchange of ideas. Wants people to focus on their authority. Does not want an alternative pose. Hollowness of nature no real depth of emotions.
- Jumps to conclusions with no real evidence. Wants the safety found in those conclusions, as they render the world defined. Change is dangerous and is judged accordingly. Inflexible. Has a high regard/fear for/of authority, even if it is wrong. Uses the ideas from that authority as their foundation for their conclusions/judgment. Heaviness of nature–energy tends to be heavy–negative thoughts; negative judgments–does not see the light in life. Feelings that life is unjust when it goes against them. Anger is directed at people in authority. Resents authority, sees it as being unjust which reflects their fear of authority.
- Justification for everything they do couched in the criticism of others or in the fear of being criticized by others. Denial of self…their inner truth is ignored. The rigidity of ideas is injurious to self. This injury creates an anger which is vented in the wrong direction. Unwilling to let go of the idea that they are wrong. Wants to be seen as helpless when in reality their rigidity prevents them from being flexible in life situations. Feels that life is unjust when things do not go their way.

Cross Indexing: Foot Problems, Fascia Problems

*This would be cross indexed to second chakra stuff (and in some disciplines 3rd chakra) and heart issues. There will be a reflection of a lack of creativity. Issues of impaired fertility. Sex organ dysfunction. A person that is rigid in the path they walk will have very little creativity and an out of balance feminine (creative energy). Suppression of feelings create the heart issues. Lower back and hips are affected also. Wounded Creative Core.

Created Patterns

1. Change is dangerous.

EMOTIONAL PATTERNS

2. Change must be done slowly.
3. Everyone else is to blame for my problems.
4. Feelings will get you hurt (I will give you something to cry about–heard this as a child).
5. I am afraid of criticism.
6. I am always right.
7. I am angry at _____.
8. I am helpless.
9. I am weak.
10. I can't be wrong.
11. I can't change directions–I must stay the course.
12. I can't forgive.
13. I can't let go.
14. I can't let go of what is not good for me.
15. I must be in charge to be in control.
16. I must be right to be safe.
17. I must blame others to be safe.
18. I must do it all myself for it to be done right.
19. I must do what people in authority say to be accepted/loved/wanted/safe.
20. I must judge other before they judge me.
21. I must judge others to be safe.
22. I must stay in control to be safe.
23. I will be punished if I am myself.
24. If I am right I am loved.
25. If I am wrong I will be punished.
26. If I'm not in control I will be hurt.
27. I'm not creative.
28. I'm not good enough.
29. I'm not safe.
30. It hurts to be me.
31. It's dangerous to feel.
32. Life is hard.
33. My father cannot be trusted.
34. My father is selfish and unjust.
35. My father is stupid.
36. My mother cannot be trusted.
37. My mother is selfish and unjust.
38. My mother is stupid.
39. Nothing happens over night.
40. Other people's ideas are not as good as mine.
41. Others are to blame for the bad thing that happen to me.
42. People in authority are only out for themselves.
43. People in authority are to be feared.
44. People in authority cannot be trusted.
45. People in authority don't get hurt.
46. People in authority take advantage of you.
47. People in authority will hurt you.
48. People take advantage of me.
49. People who create are flighty.
50. The world is dangerous.

51. The world is not safe.
52. Things must be done a certain way.
53. When I am criticized I am rejected.
54. Why should I change? This is how its always been done.
55. You can't make a living being creative.
56. You can't make change for the sake of change.
57. Nothing I do will ever be good enough.

Plantar Wart

Fears

- Fear of rushing to judgment
- Fear of holding ones ground for the wrong reason
- Fear that where they have headed in life is a waste
- Fear of changing direction
- Fear of being someone

Emotional States

- RIGHT – Feels like they are not doing a good enough job. They keep going in the wrong direction. They then have trouble changing direction that they feel will not be good enough any way.
- LEFT – Their spiritual quests have yielded no fruitful information or changes. They feel like they have wasted their time. Those prior efforts have left them feeling defeated.

Cross Indexing: Growths, HPV (herpes), foot problems, skin problems, virus, Right and Left sided negative tendencies, spurs

Created Patterns

1. I angry at _____.
2. I am frustrated with my life/the future.
3. I feel defeated.
4. I am useless.
5. I am worthless.
6. Whatever I do I fail at.
7. My inner compass is never right.
8. I don't seem to ever get anywhere.
9. I'm not good enough.
10. I can't ever seem to get it right.

Pleurisy

Fears
- Fear of there being no hope
- Fear of change
- Fear of knowing
- Fear they are wrong

Emotional States
- They are using their power in a way that goes against their soul purpose. They have not learned the proper/ balanced use of their power.
- The progression of life is change and change is scary and hurtful. Shuts down the influx of new experiences and new life. They like things just the way they are.

Cross indexed: lung problems, inflammation, pneumonia, bronchitis, virus, tuberculosis

Created Patterns
1. Who do you have strong feelings of antagonism and hostility toward?
2. I am apathetic about my life.
3. Life is painful.
4. Living is painful.
5. Change is painful.
6. Change is scary and means life is out of control.
7. When change happens I hold my breath until it is done.

Plum Pit Throat

Fears
- Fear of the harm they might do
- Fear of losing someone with their truth
- Fear of being forced against their will
- Fear of being blamed by others
- Fear of being trapped
- Fear of losing their freedom
- Fear of having to keep what no longer serves
- Fear of not being able to keep what they want to keep
- Fear of enjoying joy

Emotional States
- An intensity of words stuck in their throat that they could not say and must swallow.
- Hard on themselves. Feels that things that go wrong are their fault. They rarely see that others are participating in a failure.
- Many of the things in their life have been hard to swallow. They have not wanted to take on or

take in those things. What has been thrust at them has been couched as this is the way it is supposed to be. They have pushed back and rejected but in the end they feel forced against their will.
- They desire more freedom in their life. They want to let go of what has not helped. They feel stuck in this act of letting go. There are forces around them that say 'stop you can't do this'. They want to let go of the hardness they feel for those trying to stop them but that letting go is stopped too.

Cross Indexing: Swallowing – Trouble, Throat Problems

Created Patterns
1. I am stuck.
2. I am forced to do things against my will.
3. I have no freedom.
4. I have to do what others tell me to do.
5. I must punish myself.
6. When things go wrong it is my fault.
7. I get set up for failure.
8. I set myself up for failure.
9. Life is hard and hard things happen.
10. I am blamed for the bad stuff that happens.
11. I am trapped in a life I don't want.
12. I never get my way.
13. I can't have nice things in my life.
14. I am afraid to let others see me when I am happy.
15. I must keep my joy to myself.
16. If I say what I want to say I will hurt someone.
17. I will lose my friends if I say my truth.

Pneumonia

Fears
- Fear that they won't be sick enough to stop
- Fear that there is no hope of stopping the onslaught
- Fear that if they don't make things happen, they won't happen
- Fear of letting go of the stress cycle

Emotional States
- Go-go-go push-push-push forces things to happen. Does not engage in flow. Pushes life into happening. That version of life has no joy. Because they feel not good enough.
- Holds their breath in the face of stress. They freeze. Doesn't seem to know how to break out of the cycle of intense demands. They also acknowledge they created the stress. But need the cycle to stay safe.

Cross indexing: lung problems, infection, bronchitis, pleurisy, wounded creative core, asthma, cold, tachycardia, emphysema, flu

Created Patterns

1. I am tired of living.
2. I feel like it's no use.
3. I can't make any changes.
4. I can't stop to be sick.
5. What deep emotional hurts have not healed?
6. If I don't keep moving someone will think I am not good enough.
7. I have no joy, joy only gets taken away.
8. I am stress out.
9. I don't know how to stop and just breathe.
10. I don't know how to just be.
11. If anything is going to happen I have to make it happen.
12. I'm not good enough.
13. I am not free to just breathe.
14. I hold my breath to stay safe.

Polyarteritis

Fears

- Fear of having to be the rescuer
- Fear of no one being there to rescue them
- Fear of being alone
- Fear of trusting themselves
- Fear of living

Teachings

- Be connected to source / god / creator
- Be good enough
- Be in the flow
- Be seen and be safe
- Be supported
- Be worthy
- Deserve
- Feel emotions and be safe
- Forgiveness
- Fun
- Happiness
- Joy
- Letting go
- Letting go of anger
- Live being supported
- Live knowing which decisions are mine to make
- Live trusting myself
- Live without being guilty of enjoying life
- Live without judging others
- Live without looking to others for guidance
- Live without looking to others for the

- answers
- Live without needing permission
- Love myself
- Relax
- Trust
- Unconditional love

Emotional States

- Half way living life. Hindered by lack of support and feeling unsupported. Looking for answers to their problems in all the wrong places. Looking to others to solve their issues. They don't trust themselves to get the answers.
- They feel as if they are not allowed to enjoy life and blame that feeling on others.
- All is hindered. Nothing flows their way — abundance, love, luck — feels shut off from the flow of life. Holding on tightly to the past — fear of living their life. Wants someone else to live it for them. They will often say 'I am living my life vicariously through others'.

Cross indexing: Wegener Granulomatosis, Vasculitis, Inflammation, Autoimmune Disorders, Joint Problems, Intestinal Problems, Nerve Problems

Repeating Patterns: not feeling good enough, doesn't feel safe being seen, feels unsupported, doesn't feel worthy or deserving, won't let go of anger, doesn't trust themselves to make the right choices, is often judgmental, looks to others to make their decisions for them, feels like they have to get permission for everything

Created Patterns

1. Being seen is dangerous.
2. Everyone else gets all the luck.
3. Good things don't happen to me.
4. How are you served by letting others live your life?
5. I am angry at _____.
6. I am disconnected from creator/ god.
7. I am disconnected from life.
8. I am invisible.
9. I am never right.
10. I am stopped by others in doing what I want.
11. I am stupid.
12. I can't enjoy myself.
13. I can't let go.
14. I can't relax.
15. I don't deserve.
16. I don't have permission to _____.
17. I don't love myself.
18. I don't trust my inner voice.
19. I don't trust myself.
20. I never get a lucky break.
21. I never have any fun.
22. I will be punished if I _____.

23. I will be punished if I enjoy myself.
24. I'm not good enough.
25. I'm not loved.
26. I'm not supported.
27. I'm not worthy.
28. It is safer to let someone else do it first.
29. It is wrong to be good enough.
30. It is wrong to be seen.
31. It is wrong to enjoy myself.
32. Nothing goes my way.
33. Others stop me from having fun (who are the others?).

*Look at themes of self-worth, self-esteem, flow, loving yourself, unconditional love, anger, letting go, forgiveness, acknowledgement, allowing, authenticity, blockages, blame, co-dependence, confidence, control, disassociation, feeling, judgment, guilt, identity, self respect, self knowledge, trust, unmet needs, true self, conflicting motivations, approval, confidence, control, letting go, decision making, freedom, guilt, intuition, joy, power, truth and authenticity.

Polymyalgia Rheumatica

Fears
- Fear of weakness
- Fear of needing more strength than they have to prevail
- Fear of feeling

Teachings
- Accepting
- Allowing
- Ask for support and be safe
- Be loved
- Be supported
- Connect with others
- Creator's definition and perspective on freewill
- Embrace life
- Feel emotions and be safe
- Forgive
- Go with the flow
- Grieve and be safe
- Joy
- Let go
- Let people in
- Live feeling supported
- Live understanding your responsibility in your choices
- Live without expecting others to hurt you
- Live without needing to hold onto pain
- Live without shutting down communication to the heart
- Loving myself

- Set appropriate boundaries
- Unconditional love

Emotional States
- Heartache, heartsick – shutting off communication to the heart, missing life, stone like deadness in their actions. Hollow feelings. What they do or say is only done to appear as if they care. Their feelings have gone dead. Can't hold what life offers. The fear of dealing with a shut down heart too great. Create physical pain to feel something and detract from the issues of the heart.

Cross Indexing: Temporal Arteritis, Shoulder problems, hip problems, heart problems, Joint Problems, Shoulder problems, Inflammation

Repeating patterns: doesn't feel accepted, feels that if they ask for support they will be unsafe, feelings of being unloved and unsupported, doesn't know how to connect with others, hangs onto to things and situations way beyond the time when they should have let go, they do not know how to feel supported, they feel as if people will always hurt them, they don't take responsibility for their choices, they deaden the heart when they have been hurt, boundaries are weak, they don't get unconditional love they have never felt it.

Created Patterns
1. Being alone is better than being hurt.
2. Feelings are dangerous.
3. I am alone.
4. I am dead inside.
5. I am depressed.
6. I can't accept what has happened to me.
7. I can't allow myself to feel anything.
8. I don't let anyone near my heart.
9. I have no life.
10. I have nothing to look forward to.
11. I must put on a façade to keep people from knowing the truth.
12. I'm not lovable.
13. I'm not responsible for what has happened.
14. I'm not supported.
15. If I feel I will die.
16. If I feel I will fall apart.
17. If I feel I will hurt.
18. If I let anyone near me they will hurt me again.
19. Love is pain.
20. My heart is broken.
21. People hurt me.
22. People who get close to me hurt me.

*Look at themes of blockages, boundaries, spiritual growth, flow, loving yourself, unconditional love, denial, depression, disassociation, emotions, joy, enjoying life, forgiveness, giving, receiving, happiness, life, oneness, relationships, self-esteem, self-worth, trust, broken heart, unmet needs, defenses, feelings, grief, joy, judgment, relationships, truth and authenticity.

Polymyositis

Fears
- Fear that no one is there for them
- Fear of being unsupported
- Fear of being overrun
- Fear of being attacked
- Fear of powerlessness

Emotional States
- Weakened by emotions of heat (anger, irritation, bitterness, etc.). They have no strength in the face of their boundaries being invaded. They cannot show their emotions and they get very rigid (freeze) to endure any onslaughts.

Cross Indexing: Autoimmune, Muscle Problems, Inflammation, Joint Problems, Trouble – Swallowing, Tachycardia, ancestral/genetic

Created Patterns
1. My anger must be hidden from others.
2. When I am confronted I freeze. I can't move or defend myself.
3. I am weak.
4. My anger weakens me. I feel as if I must take the anger into me and take it out on me to not be attacked by others.
5. I have been repressing strong feelings of _____ for a long time (These are negative emotions of fear and anger-which is fear).
6. What do you not have to contend with because of the disease?
7. I am powerless.
8. What issues of masculine energy are not being dealt with (See Right-Sided Negative Tendencies)?

Post Mastectomy Problems

Fears
- Fear of not knowing who they are
- Fear of being seen by others
- Fear of self-rejection
- Fear of rejection
- Fear of being alone
- Fear of no longer being able to give
- Fear of being a woman/man
- Fear of sex
- Fear of isolation
- Fear of their body
- Fear of how they will be redefined

- Fear of intimacy
- Fear of being unloved/ unwanted
- Fear of betrayal
- Fear of having made the wrong decision
- Fear of letting go
- Fear that creative core is gone

Emotional States
- A sense that they have died to their pre-mastectomy identity. There is a feeling of lost and asking the question 'who am I?'. The feminine identification with the body had been strong and now that identity has been redefined for what feels like an outside force…forced upon them. They are grieving the loss and all that the pre-mastectomy femininity represented.

Cross Indexing: Cancer – Breast, Breast Problems, depression

Created Patterns
1. _____ is a burden.
2. Change hurts.
3. Change is dangerous.
4. I am a disappointment to others and hence a failure.
5. I am a failure.
6. I am alone.
7. I am angry at _____.
8. I am angry at having so much responsibility.
9. I am angry at my body.
10. I am angry at people that take advantage of me.
11. I am disfigured.
12. I am maimed.
13. I am only loved when I am needed.
14. I am responsible for _____.
15. I am ugly.
16. I can't let others help me.
17. I can't say no.
18. I don't know how to be loved.
19. I don't know how to be loved without being taken advantage of.
20. I don't know what it feels like to be loved.
21. I don't know what it feels like to be loved without being taken advantage of.
22. I must stay unbalanced to stay out of a relationship.
23. I'm not safe in a relationship.
24. If I let go of everything I will die.
25. If people/men get too close they may not like me.
26. If things are out of control I am a failure.
27. Intimacy is dangerous.
28. Intimacy is pain.
29. It isn't safe to say no.
30. Life is a struggle.
31. Life is hard.

32. Life is unfair.
33. Men abuse me.
34. Men don't listen to me.
35. Men use me.
36. My body betrayed me.
37. My body is ugly.
38. No one will ever want me.
39. People I love take advantage of me.
40. People I trust take advantage of me.
41. People take advantage of me.
42. Taking a risk is never worth it.
43. Since my breasts are gone I am not needed.
44. The cancer will come back.

Post-Nasal Drip

Fears
- Fear of life
- Fear of what has been said will force them to hold their breath
- Fear of being held responsible
- Fear of blame
- Fear of meaningless relationships
- Fear of purpose and being held accountable

Emotional States
- Holds head up above the fray of discontent only to be pulled down into it with their own pain of discontent. Hollow expectations of honor and respect are acknowledged and then relentlessly denied. Core elements of life are unseen and unwritten in their life story.
- Warmth warns of 'mean' expectations in their relationships. Held in a nuanced state of sublime knowledge there is false laughter and falseness to their affectations of joy in life.
- Hollowness of purpose meets the glorified expectations of others replaces true self-love. Self-knowledge is subjugated to the praise that others give to feel a sense of self-purpose. The concept of self-love is illusive and has not been felt in this life. Purpose is their substitute.
- Follow through becomes the purpose. Instead of joy in the work the stream of activity in the work becomes the 'raison d'être'. There is no sense of freedom in what they do — there is only a sense of keeping the activity between two ends going to have a purpose.
- Hard hold on the story of and in the past. The story (ies) creates the foundation from which all information is sourced. These foundations are old, have cracks, are crumbling and will not sustain. So the stories that have built their reality are now fraught with holes. The person creates words and actions to fill the holes. Ever ignoring a greater 'T' truth. Actually running away from the big 'T' truth.

Cross Indexing: Sinus problems, Lung problems, Allergies, Colds, Virus

Created Patterns
1. I am a victim.
2. I feel always sad inside.
3. I feel like I need to cry.
4. What loss have you not let yourself feel?
5. What are you grieving?

Post-Partum Depression

Fears
- Fear of loss of life as it was
- Fear of what they must be now
- Fear of no identity
- Fear of becoming nothing
- Fear of loss of life
- Fear of hopelessness

Emotional States
- Locked in a paradigm of safety before the baby was born. Now the infant represents anything but safe. The infant represents the unknown and they are now responsible for this life. There is a deep fear of the darkness of becoming nothing…the phrase 'at the edge of the abyss' came up during the information gathering. This person is trying to hold onto the way things were before the infant was born. This person wants to know and predict their world. The infant represents the unknown. The baby cannot articulate so the experience created by the new infant is not predictable. The paradigm of the world as they know it is lost.
- Their sense of beingness is shattered. People now see the baby…not them. They become the mother of _____ (old Greco-Roman-Hebrew). They disappear into the role of being only the caretaker of the infant. Parenthood has become a loss of identity.
- What they believed to be their source of happiness has gone away with the advent of parenthood. This person hears only the negative. This person actually shuns happiness, feels wounded from the act of birth instead of a sense of life flowing through. There is a sense that they should have died as a release – past life memory of death at childbirth and the release from pain and struggle left a psychic imprint of joy and bliss– that did not happen with this act of childbirth. Old program that sex was sinful and childbirth was the punishment for sex – a sense that the infant represents their sinful nature – prior beliefs of being bad / no good/ cursed.
- Holding to past ideas about how life should be or would be or needs to be. Competitive nature has been sidelined / sublimated to the task of parenthood. Lack of selflessness in the role. Ego identification has been narrowed. Struggling with the new definition- does not have an identification that supports the new role.
- Sees no end to the struggle. Feels hopeless. Regrets choices that have led to the decision of childbirth feels their life is at end. Old life has died and they do not see that they are embarking on a new life. In essence they have been born to a new life and don't know how to define it within the context of the old. Does not believe that life will get easier / better. Feels that they are in the

midst of a struggle for dominance and control of their life. Parenting skills are limited by prior parenting role models that were ignorant.
- Happiness at the birth of the baby is overshadowed by a past loss. They are afraid the loss will happen again. There was an expectation that the birth of an infant would resolve a prior unresolved grief. There was an expectation that the child's birth would dispel a sense of loss and loneliness. This person feels very much alone and abandoned. Their needs were not being met before the baby was born but those feelings were suppressed. With additional physical duress the veil of suppression and grief has been removed. The loss felt by this person is one of the heart. This person won't allow themselves the feeling of joy. They are afraid that the joy and happiness will be taken away from them.

Cross Indexing: Depression, Anxiety, Insomnia, Suicidal, Panic Disorder

Created Patterns
1. I will be like mother.
2. I am a second class citizen.
3. I am a nobody.
4. I don't want to be a mother/ father.
5. I am no good at this.
6. I hate my life.
7. Having a baby was a bad idea.
8. I can't handle being a mother / father.
9. I am afraid the baby will die.
10. If the baby dies I will kill myself.
11. If I kill myself I will become nothing / I will cease to exist.
12. The baby has ruined my life and I want nothing to do with it.
13. I can't be a mother / father.
14. I am overwhelmed by grief.
15. I am my grief.
16. I have given up everything for this baby.
17. My mother was always depressed.
18. Life is hard.
19. Life is a struggle.
20. I am hopeless.
21. Everything is hopeless.
22. No one cares.
23. I am angry at myself for giving up _____.
24. I am angry.
25. I am angry at myself.
26. I am angry at _____.
27. I have been deceived / betrayed by _____.
28. My heart is broken.
29. My life is out of control.
30. I am powerless.
31. I can't make things better.
32. Having a baby means that I am sinful.
33. I want to die.
34. I must be punished.

EMOTIONAL PATTERNS

35. Life has betrayed me.
36. I should have died.
37. I don't want to be here.
38. The world owes me.
39. I am depressed.
40. Children are a curse.
41. My life is over as I know it.
42. No one cares for me.
43. I have been abandoned by _____.
44. I need to die to be happy.
45. I am nothing.
46. I am invisible.
47. Having a baby is wrong.
48. I am guilty of _____.
49. I am guilty of the original sin.
50. I am lost.
51. I do not know where I belong.
52. I am trapped.
53. I want to give up.
54. It is hopeless to go on.
55. The child will be better off without me.
56. Good things are taken away from me.
57. I don't deserve good things.
58. Change is dangerous.
59. When things change I will be hurt.
60. I am shamed.
61. I am humiliated.
62. Children only bring unhappiness.
63. I am evil.
64. Nothing I do will ever be good enough.
65. The work is never done.
66. I alone.
67. God/ creator abandoned me.
68. Nobody helps me.
69. I'm not wanted.
70. I have to be what others want me to be (who are the others?).
71. I punish others by being depressed.
72. I get the attention I need by being depressed.
73. I use my depression to get my needs met.
74. I need my depression.
75. My depression serves me.
76. I control others with my depression.
77. I never get what I want.
78. I'm not loved.
79. I am not good enough so I must be punished.
80. Childbirth is a wound.
81. I will never be free.
82. Having a child was forced on me.
83. I have no choices.

84. I must stay in control to be safe.
85. Motherhood/ Fatherhood means giving up who I am.
86. I am a failure.
87. I created someone to love me and all they do is cry.
88. I hate myself.
89. I'm not loved, I am used.
90. My baby will die and then I will die of a broken heart (past life stuff).
91. I'm not good enough.
92. I can't let go.

Post Traumatic Stress Disorder (PTSD)

Fears
- Fear of the fear
- Fear of being powerless to stop bad things from happening
- Fear of dying
- Fear of not dying
- Fear of not being in control
- Fear of not being able to run
- Fear of the unexpected
- Fear of the triggers (dogs, sirens, helicopters, loud sounds, etc.)
- Fear of letting go
- Fear of the guilt

Emotional States
- A repetitive pattern triggered by a triggered memory of trauma(s) that triggered an instinctual response to stay safe, fight-flight response gets stuck in a loop. A feeling of guilt that somehow the originating event was their fault. They feel they could have done something to stop what happened. A sense that if you had had more control or been in control nothing would have happened. A feeling that they brought the event to themselves. No support following the trauma.

Cross Indexing: ACOA, epigenetics, Addictions, depression, anxiety, Panic disorder, nervous breakdown

Created Patterns
1. I am always on guard.
2. I am overwhelmed by anxiety.
3. I am overwhelmed by fear.
4. I am stuck in the past.
5. I can't forget.
6. I can't forgive.
7. I can't let go.
8. I can't remember.
9. I can't stand up for myself.
10. I could have stopped _____ (What is the trauma they could have stopped?).

11. I don't know how to be happy.
12. I don't know how to protect myself.
13. I don't know what is dangerous.
14. I don't know what it feels like to be respected.
15. I don't know what joy feels like.
16. I don't know who is dangerous.
17. I don't trust _____.
18. I have been betrayed by _____.
19. I must _____ (What must you do to keep from feeling shame?).
20. I must be angry to protect myself.
21. I must not tell _____ (What is the secret you must hold?).
22. I'm not respected.
23. I'm not safe when I am alone.
24. If I feel something I am in danger.
25. My anger protects me.
26. My only identity is the past.
27. Nobody is safe.
28. The only time I am safe is when I am alone.

Preemie Birth – now adult

Fears

- Fear that everything happens before you are ready – out of control.
- Fear of being forced against your will.
- Fear of self-blame for bad things happening.

Emotional States

- Holds on. Holds their breath. Won't go forward to breath in life. The breath of life is dangerous. Refuses to know that there are other ways and other points of view. Want to be seen as a 'liver' of life. So they create the illusion by doing lots that keeps them safe. It is dangerous to not be busy and not doing.
- Hopeless sense of the unknown. Constantly running scared of what might happen. 'Knows' that nothing they do will ever change the mess they feel they are in. Held accountable for what might happen by others around them.
- Just doesn't get it. At war with themselves as truths. They are hard pressed to understand the dark side of newness and the dark side of truth.
- Hard won victories to truth. Juxtapositioning of life energy to damned if you do and damned if you don't. Buried idea and buried feelings surface to create a sense of despair and chaos. Works hard to re-bury them as they pop up.
- Epigenetic/ ancestral in womb trauma.

Cross Indexing: PTSD, ACOA

Created Patterns

1. I must hold my breath so I can live.
2. I don't know how to live with joy.
3. Breathing / being seen is dangerous.
4. My ways are the right and only way, after all I survived against all odds.
5. I must worry about what might happen.
6. I can't change my circumstances, they are hopeless.
7. I am hopeless.
8. Nothing I do will change things.
9. I am clueless.
10. There is only one way of being.
11. You are damned if you do and damned if you don't.
12. My life is chaos.
13. I know how to survive in chaos.
14. I am comfortable in the chaos.
15. I must bury the past to be safe.

Premenstrual Syndrome

Fears

- Fear of a world that is hostile to the cycles that are life
- Fear of feminine nature
- Fear of being forced against her will
- Fear of the creative force

Emotional States

- Lies to themselves about being OK with being a woman/female. They secretly hate being female.
- Unaware that their actions will result in the incomplete process of creativity.
- Kills the creative urges because it is safe that way. If they engage the creative they will not be able to reach their goals.
- Nervous about what she is forced to comply with as a woman. No choice. No options. She feels forced against her will.
- Hardness in their inner core has thrown off the balance of masculine and feminine natures.

Cross Indexing: Wound creative core, menstrual problems

Created Patterns

1. Someone else must take care of me.
2. I can't take care of myself.
3. I am not doing what I want to do.
4. I will never be able to live my dream.
5. I hate what I am doing in life.

6. Love is painful.
7. Loving myself is hard to do.
8. I hate being a woman.
9. I can't be creative and be successful.
10. I must sublimate my creativity to reach my goals.
11. I have been forced against my will to _____.
12. As a woman I have no good choices.
13. I must be strong to compensate for how people see me.
14. I am judged by men and other women because of my gender.

Prolapsed Bladder (Cystocele)

Fears
- Fear of having to make adjustments or accommodation
- Fear of being used
- Fear of being forced to give birth again

Emotional States
- Heart is wounded from heartless soul wound. Someone close has led them astray and taken a feeling of self-worth with them. It was hard to see the truth around this individual. Their thoughtlessness was extremely hurtful. Cleverly being used by another who does not have their best interest at heart.
- Wants to be let go/ release from binds. Unadjusted to needs and urges – thwarted their feelings to meet the needs of others. Wants retribution/be paid back for that time spent.
- Unfinished business. Something in their life is left hanging. Issue of getting the courage to finish it.
- Left with a stuck trauma from childbirth.

Cross Indexing: Bladder problems, Menopause – Difficult, Abdominal Sacrocolpopexy

Created Patterns
1. I must sacrifice myself to create.
2. I must meet the needs of others first.
3. I am being used by _____.
4. I want revenge against/for _____.
5. I can't let go.
6. I gave birth and got no respect or praise or love from my partner.
7. I have permanent damage from giving birth and no one cares.
8. My heart is wounded to the core of my being.
9. I am devastated.
10. I have no sense of my worth. I am worthless.
11. I cannot see truth.
12. I am easily deceived by others.
13. I am afraid of _____.

Prostate Problems

Fears
- Fear of nothingness
- Fear of being nothing
- Fear of being diminished
- Fear of having no identity

Teachings
- Accepting creativity
- Act on your creativity
- Allow creative ideas
- Allow the flow of life
- Be accepted
- Be comfortable and at ease in my body
- Be comfortable with my feelings
- Be Creative
- Be good enough
- Be honored for who you are
- Be honored for your individuality
- Be in my body
- Be in the now
- Be loved without condition
- Be respected
- Be respected for who you are
- Creator's definition of judgment
- Creator's definition of sexual feelings
- Honor the differences in others
- Honoring the creative aspect of self
- Know what makes me happy
- Let go
- Live life without feeling burdened
- Live life without struggle
- Live my life's dream
- Live my life's purpose
- Live without being disappointed
- Live without blame
- Live without feeling trapped
- Live without limitation
- Live without needing the approval of others
- Love my sexuality
- Love myself
- See sexuality as a healthy part of the human experience
- Trust
- Trust Creator
- Trust women
- Trust your feelings

Emotional States
- Anger at stifled creativity.

- Lack of confidence in self — sees himself as lesser than everyone else –knows he will never be good enough.
- Repressed creative nature.
- Life feels like a heavy load to bear. Not in the flow of life. Feels like he is carrying an unfair share of the burden.
- Not living life dream/ purpose – may be unclear as to what this is.
- High degree of anxiety around life. Has never really felt relaxed into the flow of life. Creativity is stifled/ stilted and controlled. Cannot allow himself to explore in thoughts or actions his creativity. Creativity is structured (everything has a rule around it). Structured 'creativity' feels threatened by the feminine aspect of self. Repressed sexual expression is again based on society's accepted structure.
- Nothing flows freely. Speech is guarded. Keeps feelings and ideas to themselves. Rarely shares ideas or feelings that would create vulnerability in them.
- Not in their body. Feels uncomfortable with their body. Prone to bruising, falls and accidents of misstep. Gets bruises and does not remember where they came from. Unconnected to the energy systems of others that sense the impact of raw honesty (can be hurtful without really knowing a statement will hurt).
- Struggle with feeling diminished and less than. Has not lived their live dream – wanting to have done other things with their life – but now they feel like it is too late.
- There's an inner struggle of a strong masculine energy wanting to break free from the constraints of 'society', to behave without rules of conduct. Feels repressed by society 'mores' and the laws of civilization. Feels a need to prove their manhood.
- Uncertainty as to what it means to be a man. Feels like they are always guessing at what their role should be and they are constantly failing because they are not listening to the inner self. Looking for definition outside of themselves. Feels as if they are in a conflicted role and never really know what should be.

Cross indexing: Infertility, impotence, kidney problems, depression, hypertension, diabetes I & II, aging

Repeating Patterns: wounded creative core, does not allow the flow of life, has trouble being accepted, not at ease with their body or feelings, they do not feel honored for who they are, doesn't know how to be present, doesn't get unconditional love, feels disrespected, feels burdened by life, doesn't trust their feelings, doesn't love themselves, doesn't let go of situations that he should walk away from, frequently feels disappointed by their life, feels as if they are to blame, feels trapped in a life they didn't want, needs approval from others to feel wanted and loved.

Created Patterns
1. Creator doesn't listen to me.
2. Creator let me down.
3. Even ideas must have rules.
4. I am a failure.
5. I am afraid of failing.
6. I am afraid of getting old
7. I am angry at _____ *(Who are you angry at for the restriction?)*.
8. I am angry at _____ for telling me what to do.
9. I am depressed.
10. I am disconnected from creator/ source.

11. I am out of my body.
12. I am overrun by women.
13. I am pissed off.
14. I am powerless to change things.
15. I am ready to just give up on everything.
16. I am trapped.
17. I can only have so much.
18. I can't let go of _____.
19. I could have _____ *(what could you have done with your life and didn't, what stops you from living your life dream).*
20. I could have been somebody *(what stopped you?).*
21. I don't believe in myself.
22. I don't belong.
23. I don't trust Creator.
24. I don't trust my feelings.
25. I don't trust myself.
26. I give up.
27. I hate being told what to do.
28. I hate rules.
29. I have been kept from _____ *(What have you been restricted from doing in your life?).*
30. I must be under control at all times or bad things will happen.
31. I must do what others say to be accepted / safe / loved.
32. I must get my understanding of god from the priest / minister/ rabbi/ Imam.
33. I must keep my feelings to myself.
34. I must keep my thoughts to myself.
35. I must make sure people obey the rules.
36. I must obey the rules.
37. I must obey the rules of my church.
38. I need the approval of others to be loved / respected/ accepted.
39. I never get to do what I want.
40. I want to give up on life.
41. I will never accomplish my dreams.
42. I will never realize my dream.
43. I'm not accepted.
44. I'm not good enough.
45. If I am creative I will be laughed at / ridiculed.
46. If I fail _____ *(what will happen).*
47. If I have a creative idea I will be ridiculed.
48. *If you were to live your life's purpose what would happen?*
49. *If you were to realize your life's dream what would happen?*
50. Life is a burden.
51. Life is a struggle.
52. My body doesn't fit.
53. My body doesn't fit in the space I'm in.
54. My doubts are my failures.
55. My feelings don't matter.
56. My ideas are never good enough.
57. People are mean.
58. People ignore me.

59. Someone / something always stops me from realizing my dream *(who or what are you blaming)*.
60. The older I get the less I am listened to/ heard.
61. The older I get the more I am ignored.
62. The older you get the less important you are.
63. The price for being myself is too high.
64. The price of freedom is too high.
65. Things must be controlled at all times or bad things will happen *(what are the bad things?)*.
66. Thinking for myself is dangerous.
67. *What are the major issues with mother/women? (Overrun)*.
68. *What is the conflict around sex?*
69. When I ask for something I am always disappointed.
70. When you get old you start falling apart.

*Look at themes of trapped, self-respect, self-worth, self-esteem, self-knowledge, anger, approval, blame, control, excuses, failure, creativity, grounded, higher self-connection, resentment, prosperity, play, fun, unmet needs (fun, play, creativity, nurturance, approval), worthiness, spirituality, soul purpose, sex, power, manifesting, disconnection, domination, control, letting go, boundaries

Pruritic urticarial papules and plaques of pregnancy

Fears
- Fear of not being in control
- Fear of betrayal
- Fear of being hurt again

Emotional States
- Hard time has forced emotions to the surface. Unable to whisper the name of those that have hurt you.
- Difficult choices have made for rigid ideologies that protect them from feelings of guilt. Feelings that are conflicted lead to equations of guilt and sacrifices made a compromise of their own boundaries and feelings of being overrun. Ancestral.
- The wrath of a patriarch has rung like a bell through the DNA. Held accountable for their actions and shamed into submission. Warmth led to coldness. The inner conflict of push-pull — love-hate. Silent anger held in at all costs.

Cross Indexing: Hives, skin problems, ancestral/ epigenetic

Created Patterns
1. I shut down to others to punish them.
2. I must keep my feelings to myself.
3. I must not let people see I am angry.
4. I am under pressure.
5. I have been betrayed by those I love.
6. I have been made a fool of.

7. I am always right.
8. My logic is the right logic.
9. I must make sacrifices to get what I want.
10. I am not guilty for the betrayal, others are.

Pseudo Tumor – Cerebri

Fears
- Fear of not being able to hide from a hostile world
- Fear of understanding
- Fear of emotions
- Fear of feeling
- Fear of life
- Fear of their heart feelings
- Fear of peace
- Fear of being heard
- Fear of being seen
- Fear of suffering
- Fear of letting go

Emotional States
- There is no learning or understanding. Let's emotions build up without addressing them or what they mean. They keep these emotions to themselves and when more events happen that create more emotions they go into confusion to keep from having to deal with them. The confusion keeps them from having to sort through what has become overwhelming. No inner peace.

Cross Indexing: Brain problems, Addison's, Behcet's, DVT, Lupus, Kidney Disease, Polycystic Ovary, Sleep Apnea, Parathyroid Problems, Migraines, Overweight, Eye Problems

Created Patterns
1. I am overwhelmed by life.
2. I am overloaded.
3. Life is too big a challenge.
4. There is no way out.
5. The only way to get help is to get sick.
6. The only way out is to get sick.
7. I want out of my life.
8. I want out.
9. The pressures of life are too much.
10. I have no peace or clam in my world.
11. The future is scary.
12. I am unheard and when I am heard I am misunderstood.
13. I get confused to keep myself safe.

Psoriasis

Fears
- Fear of being vulnerable
- Fear of not being able to protect themselves from the slings and arrows of life
- Fear of failing
- Fear of not deserving

Emotional States
- Well intentioned changes and decisions have resulted in failure. The failures have caused a ripple effect in their life leading to a biased view of all change and decisions. Unable to let go of anger at all the people involved in the failure incurred at the hands of authority.
- Just won't let go of the idea that they are imperfect. They see nothing they do as good enough. Constant struggle to prove they are worthy of being. Wants more than they have been given. But there is a constant struggle and inner conflict of I deserve and I don't deserve. They refuse to be allowed in.
- Long term need to be held. Can never feel enough.
- Does not know that they have been misled with respect to the intentions of others. It is how they are seen and they want people to look away like the leper. The leper hides in their enclave and becomes invisible.

Cross Indexing: Skin Problems, Thyroid Problems, Autoimmune Disorders, Wounded Creative Core

Created Patterns
1. I am afraid of _____.
2. I can't tell people what I think without hurting them.
3. I give up.
4. I hate myself (What other negative feelings do you have about yourself?).
5. I resent _____.
6. I want to die.
7. I would be better off dead.
8. I'm afraid no one will like me if I _____.
9. I'm insecure.
10. No point in trying to change things.
11. Nothing will every change.
12. They made me feel that way (Who is the they and how did that happen?).
13. What were you hurt by and can't get over?

Pulmonary Fibrosis

Fears
- Fear that no one cares about your suffering

- Fear of being alone
- Fear of breathing
- Fear of mean people
- Fear of being shamed
- Fear of being humiliated
- Fear of being unworthy
- Fear of their creativity
- Fear of life
- Fear of what will happen if they move
- Fear of pain

Emotional States
- Petrified, frozen in fear — holds their breath and doesn't move. They live in an environment filled with toxic emotions and behaviors. They thicken the barriers between themselves and toxic onslaughts and find strategies for surviving their inability to lead their life.
- When they have tried in the past to live they were hurt.

Cross Indexing: Wounded Creative Core, Polymyositis, connective tissue diseases, lupus, Rheumatoid arthritis, Sarcoidosis, Scleroderma, Pneumonia, Cancer – Lung, GERD, virus, Addiction – smoking, hypertension

Created Patterns
1. People in my life are mean and hateful. There is no safe place to be me.
2. Breathing is dangerous.
3. Living is dangerous.
4. The world is a dangerous place.
5. I must make my world safe by _____.
6. I am only half alive.
7. I can't tell people how I feel.
8. I am unworthy to breathe.
9. I shouldn't be alive.

Pyorrhea – Periodontitis

Fears
- Fear of losing their dreams
- Fear of having to hold back the words indicting justice
- Fear of having no one to turn to
- Fear of becoming someone
- Fear of being wrong
- Fear of the outcome of their decisions
- Fear of being unsupported
- Fear of being not good enough
- Fear of people leaving me

- Fear of being alone
- Fear of life

Emotional States
- Their dreams have fallen away. They no longer feel like they can accomplish what they dreamed of doing. There is no support. The more resentment they build toward those that withdrew their support the more controlling they become. They take on the guilt of another as a form of gaslighting (example: It is their fault that their husband is cheating.).

Cross Indexing: Gingivitis, Periodontal Disease, Gum Disease, bacterial infection

Created Patterns
1. I can't make decisions.
2. I am angry with myself for it (What is the fear if you make decisions?).
3. I am guilty for the betrayal of others.
4. I must tighten my control of others so I won't be betrayed.
5. I have lost my dreams.
6. I am unsupported.
7. I resent those that took their support away from me.

Pyrogenic Granuloma

Fears
- Fear if having no place to live
- Fear of breathing
- Fear of an emptiness to life
- Fear of being out of control
- Fear of no support
- Fear of being alone
- Fear of change
- Fear of hurt

Emotional States
- The flow of this person's life feels as if it is going too fast and it is out of control. They are asking for help and not getting any. They feel like their voice doesn't matter and that no one hears them. This person may have feelings of desperation, self-deprecation, depression or insecurity. This person feels like they have no direction in life and they are confused about their purpose in life. There may be nervousness around living. This person feels like they can't get connected to anything in their life because it is all moving so very quickly. There's no foundation being built. They don't feel like they can use what they know to get their needs met. This person may feel a hurt inside. This person has had an event happen that hurt them deeply. This hurt has undermined their confidence and self-value.

Created Patterns

1. Change is bad.
2. Everything keeps changing.
3. Everything moves so fast.
4. I am all alone.
5. I am angry at _____.
6. I am angry at myself.
7. I am depressed.
8. I am hopeless.
9. I am invisible.
10. I am rejected.
11. I am stupid.
12. I can forgive those that have hurt me.
13. I can let go of past hurts.
14. I can't make good decisions.
15. I criticize myself to be safe.
16. I don't seem to ever know the right answers.
17. I hurt myself……why?
18. I must control relationships to keep from being hurt again.
19. I must deride/criticize myself before others do.
20. I must hold onto the pain to protect myself.
21. I must hold onto the pain to remember so I won't be hurt again.
22. I was hurt by _____.
23. If I forgive I will get hurt again.
24. My life is hopeless.
25. My life is out of control.
26. No one helps me.
27. No one listens to me.
28. No one sees me.
29. Nothing I do ever works.
30. Self-criticism is safe.
31. You can't depend on anyone/anything.

R's

Radiation Influence on Disease Creation

Fears
- Fear of conflict
- Fear of inner self
- Fear of a divine existence
- Fear of too much information
- Fear of being diminished
- Fear of being judged
- Fear of the world
- Fear of having to struggle
- Fear of someone touching their heart and soul

Emotional States
- Holding self to be valueless.
- Being unaware of true inner self.
- Knowing that there is no hope or a better way.
- Long-term inability to handle stress. Childhood was stressful and fraught with the inability to be who they truly are, had to be something/someone else. Constant state of being ware (not misspelled).
- There is no sense of a spiritual aspect to their being. There is a uni-dimensional quality to their life. What is in front of them is what they know and nothing else.

Repeating Patterns: Lives life as a facade. Just through the motions.

Created Patterns
1. I am unworthy of living my life.
2. I feel as if I live a life with no value.
3. I have no hope of a better life.
4. I have to be what someone else wants me to be.
5. I must be on-guard and stress is a way of existing for me.

Radiculopathy of Left Breast

Fears
- Fear that there is no truth in their life
- Fear of being unwanted / unloved
- Fear of not being treasured

- Fear of suffering
- Fear of pain
- Fear of not being as good as a man
- Fear of letting go of a need for revenge
- Fear of being judged
- Fear of being misunderstood
- Fears being manipulated, trapped

Emotional States

- This person has no inner peace because of the male authority in their life subjecting them to gender/sexual orientation biases and roles. They have weak boundaries and allow him to overrun them.
- They feel like they can never relax and be themselves.
- They do not extend a sense of understanding and connection to the suffering of others.
- There is a lack of discernment and not giving other people the benefit of the doubt.
- No freedom to be who they want to be and who they are.
- Does not like being around others.
- Can't be present and in their feelings
- Communicating needs for self-nurturing and giving nurturing from others is painful. May be due to lack of equality in relationships and/or being tightly wound.

Cross Indexing: Radiculopathy of Right Breast, Breast Problems, Spinal Stenosis, Nerve problems, Back-Cervical

Created Patterns

1. I am living under someone else's rules and their way of being in the world.
2. I am invisible and have no identity.
3. People make me uncomfortable.
4. Whenever I have feelings I must not be present. I don't want to be present to feelings.
5. I am trapped and have no freedom.
6. Everyone is guilty and not to be trusted.
7. People who suffer brought it on themselves.
8. I must always be on guard.

Radiculopathy of Right Breast

Fears

- Fear of differences being seen as the standard
- Fear of being unwanted / unloved
- Fear of not being treasured
- Fear of suffering
- Fear of pain
- Fear of not being as good as a man
- Fear of letting go of a need for revenge

- Fear of being judged
- Fear of being misunderstood
- Fears being manipulated, trapped

Emotional States
- Heartfelt need to be wanted, cared for and honored. Does not know how to communicate those needs to others and self. There is a pinching off of ideas and creativity.
- Feels not good enough with respect to their ideas. Holds others out to be wrong. Judging to fend off judgment.
- Long winded answers. Feels like everything they do has to be explained in a great deal of detail and depth. Heart and hearing fears being misunderstood so they use words to create their being accepted.
- Well meaning ideas and actions are misconstrued by those around them. Feels not understood. Feels like they have to be someone else, not their true self, to be loved. Won't let go of the past where the concept of love was misconstrued. Love equals manipulation and control.
- Hard on self. Won't let go of past wounds and this will sometimes hurt others. Holds self out as the paragon of behavior. That paradigm of virtue creates attitudes and images of self that does not serve them. Holds others accountable to that paragon of virtue.
- Communicating needs for self nurturing and receiving nurturing from others is painful. May be due to lack of equality in relationships and/or being tightly wound.

Cross Indexing: Radiculopathy of Left Breast, Breast Problems, Spinal Stenosis, Nerve problems, Back-Cervical

Created Patterns
1. If I ask for something I have to pay for it in emotional pain.
2. I'm not as good as a man.
3. I was hurt by someone and I can't let go of that hurt. It wasn't my fault so they have to be punished.
4. I am misunderstood.
5. I am only understood after a great deal of explaining.
6. I must judge others to not be judged.
7. I want to be nurtured my way.

Rashes

Fears
- Fear of hostile people that will have their way and say
- Fear of being caught
- Fear of being trapped
- Fear of not being given the space they need
- Fear of not being left alone
- Fear of the layer underneath being seen
- Fear of being found to be less than

Emotional States

- Hardwired to run in the face of a threat, but prevented from doing so. Consequently, the excess energy hits the skin and puts up a stay away sign.
- Hit hard by a recent loss and they want to hide but are unable to do so and the best option is to keep people away.
- Taking in a toxic energy that affects the way they are seen by others. They didn't create this situation and it irritates that others blame them.

Cross Indexing: Skin problems, Hives, shingles

Created Patterns

1. I could be killed if I am wrong.
2. I am being attacked.
3. I am irritated by _____.
4. I want people to stay away from me. I get peace and quiet.
5. I get blamed for the wrongs committed by others.

Reflexive Sympathetic Dystrophy Syndrome

Fears

- Fear of never leaving the land of no peace
- Fear of letting go
- Fear of giving in
- Fear of making a decision
- Fear of life
- Fear of doing anything

Teachings

- Be good enough
- Be honored
- Be in the flow of life
- Be listened to
- Be loved
- Be open to learning
- Be respected
- Be responsible
- Be understood for my true intent
- Be valued
- Be wanted
- Creator's definition and perspective of courage
- Embrace living
- Forgiveness
- Hear the truth and be safe
- Let go
- Let go of the past hurts
- Listen to the truth and be safe
- Live without confusion
- Live without struggle
- Live without thinking you will be punished for your choices
- Live without thinking you will be

- punished for your decisions
- Love myself
- Make choices and be safe
- Make choices and be loved
- Make decisions and be safe
- Speak my truth and be safe
- Stand up and be safe
- Unconditional love

Emotional States

- Holding the source of life to tightly. Heartache – response to a long drawn out battle – fatigue – pride kept the battle going – had the choice to let go.
- Mixed up and undesirable feelings about self.
- Really unsure of how to proceed in life. They hear lots of mixed messages. But they are hearing what they want to hear. The truth is there, they are taking the mixed message instead of the truth. This stops them from having to be responsible for anything. If they never make a decision they never have to be responsible. So communication stays jumbled up.
- Unhappy childhood. Bad choices and punished for those choices – did not understand they were bad – just knew that they were being punished for something they did not understand, now they hesitate to let any communication in – when it does come in it comes very slowly.
- Spectator in life. Looks on but doesn't commit or get involved in the stuff of life. Walks no path. Stays safe by sitting in a place and watching life. Stays safe by not learning.

Cross Indexing: Bones – Broken, Heart Problems, Infection, Carpel Tunnel, Paralysis

Repeating Patterns: No inner peace. Refuses to own their own stuff. Tends to be an observer in life instead of a participant.

Created Patterns

1. Bad things happen when you make changes.
2. Change is dangerous.
3. I am angry at _____.
4. I am confused.
5. I am not responsible for the choices others make.
6. I am tired of fighting.
7. I can't commit to _____.
8. I can't forgive _____.
9. I can't get involve.
10. I can't let go.
11. I can't move forward.
12. I don't deserve.
13. I don't know who I am.
14. I don't understand what is expected of me.
15. I don't want to listen to what others have to say.
16. I get punished for my bad choices.
17. I get punished for my bad decisions.
18. I have a broken heart.

19. I let others make my decisions for me.
20. I make bad choices.
21. I make bad decisions.
22. I must control everything around me to be safe.
23. I must fight to hang on to _____.
24. I must fight to keep what I have.
25. I must fight to keep what I love.
26. I'm not getting involved.
27. I'm not good enough.
28. I'm not honored.
29. I'm not loved.
30. I'm not valued.
31. I'm not wanted.
32. I'm not worthy.
33. If I don't get involved I never get hurt.
34. If I say anything I get into trouble.
35. If things are out of control I get hurt.
36. Life is a struggle.
37. Life is hard.
38. New ideas can get you hurt.
39. No one explains things clearly to me.
40. People don't understand me.
41. The unknown is dangerous.
42. You open yourself up for bad things to happen if you get involved.

*Look at themes of spiritual growth, clarity, communication, childhood, inner child, adventure, aliveness, anger, blockages, change, commitment, confusion, control, expression, flow, forgiveness, lessons, letting go, love, loving yourself, mistakes, self-esteem, self-worth, self-respect, trust, unconditional love, worthiness, unmet needs, defenses, denial, feelings, truth, authenticity, worthiness

Restless Leg Syndrome

Fears
- Fear of the night
- Fear of people in the night
- Fear of attack
- Fear of letting go
- Fear of relaxing
- Fear of being seen and understood by others
- Fear of being trapped
- Fear of losing their freedom
- Fear of the unknown
- Fear of the chaos
- Fear of change
- Fear of loving themselves

Teachings
- Be acknowledged and be safe
- Be comfortable in my body
- Be compassionate (peace in the face of suffering)
- Be flexible without losing your identity
- Be in the flow
- Be loved
- Be recognized and be safe
- Be responsible for my actions
- Be responsible for my choices
- Be seen and be safe
- Control my energy systems
- Feel balanced in my body

- Flexibility
- Forgiveness
- Go with the flow
- Have balanced energy systems
- Have inner peace
- Letting go
- Live connected to the Creator / God
- Live knowing you are being listened to
- Live with balanced energy
- Live without feeling life is a burden
- Live without needing to manipulate others to get your needs met
- Live without worry
- Love myself
- Move forward without needing to project into the future
- Move with comfort and ease
- Recognize and value my divinity
- Recognize my life purpose
- Sleep without discomfort
- To have enough
- Unconditional love

Emotional States

- No inner peace. Lack of substance to their life. Does not understand the relationship to things and people. Wants to let go but certain challenges make it difficult for them to let go.
- Transmitting needless energy – has a hard time containing energy – not channeling energies properly – lost in their ways. Not in time with the rest of the world. It is hard to know their inner motivation; they give no external indication of what they are feeling.
- Doesn't hear what others are saying to them. Does not hear their inner voice. Finds living really difficult. Wants to let go of all that hinders but can't find a way to do it. Feels trapped and is resisting the trap at a subconscious level – wants out. Trying to kick away the boundaries of life. Looks back at life and goes into could have / would have / should've been.
- Unmoved by the pain of others. Searching for answers to the questions of life without resolution. Refuses to see what lies in front of them. Afraid of the unknown so looks for the answers within the known – limited thinking – afraid of the chaos – afraid of change and the unknown that change will bring.
- Unyielding – unforgiving – stands their ground regardless of the influence to do otherwise. Wants to always be right. Wants to always be in control. Very solidly planted in their ideas.
- Wants to move forward but can't. The fear of what moving forward means in their mind stops them from any action. Their life is full of could have / would have / should have.
- Heavy burden felt in their whole body. Limited view of self. Stops self from action and changes. Does not love self or life.

Cross Indexing: Parkinson's, Peripheral Neuropathy, Kidney Problems, Insomnia

Repeating Patterns: Lack of inner peace – continuous mental disturbances. Out-of-body; it's not safe to be in their body and be seen. No sense of what it is to go with the flow of life, acts like the salmon swimming up stream. Does not know how to control energy. Doesn't know how to or want to have responsibility for the choices/ actions/ decisions. Manipulates people into getting their needs met instead of just asking. Continuous worry. Sources love from outside of themselves…no sense of loving themselves.

Created Patterns

1. Being seen is dangerous.
2. God does not listen to my prayers.
3. I allow others to take my energy.
4. I am lost.
5. I am out of sync with the world.
6. I am trapped.
7. I am trapped by my inability to move forward.
8. I am trapped in this body.
9. I can't forgive.
10. I can't get things done.
11. I can't hear my inner voice.
12. I can't let go.
13. I can't move forward with my life.
14. I carry a heavy burden.
15. I don't know how to do things differently.
16. I don't like myself.
17. I don't love myself.
18. I don't trust god.
19. I don't trust my inner voice.
20. I don't trust myself.
21. I don't understand people.
22. I don't want my life.
23. I have no purpose.
24. I must always have more.
25. I must be in control to be safe.
26. I must be right or I am a failure.
27. I must hide how I feel.
28. I must keep my feeling hidden.
29. I must manipulate others to get my needs met.
30. I must prove other people wrong.
31. I must put out lots of effort to be good enough.
32. I must work hard to control my world.
33. I want out of my life.
34. I want to be someone else.
35. I want to die.
36. If I express my feelings I will be attacked.
37. If I listen to my inner voice I will be ridiculed.
38. If I show how I feel I am vulnerable.
39. Life is a burden.
40. Life is a struggle.
41. Life is hard.

42. My belongings make me feel safe.
43. People bring their pain on themselves.
44. People like me for my things.
45. The more energized I am the better I will be.
46. The more I have the more important I am.
47. The more I have the more people like me.
48. The more things I have the better my life.
49. The unknown creates chaos and pain.
50. The unknown is dangerous.
51. There is never enough.

*Look at themes of inner peace, illusion, relationship, control, abundance, energy, balance, body, insomnia, letting go, beingness, worry, worthiness, self-esteem, self-worth, blockages, sabotage, acknowledgment, anger, calm, change, control, denial, enjoying life, flow, freedom, identity, letting go, love, loving yourself, right, unconditional love, consumerism, unmet needs, energy, unmet needs, abundance, peace, power, Meng Mein is on overdrive (congested, over-activated)

Reynaud's Syndrome

Fears
- Fear of rejection
- Fear of losing self
- Fear of becoming invisible

Emotional States
- Loss of face, loss of identity. What they depended on has been taken away. Feels like identity has been taken. Fighting for an identity and getting nowhere.

Cross Indexing: Scleroderma, Stress, Anxiety

Created Patterns
1. I am taken advantage of.
2. I can't give without obligation.
3. I don't know how to receive—god's definition.
4. I don't know what my heart desires.
5. I don't know who I am.
6. I have no control.
7. I must be someone else to please others.
8. I must do everything myself.
9. I must do something I do not love.
10. If someone does something for me I feel obligated.
11. Life is unfair.
12. Others take advantage of my generosity.
13. Things are taken away from me.

14. What are the real issues you are hiding from in your life?
15. What is it you REALLY want to be doing with your hands?

Rhinitis – when laying down at night

Fears
- Fear of suffocation
- Fear of a warning in the night
- Fear of fire
- Fear self
- Fear of life
- Fear of thinking you are OK
- Fear of attachment
- Fear of loss
- Fear of nothingness
- Fear of breathing
- Fear of their breathing being heard
- Fear of pain
- Fear of connection
- Fear of responsibility

Emotional States
- Adjustment to life is thwarted; maladjustment to the needs of others. Warped sense of humor – sense of what is funny is out of sync with those around them. Lack of interest in life, feels very jaded by the experiences of life – nothing has fulfilled and they feel cold and empty.
- Hard wired for unnecessary messiness and clutter. Has difficulty seeing that in their lives the clutter is a creeping kind of thing. They get a kind of safety from the things around them and the chaos is familiar. Has their own standard for cleanliness and connections. Has worn out their reception from others. Tired.
- Junked up head. Head is full of jumbled thoughts. It is not a stream, it is a cacophony of unconnected thoughts. This creates a restriction in life and living. Difficult to clear it and to create a course of action.
- Isolated by their meaning and purpose for life. Their 'way' of life isolates them from contact with others and they work to shield themselves from physical contact with too many people. They feel their life force drained when in public situations with too many people – they feel a loss of self, a loss of their being and become invisible. They make no connections in the crowd.

Cross Indexing: Nose Problems, Allergies, Wounded Creative Core

Created Patterns
1. I have no idea what others want from me.
2. I am out of sync with others and life.
3. I am depressed.
4. There is nothing I want to do.

5. I get nothing out of living. Everything is on a downward spiral.
6. I am tired of living.
7. I will clean up when the clutter gets to me.
8. I am not present to living.
9. I want to be alone. I am tired of people.
10. Confusion keeps me safe.
11. I am overwhelmed by too many people.
12. I feel invisible to the people around me that take what I have.

Right-Sided Negative Tendencies

Emotional States
Aspects
- Rigid
- Neurotic
- Anger
- Violence
- Uptight
- Attacking
- Critical
- Superiority
- Impatient
- Hate
- Revenge
- Intolerant
- Prideful
- Resentful
- Jealousy
- Selfish
- Workaholic

Created Patterns
1. I can't change.
2. I don't give in or give.
3. I can't let go.
4. I am angry.
5. I must do my work before playing.
6. I resentful.
7. I am jealous of anyone I perceive better than me.
8. I have no patience for people weaker than me.
9. People different than me are not equal.
10. I hate _____.
11. I am better than _____.
12. I must attack others before they attack me.
13. I must make sure before something bad happens.

14. I am judgmental.
15. I doubt myself.
16. I don't have time to put myself out for others.
17. I am a bully.
18. I am over self-confident.
19. I'm not able to do stuff.
20. I fail every time I try to do something new.
21. I brag about my accomplishments.
22. I distort the truth so I can win.
23. I take advantage of those weaker than me.
24. I must win.
25. I must be the center of attention.

Rosacea

Fears
- Fear of others
- Fear of connection
- Fear of touch
- Fear that someone will come near
- Fear of being outcast
- Fear of others seeing the mark
- Fear of being seen
- Fear no one will listen if they talk
- Fear of being diminished
- Fear of being known
- Fear of being in the world
- Fear of your body
- Fear of pain
- Fear of suffering
- Fear of letting go

Emotional States
- They hide behind a mask and get a look at reality. They are not seen because everyone looks at facade. They hide behind their mask because their reality makes them angry. To be angry is to be shamed, so they hide.
- Build up of toxic energy/ people/ feelings in their life. These toxic experiences create stress in their lives. They are afraid to let go of the toxins.

Cross Indexing: Inflammation, skin problems, thyroid problems, hypotension, Autoimmune disorder, pimples, acne, ancestral/genetic, colon problems, liver problems

Created Patterns
1. I am humiliated by or when _____.

2. I am stressed by/worried about _____.
3. I don't love myself.
4. What is the longstanding shame/anger?
5. I'm not good enough.
6. I am going to die.
7. How does the Rosacea serve you?
8. How would your life change without it?
9. I must hide my anger and shame so others will not know me.
10. I am angry at _____.

Rotator Cuff

Fears
- Fear of hostile forces
- Fear of people that must be resisted
- Fear of being pulling into something they don't want
- Fear of losing their freedom
- Fear of having to do everything
- Fear of succeeding
- Fear of the flow of life
- Fear of being seen as creative
- Fear of being authentic
- Fear of being vulnerable
- Fear of learning
- Fear of inner knowing

Emotional States
- Doing work with no purpose. Feeling trapped. No one to support them. Feeling of being alone. Feeling of carrying all the responsibility.
- Technical master of the skill they practice. Feel trapped by this mastery. Really trapped by their ego. Self-worth based on the skill mastery.
- Feels like they will never win. Success is illusive. Can't move forward.
- Façade hides the creative. Uses physical appearance for survival. Cut off from inner guidance. Live in a world of cold perfection created by ego. Given away their power. Without their beauty they feel they will be nothing.
- Keep getting the same experience in life. Not getting the lessons. Must adhere to an expected order. Fear creative expression will make them vulnerable.
- Gives up the inner connection to be one of the boys. Deals with life on the surface. Lack of authentic behavior and feelings. Imbalance of strong masculine energy.
- Does not solve problems. Dances around an issue. Creates distractions. Shows off their attributes to be of value.
- Lives in a fantasy. Exposure of the fantasy creates a crisis of ego with chaos and disorder.

Cross Indexing: Shoulder problems, joint problems, Right or left sided negative tendencies, arm problems

EMOTIONAL PATTERNS

Created Patterns

1. _____ lied to me.
2. Being creative is a waste of time.
3. Being creative is dangerous/not safe.
4. Being seen is dangerous/not safe.
5. Being vulnerable is dangerous/not safe.
6. Change is dangerous.
7. Change is hopeless.
8. Everyone is better than me.
9. Feelings are dangerous.
10. I am alone.
11. I am alone and there is no one to help me.
12. I am always last.
13. I am angry at myself.
14. I am depressed.
15. I am responsible for everything/bad things happening.
16. I am trapped.
17. I can never win.
18. I can't do anything except what I am doing right now.
19. I can't make change.
20. I can't move forward.
21. I can't support myself.
22. I can't trust anyone.
23. I don't know how to solve problems.
24. I don't know who I am without my job.
25. I don't love myself.
26. I don't trust others/myself/who else?
27. I feel like I'm always beating my head against a brick wall.
28. I have all the bad luck.
29. I have been betrayed by _____.
30. I have been deceived by _____.
31. I have no purpose.
32. If I make a decision people will be mad at me.
33. I must be special to be loved/liked/respected.
34. I must be tough to be a man.
35. I must do things the hard way for them to be of value.
36. I must do what I am told to be safe.
37. I must manipulate others to survive.
38. I never get picked.
39. I never get what I want.
40. I will never succeed.
41. If I just ignore _____ it will all go away.
42. If I make a change I will be hurt.
43. If my beauty fades I will be nothing.
44. I'm a failure.
45. I'm a loser.
46. It's a man's world and I will never win in it.

EMOTIONAL PATTERNS

47. It's too late in my life to start over at something new.
48. Life is hard.
49. Life is hopeless.
50. Making decisions is dangerous.
51. My life is hopeless.
52. My situation is hopeless.
53. My work is my identity.
54. Showing my feelings is a sign of weakness.
55. Something/Someone always stops me from getting what I want.
56. There is no one to help me with my burden.
57. There is no way out.
58. There is no way to make changes.
59. Things will just get better if I ignore _____.
60. When I do finally make change it isn't what I want.
61. You can't make a living being creative.

S'S

Salivary Gland Problems

Fears
- Fear of being unable to speak against hateful speech
- Fear of a heart that feel hate
- Fear of their inner voice
- Fear of being wrong
- Fear of being ridiculed
- Fear of being made out to be stupid
- Fear of being present
- Fear of knowing

Emotional States
- Doesn't trust their inner knowing enough to act on the information. Unreliable information (actually a misunderstanding of the meaning) has caused them to jump to the conclusion that only information based on the thinking-mind is reliable.

Cross Indexing: Mouth Problems, Tongue Problems, Teeth Problems, Gum Problems

Created Patterns
1. It is dangerous to listen to my inner guidance.
2. I don't trust my inner guidance.
3. My Inner guidance is wrong.
4. I don't know how to take in what I know.
5. I don't know how to be present.
6. It is unsafe to be present.

Sarcoidosis

Fears
- Fear of dismay
- Fear of disappointment
- Fear of being let down
- Fear of inner knowing
- Fear of other knowing about them
- Fear of being known
- Fear of being criticized
- Fear of failure
- Fear of change
- Fear of having to do it all over again

Teachings
- Good enough when challenged
- Good enough
- Intelligent
- Worthy
- Deserve
- Love myself
- Unconditional love

- Fear of being diminished

Emotional States
- Needs justification for everything; this is a stuck pattern – Trans generational / ancestors.
- Nothing gets beyond the justification phase of inquisition type questioning.
- Running from truth – uses justification to stop the pursuit of 'self knowing'.
- Hostility toward anyone that doubts them; seen as a direct threat to their integrity.
- Unwilling to listen to someone else's reasoning.
- There is hidden meaning to their stated goals in life; a hidden purpose. The hidden purpose in their goals takes advantage of outwardly appearing direction.
- Not truthful with others in the direction of their goals.

Cross Indexing: This inflammatory disease occurs across many body parts. Look at that body part affected.

Repeating Patterns: Doesn't accept what people say, challenges them on their sources and integrity. This challenging process alienates people and creates a stuck pattern in their life.

Created Patterns
1. I am a failure.
2. I am afraid of failing.
3. I am afraid of finding out who I am.
4. I am angry at people that doubt me.
5. I am depressed.
6. I am stuck.
7. I am stupid.
8. I am wrong if I am challenged.
9. I can only be good enough if I am right.
10. I don't know who I am.
11. I don't love myself.
12. I don't want / can't hear someone else's opinion.
13. I hate myself.
14. I look stupid when I am challenged.
15. I must be intelligent to be accepted.
16. I must prove I am good enough.
17. I must prove my intelligence.
18. I must prove myself.
19. I must take advantage of others before they take advantage of me.
20. I must understand everything that I'm responsible for.
21. I need to let go of my obligation to be here.
22. I'm not loved.
23. I'm not needed / wanted / valued / liked.
24. I'm not valued.
25. I'm not worth anything.
26. I'm not worthy.
27. I'm not worthy of being on this planet.
28. Issues of being inflexible.

29. It's OK to tell a falsehood- everyone else does.
30. My life is going nowhere.
31. People that doubt me question my integrity / intelligence / path.
32. People think I am stupid.
33. People think I don't know anything.
34. When challenged I am threatened.

Schizophrenia

Fears
- Fear of having no hope
- Fear of the darkness
- Fear of the demons
- Fear of someone trying to kill them
- Fear that they were guilty of the bad things done to them
- Fear of being punished by god

Teachings
- God's Love
- Love
- Safe
- Truth
- Acceptance
- Live without needing the fantasy for protection

Emotional States
- Heavy duty fantasies; the fantasies become the world of reasoning and the thinking adjusts to make the world fit with the fantasies.
- Fantasy created to explain a fear or trauma-based event that perpetuates the fear (possibly as a child). The fantasy creates the world the way they want it to be.
- Ego gains power from the challenge of the fantasies and the fantasies become the person's reality.
- Reasoning is aligned with the fantasies. The reasoning becomes its own reality.

Cross Indexing: PTSD, Addictions-Chemical, ACOA

Created Patterns
1. I can't trust anyone.
2. They are all lying to me.
3. People hurt me.
4. Love is pain.
5. God didn't protect me so I must protect myself.
6. I must be important to be loved.
7. I must be special to be loved.
8. I'm not safe.
9. I am disconnected from god.
10. God hates me and wants to punish me.
11. I'm not loved.
12. No one understands me.
13. I'm not accepted.

*Look at themes of love, psychosis, agoraphobia, anger, God, schizophrenia, illusion, overwhelm and trust.

Sciatica

Fears
- Fear of no support (not a leg to stand on)
- Fear of fierce opposition to who they are
- Fear of hopelessness
- Fear of being out of control
- Fear of being ignored
- Fear of being nothing

Emotional States
- Nothing is worth it anymore. There is a sense of lost. A sense that there's no real direction worth moving in. No one seems to get that. Warns others that they are not interested in the direction that others suggest but they don't seem to listen. There's a need to be where they are not. Major disappointments in life have created a feeling that they are not supported in life so they find a cause to not focus on their bone weary disappointment in living. The disappointment(s) probably broke their heart. Generalized feelings of hopelessness are suppressed. Wants others to see them as productive but, they are only just stirring the mud. Self-deprecating to the point of taking deprecation as a reason for leaving a situation.
- Trauma: (Right) Receiving Communication-shutdown of listening to the communication from others about being supported and/or their direction in life. Receiving is out of balance. Takes and takes to be in control.
- Trauma: (Left) Giving communication-telling others what you think or your truth about being supported and/or direction in life is ignored. Giving is out of balance. Giving is done to hide.

Cross Indexing: Nerve Problems, Bone Problems, Back-Lumbar, Back, Slipped Disc, Wounded Creative Core

Created Patterns
1. I must meet everyone else's needs before my own.
2. What I want is not important.
3. I never know which way to go.
4. I am worried about money.
5. If I am different/ special I am rejected.
6. Being different is dangerous.
7. Being creative is dangerous.
8. I must be responsible for everything.
9. I can't ever make a living at being creative.
10. What blocks you from being creative?
11. Who told you that you couldn't be creative?
12. What logical belief is in conflict with your emotional desires?

Scleroderma

Fears
- Fear of resistance
- Fear of flow
- Fear of obstacles
- Fear that everything isn't really rosy
- Fear of letting go
- Fear of losing identity
- Fear of not deserving

Emotional States
- Failure to let go of the past creates self abuse. Beats self up with long term maladjustment into the future. Awareness of self gets lost in the morass of the pity party. Hard core narcissism had created an inner conflict of the world is all about me, but I'm not good enough for the world. Journey into the dark night has yielded nothing but fear. When facing their darkness and demons they hid. Did not progress through this stage. They brought their life evolvement to a standstill until they re-enter the Nigredo and rebuild from the blackened bone.
- Not dealing with what life throws them. Instead of catching the balls they are ducking the pitches. Feels like the pitches are too hard and they will get hurt if they try to catch one. This is of course a metaphor for how they live their life. They create a mask to hide behind so that it appears that they are showing up in life.
- Jumps headlong into the deep end of the pool and finds out they can't swim. They are ill prepared for life. Everything is out of sync and they miss it all. They miss deadlines, communications, and skill development. Always trying to just keep their head above water. No sense of direction to the edge of the pool and a sense of control. They feel over their heads in dealing with the emotions. They literally feel they will die dealing with emotions for which they have no idea what to do with.

Additional Information
Scleroderma is an autoimmune disease that causes a hardening of the skin and other connective tissue and organs. An autoimmune disease is a self attack. A self attack could be guilt or self-judging. The skin is a boundary. Muscles are movement, strength and flexibility. The organs that are affected should be considered in understanding additional layers of emotional states. So the question would be what is the self-attack (guilt/self-judgment) about in relationship to the involved aspects?

Cross Indexing: Autoimmune disorder, Inflammation, Skin Problems, Muscle Problems, Raynaud's Disease, Pulmonary Fibrosis, Erectile Dysfunction

Created Patterns
1. I am ugly
2. People reject me
3. I'm not worthy
4. I can't change how I see things
5. Nobody believes me
6. I am powerless

7. I am locked in my body
8. What ideas are you very rigid about? Who made you feel that way?

Scoliosis

Fears

- Fear of inner being
- Fear nothing will ever be right
- Fear they will never get what they want
- Fear that life will never go their way
- Fear of always being not good enough
- Fear they will never have enough to be right
- Fear of bending to someone else's demands
- Fear of breaking
- Fear of change
- Fear of rejection
- Fear of being unloved
- Fear of not belonging

Emotional States

- This person is working to remove negativity in their life. Having encountered obstacles in working to become more positive, they feel like the harder they work at improving their outlook the worse it gets. They are actively seeks self-improvement. This person has low self-esteem and feeling of being unworthy. There may be anxieties around their sexuality. They are wallowing in their negative emotions. Thinking and/or judgment may be unclear and clouded. They are judgmental and critical of those touching their life.
- This person feels hollow inside and has been pursuing new interests and activities to find some meaning to their life. They are seeking a self-identity, knowledge, insight, and inner intellect. They are on a quest for a new understanding of their waking life and true Self. They are trying too hard in finding the truth to a problem that is nagging at their inner thoughts. There is a perception that they are frugal and thrifty in their ways. They have locked away their own feelings and emotions. Their surroundings are probably depressing, characterized by a decline in fortune and pseudo-friends.
- This person is achieving their goals quickly and with ease except they are off track and headed in the wrong direction. They are off balance and out of sync. They have ambitious ideas. There is a situation where they are going back and forth and they need to make up their mind. The decision they are struggling with has far reaching effects. There is no foreseeable end, in their mind, to the struggle and it feels as if it is spiraling out of control.
- Long-standing hopes and desires have created an imbalance and disharmony in their life. This imbalance and disharmony has created a situation where they feel as if they will never reach their goals or get what they want in life. They keep these desires hidden because of a fear of not being accepted. They feel that what they are seeking is being denied them.
- This person is floating between the unconscious and conscious. In that space the person has developed a communication between those different aspects of self. They have been willing and open to exploring their emotions. But, this person has been going in circles in their

emotional/spiritual growth. This going in circles has been created in part by being overly guarded about going beyond certain self-imposed parameters. They feel it is risky to go outside the circle. This person feels rejected and that no one understands them.

Cross Indexing: Back Problems, Hip Problems, Pelvis Problems, Cerebral Palsy, Muscular Dystrophy

Created Patterns

1. Being critical protects me.
2. Being critical/judgmental keeps me safe.
3. Change is always hard/ difficult.
4. Change is dangerous.
5. Change means I will fail.
6. Change means suffering.
7. I always make the wrong decisions.
8. I am afraid of failure.
9. I am rejected.
10. I am stupid.
11. I can't accept help from others.
12. I can't expect too much.
13. I can't let go of the past.
14. I can't let go of what is not good for me.
15. I can't stand up for myself.
16. I don't believe in me.
17. I don't believe in myself.
18. I don't deserve.
19. I don't deserve good things.
20. I don't fit in.
21. I don't know anything.
22. I don't know how to accept support/help from others.
23. I don't know how to let go of what is bad for me.
24. I don't know how to make decisions (Creator's definition).
25. I don't know how to stand up for myself (Creator's definition).
26. I don't know what it feels like to accept help from others.
27. I don't know what it feels like to let go of what is bad for me.
28. I don't know what it feels like to make decisions (Creator's definition).
29. I don't know what it feels like to stand up for myself (Creator's definition).
30. I don't know what to believe.
31. I don't trust myself.
32. I make bad decisions.
33. I make things more difficult than they need to be.
34. I must be right to be needed/ wanted/ accepted.
35. I must do what others tell me to do.
36. I must find what is wrong to be wanted.
37. I must prove I am good enough.
38. I must see what is wrong to keep from being judged.
39. I never get what I want.
40. I'm not accepted.
41. I'm not worthy.

42. It is hard for me to make big decisions.
43. It isn't safe to feel.
44. It must be hard to be worthy.
45. Letting go means I will fail.
46. Life is a struggle.
47. Life is hard.
48. No matter how hard I try I never get anywhere.
49. No matter what I do I will never be good enough.
50. No one understands me.
51. Nothing I ever do is ever good enough.
52. Nothing is ever easy for me.
53. Others always make my decisions for me.
54. Others opinions are always better than mine.
55. People don't like me.
56. People don't understand me.
57. Things never go right for me.
58. What will happen if you make a decision?
59. What will happen if you stand up for yourself?
60. When things change everything goes wrong.

Sebaceous Cysts

Fears

- Fear that others will find out about your sin of bad feelings
- Fear their true feelings will be discovered
- Fear of moving
- Fear of making the wrong decisions
- Fear of change
- Fear of the inner direction
- Fear of the inner voice

Teachings

- Be in the flow
- Be present
- Comfortable with change
- Creator's definition and perspective of trust
- Forgiveness
- Let go of anger
- Live without being judged
- Live without feeling hopeless
- Live without feeling like a failure
- Live without feeling sorry for yourself
- Live without having to meet someone else's expectations
- Live without needing to punish yourself
- Permission to feel anger
- Safe
- Safe to forgive
- Safe to release old hurts
- Secure
- Trust
- Trusting your inner voice
- Trusting your intuition

- Whole

Emotional States
- Unresolved anger very close to the surface.
- Self punishment for feeling the anger.
- Mind uses reasoning without inspiration to make decisions; the decisions are not complete and lack a higher truth.
- Self poisoning from wrong ideas.
- Always on guard- doubting all that is put into your path.
- Doubt is used as a way of controlling change in your life- stops the flow of change/ life until you allow it.

Cross Indexing: Skin Problems, Cysts, Lipoma

Repeating Patterns: Doesn't live in the flow of life – doesn't know what that feels like. Holds onto emotions that are not peaceful, doesn't let go of those. Feels like and creates the life experience of being a failure. Doesn't trust or listen to their inner voice.

Created Patterns
1. _____ hurt my feelings.
2. Anytime I lead with my heart I get hurt/ I fail.
3. Change for the sake of change is not needed.
4. Every time I believe someone I get hurt / lied to.
5. How people see me makes me sad.
6. I am a failure.
7. I am always disappointed.
8. I am angry at _____.
9. I am depressed.
10. I am never right, I am always wrong.
11. I angry at how people categorize me.
12. I can't forgive.
13. I can't trust my intuition.
14. I don't have what it takes to make things better.
15. I feel sorry for myself.
16. I have no purpose.
17. I must be punished for being angry.
18. I'm not good for anything.
19. I'm not worthy.
20. If I don't be careful I will get hurt (careful about what?).
21. If I make a mistake I will let others do (who are the others).
22. It is safer doing the same thing than making change.
23. It's hopeless.
24. It's not OK to be angry.
25. My heart is broken.
26. People are not trustworthy.
27. People don't see me for who I am.
28. People make assumptions about me that aren't true.

29. Someone is always judging me.
30. Using intuition is dangerous.
31. What happens when things change?
32. When I believe people I look like a fool.

*Look at themes of love, punishment, self-respect, self-love, self-worth, self-esteem, life purpose, anger, control, letting go, forgiveness, right/ having to be right, trust, unmet needs, broken heart, and rejection

Senility

Fears
- Fear of being alone
- Fear of becoming invisible
- Fear of becoming lost
- Fear of loss (identity, hearing, eyesight, body functions, people, purse, etc.)
- Fear of people
- Fear of losing my words
- Fear of being present
- Fear of being unsafe
- Fear of having things stolen
- Fear of people putting things in the wrong places
- Fear of no one being there
- Fear of tomorrow

Emotional States
- They cannot communicate their needs and have them met in the way they want. They surmise it is because people are not listening. They feel like they are being forced to do things against their will and then they try to maintain their identity within a different place where they do not fit in. Then when they try to communicate what they need others walk away because they feel powerless to change the situation.

Cross Indexing: Dementia, Alzheimer's, Aging, Memory Problems, Memory Loss

Created Patterns
1. I want to go back to when things were good.
2. I want out of my body.
3. I am afraid of _____.
4. I can't focus on anything.
5. I can't change my life .
6. I am powerless to fix my life.
7. I am powerless to get my needs met.
8. People don't do what I want.
9. I am unheard.
10. I do not fit in with those around me.

11. No one listens to me.
12. I am forced to do things against my will.

Sepsis

Fears
- Fear of destructive secrets
- Fear of being taken over by overriding people
- Fear of being made responsible against your will
- Fear of being overwhelmed by the responsibility of another

Emotional States
- Desire to block all contact with others so they can disappear into oblivion. Holds others responsible, blames them for the bad things that have happened.
- Hard won successes have soured. Just when they thought life was on their side, it crumbles. The attitudes reverse course or direction and they are left holding nothing.
- Jumped from the ledge — took the risk. They hurt themselves in the fall or the risky endeavor. They hurt their reputation, their life force is drained and they feel defeated and under attack.
- Jarred – they have been rattled to the core by events that shattered their concept of their world – their attachments. They feel empty, depressed and numb.
- Wants to go – die. Done with the struggle of trying to keep their body going. Every day they just want space, quiet, peace, alone time but they are not permitted.

Cross Indexing: diabetes, kidney disease, cancer, high blood pressure, HIV, pneumonia, and urinary tract infection.

Repeating Patterns: They have a life that is dogged by the mundane and it all feels so stupid, like a waste of time. They have been unable to grab the brass ring and have a life of adventure.

Created Patterns
1. Life is hard.
2. Life is a struggle.
3. I can't be alone.
4. People won't leave me alone.
5. I'm not to blame for the faults of others.
6. I'm not responsible.
7. I seem to lose the big ones.
8. When I take a risk I get hurt.
9. I want to die.
10. Peace is not achievable.
11. My time is not my own.
12. I've got to be alone to have peace.
13. I am depressed.
14. I am empty.

15. I am numb.
16. Nothing is dependable.
17. People abandon me.
18. I want to disappear.
19. Just when I think I win I lose.
20. I have not been allowed to live the way I want.

Sexual Abuse

Fears
- Fear of hurt
- Fear of love
- Fear of the unknown
- Fear of being unloved and unwanted
- Fear of being powerless
- Fear of their body
- Fear of being controlled by another
- Fear of saying no
- Fear of being in control
- Fear of the now
- Fear of knowing
- Fear of self
- Fear of others
- Fear of shame
- Fear of feeling
- Fear of mother and/or father

Emotional States
- A hollowed out sense of being creates a feeling they are not present. They live in fear of living. Their heart freezes in anxiety at all around them. They are on the look out for the bad things around them.
- No identity. No sense of beingness. A need to fill the void and be loved and understood. They need to feel special.

Cross indexing: Ancestral/ epigenetic, ACOA, PTSD

Created Patterns
1. I am frozen/can't move.
2. I am helpless.
3. I am hopeless.
4. I am intimidated by _____.
5. I am not wanted by mother/father/family.
6. I am powerless.
7. I am sinful/ shameful.

8. I can't control my body.
9. I can't say no (to sex).
10. I caused it to happen.
11. I deserve to be punished.
12. I don't have discernment about who to have sex with.
13. I don't know how to live in the present.
14. I don't know the difference between consensual sex and abuse.
15. I don't know the difference between intimacy and abuse.
16. I don't know the difference between making love and abuse.
17. I don't love my body.
18. I don't trust men/women.
19. I hate my body.
20. I have brought shame on my family.
21. I have to be alone to be close to god.
22. I have to punish myself.
23. I have to sacrifice myself to save others.
24. I'm not supposed to have pleasure.
25. If I don't feel my body I won't hurt.
26. If I tell anyone I'll be killed.
27. It is hopeless.
28. It's my fault.
29. It's not safe to receive and accept sexual love.
30. Life is dangerous.
31. Men/Women (depending on the abuser) are dangerous.
32. My father/mother/family betrayed me.
33. No one will believe me.
34. Others are more important than me.
35. Others are wrong.
36. Sex is dirty/ painful/ shameful/ sinful/ wrong.
37. Shame is my identity.
38. What are the issues around trust?

Sexual Assault – Adult

Fears

- Fear of people taking what they want
- Fear of attack
- Fear of surviving
- Fear of having to hurt to have an identity
- Fear of love
- Fear of being accepted
- Fear of being hurt to be accepted
- Fear of connecting
- Fear of having take a overwhelming burden to be accepted

Emotional States

- Searching for acceptance and love but once it is found can't accept or engage in its energy. This person has not responded to acts of love and caring. There is a feeling of distance and emptiness from their emotions. They find it difficult to engage in play for the sake of joy and physical movement. This person has chaos and frenetic activity all around them and they appear to be calm and collected when in actuality they are disconnected from the stuff of life. They have isolated themselves.
- This person feels isolated, lonely, and hopeless. Their life does not have a richness of experience. They have a sense of being overworked. They may be allowing bullying, dominating people in their life load them up with tasks and responsibilities. The tasks and responsibilities create a feeling of being overwhelmed. They have an outward façade of being peaceful and calm. When in actuality they feel as if they are being taken advantage of and run over. They have lost their objectivity in the situation and are building hatred and malice. This person may be experiencing sadness and depression.
- This individual has an unexpressed anger and rage that may go back to repressed memories of child abuse. They have an internal war going on that is trying to unconsciously protect them. This person feels torn between aspects of self. This person may vacillate between being overly assertive or not assertive enough. Part of the conflict is a struggle against perceived societal constraints. This conflict may be a need to express childhood abuse and an unspoken cultural/familial more that represses uncomfortable truth. This person feels like they are trying to hold a wild horse. They feel as if foundation and stability is being threatened. There are doubts/anxieties around their sexuality and libido.
- This individual has been attempting to protect themselves from their emotions and/or actions. They may have been projecting those onto another person. This keeps the feelings/actions distant and disconnected. They have this image of their world being a place of peace and dignity. Then something happens and this person realizes that the world they have created for themselves is an illusion with no depth or feeling. Once they acknowledge the illusion they may become depressed and angry.

Cross Indexing: ACOA, PTSD, Sexual Abuse, Wounded Creative Core

Created Patterns

1. Feelings are dangerous.
2. Good things get taken away from me.
3. I am a martyr.
4. I am a victim.
5. I am alone.
6. I am angry at _____.
7. I am bad.
8. I am depressed.
9. I am empty inside.
10. I am hopeless.
11. I am invisible.
12. I am overwhelmed by _____.
13. I am powerless to stop others from hurting me.
14. I am sad.

15. I am unacceptable.
16. I am unloved.
17. I am unworthy of being loved.
18. I am weak/ powerless to defend myself.
19. I can't forgive _____.
20. I deserve to be abused/assaulted/hurt.
21. I don't have the right to protect/defend myself.
22. I don't know how to be in a loving relationship.
23. I don't know how to play.
24. I don't know how to receive.
25. I don't know what it feels like to be cherished.
26. I don't know what joy is.
27. I don't love myself.
28. I don't matter.
29. I have no control over my life.
30. I have no options.
31. I have no purpose.
32. I have no soul.
33. I must do what I am told.
34. I must do what people tell me to do to be wanted/accepted/loved/needed.
35. I must protect myself from feeling.
36. I mustn't know too much.
37. I mustn't want good things.
38. I was born to be sacrificed.
39. I'm not OK.
40. If I get something nice it will be taken away from me.
41. If I let people in they will hurt me.
42. If I play I will be hurt.
43. It is OK for others to hurt me.
44. Knowing too much will hurt you.
45. Love is dangerous.
46. Love is painful.
47. My body is not mine.
48. My body is unsafe.
49. My life is hopeless.
50. My mother/father rejected me.
51. My opinions are worthless.
52. Pain is how I know I am alive.
53. Pain is how I stay connected to the body.
54. People are dangerous.
55. People hurt me.
56. People in authority bully/dominate/control/hurt me.
57. People push me away.
58. People run over me.
59. People take advantage of me.
60. Play is wasteful.
61. There's no meaning to life.
62. When I play I get hurt.

Sexual Assaulter

Fears
- Fear of being powerless
- Fear of the power of sex
- Fear that they will become the victim
- Fear of connection

Emotional States
- Early childhood trauma desensitized them to the needs of others. Brain filter is not developed. Feels the need to control and be superior. Hopelessly entangled in their own thoughts like a maze. They use physical action to escape the maze. Feels left out of society, there but not there.
- Searching for acceptance and love but once it is found can't accept or engage in its energy. This person has not responded to acts of love and caring. There is a feeling of distance and emptiness from their emotions. They find it difficult to engage in play for the sake of joy and physical movement. This person has chaos and frenetic activity all around them and they appear to be calm and collected when in actuality they are disconnected from the stuff of life. They have isolated themselves.
- This person feels isolated, lonely, and hopeless. Their life does not have a richness of experience. They have a sense of being overworked. They may be allowing bullying, dominating people in their life load them up with tasks and responsibilities. The tasks and responsibilities create a feeling of being overwhelmed. They have an outward façade of being peaceful and calm. When in actuality they feel as if they are being taken advantage of and run over. They have lost their objectivity in the situation and are building hatred and malice. This person may be experiencing sadness and depression.
- This individual has an unexpressed anger and rage that may go back to repressed memories of child abuse. They have an internal war going on that is trying to unconsciously protect them. This person feels torn between aspects of self. This person may vacillate between being overly assertive or not assertive enough. Part of the conflict is a struggle against perceived societal constraints. This conflict may be a need to express childhood abuse and an unspoken cultural/familial more that represses uncomfortable truth. This person feels like they are trying to hold a wild horse. They feel as if foundation and stability is being threatened. There are doubts/anxieties around their sexuality and libido.
- This individual has been attempting to protect themselves from their emotions and/or actions. They may have been projecting those onto another person. This keeps the feelings/actions distant and disconnected. They have this image of their world being a place of peace and dignity. Then something happens and this person realizes that the world they have created for themselves is an illusion with no depth or feeling. Once they acknowledge the illusion they may become depressed and angry.
- This person presents themselves as being ineffective at dealing with direct confrontation. They will often back away from confrontations or the problems/issues of life. This person may have suffered a physical or extreme emotional attack at the hands of a friend(s). But, they are the one that holds the shame/humiliation from this assault. They may even have kept it a secret. The shame of revealing what happened to them is just to overwhelming to face. This person has a shadow self that feels as if they have been rejected and holds repressed rage. They are in a constant state of feeling those negative emotions. Their thinking has become clouded by these overwhelming emotions. This person is stuck in the immature emotional reactions of a young

- boy. This person may have found it difficult to be in relationships or hold a job due to immature emotional reactions. They may often appear indifferent. They may be stuck at the emotional maturity level they had before the attack.
- This person has a lack of understanding of the unconscious to the point of fear of the unknown. Anytime they get close to something unknown they become very emotional and will lose control of their emotions or depression sets in. They fear what they believe to be the evil / shadow side of self. They fear their sexuality and as such their involvement in a life outside of a prescribed environment is almost non-existent. This is an early childhood program instilled by a fundamentally extreme parent preaching that hell was where they were bound. This emotional abuse started very early in their life. The unconscious aspect of self (spirituality) is very fearful and confrontation or opening to that aspect of self will result in becoming evil.
- This person has repressed/unexpressed emotions and feelings of frigidity. This person feels alone, indifferent and neglected. They feel they are unclean and impure. Their early life may have been marked by a loss of sexual innocence. Some aspect of self feels tainted. This person is haunted by dark moods. This person may demonstrate eruptions of emotion. They had trouble in school and found the education experience confusing. They justify their academic failures by saying 'they (the teachers) don't know what they are doing'. This same relationship to teaching institutions would also follow them into jobs.
- This person confronts one experience after another in relationships where others appear to have more power than them. This person works really hard to keep people from knowing that they see themselves as cowardly. This person is being bullied by their own inner fears. They appear to be overly controlling. They have a sense of very little power in their lives. Their inner landscape feels hostile and frustrating. This person is often depressed and/or angry. When they lack wisdom or feel confusion in a situation they will lash out with inappropriate emotions. They had trouble in school and found the education experience confusing. They justify their academic failures by saying 'they (the teachers) don't know what they are doing'. This same relationship to teaching institutions would also follow them into jobs.
- This person is dependent on others for a place to live. This person probably lives with a relative. They 'sponge' off of others for support. They are not willing to take on the responsibility of living an independent adult lifestyle. They live with someone that facilitates their dependent behavior. This person feels like stuff just falls out of the sky to knock him down. They are not to blame or accountable for the problems in their life. In fact others are to blame. They dwell on the negative that has happened to them. They use past problems as leverage for why the future won't be any better and why things won't change.

Cross Indexing: ACOA, Addictions-Chemical, PTSD

Created Patterns

1. Bad things are always happening to me.
2. Change is dangerous.
3. Confrontation is dangerous.
4. Everyone is better than me.
5. I am a coward.
6. I am a sinner.
7. I am afraid of the dark.
8. I am always wrong.
9. I am always wrong when there is a confrontation.
10. I am angry at _____.

EMOTIONAL PATTERNS

11. I am bad.
12. I am betrayed by _____.
13. I am depressed.
14. I am dirty.
15. I am discouraged easily.
16. I am evil.
17. I am going to hell.
18. I am good enough.
19. I am humiliated by _____.
20. I am judged.
21. I am powerless to stop people from hurting me/criticizing me/judging me/belittling me/calling me names.
22. I am rejected by _____.
23. I am scared to death someone will find out _____.
24. I am shamed by _____.
25. I am stupid.
26. I am unclean.
27. I can't cry and be safe.
28. I can't do anything right.
29. I can't let others know how I feel.
30. I can't make changes.
31. I can't make it on my own.
32. I can't stop people from hurting me.
33. I can't support myself.
34. I can't take care of myself.
35. I don't know how to do anything right.
36. I don't know how to live without betrayal.
37. I don't trust people.
38. I hate my mother/father/_____.
39. I must be in control at all times.
40. I must keep the bad things that happened a secret.
41. I must keep the secrets.
42. I never win.
43. I will go to hell.
44. I'm not accepted.
45. I'm not respected.
46. I'm not worthy.
47. If I don't control everything bad things will happen.
48. If I have sex I will die.
49. If I think of sex I will go to Hell.
50. It is dangerous to question.
51. It's easier to let others do it (do what?).
52. It's not my fault.
53. My feelings are overwhelming.
54. My mother/father/_____ hurt me.
55. No one can help me.
56. No one cares about me.
57. No one understands me.
58. People always blame me.

59. People are dangerous.
60. People attack me.
61. People reject me.
62. Sex is bad.
63. They owe me.
64. They ruined my life (who is the 'They'?).
65. Things will never get better.
66. Why try? I never do anything right anyway.

Shin Problems

Fears
- Fear of getting close to the edges/ outlines of the box they are in
- Fear of their heart
- Fear of listening to their inner voice

Emotional States
- LEFT – Not paying attention to their heart. Their heart is giving them information that needs to be listened to. That information will help in their journey to consciousness.
- RIGHT – Listening to others telling them what to do when their inner voice is giving them a different direction.

Cross Indexing: Leg Problems, Left & Right-sided negative tendencies, Wounded Creative Core

Created Patterns
1. I have betrayed my values/ideals.
2. I have done what others said and sacrificed myself.
3. I must sacrifice my life for others.
4. I have to help others.
5. I have listened to my heart before and it has betrayed me.
6. I don't need to be more aware. I am fine.
7. I am in control of me.
8. My inner voice is unreliable.
9. Listening to others keeps me from being responsible for my actions.

Shingles

Fears
- Fear that they have broken the rules
- Fears that what they have is failing
- Fear of giving

- Fear that if they give they are less than
- Fear of life
- Fear of being out of control
- Fear that someone is out to get them

Emotional States

- Worthlessness, heart is hardened in the worthiness of others and how they relate to them. Wants to be seen as good and righteous but doesn't cut the mustard and displays hypocrisy as what people really see. Hurts people in the process. Does this to push people away. Has a hard time relating to others. Holds self above others. Unwilling to be happy for others and support the good things happening to others and self. They blow stuff off –as if it were meaningless – when it is important to others. Willingness to see the good in others is small – diminishes the good with a judgment of smallness. There's a feeling that if I'm not worthy of being seen in that way then other's aren't either.
- Hates living. Nothing about life has made them happy. Doesn't want to commit suicide just doesn't want to 'be'. Doesn't see that they have control of their attitude and feels that anybody who says they do is full of B.S. and does not face reality and below the surface they feel the same way.
- Hyper-vigilance in watching others—will they take advantage of me, will I get 'burned'. Makes others think he is just watching out for their best, when this is really about staying in control to be safe. Quickly judges a situation to push away what does not feel safe.
- Has wild ideas that have fallen apart (they seemed like a good idea at the time), unwilling to part with their demise and follows the energy until it has gone into the negative range and causes harm to the person with the idea. The cascading effect of the negative energy creates a problem throughout other parts of their life. Sees outside forces as the reason it didn't work and that others are at fault for causing their problems.
- Thoroughly bored with life. No challenge, the boredom feels more like an irritation that keeps reminding them of how unhappy they are – unwilling to let go of the boredom because this is what they know (this is how they are safe). Stifled communication erupts and is sometimes angry in its delivery. Person is seen as angry/acerbic by others.
- **Trauma:** Angry and irritating communication, stemming from feelings of worthlessness, with a feeling that nothing good ever happens to them. *This trauma translation would be different for each different body location of inflammation.*

Cross Indexing: Rash, Skin Problems, Herpes, Hives

Created Patterns

1. Nothing will ever work out the way I want it to.
2. What is the source of ongoing tension in your life?
3. I am unworthy/ worthless.
4. Every little thing bothers/irritates me.
5. I am not good enough.
6. What are you angry about?

Shoulders

Fears
- Fear of having a burden greater than others
- Fears that their life is nothing more than serving others
- Fear of being pushed down
- Fear of not being responsible
- Fear of rejection
- Fear of living

Emotional States
- LEFT – a sense of burden keeps you from knowing yourself. An identification with 'I must be the one responsible' keeps them from reflection and understanding of their own nature.
- RIGHT – A sense of burden causes them to shrug off a compliment, a kudo, payment or recognition of efforts.

Cross Indexing: Rotator Cuff, Arm problems, Left & Right sided negative tendencies

Created Patterns
1. I have lost the love and respect of _____ (Usually a family member-daughter, son, father, *mother, etc.).
2. I am rejected by _____ when I reach out to them.
3. Left shoulder is about family.
4. Right shoulder is about financial problems.
5. I can't trust life.
6. I must bear the burden.
7. I don't have the courage to _____.
8. I carry the burden of _____ (This is a burden that does not belong to you).
9. Life is too great a burden to bear.
10. I am helpless to change _____ (What is it that you are helpless to change that is a heavy burden/responsibility?).
11. It is hopeless (What is the hopeless feeling about?)
12. _____ is just too stressful (What is the stressful responsibility in your life?).
13. I must push away _____.
14. I must push people out of my space(Who? And Why?).
15. What issues do you push away?
16. I must carry the burden of responsibility for everything around me so that things don't go bad.
17. I must be the one to take care of _____(family member).
18. I'm not good enough to be acknowledged .
19. I'm unworthy of good things.

Sickness and Love

Emotional States
Associations:
Sick = Attention
Sick = Love
Sick = Being Wanted
Love = Being Stoic
Acceptance = Being Stoic

Meta-Information
Early family life where someone was ill, the person was in competition for resources – emotional and physical.

Made connections to sickness or weakness: if a person was sick they were important, without the illness the person would lose their identity, they didn't exist. The person would have no power or visibility within the family structure.

Display of emotions is met with a lack of respect, rejection, loss of power and the person displaying the emotions became the bad one. Illness is acceptable. Illness becomes the vehicle for resolving emotions. Family or Group Consciousness leads to feelings of trapped, anger, disrespect, becomes fatigued at trying to get free of the culture (Any family culture where staying in that hierarchy of behavior is required to stay connected to the family.) The resignation leads to someone that doesn't have to deal with the outside world. They resign to the required behavior and keep the consciousness going. They just numb out to the inner voice that is screaming to get out. Rejection of happiness because being sad allows them to punish the ones around them for forcing them to live this way.

Relationships within this paradigm don't last if they come from outside the group consciousness.

Sidedness

Emotional States
- When there is an issue of survival, we look at the elements that are part of survival any threat to those and a trauma has been created. If you are confronted by anger and you cave in, you allow your boundaries to be overrun. So what are the organs affected by overrun boundaries – skin and/or liver. You have given up your power. A balanced feminine would be to have boundaries that in the face of someone's anger do not feel threatened or that their survival is at risk. That anger is allowed to flow through. Over-corrected or imbalanced boundaries would give rise to anger confronting anger.
- The out of balance feminine takes the anger into themselves, the out of balance masculine triggers a confrontational response.
- We often refer to our dominant side as the side that receives the injuries or bears a malady. For example when I sprain my ankle it is always the right side, never my left. Traditional definition of dominant side is the side of the body that is stronger. It is also the side of the body that is most often used to articulate body movement in space, pick up an item, listen to the phone, stepping

forward, writing, etc. What we call our dominant side is also our defined sidedness. Left side = feminine= right side of brain, right side = masculine = left side of brain.
- The masculine is easily angered, giving too little.
- The feminine boundaries easily overrun, giving too much.
- An over-activated masculine, right sidedness, will typically see right side injuries and maladies.
- An over-activated feminine, left sidedness, will typically see left side injuries and maladies.

Cross Indexing: Left Sided Negative Tendencies, Right Sided Negative Tendencies

Created Patterns
1. I always injure by left/right _____.
2. My left/right eye is the weakest.
3. I give too much to be wanted or liked.
4. I must be strong to be safe.

Sinus Congestion – Chronic

Fears
- Fear of being with people that reflect me back to me
- Fear of flow
- Fear of seeing
- Fear of looking
- Fear of freedom
- Fear of living
- Fear of being stopped from what they want to do
- Fear of not having stuff
- Fear of emptiness
- Fear of being nothingness
- Fear of not being defined by their stuff
- Fear of summer
- Fear of harvest
- Fear of being present (congested thinking)
- Fear of knowing the inner presence
- Fear of being lost in someone else's success
- Fear of not being good enough
- Fear of failure
- Fear of breathing in life

Emotional States
- Forethought is not their strong suit. They can't seem to understand that if they do X then Y will happen. Led them to a place of constantly being mystified by their actions/reactions. Wants everyone else to understand that they didn't see "that" coming. That is the story of their life. Hoards in a minor way. Has lots of stuff all around. Lots of energetic congestion with the stuff. Example: has lots of books they will never read and outgrew their usefulness long ago.

- Warm weather makes them anxious. There's a DNA memory (ancestral) of a trauma or hardship that happened repeatedly during the times of warm weather. That DNA memory triggers a desire to retreat and muffle any sounds they might make. They hold their life in an odd balance of live and don't live (this is not life or death) it's about being present in their life …smelling the air, feeling the air…because life is breath and breathing.
- Nothing seems to satisfy their need to know. 'Knowing' is a driving force. They reach outside of themselves for wisdom that is within. They are constantly searching for the latest greatest wisdom and latest greatest teacher selling their wisdom for a few schillings.
- Joyful at the site of others success but inward they feel defeated by it. This is not envy or jealousy. It's a sense that somehow they have failed even though that person's success had nothing to do with them nor anything to with what they do in life. They may have heard the phrase "why can't you be more like your brother/sister". There's always a sense that they will never be successful in that way. It was a way of getting noticed in the chaos of family life. They would never be successful enough so they were always a failure.

Cross Indexing: Sinus problems, Colds, Flu, Allergies, Post Nasal Drip

Created Patterns

1. I do not see the consequences of my actions. I am totally confused by the outcomes of my decisions.
2. I have too much stuff but I don't know how to get rid of it.
3. I am afraid to breathe but I must breathe or I will die.
4. I feel under attack. I can't breathe.
5. I am constantly searching for the answers, with no results.
6. I am dissatisfied with life.
7. I feel defeated when I see that others have succeeded.
8. I am a failure.
9. I will never be good enough.

Sinus Polyps

Fears

- Fear that what you have been forced to believe is wrong
- Fear of injustice
- Fear of letting go

Emotional States

- There's a lack of justice. A sense that their world is in a state of imbalance. Wrongs are never righted. Those that harm them never put it right. Obscure minutiae haunt the waking hours in the effort to find justice for those that have been wronged. Holds onto past hurts inflicted in the name of making them a better person. Justice demands a re-balancing. Haunted in the night by the wounds of a time long past as the biology seeks a balancing of the energies. Anger at injustice will never find a balance point. Longing in a place of no satisfaction.

Cross Indexing: Growths, Asthma, Fungus, Allergies

Created Patterns
1. I have been wronged.
2. My life will never be whole until justice has been done.
3. I have been harmed with no balancing of the scales.
4. There is no justice.
5. I can't get the justice I deserve.
6. I can't let go of the harm that has been caused me.
7. No one is helping me get justice.

Sinus Problems

Fears
- Fear of truth
- Fear of leaving the stories they tell themselves
- Fear of a different identity
- Fear of rejection
- Fear of abandonment

Emotional States
- They feel like they are the bottom of the pecking order, bottom of the totem pole, feels criticized and rejected.
- They stuff the energy of chaos from the heart.

Cross Indexing: Nose Problems, Allergies – Hay fever, Allergies, Post Nasal Drip

Created Patterns
1. Whose life are you trying to run?
2. I am irritated by _____.
3. I have been expressing/feeling strong emotion of _____ for a long time (these are negative emotions: hatred/resentment/anger/rage/bitterness/grief/sorrow/revenge/etc.)

Sjogren's Syndrome

Fears
- Fear of someone else's expectations
- Fear of attack
- Fear of people close to them
- Fear of being vulnerable

Emotional States
- Under attack from a friend. The friend has turned on you and you don't know why. No end in sight to the abuse from the people that are supposed to love you. They have no decency and keep up the attack even when you are sick.

Cross Indexing: ACOA, Autoimmune disorder, Chronic Fatigue, Fibromyalgia, Arthritis-Rheumatoid, Lung Problems, Joint Problems, Lymphatic system, Left-sided negative tendencies, Right-sided negative tendencies, sarcoidosis, dry eye, amyloidosis, Non-Hodgkin lymphoma, lupus, multiple sclerosis

Repeating Patterns: Weak boundaries, trying to please and take care of every one.

Created Patterns
1. Things are going too fast.
2. Nothing I do will help.
3. It is hopeless/the situation is hopeless.
4. I am overwhelmed by _____.
5. My problems are bigger than I can handle.
6. I am angry/bitter/hate _____.
7. I'll be devoured by _____.
8. I must run from what is bigger than me.
9. I can do nothing to fight back.
10. The world is dangerous.
11. The unexpected is dangerous.
12. It was wrong to be born.
13. My worst fear is happening (what is your worst fear?).
14. I have lost my honor.
15. I am dishonored.
16. I am unhappy/sad (This is a profound sadness- What is the cause?).
17. There is no rest for the wicked.
18. I am under attack by the people that are supposed to love me.

Skin Problems

Fears
- Fear of destiny
- Fear that their struggle is a waste
- Fear of being judged
- Fear of being predetermined
- Fear of self
- Fears being violated
- Fears being helpless to change
- Fears for their safety

Emotional States

- They hold within their skin the judgment of their worth. Their character and safety to be in the company of others is held by their skin. Judgment as to their intelligence is made by their skin. Their personality and value system is determined by their skin.

Cross Indexing: Acne, Angiolipoma, Blisters, Bruises, Calluses, Cancer – Basal Cell, Cancer – Melanoma, Cancer – Squamous Cell, Cysts, Dandruff, Diverticulitis, Eczema, Facial Dandruff, Fingernails, Fingernails – Biting, Growths – Skin, Henoch Schonlein Purpura, Ingrown Hair, Roseacea, Skin Problems, Stye, Warts, liver, digestive system

Repeating Patterns: They are invisible. They do nothing that defines them. This sets up the dynamic for very poor boundaries. As long as they are invisible they must hide or be overrun.

Created Patterns

1. Nothing I ever do is good enough for _____ (Who in your life criticizes you?).
2. I am irritated by _____.
3. The smallest things irritated me (Why do you think that happens?).
4. I am afraid of _____ (What things/people in your life make you insecure?).
5. I am bored.
6. I must hide to be safe.
7. I am invisible.
8. I am powerless to stop _____.
9. I have no identity.
10. No one sees who I truly am.
11. I am accepted.
12. I am unworthy.
13. I am judged by others.

Sleep Apnea

Fears

- Fear of not meeting expectations
- Fear of being wrong
- Fear of not being good enough
- Fear of showing how they feel

Emotional States

- Failure to hold oneself upright – always crumpling under the pressure of needing to figure out what's right – make the right decision, be the right person for …, feeling that you can't do that. Imbalance in communication – lack of. Must hide feelings until they become overwhelming.

Cross indexing: sinus problems, snoring, sleep problems, restless leg syndrome

Repeating pattern: Portrays themselves as always having to prove themselves in jobs, relationships, etc. Victim energy – stuff happens to them. Wounded Creative Core. Masculine energy/father was highly critical.

Created Patterns

1. I'm not good enough.
2. I'm unworthy.
3. I must over think everything to be right.
4. I must always prove myself.
5. I must hold my thought to myself.
6. I can't be open with people.
7. People will hurt me.
8. I am a victim.
9. I must hold back to keep from being hurt.
10. I can't let go of the past.
11. I am overwhelmed by life.
12. I can't relax.

Slipped Disc (Herniation)

Fears

- Fear of the rug being pulled out from under them
- Fear of a sudden lack of support
- Fear of being the outcast
- Fear of rejection
- Fear of overwhelm

Emotional States

- Justified in feeling that they don't fit in with any group – family, work, community, etc. In fact they would rather not be with any of those groups. Always made to feel like the odd person out. Doesn't reach out to anyone for support, afraid they will be rejected.
- They feel like they are being pulled in multiple directions all at one time. They start to go in one direction and then there is suddenly a call to go in another direction while they are still in motion. They are not listened to or supported in their request to allow for transition or a slow down.

Cross Indexing: Overweight, fascia, abscess, spinal stenosis, spondylosis, sciatica

Created Patterns

1. I can't make a decision about _____.
2. I am not supported in my life.
3. I don't know how to protect myself.
4. No one cares what I think or feel.
5. I don't belong in this life.

6. I am unwanted.
7. People jerk me around.
8. I am different and I don't fit in with the people around me.
9. I don't know why I am here.
10. I am being pulled in many directions.
11. No one values my opinion or listens to me.
12. No one has regard for 'me'.

Smoking – problems with quitting

Fears
- Fear of being present
- Fear of having no escape
- Fear of being attacked

Emotional States
- Inability to let go of a habit that keeps them safe. Longs to be connected to others but the cigarettes are safer than people. *Highly concerned that their life will be a failure. Yet they continue stalling the engagement into life. They bring the energy of failure to everything they do.
- Won't honor the truth of the addiction. Holds the addiction as an idealized model of living. Unwanted reactions are met with scorn. Wants to be allowed the magical thinking. Resents those that try to thwart the magical thinking.
- Helpless in the face of adversity. Goes into overwhelm and retreats into the addiction. Does not know how to live or respond in the face of adverse needs.
- Smokers are wet…that means they have a lot of water energy (emotions). They try to dry themselves with the internal artificial heat of the smoke. There are emotions carried in the blood that they want to go away. Lost opportunities haunt them always bringing them back to an unwanted space. Joy is gone.

Cross Indexing: PTSD, ACOA, Addictions, Lung Problems

Repeating Patterns: In the face of adversity they crumble and run away. Love is settling so you don't need to feel failure again. Can't be present in the moment.

Created Patterns
1. If I let go I will be anxious.
2. If I let go I will be afraid.
3. If I let go I will be found wrong.
4. People are dangerous, they will hurt you and you can't trust them.
5. I fail at everything I try.
6. I'm not addicted, I can quit any time I want.
7. Anyone who tells me otherwise is just a hater / mean / doesn't know what they are talking about.
8. I am overwhelmed whenever things get hard.
9. I can't feel joy.

10. I can't get rid of the past, it haunts me.

Snoring

Fears
- Fear of what they say/ do / see will be construed as wrong
- Fear of attack
- Fear of being vulnerable
- Fear of expanding their boundaries
- Fear of living

Emotional States
- A sense that when feeling vulnerable (laying on back) you cannot be safe or relax and enjoy life. Can't bring in joy, cannot bring in the life you want to experience. Life is restricted.

Cross Indexing: Thyroid, Pituitary Gland, Overweight, Sleep – Apnea, nasal congestion, Throat problems, Adenoid problems

Created Patterns
1. I can't have joy.
2. I can't have the life I want.
3. I can' relax and be safe.
4. Being vulnerable is unsafe.
5. I can't change _____.
6. I don't care about myself.
7. I am not being listened to.
8. If I speak up I will be rejected / made fun.
9. I am rejected.
10. I reject myself.
11. I don't love myself.
12. I'm not acceptable.
13. I don't get enough attention.
14. I'm not important.
15. No one listens to me.
16. I can't listen to others.
17. I don't know how to listen to others.

Spasmodic Dysphonia – (Laryngeal)

Fears
- Fear of speaking
- Fear of attack

Teachings
- Creator's definition and perspective of truth

- Fear of losing face/honor
- Fear of being judged
- Fear of stupid people
- Fear of rejection
- Fear of being abandoned
- Fear of hopelessness
- Fear of receiving

- Be listened to without whispering
- Be understood
- Live being listened to
- Live being valued
- Let go of anger
- Forgiveness
- Live without being the scapegoat
- Live without being attacked for the truth
- Live without being attacked for speaking
- Live without being blamed for the truth
- Live without being shamed for the truth

Emotional States

- Holding back the words so they won't be judged / criticized for their opinions. When they speak their truth they are punished.
- Feels that they work with and for stupid people. They feel they will not hear or understand what they have to say – so why say it.
- Holding onto the truth – their truth. Their truth is based in insecurity and they fear saying anything because they fear rejection.
- Hollow words – the words have lost all meaning. Feeling of hopelessness. The words don't change things so why say them?
- Anger stuck in the larynx, won't release the anger. Anger closes off communication.
- Communication is an effort no one listens to me, what's the use in talking. Listens to others but no one listens to them. Feels as if they are giving and giving but not getting anything in return. They feel disregarded and disrespected.

Cross Indexing: Stuttering, Upper Respiratory Infection, depression, anxiety, stress, Throat problems, laryngitis, heart problems

Repeating Patterns: Have repeated encounters with relatives or friends that shame/ attack them for their truth. They take on the role of scapegoat. They use the halting voice to get people to listen to them. The fact that they are difficult to understand when they speak works in their favor.

Created Patterns

1. If I talk with effort people will make an effort to listen.
2. People have a hard time hearing me.
3. I am angry at _____.
4. I am depressed.
5. I am the scapegoat.
6. I get blamed for the failure of others.
7. I have no say.
8. I have no voice.
9. I must speak in a whisper to be heard.

10. I speak the truth I will be ridiculed / rejected / laughed at.
11. If I speak up I could be hurt.
12. If I speak up I will be shamed.
13. If I speak up I will get blamed.
14. It's hopeless.
15. If I speak the truth I will be attacked.
16. It's too much effort to get people to understand.
17. No one understands me.
18. No one wants to hear what I have to say.
19. No one listens to me.
20. Nothing I say will change anything so why say it.
21. People are stupid.
22. People don't want to hear the truth.
23. People use the truth to hurt me.
24. The truth becomes whatever people want it to be.
25. The truth is not important to people.
26. I have to say is more intelligent than anyone here so why talk.
27. What I say has no value.

Sphenoid Bone Misalignment

Fears
- Fear of being wrongly accused
- Fear of being halted
- Fear of inner voice
- Fear of knowing
- Fear of psychic information
- Fear of breathing

Emotional States
- Doesn't direct their inquiries inward, to see in their innerverse. They look outward for answers.

Cross Indexing: accidents, sinus problems, PTSD, Headache-Migraines, bedwetting, memory problems, asthma, scoliosis

Created Patterns
1. I must block my inner vision.
2. I can't breathe easily.
3. There is no joy in life.
4. I don't know how to "live".
5. It is dangerous to be heard breathing.
6. I must block my sense of clairalience (sense of smell).

7. I must stay weak and helpless.
8. I am powerless to change things.
9. All of my plans fall apart.
10. I have no idea where I am going.
11. I am lost.

Spinal Stenosis

Fears
- Fear of too much
- Fear of overwhelm
- Fear of too many words
- Fear of people putting too many expectations on them
- Fear of change
- Fear of going forward in their lives
- Fear of having to deal with life
- Fear of living
- Fear of being unsupported
- Fear of being grounded

Teachings
- Be honest with myself
- Be honored
- Be in the now
- Be listened to
- Be open to communication with the creator/ god
- Be respected
- Being in my body and be safe
- Change easily
- Communicate your pain without alienation
- Communicate your pain without blame
- Connect to the creator / god
- Hear your inner guidance
- Integrate easily with others
- Let go
- Live knowing how to respond to others
- Love myself
- Safe
- Unconditional love

Emotional States
- Unguarded connections to the cosmos. Makes random connections to saints, angels, ancestors, etc. without an understanding. Unyielding in compromise – holding onto the past. No one to talk to. A readiness to release but doesn't know how. Lack of inner awareness and awareness of the environment (surroundings). Takes it for granted.
- Argues with god in an attempt to negotiate their way out of pain. Backed themselves into a corner and have tried to negotiate out of the corner by negotiating with god, angels, etc. Has tried going around god, working with angels. They want the truth to be something it's not. Thinking situations a certain way would make them that way – when the physicality was undeniable.
- Feels communication is being closed off and you feel unsupported. Needs support. Feels unable to stand up on their own. [Intense heaviness in their upper body] They give up a sense of independence for the support of someone else. They become dependent and can't see their life as an independent person.

EMOTIONAL PATTERNS

Cross Indexing: Back, pain, Nerve Problems, Skeletal System

Repeating Patterns: Makes up the story they want to believe about their life and presents that as truth. Does not live in the now…life is chaos. Bills are ignored. Medical needs are ignored. It's not safe to be in their life. Refuses to take the advice of their inner guidance.

Created Patterns

1. Being in my body is unsafe.
2. Change is dangerous.
3. Everything I do is a dead end.
4. God doesn't listen to me.
5. I am alone.
6. I am depressed.
7. I am desperate.
8. I am disconnected from god.
9. I am not connected to my body.
10. I am unsupported.
11. I can't figure out the rules for being a human.
12. I can't give in.
13. I can't go forward.
14. I can't let go.
15. I can't let go of the past.
16. I can't listen to my inner voice.
17. I can't talk to god.
18. I don't love myself.
19. I give everything and get nothing in return.
20. I hate myself.
21. I have no choices.
22. I have no friends.
23. I have shut down communication with the creator /god.
24. I have to hide my feelings.
25. I have to hide my pain.
26. I must guard myself.
27. I'm not good enough for god.
28. I'm not lovable.
29. I'm not respected.
30. I'm not responsible for _____.
31. It has to be my way.
32. No one listens to me.
33. No one wants to hear how I feel.
34. Nothing works for me.
35. People don't care about me.
36. Something is draining my energy.
37. When I need help no one is there for me.
38. I can't support myself.
39. I can't stand up by myself.
40. I need someone to take care of me.
41. I must be dependent on others.

42. I can't talk to _____ and get them to understand.

*Look at themes of boundaries, ego, denial, relationships, communication, loving yourself, unconditional love, aliveness, awareness, blockages, intuition, control, body, change, connection, disassociation, forgiveness, god, letting go, love, now, oneness, self-esteem, self-worth, spiritual growth, truth, denial, communication, unmet needs, control, letting go, disconnection, truth and authenticity

Spleen Problems

Fears
- Fear of the lack of integrity
- Fear that they can't fulfill a promise
- Fear of failing
- Fear of the future
- Fear of being unwanted
- Fear of rejection
- Fear of being unloved
- Fears being passed over
- Fears not being good enough

Emotional States
- They over think everything which looks a lot like worry. The worry creates anxiety and non-peace. They think too much about an issue and then it loses its perspective. The over thinking creates a toxic view of the topic — distorted by what-ifs.
- Feels like they are passed over and are not perceived as good enough. So they 'prostitute' themselves to be accepted. They feel unappreciated for their efforts. Their focus is on themselves and they never express appreciation to others.

Cross Indexing: Rheumatoid arthritis, Lymphoma, Leukemia, Hodgkin's disease, anemia, sarcoidosis, lupus

Created Patterns
1. I am worthless.
2. I'm not worthy.
3. I don't love myself.
4. No one loves me.
5. I am rejected.
6. I'm not respected.
7. I give myself away to be loved/ wanted.
8. I must let others take advantage of me to be loved/ wanted.
9. I am too tired to resist being taken advantage of.
10. I am angry at _____.
11. I have been sad for a long time (Why have you had this long-time sadness?).
12. I worry to stay safe.
13. If I don't ponder a decision or topic before acting I will make a terrible mistake.

14. My perspective might be skewed but at least I am safe.
15. The over thinking is deluded thinking.
16. I won't be able to be loved by others or myself with deluded thoughts.
17. I am unappreciated for what I do.

Sprains

Fears
- Fear of having to make do
- Fear of being forced to go alone
- Fear that there is nothing more
- Fear of feeling
- Fear of relationships
- Fear of going the wrong direction
- Fear of being hurt

Emotional States
- They don't trust their heart (feelings) to give them the right direction. They feel betrayed by the feelings, they feel betrayed by love. They have made relationship decisions that have failed and instead of seeing what they learned about themselves they have shut down referral to the heart. They yield control of feeling decision to their thinking mind. Every time becomes an exercise of value on a spreadsheet.

Cross Indexing: Ankle Problems, Sarcoidosis, Leg Problems, Right-sided negative tendencies, Left-sided negative tendencies, foot problems

Created Patterns
1. I must fight against _____.
2. Nobody tells me what to do.
3. I can't change direction now (What needs to change in your life?).
4. What are you resisting in your life?
5. What in your life is not supporting you?
6. I don't trust my heart to give me reliable information.
7. I feel betrayed by my heart.
8. My relationship ended in failure.
9. A spreadsheet is more reliable than feelings.
10. My feelings send me in the wrong direction.
11. I will not be controlled by my feeling.

Spurs

Fears
- Fear of being taken advantage of
- Fear of what you do being taken
- Fear of identity being usurped
- Fear of being responsible

Emotional States
- Holding others responsible for your failure and then building resentments and anger when they push back.
- Lots of anger toward someone has turned into a deep resentment that. That anger and resentment has adjusted their life path and direction.

Cross Indexing: Bone Problems, affected body part and then look at the kind of resentment that would be held there, Left-sided negative tendencies, Right-sided negative tendencies, Arthritis, Inflammation, Osteoarthritis

Created Patterns
1. What is the resentment that has built up in your life?
2. I resent _____.
3. Others are to blame for my failures.
4. I'm not responsible for what others have done to me.
5. I feel ripped off by life.

Stargardt's Disease

Fears
- Fear of not being enough
- Fear of shortages
- Fear of conflict
- Fear of nothingness
- Fear of being unwanted
- Fear of life

Teachings
- Accepted
- Be present in the now
- Create my own inner vision of the future
- Create your own destiny
- Live without ancestral fear of the future
- Live without fear of the future
- Loved
- Release ancestral obligations of suffering
- Release ancestral obligations to not see truth
- Release ancestral obligations/ commitments to not see the future
- Worthy

Emotional States

- Person is people pleaser; this is an issue of using humble or obsequious behaviors to perpetuate an attitude of self-sacrifice or humility.
- Uses humility to be liked / loved/ accepted.
- Feels like nothing; living life on the edge of nothing; this is very painful.
- This person feels unrecognized, unaccepted and/or unloved.
- Fear of the future.
- An ancestral lack of focus, ancestor unable to focus or see what was happening before it was too late to fix the problem. Intensely blamed themselves for the disaster that befell them. They turned away from a truth that was presented. They did not want to look at it.

Cross Indexing: Eye Problems, Macular Degeneration

Repeated Patterns: Not present to the now, feels hopeless about a future, keeps reenacting their families fear of the future, doesn't feel worthy or loved.

Created Patterns

1. How does the loss of vision serve you?
2. I am a burden.
3. I am broken.
4. I am dangerous if I see the future.
5. I am nothing.
6. I am worthless.
7. I can't do what needs to be done and I need to get others to do it.
8. I can't say what I feel.
9. I can't see how things are going to get any better.
10. I can't see the future.
11. I don't see the good in things.
12. I don't want to see _____.
13. I must manipulate others to get what I want.
14. I'm not accepted.
15. I'm not lovable.
16. I'm not loved.
17. Nothing good ever happens to me.
18. Only bad things happen to me.
19. People are threatened if you see the future.
20. Seeing the future is dangerous.
21. The future is dangerous.
22. What images in the now do you want to block out?
23. If I ignore bad things they will go away.
24. I am guilty of the bad things that happen in the future.
25. I can't see how things will fall apart.

*Look at themes of self-esteem, self-pity, self respect, self worth, future, unmet needs

Stills Disease – Juvenile

Fears
- Fear of isolation
- Fear of being denied love
- Fear of abandonment
- Fear of being trapped
- Fear of no purpose
- Fear of being controlled

Teachings
- Be accepted
- Be honored
- Be in the flow of my life
- Be respected
- Be wanted
- Creator's perspective and definition on the actions of my parents
- Have private time
- Know I am aligned to my life purpose
- Live being listened to
- Live having my opinion respected
- Live having my space respected
- Live with the freedom of being able to move as I desire
- Live without feeling forced to do what others say
- Live without feeling like a burden
- Live without feeling my boundaries are being encroached
- Live without feeling trapped
- Live without needing an illness to stay until I can align with life purpose
- Live without needing to be invisible
- Live without resentment
- Speak my truth and be heard
- Speak my truth and be safe

Emotional States
- Had it with parents, they have pushed them to feel trapped. There is no escaping their persistent interference in their thoughts, friends, school, etc. Feels as if they can't escape from them and they want their privacy.
- Trying to hold self really still so no one will see them. They want nothing more than to be left alone. Seen as lazy and uncooperative. Feels as if parents are controlling and domineering.
- Being forced to go where they don't want to go – hates school, forced to go to outside school activities. Doesn't feel like he/she has any say in their life, not allowed to protest or talk back.
- Pampered existence. No responsibilities. Needs challenges to stay on this side. No real purpose to living since it is all so easy. Disease gives them something to struggle against. Gives them a purpose without challenging the ego…until they grow up and create challenges in alignment with life purpose.
- Left / abandoned early in life by parent(s).
- Grandmother or matriarchal lineage was controlled and dominated…abused. Every part of her life objectified her and kept her from her humanness. Her movements were tightly controlled. She was forced to serve large groups of people. Her role was to never be in positions of receiving recognition.

- Feels unwanted and unloved. Treated as a servant at a very young age and forced to take care of the members of the family: they were the nanny, cook, housecleaning if female, if male forced to do chores and take a job very early in life, they were expected to still perform all chores on top of job and school. Their grades in school were expected to be representative of their parents.

Cross Indexing: Arthritis, Arthritis – Rheumatoid, Autoimmune Disorder, Eye Problems, Bacteria, Joints, genetic (?), inflammatory diseases

Repeating Patterns: holds back speaking because they don't feel safe or that they will be heard, when they don't speak they are also not seen…so they become invisible and their needs for love are not met, their illness creates a sense that they are a burden and feel rejected, they have a sense that they are trapped and have few options.

Created Patterns

1. I am a burden.
2. I am alone.
3. I am angry at _____.
4. I am constantly being told to shut up.
5. I am constantly being told what's best for me.
6. I am forced to do things I don't want to do.
7. I am not allowed to find my own answers.
8. I am not respected.
9. I am trapped.
10. I can't make a move without it being questioned, so I don't move.
11. I can't speak my truth.
12. I hate being told what to do.
13. I hate school.
14. I have been violated.
15. I have no life.
16. I have no life purpose.
17. I have no privacy.
18. I have no say in what I want.
19. I need my disease to stay here.
20. I resent _____.
21. I want them to go away (who?).
22. I want to die.
23. I will never get away.
24. I'm not acceptable.
25. I'm not wanted.
26. My disease is a burden.
27. My father abandoned me.
28. My mother abandoned me.
29. My parents don't have time for me.
30. My parents think I am lazy.
31. My parents think I'm an idiot.
32. My parents/ teachers think I am uncooperative.
33. No one knows who I am.
34. No one leaves me alone.

35. No one listens to what I want.
36. Nothing I do will make them go away.
37. Somebody is always making my decisions for me.
38. The more I don't want to be seen the more I am harassed.
39. There is no reason for me to be here.
40. Hate, anger and resentment of parents.
41. I am a slave.
42. Everything I do is controlled.
43. I don't get to do what I want; I must do what others tell me to do.

*Look at themes of authority, life purpose, loving yourself, unconditional love, abandonment, acceptance, anger, approval, blockages, body, boundaries, control, feelings, freedom, life purpose, lonely, resentment, truth, movement, unmet needs, true self, conflicting motivations, confidence, defenses, domination, expression, feelings, power, sabotage

Stomach Problems

Fears

- Fear of not being strong enough to handle what happens next
- Fear of not having enough
- Fear of the mother
- Fear of receiving
- Fear of change
- Fear of new things
- Fear of doing what makes them happy
- Fear of taking care of themselves (self-nurturing)
- Fears rejection
- Fears being made to feel bad
- Fears feeling vulnerable
- Fears feeling unworthy
- Fear of no control

Emotional States

- From a summarized viewpoint, if you look at the stomach and what it does; it breaks down what nurtures us so that the gut can absorb the needed nutrition. So if a person refuses nutrition, they are refusing what nurtures because what nurtures is unsafe.
- Duodenal area- Angry at what is supposed to be nurturance and feels like they're not going to take it anymore and call it 'good enough'.

Cross Indexing: Spleen Problems, All digestive disorders

Created Patterns

1. Nothing makes me happy.

2. Nothing fills me up.
3. I'm not good enough.
4. No one is here for me.
5. I have no control over what is happening to me.
6. I don't know what I want.
7. I can't take care of myself.
8. I'm not worthy.
9. I don't deserve.
10. I'm not protected.
11. I'm not nurtured.
12. Other people's success makes me angry.
13. I can't feel/be safe.
14. I am going to die.

Stomach Ulcer (Peptic Ulcer Disease-Gastric)

Fears
- Fear of not knowing how to react
- Fear of not knowing how to act
- Fear of being wrong
- Fear of the future
- Fear of forgiving themselves
- Fear of forgiving others
- Fear of hopelessness
- Fear of bad things happening
- Fear of powerlessness

Emotional States
- Chewed down by worry and disabled by guilt. Long lost hopes of a better tomorrow continually elude them. There does not seem to be any rest in the relentless gnawing. There is always something that sets off the pulling within and hiding. A history of bad things have made them think that their future holds more bad things and they can't imagine life without living on that edge of anticipation. They stay safe in the bad things. Nothing is taken in without pain and guilt and then denied. This sets up the spiral of continually revisiting the past across the time continuum.
- Chalk dry dusty white hard gritty…helpless to stop the breakage. They crumble at the slightest pressure but still trying to make their mark on the world. But all turns to dust and falls apart. The things they look to seem to get wiped away in lost memories and lost connections. All seems to blow away in the winds of life. Rapid changes leave them with no sense of feeling or depth of emotion. There is a powdery dryness to their being.

Cross Indexing: Duodenal Ulcer, Digestive Disorders, GERD

Repeated Patterns: Lives in a contracted state, afraid of what might happen next.

Created Patterns

1. I must worry to be safe.
2. I am guilty.
3. I am hopeless.
4. I have no hope that things will get better.
5. I hide to be safe.
6. Bad things happen to me.
7. Life is painful.
8. Life is hard.
9. I must worry to stay safe.
10. I have no peace – my memories are always there to hurt me.
11. If I am seeing I will be hurt.
12. If I get noticed I will be hurt.
13. I have been expressing/feeling strong emotion of _____ for a long time (these are negative emotions: hatred/resentment/anger/rage/bitterness/grief/sorrow/revenge).
14. I worry all the time *(What is the worry about?)*.
15. *What is eating you up inside?*
16. I must worry to keep bad things from happening.
17. Bad things are going to happen.
18. I am worthless/ unworthy.
19. I must please everyone.
20. I am responsible for making everything good.
21. I am helpless.
22. I have to make sure everything is done.
23. I am powerless.
24. I resent _____.
25. I want revenge against _____.
26. I'm not capable of _____.
27. I can't _____ *(What can't you do that is causing you concern?)*.

Strep Throat

Fears

- Fear of being unhappy
- Fear of being happy
- Fear of induced anxiety
- Fear of being put in situations that are stressful
- Fear of failing
- Fear of never amounting to anything
- Fear of being anything other than small
- Fear of disappointment

Emotional States

- Warned to not go forward with idealized concepts. Can't shake the voice that keeps them in the trough. Warned by that voice that they will just slide back into it. Has written about long dark passages of time where they were in a limbo of punishment and no life.
- Harsh forces have driven them into a place of little. Instead of seeing the forces are of their own creation they stay in the little. Driven by not knowing that they have the power to create a different reality.
- High expectations that are unmet. Continual disappointment and separation. Loose commitments to life bonds. Keeps them safe and wounded. They watch the waves from the shore but choose not to swim.

Cross Indexing: Sore throat, Throat Problems, Bacterial Infection

Created Patterns

1. I am small. I am little.
2. I am worthless.
3. I will never be right.
4. It's wrong to dream.
5. I am depressed.
6. Life is punishment.
7. Security is punishment.
8. The night is an endless hell.
9. Anything I do will be wrong.
10. I don't deserve to have.
11. I get just enough to get by.
12. People fail me.
13. I have really bad luck.
14. Nothing ever goes my way.
15. I can't trust people.
16. I am alone.
17. It's dangerous to be out of control.
18. New things are dangerous.
19. If I lose control I will be hurt.
20. You've got to do what you've always done or you will be hurt.

Stroke

Fears

- Fear of having a lack of value
- Fear of love
- Fear of overwhelm
- Fear of living/ life
- Fear of failing

- Fear of learning
- Fear of evolving

Emotional States

- Lack of self confidence in being able to love themselves. Love is stopped. Feels irritable with all around them. Wanting to let go of the feeling of injustice but feels like if they do they will betray that part of their life. Living in the past. They have not grown with life experiences. There has been a sense of overwhelm and they just stop — can't deal with it any more.

Cross Indexing: Aging, Hypertension, Blood Clot, Veins, Arteries

Created Patterns

1. I feel like giving up.
2. I am overloaded and overwhelmed by _____.
3. I am being punished for _____.
4. I have no patience with myself.
5. I can't make myself better.
6. I want to die.
7. There is no reason for living.
8. Life is just too hard to continue.
9. I don't love me, I will never love myself. What's to love.
10. I am a failure.
11. I am overwhelmed at all of the stuff going wrong. I need to escape.
12. I know all there is to know – there's nothing left to learn.

Stuttering (non-developmental)

Fears

- Fear of being heard too quickly
- Fear that harm will happen if they are heard
- Fear of the transition from silence and nothing to action
- Fear of standing up
- Fear of speaking

Emotional States

- Harsh lesson about the cruelty of people was learned long ago (maybe by ancestors). Fear of that cruelty for standing up, being seen caused them to freeze. Called to answer in harsh terms for something that had no meaning but was intended to create compliance and fear. There is a shutdown of communication. A place of no voice. Fear of speaking is very intense. It is so intense it shuts down a part of the brain.

Cross Indexing: stroke, anxiety, brain injury, emotional trauma, stress, spasmodic dysphonia, ancestral

Created Patterns
1. I don't dare speak my truth (What will happen if you do?).
2. I have nothing of value to say.
3. If I talk I will be hurt.
4. I must always please those in authority.
5. I can't say what I want to say.
6. I am worthless.
7. I am unworthy.
8. I'm not good enough.
9. I am going to die.
10. I'm not good enough to talk.
11. People are cruel and if you say the wrong thing they will hurt you.
12. I must keep my words to myself.
13. I freeze when I must speak.

Stye

Fears
- Fear of seeing hostile actions – can't shut them out – trauma

Emotional States
- Unwavering support for old ideas of resentment that want to "boil" over. The old idea has been deemed worthless and unworthy of merit. Yet it persists.

Cross Indexing: Pink eye, allergies, boil, infection, inflammation

Created Patterns
1. I can't see the good in _____.
2. I am critical of _____.
3. I have strong emotions of resentment / hatred / grief / revenge / etc.

Suicidal

Fears
- Fear of the pain
- Fear that the pain will never end
- Fear of the inner darkness
- Fear of the abyss
- Fear that life is the abyss
- Fear that there is nothing else but pain and darkness

Emotional States

- A dark night of the soul has enveloped their being. In this state there is a sense of the only life options are hopeless and a bottomless well of pain and darkness. A feeling that they can't cope and feel as if death is the escape from the tidal wave of crushing darkness and overwhelm. There is a deep sense of worthlessness, destruction of their identity was done in an effort to control them so that the abuser could feel in control. There is a deep wounding of the creative core and empathic sense.

Cross Indexing: ACOA, Post Traumatic Stress Disorder, Depression, Nervous Breakdown

Created Patterns

1. Nothing will ever be better.
2. What's the use?
3. Everyone would be better off without me.
4. My living will not make anything better.
5. I want to die.
6. I am in so much pain I want to die (What is the emotional pain about?).
7. I am depressed.
8. I hate myself.
9. The creator doesn't love me.
10. The pain is too much.
11. There is no way out.
12. There's no solution.
13. The creator has abandoned me.
14. I feel abandoned.
15. I am overwhelmed with pain.

Swallowing – Trouble

Fears

- Fear of having to take in too much
- Fear of having to take it
- Fear of not knowing what is good or bad
- Fear of rejection
- Fear of saying the wrong things and having to take them back
- Fear of having to swallow your words
- Fear of conflict and anger
- Fear of being wrong
- Fear of disappearing

Emotional States

- This person is seeing the world through a veil and things are not what they appear to be. The created illusion has a world that is as idyllic as 'Tele-Tubby' land. The fields are covered in rich green grass that is all the same height and everything is perfect. The sun shines and rainbows are everywhere. They believe they are doing a great job of everything. Events/people/situations all appear to support that view of the world. They get lots of recognition in the form of money, prestige, success or fame. But their connection to the grounded self and the higher, spiritual self is an illusion. It has no basis. If they venture outside of the world they have created for themselves they believe they will disappear/drop into oblivion. So they keep their world safe. And they keep all the structures in place that keep that world view intact, not letting anything else in to disturb the perfect balance they have created.
- This individual has a barriers and obstacles obstructing their progress. They have become accustomed to old habits and ways of thinking. They are locked into rigid ways of thinking due to fear. This person is unyielding in their thought processes. They are firmly anchored in a duality approach to their thinking. Everything is either black or white. This 'way' of being in the world is all they can see. They have denied themselves the opportunities to be receptive to new ideas/concepts. They may have gotten some harsh lessons about the rigidity of their thinking by alienating people they love. They have shut themselves off from people and experiences. There is a low self-worth.
- This person is meddling in other people's affairs while at the same time unwilling to take responsibility for their own life. They have issues they are trying to avoid and not taking responsibility for their actions. They have fears they are not confronting and this fear is driving them to forms of self-destruction. The person is afraid of aggression and anger in others. Yet they have their own anger they are not dealing with. They present an inability to discriminate between what can and cannot be changed. They can't release the past.
- Guilt from saying insults, critical, or judgment statements that alienated loved ones. Words were ancestral words.

Cross Indexing: Throat problems, Parkinson's disease, Esophageal Cancer, Polymyositis, ALS

Created Patterns

1. _____ is to blame for my problems.
2. Angry people are dangerous.
3. Assertive people are dangerous.
4. Change is dangerous.
5. Feeling compassion is dangerous.
6. I am afraid to make decisions.
7. I am angry at _____.
8. I am angry at myself.
9. I am dangerous if I express my anger.
10. I am disconnected from the creator/ I AM/ source/ god.
11. I am going to die.
12. I am guilty.
13. I am guilty of _____.
14. I am jealous of _____.
15. I am sad/ depressed.

EMOTIONAL PATTERNS

16. I am unhappy.
17. I can't be happy by myself.
18. I can't express my anger.
19. I can't fight back.
20. I can't make my own decisions.
21. I can't release past hurts.
22. I can't see the other person's point of view.
23. I can't speak my truth and be safe.
24. I don't get to tell people I am angry.
25. I don't how to/what it feels like to experience life without guilt.
26. I don't know how to tell the difference between people that are safe and people that are bad for me.
27. I don't know how to/what it feels like detach from the influence of others and from the need to control others.
28. I don't know how to/what it feels like let go of what is bad for me.
29. I don't know how to/what it feels like let go of what is toxic.
30. I don't know how to/what it feels like to be compassionate toward myself.
31. I don't know how to/what it feels like to be compassionate toward others.
32. I don't know how to/what it feels like to negotiate.
33. I don't know how to/what it feels like to relate to others.
34. I don't know how to/what it feels like to see the other point of view.
35. I don't know what compassion is.
36. I don't like myself.
37. I don't love myself.
38. I don't see the good in life.
39. I don't see the good in others.
40. I hate _____.
41. I hate myself.
42. I live in the past.
43. I make bad decision.
44. I must always see the negative to protect myself.
45. I must control others to be safe.
46. I must judge others to be safe.
47. I must meet the expectations of others.
48. I must put up with what comes my way.
49. I must take what others do to me.
50. I never know where to turn when confronted with a problem.
51. I will be seen as weak/at fault if I am compassionate.
52. I worry about what others think.
53. I'm not accepted.
54. I'm not at peace.
55. I'm not good enough.
56. I'm not responsible for my decisions.
57. I'm rejected.
58. If I do something creative I am always criticized.
59. If I don't get my way I am unhappy.
60. If I don't meet the expectations of others I am a failure.
61. If things change I will be hurt.
62. Making decision is dangerous.

63. My happiness depends on others.
64. My life is not my own.
65. Other people opinions are not as good as mine.
66. Others are to blame for my problems.
67. Someone else is blame for my problems.
68. Someone else must make my decisions for me.
69. The unknown is dangerous.
70. What is the source of feeling constricted?
71. What other people think is important/matters.
72. What person/situation can't you swallow.
73. What pressure are you under?
74. Who grabbed you by the throat to force you to say or do something?

Swollen Feet

Fears
- Fear of being forced to go in a direction they don't want
- Fear of nothing being there for them
- Fear that their foundation is built on sand
- Fear of feelings
- Fear of the inner knowing
- Fear of moving
- Fear of change
- Fear of the future

Emotional States
- LEFT – Not moving in the direction of being aware of the gifts of their soul. Emotions or concepts that create feelings keep them from asking, exploring and being present. These concepts keep them from the deep knowing of soul.
- RIGHT – Not moving in the direction of physical health by taking care of their physical body. There is a fear of moving. Movement (exercise) feels dangerous. Staying in one place they get more done. Movement is frivolous.

Cross Indexing: foot problems, leg problems, heart, kidneys, liver, blood clot, infections

Repeating patterns: not present, out of the flow

Created Patterns
1. I can't see the good in _____.
2. _____ causes me to feel critical.
3. I strong emotions of rage/ hatred/ grief/ bitterness/ sorrow/ resentment/ etc.

T's

Tachycardia

Fears
- Fear of being seen as different
- Fear of not fitting in
- Fear of being irrelevant
- Fear of letting go
- Fear of going with the flow
- Fear of listening to the inner wisdom
- Fear of the secular identity being shattered
- Fear of being unsupported

Teachings
- Whole
- Complete
- Trust
- Allowing the flow of the Universe
- Living in the Now
- Feel accepted
- Live without expecting persecution
- Feel respected
- Feel loved
- Allowing others to help you
- Supported
- Recognize support

Emotional States
- Conflict between ego and higher self as the higher self wants to move to let go of limiting beliefs and identity.
- Consciousness is evolving and ego is anchored in its needs for security, survival, love, and protection.
- Ego goes into fear at the awareness of letting go of the 'old' ways.
- Resistance to the flow of the universe.
- They are divided between a choice of security based on fear and truth of their spiritual path. They have been in the world in a 'sensible' way and now they have been moving along a path of spiritual growth. As they step forward along that spiritual path they become afraid of letting go of the beliefs they think have kept them secure in a sensible way…they have felt supported and protected by being 'sensible'. They are in conflict with the pull of the Higher Self/Soul and the Ego. Ego wants security, survival, love, and protection in all the ways that have been part of its identity. The Higher Self yearns to let go of the limitations of beliefs and identity that limits the evolution of consciousness. The insecurity of moving along that spiritual path will overwhelm the individual and in that overwhelm they pull back into Ego's comfort zone. There is a reluctance to see and accept the other ways the universe is providing for support needed to move fully into their spiritual path and life purpose.

Cross indexing: Adrenal fatigue, heart problems, congestive heart failure

Repeating patterns: Doesn't feel whole, has trouble with trust, does not allow life to flow tries to force it, does not feel accepted, expects to be persecuted, disrespected, unloved, won't allow others to help them, unsupported, doesn't see how others are supporting them

EMOTIONAL PATTERNS

Created Patterns
1. Being helped by others is a sign of weakness.
2. Being spiritual is risky.
3. Being spiritual means giving up/losing your identity.
4. Being spiritual means losing/giving up everything you love.
5. God will abandon me in my time of need.
6. I am going to die.
7. I am ridiculed on the spiritual path.
8. I can't accept help from others.
9. I can't be spiritual and be abundant.
10. I can't depend others.
11. I can't let go of what makes me feel secure.
12. I can't live my life purpose and be abundant.
13. I can't make money on the spiritual path.
14. I don't know how to receive.
15. I don't trust the universe to provide.
16. I must always do it myself.
17. I must always give.
18. I must conform to an accepted spiritual path to be loved.
19. I need money to be secure.
20. I need money to feel secure.
21. I'm not good enough if others help me.
22. I'm not respected for my spiritual work.
23. I'm not supported (This may also be a dual belief of I am supported).
24. If I follow my spiritual path I will be alone.
25. If I follow the spiritual path I will be poor.
26. It is difficult/ hard/ impossible to make money on the spiritual path.
27. My children accept don't my spiritual work/ life purpose.
28. My family doesn't accept my spiritual work/ life purpose.
29. My life purpose is a waste of time and money.
30. My life purpose/Spiritual work is seen as a hobby by loved ones.
31. My life purpose/Spiritual work is seen as a hobby by me.
32. My life purpose/Spiritual work is seen as a hobby by others.
33. No one makes money on the spiritual path.
34. No one supports me.
35. People let me down.
36. People on a spiritual path are ridiculed.
37. Receiving help from others means I'm not good enough.
38. Somebody is always going to let me down.
39. The spiritual path is not respected.
40. The spiritual path leads to poverty.
41. The spiritual path means being alone.
42. The spiritual work is not honored.
43. When I need help no one is there/I am alone.

*Look at themes of spiritual growth, god, trust, receiving, abundance, manifestation, self-esteem, self knowledge, loving myself, self respect, self worth, relationships, receiving, overwhelm, insecurity, flow, ego, higher self connection, identity, spirituality, stress, manifesting

Teeth – Upper Left 1st Incisor

Fears
- Fear of the future
- Fear they will be short of success
- Fear they won't make it
- Fear of being forced against their will
- Fear of change
- Fear of being unacceptable and unwanted
- Fear of being devalued
- Fear of chaos
- Fear of not being good enough
- Fear of having to tell their secrets
- Fear of feeling judged and vulnerable
- Fear of making decisions
- Fear of speaking

Teachings
- Be accepted
- Be honored
- Be trusted
- Be valued
- Creator's definition of trust and mine are the same
- Creator's definition of truth and mine are the same
- Feel safe in chaos
- Feel safe without rules
- Be safe
- Good enough without all the facts
- Hear truth
- Honor other people's ideas
- Know truth
- Live without secrets
- Make decisions and feel safe
- Make decisions without all the facts
- See truth
- Share my ideas and be safe

Emotional States
- Short sighted vision of the future can't see that things will happen as a consequence of their inaction in what is needing to be done.

Cross Indexing: Teeth, Mouth Problem, Bone Problems, Anxiety, Kidney Problems, Bladder problems, UTI, edema

Created Patterns
1. I can't see that there is a future.
2. I can't make progress on stuff I can't conceive of.
3. I can't do what is expected of me. It will get done some day.
4. All my ideas are wrong.
5. Change is dangerous.
6. Chaos is dangerous/ unsafe.
7. Chaos means I will be hurt.
8. Everything is wrong until all the facts are known.
9. I am blocked from getting the answers.
10. I am blocked from the knowing.
11. I am happy when everything is controlled.

12. I am lost without all the facts.
13. I am unable to see/hear/know truth.
14. I can't make a decision until I have all the facts.
15. I can't win.
16. I do not know the difference between truth and fiction.
17. I don't trust myself.
18. I don't trust others (who?).
19. I must have all the facts before I make a decision.
20. I must keep my ideas to myself.
21. I must know all the facts to be safe.
22. I trust my ideas.
23. I will never know the truth.
24. I will never know the truth of why things happen.
25. I will never measure up.
26. I'm the only one with the right idea.
27. If I don't have all the facts things are out of control.
28. If I share my ideas I am ridiculed.
29. If you don't have rules you have chaos.
30. Knowing all the facts prevents chaos.
31. Only my ideas are the right ideas.
32. People keep things from me.
33. People lie to me.
34. The rules are truth.
35. The rules must always be followed.
36. The truth is covered over.
37. The truth is hidden from me.
38. The truth is kept from me.
39. When I don't know all the facts I am in trouble.
40. Without knowing the facts I can't go forward.

Teeth – Upper Right 2nd Molar

Fears
- Fear of being unable to adjust to change
- Fear of letting go
- Fear of the flow of life
- Fear of inner peace
- Fear of having too much
- Fear of losing identity
- Fear of listening to inner voice
- Fear of the future
- Fear of becoming irrelevant
- Fear of trusting others
- Fear of being let down
- Fear of letting others take charge
- Fear of being out of control

Teachings
- God's plan feels like
- Let the greater path unfold
- Allow others their path in life
- Allow others their life path without judging
- Trust the creator
- To have creator's definition of trust
- Allow others their power

Emotional States

- Distressed at the path of others.
- Holding onto the pain of separation created by not seeing the overall picture.
- Misunderstanding with children/others.
- Feeling as if your children/others do not meet your expectations.
- A sense that you are biting the bullet (grin and bear it).
- Children of the person with this problem have stopped their dreams to heal the past.
- Trans-generation healing by your children…children will hold the beliefs to be held from their ancestors/past generations.
- Only giving yourself so much and then stopping.
- Soul sees the overall but the ego is in fear of what it may lose so it stops just short of total commitment and involvement.
- Thoughts become short sighted and don't embrace the bigger picture.
- Connection to the divine plan is lost.
- Lack of hope that the future will be any better.

Cross Indexing: Teeth Problems, vision problems, Stomach problems, Spleen Problems, Stomach Ulcer, GERD

Repeating Patterns: doesn't allow others to live their lives the way they want…interferes in their decision making and judges them for trying to live their own lives, doesn't trust the flow of the universe, doesn't allow others their power.

Created Patterns

1. I am disappointed in others.
2. I am disappointed with my children
3. I am rejected when people/my children don't listen to me.
4. I can't see how things are going to work out.
5. I can't see the big picture.
6. I don't trust that there is a greater plan.
7. I don't trust that things will work out.
8. I don't trust the Creator.
9. I don't trust the decisions of others/my children
10. I don't understand my children
11. I must be obedient to be a good daughter/son.
12. I must grin and bear it.
13. I must make things happen the way they are supposed to.
14. I must see it for it to be real.
15. If others would listen to me they would have an easier life.
16. It hurts when people don't take my advice.
17. My children/ others are a disappointment.
18. My children/others/*What situation (?)* did not turn out how you expected.
19. Others/My children make bad decisions.
20. People don't meet my expectations.
21. The future is not going to be any better.
22. When I see/say what's wrong I stop bad things from happening.

23. When I tell people what I think I am rejected.

Teeth Problems

Fears
- Fear of the future
- Fear that they will die without answering your calling
- Fear of making decisions
- Fear of being judged
- Fear of moving
- Fear of dying
- Fear of weakness

Emotional States
- Doesn't see how things are going to be any better and gets stuck in a place where they can't conceive of a different way to get unstuck.

Cross Indexing: Mouth Problems, Bone Problems, Anxiety

Created Patterns
1. I can't make decisions.
2. I don't trust my decisions.
3. I never seem to get anything done.
4. I make lots of plans but never seem to get anything done.
5. *What is the impatience about*?
6. I am not connected to God.
7. I am weak.
8. I am stuck.
9. I can't let go of what's not working.
10. Things are never going to be any better.

Temple Pain or Pressure

Fears
- Fear of knowing their source
- Fear of knowing their spiritual self
- Fear of getting too close to an inner truth that will take them into the unknown
- Fear of not being good enough
- Fear of being unwanted
- Fear of trusting someone unworthy of

Teachings
- Allow the flow of the universe
- Be in the presence of the creator without fear
- Be wanted without being good at everything
- Believe in the creator without shame / humiliation / ridicule
- Creator's definition and mine are the

- their trust
- Fear of flow
- Fear of not being good enough for god
- Fear that when entering an altered state they will be alone and dying

- same for god's love
- Creator's definition of depending on others
- Creator's definition of perfection
- Creator's definition of purity
- Depend on others
- Difference between the Universal Wisdom and my thoughts
- Enter the 7th plane easily
- Enter the 7th plane without fear
- Enter the 7th plane without feeling you have broken the bodhisattva vow
- God's love
- Be wrong without shame / humiliation / ridicule
- Live being able to talk about the creator and be wanted
- Live my life without the threat of humiliation
- Live without always having to have the answers
- Live without getting love by meeting the expectations of others
- Live without needing force to make things happen
- Live without needing to get love and recognition for my work
- Live without struggle
- Live without the need to be good at everything
- Live without the need to be perfect
- Make things happen without force
- Matter without the struggle
- Talk about my beliefs without shame / humiliation / ridicule

Emotional States

- Lack of recognition has caused deep emotional hurt. Will never have enough recognition- wants more than can be gotten. Holds self to a higher standard than everyone else. Works hard to be good enough.
- Heart is broken by failures, no matter how hard they try they will never be good enough, feels unwanted. Took criticism and judgmental emotional abuse as a personal failure and they are therefore unworthy of love or being wanted. Feels unwanted in a world that is superficial and wants to leave it. Inner anger at still being here.
- Lack of love. No understanding of what love is. Always doubting love's sincerity. Continually enmeshed in the trap of trying to force it to their expectations when their expectations are unrealistic. Sets up a cycle of failures in relationships based on the standard of trust. The standard for trust is broken and the relationship fails.

EMOTIONAL PATTERNS

Cross Indexing: TMJ, Headaches, Headaches-Migraine, Sleep problems, ear problems, vision problems, thymus problems

Repeating Patterns: Does not allow the flow of the universe, fears a divine connection, must prove themselves to be the best to be love, doesn't ask others for help, when they are wrong they feel shame/humiliation/ridicule, fears being humiliated, meets the expectations of others to be loved, makes things happen by force, they must have all the answers, live a life of struggle, they need to get recognition for being good, they need recognition to be loved.

Created Patterns

1. _____ blocks the beauty of the universe.
2. Being in the presence of god is dangerous.
3. Being in the presence of god means I will be killed.
4. Change can't happen without brute force.
5. For something to happen I must make it happen.
6. God demands perfection.
7. God only listens to those that are perfect / pure.
8. I am insignificant.
9. I am trapped in the earth plane.
10. I am trapped on Earth.
11. I break the vow of the Bodhisattva if I go to the 7th plane.
12. I can't allow the wisdom of the universe to come through me and not own it.
13. I can't believe in the creator without humiliation / shame / ridicule.
14. I can't depend on others.
15. I can't enter the presence of the creator, safely.
16. I can't leave the earth plane safely.
17. I can't talk about my beliefs without shame / humiliation / ridicule.
18. I don't know how to _____ and not be responsible for it.
19. I have a vow to never leave the earth plane.
20. I have to force everything to happen.
21. I have to get love from my parents.
22. I have to struggle to matter.
23. I lack faith in me.
24. I make things happen.
25. I must achieve recognition even if costs.
26. I must always have the answers.
27. I must be better than others.
28. I must be good at everything so I don't depend on others.
29. I must be good at everything to be wanted / needed / loved.
30. I must be pure.
31. I must be pure and perfect.
32. I must be recognized to be loved / wanted / needed.
33. I must be right or I am in trouble / hurt / disgraced / shamed.
34. I must criticize myself before someone else does.
35. I must hide my belief in the creator from _____.
36. I must hide my belief in the creator to not be humiliated by _____.
37. I must hold myself to another standard

38. I must know where the Universal Intelligence that comes through me comes from.
39. I must meet the expectations of others to be loved.
40. I use extraordinary work effort to get love.
41. I use extraordinary work effort to get recognition.
42. I use work to get love and recognition.
43. I will be ridiculed by _____ if I believe in the creator.
44. I will die if I enter the 7th plane of existence.
45. I will die if I leave the earth plane.
46. I'm not worthy of god's love.
47. If I am good at everything people want me.
48. If I am wrong I will be shamed / humiliated.
49. If I believe in _____ my father will not want me.
50. If I have hurt someone it means I have shamed myself.
51. If I merge with god I cease to exist.
52. If I write / say something wrong I am will be shamed / humiliated / ridiculed.
53. It is wrong for others to know you have been shamed.
54. My work must be perfect.
55. Talking about the creator to _____ is dangerous.
56. The Bodhisattva cannot go to the 7th plane until all suffering ceases one earth.
57. The more the effort the more I am worth.
58. The only way to receive attention is to help others.
59. To know god I must be perfect and pure.
60. To talk to god I must be perfect.
61. To talk to God I must be pure.

*Look at themes of criticism, perfectionism, god, self-esteem, self-knowledge, self-respect, self-worth, unmet needs (recognition, feelings validated, attention, being seen /heard/ held)

Temporal Arteritis

Fears
- Fear of life
- Fear of being
- Fear of knowing
- Fear someone will take what they have and claim it as their own
- Fear of being imperfect
- Fear of being out of control
- Fear of hearing / knowing new information
- Fear of change

Emotional States
- Holds themselves to a different standard than everyone else, unable to let go of the concept of 'I must be perfect'. What they see and think must be perfect. Imperfect thoughts make a bad person. This is how they control their world. The perfectionism is a form of keeping everything

in line. Their status quo has been challenged – can't keep things perfect so they scramble to put it all back in perfect order to make sense of the world.
- They won't listen to what they are being told. There's an emotion charged situation in their life that is festering and they refuse to listen to the inner voice giving them information. This energy is building in energy and intensity.
- Lack of tolerance. Lack of receptivity. Closed off to new information.

Cross Indexing: Vasculitis, Polymyalgia Rheumatica, Lupus, Arthritis-Rheumatoid, Temple Pain/ Pressure, Face/ Head problems

Created Patterns
1. I must be perfect.
2. I must be better than everyone else.
3. I am a bad person.
4. I must be perfect to be loved.
5. Being perfect keeps the world in control.
6. Chaos is dangerous.
7. I can't hear my inner voice.
8. I don't trust myself.
9. Listening to my inner voice leads to chaos.
10. New ideas are dangerous.
11. The old ways are safe and predictable.
12. I don't trust others.
13. I expect more of myself than others.

Temporo-Mandibular Joint (TMJ)

Fears
- Fear of being too powerful
- Fear that they can't hold back their intense emotions
- Fear of their anger
- Fear of accepting new ideas
- Fear that they will never see justice
- Fear that others will see their anger as wrong
- Fear of being alone
- Fear of myself
- Fear of being healthy
- Fear of being unloved
- Fear of being abandoned

Emotional States
- They are tearing themselves apart for not saying or holding back their words. They are holding intense emotions in their mouth.

- They keep cycling through ideas of resentment/ revenge / rage/ anger. The ideas never make it out of their mouth and tension builds.

Cross indexing: anxiety, jaw problems, dizziness, back (cervical), PTSD, Arthritis, Pelvis Problems, Ancestral/ Genetic

Created Patterns
1. I am angry at the unfair situation I am in.
2. I am powerless to stop the bad stuff from happening.
3. I must hold it all in.
4. I can't express myself safely.
5. *What is the stress/going wrong in your life?*
6. It's tearing me apart to not say what I want to say.

Tendon Problems

Fears
- Fear of the joints
- Fear of being the one that's supposed to keep it all together and under control
- Fear of being unsupported
- Fear of being unable to move
- Fear of having your freedom taken
- Fear of being too weak to do what needs to be done
- Fear of change
- Fear of losing power and control

Emotional States
- They resent others for not supporting them. They needed the others to be flexible and instead hit obstacles that did not help.

Cross Indexing: Joint Problems, Muscle Problems, Ligament Problems

Created Patterns
1. I can't forgive myself (Why can't you forgive yourself?).
2. *Why do you always see the negative?*
3. *What in your life causes you to become rigid and inflexible?*
4. I can't change my mind on _____ *(What happens if you do?)*.
5. I am unsupported.
6. I resent _____ for not supporting me.
7. People put obstacles in my way.
8. *What is being reflected back to you?*

Testicle Problems

Fears
- Fear of being vulnerable
- Fear of being disrespected
- Fear of being diminished
- Fear of isolation
- Fear of rejection
- Fear of being emasculated
- Fear of being found to be lacking
- Fear of being shamed
- Fear of being hurt
- Fear of pain
- Fear of being alone
- Fear of being exposed
- Fear of not being good enough
- Fear of not being enough
- Fear of having to depend on others

Emotional States
- Harbors a deep resentment toward those that have hurt him. He feels vulnerable and abandoned. Was exposed to harm.
- Hardship and hard heart-ship has caused him to feel beat up by the world. There doesn't seem to be anyone standing up to help and he feels all alone. Creative efforts have been diminished or destroyed.
- Guilt and/or shame when expressing himself sexually.

Cross Indexing: Endocrine System Disorders, Kidney Stones, Cancer, Virus, Wounded Creative Core

Created Patterns
1. All men are *bad (Who made you feel that way?)*.
2. I don't trust other men.
3. I wish I had never been born.
4. I am vulnerable to attack.
5. I'm vulnerable to being hurt.
6. I have no place to call home.
7. I am abandoned.
8. I am alone
9. I feel defeated and powerless to protect myself.

Thalamus Problems

Fears
- Fear of making decision

- Fear of being present
- Fear of nothingness
- Fear of being nothing
- Fear of inner peace
- Fear of knowing what is important
- Fear of making a mistake
- Fear of being responsible
- Fear of knowing what is real and what isn't
- Fear of not knowing what to bring in and what to filter out
- Fear of feeling guilty
- Fear of being overwhelmed
- Fear of being criticized and judged
- Fear of getting it wrong
- Fear of saying the wrong thing
- Fear of not being right
- Fear of their history

Emotional States

- Disconnected from what their body is telling them. Disconnection was created by an overload of information, they do not know how to handle the overwhelm and they created "literally" a short circuit that stopped the overwhelm. They don't know how to interpret the information coming in. It feels as if information is getting lost.

Cross Indexing: Wounded Creative Core, Stroke, Parkinson's, Narcolepsy, Insomnia, Aging, Memory problems, Vision Problems, Hearing Problems, Skin Problems, Tongue Problems, Ancestral / Genetic

Created Patterns

1. I am constantly being criticized/ put down.
2. I am impatient with others *(What happens to cause that feeling?)*.
3. I am out of touch with my body.
4. It's not safe to feel.
5. I get overwhelmed by too much happening.
6. I must shut down to be safe.
7. I don't know what to do when there's too much happening. I know what decisions to make.

Thigh Problems

Fears

- Fear of identity annihilation
- Fear of death
- Fear of hurt
- Fear of being overpowered
- Fear of not being alignment with purpose

Emotional States
- Held in place by an overriding sense of duty and responsibility. Constantly pushing against that duty. Strains against the inner need to let go of the duty. A dogged sense that they have not gone in the direction they need to. There is a welling power within to shift who they are and where they are going.

Cross Indexing: Left and Right sided negative tendencies, hip problems, leg problems

Created Patterns
1. I am afraid of the future.
2. I can't stand on my own.
3. Bad things are going to happen *(Who/What makes you feel that way?)*.
4. I am losing me.
5. I am afraid of dying.
6. I am being overrun.
7. I am not living my purpose.
8. I must do my duty.
9. I must be responsible.

Throat Problems

Fears
- Fear of being desperate
- Fear of judgment
- Fear of indecision
- Fear of others
- Fear of speaking
- Fear of the self(s)
- Fear of those that would manipulate them
- Fear of revealing too much about themselves
- Fear of expressing their anger
- Fear of creating a scene

Emotional States
- Words not said, words then said harshly equals the same thing. Putting the brakes on words holds power in check to keep people from knowing who they are. They feel that if they don't they will be overrun and lose all power. Boundaries will crumble.
- Safe to express power in pecking little comments that become annoying and not valued or listened to. Then when the words do come they have a lot of power that can hold the anger of having to hold your tongue. Feminine energy is out of balance.
- Resentment at being a woman and not being able to speak. If you do speak your truth then you become the bad person. The one that has disturbed the harmony or balance.

Cross Indexing: Vocal Cord Problems, Strep Throat, Laryngitis, Spasmodic Dysphonia, esophagus problems

Created Patterns
1. I have been suppressing a strong feeling of anger for a long time *(What's the anger about?)*.
2. I just 'take it' when I am hurt.
3. I am angry at _____.
4. I swallow the pain.
5. I can't forgive myself for saying hurtful things to others.
6. I never know what the right thing to say or do is.
7. I never get my own way *(What prevents you from having your own way?)*.

Thrombosis

Fears
- Fear of feeling
- Fear of knowing what could hurt
- Fear of being told what you must know
- Fear of peace and calm
- Fear of being seen
- Fear of being responsible for making decisions
- Fear of receiving
- Fear of not giving
- Fear of living
- Fear of flow

Teachings
- Live with being able to trust people
- Know truth when it is heard
- Truth
- Live without drama
- Live without a continual crisis
- Make decisions safely
- Feel safe when making a decision
- Trust
- Feel confident
- Joy
- Live without betrayal

Emotional States
- Person has lots of drama/ crises in their life.
- Frenetic energy of drama doesn't really accomplish anything; keeps issues at the surface level.
- Hold narrowly focused ideas and when situations/ concepts deviate there is an over-reaction.
- Limited ability to judge a decision as right or wrong; stops them from making decisions. They turn a decision inside out and upside down. This stops them from doing which stops the flow of life.
- Allows others to run over them and take advantage of them.
- Limited life skills to stop people from taking advantage of them.
- Hates life; stopped living life.
- Do not feel like they can trust people around them; lack of confidence in what is being told to them.
- Doesn't know who to trust.

Cross Indexing: Deep Vein Thrombosis, Arteriosclerosis, High Cholesterol, Heart Problems, Headaches, Headaches-Migraine

Created Patterns

1. _____ betrayed me.
2. Change is dangerous.
3. I am a doormat.
4. I am angry at _____.
5. I am anxious about everything.
6. I can't believe what people tell me.
7. I can't ever seem to get anything done.
8. I can't go forward with my life something always stops me.
9. I can't make decisions.
10. I can't trust people.
11. I don't believe anyone.
12. I don't care about anything anymore.
13. I don't know how to have fun.
14. I don't know what joy is.
15. I don't know what the truth sounds like.
16. I don't know who I can trust.
17. I hate life.
18. I hate myself.
19. I must always be on guard.
20. I need the drama to protect me from myself.
21. I need the drama to protect me from others.
22. I want to die.
23. I'm not going anywhere with my life.
24. Life is hard.
25. Life's not worth living.
26. New ideas are dangerous.
27. People never mean what they say.
28. People take advantage of me.
29. People tell me whatever they want me to hear.
30. The way I do it has always worked -why change.
31. There's no point.
32. Truth is whatever someone wants to make it.
33. *What is stopping you from living your life?*

*Look at themes of boundaries, trust, power, drama, truth, decisions, self-worth, self-love, joy, struggle, unmet needs

Thrombotic thrombocytopenic purpura

Fears

- Fear of joy
- Fear of life
- Fear of inner peace
- Fear of balance

- Fear of being loved
- Fear of letting go
- Fear of seeing the big picture
- Fears that what they see will be different than their world view
- Fear of seeing outside their narrow focus of life

Emotional States

- Hopeless sense that life will be a continuous chaos. They are tired from moving from one trauma-drama after another that stops the flow of living. There no sense of joy or inner peace. Life always feels off balance.

Cross Indexing: Autoimmune disease, bacterial infection, genetic disorder, AIDS & HIV, Circulatory Problems, Artery problems, Vein problems, blood disorders

Created Patterns

1. I am bound by _____. *(Something old: a tradition or a way of being in the world)*
2. I can't share the load.
3. I am all alone in handling this *(What is the this?)*.
4. Nothing will ever help me.
5. I am doomed/a failure.
6. I out of alignment with god/divine purpose.
7. I can't let go of the past *(This is a heart hurt that has not been let go of)*.
8. I will never heal/get better.
9. I am unhappy/sad *(This is a profound sadness- What is the cause?)*.
10. I have been poisoned by _____.
11. If I am happy someone will take it away from me.
12. God Beliefs: I am disconnected from god-god has abandoned me-god has betrayed me-I don't believe in god.

Thrush

Fears

- Fear of getting sick
- Fear of illness
- Fear that what they take in will make them ill
- Fear of being different
- Fear of liking yourself
- Fear of being upbeat

Emotional States

- Can't fight back, old ideas keep you locked into what you can say and what you can't. Forced to give into others that have more power and control over their life. Resentment builds and goes unexpressed for many years. Negative feelings of self become the pattern of speech. These feelings are old patterns from their early life and ancestry.

Cross Indexing: Yeast Infection, Candida, Athlete's foot

Created Patterns
1. I am angry with myself for making wrong choices.
2. I don't know how to live without anger/ resentment.
3. I don't know how to safely express my anger/resentments.
4. I feel powerless to fight back against the old constraints of old ideas.
5. I must keep my resentment to myself.

Thyamine Deficiency

Fears
- Fear that the given truth is a justification for a lie
- Fear that information is forced to look like the truth
- Fear of being seen
- Fear of being found
- Fear of following through
- Fear of doing
- Fear of responsibility
- Fear of giving
- Fear of being made fun of
- Fear of being present to themselves
- Fear of staying in one place
- Fear of the truth

Emotional States
- Shifting Priorities have left them feeling empty and devoid of feeling excitement or enthusiasm for life. A long standing agreement or understanding was broken. The agreement/understanding died from neglect. Because they let it die. They somehow think they are owed its resurrection.
- Bewilderment. There is total bewilderment as to how they got to this place in life. They don't see the path of conclusion. They don't see the road that brought them here.
- The truth yields little support. It dances around them like a group of school children dancing and chanting a nursery rhyme. The truth feels mocking and hateful as if trust is out to get them.
- Instead of walking through life they hop through life, hopping from one thing to another. Not following a path but a point or dot. Nothing connects. There is not an energetic flow from one point to another. Just random jumping. Shiny object syndrome.

Cross Indexing: Heart Problems, Addiction – Alcohol, Peripheral Neuropathy, Edema

Created Patterns

1. I need to go on to the next thing to be safe; the other stuff is not working.
2. Life is dull and boring, I feel empty and tired.
3. I have no purpose.
4. People won't support me in my efforts.
5. I feel abandoned and unwanted.
6. I don't understand the world – nothing makes sense.
7. Even when I try to live my truth the world leaves me behind.
8. I am ridiculed for who I am.

Thymus Problems

Fears
- Fear of being attacked
- Fear of not being able to fight back
- Fear of confrontation
- Fear of being overrun
- Fear of love
- Fear of the divine
- Fear of divine retribution
- Fear of moving
- Fear of their own power
- Fear of isolation
- Fear of being weak
- Fear of being good enough
- Fear of owing others
- Fear of being taken advantage of
- Fear of someone revealing victim identity

Teachings
- Acknowledge your beauty
- Acknowledge your divinity
- Balance
- Be loyal to myself
- Be worthy
- Complete
- Deserve
- Feel safe
- Inner peace
- Learn from what you do
- Let others help you
- Listen to my inner voice
- Live without being overwhelmed by life
- Live without condemning myself
- Live without judging myself
- Love myself unconditionally
- Not be taken advantage of
- Nurture myself
- Put my needs before the needs of others
- Put myself first
- Stand up for myself
- Take care of myself
- Trust other to carry some of the load
- Trust others to support you
- Be in the flow of life
- Be present

Emotional States

- Inappropriate response to having boundaries overrun attacks or lashes out at the wrong party. Feels overrun and under attack. Attacks self when the attack is coming from outside of self.
- Worries that an attack is imminent so they overreact. Constantly on watch for the imminent attack.
- Does not have a love of self. Puts themselves down in a derogatory way. Puts others before themselves.
- Depressed and feels as if life is a constant battle to stay safe and still they don't believe they can defend themselves.
- Maintains control and power while not being seen or heard, which is about protecting self. If you lock it into place and get rigid then you survive.
- Someone told them they were not good enough. They used that to stop themselves and retreat into a sense of powerlessness bringing down the shields/protection to be that identity. As long as there is weakness then there's an opportunity for connection.
- Feeling in danger. Being on alert to protect themselves. The message is don't get sick. On alert trying to defend themselves from attack. They hold this energy for some time but then can't hold it any longer. They give up fighting it.
- People are always "after me". They don't understand and they think I have time "to do". They don't talk "to me" they talk "at me". Not letting go of my resentment for the lack of appreciation.
- Can't hear the inner voice. Can't hear the good meaning advice given from others. Belief systems of being unworthy won't let them take it in.
- Reluctance to let others help them. They have to do it all themselves. Over extend self to do for others. Give, give, and give with no inflow of energy from self-giving. Won't allow the energy from others in. Inflow of energy is blocked.
- Just too much stuff to do. They bury themselves with activities. This keeps them from looking the issues of self. They then stress out when they can't get it all done. Stress keeps them out of the now.
- They have a big heart for others but not for self. Gives love and caring to others as a way of getting recognition. Has no sense of self in the process so the love and caring is a well meant illusion.

Cross Indexing: Myasthenia Gravis, Endocrine System Disorders, Lymphatic System Problems, Autoimmune disorders, Virus, AIDS & HIV, Temple pain/ pressure, Ear Problems, Labyrinthitis

Created Patterns

1. I am under attack.
2. I do not love myself.
3. I always feel unsafe.
4. I am stupid.
5. If I attack those that attack me I will be hurt, so I attack myself.
6. I am the victim.
7. I resent myself.
8. I resent those that attack me.
9. I can't respond to those that attack me.
10. I can't fight back.
11. I can't defend myself.

12. I always seem to attract mean people into my life.
13. I am an easy target for abuse.
14. I am picked on.
15. I am powerless.
16. I am powerless to stop others from hurting me.
17. I am taken advantage of.
18. I am unworthy.
19. I can't defend myself.
20. I can't get it all done.
21. I can't love myself.
22. I can't stand up to life.
23. I don't deserve.
24. I don't know when to defend myself.
25. I don't love myself.
26. I don't trust others to get thing done.
27. I have to please others to be loved.
28. I must condemn myself.
29. I must condemn myself for doing things wrong.
30. I must judge myself.
31. I shut down to survive.
32. I'm not safe anywhere.
33. It is dangerous to listen to my inner voice.
34. It is wrong to listen to my inner voice.
35. It is wrong to put myself first.
36. Life is overwhelming.
37. Life is unfair.
38. No one stands up for me.
39. Other people's needs before mine.
40. People always drop the ball and don't follow through.
41. People are out to get me.
42. The only way I am safe is to do nothing.
43. There's never time for my needs to be met.

* Look at themes of boundaries, self-esteem, criticism, power, worthiness, self-love, workaholic, needs (recognition, boundaries, love, nurturing, accepted), control, letting go, stress)

Thyroid Problems

Fears
- Fear of being overwhelmed
- Fears being forced to be quiet or not speak
- Fears being powerless in the face of injustice
- Fear of being overlooked
- Fear of not being able to speak
- Fear of being alone
- Fear of being unimportant and being forced to sacrifice

- Fear of my body
- Fear of not being enough
- Fear of carrying the burden
- Fear of myself (constantly attacking one's self)
- Fear of being judged
- Fear of shame
- Fear of guilt
- Fear of regret
- Fear of humiliation
- Fear of betrayal

Emotional States

- They have no control or voice in the face of injustice. They don't have the freedom or power to talk back. They feel intense anger injustices that must be endured and swallowed. When they have to swallow the injustice they feel humiliated and shamed. What they are feeling and experiencing presses in on them and builds a pressure. They feel overwhelmed by having to carry the burden.

Cross Indexing: Endocrine System Problems, Restless Leg Syndrome, Chronic Fatigue, Hashimoto's

Created Patterns

1. I always attach myself.
2. I am a pessimist.
3. I am a savior.
4. I am humiliated and can't say anything.
5. I am in danger.
6. I am misinterpreted.
7. I am never enough.
8. I am unjustly accused of….
9. I can't complain and be safe.
10. I can't defend myself against injustice.
11. I don't know how to live without drama.
12. I don't let people hear me.
13. I have to do things to be important.
14. I have to shut up.
15. I have to speak my truth.
16. I have to suffer in silence.
17. I must hold onto my anger.
18. I must swallow my words.
19. I'm not at peace.
20. I'm not relaxed.
21. If I say anything I will make it worse.
22. Life is dangerous.

Tibia – Left

Fears
- Fear that where they are in life is not reliable
- Fear of being in the right place at the wrong time
- Fear of attack
- Fear of being blamed
- Fear of losing their victim identity
- Fear of not being good enough
- Fear of change

Teachings
- Allowing
- An identity that takes responsibility for your choices
- An identity without prejudice toward _____
- Be good enough
- Be in the flow
- Be responsible for my choices
- Be true to myself
- Be who I am and be safe
- Be within my power without needing to diminish others
- Forgiveness
- Let go of the ancestral roles
- Let go
- Live without being a martyr
- Live without being a victim
- Live without being better than someone else
- Live without being imprisoned by ancestral roles / drama
  Live without needing to compare myself to others
- Live without resenting others because they have more
- Live without using martyrdom to feel powerful
- Live without using victim-hood to feel powerful
- Love
- Release resentment
- Unconditional love
- Whole

Emotional States
- Holding onto ungrounded fears based in an ancestral conflict / strife (could be gender, race, religion, groups, outsiders, etc.). One group against another – looking to hold the other accountable for all the bad things that happen. Not taking responsibility for making the decisions that led to events in their lives.

Cross Indexing: Leg Problems, Left-sided negative tendencies, Tibia – Right

Created Patterns

1. Bad things happen to me.
2. _____ is to blame for _____.
3. I'm not responsible for what happens to me.
4. I don't trust my inner voice.
5. I don't trust others.
6. I am disconnected from creator / god.
7. I am better than _____ (the prejudice you hold).
8. I am angry at _____.
9. I blame _____.
10. I resent _____.
11. I hate _____.
12. Others are out to get me.
13. People are out to get me (what people?).
14. Change is dangerous.
15. I can't change.
16. I can't be myself.
17. My life would be great if _____.
18. People who take responsibility are wrong.
19. I'm not good enough.
20. What prejudices are you holding? (gender, race, religions, groups, etc.)
21. I'm not good enough.

*Look at themes of responsibility, prejudice, allowing, ancestors, class systems, equality, judgment, love, oneness, self-respect, trust, boundaries, control, letting go, disconnection, jealousy, judgment

Tibia – Right

Fears

- Fear that where they are moving towards is not reliable
- Fear that their direction is out of sync
- Fear of being blamed
- Fear making decisions
- Fear of being responsible
- Fear of what others might have to say

Emotional States

- Unable to make decisions. Decision-making is stressful. Chaos gets created to divert from the real issue needing attention in the moment.
- This person does a lot of fault finding as a means of staying away from being responsible or making decisions themselves

- Doesn't really hear what others are saying to them. Hears what they want to hear and makes up the rest. This allows them to not understand the other person and stay safe in their own reality.

Cross Indexing: Leg Problems, Right-sided negative Tendencies, Tibia – left

Created Patterns
1. I must let others make my decisions for me.
2. Others tell me what to do.
3. Life is hard.
4. I must be something I'm not.
5. I can't let go of what stops me from going forward.
6. If I make my own decisions then I will be responsible.
7. Responsibility is dangerous.
8. I must do it my way or not at all.
9. My way of doing things is the best way.
10. I don't trust the direction of other people.
11. By finding fault in others I stay safe.
12. I know what is best for others.
13. Chaos keeps me safe.
14. I don't understand.

Tinnitus

Fears
- Fear of hearing criticism
- Fear of being judged
- Fear of knowing
- Fear of new
- Fear of information that will change their foundation
- Fear of change
- Fear of the future
- Fear of life / living
- Fear of being present

Teachings
- Allow for the flow of the universe
- Be comfortable in the silence
- Be ecologically balanced
- Be open to listening to the ideas of others
- Be safe in the silence
- Complete
- Create and be safe
- Create the time for creativity
- Create the time for fun
- Creator's definition of compassion
- Creator's definition of control
- Fun
- Hear your inner voice
- Listen and feel safe
- Listen and stay emotionally open
- Listen to others with discretion
- Listen to your inner voice and be safe
- Live an authentic life
- Live in the now
- Live without worry
- Make change with ease

- Make changes and be safe
- Make decisions and stay true to yourself
- Make mistakes and be safe
- Nurturance
- Nurture others
- Play
- Whole

Emotional States

- Does not hear information that is new or contrary to their beliefs.
- Creates an inner noise to not hear inner voice.
- Creative is struggling to survive inner voices from the past.
- Old burden has stopped spiritual growth.
- Stuck in the past.
- Brute forces their way through situations using old tools and skills.
- Rationalizes emotional turmoil, hides from emotional challenges.
- Worries…fears are out of proportion and out of control.
- This individual is making their own noise so they can't hear what is being said either by the inner voice or by others. They pretend to listen but they are not letting what is being said be really heard. They throw up a wall to information that is new or contrary to their already established ideas.
- This individual is not growing, they are going in circles. They are carrying an old burden. They are stopped in their spiritual growth. They are stuck in the past and won't let go of what no longer serves them. They have a rationale that they must do things the way they always been done. This individual will push their way through situations by sheer will and assertiveness using the same tools/ skills as they have always used. They refuse to try alternative or new approaches when confronted with an obstacle that clearly says this way of being in the world is not working.
- This person is trying to run away from emotional turmoil by using their intellect and rational thought. They do this by attempting to find a sanctuary from their emotional storm. The emotional turmoil follows them and keeps coming back, The worries feel as if they are getting bigger and impossible to control. The emotions related to the worry (futurization of 'what if') flatten the person. They feel overwhelmed as if the life force has been knocked out of them. The fears are out of proportion and out of control. This person does not know how to be any other way in the world than in this state of continual worry. The worry is a smoke screen to keep them from having to deal with their own issues of an immature consciousness that is striving to grow into what is unknown.*This person probably had a parent whose main emotion was continual worry about what might happen.

Cross Indexing: Circulatory disorders, Brain problems, Aging, TMJ, Acoustic Neuroma, Hypertension, Arteriosclerosis, Addiction – smoking

Repeated Patterns: Doesn't like being with themselves alone, Out of sync with the flow of life, Is not open to listening to the ideas of others of it they go up against what they believe, Never enough time in their lives for creative expression, Listening is a dangerous endeavor

Created Patterns

1. Bad things always happen to me.
2. Change is dangerous.
3. I am blocked from hearing my inner voice.
4. I am depressed.
5. I am disconnected from creator.
6. I am overwhelmed by worry/fear.
7. I am paralyzed by worry.
8. I can face my fears and be safe.
9. I can't let go of what no longer serves me.
10. I can't play.
11. I can't stop worrying about things.
12. I can't throw anything away.
13. I can't trust my inner voice.
14. I don't listen to others.
15. I hate waste.
16. I MAKE things happen.
17. I may need that someday.
18. I must do things the way they have always been done.
19. I must listen to mom/ dad and worry about the future.
20. I must worry to keep others safe.
21. I must worry to stay safe.
22. I need to run away from my life.
23. I'm abandoned by god.
24. I'm afraid of my inner voice.
25. I'm not creative.
26. Listening to my inner voice will get me killed/locked up.
27. Listening to others will get me in to trouble.
28. My life is out of control.
29. My problems are just too big for me to handle.
30. Nurturing others is weakness-people should just suck it up.
31. The old way has always worked so why try something new.
32. Things must be done my way I know best.
33. Things will never change.
34. Waste not want not.
35. What sound/ voice are you trying to hide from?
36. Whose voice is in your ears?
37. You must be practical about things.
38. You never know where the next meal will come from.

*Look at themes of denial, allowing, anger, boundaries, overwhelm, clairaudience, control, higher self-connection, listening, loving yourself, mistakes, now, peace, self-knowledge, spiritual growth, trauma, creativity, control and letting go, defenses, trust and authenticity.

Toes

Fears
- Fear of being run over by someone else
- Fear of losing position
- Fear of being taken over
- Fear of being shown to be less than
- Fear of going in the wrong direction
- Fear of being destroyed by criticism
- Fear of being shamed / ridiculed
- Fear of being unloved
- Fear of being abandoned
- Fear of obstacles

Emotional States
- Lack of respectful attitude. Instead of respecting someone else's truth they want to beat down and go through their position instead of honoring and finding common ground or a way to accomplish both ends, find a new path. The want to build a highway of their design through the wall.
- Lofty goals have them wanting to float off instead of honoring the needs of a foundation and then building on top of that. Trying to float away keeps them out of balance.

Cross Indexing: Foot Problems, Bunions, Athlete's Foot, Spurs, Plantar Fasciitis, Wounded Creative Core

Created Patterns
1. If I don't take care of the little stuff _____.
2. I am afraid of being seen as wrong.
3. If I make a mistake I will die/be hurt.
4. I know best.
5. I know what needs to be done.
6. I know more than others.
7. My way is the best way.
8. I can do what I want.
9. Everyone knows I am always right.
10. People will support me. Whether they want to or not.
11. I am off balance.
12. I am in control when I am doing what I want to do.

Tongue Problems

Fears
- Fear of saying what I think
- Fear of speaking
- Fear of tasting the joy of life

- Fear of enjoying food
- Fear of taking what is needed to savor
- Fear of upset
- Fear of their anger
- Fear of causing more suffering
- Fear of people that are untrustworthy
- Fear of betraying themselves

Emotional States
- They hold their words to keep harmony / peace. The energy of those words are stopped in the tongue. If they are angry words, then an inflammation will result.
- They have shut down their enjoyment of life. What they take in for nurturance is perfunctory to sustaining the body. They are punishing themselves for the suffering they think they caused.
- Their words get jumbled up when they need to speak their truth to people that they don't trust.

Cross Indexing: CTE, Concussion, Parkinson's, Alzheimer's, Mouth Problems

Created Patterns
1. I can't taste the good things of life.
2. I don't deserve good things.
3. I don't know what the truth is.
4. If I tell the truth I will be hurt.
5. I must bite my tongue to not hurt people.
6. I can't say what I want to say.
7. I can't express anger when I want.
8. I must punish myself for the suffering of others.

Tonsil Problems

Fears
- Fear of people not like me
- Fear of not letting my anger out
- Fear of talking back
- Fear of taking in something not good for me
- Fear of the unknown
- Fear of angry people
- Fear of saying what I think
- Fear of standing up to abusive people
- Fear of being attacked
- Fear of defending myself
- Fear of being hurt

Emotional States
- Taking in what may not be good for you. No discernment in what may be perceived as anger and they take it into themselves. They may hold the energy of angry words unsaid.

Cross Indexing: Throat Problems, Sore Throat

Created Patterns
1. I have been suppressing a strong feeling of anger/fear for a long time *(What's the anger/fear about?)*.
2. I am irritated at _____.
3. I never get my own way.
4. *Why do you need to block the flow of life?*
5. I have to swallow / take on someone else's abuse.
6. I have to put up with angry people.
7. I can't talk back.
8. I am under attack and I cannot defend myself.

Tooth Infection

Fears
- Fear of my intuition
- Fear of listening to my inner voice
- Fear of trusting myself
- Fear of change
- Fear of moving
- Fear of doing
- Fear of not doing what others tell me
- Fear of being wrong

Emotional States
- Wrong ideas about people's intentions hold little value but are given immense (out of proportion) importance in deciding direction. Out of coherence with your own inner compass.
- Holding out for the brass ring and ends up not doing anything.

Cross Indexing: Teeth, Abscess

Created Patterns
1. I must do what others tell me even if my intuition says something else.
2. If I just wait I will get the good stuff.
3. I never get anything done because I am waiting for things to change.
4. I don't listen to my intuition, I don't trust myself.

5. Change is dangerous.
6. If I get what I want bad things will happen.

Tourette's Syndrome

Fears
- Fear of their anger (ancestral) in a hyper-state of awareness
- Fear of others controlling them
- Fear of being explained away
- Fear of being made invisible
- Fear of being trapped

Emotional States
- Lack of nurturing. Nourishment is not being taken in. Outside influence controlling life force. Growth has stopped. Lack of creativity and desire for life. Doesn't know how to stop others from controlling life force.

Created Patterns
1. I am controlled by others.
2. I don't know what it feels like to be nourished.
3. I am overwhelmed.
4. I am overrun.
5. My rights are being violated.
6. I am not protected.
7. I am imprisoned.
8. I am a prisoner.
9. My privacy has been taken from me.
10. No one will leave me alone.
11. My mother/father control me.
12. I have no privacy.
13. I resent my mother/father.
14. Others make my decisions for me.
15. I am no good.
16. I am worthless.
17. I am a nobody.
18. I don't know how to take in nourishment.
19. I don't know how to accept/receive love.
20. I don't trust myself.

Toxins – Aluminum

Fears
- Fear of losing my identity
- Fear of being lost
- Fear of feeling guilty
- Fear of no purpose
- Fear of not belonging
- Fear of being unheard
- Fear of being invisible

Emotional States
- Perception of their life purpose is wrong. Loss of identity. They are in a state of non-peace. Communication is blocked. They have old habits that hurt their bodies. Feels guilty and fearful.

Cross Indexing: Alzheimer's, Kidney Problems

Created Patterns
1. I never do anything right.
2. I am always at fault.
3. I hate myself.
4. I am no good/worthless/not worthy.
5. I am powerless.
6. I don't know who I am.
7. I have no way of knowing my life purpose but I feel as if all I do is wrong.
8. I am afraid of _____.
9. I am guilty of _____.
10. I have no inner peace.
11. No one hears me.
12. When I speak I become invisible.
13. I keep doing the same thing over and over even though it is bad for me.

Toxins – Asbestos

Fears
- Fear of happiness
- Fear of not being punished
- Fear of letting go
- Fear of not having not having purpose
- Fear of being alone
- Fear of being abandoned
- Fear of open space
- Fear of being with themselves

Emotional States
- Stuck negative emotional feelings

Cross Indexing: Cancer – lungs

Created Patterns
1. I never do anything right.
2. I am always at fault.
3. I hate myself.
4. I am no good/worthless/not worthy.
5. I am powerless.
6. I am unhappy with life.
7. I absorb the bad feelings of others.
8. I must take on the troubles of the world.
9. I can't forgive and let go of bad things that have happened to me.
10. I resent _____.
11. I am overwhelmed by _____.
12. I regret _____.
13. I am guilty so I take the anger of others to be punished and feel better about myself.

Toxins – Cadmium

Fears
- Fear of being out of control
- Fear of being seen as vulnerable
- Fear of joy
- Fear of peace
- Fear of failure
- Fear of being seen as wrong
- Fear of being hurt

Emotional States
- Loss of control creates a hard method of being in the world to appear in control.

Cross Indexing: Kidney Problems, Cancer, Skin Problems, Adrenal problems, Aging, Addiction – Smoking, Chronic cough

Created Patterns
1. I never do anything right.
2. I am always at fault.
3. I hate myself.

4. I am no good/worthless/not worthy.
5. I am powerless.
6. I am out of control.
7. I must be tough to be in control.
8. I am hard on people because they need it.
9. I have no joy.
10. I have no inner peace.

Toxins – Glyphosate

Fears
- Fear of their mother
- Fear of nature
- Fear of their power
- Fear of their divine nature
- Fear of the unknown
- Fear of being at peace
- Fear of the system
- Fear of being crushed by the system
- Fear of going against the system

Emotional States
- Lack of connection with our foundations. Hardcore resistance to the truth of one's existence. Not acknowledging your true nature an illusion in the field of soul. Anchored in ego-identity of a global state of non-peace and helpless in the face of that information to do anything except be carried by the wave of connection in the matrix of fear and manipulation.

Cross Indexing: Alzheimer's, Lymphoma, Overweight, skin problems, Parkinson's, Intestinal Problems, Allergies – Gluten Intolerance, Irritable Bowel Syndrome, Colitis, Autism, Cancer (Breast, Lymph, brain), Celiac, Diabetes

Created Patterns
1. I never do anything right.
2. I am always at fault.
3. I hate myself.
4. I am no good/worthless/not worthy.
5. I am powerless.
6. There is no soul.
7. There is no divine nature.
8. I have no inner peace.
9. I am afraid of _____.
10. I must do what the system wants even if it hurts me.

Toxins – Lead

Fears
- Fear of growth (spiritual)
- Fear of change
- Fear of death
- Fear of abandonment
- Fear of the man (authority)
- Fear of betrayal
- Fear of not getting what is needed to survive
- Fear of having to rely on others
- Fear that others will let them down
- Fear that will be hurt/killed by those in authority

Emotional States
- Soul's journey of evolution under attack. Lack of discipline and patience. Feeling unprotected and vulnerable from those you should trust. Betrayed by the system (education, government, community, etc.)

Cross Indexing: Brain Problem, Developmental Disorders, Abdominal Problems, Hypertension, Joint Problems, Infertility

Created Patterns
1. I never do anything right.
2. I am always at fault.
3. I hate myself.
4. I am no good/worthless/not worthy.
5. I am powerless.
6. I am in danger.
7. I am unsafe/ vulnerable.
8. I have been betrayed by the people I depend on.
9. I have been assaulted by the system.
10. I have nothing I can rely on in my life.
11. I am impatient, I need things done now.

Toxins – Mercury

Fears
- Fear of knowing
- Fear of attaining knowledge
- Fear of being in one place for any length of time
- Fear of being found
- Fear of having their truth reflected back to them
- Fear of their imagination

- Fear of the creative part of themselves
- Fear of being criticized
- Fear of the truth of life
- Fear of being seen
- Fear of people getting too close

Emotional States
- They do not want to learn about the world they are in. They do not want to learn new information. They have low self-esteem and hide in the background as much as possible. They tend to anger easily.

Cross Indexing: Autism, Neural Disorders, cardiovascular diseases, diabetes, Attention Deficit Disorder, Pineal Gland problems, Endocrine System Disorders, Kidney problems, Mouth Problems, Gum problems and Teeth Problems

Created Patterns
1. I never do anything right.
2. I am always at fault.
3. I hate myself.
4. I am no good/worthless/not worthy.
5. I am powerless.
6. I don't want to learn new stuff.
7. I am tired of learning.
8. I don't want to know _____.
9. I must keep on the move to be safe.
10. I don't use my imagination, it just gets me in trouble.
11. I am afraid of living.
12. I am afraid of being seen.
13. If I let people close to me they will hurt me.
14. If I let people see me they will criticize me.

Toxins – Polychlorinated Biphenyls (PCBs)

Fears
- Fear of peace
- Fear of life
- Fear of hearing the truth
- Fear of being hurt by the truth
- Fear of joy
- Fear of belonging
- Fear of fitting in
- Fear they will lose themselves
- Fear they will become nothing

Emotional States
- Odd resonance – disharmonious – doesn't feel like they fit in with the environment. A sense of not belonging and out-of-sync.

Cross Indexing: Acne, Rash, Lungs, Cancer

Created Patterns
1. I never do anything right.
2. I am always at fault.
3. I hate myself.
4. I am no good/worthless/not worthy.
5. I am powerless.
6. I am out of sync with the world.
7. Everything is out of harmony.
8. I don't fit.
9. I don't belong.
10. Life is not joyous.
11. I ignore the hard answers to hard questions.
12. I don't listen to the advice of others.

Trigeminal Neuralgia

Fears
- Fear of pain
- Fear of losing their freedom
- Fear of my heart
- Fear of being alone
- Fear of rejection
- Fear of shame
- Fear of humiliation
- Fear of being revealed
- Fear of living
- Fear of others

Emotional States
- Secrets that touch their identity have been revealed. These are secrets that hold the most vulnerable part of their identity, aspects that have never been revealed. There was a communication leak that caused deep pain, shame and humiliation resulting in them not being able to show their face.
- Painful communication.

Cross Indexing: Neuritis, Nerve problems, Face/head Problems, Multiple Sclerosis, ancestral

Created Patterns

1. Facing the world is painful.
2. It is painful to face the world.
3. There is no way out.
4. I need my pain to keep people away.
5. My secrets have been violated.
6. I must keep the secrets.
7. It is safer being in pain than facing the world.
8. Without the pain I am nothing.
9. I have lost the reason to live.
10. Life is too painful to continue.
11. I want to die.
12. I am afraid of pain.
13. I am afraid of being enslaved.
14. I must run away or they will catch and trap me.
15. I am shamed and humiliated.
16. I must hide and crumble.

Tuberculosis

Fears

- Fear of guilt
- Fear of living
- Fear of not dying
- Fear of feeling more regret
- Fear of losing their home
- Fear of not knowing where they belong
- Fear having made a mistake
- Fear of change
- Fear of moving
- Fear of never being able to go back home

Emotional States

- Lost in a sea of confusion and loss they can't seem to figure out how to get out of the mess they are in. Being held hostage to their guilt. Feels overwhelming grief and sorrow. Every breath hurts and aches with regrets and the guilt they feel.

Cross Indexing: Lung Problems, Bacteria, Infection, Virus, Cancer – Lung

Created Patterns

1. I must hurt others before they hurt me.
2. I must take advantage of others before they take advantage of me.

3. People are going to take things from me.
4. My needs must always be met first.
5. I must get them before they get me.
6. I must be first.
7. I don't care what other people say I will do what I want.
8. I am guilty.
9. I regret _____.

Tumors – Lipomas

Fears
- Fear of being left/ starvation
- Fear of needing to hide what they have
- Fear of not having what you need to survive
- Fear of letting go
- Fears vulnerability
- Fear of injustice

Teachings
- Accept and receive love
- Be honored
- Be respected
- Be valued
- Being in the flow
- Being in the now
- Being present
- Creator's definition and perspective of trust
- Difference between what belongs to me and what belongs to others
- Forgive
- Let go
- Live without anger
- Live without betrayal
- Live without feeling abandoned
- Live without feeling left behind
- Live without holding onto anger
- Live without holding onto betrayal
- Live without indulging in fault finding
- Loving yourself
- Trust
- Unconditional love

Emotional States
- Finds life moving way to fast. Can't absorb the changes fast enough to keep up. This creates confusion and anger. Feels left behind and ignored.
- Unable to let go of what has happened in the past. Is still trying to figure out what happened and why. Wants an explanation that satisfies the ego. Keeps demanding an explanation. Feels ignored because no one is giving them sufficient information. The answers are not being heard because they don't fit within their reality or what they want to hear.
- Weeping under the skin. Holds in regrets and remorse. Heart feels abandoned and betrayed.
- Unable to let go of what does not belong to them. An injustice against someone becomes their cause célèbre. They are taking someone else's energy into their body.

Cross Indexing: Sebaceous Cysts, Cysts

Created Patterns
1. I am angry at _____.
2. I am jealous of _____.
3. I am left behind.
4. I am not honored.
5. I am not respected.
6. I am out of sync with the world.
7. I am unloved.
8. I can't forgive _____.
9. I can't forgive myself for _____.
10. I can't let go.
11. I can't understand because no one is telling me what I want to heart.
12. I don't matter anymore.
13. I don't trust myself/ others.
14. I don't understand _____.
15. I don't understand the world.
16. I hate _____.
17. I have been abandoned by _____.
18. I have been betrayed by _____.
19. I have been repressing/feeling a strong emotion of hatred/anger/resent for a long time.
20. I must fight the battles for those weaker than me.
21. I must have the answers.
22. I must protect others in the face of injustice.
23. I must take the pain of others.
24. I need the story to feel complete.
25. I need the story to feel valued.
26. I regret _____.
27. I should have _____ *(what is the remorse in your life)*.
28. Life moves to fast.
29. My father doesn't love me.
30. My mother doesn't love me.
31. No matter what I do I am always behind.
32. No one cares.
33. No one listens to me.
34. The anger protects me from _____.
35. The hate protects me.
36. There is no love lost between me and my parents.
37. *What is the emotional hurt you have been suppressing?*

*Look at themes of boundaries, power, Father, Mother, anger, betrayal, jealousy, control, envy, forgiveness, letting go, love, loving yourself, regret, rejection, unconditional love, unmet needs, abandonment, anger, boundaries, control and letting go, disconnection

U's

Umbilical Hernia

Fears
- Fear of being alone
- Fear of losing their mother
- Fear of losing love
- Fear of losing their identity
- Fear of not meeting the needs of others and losing their love
- Fear of losing their strength
- Fear of losing themselves in the needs of others

Emotional States
- A weakened connection to the female-mother figure. There is a conflict between the two where their needs for support are at odds with each other. They can't let go of the female figure and they can't get their needs met.

Cross Indexing: Hernia

Repeating Patterns: Victim

Created Patterns
1. I am unsupported by my family/friends.
2. I am being pulled in many directions.
3. Everybody is angry at me for not taking care of them.
4. All people want to do is take from me.
5. I don't have any way of having inner peace.
6. I am afraid of losing my family/friends.
7. I will be alone if I get my needs met.
8. Everyone comes before me.

Upper Respiratory Infection (URI)

Fears
- Fear of not being good enough
- Fear of being alone
- Fear of being forgotten
- Fear of the feeling of injustice being found wrong
- Fear of forgiving only to be hurt again
- Fear of not working hard enough

- Fear of saying the wrong thing
- Fear of not being liked
- Fear of injustice
- Fear of being blamed for something they didn't do

Emotional States
- Running their life as if they have to constantly prove they're worthy of their position in life. Never quite worthy enough, always believing they are not good enough. So they work harder than everyone else. Never speaking up against injustices and never feeling like they can be themselves. They feel guilty for all things that have gone wrong and then they work harder to make it better.

Cross Indexing: Lung problems, Throat Problems, Pneumonia, Bronchitis, Virus, Nose Problems, Cough – Chronic, Sore Throat, Cold

Created Patterns
1. I'm not worthy.
2. I can't forgive myself for what I have done.
3. I can't speak up about injustice, I will be found guilty if I do.
4. I'm not good enough to be doing what I am doing.
5. I must push myself until there is nothing left.
6. I must present a different face to be loved.
7. I am guilty of _____.
8. I am depressed.
9. I must judge others before they judge me.
10. I am forced to do what others tell me to do.
11. I don't understand the points of view of others.
12. I can't forgive what has been done to me.
13. I can't be myself with others.

Urinary Tract Infection (Cystitis)

Fears
- Fear of having nothing to give
- Fear their perception will misinterpret – lead them astray and they won't be able to pivot
- Fear of not being good enough
- Fear of rejection
- Fear of being controlled
- Fear of being manipulated

Emotional States
- Warm exclusions, deceptive rejections, create needless anxiety of inferiority. Hollow promises to do more yield uncompromised rejections. Unwillingness to let go of the things that should have

been wiped out of their inner vision a long time ago. Hollow first impressions. Ancestral rejections are relived in relationships.
- Weak impressions of the past haunt their waking hours. These impressions have no value, they are but illusions that are held sacrosanct and given an uncompromising power in the here and now. The past they remember never existed. It was all lies told to them to manipulate them and now it is held as true history. They know this and still play a bit part in keeping the lies alive. They have been manipulated to anger which when they find out perpetuates the anger at the deception and manipulation. Every word has an edge. Even words of love feel as if they could but with little warning that the person had crossed a line. Underlying anger can be set to erupt. Heart has been broken and anger has replaced the hurt heart and never resolved.

Cross Indexing: Bladder Problems, Bacteria, Kidney Problems, Excretory System, Venereal Disease, Cytomegalovirus, Arthritis – Reactive, Symptoms

Repeating Patterns: Wounded Creative Core, relationships are untrustworthy. Doesn't see beyond the surface of others, memories that are untrue – live as if they were. Feels wronged by those in authority.

Created Patterns

1. I will never get what I want.
2. Why are you so angry inside?
3. Everything is wrong.
4. I am sad.
5. I angry at the world.
6. I can never be happy.
7. I am powerless to change things.
8. People manipulate me.
9. You can't trust people who say they love you.
10. Can't let go of events that inflame.
11. I am worthless.
12. Others are better than me.
13. _____ is to blame for my problems *(Why are you blaming someone else?)*.
14. I am pissed at _____.
15. I am bitter at _____.
16. I must control myself.
17. I must control those around me.
18. I must be in control at all times to be safe.
19. I must control others to be important.
20. People who control me hurt me.
21. I don't trust myself.
22. I don't trust others.
23. I am being controlled by _____.
24. I am in charge.
25. I can't forgive _____ for lying to me.
26. I reject people that don't do it my way.
27. People in authority over me hurt me *(who?)*.
28. I am angry at _____.
29. *Who irritates you and why? How does that irritation serve you?*

V's

Vaginitis

Fears
- Fear of their creative ideas being corrupted by others
- Fear that their creativity will be shot down
- Fear of being shamed
- Fear of their inner voice
- Fear of knowing

Emotional States
- Warmth is lost. They feel nothing that makes or gives them the feeling of loves warmth. Love has been lost to a cold dark forest of the night.
- A fire rages in blocked sexuality. Shame and hatred of what is creative by parental figures.
- Obscured curses from unknown sources. Takes the opinions of others instead of listening to their inner direction.

Cross Indexing: Inflammation, Infection, Bacteria

Created Patterns
1. I am shameful.
2. Creativity is shameful.
3. Sexuality is anger and hatred.
4. Sexuality is shameful.
5. Love is nothing but a cold scam.
6. I am unloved.
7. I am cursed.
8. Others know better than me.
9. I hate sex.
10. Sex is wrong.
11. Creativity is wrong.
12. I must be who I am told to be.
13. My very existence is wrong.
14. I am worthless.
15. I am stupid and I don't know anything worth knowing.

Varicose Veins

Fears
- Fears joy being stopped
- Fear of giving not being returned

- Fear of expectations
- Fear of being present
- Fear of joy
- Fear of bad things happening

Emotional States

- Giving is corrupted and not returned. The flow of joy has been broken. They are now expected to give and that becomes a heavy burden. Not allowed to play and experience joy as a child. As an adult joy is blocked because of the fear of what will happen it if they put down the burden and allow themselves joy.

Cross Indexing: Wounded Creative Core, Leg Problems, Thrombosis, Deep Vein Thrombosis, Aging, Vein Problems

Created Patterns

1. I want to run away *(What do you want to run away from and why?)*.
2. It's useless.
3. Nothing works out.
4. I am overburdened/ overwhelmed.
5. My burdens stop me from joy.
6. It will never be any better.
7. Nothing works for me.
8. *Why are you afraid to be present in your body?*
9. I can't have joy.
10. Joy is for others not me.
11. I can't play because I will be stopped.
12. When I give love it is never returned in kind.
13. I am sad all the time.

Vasculitis

Fears

- Fear of heart break
- Fear of knowing
- Fear of connecting to their soul
- Fear of the future
- Fear of bad things happening
- Fear of being invisible
- Fear of being seen as weak
- Fear of expressing compassion
- Fear of living
- Fear of joy

Emotional States

- Locked into a dogma (religious or person in authority's view) that created a hardened world view. Disconnected from their heart and the expression of compassion.
- Not listening to their higher self. Refuses to let go of ways that are conflict with higher self. Self-acceptance issues. Disconnected from Creator. Closed off from others. Imbalance in the feminine.
- Workaholic behaviors to avoid dealing with heart/ purpose. Worries about small problems. They are miserable.
- Feels like they have a meaningless life. Expression in the world is a wooden response. They feel anonymous.
- This person was concentrating on a path of self-development and individuation. They had new hopes and desires. They felt strong and stable. This person was talented and had numerous opportunities for self-expression. Then they took on a set of beliefs, possibly religious dogma or from a person in authority that limited their self expression and harden their worldview. The numerous opportunities for growth became only surface expressions that worked to cover over the hardened feelings and rigid viewpoint. The hardening was an effort to reduce what the perceived authority would know about them. This started off as an avenue for protection and led to long term hardening of their outlook. They have lost touch with a heart that feels compassion for others. Their hardened exterior projects a hardened heart.
- This person is receiving guidance from the divine light of their soul and they are not listening. They don't listen to anything that seems to come from the outside. They do not recognize the presence of their higher self and reject that information as coming from another source…not self. They have been told that they are 'all wrong' but they are not listening and they are refusing to change direction. This person has issues of self-acceptance. Self-acceptance is about being comfortable enough with self to listen to and recognize wisdom from whatever source it may come from. This person has compromised some aspect of their own beliefs and values. They are feeling numb or out of touch with those around them. They may also feel disconnected from God/Creator/Source. There is an imbalance in the feminine. This person is closed off from others. This person may be seen as domineering and selfish.
- This person is headed in a direction that is cutoff from their heart and spirit so they are standing still in a situation that they hate. This person takes on a lot of work so that they don't have to reconnect with their purpose/heart. The joy that this person would feel is filled with worry about small problems. This person does not know what it is to work with joy in their heart. Having to work is a burden. They are miserable.
- This person is feeling dead inside and emotionless. Their behavior is automatic; they just go with the flow. They feel like they have been buried alive. Their expression in the world is a wooden response. They feel anonymous and as if they have no purpose or significance in this world. They feel as if they have led a meaningless life and what little they have accomplished has disappeared and been covered over…buried never to be seen or recognized.

Cross Indexing: Thrombosis, DVT, Heart Problems, Circulatory disorders, Behcet's Syndrome, Henoch-Schonlein pupura, Polyarteritis, Multiple Myeloma, Lupus, Wegeners Granulomatosis

Created Patterns

1. I don't trust my intuition.
2. I don't trust myself.

EMOTIONAL PATTERNS

3. Life is a struggle/hard.
4. I am miserable.
5. Work is not supposed to be fun.
6. Feelings are dangerous.
7. I can't move forward.
8. I must do what others tell me to do.
9. I must be sensible.
10. I must conform to what people want to be loved/wanted/employed.
11. I must protect myself from others.
12. If people saw who I truly am I would be hurt.
13. I don't know what joy is.
14. I don't know what joy feels like.
15. What others think of me is important.
16. I can't be myself and be safe.
17. Compassion is weakness.
18. If there is a religious dogma the person practice, look at the beliefs that lack compassion, based in fear, and project intolerance.
19. Pantheism is evil.
20. Pantheism is pagan.
21. Pagans are evil.
22. I'm not loved.
23. I don't love myself.
24. Listening to your inner voice is dangerous.
25. I don't accept myself.
26. I'm not good enough.
27. I am disconnected from god.
28. I am disconnected from the people around me.
29. I am disconnected from my life.
30. I am only going through the motions.
31. I'm not accepted.
32. I'm not really engaged in life.
33. I hate what I do.
34. Life is a burden.
35. I am miserable.
36. There is no time to play.
37. There is no time for me.
38. I must sacrifice myself so that everything is in control.
39. Chaos is dangerous.
40. I am invisible.
41. I am depressed.
42. No one loves me.
43. I don't know what love is.
44. I have no life purpose.
45. I have no reason for being here.

Vein Problems

Fears
- Fear of heartlessness
- Fear of having no one care
- Fear of giving and giving with no return
- Fear of being taken advantage of
- Fear of betrayal
- Fear of being present

Emotional States
- There is no flow to giving and receiving. They feel that if they give they will be rewarded in kind. That doesn't happen. They look for love outside of themselves and are not looking to themselves for a centering self-love that is balanced by the act of giving. They are fearful of being lied to by people that are supposed to love them.

Cross Indexing: Vasculitis, Artery Problems

Created Patterns
1. I was never allowed to be a child / boy / girl.
2. There is no way out.
3. I was never a child.
4. I am responsible for everything.
5. I am stuck and have to accept this.
6. I am forced to lie.
7. I'm not free to feel.
8. There is no joy in living.
9. I am stopped from getting what I want.
10. I give and give and never get anything back.
11. People who love me lie to me.

Venereal Disease

Fears
- Fear of guilt being seen
- Fear of having their heart broken
- Fear of being alone
- Fear of being shamed
- Fear of their bodies

Emotional States

- Creative expression has been stopped because of criticism by people that are supposed to love them. They feel under attack. Their life is out of balance in an effort to get what they think they don't have.
- Shamed as a child when they became aware of their bodies. The child had no understanding of the shame that they had been forced to take on. This left them with the sense that their bodies were shameful.

Cross indexing: Wounded creative core, Herpes, AIDS & HIV, Virus, Ancestral

Created Patterns

1. I must be punished.
2. I am shameful/ sinful.
3. Sex is bad.
4. I am guilty of _____.
5. I am powerless.
6. People criticize what I do.
7. I'm not good enough.
8. Relationships are hurtful.
9. I must disguise my sexuality.
10. I am out of balance.
11. I am unwanted.
12. I am being used.
13. There is no balance in my relationships.
14. I am humiliated.

Vertigo

Fears

- Fears being out of balance
- Fear of falling
- Fear of failing
- Fear of being forced to take on too much
- Fear of being forced to give and give
- Fear of asking for help
- Fear of being seen as not good enough
- Fear of hearing their personal truth

Emotional States

- Working hard to keep things on an even keel. Won't ask for help. Has placed heavy demands on themselves.

- Concerned about how they appear to others (materially). Life feels repetitious and monotonous. Act without thinking things through.
- In pain; caused by the heavy burdens place on them. Hides the emotions of anger and frustration. They fake compassion, gentleness and kindness. The source of nurturance has become a source of destruction.
- Lost their sense of direction in life. Fear self-evaluation. Fears going into the silence and hearing the answers they seek.
- Life is associated with service; high personal standards and ethics. They have put on a facade for others to see. They can be harsh and judgmental to distract from their personal truth.
- An aspect of self is not functioning/has shut down (masculine or feminine). Another aspect of self has taken over and is working frenetically to keep everything on an even keel. There is a need for outside help or assistance but this individual insists on doing it themselves and not asking for help. This person has placed heavy demands on themselves. This person's life is passing them by while they believe they have to work very hard just to keep everything 'afloat'
- The creative-intuitive-feeling aspect of self is obscured by a concern about how they appear to others especially around the material body. This individual is going in a circle and their life feels like it is one of monotony and endless repetition. In much of their life they are behaving automatically. They act without thinking things through.
- This person is in a degree of discomfort and pain (inner and maybe physical) by the heavy burdens placed on them. They are angry and frustrated. For the most part the anger and frustration is hidden away from those around them. They cover over that aspect of themselves by demonstrating compassion, gentleness, and kindness. What is supposed to nurture them and make them happy has actually become a source of destruction of those aspects of self they work so hard to show the outside world: compassion, gentleness, beauty, and kindness. What was supposed to nurture has proved to be rigid and unyielding…lacking compassion.
- This person had made choices in their life that have proven to be frightening and uncomfortable. They made these choices because of confusion, troubles and/or worry. They feel as if they have lost their sense of direction in life. They have been shown the higher path of light. They know that they need to develop a higher awareness in their decisions but the ability to do that seems to dissolves into darkness when they get close to their fears. They are afraid of entering that space between the conscious and unconscious to get the answers. They are afraid of what they will find there. They fear self-evaluation.
- This person's life has been associated with service. They are seen as having high personal standards and ethics. They may appear to strive for perfection and order. They have put on a facade for others to see. It is a beautiful facade that dazzles and distracts from the honest truth of who they are underneath. They are not completely honest with people. This person can be harsh, critical and judgmental of others to distract from their personal truth(s). This person is dancing in circles around who they truly are instead of dealing with their own inner truths.

Cross Indexing: Hip Problems, Ear Problems, Labyrinthitis, Dizziness, Ear Problems, Brain disorders, Circulatory disorders

Created Patterns
1. I don't know how to receive.
2. I don't know what it feels like to receive.
3. I must do everything myself.
4. I can't trust others to be there when I need them.
5. I don't trust others.

EMOTIONAL PATTERNS

6. _____ betrayed me.
7. I must work hard to get anywhere.
8. I must always work hard to be of value.
9. I don't know what balance is.
10. I don't know what balance feels like.
11. People judge me based on what I look like.
12. I must be perfect.
13. If I'm not perfect people will not like me/love me/ respect me.
14. If I'm not perfect I will be rejected.
15. I make the wrong choices.
16. People judge me.
17. Life is boring.
18. I see no purpose in living.
19. I am angry at _____.
20. I am frustrated by _____.
21. I have no purpose in life.
22. I don't know where I am going.
23. People don't want to know the truth.
24. The truth will hurt me.
25. I am bad.
26. I am sinful.
27. I don't know how to take care of myself.
28. I don't know what it feels like to take care of myself.
29. If I ask for help I am weak.
30. You must never let them see you cry.
31. Crying makes you weak.
32. I can't be vulnerable and be safe.
33. Being vulnerable is being weak.
34. I listen to what people think about me.
35. What people think about me is important.
36. People are mean (this is an 'all' versus a 'some').
37. Compassion is a wasted emotion.
38. If I slow down, bad things will happen.
39. I can't slow down.

Viruses

Fears
- Fears being worthless
- Fears powerless anger and/or hatred
- Fear of letting go of old hurts
- Fear of joy
- Fear that if they feel joy it will be taken away
- Fears not deserving

Teachings
- Forgiveness
- Letting go of grudges
- Letting go of resentment
- Letting go of bitterness
- Safe when other people are fighting
- Getting my needs met without getting sick
- Complete
- Whole

- How to receive the tone / vibration that transforms the (name of virus) virus
- Teach body exactly what to do to clear virus (focus on base of spine)
- Difference between my worthiness issues and the viruses' issues
- Difference between my abandonment issues and a virus' abandonment issues

Emotional States
- Holding onto negative thoughts – bitterness / mean / resentment.
- Negative thoughts fester and may become worthiness issue.
- Something in life is creating a block of negative energy.
- Negative issue just keeps getting reinforced.
- Taking in the negative energy stops the joy flowing.

Cross Indexing: Associated body part infected by the virus, specific viral infection, other symptoms

Repeating Patterns: There social interactions are restricted based on the resentments they hold. Their intimate relationships are fraught with arguments. They then get sick to get their needs met within that relationship. Early feeling of abandonment and low self-worth has also dominated their adult life.

Created Patterns
1. I always come last.
2. I am going to die.
3. I get everything that comes along.
4. I have a grudge against.
5. I must meet everyone else's needs first.
6. I never have time to take care of myself.
7. I only get a day off when I am sick.
8. I see only the bad things of life.
9. I'm not good enough.
10. I'm not worthy.
11. I'm not worthy of being loved / respected.
12. I'm rejected by my mother / father.
13. My father has no time for me.
14. My mother has no time for me.
15. My needs are not being met.
16. The only time I can let down is when I am sick.
17. The only time I get attention / love is when I am sick.
18. The virus is triggered every time I feel unworthy.
19. The virus is triggered every time I feel worthy.

*Look at themes of letting go, loving myself, self-esteem, self-pity, self-respect, self-worth, unmet needs

Vitiligo

Fears
- Fears never being accepted
- Fears violence/ harm to be good enough
- Fear of people
- Fear of people coming into their space
- Fear of being bullied
- Fear of being dominated
- Fear of being seen
- Fear of children

Emotional States
- Strong; need to be seen as complete, feels as if they are less than for who they are. Shows a different aspect of self to others depending on who it is. They warn people to stay away, because they can't handle them being too close. Boundaries appear to be transparent or non-existent. Cannot defend themselves against people in authority. Their survival is achieved by not having boundaries.
- Hardly know where to start with life. Overwhelmed. Head/thinking is in a constant state of confusion. Doesn't understand why they are here and wishes to achieve true invisibility. Wants to fade into the background – has chameleon qualities in their personality. Chokes at decision involving stepping out – or being seen – feels threatened by those that are seen. Allows others to run over them. Victim energy.
- Cough – may well have a pairing of upper respiratory ailment where they cough a lot. Appears unrelated to the disease by allopathic practitioners. A gentle person, where kindness is their defense. Kindness is the only boundary they have and they use it as a deflection. They hide in the kindness.
- Runs away from children. In their childhood they ran away from other children that were bullies. So they continue running to be safe. Held up as an example of perfect behavior by authority and then punished by others later. Ostracized. Afraid of people.

Cross Indexing: Skin problems, Autoimmune diseases, Addison's disease, Hashimoto's Disease, and Diabetes Mellitus 1.

Created Patterns
1. I am ashamed.
2. I am ashamed of where I come from.
3. I am rejected.
4. I am insecure.
5. I'm not loved.
6. I am afraid of _____.
7. I am anxious about _____.

Vocal Cord Problems

Fears
- Fear of being wrong
- Fear of not knowing
- Fear of speaking
- Fear of standing up
- Fear of being taken advantage of
- Fear of having their voice heard
- Fear of being judged
- Fear of rejection
- Fear of crumbling

Emotional States
- The person feels it's not fair that they have to go in and clear up someone else's mess.
- Deeply wounded in an effort to do something that would have brought them attention or recognition. Their words were destroyed.
- When talked "at" I have to challenge them, to engage them. If I engage instead of challenge my toes would be stepped on. So talking is always a 'challenge' to have my words heard.
- Their anger is weakened in the face of being judged.

Cross Indexing: Laryngitis, Throat Problems, Strep Throat, Spasmodic Dysphonia

Created Patterns
1. I am always cleaning up after people.
2. I get blamed for the messes made by others.
3. It's unjust that I am made to pay for the mistakes of others and I can't complain or push back.
4. People put me down when I am seen.
5. I am criticized for trying to help others.
6. I have to push my words at others to be taken seriously.

Vomiting

Fears
- Fears being overrun by what's bad for you
- Fears being deceived by what is supposed to be good
- Fear of inner wisdom
- Fear of wrong information

Emotional States
- Rejection of what is coming in from a sense source — the creative senses. There is a need to reject the inner self and the wisdom it brings. Rejects the information from the sense source because it brings change. They view change as potentially dangerous.

Cross Indexing: Nausea, Stomach Problems, Bulimia, Symptom

Created Patterns
1. I am disgusted by _____.
2. I need to get rid of _____.
3. What in your life can't you accept?
4. I need to reject my feelings.
5. My feelings don't pay the rent.
6. My creative senses are not reliable.
7. I don't know how to integrate my feelings safely.

W's

Warts

Fears
- Fears being lied to and having to hide the lies
- Fears being seen
- Fears seeing themselves
- Fears shame
- Fears guilt

Emotional States
- Holds themselves out as exemplary. They are sterling yet there is a piece of them that wants to tell the world how unhappy they are. No sense of justice or direction when it comes to knowing who they are. They are ugly. They feel ugly. Nothing should get in the way of this perception of their ugliness. They hide behind it and use any reinforcement of that as an excuse to not be seen. They just keep digging that hole deeper.
- Hiding the truth. They see their truth and themselves as ugly. They make themselves ugly on the inside. They bring to the surface all the slights and instances of poor behavior so they can make themselves ugly to themselves. They feel guilt at those misbehaviors and acts of poor judgment. They have tried forgiving themselves. They don't know how to forgive and if they aren't ugly then they become seen. The shame of having their guilt and ugliness seen is unbearable.

Cross Indexing: Skin Problems, Plantar Warts, Growths, Moles

Created Patterns
1. Life is ugly.
2. I hate _____.
3. I am inadequate.
4. I am ugly.
5. I am worthless/ unworthy.

Wegeners Granulomatosis

Fears
- Fears that if they don't step up they will be flattened
- Fear of letting go
- Fear of joy
- Fears bad things are going to happen
- Fears begin blamed

Teachings
- Allow others their power
- Appropriate use of Power
- Be loved
- Being vulnerable without being weak
- Boundaries
- Complete
- Forgive yourself

- Forgiveness
- Fun
- Go with the flow
- Inner peace
- Joy
- Live feeling respected
- Live without feeling betrayed by others
- Live without needing anger to protect yourself
- Live without needing to be punished
- Live without pain
- Live without shame
- Live without suffering
- Love
- Loving myself
- Make decisions and be safe
- Permission to forgive yourself
- Permission to have fun
- Receive
- Release Anger without hurting myself
- Respect
- Whole

Emotional States
- Off-target in an attempt to enjoy life – they keep doing things that bring them pain.
- Holds onto past hurts so that they prevent joy / fun from entering their life.
- Angry at others for not having the same fear of what might happen.
- Feeling of hopelessness are turned into inward anger; angry at the world for the wrong choices made early in life.
- They feel like they are being punished for the rest of their life.
- Critical of others.
- Blames others for the bad things that happen to them.

Cross Indexing: Vasculitis, Lung Problems, Kidney Problems

Repeating Patterns: Has a tendency to tell people what to do instead allowing them the space to solve their own problems. They have no inner peace. They don't know how to go with the flow. They want to control the outcomes so they stay safe. Judgmental of others that don't let them control the decisions.

Created Patterns
1. _____ betrayed me.
2. Anger protects me.
3. Bad things happen to me.
4. Everyone ends up disappointing me.
5. God is a punishing god.
6. How can I have fun when _____ .

EMOTIONAL PATTERNS

7. I am a disappointment.
8. I am a failure.
9. I am angry at _____.
10. I am angry at myself.
11. I am ashamed of _____.
12. I am being punished by god.
13. I am disappointed in life.
14. I am going to die.
15. I am powerful when I am angry.
16. I am sad.
17. I am vulnerable.
18. I can't ever seem to do things right.
19. I can't let go of _____.
20. I can't receive.
21. I don't deserve.
22. I don't know how to have fun.
23. I don't know how to receive love.
24. I don't love / like myself.
25. I don't love myself.
26. I don't want to be seen.
27. I have paid for making a wrong choice all my life.
28. I let god down
29. I make wrong choices.
30. I must be punished.
31. I must be punished for making wrong choices / decisions.
32. I must be punished for the bad things I have done.
33. I must suffer to be good enough for god.
34. I see bad things happening to others.
35. I will always suffer.
36. I will never be at peace.
37. I will never be good enough.
38. I'm no good.
39. I'm not good enough.
40. I'm not loved.
41. I'm not respected.
42. I'm not worthy.
43. If I don't worry bad things will happen.
44. If I suffer I will be good enough.
45. If I'm not angry I will be seen as weak.
46. It's hopeless.
47. Love is pain.
48. My soul is being tortured.
49. No one sees the truth the way I do.
50. Nothing will every change.
51. People don't bother me when I am angry.

*Look at themes of fun, boundaries, trust, self-esteem, self-knowledge, self-love, self-respect, self-pity, happiness, judgment, decisions, allowing, peace, friendship, unmet needs, disconnection

Weight – Overweight

Fears
- Fear of never enough
- Fear of being vulnerable or truly seen by others
- Fear of showing their pain
- Fear they will never be enough
- Fear of the flow of life
- Fear of living
- Fear of learning and understanding the higher nature of our lives
- Fear of injustice
- Fear of letting go
- Fear of losing (identity)
- Fear of feeling
- Fear of love
- Fear of emptiness
- Fear of being nothing

Emotional States
- Eating is out of balance. Eats carbohydrates to have pleasure but no real sense of inner joy. Carbohydrates create a cycle of feel good – no feel good. Flow in their lives is replaced with a craving for carbohydrates.
- Doesn't listen to themselves. They still have the story of injustice. Can't let go of it. Feels that the injustice supports their victim identity.
- Can't draw the curtains on an aspect of their life. They work to bury the uncomfortable feeling caused by the event(s). The experience of eating draws their focus from those uncomfortable feelings.
- Loves eating. Enjoys the sensual nature of food when no other source of sensual pleasure is possible. The love of eating has replaced the other possible loves in their life. Feels alive when they are eating.
- They have a hole in their heart that can never be filled. There will never be enough of the right thing to fill it. Lost opportunity lost to time. They feel an aching emptiness that they try to fill.

Cross Indexing: Overeating – Compulsive, Weight Loss panic, Weight Loss – Insulin Resistance, Weight Loss – Fear of Starvation, Weight Loss – The Magical Thinking Diet, Weight Loss – The Family Money Story and Weight, Bulimia, Anorexia, Ancestral/ Epigenetic, Weight-Under

Created Patterns
1. Being fat makes me safe.
2. Being fat protects me from evil.
3. Chores before play.
4. Chores before taking care of myself.
5. Eating is how I declare my independence.
6. Eating is how I get revenge on _____.
7. Eating is how I show I am free.
8. Exercise is a chore.

EMOTIONAL PATTERNS

9. Exercise is no fun.
10. Exercise is work.
11. Fat men are _____.
12. Fat people are powerful / successful.
13. Fat women are _____.
14. Food is Love.
15. Good things are kept from me.
16. Hunger is pain.
17. Hunger is punishment.
18. I am a gorilla.
19. I am a victim.
20. I am afraid I will lose my mother.
21. I am always hungry...*(this leads to the question of what is the void the food is trying to fill)*.
22. I am angry at _____.
23. I am angry at my father.
24. I am angry at my mother.
25. I am angry at myself.
26. I am fat.
27. I am going to die.
28. I am guilty if I have sex.
29. I am never full.
30. I am too fat.
31. I am worthless.
32. I can eat all I want and no one can tell me what to do.
33. I can't be trusted with food.
34. I can't forgive _____.
35. I can't get enough to eat.
36. I can't let go of what is bad for me.
37. I don't know how to recognize a feeling of being full.
38. I don't know how to relax without food.
39. I don't know how to take care of myself.
40. I don't know what full feels like.
41. I don't know what it feels like to be comfortable in my body.
42. I don't know what it feels like to have enough food.
43. I don't know what it feels like to relax without food.
44. I don't know what it feels like to take care of myself.
45. I don't love myself.
46. I don't know how to stop eating.
47. I don't know what it feels like to be full.
48. I get love from food.
49. I hate/resent skinny people.
50. I have no purpose.
51. I must be fat to be faithful.
52. I must be fat to be trusted by _____.
53. I must be punished for secrets.
54. I must constantly protect myself.
55. I must do my chores before I play.
56. I must eat to fill the void.
57. I must not show my feelings.

58. I must punish myself by being fat.
59. I use food to fill the voids left by _____ in my life.
60. I'm not good enough.
61. I'm not good enough for God.
62. I'm not good enough for the good things in life.
63. I'm not loved.
64. If I am skinny I will die.
65. If I lose weight, I betray _____ (often mother/grandmother).
66. If I'm attractive, I betray_____.
67. If I'm more attractive/thinner than_____, I betray them.
68. Life is boring.
69. Loving mothers are fat.
70. My chores are never done.
71. My fat protects me.
72. My father/mother abandoned me.
73. My father/mother betrayed me.
74. My mother hates me.
75. My mother rejected me.
76. My power is in my being fat.
77. My weight protects me.
78. Sex is shameful/ sinful / dirty.
79. Skinny grandmas are mean.
80. Taking care of myself is play/selfish.
81. Thin people cannot be trusted.
82. Thin people will betray you.
83. When I am hungry I am bad.
84. Who wants to see you punished?
85. Women are beautiful furniture.
86. Women must be beautiful and thin.
87. Women must be thin.
88. Work before play.

Weight – Under

Fears

- Fear of instant success
- Fear of being over weight
- Fear of being unloved
- Fear of being unwanted
- Fear of not suffering

Emotional States

- They can't let go of the idea that being under weight is how they stay wanted and loved. They feel you can never be too thin.

Cross Indexing: Overeating – Compulsive, Weight Loss panic, Weight Loss – Insulin Resistance, Weight Loss – Fear of Starvation, Weight Loss – The Magical Thinking Diet, Weight Loss – The Family Money Story and Weight, Bulimia, Anorexia, Ancestral/ Epigenetic, Weight-Over

Created Patterns
1. No matter what I do I can't gain weight.
2. I must be thin to be loved/ wanted/ seen.
3. If you are heavy people make fun of you.
4. Fat people are never seen as important or capable.
5. I must be hungry to suffer.
6. Suffering is how I punish myself for being sinful.
7. Nobody want a fat person.
8. I am afraid of _____.
9. I distrust _____.
10. I am worried about/that _____.

Weight Loss – Fear of Starvation

Starting in the early to mid-2000's I had put on an extra 40 pounds that needed to come off. As the pounds crept in I bought a larger clothing size. I found comfortable jeans and I figured I could live in them. The 40 pounds was primarily the result of being very sick for a few years and I had no energy for exercise. I would eat anything that gave me a quick burst of energy…sugar and lots of it. I had this very special relationship with a sweet roll I nicknamed the 'Ooey Gooey Wonder'.

Dieting did not work. I would get to about 10 am in the morning and I would be so hungry I could not think. The hunger pangs took over my entire body. The same routine developed in the afternoon around 4:00 pm. I would go to the kitchen (one of the big disadvantages of working from home) and snack. I would snack on healthy food items. But nuts, pepper dip and chips made of edamame, flax seed, blue corn meal, etc. are not low in calories and I could not face one more raw vegetable.

I was triggering a feeling in my body that if I didn't get that handful of nuts or chips I was going to starve, there was a panic. My body hunger was overriding my goals for a healthy weight. I had never experienced food deprivation so the fear of starvation was not from my current life experience. I would experience this same life-threatening sense of hunger when I got in the car to go on a long road trip. I had a steady stream of food going in my mouth while I drove.

As I sat in reflection on this aspect of my dieting experience I remembered stories told by my ancestors of deprivation during the Depression Era of having only one small meal a day and often going to bed hungry. There was no food. Farmers were not growing food because they could not sell it.
Had that feeling of an empty stomach, experienced by my ancestors, created an association that was passed to me via epigenetics that was now linked to my instinctive fear of starvation?

Fears
- Fear of starvation
- Fear of never enough

- Fears there will not be enough
- Fear of deprivation
- Fear of no food
- Fear of dying
- Fear of seeing others suffer

Emotional States
- A sense that starvation will happen unless you stay in close proximity to a steady source of food at all times.

Cross Indexing: Overeating – Compulsive, Weight Loss panic, Weight Loss – Insulin Resistance, Weight Loss – Fear of Starvation, Weight Loss – The Magical Thinking Diet, Weight Loss – The Family Money Story and Weight, Bulimia, Anorexia, Ancestral/ Epigenetic, Weight-Over, Weight-Under

Created Patterns
1. There is not enough.
2. I will starve.
3. I panic when I am hungry.
4. I must eat or I will die.
5. I must have food around me at all times or bad things will happen.

Weight Loss – Insulin Resistance

Fears
- Fears having too much power
- Fears being responsible
- Fears being shamed
- Fear of being forced to give more than they have
- Fear of the future
- Fear of letting go
- Fear of being out of control
- Fears being connected

Emotional States
- Held up to others as an example of what you should and shouldn't do. Shame and humiliation is the result. Laughing on the outside but crying on the inside. Joined by others in the laughter and wants to hide. No boundaries – overrun by life and all relationships. Feels depleted with no more to give but keeps giving.
- Long the embodiment of an idealized way of being in the world that does not meet reality. Hopes at some point the world will give way around them and they can stop living the idealized format for existence. Living that way is compulsive. They feel like they have no choices.
- Worried about everything around them. They can't let go of the past stuff and that becomes the foundation and justification for the worry. The worry distorts their image of their life reality.

- Runaway thoughts about life. They can't stop the thinking. It's like a train that just keeps going. There's this outward sense of being in control but inside they feel completely out of control.
- Decreased sense of ownership for the stuff around them – a loss of connection to the world around them – a disconnectedness. There is an emptiness in their movements and sense of duty-bound.

Cross Indexing: Overeating – Compulsive, Weight Loss panic, Weight Loss – Fear of Starvation, Weight Loss – The Magical Thinking Diet, Weight Loss – The Family Money Story and Weight, Bulimia, Anorexia, Ancestral/ Epigenetic, Weight-Over, Weight-Under

Created Patterns

1. I am disconnected from the people around me.
2. I am ashamed.
3. I am humiliated.
4. I am used as a scapegoat.
5. I am blamed for the faults of others.
6. People laugh at me.
7. I have nothing. I am depleted.
8. People run over me.
9. I am disconnected from the world around me.
10. They work hard, they accomplish, they are referred to as 'be like your sister' or 'be like your brother' by their parents. They are held up as the example.
11. I must worry about everything.
12. I can't let go of the worry. If I do bad things will happen.
13. I appear to be in control but I am really a runaway train.

Weight Loss – The Family Money Story and Weight

Fears
- Fear of having and not having
- Fear of eating
- Fear of having more than others
- Fear of getting caught
- Fear of the secrets being known

Emotional States
- "Lose it all and then gain it back", the roller coaster money story. The family history may have stories of several reversals of fortune so this became a pattern of survival. This could also parallel the pattern of yo-yo dieting. This pattern plays out as a person constantly looking for that next great diet. They lose the weight and then feel a sense of panic as they lose the weight. The panic creates the need to start eating again to ease the panic.
- There was continual confusion around the family's economics. There was not enough money to pay the bills and put food on the table yet there was money to put new carpeting in the house. This was a repeating pattern all through childhood. As a result they may not have a sense of how

to balance a budget and live within their means. This may well have translated to a diet of "I can have all the good stuff (sweets and fats) without having to pay for it (calorie reduction)". There is not a balance in their diet. If there is a need to cut back on the sweets/high caloric content foods to maintain a balanced weight then confusion and stress may be result.

- Keeps money a secret. They must never let anyone know how much they have. Grandma may have kept the money in a shoe box hidden under a floor board in the back of a closet. They have the same pattern of making sure no one has an understanding of their wealth. Discussing money is forbidden in the family. In times of hardship food was secreted to survive. There is a need to secretly eat. There is a need to compulsively keep stashes of food in their car, purse, backpack, desk drawer, bookshelves, etc. Yet, they eat their three meals with small portions declaring they don't know how they gain weight because they don't eat that much, all the while secretly eating from their stashes. They compulsively have these food sources available wherever they are. When they eat one of these secret stashes there is a feeling of stress relief. Everything is going to be OK. Or in times of stress they go to these secret stashes of food.
- Their family can't throw anything away because it may be needed some day. They keep every margarine tub and actually buy more of them at garage sales. They have a closet(s) full of Tupperware where there is no matching lid and the Tupperware is useless. They have piles of magazines that have a good idea for something they will never make (recipe, wood project or craft). The idea of throwing out leftover food whose shelf life has expired creates stress, anger and anxiety. They will then eat the leftovers even when they have expired.
- They have this overwhelming need to buy stuff…anything. They buy clothes or other items they don't need and they don't particularly like because they feel this need to spend money. Then they dislike themselves and question why they did that to begin with. This may have also played out in large families where there was barely enough food to go around and they would leave the table still hungry. So they would get as much as they could get when they could get it. Money-wise this would translate into over spending on the credit cards. They've got the credit so they need to spend it while they can because they may not have it tomorrow.
- A pattern of people taking what is theirs (money, belongings, etc.)? Their family money and relationship patterns were without clear boundaries. There was a sense that if they had it then it was available to anyone in the family to take and call their own without any ramifications. They saw their parents take money and belongings from their parents or siblings. This lack of boundaries would also play out in terms of food. Food would be taken off their plate if someone wanted it. Protest would have brought them punishment. Having boundaries in this family structure was dangerous. If they had boundaries they would have been punished, rejected and love would have been withdrawn. They play out this lack of boundaries when it comes to their eating habits. If they want it they eat it. Restraining themselves or having proper boundaries around food creates an abnormal amount of stress that becomes overwhelming.
- There is embarrassment and shame around money. This could go back to ancestral trauma that if they had enough or more than others then they had to hide it. It was shameful to be more prosperous than the neighbors or other family members. This may have had its roots in religious or cultural mores. In some countries it may have been politically or legally punishable if they seemed to have more than others. So eating becomes stressful. Eating and enjoying food could be wrong and creates anxiety around surviving.

Cross Indexing: Overeating – Compulsive, Weight Loss panic, Weight – Under, Weight Loss – Insulin Resistance, Weight Loss – Fear of Starvation, Weight Loss – The Magical Thinking Diet, Bulimia, Anorexia, Ancestral/ Epigenetic, Weight-Over, Weight-Under

Created Patterns

1. If I lose weight I must gain it back or I will be in danger.
2. When I lose weight I panic.
3. There is not enough so I have to eat it all.
4. I can eat all I want without gaining weight. It's just _____ that puts on the pounds.
5. Diets confuse me. When I am on a diet I go into confusion to be safe.
6. I must keep my money a secret.
7. Discussing my money is dangerous.
8. When I eat in secret I feel better about myself. I feel safe.
9. I can't throw anything away.
10. I buy stuff I don't need.
11. When I buy stuff I then feel bad about myself.
12. People take what belongs to me.
13. It's dangerous to stop people from taking from you.
14. To be loved you must not have boundaries.
15. If I eat more than others I will be shamed/hurt. So I eat secretly.
16. If I enjoy my food I will be punished.

Weight Loss – The Magical Thinking Diet

A few days ago I went to Trader Joe's to purchase the yummy treats that only they offer. One of my favorite snacks is the peas in a pod that have been turned into these crunchy tidbits. After getting to the car with my precious cargo I opened the bag of peas. As an afterthought I looked at the back of the bag to see what the calorie content was. 10 peas were 160 calories. OK, I would allow myself 10 peas. 160 calories would be OK. I rationalized that the extra 160 calories of this treat would not hurt. By the time I got home I had rationalized myself to an empty bag that had once held pea pods. I had eaten the whole bag and probably about 1000 calories and way too much sodium for a day's intake. Then I make myself another undeliverable promise 'I'll just go to the gym an extra day'. ARGH. I had sabotaged myself, again, with the magical thinking that the calories would just go poof and they would have no impact on my poundage.

I stopped and contemplated that pattern of 'I'll just have this one little piece of [you fill in the blank] and then I'll cut back at dinner or I'll eat a salad for lunch.' I was living the Magical Thinking Diet. My whole calorie intake was based on magical thinking. It was like those many moments of 'I'll just have a little more [you fill in the blank]' had become my diet. These moments were magical because those calories apparently didn't get counted because they would get countered by a decrease at some point in the future. The problem was those excess calories never got balanced out. They just conveniently slipped into oblivion. The memory of that bag of pea pods lingered when I stepped on the scales but not in my mind. The Magical Thinking relegates responsibility to a time in the future. When you are thinking magically you create an imaginary world where at some point, very soon, you will do what you promise. The future world is never in the present and those changes never happen. Since the imaginary world is in the future you don't have to take present responsibility for your actions in the present.

The Magical Thinking Diet is a serious problem. The Magical Thinking Diet does not create weight loss or good health. While I don't have health issues now, carrying an additional 30-40 pounds could be an issue in the future that could severely limit me. So, the question becomes 'what keeps me from taking present responsibility for my diet choices'. What happens if I take responsibility for those diet choices in each moment? When I feel into the answer I heard 'alone' and I had a knowing of what I was doing. I am not making choices to please others as I did in the years between 19-50 years of age. I learned very quickly at age 19 that the thinner I was the more sexually appealing I was and the more sexually appealing I was to men the more acceptance I found. I found 'love' and acceptance by being thin. It was at age 50 that the pounds starter to creep in. I had healed the dysfunctional motivation of needing to be thin to be loved. I had not healed the very deep feeling of being alone to be safe. I had learned that after 'love' and acceptance I was still alone and I learned to survive in that aloneness. As I look over my past patterns of relationships, I would treasure those moments of aloneness. I would feel my best and happiest when I was alone. Then the cycle would repeat itself. I would feel a need to go back to the cycle of seeking out 'love' and acceptance and then pull myself away to get to the place of feeling alone.

Then another question appears 'what motivates me right now to lose weight and make diet choices without magical thinking?' I had not replaced that survival based motivation with a healthy and healing approach to maintaining my weight. I am stuck in a place of no motivation to have a holistically healthy body.

Fears
- Fear of being unloved
- Fear of being unaccepted
- Fear of being responsible for my health
- Fear of being enslaved by others to be accepted

Emotional States
- Responsibility is relegated to a time in the future. They are thinking magically and they create an imaginary world where at some point, very soon, they will do what you promise. The future world is never in the present and those changes never happen. Since the imaginary world is in the future they don't have to take present responsibility for their actions in the present. As a child they probably were subjected to promises made by a parent(s) that were never kept. There was always a place in the future where the good things would happen and you would be special.

Cross Indexing: Overeating – Compulsive, Weight Loss panic, Weight Loss – Insulin Resistance, Weight Loss – Fear of Starvation, Weight Loss – The Family Money Story and Weight, Bulimia, Anorexia, Ancestral/ Epigenetic, Weight-Over, Weight-Under

Created Patterns
1. I'll start my diet in earnest next week/ after the holidays/ after the wedding (you name the event).
2. I'm not responsible for overeating.
3. I must be alone to be safe.
4. When I am alone no one expects me to serve them.
5. When I am alone I don't have to be on guard.
6. What cycles do you repeat to keep you from being a healthy weight.
7. I am loved when I feel disappointed.
8. People promise me things that they never deliver.
9. Life is one dead end promise after another.

Weight Loss Panic

Fears
- Fears dying first when there is nothing
- Fears weight loss
- Fears people
- Fears being harmed if thin

Emotional States
- Feels a sense of frenzy creep into their psyche at a drop in weight. Cannot stay out of the kitchen. They drop the weight and then go into a feeding frenzy. The feeling is compulsive to the point of panic. A feeling that weight loss is dangerous. They have to gain the weight they lost back, quickly. There is a sense that thin is dangerous. Being thin meant they would bring in people they could not trust. They would then go cold and empty at that idea. It felt like a wall of protection. The cold and empty kept them safe from people that would betray them.

Cross Indexing: Overeating – Compulsive, Weight-Under, Weight Loss – Insulin Resistance, Weight Loss – Fear of Starvation, Weight Loss – The Magical Thinking Diet, Weight Loss – The Family Money Story and Weight, Bulimia, Anorexia, Ancestral/ Epigenetic, Weight-Over, Weight-Under

Created Patterns
1. If I lose weight I will die.
2. If I am thin people will take me over.
3. If is dangerous to be thin.
4. I will be raped if I am thin.
5. I will be hurt if I am thin.
6. When I am thin people use me and then discard me.
7. I am unloved/ uncared for.
8. As long as I am disregarded, I am not responsible and can't be blamed.

Wilson's Syndrome

Fears
- Fear of failing
- Fear of succeeding
- Fear of being judged
- Fear of intimacy
- Fear of connection with others
- Fear of letting go
- Fear of power
- Fear of not being good enough
- Fear of loving self
- Fear of being judged/ criticized

Teachings
- Loving yourself
- Live without needing to be perfect
- Live without needing to be critical
- Live without needing to be judgmental
- Forgiveness
- Live without blaming others
- Take care of yourself
- Nurture yourself

- Live without needing the approval of others
- In the flow
- Live without protecting yourself with negativity
- Comfortable with change

Emotional States

- Farfetched ideas have yielded profound disappointment. They thought these ideas would take them to their dream, which did not include working to make it happen. It would just happen. Puts others down that don't go along with them.
- There's a hollowness in their being where disappointment has decided to take up residence. Unrealistic expectations were cast as reality in their mind and when they didn't materialize they also didn't move on to something else. They have a distance or a coldness toward others.

Cross Indexing: Thyroid problems, Fatigue, Endocrine System Problems, ACOA, Hyperthyroidism, Laryngitis

Created Patterns

1. Change is bad/ dangerous.
2. Everything is *bad (what is bad in your life?)*.
3. Everything is wrong *(what is wrong in your life?)*.
4. I am afraid of what other's think of me.
5. I am jealous of _____ for _____.
6. I am never satisfied with what I have.
7. I blame _____ for _____.
8. I don't know how to take care of myself.
9. I don't know what nurtures me.
10. I don't love myself.
11. I hate/am angry/bitter toward _____.
12. I must be perfect *(What happens when you aren't?)*.
13. I must criticize/judge others to show them how to be better.
14. I want what others have.
15. I worry about what others think of me.
16. I'm not good enough.
17. Others are to blame for _____ in my life.
18. *What happens when there is change?*
19. *Why should I change when others are wrong?*
20. The world is unfair.
21. I am powerless to make things happen.
22. When I fail I am humiliated.

Wounded Creative Core

We are born with the ability to create and access that inner wisdom of inspiration, our creative core. Institutions (schools, governments, etc.), cultures and religious dogma create conform and perform structures of behavior. These structures constrain the creative core through punishment. These punishments are designed to reinforce control over the individual and groups through the use of physical, emotional, mental, financial and spiritual violence.

The institutions put you in a box. The religious dogma may say that you can't step outside of their moral box and love who you want without being condemned or worse. A culture or religion may define your life in terms of your gender. If you are a woman you may be expected to marry at age 16. Yet your heart yearns to become an astrophysicist. If you listen to your heart's yearning, creative core, you may lose your family, your freedom and possibly your life. As a woman born in the early 1950's it was determined that I had a specific set of options for a job; teacher, nurse or secretary. I was expected to get married and have children, in that order. When creativity was expressed it had to be confined to acceptable forms that adhered to the expectations of the institutions.

When the Creative Core is wounded a plethora of trauma is experienced. That trauma translates to rejection, feeling unwanted, fear of authority, fear of your parents, fear of being unloved, and more. These fears and feelings become emotional states and created patterns that become our identity. This wounding is also reflected in the wounding of the feminine and masculine aspects of who we are.

Fears
- Fear of my own creative abilities
- Fears sexuality
- Fears their body
- Fear of rules
- Fear of breaking the rules
- Fear of authority
- Fear of standing up for what you believe
- Fear of feeling
- Fear of having your creativity seen
- Fear of having my creativity questioned
- Fear of being diminished
- Fear of judgment
- Fear of being forced to give up creative efforts
- Fear of not being able to defend my creativity
- Fear of not being able to follow through with my creative ideas
- Fear I am going the wrong way
- Fear of having creativity destroyed
- Fear of having ideas stolen
- Fear of being destroyed by criticism
- Fear of being shamed / humiliated for my creativity
- Fear of being ridiculed
- Fear of being vulnerable and open
- Fear of being seen

Wounding of the Empathic Sense
One of the intuitive abilities that we are born with is our empathic sense. The empathic sense allows us to feel the emotions and feelings of others. Those feelings may encompass physical feelings as well as

emotional. The empathic sense sends physical feelings to the body and those signals are interpreted within the framework of other intuitive senses and beliefs. For some people this is their primary intuitive sense. The mature developed response to empathic feelings is to acknowledge the feelings and their source. The mature response knows that these feelings are not theirs but empathic information. The mature response sees their empathic sense as the catalyst for a compassionate response; inner peace in the face of suffering.

The immature response to empathic feelings is to take in the feelings of others and make the responsibility for someone's physical pain, anger, disappointment, failure, etc. their own. The immature empathic response was developed as a finely honed survival skill in response to an environment that appeared threatening. The energies of others may cause a highly sensitive person to feel physical and/or emotional pain.

The empathic sense becomes wounded when a child is highly sensitive to the stimuli in their environment. Anger, depression, sadness, loud voices by anyone will be terrifying for a highly sensitive child. The reaction is a wounding of the empathic sense. The highly sensitive child takes the energy of these emotions and believes it is their fault the adult is unhappy.

The highly sensitive child may feel crowded out in a household with lots of children and/or chaos. They may not feel there is a safe place to be themselves. The chaotic energy of a large household can wound the empathic sense. The child goes unrecognized and begins to believe that all they do is wrong.

A professional healer in any field (allopathic, energetic, or consciousness) that has poor boundaries as a consequence of a wounded empathic nature can find themselves energetically drained at the end of a day of working with others. These weakened boundaries may also contribute to a misunderstanding of the information being received. This person can lose track of their own needs in the face of working to meet the perceived needs of others. The filter through which this empathic information is received is colored with their own unmet needs. This healer is attached to the outcome. In a few years/months they may burn out.

Fears

- Fears feeling bad
- Fears other people's feelings
- Fear of knowing too much
- Fear that they won't know in time
- Fear of harm/ hurt
- Fear of being blamed
- Fear of failing at the responsibilities
- Fear that they can't help or heal another

Emotional States

- Hide in the middle- This could be likened to hiding in plain sight. The person with a wounded empathic sense makes decisions based on not creating controversy or comment. They adjust what they say and do to stay safe. They stay safe by making sure they have pleased the people around them. They have spent so much time in this place they have lost touch with their authentic self. They no longer know what they believe or feel. They have taken on the beliefs of others to be safe. Their own needs are suppressed. They may find that when they have taken on too much of

the energies of others they start to cry. If the person is asked the reason for their crying, they will not know. They just know that they have a deep inner sadness.
- Can't say no-They have an inability to say 'no'. They take on more and more responsibility or tasks because if they say 'no' they may hurt someone's feeling or make someone angry. If they hurt someone's feelings or make someone angry then they will be hurt. They work very hard to please others. To them an angry person is very dangerous. They work to avoid confrontation with others.
- Always a feeling of being in trouble-There is a nagging feeling in the center of their chest that they have done something wrong and they are about to get into trouble. This feeling is with them all the time. They have a constant feeling of living on the edge of disaster. They carry a projection that everything that goes wrong is their fault.
- Sexual feelings are confused for love-Love based relationships have at their core confusion between sexual feelings and feelings of love from the heart. They commit themselves very quickly into relationships with no real understanding of the other person. They have come into the relationship with a distrust of their intuition so they don't trust that level of information. The closeness brought about by a sexual relationship becomes their basis for love. This in time often leads to disillusionment. When the relationship fails or they can't seem to do enough to please the other person they have just received validation that their feelings are dangerous and can't be trusted. This results in the creative aspect being denied or shut down.
- Masculine and Feminine out of balance-The feminine aspect is strong and reflects an over active anticipation of the needs of others. The masculine is weak and the person doubts themselves. They are certain they will fail and they are afraid to put themselves out there.
- Skewed sense of appropriate social reactions- Family may have had drama queens/kings that were dominant in the family structure; mother, father, grandparent, etc. They dominated the conversation and energy in the household with their physical/emotional needs. The family dynamics led to no one else being allowed to express their own physical or emotional feelings safely. The expression of feelings was met with ridicule or shame. They learned early that it was risky to express your feelings. They also learned not to trust what they were feeling. Their feelings became a source of self-betrayal that would lead them to ridicule or shame. Intuition is not trusted and is suppressed. They may not know how to appropriately communicate their own feelings of physical or emotional discomfort. The ability to react appropriately to someone else's physical or emotional discomfort has become dampened and may not be appropriate.
- Always in a state of analysis- The mind of a person with a wounded empathic sense is constantly searching for the right answer, the right thing to say, and the appropriate reaction to external events. Their responses must be based on a logical thought process and not their feelings. Everything must be backed up by an analytical sequence of thought. If they are wrong there is no shame in a faulty logic process. The shame is felt if their response was based in feelings. If they made a mistake they will go back over every step in the sequence until they know exactly where the error occurred.
- Sense of being alone- This person is in a constant state of inner turmoil. They have a feeling of being alone and that no one understands them. They have no inner peace.

Cross Indexing: Attention Deficit Disorder, PTSD, ACOA, Addictions, Nausea, Headache, Headache-Migraine, Headache-Tension, Shoulder Problems, Anxiety, Depression, Wounded Creative Core

Created Patterns
1. Bad things happen when I'm not looking.
2. Crying is for babies.

3. Everything is my fault.
4. I am always wrong.
5. I am depressed.
6. I am guilty for everything.
7. I am in trouble.
8. I am responsible for all bad things that happen.
9. I am responsible for everything.
10. I am shameful.
11. I am to blame for everything.
12. I am to blame when things go wrong.
13. I can never let my guard down.
14. I can speak my truth and be safe.
15. I can't let go of _____.
16. I can't make a decision unless I have all the facts.
17. I can't paint/write/draw/_____(creative efforts).
18. I can't say no.
19. I can't shut my brain off.
20. I can't speak my truth and be safe.
21. I can't trust my family/people.
22. I can't trust my mother/father/brother/sister.
23. I don't know what it feels like to say no.
24. I don't know god's definition of compassion.
25. I don't know god's definition of love.
26. I don't know god's definition of my authentic self.
27. I don't know how to feel.
28. I don't know how to feel safe in my body.
29. I don't know how to say no.
30. I don't know how to trust my feelings.
31. I don't know the different between my feelings and someone else's.
32. I don't know what it feels like to trust my feelings.
33. I don't know what love feels like.
34. I don't know who I am.
35. I don't trust myself.
36. I don't understand the difference between sexual feelings and love.
37. I don't/ can't trust my feelings.
38. I must always be on alert.
39. I must analyze everything before making a decision.
40. I must do what others want me to do.
41. I must take care of everyone else first.
42. I must take care of others to be love/wanted/accepted.
43. I must tell myself what to feel.
44. I need permission to feel.
45. I want to die.
46. I will never be good enough.
47. I'm no good at creative things.
48. I'm not good enough.
49. I'm not loved.
50. If I relax someone will hurt me.
51. It is safe to be in my body.

52. It is safer to be analytical.
53. It is weak to feel.
54. Listening to my inner voice is dangerous/wrong.
55. Love is pain/hurtful.
56. My feelings are irrelevant.
57. My feelings are wrong.
58. No one will believe me if I tell them how I feel.
59. No one will believe me if I tell them the truth.
60. Others tell me what to feel.
61. People are mean.
62. People hurt me.
63. People think I am lying.

Wrists

Fears
- Fear of being bored to death
- Fear of no learning/ no growth
- Fear of not being wanted unless they give
- Fear of being creative

Teachings
- Acceptance
- Allow myself to play / have fun
- Allowing
- Flow
- Balanced
- Be good to myself
- Comfortable with change
- Giving
- Good enough
- Have fun
- Joy
- Let go
- Live without being threaten by the ideas of others
- Live without guilt
- Live without needing to be perfect
- Make a mistake and be safe
- Move with ease
- Play
- Receiving
- Unconditional love
- Use your hands to do the work you love
- Use your hands to give with love
- Use your hands to receive with love
- Valuing others
- Work from a place of love

Emotional States

- Wrists represent movement and ease in the realm of emotional, mental and spiritual flexibility.
- Not acknowledging the right to use their hands for pleasure for fear of making a mistake or not being capable.
- They only do with their hands what is worthwhile and prove your worth.
- They ask too much of themselves. They don't deserve a job that is fun and enjoyable. They feel guilty if they have fun. They must work their fingers to the bone – give your utmost.
- Holds onto outmoded beliefs about life and self.
- Imbalanced in giving or receiving.
- Right = Ability to give
- Left = Ability to receive

Cross Indexing: Carpal Tunnel Syndrome, Arm Problems, Right Sided negative tendencies, Left sided negative tendencies, Wounded Creative Core

Repeating Patterns: When working on a new idea or project they fear being usurped by someone else or having their ideas taken and claimed by someone else. They do not love their work. The use of their hands to do their work becomes a place where they hold their negative feelings toward their work. It reflects their inflexibility at making choices toward moving into work that they love to do. They are out of alignment with their inner peace. They are choosing not to look at who they are and how that might translate into a love for themselves.

Created Patterns

1. Being creative is a waste of time.
2. Change is dangerous.
3. I am guilty.
4. I am never good enough.
5. I am not allowed to be creative.
6. I am not good enough so I must work harder than everyone else.
7. I am stuck.
8. I can't make a mistake and be safe.
9. I can't give.
10. I can't move forward.
11. I can't receive.
12. I demand excellence from myself.
13. I feel guilty if I have fun when there is work to do.
14. I give everything I have to be good enough.
15. I know what is best.
16. I must always give to others first.
17. I must be what others want me to be.
18. I must do it my way to be safe.
19. I must do my absolute best with everything I do.
20. I must do my very best at everything.
21. I must do things my way.
22. I must give to be good enough.
23. I must use my hands for work.

24. I must work hard to prove I am good enough.
25. I over give/receive (What is out of balance with either giving or receiving in your life?).
26. I work my fingers to the bone.
27. I'm not good with my hands.
28. If I have fun/ play I am guilty.
29. It is wrong to be creative.
30. It is wrong to play when there is work to be done.
31. It's wrong to change your mind.
32. My way is the best way.
33. The old ways are best.
34. What are you holding onto that you need to let go of?
35. Why change if it's not broken.

*Look at themes of acceptance, approval, balance, blockages, control, enjoying life, flow, freedom, joy, fun, giving, receiving, guilt, right, self-esteem, self-worth, worthiness, letting go, boundaries, guilt, and receiving

Y'S

Yeast Infection

Fears
- Fear of responsibility
- Fear of being forced to carry an unwanted load that belongs to someone else
- Fear that people will see them running away from responsibility
- Fear of a heart wound
- Fear of feeling unworthy
- Fear of being lost
- Fear of having joyless life

Emotional States
- Yearning of the heart to heal all wounds that narrow the heart. Holds grudges toward those that have created that narrowing. Unwanted sexual energies become annoying. Instead of channeling the energy into creativity the energies are ignored or tamped down. The warmth of the rise of those energies creates an inner chaos.
- Gentle outward nature belies an anger below the surface that causes an inner fire that will eventually burn the inner organs. The anger is at one's self. They needle themselves. They poke at little things that are insignificant and unworthy of recognition in an effort to deflect from the core of their irritation. The core of inner agitation is a hatred of self of having been born unworthy.
- Unyielding evidence that they lived a wrong life. A life that brings them no joy. They have forgotten the purpose and feel lost in the wilderness of their life.

Cross Indexing: Thrush, Candida, Vaginitis

Created Patterns
1. I am angry at myself.
2. My heart is wounded.
3. I have been wronged by the people I love.
4. Sexuality is chaos.
5. Creativity only makes a mess.
6. I am unworthy.
7. I am wrong.
8. I do not belong in this life.
9. I am joyless.
10. I have no purpose.
11. No one loves me.
12. I am lost.
13. I do not know where I am going.
14. I must punish myself for being wrong.

ABOUT THE AUTHOR

Valeria Moore is a consciousness researcher and journeyer. Valeria has explored the foundations of our consciousness for over 50 years and shared her explorations with people around the world. Valeria has never used just one path to discover the wisdom of the ancients. Instead, she believes that all traditions hold foundational wisdom that moves us forward along our path of understanding our nature. Valeria trained in a plethora of healing methods both as a practitioner and as a teacher. Each one of these healing methods added to her understanding of our nature.

Valeria holds a degree in computer and information sciences from the University of California.

Valeria retired in 2017 and immediately started writing. She has many personal transformation and children's books planned in the coming years. She recently published The Remen Q̄ Method: An Easy Do-It-Yourself Process to Create Inner Peace and Change Your Reality and Billy Visits the Farmer's Market: Adventures of Billy, Lilly, Milly and Mr. Ely. The children's books will offer a brief science of an aspect of our environment at the end of the book. The Remen Q Method is a simple process for reaching inner peace in the moment. You can check her website at valeriamoore.com to see what books are in the works and expected publishing dates.

Valeria lives in Oregon with her life partner and sweetie, Mike Read. She has two daughters and four fantastic grandchildren.

INDEX

A's, 27
Abdominal Aortic Aneurysm, 27
Abdominal Pain and Problems, 28
Abdominal Sacrocolpopexy, 30
Abortion Complications, 31
Abscess, 32
Abused Child, 33
Accidents, 34
Aches, 36
Achilles Tendonosis-left, 38
Achilles Tendonosis-right, 39
Acne, 40
ACOA-Adult Children of Alcoholics, 42
Acoustic Neuroma – Left Side, 49
Acoustic Neuroma – Right Side, 50
Addiction – Alcohol, 51
Addiction – Chemical, 53
Addiction – Cocaine, 58
Addiction – Food, 59
Addiction – Gambling, 62
Addiction – Shopping, 63
Addiction – Smoking / Nicotine, 65
Addison's disease, 67
Adenoid Problems, 69
Adrenal Fatigue, 70
Adrenal Problems, 72
Aging – Difficulties, 74
Agoraphobia, 76
AIDS and HIV, 79
Allergies – Dairy, 82
Allergies – General, 84
Allergies – Gluten Intolerance, 85
Allergies – Hay Fever, 86
Allergies – Wheat, 88
Alopecia, 91
ALS or Amyotrophic Lateral Sclerosis or Lou Gehrig's Disease or Motor Neuron Disease, 93
Alzheimer's, 94
Amenorrhoea, 96
Amyloidosis, 97
Anemia, 98
Anemia – Pernicious, 100
Anemia – Sickle Cell, 101
Aneurysm, 102
Angiolipoma, 104
Ankle Problems (pain, sprain, swelling), 105
Ankylosing Spondylitis, 107
Anorectic Bleeding, 107
Anorexia, 108
Anus Problems, 110
Anxiety, 111
Appendicitis, 113
Appetite – Excessive, 115
Appetite – Loss, 116
Arms – Left, 117
Arms – Right, 118
Arteriosclerosis (Atherosclerosis), 119
Artery Problems, 120
Arthritis, 121
Arthritis – Infectious or Septic, 122
Arthritis – Osteoarthritis, 124
Arthritis – Psoriatic, 125
Arthritis – Reactive (Reiter's Syndrome), 127
Arthritis – Rheumatoid, 128
Asthma, 130
Athlete's Foot, 132
Atrial Fibrillation, 132
Attention Deficit Disorder, 134
Autism, 137
Autoimmune Disorder, 139
Autoimmune Hemolytic Anemia, 142
B Cell – Abnormal Recognition, 145
B's, 145
Back, 145
Back – Cervical (neck), 146
Back – Coccyx Pain – Tailbone, 147
Back – Lumbar (middle), 150
Back – Sacral – Lower, 150
Back – Thoracic (Back High heart), 151
Bacterial Infection, 153
Baker's Cyst, 154
Bedwetting, 155
Behcet's Syndrome, 156
Biliary Colic, 160
Bi-Polar Syndrome, 158
Bladder Infection, 162
Bladder Problems, 163
Blisters, 164
Bloating, 165
Blood Disorders, 167
Boils, 168
Bone Problems, 169
Bones – Broken, 170
Brain Problems, 172
Brain Tumor, 173
Breast Problems, 176
Bronchitis, 177
Bruises, 178
Bulimia, 179
Bunions, 180
Bursitis, 181
C's, 183
Calluses, 183
Cancer, 183
Cancer – Basal Cell, 184
Cancer – Bladder, 186
Cancer – Breast, 188
Cancer – Cervical, 190
Cancer – Colon, 193
Cancer – Esophageal, 195
Cancer – Hodgkin Lymphoma, 196
Cancer – Leukemia, 197
Cancer – Liver, 198
Cancer – Lung, 199
Cancer – Medullary Thyroid, 200
Cancer – Melanoma, 201
Cancer – Multiple Myeloma, 202
Cancer – Non Hodgkins Lymphoma, 203
Cancer – Osteosarcoma, 205
Cancer – Ovarian, 207
Cancer – Pancreatic NeuroEndocrine, 208
Cancer – Prostate, 210
Cancer – Squamous Cell, 211
Cancer – Stomach, 212
Cancer – Urethral, 213
Candida, 214
Canker Sores, 216
Cardiovascular Disorder, 217
Carpel Tunnel, 218
Cartilage Degeneration, 219
Cataracts – Left, 220
Cataracts – Right, 222
Celiac Disease, 223
Cellulite, 226
Charcots Joints, 228

Chest Problems, 230
Cholesterol – High, 231
Chronic Fatigue Syndrome, 232
Chronic Illness, 233
Chronic Traumatic Encephalopathy (CTE), 234
Circulation Problems, 235
Cirrhosis, 236
Clavicle Problems, 237
Colds, 238
Colitis – Ulcerative, 239
Colon Problems, 242
Concussion, 243
Congestive Heart Failure, 244
Conjunctivitis, 248
Constipation, 249
Cough – Chronic, 250
Coughing, 251
Crohn's Disease, 253
Cysts, 255
Cytomegalovirus, 256
D's, 258
Dandruff, 258
Deep Vein Thrombosis(DVT), 258
Dementia, 259
Depression, 260
Depression with history of abuse, 264
Diabetes, 265
Diabetes Mellitus Type 1, 267
Diabetes Mellitus Type 2, 270
Diabetes: A Global View, 272
Diarrhea, 273
Diverticulitis, 274
Dizziness, 274
Dry Eye, 275
Duodenal Ulcer, 277
Dupuytren's Contraction, 278
Dysmenorrhea, 279
E's, 281
Ear Infection – Chronic, 281
Ear Problems, 282
Ears – Hearing Problems, 283
Eczema, 284
Edema, 286
Ehlers-Danlos Syndrome, 287
Elbow Problems, 288
EMF Sensitivity, 289
Emphysema – COPD, 290
Endocrine System Problems, 291

Endometriosis, 293
Epigastric Hernia, 294
Epilepsy, 294
Epstein Barr Syndrome, 296
Erectile Dysfunction, 297
Esophagus Problems, 299
Ethmoid Bone, 299
Eye Problems, 300
Eyes – Nearsightedness and Farsightedness, 302
F's, 307
Face/Head Problems, 307
Facial Dandruff, 308
Fallopian Tube Blockage, 309
Fascia Problems, 310
Fatigue, 310
Fear of Mold, 312
Fever, 312
Fibroid Tumors and Cysts, 313
Fibromyalgia, 314
Fibula – Left, 316
Fibula – Right, 318
Fingernails, 319
Fingernails – Biting, 320
Floaters – Left Eye, 321
Floaters – Right Eye, 321
Flu, 322
Focal Dystonia, 323
Foot Problems, 324
Frontal Skull Bones, 325
Fungus, 326
G's, 329
Gall Bladder Problems, 329
Gallbladder Polyps, 329
Gallstones, 330
Ganglion Cyst – Left wrist, 332
Ganglion Cyst – Right Wrist, 332
Gastritis, 333
Gingivitis, 335
Glaucoma, 336
Good Pasture's Syndrome, 337
Gout, 338
Graves Disease, 339
Growths – Skin, 340
Gum Problems, 344
Gums – Bleeding, 345
H's, 346
Hair – Balding, 346
Hair – Falling Out, 346
Hair – Ingrown, 347

Halitosis, 348
Hand Problems, 349
Hashimotos Disease, 350
Headache, 351
Headache – Migraine, 352
Headache – Tension, 354
Hearing – Hyper Acute, 355
Hearing Loss (Deafness) – Left, 355
Hearing Loss (Deafness) – Right, 356
Heart Problems, 357
Hemorrhoid, 360
Henoch Schonlein Purpura, 360
Hepatitis, 361
Hepatitis C, 362
Hernia, 363
Herpes Simplex (Cold Sores), 363
Herpes Virus Simplex II, 364
Hiatus Hernia, 366
Hiccups, 367
Hip Problems, 368
Hives, 369
Human Papilloma Virus (HPV), 370
Huntington's Disease, 371
Hyperactivity, 373
Hypertension, 373
Hyperthyroidism, 377
Hyperventilation, 378
Hypoglycemia, 379
Hypotension, 380
Hypothalamus, 381
Hypothyroidism, 382
I's, 384
Impetigo, 384
Incontinence, 385
Indigestion, 385
Infection, 386
Infertility, 387
Inflammation, 393
Ingrown Toenail Left Big Toe, 394
Ingrown Toenail Right Big Toe, 395
Insomnia, 396
Insulin Resistance, 398
Intestinal Problems, 399
Intestine – Large Problems (Bowel), 400
Intestine – Small Problems, 401
Intestines – Blocked, 402
Irritable Bowel Syndrome, 403
Itching, 404

EMOTIONAL PATTERNS

J's, 406
Jaw Problems, 406
Joint Problems, 406
K's, 408
Kidney Problems, 408
Kidney Stones, 409
Kidneys – Amyloidoisis, 410
Kidneys – Polycystic, 411
Knee – Left, 413
Knee – Right, 414
Knee Problems, 415
L's, 417
Labyrinthitis, 417
Lack of focus (in school/studies), 418
Laryngitis, 419
Lasik Surgery Reversal – Left Eye, 420
Lasik Surgery Reversal – Right Eye, 421
Leaky Gut Syndrome, 421
Leg Edema, 424
Leg Problems, 425
Leg-Paralysis, 426
Leucorrhea, 427
Libido – Under Activated, 427
Ligament Problems, 429
Lip Problems, 430
Liver – Jaundice, 430
Liver Problems, 431
Long Term Illness, 433
Low Progesterone Levels, 433
Lumbar Hernia, 434
Lung Problems, 435
Lupus, 436
Lymes Disease, 438
Lymphatic System Problems, 441
M's, 443
Macular Degeneration, 443
Marfan Syndrome, 443
Mastoiditis, 445
Maxilla, 446
Measles, 447
Memory Loss non-physical trauma, 448
Meningitis – Bacterial, 450
Meningitis – Fungal, 450
Meningitis – Viral, 451
Menopause – Difficult, 452
Menstrual Problems, 453

Mitral Valve Prolapse, 454
Mold Sensitivity, 455
Moles, 456
Mononucleosis, 457
Morning Sickness, 458
Mouth Problems, 458
Mucormycosis, 459
Multiple Sclerosis, 460
Muscle Problems, 461
Muscles – Cramps, 462
Muscular Dystrophy, 463
Myasthenia Gravis, 463
N'S, 465
Narcolepsy, 465
Nausea, 465
Nephritis, 466
Nerve Problems, 467
Nervous Breakdown, 468
Nervousness, 469
Neuritis, 470
Neurosis, 471
Nose Problems, 472
O'S, 473
Osteomyelitis, 475
Osteoporosis, 476
Ovarian Cyst, 476
Ovarian Fibroids, 477
Ovaries – Polycystic, 479
Ovary Problems, 481
Overeating – Compulsive, 482
P'S, 485
Pagets Disease, 485
Pain, 487
Pancreas Problems, 488
Pancreatic Insufficiency, 489
Pancreatitis, 490
Panic Disorder, 491
Paralysis, 492
Parasites, 493
Parathyroid Disease, 494
Parkinson's Disease, 496
Peacemaker, 497
Pelvic Organ Collapse/ Prolapse, 498
Pelvis Problems, 499
Periodontal Bone Loss, 500
Peripheral Neuropathy, 501
Phlebitis, 504
Physical Abuse, 505
Pimples, 506

Pineal Gland, 506
Pinguecula, 508
Pituitary Gland Problems, 508
Pityros, 509
Plantar Fasciitis, 510
Plantar Wart, 513
Pleurisy, 514
Plum Pit Throat, 514
Pneumonia, 515
Polyarteritis, 516
Polymyalgia Rheumatica, 518
Polymyositis, 520
Post Mastectomy Problems, 520
Post Traumatic Stress Disorder(PTSD), 526
Preemie Birth – now adult, 527
Premenstrual Syndrome, 528
Prolapsed Bladder (Cystocele), 529
Prostate Problems, 530
Pruritic urticarial papules and plaques of pregnancy, 533
Pseudo Tumor – Cerebri, 534
Psoriasis, 535
Pulmonary Fibrosis, 535
Pyorrhea – Periodontitis, 536
Pyrogenic Granuloma, 537
R'S, 539
Radiation Influence on Disease Creation, 539
Radiculopathy of Left Breast, 539
Radiculopathy of Right Breast, 540
Rashes, 541
Reflexive Sympathetic Dystrophy Syndrome, 542
Restless Leg Syndrome, 544
Reynauds Syndrome, 547
Rhinitis – when laying down at night, 548
Rosacea, 550
Rotator Cuff, 551
S'S, 554
Salivary Gland Problems, 554
Sarcoidosis, 554
Schizophrenia, 556
Sciatica, 557
Scleroderma, 558
Scoliosis, 559
Sebaceous Cysts, 561
Senility, 563
Sepsis, 564

EMOTIONAL PATTERNS

Sexual Abuse, 565
Sexual Assault – Adult, 566
Sexual Assaulter, 569
Shin Problems, 572
Shingles, 572
Shoulders, 574
Sickness and Love, 575
Sidedness, 575
Sinus Congestion – Chronic, 576
Sinus Polyps, 577
Sinus Problems, 578
Sjogrens Syndrome, 578
Skin Problems, 579
Sleep Apnea, 580
Slipped Disc (Herniation), 581
Smoking – problems with quitting, 582
Snoring, 583
Spasmodic Dysphonia – (Laryngeal), 583
Sphenoid Bone Misalignment, 585
Spinal Stenosis, 586
Spleen Problems, 588
Sprains, 589
Spurs, 590
Stargardts Disease, 590
Stills Disease – Juvenile, 592
Stomach Problems, 594
Stomach Ulcer (Peptic Ulcer Disease-Gastric), 595
Strep Throat, 596
Stroke, 597
Stuttering (non-developmental), 598
Stye, 599
Suicidal, 599
Swallowing – Trouble, 600
Swollen Feet, 603
T'S, 604
Tachycardia, 604
Teeth – Upper Left 1st Incisor, 606
Teeth – Upper Right 2nd Molar, 607
Teeth Problems, 609
Temple Pain or Pressure, 609
Temporal Arteritis, 612
Temporo-Mandibular Joint (TMJ), 613
Tendon Problems, 614
Testicle Problems, 615
Thalamus Problems, 615
Thigh Problems, 616
Throat Problems, 617
Thrombosis, 618
Thrombotic thrombocytopenic purpura, 619
Thrush, 620
Thyamine Deficiency, 621
Thymus Problems, 622
Thyroid Problems, 624
Tibia – Left, 626
Tibia – Right, 627
Tinnitus, 628
Toes, 631
Tongue Problems, 631
Tonsil Problems, 632
Tooth Infection, 633
Tourette's Syndrome, 634
Toxins – Aluminum, 635
Toxins – Asbestos, 635
Toxins – Cadmium, 636
Toxins – Glyphosate, 637
Toxins – Lead, 638
Toxins – Mercury, 638
Toxins – Polychlorinated Biphenyls (PCBs), 639
Trigeminal Neuralgia, 640
Tuberculosis, 641
Tumors – Lipomas, 642
U'S, 644
Umbilical Hernia, 644
Upper Respiratory Infection (URI), 644
Urinary Tract Infection (Cystitis), 645
V'S, 647
Vaginitis, 647
Varicose Veins, 647
Vasculitis, 648
Vein Problems, 651
Venereal Disease, 651
Vertigo, 652
Viruses, 654
Vitiligo, 656
Vocal Cord Problems, 657
Vomiting, 657
W'S, 659
Warts, 659
Wegeners Granulomatosis, 659
Weight – Overweight, 662
Weight – Under, 664
Weight Loss – Fear of Starvation, 665
Weight Loss – Insulin Resistance, 666
Weight Loss – The Family Money Story and Weight, 667
Weight Loss – The Magical Thinking Diet, 669
Weight Loss Panic, 671
Wilson's Syndrome, 671
Wounded Creative Core, 672
Wounding of the Empathic Sense, 673
Wrists, 677
Y'S, 680
Yeast Infection, 680